# TRAVELS

IN

# THE UNITED STATES,

ETC.

During 1849 and 1850.

BY THE

LADY EMMELINE STUART-WORTLEY.

NEW YORK:
HARPER & BROTHERS, PUBLISHERS,
82 CLIFF STREET.
1851.

This Volume is Dedicated

TO THE

COUNTESS OF CHESTERFIELD,

BY

HER MOST AFFECTIONATE COUSIN,

THE AUTHORESS.

# PREFACE.

I LEFT England fully determined against writing a book of travels, nay, I would not even keep a Journal during our wanderings, lest I should be tempted to jot down, and ultimately to publish, my impressions of the society and institutions in those countries which it was our good fortune to visit; but since our return to England, friends, to whose better judgment I am bound to defer, have pressed me so strongly to print the letters which I had written during our excursion, that I have consented to do so, after adding somewhat, to give them the usual narrative form, and dividing them into chapters. This will account for the familiar tone of the Work, and for occasional repetitions.

For the politician or philosopher these pages will, I fear, have little or no interest; written familiarly to relatives and friends at home, their staple is the gossip of travel; and if they amuse that large class to whom gossip is welcome, and tend in any way to strengthen kindly feelings in the breasts of my English readers toward the people from whom their wandering countrywoman received so much and such constant courtesy and hospitality, I shall not regret giving to the world this Work.

BELVOIR CASTLE, 1851.

# CONTENTS.

CHAPTER XVI.



CHAPTER XVII.



CHAPTER XVIII.



CHAPTER XIX.



CHAPTER XX.



CHAPTER XXI.



CHAPTER XXII.

CHAPTER XXIII.



CHAPTER XXIV.



CHAPTER XXV.



CHAPTER XXVI.



CHAPTER XXVII.



CHAPTER XXVIII.

CHAPTER XXIX.



CHAPTER XXX.



CHAPTER XXXI.



CHAPTER XXXII.



CHAPTER XXXIII.



CHAPTER XXXIV.



CHAPTER XXXV.

# NARRATIVE

OF

# TRAVELS IN THE UNITED STATES.

## CHAPTER I.

Arrival at New York—First View of Broadway—Summer Costume of the Ladies—Description of New York—Its Suburbs and Islands—Its Fortifications—Prepare to start for Niagara.

The Bay of New York looked beautiful on the morning of our arrival (May 16th, 1849). It was a bright, warm, splendid morning; the sun shone gloriously, and the sky reminded me of Italy. We took leave of Captain Judkins, the obliging and excellent captain of "The Canada;" but before we went on shore, we witnessed the disembarkation of the mails—it is quite an interesting spectacle. There were about thirty thousand letters—white-winged messengers of peace!—one could not but rejoice at the sight. Those numerous letters of business, of friendship, of mutual interest, seemed so many links uniting the two countries in a concord not to be easily, if ever, broken.

One of the first things that struck us on arriving in the city of New York—the Empress City of the West—was, of course, Broadway. It is a noble street, and has a thoroughly bustling, lively, and somewhat democratic air. New York is certainly handsome, and yet there is something about it that gives one the idea of a half-finished city, and this even in Broadway itself; for the street was literally littered with all imaginable rubbish which, we should imagine from appearances, is usually shot in that celebrated thoroughfare; indeed it seems a sort of preserve for this species of game. Piles of timber, mounds of bricks, mountains of packing-cases, pyramids of stones, and stacks of goods, were observable on all sides. The New Yorkers themselves grumble much at the inconvenience, and their newspapers often contain pathetic remonstrances with the authorities, for allowing such obstructions to crowd the thoroughfare.

Besides this, it appears from their published complaints, that their streets are very much too often torn up for sewage purposes, &c., and, in short, that this tiresome performance is frequently *unnecessarily encored*, without their consent, and certainly to their manifest inconvenience. They ask if their time is to be taken up (as their streets are) continually, by having to stop every two or three steps, and sit down on the next door-step to take the paving-stones out of their boots? Cart-loads of these same paving-stones, adding to the confusion, were to be seen on all sides, and sometimes felt, as our handsome, heavy, crimson-velvet-lined, hired vehicle (rather a warm-looking lining for New York, near the beginning of June), swayed from side to side, and rolled and rattled ponderously along.

We went to the Astor House, or rather Astor *Town*, for its size is prodigious: there we had comfortable bedrooms, and a nice sitting-room; and we dined in private;—and I was glad to find no objection was made to this arrangement. There is a perfect colony of Irish at the Astor House; but till the accent betrayed them, I took the waiters, at first, for French or German, so carefully had they followed the example of their American fellow-citizens (of whom, be it remembered, I had as yet beheld next to nothing), and were so be-bearded, imperialed, and, I believe, in many instances, mustachioed too, that Paddy seemed quite transmogrified into a "whiskered Pandour or a fierce hussar," which seemed unnecessary for the peaceful occupation of laying knives—not without forks—and handing cream-ices.

What a glorious sunny day it was! We had a glimpse of busy Broadway from our windows. We soon saw some evidence of the warmth of a New York summer, in the profusion of light cool bonnets furnished with broad and deeply-hanging curtains, shading and covering the throat and part of the shoulders—a very sensible costume for hot weather. The fashion, or the custom, just now seems to be for all the ladies to wear large white shawls. I never beheld such a number of white shawls mustered before, I think: the female part of the population seem all *vouée au blanc.* It had rather too table-clothy an appearance, and from its frequency, the snowy shawl became quite tiresome; besides, they made one think of "weird white women," sheeted spectres, and Abd-el-Kader's scouring Arabs, in their "burnooses." This is, I dare say, however, only a temporary fancy; and probably, when I return to New York, they (the shawls, not the wearers thereof) will all have been swept away, like so many light fleecy clouds, to the four winds of heaven.

I will say but little of New York itself now, as this is only a flying visit, and I shall return, ere long—merely observing, *en passant*, that every thing around me betokens energy, industry, and prosperity, and also the impetuous go-aheadiness, which will hardly allow time for completing all that is begun, or for contriving that order and comfort which should keep pace with improvement and innovation.

New York is situated on Manhattan Island, at the confluence of the bright and beautiful Hudson, with the East River (or Strait of Long Island). It is the centre of an imposing panorama, and is screened from the tumultuous ocean by an assemblage of intervening, protecting islands. Its harbor is safe, easy of access, very spacious, and is said to be capable of accommodating the combined navies of the world. This noble harbor occupies a sweeping circuit of twenty-five miles: on every side it is gracefully bounded by ever-varying scenery, country seats, and scattered hamlets, while the above-mentioned lovely islands shine like precious jewels on its radiant bosom.

The busy metropolis of the United States has almost constant communication, by steam and sailing-packets, with all the seaports of America, Asia, Africa, Europe, the East and West Indies, and the islands of the Pacific. Its progress in commerce, population, and wealth is indeed astonishing. The population in 1800 was 60,489; in 1820, 123,706; in 1840, 312,710; and in 1849, 400,000.

Manhattan Island is thirteen and a half miles long from north to south, ranging from half a mile to somewhat more than two miles in width—the greatest width being at Eighty-eighth-street, and it contains about twenty-two square miles. Incessant communication is kept up between the city and its picturesque, prosperous, and rapidly increasing suburbs, by means of steam ferry-boats, the Harlem Railroad, and omnibusses; the fares being exceedingly reasonable, and the accommodations extremely good.

In approaching New York from "The Narrows," one can hardly fail to be struck by the beauty of the bay: the scenery on its shore, as I have already mentioned, is very striking. The outer harbor, or bay, extends from the "Narrows" to Sandy Hook, where is a light-house at the distance of eighteen miles from the city. In the harbor, adjoining the city, are Bedlow's,

Governor's, and Ellis's islands, all of them strongly fortified. The first, and most important, includes seventy acres of ground, and is situated three thousand two hundred feet from the Battery. Fort Columbus occupies its centre, and on the northeast point is Castle William, a round tower six hundred feet in circumference and sixty feet high, with three tiers of guns. There is a battery likewise, on the northwest side, commanding the entrance through Buttermilk Channel, a strait which separates it from Brooklyn, Long Island.

In addition to these fortifications, New York harbor is well defended by similar works on Bedlow's and Ellis's Islands; at the Narrows, on the Long Island shore, by Fort Hamilton and Fort Lafayette (formerly Fort Diamond), which is built on a reef of rocks about two hundred yards from the shore; and on Staten Island, opposite, by Fort Tompkins and Fort Richmond. Here the "Narrows" is about two-thirds of a mile wide. The entrance from the Sound, on the East River, is defended by Fort Schuyler, on Throg's Neck.

So much for the defenses of the great emporium and metropolis of the United States, and so much for itself for the present—for I am off to the great Niagara. Every facility for our journey has been afforded us by the kindness of the English Consul and Mrs. Barclay, who have amiably given me all the necessary instructions, directions, &c. It may easily be guessed how eagerly I long to hear and see the waters of Erie, Superior, Huron, and Michigan, all thundering down one mighty steep in their awful greatness and power!

## CHAPTER II.

Detained at Albany—Wreck of the "Empire" Steamer—American Indifference to human Life—The theatrical Riot and Massacre caused by Mr. Forrest's Jealousy of Macready—Sympathy of the Lady for the Captain of the "Empire"—High-sounding names of Towns—The Hudson—Hotels at Albany—Description of Albany.

We came to the handsome town of Albany in a fast and beautifully-decorated steamer; but we might almost as well have been on board a slow one, as we find we can not go on till to-morrow to Buffalo. The steamboats and railroads do not communicate as conveniently as they might do for travelers, and I hear this is done expressly to please the hotel-keepers, by forcing travelers to remain a night at Albany. I was much disappointed; and so full were my thoughts of the great cataract, that I might well expect to have a nightmare of Niagara to-night, which would not be a pleasant introduction, or preface of an introduction to "the Falls."

The Hudson is a beauteous river; but, in the midst of its loveliness, it was very *triste* to come upon the wreck of the splendid "Empire" steamer, which was lost two nights before we started. I believe she ran foul of a large merchant vessel in the dark, and went down very shortly afterward. Numbers of lives were lost; many dead bodies had been picked up, and as soon as they can penetrate into her sleeping cabins they expect to find many more. They were slowly attempting to raise the steamer when we passed.

Then was I a second time struck by the American indifference to human life, which I had before observed at New York. The first time, it was on occasion of the frightful massacre of citizens at the miserable theatrical row occasioned by Mr. Forrest's professional jealousy of our Macready. It seemed to excite wonderfully little horror, indignation, or regret. One or two of the newspapers kept up an agitation about the matter; but I do not think I have yet heard a single person stigmatize the shooting some five-and-twenty citizens on such an occasion, as uncalled for or severe. I have heard some say it was perfectly right; and that it was a pity so few had paid the penalty of their misconduct; I heard even harsher things said than that, but forbear to repeat them, lest it should be thought that I exaggerate.

After all, I believe most of those who suffered were merely idle spectators, drawn there by curiosity, or mixed by chance in the crowd. However, that is very often the case in less severe encounters between the mob and the preservers of order. When I expressed my horror at such a frightful massacre in the streets of a peaceful city, I found none to sympathize with such sentiments, if I except the columns of the *Herald*. In the crowded steamer, where one heard people talking over the topics of the day, I do not remember to have once heard the subject alluded to, though the affair had so recently happened. What a sensation would such a slaughter have excited in London!

When we passed the melancholy wreck of the ill-starred "Empire," whose fate had caused the destruction of so many lives, scarcely any one manifested any interest in the catastrophe. They sauntered to that side of the vessel in crowds—to look very indifferently, it appeared to me, at the mournful spectacle, as they might and would have done at any other sight. Yet in addition to the great number of corpses that had already been found, it was almost certain that the still submerged cabins were so many coffins; and those who were prosecuting the melancholy search were constantly, we were told, finding fresh bodies in different parts of the vessel.

The only person who seemed to me at all to feel any commiseration and regret was a lady who stood near me, and all hers was reserved exclusively for the captain of the ill-fated steamer, who was her cousin, and who, however, was alive and safe. But, she said, some people blamed him, which was very hard, as it was no fault of his; and he had been quite "sick," she assured me, ever since, from the annoyance he had undergone. Thus the only one who was pitied, it seemed, was one who survived. She added, however, he was much shocked at all that had happened. It was really consolatory to hear, that there was such a thing as compassion, in this busy, go-ahead world of the West, for unfortunates, who had been so suddenly and unexpectedly launched into eternity; for one began, almost unconsciously, to lower even one's own opinion of the value of existence, and to think life a very twopenny-halfpenny possession, after all. I will not be sure, however, but that what so shocked the captain, was the amount of property lost; but I would not too curiously inquire touching the point, preferring to think the sorrow arose from more humane feelings.

Whence arises this indifference to human life in so flourishing and prosperous a community? One has always understood that existence is of little account in China, because the over-crowded, half-starved, hard-worked, oppressed, and tyrannized-over population, are so wretched in this world, that any change must, they feel, be a beneficial one for them; but how different is the case here? Yet true it is that they are tyrannized over by a very despotic task-master, and a very exacting and spirit-grinding ruler —Mammon; and I can well imagine that ceaseless toil in his service, with all the cares and troubles incident to it, must make a man find life somewhat of a wearisome burden. Indeed, money-getting, which is certainly in most countries a great business, appears here to me almost a battle. It seems as if they must win, do or die, and the dead on the field are trodden under foot by their eager comrades and competitors, hurrying onward, and having no time to stay, however they might be disposed. That they are a very kind-hearted people, I fully believe; but to make money seems a sort of duty in America—the great object of living; and this paramount feeling, to a certain extent, like Aaron's rod, swallows up all the rest.

On our road to Niagara, to-morrow, we shall come to a great many very high-sounding places: Rome, Syracuse, Egypt, Athens, Geneva, Utica, Amsterdam, Batavia, and Palmyra, among them, I believe. A noble line of places indeed, and worthy of forming the road to the great, glorious Niagara, if their actual state, circumstances, and proportion harmonized with their pretensions. What a pity the Americans do not choose Indian names for their rising towns and cities, which are generally as sonorous and noble-sounding as they are impressive and poetical! Setting aside the inadequacy of the towns in general, for the present at least, to do justice to such splendid appellations, and the sometimes ridiculous juxtaposition in which they are placed with regard to each other (the most different, and distant, and hostile places in the Old World being forced into a sort of happy-family brotherhood in the New), in their immediate neighborhood are too often found other flourishing villages and towns rejoicing in the very homely designations of Smithsville, Brownsville, Onion, Jacksontown, &c. In one place I see they have an infant Troy (not the one almost close to this place, but some diminutive rival)—then Highgate, Canaan, Guildhall, Milton, Hyde Park, and Columbia, are all tolerably near to one another; but I believe this is nothing to the greater incongruities which the West presents in its more out-of-the-way districts.

We were quite charmed with the extreme beauty of the Hudson and its banks, especially at West Point. I shall not go into any particulars on the subject till my return, but only say the river reminded me of the Rhine in many parts, *minus* the old feudal castles.

When we arrived at Albany we first tried a very handsome-looking hotel in a high situation, from whence I thought we should have a fine view, which our driver recommended, the one I had been advised to go to in New York being quite full. It was closed, and this, I suppose, our cunning driver knew right well, but it gave him the opportunity of asking about twice as much more for our short but rather steep drive, as we had paid for our passage the whole way from New York; the one being remarkably cheap, the other rather more remarkably dear. Of course we soon found another hotel, for Albany abounds with them. Here are some of their names—Stanwix Hall, the American Hotel, the City, the Clinton, Columbian, Congress Hall, Delavan House, Temperance Hotel, Eastern Railroad Hotel, Franklin House, Mansion House (where we are staying), United States Hotel, and Washington Hall.

The proprietor and people here are extremely civil and obliging, and we are very comfortable. The street in which our hotel is situation is particularly handsome; it is exceedingly wide with excellent and very broad *trottoirs* (which they call here side-walks).

This town was founded by the Dutch in 1623, and called Fort Orange, and in 1686 it was chartered as a city. Next to Jamestown in Virginia, it was the earliest European settlement within the thirteen original States; it has not, however, at all an ancient air, at least as far as I have seen of it; but, in fact, it was almost entirely rebuilt not long ago; I believe after one of the dreadful fires so frequent in the United States.

When the English captured New York this town was named Albany, a compliment to the Duke of York and Albany, afterward James the Second. Its position makes it necessarily a great thoroughfare: it is placed near the head of tide navigation, and on the direct line of communication from the east and the south with the River St. Lawrence, with the Saratoga Springs, and with the country of the great Lakes.

The city has acquired great additional commercial importance since the completion of the Erie and Champlain canals: this has made it the *entrepôt* for a large proportion of the products of the State destined to the New York markets. A fine basin is constructed upon the river to accommodate this large trade: in this all the boats employed on the northern and western canals are received. This consists of part of the river included between the shore and a noble pier, whose proportions are magnificent. It is, indeed, a stupendous work, containing several acres, on which large stores have been built, where enormous quantities of "lumber," and other articles of trade are collected. Drawbridges connect it with the city.

The public buildings here are said to be handsome: the population is forty-five thousand, or thereabouts. The town appears very clean, and is altogether a very striking-looking, bustling, thriving, and admirably-situated place. The Capitol looks imposing at the head of State-street, one hundred and thirty feet above the Hudson.

---

## CHAPTER III.

Difficulty of conveying the Impression caused by a first View of the Falls of Niagara—An Attempt to do so—The Falls described—A Thunder-storm over the Great Cataracts—The Rainbow—Kindness and Courtesy of the Americans—Their Spirit of Enterprise—Luxurious Appointments of American Steamers—The Dimensions of the Falls—Goat Island—Quantity of Water precipitated over the Falls—Grand and Navy Islands.

We arrived at Niagara to-day from Buffalo, and put up at the Clifton House. It will not be expected that I should tell what my first feelings and impressions were on beholding this thrice-glorious cataract, for I hardly am in the least conscious of what they were myself. I only know this; it scarcely seemed to me at all like what any painting or any description had represented it to be, except only in the shape of the great Canadian Fall.

When the train we were in stopped, the roar of the cataract burst on our ears most majestically. It was a moment of intense excitement, and on we hastened, and stood very shortly within a few feet of the verge of the American Fall, and looking on to the magnificent Horse Shoe. There we were in the audience-chamber of the great Water King. If one saw the sun for the first time, could one describe it? Do not expect me yet to say any thing of Niagara; at least any thing to the purpose. The garrulous mood will very likely come on me presently; when, perhaps, I shall quite tire the reader with my rhapsodies, so that he may have cause to wish all my powers of expression were still frozen up by awe and admiration, like the notes in the horn, as related of Baron Munchausen.

What a wonderful thing can water become! One feels, on looking at Niagara, as if one had never seen that element before. Were I to try and tell what I felt at my second and third look at the Mighty Wonder, I think it was still confusion and bewilderment, mingled with a slight disappointment at the apparent height of the cataract, and very much the reverse with regard to the general features and breadth; and now I can most truly say it is far more magnificent than I had anticipated it to be, though my expectations were of the very highest order.

For the spray (I can already find courage to speak of that)—it is what enchants me the most in the whole stupendously magnificent scene. It is a very stormy windy day, carrying the huge columns of that beauteous spray to an immense height, so it is seen to the greatest advantage. I think it sometimes seems really celestial! it looks like something not of this world. This hotel is very close to the Falls, and, as I write, I have only to look up, to see them. The noise is extremely fine, like the stormy roaring of a tempest-shaken sea, only the sound is more measured, and conveys an idea of a calm, kingly defiance, altogether inexpressibly grand and solemn.

Besides feeling as if it were a presumption to attempt to write about Niagara, thus in its overpowering presence, as it were, I find it very difficult to write at all now, as I am drawn to the window and balcony constantly (whence one sees both Falls fully), by the irresistible fascination of this most wonderful water; and the changes that take place almost momentarily are a source of great interest. At one time it looks enveloped and almost hidden in spray; an instant afterward, perhaps, it shines forth fully revealed; now it seems covered with gloom, and looks black and frowning, and full of wrath and terror; and now the sun (which alone appears worthy to be its comrade and compeer) breaks forth, and makes it all one glory.

V—— is enchanted, and independently of the intense enjoyment Niagara affords her, she is delighted to find herself once more in the country, where all looks beautifully green and fresh. Her bedroom window opens on the American Fall. I went there just now, to have a view from that side, and I can not tell how much one delights in the immense variety and diversified points of view these matchless cataracts present.

Though I have been here so short a time, I think I have

already seen them display a hundred different aspects. From V——'s window I saw a wonderfully beautiful rainbow on the water; one-half of the American Fall was in deep shadow, and the other in dazzling sunlight. A small cloud was just passing over the sun above it.

I must now—the first overpowering impression having been conquered—try to speak a little of what I think and feel about this glorious Fall. But what language could ever do justice to its more than magnificence? It seems to belong really to some grander world, of more gigantic proportions and sublimer features than our own.

Before I came here, I erroneously supposed that one should be immensely struck, and overpowered, and enchanted at first, but that afterward there would be a certain degree of monotony attached to that unvarying sublimity, which I wrongly believed to be the great characteristic of Niagara. But, how miserably did I do it injustice! Perhaps the most peculiar and transcendent attribute of this matchless cataract, is its almost endless variety. The innumerable diversities of its appearance, the continual countless rapid alterations in its aspect; in short, the perpetually varying phases which it displays, are indeed wondrous and truly indescribable. This is a great deal owing to the enormous volumes of spray which are almost incessantly shifting and changing their forms like the clouds above. Niagara, indeed, has its own clouds, and they not only give it the great charm and interest of an ever-beautiful and exquisite variety, but also environ it with a lovely and bewildering atmosphere of mystery, which seems the very crown of its manifold perfections and glories.

Niagara has its changes like the sea, and in its lesser space circumscribed, they seem fully as comprehensive and multitudinous. I have dwelt long on this, because I do not remember to have seen this mighty and transcendent feature of Niagara particularly noticed in any of the descriptions I have ever read of it, and it has most especially delighted and astonished me.

We were so very fortunate as to have a tremendous thunder-storm here on Tuesday night, and it may be guessed what a tremendous thunder-storm *must* be here! The heavens seemed literally opening just over the great cataracts, and the intensely vivid lightning, brighter than day, lit up the giant Falls, and seemed mixed and mingling with the dazzling mountains of spray, which then looked more beautiful and beatific than ever. It was a wild windy night, as if all the elements were revelling together in a stormy chaotic carnival, of their own, till it really presented altogether a scene almost too awfully magnificent.

The deafening roar of the crashing thunder was yet louder than the roar of the cataract, and completely appeared to drown it while it lasted; but the moment the stormy roll of the thunder died away, it was grand indeed to hear again the imposing, unceasing sound of Niagara—like the voice of a giant conqueror uttering a stunning but stately cry of victory. Then soon the bellowing thunder broke forth again, fiercer and louder than before; and oh, the lightning! it seemed like a white-winged sunbreak when it blazed on the snowy glare of the ever-foaming cataracts.

I hardly ever saw before such dazzling lightning; and those reverberating peals of Niagara-out-voicing thunder were truly terrific, and appeared quite close. Heaven and earth seemed shouting to one another in those sublime and stupendous voices; and what a glorious hymn they sang between them! At first, the lightning was only like summer flashes, and it kept glancing round the maddened waters as if playing with them, and defying them in sport; but, after a little while, a fearful flash, updarted really like a sudden sun, behind the great Horse Shoe Fall, and the whole blazed out into almost unendurable light in a moment. The storm continued during the whole night.

From our drawing-room windows we have a magnificent view of the Horse Shoe Fall, and almost the whole of the American one besides; and what a sublime pomp and pageant of Nature it is! What a thrilling, soul-stirring sight; and, ever new and ever changing, and eternally suggesting fresh thoughts, fresh feelings and emotions. Just now, a violent gust of wind drove a huge cloud of spray quite on our side of the Canadian Falls, and it was hovering between the two glorious cataracts like a mighty, suspended avalanche, till it dispersed. This transcendently beautiful spray is generally most brilliantly white, like sunlit snow. We saw a vast resplendent rainbow on the water itself on Tuesday afternoon, of colors quite unimaginably bright, and we had a marvelously glorious sunset last evening. There were flaming, blood-red reflections on the rocks, trees, and islands; but the most delicate suffusions only, of a rich soft rose color, rested on the fantastic forms of the matchless spray—as if it softened and refined every thing that came near it, and made all that touched it as rare and exquisite as its own etherialized self. He who has not seen, can have no idea of the absorbing nature of the admiration excited in one's mind by this surpassing and astounding marvel of creation: I feel quite enthralled and fascinated by it, and time seems to fly by at an electric-telegraph pace here, while I am watching it.

I feel so rooted and riveted to this spot by the unutterable enchantments of this master-piece of Nature, I can scarcely believe that two days have passed since I first arrived. One becomes here, indeed, utterly Niagarized; and, the great cataract goes sounding through all one's soul, and heart, and mind, commingling with all one's ideas and impressions, and uniting itself with all one's innermost feelings and fancies. The sounds of the Fall vary nearly as much as their aspect: sometimes very hollow, at other times solemn and full-toned, like an host of organs uttering out their grand voices together; and sometimes, as I heard it said, the other day, with a rolling kettle-drum, gong-like sound, in addition—as if it were a temporary and accidental accompaniment to their majestic oceanic roar. I have come *patriotically* to the British side, but not from any want of liking for the mighty neighbors of the Canadians.

Great injustice has been done to the Americans, and we have been accustomed too implicitly to believe the often unfair and unfounded reports of prejudiced travelers. Instead of discourteous and disobliging manners we find them all that is most civil and obliging. Among the less educated, no doubt, occasionally, some of the faults so unsparingly attributed to them, may be found; but they appear to me, as far as I have had any opportunity of judging as yet, a thoroughly hospitable, kind-hearted, and generous-minded people.

And, then, what a noble, enterprising people they are! What miraculous progress and improvement is visible on every side in the United States. One town we came through, Buffalo, was, not many years ago, I was told, a mere Indian village: it is now a mighty city. Albany is also a magnificent town; the streets are strikingly broad and straight;—the *trottoirs* are about the width of Dover street! The steamers on the Hudson are perfect palaces, and *fairy* palaces to boot! being the most delicate and finished creations of art, and fancy you can imagine; larger than the far-famed "Great Britain," and apparently lighter than the rainbowed coracle of a nautical sylph: a floating island of painting, marble, gilding, stained glass, velvet hangings, satin draperies, mirrors in richly-carved frames, and sculptured ornaments, with beautiful vases of flowers, Chinese lamps of various indescribable fantastic forms, arabesques, chandeliers—in short, you might fancy yourself in Haroun Alraschid's palace.

It was very agreeable, steaming along in the Bucentaur-beating vessel, and looking on the fine scenery of the lovely Hudson, in the most charming, warm, soft, sunny weather. And now the potent wondrous magnet, the mighty mystery that mortals call Niagara, draws me to the windows, and I *must* go and watch that world of wonders. By the way, what a fortunate thing it was that the noble old Indian name was retained for *this*. How distracting it would have been, to have had it named Smith's Fall, or Patch's Plunge.

It rains a little now, and the vast black clouds hovering near the snowy spray, have a truly noble and striking effect; like the shadowy Angel, Death, about to bound on his pale courser; but every thing is noble and beauteous here! there is scarcely a cloud in the sky that does not pay its tribute, and fling its fresh fairy-gift on these magical waters. I have, as yet seen nothing of moon-light and star-light on them.

We see, constantly, a small steamer, called "The Maid of the Mist," going almost close to the foot of the Falls. The River Niagara forms the outlet of the waters of Lake Erie, and of all the great Upper Lakes, which, together with Erie and Ontario, are estimated to contain nearly one half the fresh water on the surface of the globe! At the distance of about three-fourths of a mile above the Falls, the river begins a rapid descent, making, within this distance, a constant succession of slopes equal to about fifty-two feet on the American side, and fifty-seven on the Canadian. It forms an impetuous current just above the Falls, and turns a right angle to the northeast, and then its width becomes suddenly contracted, from three miles to three-quarters of a mile. The river's depth below the cataract exceeds three hundred feet. Goat, or Iris Island (containing somewhere about seventy-five acres) divides the gigantic cataract into two parts, but on the western, or British side, is the principal channel. The channel between Goat Island and the eastern shore is also divided by a small island.

The noble river falls perpendicularly over the precipice from a hundred and seventy to two hundred feet. The Horse Shoe, or Crescent Fall is so called from its shape: it looks to me like a mighty scooped-out throne for some King of the oceans of a hundred worlds. In the eastern channel, between Goat and Luna Islands, the stream's breadth is only about ten yards: it forms a lonely, separate cascade, and assists one to form a due estimate of the enormous width of the awful cataracts thundering near it.

Between Luna Island and the shore, with a comparatively shallow stream, the descent of the Fall is said to be greater by several feet than at the Horse-shoe Fall. An ingeniously constructed bridge connects Goat Island with the shore, from whence you have an excellent view of the rapids; indeed the bridge crosses the American branch of the river in the midst of them. You look on your right hand, and there is the roaring American Fall, almost close to you.

Goat Island is a gem of beauty, and its lovely foliage and bowery walks seem to charm away a little of the overpowering awfulness from its tremendous neighbor. It is said that if, as is supposed, the cataract has backed all the way from Queenstown, it must have taken about forty thousand years for it to recede to its present situation.

The quantity of water precipitated over the Falls is estimated by Professor Dwight to be 11,524,375 tons per hour; by Darby at 1,672,704,000 cubic feet per hour, and by Pickens at 113,510,000, or 18,524,000 cubic feet a minute.

Among the islands which diversify the surface of the Niagara River, is Grand Island, which contains 18,000 acres of good and fertile soil, covered with rich forests. Navy Island is another, and it terminates in a beautiful point about a mile and a half above the Fall.

---

## CHAPTER IV.

Port Talbot—Canadian Carriages—Vast Extent of American Woods—The Hotel at Port Stanley—Lake Erie—Mr. A—— and his Family—Col. Talbot, the "Last of the Mohicans"—Instance of the Memory of North American Indians—Another Story of the same Kind—A Recurrence to Niagara—A second Thunder-storm—American Forests—Lake Erie by Sunset—The Maple and the Sugar made from it—Coldness of Canadian Winters.

We arrived at Port Talbot, Canada West, a day or two ago from Niagara, where we staid a fortnight. This is a delightful place. We went back to Buffalo, then crossed a part of Lake Erie (we were a day and a night on board the steamer "London"), and, landing at Port Stanley, we had some refreshments at the little hotel there, where we were well taken care of, by the particularly attentive and obliging proprietors; and then we came on in a hired carriage, through beautiful woods to this beautiful spot.

The road, however, was not equally beautiful, and we broke down, which apparently not unforeseen accident our driver took very unconcernedly and philosophically, and immediately set about repairing the damage. A carriage breaking down is of little moment indeed in the woods of Canada, where they are usually of a tough and rough kind, and where the charioteer (who, I believe, is generally expected to be somewhat experienced in this way), speedily rectifies the injury by cutting down the first likely tree by the road-side, and adapting it to his purpose by some "rough and ready" kind of craft.

In this instance I had little doubt but that our damaged vehicle would come out of the hands of our Jehu nearly, if not quite, as good as new; for its "build" was such, that he might very probably have been himself the coach-maker originally, as well as coach-driver and coach-breaker. We were soon jolting and pitching along as merrily as ever, and arrived without any bones broken, as we flattered ourselves, at the hospitable door of Port Talbot. Its kind and friendly proprietor, with Colonel and Mrs. A——, his nephew and niece, received us with the most amiable cordiality, and we are quite enchanted with the place.

The house is beautifully situated on a high bank close to Lake Erie, of which I have a magnificent view from my window. Within view of the house (which has splendid groups of trees close to it), stretch away mighty woods, which probably continue without interruption, except from the lakes and the strides of American civilization in Michigan and Wisconsin, to the very shores of the Pacific. I could not have "realized" such enormous worlds of woods as I have even already seen, without beholding them with my own eyes.

On our way from Port Stanley here, we passed numbers of neat, newly-erected wooden houses of emigrants, looking generally very comfortable, and occasionally exceedingly pretty; with the bright cheerful-looking clearings about them, and the grandeur of the fine sombre old forests stretching away around them, as if to shut out the every-day *worldly* world. Colonel and Mrs. A—— have made this house delightfully comfortable, and there is an air of true English comfort and of that indescribable refinement, which the gorgeously-furnished saloons and chambers of the hotels we have lately been at in New York and other places, did not possess. Every thing is in the perfection of good taste. The drawing-room is a most charming apartment, with large windows reaching down to the ground, presenting a lovely view of that fresh-water sea, Lake Erie.

My own room is really quite luxuriously appointed in some particulars; first and foremost with regard to some splendid decorations and draperies of beautiful old Greek lace, which our fair hostess brought with her from the Ionian Islands, where she had resided for some time (what a change from such an ancient world as grand old Greece, to this grand young one, Canada!) but there is nothing gaudy, and nothing that looks out of place here or unsuited to the general character of simplicity of the house, owing to the exquisite arrangement of all the subordinate parts, and the graceful tact with which every thing has been ordered and contrived.

The amiable lady of the house tells me she went through a great deal of discomfort when they first established themselves here, which I can readily believe; but she seems to make a capital and very contented emigrant now. Her charming children—one or more of whom are little Greeks, that is, born in Corfu—seem to have suffered nothing from the rigor of a Canadian winter, and they appear thoroughly to enjoy a Canadian summer. Colonel Talbot does not live in this house, but in a sort of shanty, which agrees extremely with my idea (probably a very imperfect one) of an Indian wigwam, close by. He is going, almost immediately, to rebuild it, and make a good-sized comfortable house of it.

His life has been replete with adventures, since he came out here as a settler between forty and fifty years ago. He has performed almost prodigies here, and possesses immense tracts of country in these wild regions. In former days he used to milk his own cows, and drive them home from their pasturing places, for many miles sometimes; and besides, he did all the household work in his establishment; cooked, churned butter, washed, &c. His energy and perseverance were finally rewarded with great success; and he is lord of almost a principality here, and of a very flourishing one, apparently, too. He tells me he is in reality "the last of the Mohicans," having been adopted many years ago into this gallant tribe, and called by them by an Indian name, which I will not attempt to spell. He told me a remarkable instance of the accurate memory of the North American Indians. It seems that, having been away, and not having seen any of the tribe for a great many years, one day, on his return, he met an Indian, whom he did not in the least recognize, but who, the moment he saw him, repeated softly his Indian name in the usual, calm, impressive manner of the red man. Another story, not of a Mohican, but of a gentleman, apparently quite as cool in his proceedings, amused me much. It appears, some years ago, the colonel called to his servant to bring him some warm water for shaving purposes. The servant did not answer; and after repeatedly calling in vain, Colonel Talbot ascertained at length that the man had marched off, having, I believe, spoken before of feeling discontented where he was, but without giving any reason to think he would shake the dust of Port Talbot from his shoes so suddenly. Some years afterward, Colonel Talbot one morning called for warm water, and in walked the truant, most demurely, jug in hand, and proceeded to take upon himself all his once repudiated valet duties, in the most quiet and regular manner imaginable, as if he had never been absent from his post for an hour. He alluded not to what had occurred; nor did Colonel Talbot. The Mohican could not easily surpass that, I think, in coolness and self-possession, and Colonel Talbot, too, was evidently not made one of the tribe for nothing. It reminds me of a Yankee story of a man who sent his young son for a log to put on the fire. The son brought a mere stick, and papa whipped him; so the young gentleman went out again for a large log, and—never returned; at least not till twenty-five years afterwards, when, one evening, the choleric, corporal-punishment-loving old gentlemen, was calling to one of his grandsons to bring in a "large log for the fire," and in stalked son number 1, 2, or 3, as the case might be, who had so unconscionably absented himself, with a Brobdignagian log in his dexter hand. The old gentleman looked quietly up, examined the log, threw it carelessly on the fire, and then addressed his returned runaway: "*This* 'ere log 'll do; but you've been a darned long time a-fetching it."

Let me go back to Niagara. The reader may imagine our good fortune; we had a second thunder-storm there, far finer than the first. It continued through the whole night, and the lightning was unspeakably terrific, like a long succession of rising suns behind the falls, dazzling, bewildering, almost blinding it was; but most inconceivably, incommunicably glorious. A church was struck not far off, and severely damaged. V—— is much afraid generally, during a thunder-storm; but we both fortunately happened to think it was sheet lightning (for till it comes very near, you can not hear the thunder for the chorus of the cataracts). But for this I think she would have been much alarmed, for the sight was awfully tremendous.

As it was she even ventured to look at it from the balcony. How almost supernaturally sublime it looked! Between all the flashes, for a moment or two it was pitchy dark; then, when out-leaped the piercing lightning, the cataracts burst into full view, instantaneously of course, in all their overwhelming majesty and grandeur. V—— exclaimed that it looked like Vesuvius in vast eruption (which she saw last year), hovering and blazing over Niagara; and really it was a very fair simile, if you can imagine an intermittent Vesuvian eruption.

I think, next to Niagara, I admire these enormous forests, with their wild wondrous luxuriance of foliage, of every exquisite shade of the most lustrous and resplendent green: they are sublime. Lake Erie looked splendid in a very fine sunset the other evening. It seemed almost paved with many-colored jewels, and long bars of light, of divers and brilliant hues, crossed it. At another time, it appeared strewn all over, from the horizon to the shore, with myriads of all sorts and species of roses!

Among the many beauteous trees here, I have admired much the sugar maples. By the way, I tasted some of the sugar the other day, and thought it excellent. In tea or coffee I should not know it from the cane sugar; but alone, it tastes, I think, very much like sugar-candy. The children had a little pic-nic in the woods. V—— was superlatively happy, superintending various cookings and contrivings.

Our charming hostess says this place is so cold in the winter, that even with an enormous fire in her room, her ink has frozen in the inkstand while she has been writing a letter. I suppose this is owing to the isolated situation of the house, and to the immense forests almost contiguous to it, for I believe no such intensity of cold (or very rarely) is experienced in the cities and towns of Canada.

## CHAPTER V.

Return to New York—Courtesy and Hospitality of the Americans—Butterflies and Humming-birds—Railroads through American Forests—Rapid Progress of American Civilization—Port Stanley—Captain Bawbee—Description of Buffalo—Trading Facilities of that City—The United States' Military Academy—Monument to Kosciusko—His Garden—West Point—The Traitor Arnold and Major André—Constitution Island—Oppressive Heat of the Weather.

We again find ourselves, on the 25th June, in the busy, stirring, populous, go-ahead State of New York. We have suffered much from the heat: it was really intense during our journey. The number of people who are said to have died from the effects of *coup de soleil* here, is quite extraordinary.

I like the Americans more and more: either they have improved wonderfully lately, or else the criticisms on them have been cruelly exaggerated. They are particularly courteous and obliging; and seem, I think, amiably anxious that foreigners should carry away a favorable impression of them. As for me, let other travelers say what they please of them, I am determined not to be prejudiced, but to judge of them exactly as I find them; and I shall most pertinaciously continue to praise them (if I see no good cause to alter my present humble opinion), and most especially for their obliging civility and hospitable attention to strangers, of which I have already seen several instances.

I have witnessed but very few isolated cases, as yet, of the unrefined habits so usually ascribed to them; and those cases decidedly were not among the higher orders of people; for there seems just as much difference in America as any where else in some respects. The superior classes here have almost always excellent manners, and a great deal of real and natural, as well as acquired refinement, and are often besides (which perhaps will not be believed in fastidious England) extremely distinguished looking. By the way, the captains of the steam-boats appear a remarkably gentlemanlike race of men in general, particularly courteous in their deportment, and very considerate and obliging to the passengers.

I must not forget to mention the delight with which, at Port Talbot, we beheld some beautiful humming-birds flying about in the garden, and such gorgeous butterflies ; it was quite a pleasure to look at them ! It seemed so strange to see these tropical-looking humming-birds fluttering about amid the bowers and trees, that we know are doomed to be stripped of all their beauty by the icy terrors of the severe Canadian winter. But these little, delicate, diminutive winged "flowers of loveliness" migrate. They leave the winter behind them : those lovely, tiny, glittering wings bear the little feathered miniatures to the sunny south, to revel among magnolias and roses, when here all is snow or storm.

Though we had a very hot journey from Buffalo to New York, yet we had the advantage, for a considerable part of the way, of going through charmingly shadowy forests. Railroads in the United States are not like railroads in other countries, for they fly, plunging through the deep umbrageous recesses of these vasty, widely-spreading woods, whose sweeping verdure-loaded boughs, go arching and branching about the "cars" in all directions, shedding a deep, delicious, intensely-green light around, which bathes every thing and every body in a sea of molten emerald, and is excessively refreshing to the passengers' eyes, though eminently unbecoming to the said passengers' complexions ; for they all look there exactly as if they were playing at "snap dragon," and the very ruddiest, and most rubicund turn to a sort of livid, ghastly, plague-struck looking green ; but this may serve to give you an idea, peradventure (and, I assure you, not an exaggerated one), of the cool, and verdant, and deeply-tinted reflections from these overshadowing masses of forests.

Every thing in nature and art almost seems to flourish here. Schools, universities, manufactories, societies, institutions, appear spreading over the length and breath of the land, and all seem on such a gigantic scale here too ! Lakes, forests, rivers, electric telegraphs, hotels, conflagrations, inundations, rows, roads, accidents, tobacco, juleps, bowie knives, beards, pistols, &c. ! moderation or littleness appear not to belong to America, where Nature herself leads the way and seems to abhor both, showing an example of leviathanism in every thing, which the people appear well inclined to follow.

We were quite sorry to leave charming Fort Talbot. V—— intensely regretted the poultry, the pic-nics, the sweet pickaninnies, and the ponies, besides divers other bewitching delights ; and I lamented over my beauteous bower of old Greek lace, my splendid view of the lovely Lake Sea, and, above all, the kind friends who had made our sojourn there so exceedingly enjoyable.

We had an enchanting drive through the glorious forest on our return to Port Stanley in Mrs. A——'s carriage, Colonel A—— driving us. It was very different from the bumping, thumping, break-bone, and break-down vehicle we had made our last little journey in through those noble woods. By the time we got to Port Stanley the steamer was ready to start; and after inquiring concerning the health of our kind hostess at the hotel, we put ourselves on board the "London," under Captain Bawbee's obliging care. This singular name is pronounced Baby, which had a rather curious effect when you heard it addressed to a very manly-looking and tall person, which the captain of the good steamer "London" happened to be. Our voyage over, we stopped at Buffalo, which is situated at the northeast end of Lake Erie. It has altogether a commanding position as a place of business, being at the western extremity of the Erie Canal, and at the eastern termination of the navigation of those mighty lakes, Erie, Huron, and Michigan. The city is partly built on high ground, and commands extensive views of the Lake, Niagara River, and the Canadian shore. Its population is about forty thousand. Main-street is a very handsome street, more than two miles long, and 120 feet broad.

Buffalo has a court-house, a county clerk's office, a jail and two markets, in the upper story of one of which is to be found the common council chamber and city offices. There are about twenty churches, several banks, a theatre, and numerous very excellent and capacious hotels. The one we were at, the Western, was an exceedingly good one, and we experienced there the greatest civility and attention.

A pier, extending fifteen hundred feet, on the south side of the mouth of Buffalo Creek (which creek forms the harbor of Buffalo), constitutes a substantial breakwater for the protection of vessels from the furious gales occasionally experienced there. There is a handsome lighthouse, forty-six feet high, and twenty in diameter, placed at the head of the pier, built of a yellow-tinged lime-stone.

Buffalo, from the trading facilities it enjoys by the canal and railroad, in connection with the lake navigation, is a great commercial mart, that lake navigation having an extent of some thousands of miles. With Albany it has communication on the east by canal, and thence by a regular chain of railroads five hundred and twenty-five miles long, on with Boston. And on the northeast it is also connected by railroad with the Niagara Falls and Lewiston. What a mighty city will this most likely be twenty years hence!

We came from Albany in a rapid and beautiful steamer called the "Alida;" the day was almost insufferably hot, and the quantity of ice-water consumed by the passengers was truly prodigious. We took up some very military-looking students at West Point, from "the United States Military Academy" there. Their uniform was handsome, though very simple, and they were as upright as Prussian soldiers. The academy was established in 1802. There are, I understand, two stone barracks, a building for winter exercises, two hundred and seventy-five feet long; a Gothic building, one hundred and fifty feet long, with three towers for astronomical apparatus, and an observatory; a chapel, an hospital, a mess-hall; seventeen separate dwellings for officers connected with the institution; workshops, cavalry-stables, store-rooms, laboratory, and a magazine, with various other buildings, including twenty-five dwellings, for families belonging to the establishment. There is a monument on the grounds, erected to Kosciusko, by the cadets, at an expense of five thousand dollars. On the river bank is "Kosciusko's garden," whither the Polish chief was wont to retire for meditation or study.

West Point was one of the most important fortresses during the great Revolutionary War: it was considered the key of the country, as it commanded the river, which admitted vessels of heavy burden as far as Hudson, and hindered the English from holding communication with Canada. The English commanders, on this account, were very desirous of obtaining it, and its surrender was to have been the first fruit of the treason of Arnold; but in this he was balked by the arrest of the unfortunate Major André.

On the east shore, opposite to West Point, is "Constitution Island," where are the ruined remains of a fort, erected during the Revolution. A huge chain was extended from the island to West Point, to obstruct the passage of the river by the troops. Part of this identical chain is said to be shown now at West Point.

The scenery was extremely lovely all about there—the Hudson Highlands wearing all their sunny, summer beauty. One can hardly imagine that blackest of all demons, War, flinging his hideous shadow over such a charming, smiling, lovely prospect; but what scene of beauty or gracefulness does he ever respect?

A mile above West Point, is the "West Point Iron Foundry," which claims to be the most extensive establishment of the kind in the country. I think of going to Washington when this blazing weather moderates a little, taking, *en route*, Philadelphia and

Baltimore. The thermometer here and in the neighborhood has been 98° and 100°, they say, in the shade, and people declare it was never so hot in New York before—at least not for many years. At Albany we found the heat, if possible, more oppressive: not a breath of air seemed stirring. Suddenly we hailed with delight a gentle movement of the light muslin curtain round the window, indicating a soft wind. V—— rushed to the window to inhale it, but as speedily rushed back again, declaring it was as hot as the air of ten furnaces. The present is a broiling morning: a sky like a great turquoise roof *on fire*, a sun like a hundred suns, a breathless clear atmosphere, without the least dream of any thing that reminds you of air—and there is a thundering salute going on now (for what, I know not, unless they are saluting the sun, who certainly seems victorious over every thing and every body just now, striking down man and horse) which cruelly makes one think of "villainous saltpetre," and such hot compounds, when Wenham Lake ice, and the expedition to the North Pole, are the only fit and pleasant subjects for reflection at present.

---

## CHAPTER VI.

Boston—The Park—The Tremont Hotel—Its luxurious Appointments—Mr. and Mrs. Abbott Lawrence—The "Book of the World"—Description of Boston; The Bridges—Their Immense length—The Western Avenue—Boston Harbor—Anticipated Rejoicings on the Anniversary of American Independence—Boston Newspapers and Reviews—Supply of Water to the City—Its Docks and Wharves—Public Buildings—The State House—The Custom House—The Athenæum—The Exchange and Lowell Institute.—The crowded Stores—Constant Alarm of Fires.

On July 3d we arrived at Boston, and took up our quarters at the Tremont House.

Boston is a very handsome, very large, and very clean town, apparently kept in admirable order: it has a pretty little park, called by the modest name of "the Common," and a splendid State House, magnificently situated on Beacon Hill; this is a very imposing looking structure, and crowns the height superbly. The town reminds me of an English one in many respects, but yet more of a Dutch one.

To-morrow they have a grand commemorative festival, in honor of their independence, and we, poor English, must make up our minds to hear them "Yankee-doodling," and "Hail Columbia-ing," all day long. I shall shut myself up pretty closely on the occasion to save my feelings of nationality, especially as I have no idea of seeing "the Crown of England" burnt in a fire-work and consumed to ashes, as it is announced in a pompous advertisement it is going to be, for the pleasing recreation of Brother Jonathan. I hope, I must confess, that just at that moment it will rain in torrents, and put out their very impertinent and presumptuous pyrotechnics without loss of time: the English crown thus may not be consumed to a cinder after all.

It will be suspected that I am exceedingly wroth against said Brother Jonathan just now! but it is a spite and anger confined exclusively to the 4th of July! and on the 5th I shall be quite friends with him again; nay, I almost think my fury may be hushed before the 4th itself dawns; though, if what I hear is correct of the immense and noisy excitement in general through the whole night preceding "Independence day," the lullaby will be of a rather rough description! But our American cousins are such a good-humored, kindly-dispositioned people, that I think one could not well be sulky with them long. *Apropos* of noise—I believe, to keep our tempers a little, it would be a good plan to stuff our ears with cotton, and so be "*independent*," in our turn, of their uncivil serenadings, salutings, drummings, trumpetings, and fireworkings.

The Americans are very busy just now abusing the French for their Roman war: they call them cowards, and all sorts of hard names. As they are in this mood they might as well, for variety's sake burn the Gallic liberty-cap to-morrow instead of the crown of England. They are, evidently, very indignant at the anti-republican turn affairs are taking in France. However, France has become lately such a spinning, twisting-about, volcanic tee-to-tum, that who can guess what news the next steamer may bring out?

To-day is a beauteous day—not too hot, yet sunny-bright, and with a charming fresh breeze. We have comfortable, quiet, private apartments in this huge hotel: our drawing-room is a very nice one, and is quite away from all the bustle of visitors arriving and departing. The master, or rather masters (for there are two, if not more), are extremely civil; and the attendance is very good. Finger-posts are placed in some of the passages to direct bewildered and foot-sore wanderers to their own rooms. I think a few light omnibuses might run on the different lines of passage with much profit. Immense as the hotel is, our apartments are so secluded that we hear but little noise, and suffer no inconvenience whatever from the house being very full. I have not yet dined one day in public since my arrival in America—it must be extremely unpleasant for ladies.

We have made acquaintance with Mr. and Mrs. Abbott Lawrence (Mr. Bancroft was good enough to give me letters to them at Lady J——'s request, as I had not the pleasure of knowing him); they leave America in October. They are most kind and friendly; he is one of the great merchant princes of this wonderful land, and a very distinguished man; and Mrs. Lawrence appears to be every thing that is amiable and kind. Mr. Lawrence has just given me a very interesting book, called "The Book of the World:" it is replete with information, and is written nearly up to the present day, and it really seems to be almost what it *calls itself*, which is a pretty "considerable deal."

This good city of Boston is connected with the surrounding country by bridges and artificial avenues, being built upon a peninsula of nearly three miles in length, with an average breadth of a mile, and with many elevations from fifty to one hundred and ten feet above the sea, giving the city a remarkably noble appearance, particularly, I am told when beheld from the sea, which view of it I have not yet seen. The population is one hundred and twenty-five thousand. Its Indian name was Shawmut, but the first settlers called it Trimountain, from the three hills on which it is built.

Boston communicates with East Boston (formerly Noddle's Island) and Chelsea by means of steam ferry-boats, which ply regularly during the day. Among the most peculiar curiosities of the place are the bridges, which differ in their construction from any thing of their kind elsewhere, and their immense length and the lovely views they present, make them very interesting and attractive, especially to foreigners. With Roxbury, Boston is connected by the neck which forms the peninsula on which the city is built. With Charlestown it is united by the Charles River, or Old Charlestown Bridge, and by Warren Bridge. The former is one thousand four hundred and three feet long, forty-two in breadth, and cost more than fifty thousand dollars. Warren Bridge is one thousand three hundred and ninety feet; breadth, forty-five. No toll is taken on these bridges: there was one formerly; but on their becoming state property it was done away with.

West Boston Bridge, leading to Old Cambridge, rests on one hundred and eighty piers, and, with causeway and abutments, is six thousand one hundred and ninety feet long. Craigie's or Canal Bridge, leading to Lechmere Point, in East Cambridge, is two thousand seven hundred and ninety-six feet long and forty feet broad: a branch extends from it to Prison Point, Charlestown, one thousand eight hundred and twenty feet long, and thirty-five feet wide. The western avenue or mill-dam reaches from the foot of Beacon-street to Sewell's Point in Brookline. It is strongly constructed of stones and earth, and is a mile and a half long, and from sixty to one hundred feet broad.

This incloses about six hundred acres of flats, over which formerly the tide flowed. This inclosure is divided by a cross dam, which, aided by flood and ebb-gates, forms a receiving basin, producing thereby a great extent of water-power at all periods. This work cost about seven hundred thousand dollars. Boston Free Bridge, to South Boston, is five hundred feet long, thirty-eight wide. South Boston Bridge, leading from the "Neck" to South Boston, is one thousand five hundred and fifty feet long; width forty feet.* They are all well lighted by lamps, and in addition to them, numerous as they are, there are various railroad bridges or viaducts over the river. Does not Boston deserve to be called the City of Bridges?

It possesses one of the best harbors in the United States. The harbor extends from Nantasket to the city, and spreads from Nahant to Hingham, containing seventy-five square miles: it contains many islands, among them some beautiful ones: it is safe and spacious. The inner harbor has a depth of water sufficient for five hundred vessels of the largest class to ride at anchor in safety, with so narrow an entrance as scarcely to admit two ships abreast. Boston consists of three parts: Boston on the Peninsula, South Boston, and East Boston. The "Neck," or Isthmus, which formerly constituted the only connection of the Peninsula with the main land, still forms the main avenue to the city from the south. Boston harbor is defended by forts Independence and Warren, the latter of which is on Governor Island, and the former on Castle Island. The outside harbor is protected by a strong fortress on George's Island.

Of course sight-seeing to-morrow is out of the question, and from the moment when the sun rises on seas of sherry-cobblers and cataracts of mint-juleps, miles of flags, wildnernesses of crackers, pyramids of edibles, mountains of lollypops, and monster-trains, and legions

* These figures are taken from "Appleton's Railway Companion."

of little boys (and little girls, too, if my information be correct), who, I hear, generally shoot with pistols at friend, or foe, or each other, during the day, and frequently end by maiming themselves severely—there will be no peace in Boston. But though I did not like their promised entertainment of fireworks, yet, when I recollect how abominably ill England behaved before she forced this country into a revolution, I can—nationality notwithstanding—rejoice with them a little in their joy at the return of the Anniversary of their Independence, and feel a slight something of their exuberant exultation, and, therefore, not only endure philosophically, but greet cordially, their festive demonstrations—except the fireworks and that thrice villainous and atrocious device. They stick in my throat terribly. I wonder whether it will rain to-morrow evening!

In my transatlantic travels, I do not feel so far away from home as I thought I should; the Cunard steamers are so regular and rapid in their passage, they are now generally here to the day they are expected. What a fast age we live in!

The American newspapers amuse me much; they are so unlike any thing else of their kind. There are thirty-six newspapers published here, of which twelve are daily, the rest are semi-weekly and weekly. In addition to these, there are a good many reviews and magazines. "The North American Review" is, I believe, the most distinguished of the former.

Boston is capitally provided with water from Long Pond, now named Cochituate Lake. This lake covers an area of six hundred and fifty-nine acres, and drains a surface of eleven thousand four hundred acres. In some places it is seventy feet deep, and is elevated one hundred and twenty-four feet above tide-water in Boston harbor: the Boston reservoir, situated on Beacon-hill, covers an area of forty thousand feet. The water is brought in an oval aqueduct, in height six feet four inches, and five feet in width, laid in brick (with the hydraulic cement), about fourteen miles and a half from Cochituate Lake to Brookline, where it discharges itself into a reservoir of thirty acres in extent.

The water from Brookline is forced by its own pressure through pipes of thirty and thirty-five inches in diameter, to the two reservoirs in the city; that on Mount Washington, at South-Boston, which will contain a superficies of seventy thousand, and that on Beacon Hill, of thirty-eight thousand feet. When full, the latter will contain three millions of gallons. These reservoirs will deliver to the city of Boston ten millions of gallons a day of the purest and best water. Wise Bostonians!

The entire cost of the construction I have heard will probably fall within three millions of dollars. Wise Bostonians! I say again: they will probably save that much in drugs and medicine ere many years pass over their heads. The doctors must be the only people who will suffer from this liberal supply of the pure element.

The docks and wharves surrounding the city form one of its distinctive features. There are about two hundred of them. Long Wharf is one thousand eight hundred feet long, and two hundred feet wide, and contains seventy-six spacious stores. There are numbers of fine public buildings here. The State House is among the finest: its foundation is one hundred and ten feet above the level of the sea. From the dome there is a splendid view of the city, the bay, with its lovely islands, and the wide expanse of surrounding country: the Bostonians boast that it is one of the finest views in the Union, if not in the world. The last is saying too much. Here the State Legislature holds its annual session.

The new Custom House is handsome: it is in the form of a cross, and has very superb porticoes. The Court House is a fine building: the material is Quincy granite. The Athenæum, in Beacon-street, has a library of about forty-five thousand volumes, and a rich cabinet of coins, medals, &c. The Exchange is a fine structure; it was finished in 1842. The Lowell Institute was founded by a Mr. Lowell, who died at Bombay, in 1836. He bequeathed about two hundred and fifty thousand dollars for the support of regular courses of popular and scientific lectures: by his will he provides for the maintenance and support of public lectures on natural and revealed religion, physics, chemistry, with their applications to the arts, geology, botany, and other useful and interesting subjects. These lectures are all free; they are delivered from October to April, during which period four or five courses (of twelve lectures each) are usually delivered.

This town has a multitude of stores teeming with goods of every description, which are actually running over from their crammed and loaded shelves and counters, and often blockade the foot-pavements: they told us the people were so honest, that those unprotected goods, literally thrown at their feet, were never carried off; but I have seen complaints of the custom in the papers occasionally—accounts, not of shop-lifting exactly, but side-walk-lifting, with observations as to the impropriety of thus almost tempting poor people to be dishonest. I recollect when I first visited Genoa, thinking art and fancy seemed to overflow there from the very windows of its stately palaces, so gorgeous were the richly-coloured paintings of saints, historical personages, and other subjects on their walls. Here more suitably to the character of the people, it is industry and utilitarianism that can hardly be contained within bounds and limits.

There are constant alarms of fires here. I think hardly a night has passed, without our hearing the engines going full speed somewhere or other; but in general it proves a false alarm, and after posting along in "hot haste," on finding all cool and quiet where they were bound to, they come deliberately back, to make the same little "promenade" again on the following night.

The first night, V—— and I were quite anxious to ascertain where the dreadful fire could be, for the engines went thundering through the streets at a terrific pace, making a prodigious noise: we soon found that we might sit up all night, and every night at Boston, if we paid any attention to these gad-about engines taking their gallops about every half-hour.

## CHAPTER VII.

Plans for the Future—Musical Taste of the New Englanders—Cholera in New York—Transparency of the American Atmosphere—American Newspapers—Their Personalities—A signal Instance—Mrs. S. M—— of New York and her Family—Miss G—— of Boston—The Loud Talking ascribed to American Ladies—The Town of Gloucester—Its Trade.

On the 27th July we came to Cape Ann Pavilion, Gloucester, Massachusetts. The place is truly charming. The hotel is almost in the sea, like a very huge and gayly-decorated bathing machine—(the only one here by the way!) There is a wide, beautiful covered veranda all round the house; then comes a *wee* narrow strip of beach, then a low stone wall, some rocks, and then the Atlantic, so close, that I can not imagine the house can be quite safe in winter, unless they intend to strengthen and heighten the defensive wall. The hotel is quite new. It may be imagined how clean, and fresh, and nice it is.

As to traveling about, and seeing sights, in so hot a climate as America is in the summer, it is out of the question, I find; but, this I believe is an unusually hot summer—the hottest, I am told, but one, they have had for twenty-four years. I think of staying quietly at the sea, till summer is over, and it is safe and pleasant to travel; of course, this will necessarily prolong my stay: every body assures me I must not think of going southward till October, particularly this year, considering cholera and the great heat.

I think we have fortunately found a very quiet and healthy spot here. I was going to Newport, but heard of this being so very nice, that I thought I would try it first, and I think I shall remain here for some time. We have delightful rooms on the ground floor, opening on the sea. It is very much like being afloat in a line-of-battle ship, we are so close to the grand old Atlantic.

The New Englanders appear to me generally a very quiet people, and very fond of music: we hear them playing and singing a great deal. Some of them sing exceedingly well, too, airs out of Italian operas, &c. They have a good piano-forte in the ladies' public drawing-room, which has plenty of work on its hands, or rather plenty of hands on its keys from morning till night. They have an excellent piano-forte maker at Boston named Chickering.

I hear from New York of a sad increase of cholera in that city. My correspondent, poor Mrs. Barclay, who writes in evident low spirits, tells me of the death of some of their friends from this terrible disease: one of her own family had had it slightly. I believe the wisest thing to do is to dismiss the subject from the mind as much as possible, putting one's whole trust where safety and protection can alone be found. At the same time, of course, it is right to be properly prepared, and to use the necessary remedies at the very first moment of alarm, and to be prudent and careful in diet. From all I can learn of the spread of cholera on this side of the Atlantic, I believe most of the fatal cases arise from carelessness and neglect at first, and total disregard of the premonitory symptoms.

The weather is lovely in this delectable place. I think the atmosphere in America is much like that in beauteous Italy, it is so exquisitely clear and transparent. Thus the grand features of this country are presented to the eye through a lovely lucid medium, and it is indeed a country of "magnificent distances," as some one named its unfinished capital. As yet, however, we have seen but little of it, and that little seems less when we recollect *how much* there is to be seen.

Pine-apples and newspapers are rather cheap here! The first (and *fine* ones) at a penny apiece (owing a good deal to the prevalence of cholera, which makes people afraid of eating them), and the second, I am told, many of them at a *half-penny* (English)—these are of course small, but really sometimes full of information and news. Some of their most distinguished papers are admirably written, and replete with varied and extensive information and tidings from all the corners of the earth; there seems in general in their tone, I think, more heartiness of feeling and more freshness and originality than in ours. What I do not like in the daily American press, is the perpetual and sometimes puerile and paltry attempts at wit and humor, which they seem to think indispensable, whether in season or out of season. They sometimes mingle this often rather ponderous pleasantry with the most serious accounts of accidents and disasters. Then their abuse of the authorities and people in office is beyond all idea violent. In the opposition papers, the most unmerciful vituperations are poured forth against some of their most eminent men; *really* if you did not see their names you would sometimes think they were speaking of the most atrocious criminals. It might almost make one imagine that three-quarters of the population are in a state of perpetual irritation and disappointment at not being President themselves, or at least, Secretary of State.

Taylor is one of the most popular of men, and all seem to be proud of, as well as attached to, their far-famed "Old Zack;" yet I have seen such epithets as these applied to him in their public prints—"Journeyman butcher," "Moloch," "Monster," "Nero," "Tyrant," "Ignominious cheat," "No three men could be found on a jury to credit him on his oath," "dolt," "tool," "fool," "cipher," "Cyclops," "fly on a coach wheel," "disgrace to the country," &c. Still this is only an ebullition of, perhaps, quite transitory wrath; and the next day their good "Old Zack" will be forgiven.

We have made acquaintance with a very agreeable lady here, Mrs. S. M——, of New York. She has charming unaffected manners, and appears to be very accomplished: she sings remarkably well, and has a handsome Italian-looking face. Her husband and daughter in-law are here with her; the latter, I believe, older than herself. Her little grandson-in-law is a pretty, dark child, and his youthful grandmamma appears excessively attached to him. A friend of Mrs. M——'s, a Miss G——, of Boston, is one of the loveliest young American ladies I have yet seen: she is fair, and a little reminds me of our own beautiful Lady C. V——, in the cast of her countenance and the line of feature. She looks particularly pretty in the *bathing* hat, a large Swiss-looking straw hat which she sometimes wears also out walking. She appears to have the softest and sweetest manners imaginable; and all she does and says seems characterized by extreme grace and gentleness.

There is no loud talking and constant giggling, of which travelers have so often accused American young ladies, and which, I believe, wherever it is to be found, is greatly owing to their being partly educated at large public schools, which, perhaps, gives them a habit of pitching their voice high, in order to make themselves heard among numbers. I am happy to say I have not yet met with any who have that unrefined disagreeable habit.

The town of Gloucester, where we are, has a population of about six thousand: its trade is entirely maritime. The harbor is reckoned one of the finest on the whole coast of the Atlantic. The town contains seven churches and various public buildings; the inhabitants are mostly employed in the halibut, cod, and mackerel fisheries; and there are about seventeen thousand tons of shipping here. Quite a little navy (chiefly from Newfoundland station) came in the other day to take shelter in the harbor from a gale at sea. If it is true that Newport is very foggy, which I am told it is, I think this must be a far preferable place of summer residence. Colonel Green and his lady called on me the other day. He is the accomplished editor of an excellent Boston paper.

---

## CHAPTER VIII

Return to Boston—Fire Engines and their Horses—The Cradle of American Liberty—Faneuil Hall—Boston Prohibition of Street-smoking—Statue of Washington in the State House—Anecdote connected with it—A Drum preserved in the State House—Visit to Cambridge—Mount Auburn—Harvard University—Professors Pierce, Silliman, Guyon, Sparks, and Agassiz—Live Coral Insects preserved by Professor Agassiz—Reflections suggested by them—Museum of Professor Agassiz.

The weather on this 16th of August, is very pleasant at Boston. I hear it *has been* terribly oppressive, and we were fortunate to be at charming, breezy Cape Ann.

I was surprised the other day at my nephew-in-law, E. W——, suddenly making his appearance here. He is going to visit Newport *instanter*, and then is off to Canada. He introduced the other day a friend of his to me, Mr. C. S——, a most agreeable and highly-informed person.

The thunder-storms have been as rare in America as in England this year: we had one however, the night before last. I hope it will do good, and clear away the cholera a little.

We had a disagreeable little fright some time ago here, occasioned by the passage being on fire close to V——'s room (it was owing to something wrong about the gas-pipes). It was early in the night fortunately, and as I thought most likely some of the numerous fire-engines would be within call, taking their usual constitutional walk or canter (in short, taking the air if there was no fire to take), I did not feel much trepidation. The fire was easily overcome, and thereafter I felt for some time more secure than usual, thinking that for a fortnight or more people would be particularly careful hereabout concerning fire, in consequence of this little warning, and that I should hear those fidgety engines at exercise without much apprehension of their being called into requisition by us.

By the way, there is a team of ghostly-looking white horses attached to one of these engines, that truly seem to have no repose. Like the restless phantoms of wicked horses, they haunt the streets at the witching hour of night, and seem to wander over the face of the granite city, without object or aim, as if disturbed in their graves by the proximity of so many railroads here, and feeling, like *Othello*, their "occupation gone"—at least that of their fellows.

I saw the other day the place where the first blood was shed in the great Revolution—the righteous Revolution, if ever there was one deserving to be so called; yet my English feelings make me dislike always to dwell on the details of it. Faneuil Hall is the American cradle of liberty. Would the reader like a slight sketch of the cot where so sturdy and chopping an infant first began to crow and squall? This, in America, universally-venerated structure has stood for about one hundred and nine years, and was presented to the city of Boston by Peter Faneuil, a respected merchant. Here the chiefs of the Revolution harangued the people in those troublous and perilous times, and here often some of the most distinguished orators of America pour forth the living fire of their eloquence.

It is a large building, but not architecturally remarkable. The lower story is occupied by stores. The hall on the second story is seventy-six feet square and twenty-eight high, having galleries on three sides, supported by two ranges of Ionic columns. Portraits of Washington and Mr. Faneuil hang on the walls. Above this hall is one of about the same dimensions, devoted to military exercises.

There is a regulation here that reminded me of Vienna. People are not permitted to smoke in the streets. (I know not whether this is still in force at Vienna, after the various changes there.) This they appear to submit very patiently and unmurmuringly to, albeit the Cradle of Liberty lifts its protecting walls so near them.

The State House, on its noble site, with its handsome dome, is very striking; its colonnade is fine. There is an excellent statue of Washington in the large hall: it is enveloped in folds of massive drapery, and so easily do the graceful robes hang, that it is related of a countrywoman coming one day to see it, that she exclaimed she could not judge of the statue till they "tuk that sorter sheet off of it." It was a more natural mistake than that of a purblind lady visiting at ——, who, on entering the hall, gazed with respectful admiration at the representation of an Egyptian mummy, and it was found afterward she had imagined it to be a former Bishop of Norwich in his full canonicals, and as such thought it a remarkable likeness, and a work of great excellence!

In the interior of the State House are the two chambers of the Legislature. The House of Representatives has accommodation for about four hundred persons, and the Senate-chamber is rather smaller. An ancient drum is to be seen there taken in one of the earlier revolutionary battles: did it hear the glorious words Mr. Webster once spoke, concerning its brother-drums of Britain? If it did, I marvel almost it did not burst out into an extemporaneous and self-beating rub-a-dub in echo to those noble, generous, and spirit-stirring strains; if a drum had a heart in its skin, it would surely have done so. "England, the beat of whose drum, keeping company with the hours," &c.,—would that my memory could serve me to repeat some of this eloquent outburst—but, alas! I am far from sure that even these few words are correct.

The first time we went to Cambridge we went to see our amiable friends Mrs. and Miss Everett. They are in the President's house, and are to continue there for the present. After sitting a little while with Mrs. Everett, we went with Mr. and Miss Everett, in their carriage to Mount Auburn, the spacious and beautiful cemetery. The finely diversified grounds occupy about one hundred acres, in general profusely adorned with a rich variety of trees, and in some places planted with ornamental shrubbery: there are some tombs graced with charming flower-beds. There are also some pretty sheets of water there: it is divided into different avenues and paths, which have various names. Generally they are called after the trees or flowers that abound there, such as lily, poplar, cypress, violet, woodbine, and others. It is, indeed, a beauteous city for the dead. The birds were singing most mellifluously and merrily—it was quite a din of music that they kept up in these solemn but lovely shades. The views from Mount Auburn are fine and extensive. There are some graceful and well-executed monuments within its precincts.

Afterward we went with Mr. Everett to see a little of the colleges, and then visited the mineralogical cabinet. Harvard University is the most ancient, and is reckoned the best endowed institution in the Union. It was founded in 1638, and from a donation made to it by the Rev. John Harvard it was called after him. We paid a brief visit to the great telescope, merely to look at it, however, and not through it, for it was then dull, and very cloudy, with no prospect of its being otherwise during the evening —it is a refracting telescope. Mr. Bond himself was not there, but his son was, who is already a distinguished and enthusiastic astronomer. Mr. Bond, senior, was one of the discoverers of the eighth satellite of Saturn.

Another time we went to the *soirée*, which Mr. and Mrs. Everett gave on the occasion of the meeting of the American Association of Science at Cambridge.

There I saw, of course, many learned celebrities. Among them—Professor Pierce, Professor Silliman, Professor Guyon, Professor Sparks (the new President of Harvard University), and Professor Agassiz, the celebrated naturalist (I found he was a cousin of my old governess, Mademoiselle Anne Agassiz).

This very distinguished man—one of the great contributors to the world's stores of science and knowledge—is an extremely agreeable member of society, and a very popular one. His manners are particularly frank, pleasing, cordial, and simple; and though deeply absorbed, and intensely interested in his laborious scientific researches, and a most thorough enthusiast in his study of natural philosophy, yet he rattled merrily away on many of the various light topics of the day with the utmost gayety, good-humor, and spirit.

He has succeeded, after great trouble and persevering indefatigable care, in preserving alive some coral insects, the first that have ever been so preserved, and he kindly promised me an introduction to those distinguished architects. We accordingly went, accompanied by Mr. Everett, the following day. M. Agassiz was up-stairs very much occupied by some scientific investigation of importance, and he could not come down, but he allowed us to enter the all but hallowed precincts devoted to the much-cherished coral insects.

M. Agassiz had been away a little while previously, and left these treasures of his heart under the charge and superintendence of his assistant. This poor care-worn attendant, we were told, almost lost his own life in preserving the valuable existence of these little moving threads, so much did he feel the weighty responsibility that devolved upon him, and with such intense anxiety did he watch the complexion, the contortions, all the twistings and twirlings, and twitchings, and flingings and writhings of the wondrous little creatures, and assiduously marking any indications of *petite santé* among them. They were kept in water carefully and frequently changed, and various precautions were indispensably necessary to be taken in order to guard their exquisitely delicate demi-semi existences.

Glad enough was the temporary gentleman-in-waiting, and squire-of-the-body to these interesting zoophytes to see M. Agassiz return, and to resign his charge into his hands. With him this exceeding care and watchfulness was indeed nothing but a labor of love, and probably no nurse or mother ever fondled a weakly infant with more devoted tenderness and anxious attention than M. Agassiz displayed toward his dearly-beloved coral insects.

As to me, I hardly dared breathe while looking at them for fear I should blow their precious lives away, or some catastrophe should happen while we were there, and we should be suspected of *coralicide!* However, the sight was most interesting. We watched them as they flung about what seemed their fire-like white arms, like microscopic opera dancers or windmills; but these apparent arms are, I believe, all they possess of bodies. How wonderful to think of the mighty works that have been performed by the fellow-insects of these little restless laborers. What are the builders of the Pyramids to them? What did the writers of the "Arabian Nights" imagine equal to their more magical achievements? Will men ever keep coral insects by them to lay the foundations of a few islands and continents when the population grows too large for the earthy portion of earth? People keep silkworms to spin that beautiful fabric for them: and M. Agassiz has shown there is no impracticability. I looked at the large bowl containing the weird workers with unflagging interest, till I could almost fancy minute reefs of rock were rising up in the basin.

What a world of marvels we live in, and alas that the splendid wonders of science should be shut out from so many myriads of mankind; for that the marvelous is inalienably dear to human nature, witness all the fairy tales, ghost stories, and superstitions of all kinds that have abounded and been popular from age to age. Penny Magazines and such works have done much, but much there remains to be done to bring the subjects not only within reach, but to make them more universally popular and attractive, and less technical.

At last we took leave of those marine curiosities, and wended our way back, sorry not to have seen M. Agassiz (who was still absorbed in dissecting or pickling for immortality some extraordinary fish that he had discovered), but delighted to have had the opportunity of seeing his *protégés.*

"M. Agassiz ought indeed to have an extensive museum," said —— "for I believe every body in the States makes a point of sending off to him, post haste, every imaginable reptile, and monster, and nondescript that they happen to find." I should, assuredly not like to have the opening of his letters and parcels if that is the case.

---

## CHAPTER IX.

Plymouth—The Pilgrim Fathers—Mrs. Warren, a Descendant of one of the Pilgrims—Visit from Mr. Prescott the Historian—Graves of the Pilgrim Fathers—Visits from Daniel Webster and from Mr. N. P. Willis—Samoset the Indian Chief—Energy of the Pilgrim Fathers—Altered Face of their Country.

We have come to famous Old Plymouth, to see the interesting spot where the first Pilgrim Fathers landed. We paid a visit to the rock which it is said their feet first touched: it has been conveyed to the centre of the village. Here they landed after their perilous voyage in the "Mayflower," on the 22d of December, 1620. Plymouth boasts of being the first town built by civilized beings in New England. The inhabitants celebrate the interesting anniversary of the landing every year.

We visited one of the lineal descendants of the pilgrims, soon after our arrival here. Mrs. Warren is the mother of Judge Warren (with whom we went); she is a most charming, delightful old lady, with the most gentle, amiable, and polished manners imaginable; her house was as delightful as herself! and was, I believe, certainly one of the original houses built by the Pilgrim Fathers. Mrs. Warren seated me on a precious old-fashioned chair, that actually had come over in the "Mayflower." I fancy there are pseudo-Mayflower chairs enough in various parts of Massachusetts to set up a score of upholsterers in business; but this, there is no doubt, really came over with the venerable voyagers, as it belonged to the descendant of one of the earliest governors. There were a number of old family pictures in the room, some of them by Copley, father of our greatly-distinguished Lord Lyndhurst (who was born, I think, in Boston).

I had the great pleasure of a visit from Mr. Prescott before I left Boston; he came from Nahant to see me with his daughter. I was delighted to have an opportunity of making acquaintance with this justly celebrated historian, whose works I had read with such lively interest. Even by the side of his handsome (and, by the way, very English-looking) daughter, he still looks quite a young man, and he seems to have a flow of spirits equal to those of Lord Stanley: there is not a particle of pomposity about him, and his style of conversation is of the most fresh, original, agreeable, and striking kind; and with all his stores of learning, and varied knowledge, there is the most complete absence possible of any thing approaching to pedantry. His eyesight is, unfortunately, defective, but no one would observe this in society.

He appeared rather absent. A short time after he had taken leave and left the room with his daughter, we heard a knock at the door; on saying, "come in," Mr. Prescott appeared again, and said he had left his cane there. He looked, and we looked, chairs were inspected, sofas pushed about, and tables trotted out from their places, when presently I heard a subdued exclamation from Mr. Prescott, who had found the cane—in his hand, where I certainly did not think of looking for it. He laughed good-humoredly at his forgetfulness, and he and his cane vanished presently together.

We have visited the church-yard here, which contains some interesting graves of the old Pilgrims. Altogether, there is much to attract and to please in Plymouth, and I am very glad I came here.

I have just seen that great man, Mr. Webster, and also Mrs. Webster who, I find, are now staying in this hotel. He is a friend of my father's; but as I was abroad when he was at Belvoir Castle, I had never before seen him. I was, as every body must be, I should think, very much struck by his magnificent countenance—that prodigiously massive brow, those mighty eyes, that seem as if they were calmly looking down the depths of ages, and that grand air of *repose* (which especially appeared to me to characterize his aspect) have a sort of quiet *mountainous* grandeur about them that makes one think, that old Homer, had he not been blind, might so have looked, or the awful son of Cœlus and Terra! His features have more, I think, of the Oriental than the Occidental cast; but then you seldom see so much intellect in an Eastern countenance. It is, indeed, a very un-American face, for their features are ordinarily rather sharp and delicate.

Mr. and Mrs. Webster have kindly asked me to go to Green Harbor; the invitation was most cordial and friendly. "Come, pray, and remain there as long as you can—we shall do all we can to make your stay agreeable," &c. I look forward very much to going and seeing this great man in his own house. I hear he occupies himself much with farming and various country pursuits.

I am afraid there will be no change in American policy with regard to protection. The South are for free trade, and if they can carry the day they will have it.

I have just had a very agreeable visit from Mr. N. P. Willis. V—— was highly delighted to see this well known and popular American author, of whom she had often heard. I hope to see Mrs. Willis to-morrow; she is the niece and adopted daughter of Mr. Grinnell, brother to the Mr. Grinnell to whom I have letters from Mr. C——.

There are six churches in this small town, and two academies. The hotel is called Samoset House, after the friendly Indian chief whom the settlers found here in the olden time. It sounds so like Somerset that I begin to think my cousin the Duke of Beaufort must claim some very distant relationship with this old chieftain of Massachusetts, and we, of course, too! I remember finding something like traces of the De Rooses in Africa: so at this rate, it seems, I shall establish very amicable relations of my own between far-apart and widely extended countries. I believe there is some curious tradition of this identical old Samoset accosting the newly-arrived pilgrims with some words of broken English; but I do not exactly recollect the story.

What energy and determination those old Pilgrim Fathers showed, and the poor Pilgrim mothers too (who, as some one justly observed the other day, seemed usually consigned to an unmerited oblivion). What hardships and heart-quakings must they not have gone through when all this now cheerful and cultivated and inhabited country, with its profusion of towns and villages, and its multiplicity of railways, was one huge wild-waving pine forest! Fancy their surprise if they could look upon it *now;* and the iron trains, and the electric telegraphs, and their dandy, French-costumed, mustached sons, and their polka-dancing daughters; what would great-grandmamma think of that? Mrs. Hemans's lovely lines on the Landing of the Pilgrim Fathers, and the beautiful music poor Mrs. Arkwright wedded to them, have often lately recurred to my memory!

---

## CHAPTER X.

Green Harbor, the seat of Daniel Webster—His Guests—Description of his Mansion—The Militia General—Enterprise of American Lady-travelers—An instance—Mrs. C—— from China—Great intellectual Powers of Mr. Webster—A Storm—"My Kingdom for a Pin"—Anecdote of Lady ———The sole American with an aristocratic Title—Extraordinary Popularity of Mr. Webster in New England—Anecdote of Mr. Webster—That Statesman and Mr. Clay never Presidents of the United States—A Cause assigned—Appointment of illiterate political Postmasters—Mode of Living at Green Harbor.

We have been much charmed with our visit to Green Harbor, Marshfield, the beautiful domain of Mr. Webster. It is a charming and particularly enjoyable place, almost close to the sea. The beach here is something marvelous, eight miles in breadth, and of splendid hard floor-like sand, and when this is covered by the rolling Atlantic, the waves all but come up to the neighboring green, grassy fields. Very high tides cover them.

There is a very agreeable party in the house, including Mr. and Miss Everett, &c., and in addition to the guests here, those staying at Mr. F. Webster's (Mr. Webster's son) generally assemble here in the evening; among them was Miss S——. She was an exceedingly pleasant and agreeable young lady, full of life, spirits, information, and good-humor, joined to mild and amiable manners. Miss F—— was another very pleasing specimen of an accomplished American young lady.

This house is very prettily fitted up. It strikes me as being partly in the English and partly in the French style, exceedingly comfortable, and with a number of remarkably pretty drawing-rooms opening into one another, which always is a judicious arrangement I think; it makes a party agreeable and unformal. There are a variety of pictures and busts by American artists, and some of them are exceedingly good. There is a picture in the chief drawing room of Mr. Webster's gallant son who was killed in the Mexican war. The two greatest of America's statesmen each lost a son in that war, Mr. Clay and Mr. Webster. There is also a fine picture of Mr. Webster himself, which, however, though a masterly painting, does not do justice to the distinguished original. It was executed some years ago; but I really think it is not so handsome as the great statesman is now, with his Olympus-like brow, on which are throned such divinities of thought, and with that wonderful countenance of might and majesty.

The dining-room here is a charming apartment with all its windows opening to the ground, looking on the garden; and it is deliciously cool, protected from the sun by the overshadowing masses of foliage of the most magnificent weeping (American) elms. These colossal trees stand just before the house, and are pre-eminently beautiful: they seem to unite in their own gigantic persons the exquisite and exceeding grace of the weeping willow, with the strength and grandeur of the towering elm. I was told a curious fact last night. Every where, through the length and breadth of the States, the sycamore trees this year are blighted and dying.

The walls of the dining-room are adorned chiefly with English engravings, among which there is one of my father. My bedroom is profusely decorated with prints of different English country houses and castles. The utmost good taste and refinement are perceptible in the arrangements of the house, and a most enchanting place of residence it is. All the domestics of the house are colored persons, which is very seldom indeed the case in this part of the United States. Mr. Webster tells me he considers them the best possible servants, much attached, contented and grateful, and he added, he would "fearlessly trust them with *untold gold*." They certainly must be good ones to judge by the exquisite neatness and order of every thing in the establishment.

Mr. Webster's farm here consists of one thousand five hundred acres: he has a hundred head of cattle.

Mr. F. Webster has been a good deal in India, and he was mentioning the other evening that he was struck, in several of the English schools in that country, by the tone of some political lessons that were taught there. For instance, with regard to freedom and representation of the people, &c.; the natives were forcibly reminded of their own unrepresented state, by questions bearing on the subject—the United States being instanced as an example of almost universal suffrage; Great Britain itself of a less extensive elective franchise; France, of whatever France was then; and Hindostan *especially* pointed out as having nothing of the kind, as if they really wished to make the poor Hindoos discontented with their present state. To be sure, they might as well go to Persia and Turkey for their examples. Mr. F. Webster seemed to think the Hindoos were beginning a little to turn their thoughts to such political subjects.

While we were at dinner a day or two ago, a new guest, who had arrived rather late from New York, walked in, being announced as a general. He was a very military looking man indeed with a formidable pair of mustaches. Some turn in the conversation reminding me of the Mexican war, I asked if General —— had served in Mexico. Mr. —— laughed, and told me he was in the militia, and had never smelt powder in his life.

What enterprising travelers American ladies sometimes are! My Atlantic-crossing performances seem very little in comparison with some of their expeditions. It would not surprise me that any who have ever gone to settle in the far-off portions of the country, and been doomed to undergo such rugged experiences as those described in the American work (by a lady) called "A new Home, Who 'll·Follow?" should laugh at hardships and discomforts which might reasonably perhaps deter less seasoned and experienced travelers; but it must be a very different case with those habituated only to refinements and luxuries. Mr. Webster had told me he had expected for some little time past the arrival of a lady, a relative of his, who had lately left China for the United States; she was to leave her husband in the Celestial flowery land, her intention being, I believe, to see her relatives and friends at home, and then to rejoin him in the course of some months in China.

Like the gallant chieftain spoken of before, she arrived late, and during dinner the doors were thown open and "Mrs. P——, from China," was announced. She came in, and met her relatives and friends, as quietly as if she had merely made a "petite promenade de quinze jours" (as the French boasted they should do when they went to besiege Antwerp). She seated herself at table, when a few questions were asked relative to her voyage.

"Had you a good passage?"

"Very—altogether."

"How long?"

"About one hundred and three days" (I think this is correct, but I can not answer to a day).

"Pleasant companions?"

"Very much so, and with books the time passed very agreeably."

All this was as quietly discussed as if the passage had been from Dover to Boulogne, and the length of the time of absence a fortnight.

American ladies, perhaps, on the whole, do not travel about as much as we do, but when they do set about it, the uttermost ends of the earth seem scarcely to alarm them. The fact is, I think, that foreign travel to American ladies is rather a different thing to what it is with us. Living so close, comparatively speaking, to all the most interesting places in the world—Italy, with its countless associations and glories of art—Switzerland, with its crown of mountains and enchanting scenery, and other classic lands—we can so easily and so quickly indulge ourselves with these glorious and interesting spectacles; but if our transatlantic sister wishes to gaze on the time-honored monuments and transcendent works of art of Old Imperial Rome, or the magical enchantments of Naples, or the Arabian-Night-like glories of the Alhambra and Granada; or to speed to that Mecca of the Americans—Paris; there rolls the broad Atlantic, and she must prepare for the fatigues of a regular sea voyage before she can hope to accomplish it. Thus their ideas of foreign travel are necessarily more comprehensive, and, perhaps more expansive than ours. Without doubt, after crossing the Atlantic the Pacific becomes less formidable; but I need not talk of foreign travel, when part of their own America—California—is at such a mighty distance from them.

"Mrs. P——, from China," I found to be a delightful person, and I was excessively interested in many things she told me during a long conversation we had in the evening. Some of her accounts of Chinese proceedings amused me greatly. Together with other things, she told me that at Canton, among the crowded population who live in boats, it was a regular custom, as soon as a boy could crawl about on his hands and knees, to fasten carefully around his head a sort of life-preserving apparatus, in case little Master Chinaman should, when occasionally left to his own inventions, pop overboard, and the brother of the sun and moon lose a valuable subject. But no such tender precautions are ever taken with regard to the poor little Celestial misses. Their brows and waists are left unbound by the guardian bladder, and if they become a morsel for the fishes, so much the better for the finny *bon-vivant*, and also for the affectionate parental *non*-barbarians! It is not unlikely, if this is the case, that these poor little supernumerearies are sometimes assisted by a sly push in their aquatic excursions.

Mr. Webster was good enough to drive me out yesterday, and a most splendid drive we had. At one part, from a rather high eminence, we had a glorious panoramic view: it was really sublime: ocean, forest, hill, valley, promontory, river, field, glade, and hollow, were spread before us; altogether they formed a truly magnificent prospect. One almost seemed to be looking into boundless space. We paused at this spot a little while to admire the beautiful scene. How meet a companion the giant Atlantic seemed for that mighty mind, to some of whose noble sentiments I had just been listening with delight and veneration, and yet how far beyond the widest sweep of ocean, is the endless expanse of the immortal intellect—time-overcoming—creation-compelling!

However, while I was thus up in the clouds, they (condescendingly determining, I suppose, to return my call) suddenly came down upon us, and unmercifully. St. Swithin! what a rain it was! The Atlantic is a beautiful object to look at, but when either he, or some cousin-german above, takes it into his head to act the part of shower-bath extraordinary to you, it is not so pleasant. My thoughts immediately fled away from ocean (except the *descending* one), forest, hill, dale, and all the circumjacent scenery, to centre ignominiously on my bonnet, to say nothing of the tip of my nose, which was drenched and drowned completely in a half second. My vail—humble defense against the fury of the elements!—accommodated its dripping self to the features of my face like the black mask of some desperate burglar, driven against it, also, by the wind, that blew a "few," I can assure the reader.

How Mr. Webster contrived to drive, I know not, but drive he did, at a good pace too, for "after us," indeed, was "the deluge;" I could scarcely see him; a wall of water separated us, but ever and anon I heard faintly, through the hissing and splashing and lashing and pattering of the big rain, his deep, sonorous voice, recommending me to keep my cloak well about me, which no mortal cloak of any spirit will ever allow you to do at such needful moments—not it! "My kingdom for a pin."

I recollect Lady ——, telling me how her life had once hung on a pin. Thus it was; she was driving herself one day across a bleak, broad moor in Yorkshire, and it began rather suddenly to rain, and blow tremendously. Excepting a cloak, she was very lightly clothed, and this said cloak blew open, flew back, and made itself as odious as possible, and left her chilled by the wind, and drenched by the rain. She was delicate, and extremely afraid of cold, and was shivering from head to foot: at last a friendly pin was found, and behold—perhaps her lungs and her life were thus saved!

When we arrived at Green Harbor, we found Mrs. Webster very anxious for the poor rain-beaten wayfarers. She took every kind care of me, and except a very slight *soupçon* of a cold, the next morning, I did not suffer any inconvenience. Mr. Webster had complained of not being very well before (I think a slight attack of hay-asthma), but I was glad to meet him soon afterward at dinner, not at all the worse for the tempestuous drive; and for my part, I could most cordially thank him for the glorious panorama he had shown me, and the splendid drive through what seemed almost interminable woods: and (since we had got safely through it), I was not sorry to have witnessed the very excellent imitation of the Flood which had been presented before (and some of it into) my astonished eyes. Mr. Webster told me the drive through the woods would have been extended, but for the rain, ten miles!

He took me the other day to a room I had not before visited, and showed me a beautiful picture of a lovely and only daughter, whom he had the great misfortune to lose last year.

I am about to leave this delightful place, for I have an engagement to go and dine at Nahant to-morrow, with Mr. and Mrs. Prescott. The latter I have not yet had the pleasure of meeting. I believe she has very delicate health.

I made acquaintance at Plymouth with a charming Mrs. Thayer: her father is said to be the only American who possesses and is universally known by an aristocratic title: he is the lineal descendant of an ancient Dutch family. I believe the title is "The Patroon."

I can not describe to you the almost adoration with which Mr. Webster is regarded in New England. The newspapers chronicle his every movement, and constantly contain anecdotes respecting him, and he invariably is treated with the greatest respect by every body, and, in fact, his intellectual greatness seems all but worshiped. Massachusetts boasts, with a commendable pride and exultation, that he is one of her children. A rather curious anecdote has been going the round of the papers lately. It appears Mr. Webster was at Martha's Vineyard a short time ago, and he drove up to the door of the principal hotel, at Edgartown, the capital, accompanied by some of his family, and attended, as usual, by his colored servants. Now it must be observed that Mr. Webster has a swarthy, almost South-Spanish complexion, and when he put his head out of the window, and inquired for apartments, the keeper of the hotel, casting dismayed glances, first at the domestics of different shades of sable and mahogany, and then at the fine dark face of Mr. Webster, excused himself from providing them with accommodation, declaring he made it a rule never to receive any *colored persons.* (This in New England! if the tale be true.) The great statesman and his family were about to seek for accommodation elsewhere—thinking the hotel-keeper alluded to his servants—when the magical name of "glorious Dan" becoming known, mine host, penitent and abashed, after profuse apologies, entreated him to honor his house with his presence. "All's well that ends well."

One can not wonder at the Americans' extreme admiration of the genius and the statesman-like qualities of their distinguished countryman, his glorious and electrifying eloquence, his great powers of ratiocination, his solid judgment, his stores of knowledge, and his large and comprehensive mind—a mind of that real expansion and breadth which, heaven knows, too few public men can boast of. But what does excite wonder is, the singular fact, that neither he nor that other idol of the western world, Mr. Clay, should ever have been chosen to fill the highest office in the United States.

It has been explained to me thus: the greatest and most distinguished statesmen in America are so thoroughly identified with some particular party, that naturally all the men of other parties (and party-spirit appears to run very high in America) are violently opposed to them. A comparatively unknown politician, therefore, who has made himself popular in some other sphere—as the present President, for instance*—has a better chance to occupy the Presidential chair than the best and most renowned of their statesmen. In short, as regards the politics of their chief magistrate, they appear universally to prefer what is called in sporting circles in England, a "dark horse." Whether this peculiarity in the working of their constitutional polity be for good or for evil, where the chief magistrate for the time being has so vast an amount of power and patronage, I leave those more conversant with such subjects to decide.

Speaking of patronage, it may be well to allude to the army of postmasters whom every successive President has the privilege (of

* I need hardly point out to the reader that President Taylor died since these remarks were written.

which it is said he uniformly avails himself) of turning out on his election. In the newly-appointed legions of this class of administrators, it is not experience, I am told, or fitness in any way for the post, that is considered, but the direction their votes have taken; and I have been assured that sometimes persons are appointed—certainly extraordinarily illiterate for America—who can not read, and others who can not spell.

In one of the public prints I saw the other day an attack on a recently appointed postmaster to Indianapolis, the capital of Indiana. This functionary wrote from his then abode to some one at the place of his future labors, and spelt the name of the town thus: "Indian Apolis." Deponent sayeth not whether he added the name of the State as Indian Anna.

The mode of living at Green Harbor is exceedingly agreeable, quiet, and unostentatious, yet all is conducted with the most unbounded hospitality. Every one is judiciously allowed to follow their own tastes and inclinations, and read, walk, drive, write, or whatever else they may like, without any formality or interference.

---

## CHAPTER XI.

Visit to Mr. and Mrs. Prescott at Nahant—Paucity of Trees there—A magnificent Water-Melon—Beauty of Boston Harbor—Poetical additional Names given to American Cities—New Bedford—Its Population and Trade—Delicate Politeness of a Descendant of William Penn—Martha's Vineyard—The Hostess, her Son and Daughter—Woodsville—Naushon—Its Loveliness—The One Grave—Reflections suggested by it—An ancient Place of Indian Sepulture—Verses suggested by Naushon.

To-day we went and dined early with Mr. and Mrs. Prescott at Nahant, where they are staying for the summer. They have a charming country villa on the beautiful peninsula of Nahant. The town of Nahant is a very pleasant watering-place, about twelve miles from Boston by water, and sixteen by land. Near Mr. Prescott's house is a magnificent-looking hotel with numerous piazzas: the sea-coast view from his villa is boundless, and the perpetually high and dashing waves fling their fantastic foam, without ceasing, against the wild jagged rocks, which abound in every direction.

We started by railroad to go there, and very near us in the car was a respectable looking negro. Mr. C. S——, who was in the same car with us (also going to dine at Mr. Prescott's), pointed this man out to me, at the same time saying, that this could not by possibility have happened two years ago in this State, so strong then were the prejudices against any approach to, or appearance of amalgamation with the black race. No one could certainly appear more humble and quiet, less presuming or forward in his new position, than did this colored individual.

On our way to Mr. Prescott's, we stopped to pay a visit to Mrs. Page, the sister of Mrs. F. Webster. She has a very pretty little country house at Nahant: she made many inquiries, with much kind feeling, after those friends whom she remembers at Belvoir Castle, where she was staying with Mr. and Mrs. Webster.

I have already mentioned that Mr. Prescott is one of the most agreeable people I ever met with—as delightful as his own most delightful books: he talks of going to Europe next year. He tells me he has never visited either Mexico or Peru. I am surprised that the interest he must have felt in his own matchless works did not impel him to go to both. Mrs. Prescott is very delicate, with most gentle and pleasing manners. One of the guests was a niece of Lord Lyndhurst, her mother being Lord Lyndhurst's sister.

After a most interesting and agreeable visit, we returned by water to Boston. The sea was blue as a plain of sparkling sapphire—quite Mediterraneanic! Nahant is certainly a delightful place of summer residence, though it wants shade: trees in general most positively refuse to grow there, and there are but a few, which are taken as much care of as if they were the most precious exotics; but Nahant and they do not agree. They have quite a pouting sulky look; and it is almost as sad to look at them as it is to see the *girdled* trees, which look like skeletons of malefactors bleaching in the wind. At dessert, at Mr. Prescott's, there was a huge magnificent water-melon, that almost might have taken the place of the Cochituate Pond, and supplied Boston with the crystal element for a day.

In returning through the harbor of Boston from Nahant, we were full of admiration of its scenery: the many lovely islands with which it is beautifully studded, and the superb view of Boston itself, so nobly surmounted by its crown-like State House, enchanted us.

Since I wrote this, we have had a very agreeable little tour. We have received, through Mrs. W——, a kind invitation from Mr. and Mrs. J. Grinnell to visit them at New Bedford. That town is called "the City of Palaces," from the beautiful buildings it contains: it is also the great whaling metropolis of the North. It is about fifty-six miles from hence.

The Americans give their cities most poetical and significant designations, and sometimes one town will have a variety of these. For instance, this, I believe, is not only called the Granite City, but the Trimountain City. Philadelphia is the city of Brotherly Love, or the Iron City. Buffalo, the Queen City of the Lakes; New Haven, the City of Elms, &c. I think the American imagination is more florid than ours. I am afraid matter-of-fact John Bull, if he attempted such a fanciful classification would make sad work of it. Perhaps we should have Birmingham, the City of Buttons or Warming-pans; Nottingham, the City of Stockings; Sheffield, the City of Knives and Forks, and so forth.

Mr. and Mrs. Willis, and Mr. Willis's musical brother, were at Mr. and Mrs. J. Grinnell's beautiful mansion. We paid a visit to an immense whale-ship that is in the course of busy preparation for her voyage—to the South Seas, I believe. The whale-fishery is very extensively carried on at New Bedford. The population is about fifteen thousand, almost all engaged directly or indirectly in this trade. There are about two hundred and twenty-nine vessels engaged in the fishery, which is said to be continually increasing.

The system on which they conduct their whaling operations, seems to be a very judicious one. Every one of the crew has a share in the profits or losses of the expedition; it becomes, therefore, his interest to do all he possibly can to render the voyage a prosperous one. All are eager, all on the look-out, all are quite sure to exert their energies to the utmost, and perhaps this is one secret of the success that attends the American whaling-ships.

Mrs. Grinnell had a little *conversazione* the other evening, and among the visitors was a beautiful young Quaker lady, a descendant of William Penn. She was an extremely pleasing person and her conversation was very animated and interesting. Imagining that perhaps I had never been in the society of Quakers before, she cleverly contrived to converse in the most pleasant and delightful manner, without once bringing in either "thee" or "thou," or "you" though she was talking to me almost all the evening.

I remarked this omission, and was afterward certain of it when Mrs. Willis told me the lady informed her of the fact before going away, and gave her that reason for her delicate, scrupulous abstinence. She would not say "*you*," in short; and "thee" and "thou" she thought would appear strange to me. I was told her family are in possession of a splendid silver tea-service which belonged to their celebrated ancestor, William Penn.

We went from New Bedford to Martha's Vineyard, an island in the Atlantic not far from New Bedford. There we staid a few days at an unpretending neat hotel, of small dimensions—not the chief hotel, where the mistress, we found, was unaccommodating and disobliging—*a very rare thing* in America. On taking refuge at the other hotel, we found we had reason to congratulate ourselves, for a more kind-hearted, attentive person I never found than our new hostess. She, poor soul, was in affliction at the time; for her son was about to go off to California—indeed his departure took place for that distant region the morning after our arrival.

What misery has this Californian emigration brought on thousands of families—unknown, incalculable wretchedness! There was, as may be supposed, a melancholy chorus of wailing and sobs when the dreaded moment actually arrived; but her domestic sorrows did not make the excellent mother of the family neglect her guests. Nothing was omitted that could conduce to our comfort; and her daughter's attention and her own were unremitting.

Her daughter was a smart intelligent lassie. One day, when she was in the room, the mother hurried in to ask some question relative to dinner, or something of the kind. She had previously been baking, and her hands, and arms too, I believe, were white with flour. This very much annoyed her neat, particular, and precise daughter, who kept dusting her daintily, and trying to wipe it off, and drawing her mother's attention to it with great pertinacity. At last the mother said she hadn't had time to get rid of it—hoped the lady would excuse it, with other apologies, and the daughter was a little pacified. One should hardly have expected so much susceptibility in such matters in a little out-of-the-way town on an island like Martha's Vineyard.

When we came away I felt it was quite a friend I was taking leave of, though we had been there so short a time, so good and kind did we find her. On the table in her little parlor, instead of the horrid novels so commonly to be seen in America, were the "Penny Magazine," and other works of that species.

From Martha's Vineyard we went to Woodsville, a quiet little village by the sea. I had promised to pay a visit to Mrs. J. Grinnell, at the residence of a friend of hers, situated on an island very near this place (to which Mr. and Mrs. J. Grinnell had lately gone from New Bedford). We were at a very nice little hotel, indeed, at Woodsville, the master of which was a Mr. Webster, who had called one of his sons Daniel, after the famous statesman, the pride of old Massachusetts.

At this hotel there was an admirable specimen of an American female waiter and house-maid; in short, a domestic factotum. She was excessively civil, obliging, active, and attentive, not in the slightest degree forward or intrusive, always willing to do whatever one required of her. Altogether a very prepossessing personage is Mademoiselle Caroline—not the famous female equestrian of Paris, but the excellent and accomplished waitress and chambermaid at Woodsville, whom I beg to introduce to the reader, and to immortality. The mistress of the hotel cooked for us herself, and she was quite a *cordon-bleu*, I assure you. Her chicken pies and her puddings were of the sublimest description.

The morning was lovely, the sea sparkling with a myriad lustres, the air of Ausonian clearness and purity, when we went to Naushon, an exquisite little island (one of a cluster of the islands called the Elizabeth Group). We started in a small boat manned by the two sons of our host, and before very long we entered a little creek, and soon landed on the beautiful shore of fairy-like Naushon. (This is of course its old Indian name, and long may it retain it).

We found Mr. Grinnell kindly waiting to receive us and drive us to the island palace of the proprietor of Naushon, for to Mr. S——, the whole beauteous island belongs.—What an enviable possession! Though not given to pilfering propensities, I should like to pick Mr. S——'s pocket of this gem! We started in a somewhat sledge-like vehicle, *à la flèche* (as our old Belgian courier Marcotte used to say), for the house, and soon found ourselves seated in a large cool apartment with Mrs. Grinnell, and the kindly cordial Lord and Lady of the Isle, whose welcome had much of unworldly heartiness about it. I longed to explore the beautiful island, and when I did so, my anticipations were not disappointed.

Naushon is a little America in itself. There are miniatures of her wild, illimitable, awful old forests—a beautiful little diamond edition of her wonderful lakes, a fairy representation of her variety of scenery, a page torn from her ancient Indian associations and remains. There too are her customs, her manners, her spirit, and character; in short, it is a little pocket America (and enough to make the chief superintendent of any police himself a pick-pocket), a Liliputian Western World, a compressed Columbia. But its trees are not Liliputian, they are magnificent.

We drove under a varied shade for a long time, and saw lovely views through openings in the woods. At last after tearing and crackling along through a thick growth of timber and underwood, we emerged upon a truly magnificent prospect. We were on a height, and on either side were lovely woods, valleys, and gentle eminences; and in front the glorious Atlantic. After enjoying this beauteous view for some time, the Lord of Naushon took us to see a still, secluded part of the forest, where in the midst of a sunny clearing, surrounded by partly overshadowing trees in the heart of that sequestered island, embosomed in the mighty ocean, was a single grave, that of the only and adored son of our amiable hosts; indeed, their only child. Almost close to this simple grave was a semi-circular seat. "There often," said Mr. S——, "we come in the summer time and spend the evening, and frequently bring our friends, too, with us, and it is a melancholy happiness to feel *he* is near—almost, as it were, with us."

Here we all remained for some time: the birds were singing, the sea so calm you could scarcely just then at that distance hear its everlasting resounding voice. You might look through the opening in the woods, up and up, and the clear cloudless sky would seem almost receding from your gaze (like the horizon when you are advancing toward it), yet bluer and bluer, brighter and brighter. All was beauty and enchantment! and there lay the lonely dead—who could dare to say in unconsecrated ground? where Nature was so wild and beautiful, and Nature's Creator seemed so nigh—and where that grand untrodden ground with nothing to desecrate it, was ever bathed by the tears of hallowed parental affection? How blessed and sacred it appeared! To think, in contrast with this grave, of our dead in crowded city church-yards! But I trust that unutterably detestable system will soon be done away with.

If what I have related seems strange to you, you must recollect that in America it is often the case; at least, I have frequently heard so before I came here. In the quiet garden, or in the wood near the house, often sleep in their last slumber the beloved members of the family, not banished from the every-day associations of the survivors, and almost seeming to have still some participation in their feelings, in their woes, and their pleasures. I could almost fancy, after seeing that Eden for the dead, Mount Auburn, and remembering this affectionate custom, that is one reason why death does not seem a thing to be dreaded or deplored in America, as with us. If I recollect correctly, the only words on the modest head-stone were, "To our beloved Son."

After willingly remaining some time here, beside this simple Christian tomb, we went to see an ancient place of Indian sepulture. The corpses, I believe, had mostly been dug up—poor Indians; hardly allowed to rest in their graves! Mrs. S—— told me that the first time Naushon had passed into white men's hands from those of the red chief's, this exquisite island, with all its lovely and splendid woods, its herds of wild deer, and all its fair lands, it had been sold for an old coat. (I think a little fire-water must have entered into the bargain). After hearing this, I began to think *feu* squire and squaw Naushon of the olden time and their clan hardly deserved to rest in their graves.

Our excellent hosts most kindly pressed us to stay at Naushon, but my plans did not admit of this; so, enchanted with their delectable island, and full of gratitude for all their cordial friendliness and truly American hospitality toward us, we took leave of them and Mrs. Grinnell, in the evening, and returned to the main land. The weather became very unpropitious, and it blew and rained heavily. However, we arrived in damp safety at our hotel.

I will venture to give some verses which I wrote for an album at Naushon, begging the reader not to be severe in his criticisms; for constantly traveling, as I have lately been, is not favorable to verse manufacturing.

NAUSHON.

If falling stars were truly what they seem,
The glittering regions of a magic dream,
Then might we fancy this enchanted isle
(Where such bright, varying beauties gleam and smile),
Were even an after-gift, in mercy sent,
Straight from yon golden-fretted firmament;
Rapt from those lustrous paths, to vision bared,
A down-dropped star from yon grand circle spared;
Fallen in a gracious moment from the sky,
To charm to rapture man's earth-wearied eye,
From harsher haunts and sceneries to beguile,
To almost Eden's loss to reconcile.
A home for world-sick angel-hearts to be,
A wilder, freer Paradise at sea;
Hung, gem-like, where to stormless deeps are given
The best reflections of its parent heaven!
The loveliest likeness that this planet wears,
Of kindred glories—sister stars and spheres!

But since 'tis not so, let me hope, at least—
Kind new-made friends, by its possession blest—
That while no fallen-star hath spread for you
A bowered Elysium midst these waves of blue,
Your hearts, your hopes, your virtues yet will make
This radiant island, for your own bright sake,
A rising-star in guardian-angels' eyes,
That, better-seeing, watch the heavenward rise,
The unceasing soul-flight of its human guests,
Far, far beyond where sun or system rests
(Till they, and *thou*, in their remembering thought
Fair isle! to faith's own glorious goal are brought).

Ah, yes, a mounting world, be this hushed spot,
Where th' earthlier globe's vain mockeries are forgot,
A star of rising heaven-bound souls, that feel,
'Midst such rare scenes, fresh hopes, fresh trusts and zeal,
And, looking on this lustrous realm below—
In morn's creation-burst, or sunset's glow—
This little heaven of beauty, peace, and love,
*Who* could forget the kindred heaven above?

Though, in thyself, fair isle! thou mayst not soar
To be their bower of bliss for evermore,
Nor midst the unfading realms of splendor shine,
And hallowed fields, and mansions, all divine;
Thy deathless dwellers there may cherish yet
(Where worlds ne'er sink, nor suns of glory set),
Thy precious memory's truth, in ages bright,
That through eternity shall speed their flight.
Thus thou mayst find thy changeless home within,
The unbounded soul released from earth and sin,
As now within the unbounded sea, that smiles
Round thee, like molten skies, sweet isle of isles!

## CHAPTER XII.

The Blind Asylum at Boston, and Laura Bridgeman—New Haven, the "City of Elms"—Yale College—Its Objects of Science and Art—Professor Silliman, Jun.—Governor Yale—His Epitaph—His English Connections—Black domestic Servants—Two Opinions of them—A sable Count D'Orsay—The American Character—Scenery about New Haven—Katydids, Tree-frogs, and Crickets—Connecticut Yankees.

I HAD been very anxious to pay a visit to the Blind Asylum and Laura Bridgeman, at Boston. Perhaps the reader will remember the very interesting account given of poor Laura by Mr. Dickens, in his work on America, and Dr. Howe's wonderful and successful mode of teaching her. She is blind, and deaf, and dumb, and has hardly any sense of smell or taste.

They told us at the Asylum that if they gave her strong Cayenne pepper, or any thing equally pungent, she would appear to taste it slightly, but nothing less powerful.

After Mr. Dickens's excellent and elaborate description, I need only say say that we found Laura apparently well and contented, though she is slight and delicate-looking, and has a rather pensive, serious expression of countenance. A lady, who we understood was a governess, especially devoted to her, told us Laura Bridgeman had enjoyed a late visit into the country much; and though she could neither see the views, nor hear the merry song of birds, nor smell the sweet odor of flowers, yet she appeared to inhale the freshness of the free air with delight. She added that Laura was now learning geometry, and that she took very deep interest in it, and made great and rapid progress. Is not this wonderful?

When we first entered, the teacher was holding an open letter in one hand, while with the other she was repeating the contents of it to the poor girl, by telling it very rapidly on the fingers of Laura's lifted hand. This was a letter from her country friends, and it was extraordinary to observe each eloquent change of expression that passed over Laura's intelligent and most speaking face. Wonder, pleasure—sometimes a slight shade of vexation and disappointment—regret, affection, mirth, sympathy, doubt, anxiety, hope, expectation; all seemed to impress themselves by turns on the voiceless and sightless one's features. I could almost *read the letter* on Laura's eloquent face, which those mute signs, quick as lightning, were conveying to her mind!

I might well have been reminded of the illumined alabaster vase to which some one imaginatively compared a celebrated poet's countenance, for really Laura's face appeared almost like a crystal one, and the mighty mystery of mind seemed peering through the transparent casket. I do not think I ever saw any features that had a voice to help them, or eyes to look with, speak so impressively with their varied changes. All her features and movements seemed forced by her active mind to act as voice, tongue, and eyes. When we first entered the Asylum, the blind children were singing, in a sort of music-hall, furnished with a good organ. What a pleasure must this be to these poor bereaved beings! Their voices sounded very sweet and solemn, and they had evidently been carefully taught.

The Institution for the Blind is admirably situated, on open and elevated ground, and commands a noble and splendid prospect of the island-studded harbor, the city and circumjacent country: its lofty position, and the pure air that circulates around it, are, no doubt, highly conducive to the health of the pupils. But how mournful to think, on looking out of the vast opened windows of the establishment, that all this beauty and glory can shine not to those poor benighted eyes!

New Haven is lovely; but I must explain to what it owes its principal charm: it is to the exceeding profusion of its stately elms, which render it not only one of the most charming but one of the most "unique" cities I ever beheld. From the trees it is called the "City of Elms," and it may be imagined how delightful a place of residence they must make it in the heat of an American summer. Even now we find their shade very welcome; and wherever we go, in street or suburb, we see these umbrageous trees—in short, I think, there are multitudinous avenues of them.

We lately paid a very interesting visit to the college library, with a lady to whom I had a letter, and who has been most friendly and kind since our stay here. In this city is Yale College, which is said to have a greater number of students than any other college in the United States. Yale College was founded at Killingworth in 1701, and subsequently established at New Haven in 1717. There are several college-halls, about one hundred and four feet long by forty feet wide and four stories high; a hall for theological students, a chapel, the Lyceum, and the Athenæum. Behind the main building is another range which contains a building devoted to an interesting collection of paintings by Col. Trumbull; a chemical laboratory, and the Commons' Hall, which has in its second story a fine mineralogical cabinet, supposed to be by far the most complete in the United States. Buildings devoted to the law and medical departments are hard by. We saw in the library a likeness of poor Major André, drawn by himself, just before his execution, and a lock of his hair.

I was particularly interested in my visit to the cabinet of minerals. They boast that they have some specimens far superior to any corresponding ones in the British Museum, but this is a knotty point which I am not at all competent to decide. The specimens of meteoric iron struck me certainly as extraordinarily fine: one piece was truly enormous, and if the theory of some natural philosophers respecting their lunar origin be correct, it seems almost frightful to think of such an iron rock being lanched at us from such a distance! We had better take care and keep on good terms with the moon, if she can bombard us thus. One can hardly help wondering, when gazing on that huge projectile, how so many poets and poetasters have escaped her vengeance, making her, as they do, the target for their rhyming arrows, without mercy or compunction. Long suffering must the "Casta Diva" be indeed!

Besides my letter to Mrs. W——, I had one for Mrs. D——. They both appear highly-accomplished and agreeable persons, and are nearly related to wealthy planters in the South. Owing to Mrs. D—— being absent from New Haven during the greater part of the time we were there, I saw the more of Mrs. W—— and her daughter: I found them most particularly pleasing and amiable. It was with them we went to the colleges, the library and mineralogical cabinet. We had the advantage of meeting Professor Silliman, Jun., at the latter, who was kind enough to accompany us round, and his elucidatory observations rendered our visit far more attractive and interesting than it would otherwise have been.

The chief benefactor of the college, Governor Yale (from whom the institution received its name), died July 8, 1721. Here is the old gentleman's epitaph (in the church-yard at Wrexham):

"Under this tomb lyes interred Elihu Yale, of Place Gronow, Esq. Born 5th April, 1648, and dyed the 8th of July, 1721, aged seventy-three years.

"Born in America, in Europe bred,  
In Afric traveled, and in Asia wed,  
Where long he lived and thrived; at London dead.  
Much good, some ill he did; so hope all's even,  
And that his soul through Mercy's gone to Heaven.

You that survive and read, take care,
For this most certain exit to prepare;
For only the actions of the Just
Smell sweet, and blossom in the dust."

The last two lines are a naughty plagiarism from old Shirley, and poor Charles Lamb would have taken, perhaps, offense at the previous two. Touching the plagiarism, it is more pardonable than the almost parody I once saw in a country church-yard in England, on Lord Byron's fine lines,

"Bright be the place of thy soul," &c.

The line—

"On earth she was all but divine,"

was thus rendered:

"On earth she was all *we could wish*."

The rhyme was unmercifully sacrificed; not even did they deign to press an extraneous line, slightly altered into the service, and say—

"And the spoon ran away with the dish."

I return to old Governor Yale.* One of his daughters married a son of the then Duke of Devonshire; another, a grandson of the Earl of Guildford. It was he of whom Collins says in his "Peerage of England:"—"he brought such quantities of goods from India that, finding no house large enough to stow them in, he had a public sale of the overplus, and that was the first auction in England."

Yale College was instituted when Connecticut was in its infancy, and has exerted a powerful influence over its literary, moral, social, and religious character. A new department was established in the college in 1847, called the Department of Philosophy and the Arts. The gentleman I have mentioned, Professor Silliman, Jun., instructs in elementary and analytical chemistry, mineralogy, and metallurgy.

I was talking, the other day, to Mrs. W—— and her daughter of the capabilities of the black people for making good domestic servants, and remarking how very civil, attentive, and intelligent we had uniformly found the black waiters and attendants we had

* On the monument to Governor Eaton is a quaint inscription. He was buried here, with his son-in-law and daughter near him. It thus concludes:

"T' attend you, sir, under these framed stones,
Are come your honored son and daughter Jones,
On each hand to repose their wearied bones."

occasionally encountered. I was surprised to hear them condemn them unconditionally, and declare they carefully avoided having any of them in their house; speaking in no measured terms of their having many uneradicably bad habits. How different from Mr. Webster's expressed opinion concerning them! But it is very natural that they should, from their Carolinian antecedents, be disposed not to judge the colored race with much impartiality; and it is certainly probable that, after being accustomed to them as slaves, they would be likely to be a little impatient of them as servants. Altogether, I can easily imagine the household arrangements, under the circumstances of the case, not being conducted very harmoniously or satisfactorily to either party.

The old black waiter who attends on us here is an admirable specimen of his class. He is invaluable to the master of the establishment, and I find he is constantly spoken of by the white servants, quite respectfully, as "Mr. Williams." He speaks particularly good English, without any twang, and has the manners of a quiet, highly-respectable English butler.

We saw one very curious specimen of a dandy among his fellow-colorists, lounging down the street. He was a sable Count d'Orsay. His toilet was the most elaborately *recherché* you can imagine. He seemed intensely and harmlessly happy in his coat and waistcoat, of the finest possible materials; and the careful carelessness of the adjustment of the wool and hat was not readily to be surpassed.

The more I see of American society, the more I like it. In general, I should say, they are a peculiarly sensitive people, and yet very forbearing and not easily offended. They are generally accused of being conceited. I can only say, as far as I have seen, their candor appears to be far more remarkable than their conceit. Indeed, I have perpetually found them volunteer remarks on what they consider defects in their manners and customs, with the greatest possible good-humor and ingenuousness. Nay, I have sometimes, in common honesty, found myself compelled to take their part against themselves. In traveling, their courtesy, their good-temper, their obligingness, their utter unselfishness, are beyond all praise.

This town is delightfully situated. It is built round the head of the bay, and is partly skirted by an amphitheatre of hills, of which two, at their termination, present steep bluffs, which rise, indeed, almost perpendicularly to the height of three hundred and seventy feet. The population is about 20,500. We have had several charming drives with Mrs. and Miss W——. The country surrounding New Haven, is very picturesque and fine, and these bluffs look very imposing. They took us to see some exceedingly nice country houses, with grounds well laid out. Their own mansion was a very pretty one (as was also Mrs. D——'s), completely embowered in trees, except on one side, where there was a beautiful garden.

The noise the katydids, tree-frogs, and crickets make at New Haven, is inconceivable—almost enough to interrupt the students at their labors. The former repeat very plainly the sound that gives them their name, in a most positive and authoritative manner; and, after a little time, you will hear others apparently replying, "Katy-didn't." Of course the prodigious number of these insects at New Haven arises from the multitude of trees.

The Americans, I find, call the New Englanders Yankees in general; though, I believe, the meaning of the term varies according to the section of country you happen to be in. They tell me that almost all the Americans met with abroad, especially those who venture into remote localities, such as India, China, Australia, Polynesia, and other distant regions, are Yankees, *i.e.*, New Englanders; and that of these, by far the greater part are the enterprising, active, indefatigable, Connecticut Yankees. It is said, if you ask a Connecticut Yankee, in any part of the world, how he is, he will, if not "sick," answer "moving, sir," equivalent to saying "well;" for, if well, he is sure to be on the move.

---

## CHAPTER XIII.

Bridgeport—The Irish Housemaid—Ultra-Republicans even in America—The Great Croton Aqueduct described—Supply of Water to New York—New York Trotters—Delmonico's Hotel—Excursion with American Friends—Glorious Scenery of Staten Island—Greenwood Cemetery—Its Extent, Scenery and Monuments—Miss Lynch the Poetess and Fredrika Bremer.

In coming here (to Delmonico's Hotel, New York), on the 14th October, from New Haven, we stopped at Bridgeport, at a rather indifferent hotel—that is to say, compared with the generality of the hotels in the United States. I believe it is near that town that the well-known Mr. Barnum, of Tom Thumb and "woolly horse" notoriety, has his abode—his splendid abode, I fancy I may say, if the accounts generally given of it are correct.

We did not see Bridgeport to advantage, as it rained a good deal while we were there. Both V—— and I were quite sorry to leave the city of Elms, and our very kind friends Mrs. and Miss W——, and Mrs. D——, who had made our sojourn there so singularly agreeable. I should think Bridgeport is a pretty place when you can see it, which we could scarcely do for the cascade-like rain during our short stay.

There was a poor Irish housemaid there who touched our feelings extremely: we had watched her with compassion in the pouring rain milking the cows, her gown-skirt over her head, crouched in the wet grass. When she came in with our tea we asked her some questions about her leaving Ireland, and she appeared delighted to talk about the "ould country;" ill off as she had been there. She seemed to think it the most beauteous and charming place on the face of the globe. Every time we saw her after that, we had a little talk about "the fair Emerald Isle;" and on our coming away, when I gave her a little gratuity, she fairly burst into tears and thanked me most heartily; but, I verily believe, more for talking to her about beautiful "ould Ireland," and displaying interest in her simple history, than for the trifle I presented her with. She sobbed out as we took leave, "Och sure, my heart warmed toward ye from the first, when I found ye was from the *ould countries!*" thus cordially uniting together the land of the Saxon with her own far-off Erin.

I have been reading some extracts from late American newspapers, which I inclose, concerning the tariff. It is easily to be seen that there are radicals and ultra-republicans in the United States as well as elsewhere, which I think is scarcely well known to politicians in England. What intemperance of language there is in these extracts! To judge by the meeting described, they seem just as violent as the malcontents of Europe, and fully as discontented with their government; but if they ever did more than talk here, they would find no merciful Louis the Sixteenths, or Charles the Tenths, or hesitating, compromising, concession-making Louis-Philippes: the executive would deal with them at once with determination, promptitude, and just whatever amount of severity might be deemed necessary.

I have found those kindest of friends, Mrs. Barclay and Mrs. W. Barclay here. Mrs. Barclay most kindly invited me to spend the winter with them in Georgia, but as I wished extremely to go down the Mississippi to New Orleans, I, with great reluctance, declined their truly friendly proposal. We went with them one day to see the High Bridge of the great Croton Aqueduct. It is very magnificent indeed. This bridge crosses Harlem River and is made of stone : it is one thousand four hundred and fifty feet long, with fourteen piers, eight of which bear arches of eighty feet span, and seven others of fifty feet span, one hundred and fourteen feet above tide water at the top. It has cost about nine hundred thousand dollars. The whole cost of the aqueduct will be about fourteen million dollars.

"The aqueduct commences about five miles from the Hudson," says 'Appleton's Railroad Companion,' "about forty miles from the City Hall. The dam, which is two hundred and fifty feet long, seventy feet wide at the bottom and seven at the top, and forty feet high, is built of stone and cement. A pond five miles in length is created by the dam, covering a surface of four hundred acres, and containing five hundred million gallons of water. From the dam the aqueduct proceeds, sometimes tunneling through solid rocks, crossing valleys by embankments and brooks by culverts, until it reaches Harlem River. It is built of stone, brick, and cement, arched over and under ; is six feet three inches wide at the bottom, seven feet eight inches wide at the side walls, and eight feet five inches high ; it has a descent of thirteen inches and a quarter per mile, and will discharge sixty millions of gallons in twenty-four hours."

Then follows a description of the High Bridge, and it goes on to say : "The receiving reservoir is at Eighty-sixth-street and Sixth-Avenue, covering thirty-five acres, and containing one hundred and fifty million gallons of water. There is now no city in the world better supplied with pure and wholesome water than New York, and the supply would be abundant if the population were five times its present number." Another account I have seen proceeds to say, that the distributing reservoir on Murray's-hill, in Fortieth-street, covers about four acres, and is constructed of stone and cement, raised forty-five feet above the street, and contains twenty millions of gallons. The water is thence distributed over the city in iron pipes, laid sufficiently deep under ground so as to be secure from frost.

As we returned from the "High Bridge," we were passed by some of the famous New York trotters, who flew by at a most wonderful pace, drawing after them almost invisible little light vehicles.

Delmonico's is a most excellent hotel, admirably conducted ; it has all sorts of comforts and conveniences ; charming apartments, delightful baths of all kinds, and during the whole day a number of extremely good carriages for hire by the hour, or just as you choose, are drawn up before the door. In addition to this, the attendance is remarkably good.

We dined at Mr. H. Grinnell's,* the other evening (to whom I had letters from Mr. C——) : he is brother of Mr. J. Grinnell, at whose hospitable house we were staying at New Bedford. I like Mrs. H. Grinnell exceedingly, and her daughter seems a most thoroughly well-educated and accomplished young lady. Mr. Grinnell showed us some specimens of Californian gold that looked remarkably pure. Their drawing-rooms were adorned with some beautiful Italian paintings.

I have just returned from an agreeable little excursion to Staten Island, to dine and sleep at Mr. and Mrs. Cunard's enchanting villa in this beautiful locality. No words can describe the magnificence of American autumnal coloring. When the sun rose on the rainbow-tinted woods of the island in the morning, what a glorious blazing world we beheld! The scenery of Staten Island is superb, and not only is that well worthy of admiration, but its situation commands a glorious view of the Bay of New York, Long Island, &c.

We had, indeed, a delightful visit, though from my stupidly misunderstanding what Mr. Cunard said, I thought it was limited to a dinner invitation, and consequently, we arrived at the house, maidless, trunkless, and carpet-bag-less. Light was soon thrown upon the mistake ; but we found though we had not burned our ships, yet that no mode of retreat was open to us, for the last steamer for New York had already departed. However, Mrs. Cunard most kindly supplied us with all possible paraphernalia and caparisons and appointments, and we passed a charming evening listening to the beautiful instrumental music, with which Mrs. Cunard, who is an admirable performer, entertained us delightfully.

I must now give a brief account of Greenwood Cemetery, which we visited the other day in company with Mr. and Miss Grinnell, who obligingly insisted on taking us there, and showing us the place. It is in the south part of Brooklyn, about three miles from Fulton Ferry (you may also go to Greenwood by the new ferry, at Whitehall, which lands you in the vicinity of the cemetery on a very long pier). Greenwood contains two hundred and forty-two acres, of which a great part is beautifully covered with woods of a natural growth ; and I think the surprisingly brilliant colors of autumn are more striking and exquisite here than those at Staten

* This is the gentleman who subscribed so munificently to the American expedition in search of Sir John Franklin.

Island, or New Haven, or in the country before we came to New York. These were perfectly extraordinary—the most dazzling scarlet, the most golden and vivid yellows and Tyrian purples, and rich, deep, velvet-like crimsons, and delicate pale primrose-tints, and soft surviving greens, and rose-hues, such as flush the lips of Indian shells—all cast their sumptuous shadowings over the quiet graves, like the reflections from richly-painted windows, "blushing with the blood of kings and queens," in some mighty old cathedral. The views from the heights of the cemetery were sublime. I admired the one from Ocean Hill the most. There is a lovely variety of valleys, elevations, plains, groves, and glades, and paths. When will London have any thing even *approaching* to this magnificent cemetery? The ocean rolling and moaning, with its fine melancholy, organ-like sounds, so near, like a mighty mourner, she can not have, nor the gorgeous pall cast over the tombs by a Western autumn; but all the rest she could have, and yet has not.

The cemetery is traversed by many winding paths and avenues, all beautiful and solemn. Some of the monuments are interesting. There is one to an Iowa Indian Princess, named Dohumme; another handsome one to a young lady who was killed while returning from a ball. There is one thing which I did not quite like, and yet it is not only useful, but necessary, and that is, having "Guide Boards" given to visitors, to direct them in these solemn labyrinths. We were told that, but for this precaution, many persons would probably lose themselves in the Cemetery; still, there is something not in keeping with all the rest in these melancholy, methodical maps; but that is only fanciful.

We met, a short time since, at Mr. and Mrs. Willis's, Miss Lynch, the poetess; she is expecting Miss Fredrika Bremer to pay her a visit shortly. Miss Bremer's works are very much liked in the States. I believe she is going to remain in America some time. Miss Lynch, who has kindly sent me a delightful volume of her poems, reminded me a little of our poor L. E. L. in her manner and conversation.

## CHAPTER XIV.

Philadelphia—Incessant Uproar in that City—its Custom House and Cemeteries—Baltimore—Battle and Washington Monuments—The Catholic Cathedral—The Merchants' Shot Tower—Its Trade and Commerce—Its Increase and Population—Baltimore Clippers—Barnum's Hotel—Sensitiveness of Americans to Cold—The Deaf Gentleman and His Stentorian Friend—Anthracite Coal Fires.

We came to Baltimore, *viâ* Philadelphia; and though I very much admired the regularity of the Iron City's streets, and the beauty of many of the principal buildings, its profusion of white marble, and its perfection of cleanliness, I was glad to escape from its unearthly nightly noises, and the wars and rumors of wars which seemed unceasing and ever-increasing in the City of Brotherly Love —to Baltimore.

The Society of Friends at any rate, methinks, must gain many converts in the former place. Verily I was a Quaker all the time I staid there, and still tremble at the recollection of it. All night a sound as of a masque and procession of one hundred menageries let loose, filled one's ears. The deserts of Africa seemed to have disgorged half their denizens on the beautiful streets of fair Philadelphia; while bells, horns, gongs, and rattling fire-engines, helped to swell the hideous chorus.

I had understood there had been, some time ago, serious riots at Philadelphia, but that they were all over now, and I was, naturally surprised at this hubbub; but on inquiring the next morning, all I learnt was—it was the fashion of the dwellers of Moyamensing, a suburb of Philadelphia, called, I believe, a "district," to regale the ears of the inhabitants of that city frequently with such harmonious serenades. These gentlemen appear to indulge in very peculiar notions of music and melody, and to be resolved that at least their neighbors shall admire no rival harmonists, by leaving them completely deafened by their din. The Moyamensingists, in short, seem to look upon a riot or a row, or something resembling it, as the first necessary of life: they also would seem to entertain a new theory with regard to sleep, and to consider it as a wholly needless indulgence. To any one not participating in these sentiments, Philadelphia (while thus apparently at the mercy of this theoretical and experimentalizing suburb) can not be an eligible place of residence, I think: Sancho Panza certainly would shun it; for blessed, he declared, was the man who invented sleep.

It is said, it is the colored people residing in Moyamensing, who are the chief ringleaders of these frequent riots; but I know not how this may be. At New York I heard the authorities at Philadelphia very much found fault with for their supineness in allowing these disturbances to take place: if there was a proper amount of energy and resolution displayed, it was said, Philadelphia might be as orderly and tranquil as the other cities of the United States.

Our hotel is opposite a beautiful building, the Custom House (formerly the United States Bank), of the Doric order of architecture, built in imitation of the Parthenon at Athens, but lacking the side colonnades; it reminded me much of its glorious prototype, except in its situation, which is unfavorable to it. There are some fine cemeteries here: "Laurel Hill," "Green Mount Cemetery," and others which my brief stay did not allow me to visit.

Baltimore is a very handsome city, situated on the north side of the Patapsco River. Jones's Fall, a confluent of the Patapsco, divides it into two parts. (This is an ill-sounding conjunction of Anglo-Saxon and Indian names. Again I rejoice at the luck that spared Niagara from a denomination similar to the preceding one!) Three fine stone bridges and four wooden ones crossing this stream connect the different parts of the city.

The streets of Baltimore are, in general, very regular, clean, broad, and straight, and it has several fine monuments, among which tower conspicuously, Battle Monument, and Washington Monument. The Catholic Cathedral is a noble structure: it has the largest organ in the Union; this instrument has six thousand pipes and thirty-six stops: and the cathedral has two valuable paintings, one presented by Louis the Sixteenth, and the other ("St. Louis burying his officers and soldiers slain before Tunis") given by Charles the Tenth. The Merchants' Shot Tower here rises above all the monuments that distinguish Baltimore: it is two hundred and fifty feet high, and is said to be higher than any similar building in the world, exceeding by one foot that at Villach, in Carinthia.

Baltimore is said to be the greatest flour market in existence (within twenty miles of the city there are seventy or more flouring mills); and no city in the United States deals so extensively in tobacco. The Patapsco affords numerous valuable mill sites (falling eight hundred feet in thirty miles); and Jones's Falls also yield a considerable water-power—it has thus great advantages for manufactures, and they appear to keep pace with its commerce.

This flourishing city spreads rapidly: one thousand nine hundred and fifty-nine houses were erected during the year 1847, the assessed value of which is more than two million six hundred thousand dollars. The population, in 1840, was 102,313; it is now said to be about 125,000. The capital of Maryland contains upward of one hundred churches. The Maryland University is here: it constitutes one of the most important institutions of the kind in the country.

Canton, a skeleton suburb of the city of monuments, is waiting for nothing but—houses; like the magnificent library at E——, that had every thing complete except books.

Baltimore has an admirable harbor, which is incessantly crowded with shipping: and who has not heard of the Baltimore clippers, that start "before the wind has time to reach their sails, and never allow it to come up with them?"

We are at a magnificent hotel here, called "Barnum's," and its comforts and excellent arrangements are scarcely to be surpassed. It is admirably conducted, and if it has not quite the "*gentleman-like porters*" spoken of in some of the hotel cards, it has, at least, a set of most attentive and assiduous domestics.

In coming by the railroad here, I was struck one evening by the dread the Americans appear to have of catching cold. The car was extremely close, and V—— and I let down our window, and much enjoyed the cool, fresh air, which we thus secured in our immediate vicinity—we beheld instantly a simultaneous stir among the passengers. At first, I could not think that the fresh, but hardly cold air, I had been instrumental in introducing to the crowded and suffocating car, occasioned this movement; but I soon ascertained that such was the fact, on seeing a gentleman carefully barricading himself with a large carpet-bag against the assaults of his aerial foe. His appearance, just peeping over this gaudy-patterned, defensive wall, was rather comical.

One opened a vast umbrella, and disappeared behind its ample shade from scrutiny and the supposed severity of the elements, looking—as there was neither rain nor sun—like that Asiatic potentate above whose head, as a sign of royalty, an umbrella is reverentially and habitually carried. There was a general raising of collars and buttoning of coats, and slouching of hats, and shrinking, and shrugging; but all were too courteous and obliging to remonstrate, and I am not sure that one of the victims did not actually most politely assist us to open this terrible window, though so much to his own discomfiture.

Shall I confess it? grieved as I was to cause so much apparent annoyance, I had not the magnanimity to raise the glass—I felt so sure that, though unpalatable to them, this homœopathic dose of pure air was for their good. It must be, no doubt, the great variability and the violent extremes of their climate, that render them thus susceptible of the slightest chill. I heard some saying; "we shall all be frozen before we get to our journey's end," yet there was only a little part of the window open, and the only persons close to it were ourselves. I think I ought to have shut it, notwithstanding; but I can only hope none of the passengers suffered from this barbarous infliction of Zephyrus. We who stood the whole brunt of it certainly did not.

The room adjoining our sitting-room is occupied by an exceedingly deaf gentleman, and he has the advantage of possessing a friend who has a tremendously loud voice—a perfect Stentor: the hallooing and bawling are past description. In consequence of this proximity, we found Baltimore by day almost as noisy as Philadelphia by night. At first I could not imagine what the shouting was, and thought a caravan of lions or Moyamensingers had arrived, and were accommodated with apartments close by. Soon, however, the various friendly inquiries roared out, and the low milder answers, informed me of the truth.

I was sorry, but really could not help hearing the communications addressed to the deaf gentleman, and being enlightened by them considerably about "lots," and "sales," and "dollars." What a comical effect it sometimes had to hear the most insignificant remarks hallooed out with Apollonicon-loudness, and often with a wrong emphasis, from the difficulty of sustaining and pitching the voice properly, in speaking to the deaf in that tone of "live thunder" which people ordinarily employ under such circumstances. I believe one ought, instead, to speak *low* and distinctly. Hark! listen to Stentor!—for one *must* whether one will or no. The louder shouts are italicised. "I *guess* so, sir: that *chap* in the *pepper* and salt coat *popped* in; he *hemmed* and *hawed* at first, and then *squeaked* out—" "What?" "*Squeaked*, I say," with a roar.

The weather is beginning to get colder, and a little fire every now and then is not unpleasant. I like the anthracite coal, in which taste I am quite in a minority: it is supposed to give headaches, and to be very unwholesome; I have never suffered from its effects as yet, and it gives so little trouble, burning quietly, and lasting for an immense time. It goes on and on like a free horse, wanting not that whip the poker, and then there is no smoke. But I think its great advantage is its burning so long without any necessity for that drawing-room earthquake—the distracting uproar of flinging coals on the grate. In short, the coal-scuttle (that great institution of England) sings very small where anthracite is used, and its inner darkness is banished into outer darkness.

---

## CHAPTER XV.

The City of Washington—Pennsylvania Avenue—The "City of Magnificent Distances"—The Stentorian Gentleman and his Hogs—The Capitol described—Monument to Washington—The Navy Yard—Georgetown—A Digression to Tunis—Public Buildings—The Post Office—The Patent Office—The Treasury—The President's Mansion—The "White House" —Visit to General Taylor, the late President—His Daughter, Mrs. Bliss —Appearance of General Taylor—His Affability—His Conversation—Invitation to the Authoress—Heat of the Weather in November.

Washington would be a beautiful city if it were built; but as it is not I can not say much about it. There is the Capitol, however, standing like the sun, from which are to radiate majestic beams of streets and avenues of enormous breadth and astonishing length; but at present the execution limps and lingers sadly after the design.

This noble metropolitan myth hovers over the north bank of the Potomac (this Indian name means, I believe, the wild swan, or the river of the wild swan), about one hundred and twenty miles from Chesapeake bay and at the head of tide water. Pennsylvania Avenue is splendid: it is about three hundred feet broad; but the houses are not colossal enough to be in keeping with the immense space appropriated to the thoroughfare. They should be at least as high as the highest of old Edinburgh houses, instead of like those of London, which some one compared to the Paris ones making a profound courtesy. Now these Pennsylvania Avenue habitations seem making a very distant courtesy indeed to their opposite non-neighbors; and it made us think of people at an immensely wide dining-table, separated as "far as the poles assunder," by way of a pleasing rencontre and social intercourse. However, that is merely fancy; you do not want to talk across the streets;

and this appearance would vanish if the houses were taller and larger.

Washington is called the "City of Magnificent Distances:" it reminds one a little of a vast plantation with the houses purposely kept far apart to give them room to grow and spread: the "sidewalks" of Pennsylvania Avenue are twenty-six feet wide.

My unseen friend, Stentor, was in the same railroad car with us from Baltimore to this place, and the gentleman who was hard of hearing as well—at least I can hardly think there can be two sets of lungs of such marvelous power in the same country. Still, the theme of his discourse was very different; one subject occupied him all the way—it was hogs. The car was full, I was at some distance from him, but no other voice was heard—how could it be? Poor Stentor! he was lamenting with a most lachrymose roar, the abduction of some magnificent swine: their size was something prodigious, unparalleled (*maestoso*), their fat (in a melting tone) unheard of—they were Stentor's! The howl with which this dreadful fact was enunciated made one start.

But this was not all. Some friends, possessors of almost equally enchanting animals, had lost theirs too. "One wonderfully splendid creature of enormous dimensions (emphatically expressed in a perfect hurrah), and promising to grow much huger, was found killed (this in a lack-a-daisical bellow of grief and ire), supposed to be with a spiteful motive, but the wretches will suffer for it (a nine-times-nine, and-one-cheer-more sort of a tone)! It was the most magnificent hog quite, that ever—" and here, wonderful to relate, the noise of the railroad, together perhaps with his own emotions, overpowered the narrator. There was that terrible din that they make sometimes in the States when another train is expected. Very quickly, however, this was over, and there was Stentor shouting as loud as ever, or rather louder, as if indignant at the interruption.

"The lovely, interesting widow was much afflicted," continued he. "What," thought I, "can he mean, the widow of the pig!" I found soon she was the proprietress of the fat animal he was grieving for. He thundered on in the same way, and on the same subject, till we arrived; and if he did not leave his poor friend much more deaf than he found him, it is matter of surprise. What an invaluable "muezzin" he would make!

I have had the great pleasure since I came here of making acquaintance with Madame C. de la B——, the Spanish *ministress*, here, the authoress of a most charming and entertaining work on

Mexico, published some years ago. It made one long to go to Mexico, and I find it is not at all impracticable, from Madame C——'s account. I have a great mind to try it.

We went to see the Capitol soon after our arrival. There is a fine colossal statue by Greenough, of Washington, placed in front of it. The Capitol itself is a very noble-looking and imposing structure, though I think disadvantageously situated with regard to the city, as it seems rather to present the appearance of running away from it, while, like the flight of Louis-Philippe in the memorable days of February, there is nothing running after it. However, it is an exceedingly striking and handsome building, and is otherwise very finely situated.

It is built on an elevation that is about seventy-two feet above tide water. It is of the Corinthian order of architecture, and is built of freestone; and the front, including the wings, is three hundred and fifty-two feet long, and the depth of the wings is one hundred and twenty-one feet. The projection in the main front, which looks to the East (hardly complimentary to the West, in this world of the West), is decorated by a handsome portico of twenty-two lofty Corinthian columns. The broad steps leading to the portico are adorned by pedestals, on one of which is a group in marble, representing Columbus, with a globe in his outstretched hand, and an Aboriginal American of that New World he discovered, a female figure, in a lovely, half crouching attitude of veneration and wonder, beside him. The remaining pedestals will, in process of time, no doubt, be ornamented by groups of statuary. To the highest top of the dome, the height of the building is one hundred and twenty feet. The rotunda, which is under the dome, is ninety-five feet in diameter, and the same in height, In this rotunda there are some celebrated pictures by Trumbull, representing historical subjects.

The hall of the House of Representatives is in the second story of the south wing. Its form is semicircular; it is ninety-six feet long and sixty feet high, and has a dome supported by twenty-four columns of native variegated marble, whose capitals are of Italian marble. The chair of the Speaker occupies, so to say, the centre of the chord of the arc, the members' seats radiate back from the chair to the massive pillars. Congress is not sitting now. The Senate chamber is in the second story of the north wing, semicircular like the other, but of smaller dimensions, being seventy-eight feet long and forty-five feet high. The library is a fine room, containing thirty thousand volumes.

After seeing the Capitol, we went to have a glimpse of the Navy Yard. There we beheld two mountainous looking ship-houses, a man-of-war steamer, the Alleghany, lately dismantled, &c. Keeping guard on board the Alleghany, was an old Irish marine, with his face tied up for the tooth-ache—a most lugubrious-looking sentinel.

We saw a sadder sight after that, a large number of slaves, who seemed to be forging their own chains, but they were making chains, anchors, &c., for the United States navy. I hope and think slavery will be done away with soon in the District of Columbia, where it seems indeed strikingly out of place.*

Madame C. de la B—— kindly took us to Georgetown a day or two ago in her carriage. It is on the left bank of the Potomac River, two miles to the west of Washington, from which it is separated by Rock Creek, over which are two bridges, I think the situation of Georgetown delightful: it commands a fine view of the Potomac, of Washington, and the circumjacent country. Here you observe a number of handsome buildings and pleasant-looking country seats, and here, I believe, many of the *corps diplomatique* reside.

Dr. Heap, American consul at Tunis (whom we made acquaintance with there), called on me lately. I was glad to see him, but very sorry to learn that he had had more than one melancholy loss lately. His charming daughter, Mrs. Ferrier, was in a very delicate, indeed alarming state of health while we were there: she has since died, and she left her husband suffering from the same complaint—consumption.

Dr. Heap told me how well the Bey had behaved on the occasion of the death of my poor much-esteemed friend, Sir Thomas Reade. He sent two thousand troops to attend the funeral, and offered the Abdellia to Lady Reade for her life, if she would like to live there. I was so much reminded of Tunis by the way in which Dr. Heap shook the forefinger of the right hand before his chin, whenever he wished to say "No." This negative sign is constantly used there; and I remember little dear Peter Reade, at five years old, gravely shaking his little finger backward and forward before his innocent childish countenance, when asked any thing from which he dissented, as solemnly as the oldest Moor in the Regency.

The General Post Office here is a handsome, white marble building, classical and simple. The Patent Office is to the north of it,

* Since the letters were written this has taken place.

and is a very noble structure. The Treasury is splendid, and has a colonnade of extraordinarily great length and beauty. The President's mansion, usually called the "White House," is of ample size, and of simple architecture; it has altogether a noble effect: quiet lawns surround it, and some fine trees are grouped near: it is said to be not at all in a healthy situation.

We have just paid a visit by appointment to the hero-President. Madame C—— kindly took us there. I was much pleased at being allowed to take V——: she may never have another opportunity of being presented to a President of the United States. She was delighted at going.

General Taylor received us most kindly. He had had two councils to preside over that morning, and when we first arrived at the White House, he was actually engaged in an extra Session of Council—in short, overwhelmed with business, which rendered it doubly kind and amiable of him to receive us. Mrs. Bliss, the charming daughter of the President, was in the drawing-room when we first went in. Mrs. Taylor has delicate health, and does not do the honors of the Presidential mansion. Mrs. Bliss received us most cordially and courteously, saying her father would come as soon as his presence could be dispensed with. Presently after, the President made his appearance: his manners are winningly frank, simple, and kind, and though characteristically distinguished by much straightforwardness, there is not the slightest roughness in his address. There was a quick, keen, eagle-like expression in the eye which reminded me a little of the Duke of Wellington's.

He commenced an animated conversation with Madame C. de la B—— and us: among other things, speaking of the routes, he recommended me to follow, steam navigation, Mexico, and the Rio Grande, &c.

He was so exceedingly good-natured as to talk a great deal to my little girl about roses and lilies, as if he had been quite a botanist all his life. This species of the slight, childish, daffydown-dilly talk was so particularly and amiably considerate and kind to her, that it overcame her shyness at once, and the dread she had entertained of not understanding what he might say to her.

I was quite sorry when the time came for us to leave the White House. General Taylor strongly advised me not to leave America without seeing St. Louis: he said he considered it altogether perhaps the most interesting town in the United States: he said he recollected the greater part of it a deep dense forest. He spoke very kindly of England, and adverting to the approaching acceleration and extension of steam communication between her and America (the contemplated competition about to be established by "Collins's line") he exclaimed, "The voyage will be made shorter and shorter, and I expect England and America will soon be quite alongside of each other, ma'am."

"The sooner the better, sir," I most heartily responded, at which he bowed and smiled.

"We are the same people," he continued, "and it is good for both to see more of each other."

"Yes," I replied, "and thus all detestable old prejudices will die away."

"I hope so," he said: "it will be for the advantage of both."

He continued in this strain and spoke so nobly of England, that it made one's heart bound to hear him. And he evidently felt what he said; indeed, I am sure that honest, high-hearted, true-as-steel, old hero could not say any thing he did not feel or think.

A little while before we took leave he said, "I hope you will visit my farm near Natchez: Cypress Grove is the name—a sad name," he said, with a smile, "but I think you will find it interesting." I thanked him, and promised so to do. A short time previously, after talking about the beauties of Nature in the South, General Taylor had said to V——, that he longed to return to that farm, and to his quiet home near the banks of the Mississippi, and added, that he was sorely tired of public life, and the harassing responsibilities of his high office. The President insisted most courteously on conducting us to our carriage, and bareheaded he handed us in, standing on the steps till we drove off, and cordially reiterating many kind and friendly wishes for our prosperous journey, and health, and safety.

We afterward went to Madame C——'s, and staid some time in her pleasant house. She kindly wishes me to go to a party at her house to-night, but the sudden hot weather has given me a headache, and I fear I shall not be able. It is the Indian Summer here, now, which answers to the French "Eté de St. Martin," only it is twenty times as hot. The spacious high rooms in the White House felt quite oppressively warm, and here we are suffocated with heat, though the drawing-room is a large apartment. I think it is like a July in England, when our summer has *not* "set in with its usual severity." Fans and parasols are plentiful; and there are no fires except the apparently indispensable ones which are lit, it would almost seem, for the benefit of the very numerous fire-companies here and elsewhere in the Union.

## CHAPTER XVI.

Discomforts of Traveling over the Alleghanies—Mr. Clay—Pittsburg as sable as Sheffield—Its Population—Visit to a Glass Factory and Iron Foundry—A dingy Vehicle—Factories and Foundries in Pittsburg—The Ohio—The new Suspension Bridge at Wheeling—Accidents to Steamers caused by it—Courtesy of the Captains and Clerks of Steamers—Cincinnati—German and Irish Immigrants compared—Verses addressed to Emigrants.

We had a very cold journey to Louisville over the Alleghanies, but a safe one, which is, I find, matter of congratulation.

I think it was the day before we started from Cumberland, Mr. Clay was overturned on those rough roads: most fortunately, he was not injured. Another carriage that started about the same time we did, was detained a very long time; and the passengers had to walk a long way. I am not, in general, fond of walking, but should particularly hate such compulsory pedestrianism.

One can not wonder at accidents in crossing these mountains, for the drivers appear to be frequently intoxicated, and are rough and reckless, cruel to their horses, by over-urging them, and cruel to their passengers, driving often full gallop over the worst part of abominable roads, to the almost dislocation of their limbs and the bumping and thumping of their unfortunate heads against the hard roof of the vehicle. If there be any truth in phrenology, what changes in character must be wrought during a journey across the Alleghanies! The morose cynic may come out sweet as syrup; the humble with an ambition, that will be already practiced in "overvaulting itself" and tumbling on the other side! A Pensylvanian Quaker might be shaken out of all his trembling sectarianism, or a French novel-writer tossed into a demure Broadbrim. I can answer for our tempers being very materially changed.

I am particularly sorry to miss seeing Mr. Clay, for whom I had a letter of introduction from Mr. ——: it is the only disappointment I have yet had in America. He crossed the Alleghanies for Washington in good time to avoid bad roads and bad weather. The first he certainly did not.

We stopped at Pittsburg on our way hither at an excellent hotel called the Monongahela House. At Pittsburg we went to see some manufactories, and iron foundries, in a sort of coal-scuttle on wheels. No mourning coach was ever so thoroughly black, methinks, inwardly and outwardly; and, that we might be in keeping with our vehicle, we found it obligingly undertook (without any outlay or trouble on our part) to put us all into decent mourning.

Pittsburg has as sable a complexion as Sheffield. It is situated at the confluence of the Monongahela and the Alleghany (the latter name, I believe, means "clear water"), which by their union form the noble Ohio. These two rivers, together, avail not to cleanse the sooty Pittsburg; if they did, as Coleridge said of the Rhine at Cologne, nothing could ever wash them clean again (though it has *not* the hundred and seventy-two distinct "*mauvaises odeurs*" of that city). Nevertheless, in spite of its brunette coloring, it is a handsome town. With its suburbs, it contains about seventy-five thousand inhabitants; some say a hundred thousand.

A great number of Germans are settled at Pittsburg. In one manufactory (a glass one) we heard hardly any language but German spoken. An American in that manufactory looked rather reproachfully at us, with a glassy eye—or an eye to the glass—and said, we English were underselling them in articles of this material. I bore the "brittle" impeachment as well as I could; this glass was slippery ground, and I was fain to slide off it.

In the place we next went to, without meaning to insinuate any thing to the prejudice of Pittsburg, which is a well-principled and orthodox city, I doubt not, it really appeared to me they had dealings in the black art—(I must beg to disclaim any allusion to the half-mourning tints which seem the fashion here)—so wondrous was the rapidity of the processes, and the way in which the workmen appeared to be snowballing one another with huge lumps and blocks of red-hot iron. The noise was very great, and the glare; but in the midst of the confusion a woman stood with a mite of a baby in her arms, an infant Cyclops, or young Vulcan himself in bib and tucker—to judge by the coolness with which it surveyed the scene and listened to the noise, as if the whole were got up for its especial edification, and it would like much to have all those pretty playthings that were being tossed about on all sides.

It was late, and our "coal-scuttle" stopped the way, so we departed, still leaving the little Vulcan evidently deeply engaged in teaching his own young idea how to shoot, or to toss those nice balls of red hot iron, which he would also have liked uncommonly to stuff into his mouth, big as they were. We stepped most gingerly into our jetty coach; but in vain did we try to escape being made finished chimney-sweepers. Methinks it must have served a subterraneous apprenticeship in some coal-mine as a lowly wagon for the conveyance of that article, before it was promoted to its present office above-ground—the reverse of the fate of mortals. The driver was hopelessly black, having the features, however, of a white man, and the brogue of the Green Erin. He affected to guard our dresses from the wheel as we ascended, which delicate attention was but a refinement of barbarity, adding insult to injury. We met a number of similarly sable coaches, but I think ours bore the *belle.*

There are twenty-five furnaces, and five forges and rolling-mills in Pittsburg, besides which, there are woolen and cotton factories, machine shops, tanneries, and hardware, cutlery, and several other manufactories in abundance. The city is lighted by gas, which is produced by the bituminous coal that fills the hills which surround Pittsburgh. Most of the extensive manufactories are not *in* the city, but are distributed over a circle of about five miles' radius from the Court House, which stands on Grant's Hill. One of the suburbs of Pittsburg is called Birmingham.

The Ohio quite exceeded my expectations: the river and the scenery are both beautiful. We came under a splendid new suspension bridge at Wheeling, which is however, a bone of contention just now between various parties. It seems, the bridge is not high enough for some of the lofty funnels of the steamers, and several of these have had some very hard knocks. There are great complaints in consequence; and the poor captains of these crippled boats seem, to judge by the newspapers, to take their disfigurement and discomfiture quite to heart. Captain This has felt himself grievously wounded through the knock-down blows dealt at the splendid steamer "Explosion," by the bridge aforesaid; and Captain That thinks he will never entirely recover—indeed, will carry sympathetically to the end of his days the marks left on his beautiful steamer, the "Racer."

If there is any safety in new steamers, we need not just now be afraid of boilers bursting, or any such *foreseen* accidents, on these rivers; for, since this new and destruction-dealing bridge has been built, it is extraordinary how every steamer on the river, according to the complainants' statements (save those with low funnels) seems equally "new," "splendid," and just "come out." It must be provoking, it is true, to be knocked on the head—of your steamer, and to be forced to cut her down yourself without mercy. That bridge, in short, proves a "bridge of sighs" to the navigators of the Ohio. As for our boat, being of moderate proportions, she did not receive the slightest contusion on her crown. She was, (though not holding her head as high as some) an extremely fine and comfortable vessel.

The captains of these steamers appear universally a most gentleman-like set of persons, and the clerks are always as civil and obliging as possible. The other day, having heard one particular steamer was the best, I sent to take places in it: all was arranged and paid, but the person who had taken the tickets had mistaken a rival boat for the one specified. When I found out this misunderstanding, which was not till we went down to the wharf to embark, I went to the clerk (not liking the appearance of this boat so much as that of the opposition one to which we had been recommended) and informed him of the error that had been committed, and asked if we might be allowed to change. He most courteously complied, and returned the money. In the hurry of departure, I did not do what I *now* feel sorry I did not—return such civility by going by the smaller boat, after all; for such obliging conduct deserves to meet with reciprocal complaisance.

We only stopped a day at Cincinnati, for the hotels were all crowded, which made it extremely uncomfortable. The "Queen City of the West," is built on the north bank of the Ohio. It has floating wharves, which are rendered necessary by the continual and rapid fluctuations of the river. It is a very handsome city, and in a remarkably fine situation. In 1840, the population was 46,338; and now it is estimated at about 110,000. I asked them, at Pittsburg, and other places, how they liked the German immigrants. You almost invariably receive the same reply to this question:—"Very much. They are the best immigrants possible: industrious, generally sober and quiet—not quarrelsome like the Irish." Then they added—"but we could not do without the Irish. They build all our railroads, make our roads, canals, and do all the hardest work in the country."

"Wanderers! who come from many a distant zone,
To gaze on Nature's Transatlantic throne:—
Wanderers!—whose feet like mine ne'er trod before,
This proud, magnificently-various shore;
Ne'er lightly view the thousand scenes sublime
Of great America's resplendent clime;
But still, in thoughtful mood's observant care
Weigh well the many-mingling glories there
Since all the loftier wonders of the land
Are most admired, when best ye understand.

'Tis a glad, gracious study for the soul,
As part by part the Heaven-stamped leaves unroll,
To watch the crowing triumphs still expand,
The will, the wisdom live along the land!
  Not only all-majestic Nature here
Speaks to each kindling thought, but far and near
A large and mighty meaning seems to lurk,
A glorious mind is every where at work!—
A bold, grand spirit rules and reigns around,
And sanctifies the common air and ground;
And glorifies the lowliest herb and stone
With conscious tints and touches of its own;—
A spirit ever flashing back the sun,
That scorns each prize while aught is to be won;—
More boundless than the prairie's wondrous sweep,
Or the old Atlantic's long-resounding deep;—
And more luxuriant than the forest's crowd
Of patriarch trees, by weightiest foliage bowed;—
More rich than California's teeming mould,
Whose hoarded sunbeams laugh to living gold;—
More soaring far than the immemorial hills,
More fresh and flowing than their streams and rills.
That mind of quenchless energy and power
Which springs from strength to strength, hour after hour;
Man's glorious mind in its most glorious mood,—
That seems for aye, on every side to brood
In this empurpled and exultant land
So gladly bowed beneath its bright command.
Man's sovereign mind in its most sovereign march,
Embracing earth, like light's own rainbowed arch.
  That soul—that mind, 'tis every where revealed,—
It crowns the steep, it gilds the cultured field,
Bids science, art, and studious knowledge aid,
Till all hath heard its voice, and all obeyed.
It charms the waste, and paves the rushing stream,
And scarce allows the sun a vagrant beam;
The obsequious lightning to its service trains,
And bids the elements to wear its chains.
It tames the rugged soil of rocks, and flings
From seas to seas the shadow of its wings;
And Time and Space in that great shadow rest,
And watch to serve their ruler-sons' behest;
And still its growing, gathering influence spreads,
And still abroad its own great life it sheds
O'er mount and lake, o'er cataract, field and flood—
O'er rock, and cave, and isle, o'er plain and wood:
It lives, it lightens, and its might inspires
Each separate scene with fresh creative fires.
Where'er it moves a wondering world awakes,
And fast all nature's form its likeness takes;
It quickening thrills, and kindles and pervades——
Her startled deserts and receding shades,

Her mightiest solitudes and paths unknown,
Her deep-vailed shrines, and well-springs pure and lone.
America's great Mind, *the true* New World,
Launched like the sun, 'gainst th' elder darkness hurled;
Hung, as The Heavens are hung, above thêm all,
And holding their sublimest powers in thrall!

It must be confessed that Cincinnati, the pride of the banks of "La belle Rivière," is in fact what its nickname, "Porkopolis," implies—the Empire City of Pigs, as well as of the West; but it is fortunate that they condescendingly allow human beings to share that truly magnificent location with them.

---

## CHAPTER XVII.

Description of Louisville—Its Trade and Natural Productions—Its Soil and Rivers—The Kentucky Caves—A Visit to one—Its Avenues, Domes, Cataracts, Pits, and Rivers—A Sea in it—The vociferous Bats—Echoes of the Cave—The Cave once the Residence of consumptive Patients—The eyeless Fish—The narrow Path and the fat Englishman—Vast Extent of the Cave—Verses suggested by it.

We have had a very interesting expedition to the Mammoth Cave of Kentucky. But, first, a word of Louisville itself.

It is a fine city, and the best lighted, I think, that I have seen in the United States. I imagine the Louisvillians are proud of this, as they have their diligences start at four o'clock in the winter's morning! It is the chief commercial city of Kentucky, and lies on the south bank of the Ohio. The canal from Portland enables large steamers to come to the wharves. An extensive trade is carried on here, and there are manufactories of various descriptions, the facilities offered by the enormous water-power of the region assisting greatly in the development of this department of industry. There are numerous factories, foundries, woolen and cotton mills, flour-mills, &c. The population is about forty-seven thousand: in 1800, it was only six hundred. Kentucky is a very prosperous state.

The natural growths of the soil are—the black cherry, black walnut, chestnut, honey-locust, buck-eye, pawpaw, mulberry, sugar-maple, ash, elm, white-thorn, cotton-wood, and abundance of grape-vines, and various others. Part of the country we traversed in going to "The Cave," is called the "Barrens;" other portions looked very fertile, and reminded me exceedingly of England. "The Barrens," were bestowed some time ago gratuitously on actual settlers, as the Legislature of the State were under the erroneous impression that the tract was of little value; but it proved to be remarkably good grain land, and particularly well adapted to grazing and the successful rearing of cattle.

Below the mountains, the whole of Kentucky, it appears, rests on an enormous bed of limestone, generally about eight feet beneath the surface. Every where in this formation are found apertures, which they denominate "Sink-holes." Through these the flowing waters of the rivers disappear into the earth. Several of these were pointed out to us on our journey. Owing to this the waters in Kentucky are more impoverished and diminished during the hot and dry season, than those of any other portion of the United States, and the lesser streams vanish entirely.

The banks of the rivers are quite natural curiosities. Very profound channels are usually worn in the calcareous rock which they pass over in their course. The Kentucky River especially is said to have sublime precipices of great height, on either side, consisting of almost perpendicular banks of solid limestone.

There are several huge caves between Green and Cumberland rivers; but the one we went to see is the largest. The size of it may be guessed when I inform the reader that we walked in it the first day eight miles, four in and four out; and the second fourteen, seven in and seven out, hardly traversing any of the same ground, except just at the beginning. In fact, this marvelous cave is a little subterranean state in itself, that might almost claim to be admitted separately into the Union, if it had any population besides mummies and bats (and, alas! the former have disappeared, to our regret).

The cave contains, it is said, two hundred and twenty-six avenues! It has, besides, forty-seven domes, eight cataracts, twenty-three pits, and several rivers—one, the River Styx—and, I believe, a small sea, the Dead Sea. The Echo River (called so from its possessing a very remarkable and powerful echo) is wide enough and deep enough to float the largest steamer. The great dome is four hundred feet high. In 1813, two Indian mummies were found here, wrapped in highly-ornamented deerskins; so that it is evident, though the white men have only of late years discovered this gigantic cavern, the red warriors knew of it in days of yore. There was a great deal of saltpetre found in this cave, and the remains of the furnaces, and large mounds of ashes, are still to be seen near the entrance.

In one of the most beautiful chambers we saw in the interior of this vast underground Palace of Nature, the roof appeared to represent a firmament of stars! A comet, with its train of light, seemed sparkling in the distance. And in another place, the appearance of the roof was that of an "inverted flower-garden" (as Professor ——, at Washington, happily called it, in describing the wonders of this under-world to me). The bats, which are "located" near the mouth of the cave (where, spacious an area as it is, there are excellent lodgings for man and bat—if any of the former are tired of this very superficial earth), are the noisiest little rascals I ever met with. Jabbering like monkeys, chattering like magpies, they appear to repudiate all connection with their humble, quiet little cousins, the mice. They made such a din when we entered their chosen precincts, that it seemed as if they were hissing us off the subterranean stage on which we were making our *début*, rather agitated at our novel position; or perhaps they were intending those suspicious sounds for cheers—nine times nine, and one cheer more—and the Kentish (or, rather, the Kentuckyish) fire, at our entry.

Without caring to silence this bat-tery, we proceeded, and soon invaded the haunts of old Silence herself. Ours being almost entirely a female party, it will readily be imagined, we did little to disturb the stillness of the place! One English and one American gentleman, however, were also there; and I can not answer equally for them, especially the latter, who, however, did the honors of the cave most admirably. He knew every nook of it, brought out the echoes splendidly, with "The Arkansas Hunters," "Uncle Ned," "O! Susanna," and other far-famed works of the great masters, finishing with "Yankee-doodle," and repeated some really very fine and striking lines, author unknown. There is a magnificent natural church in the cave; and here divine service has been performed, we were assured. Of course, we had a great number of torches, or rather lamps with us. Bengal lights are sometimes used here, but we had not given due warning, and none were to be procured.

Some of the sadder things to be seen in this gloomy stronghold of Nature, are the remains of a number of small ruined houses, erected within the cave for consumptive patients, the constantly equable temperature of this solemn place being considered as of great efficacy in restoring them to health. This idea is, however,

I should imagine, almost abandoned, if we may judge by the dilapidated structures before alluded to; indeed, we understand that the depressing effect on the spirits of the sufferers tended greatly to counteract the beneficial influence of the unvarying and mild temperature. They were obliged to remove these melancholy habitations to some distance from each other, as they found the constant sound of the hollow cough reverberating through the vaulted galleries irritated the nerves, and affected the spirits of the invalids grievously. I can not imagine it doing any good in a single instance; yet it is said some apparent cures were performed; but on returning to the upper earth and the cheerfulness of day, the symptoms of the disorder immediately returned, and, therefore, the only hope of continued existence was in renouncing all its delights and charms; in perpetuating this most dreary exile, in living as much like the dead as possible, and in anticipating and rehearsing, as it were, the loneliness, the gloom, the silence of the grave. These ruined tenements made me shudder; sepulchres of the living as they must have been.

Even for the short time I was in the cave I felt a strange oppression, and a longing for the sun and the free fresh air again, that was almost painful. Notwithstanding this, you can undergo much greater fatigue in the cave than outside—owing, I was told, to the remarkable elasticity of the air there; but walking so long, and over such frightfully-rugged ground made me very thirsty. Some of the springs were of delicious water, but one that we drank of was like sulphur: we should have thought it horrible under other circumstances, but were so suffering from drought, that we found it then and there exquisite.

One of the most singular curiosities of this stupendous cave, are the eyeless fish that are found in one of the rivers: they are not only destitute of eyes, but have not the faintest, slightest rudiments of the organ, or place for it; the skull is perfectly smooth. I had heard these fish much talked of by Professors A—— and G—— at Cambridge, and was anxious to see one; there were some swimming about in the river, but I could not thus examine their peculiarities satisfactorily; subsequently, I got a preserved one in spirits. They are to be purchased of the guides.

There is in the cave an extraordinarily narrow path, between immense rocks, through which a human being can with difficulty force his way. The American gentleman I have alluded to before gave an amusing account of a fat Englishman accomplishing this feat, and emerging on the other side, all sorts of shapes—a kind of

Proteus, exhibiting at one and the same time, a pleasing variety of appearances. One arm jammed into his side, one cheek alarmingly flattened, and the other, by the contrast, apparently puffed out preposterously, as if the material of the one had been squeezed into the other. By all accounts he must have looked something like a huge pillow, of which the feathers had been displaced in one part, and huddled up in another, which, in short, had shifted its cargo of down! and that required shaking and putting to rights. By degrees the metamorphosis ceased, and he shortly regained his natural shape, but then the poor wretch had to endure a second martyrdom! I know not the end of his history, perhaps he staid on the other side for a while, practiced abstemiousness, and went into training, and so came out of the cave a "lean and slippered pantaloon," having gone in like a *Falstaff*. This "Winding Way" is popularly known as "The Fat Man's Misery."

It is the tall man's also, for even women have here and there to bend almost double. One longed to walk with one's head under one's arm, in imitation of some of the gentry who figure in ghost stories. I suffered several times from a severe concussion of my bonnet, and only narrowly escaped a compound fracture of the comb.

As to the cave altogether, it is magnificent—that is, what we saw of it; for many parts of it we did not see at all, which are already explored, and it is said people may go on exploring for three hundred miles or more; I should be sorry to try the experiment. After this under-ground jaunt—after this sort of temporary burial, I think one almost requires a dozen or so of balloon-ascensions to restore the equilibrium of one's feelings, and take away the subterraneousness of one's sensations, and ungrovelize one's self;—in short, to carry off a little of the superabundant earthliness that one feels has been acquired by walking below ground, where should be nothing but graves and gas-pipes, and cellars and worms, and Guy Fawkeses, and sorcerers, and mummies, and trains of gunpowder, and fossil Ichthyosauruses.

Stalactites and stalagmites are beautiful and interesting, but they seem to me to have a sort of magnetism of petrifaction about them, and to inoculate one with ossification. Glad was I when we wended our way from these mighty vaults, with their imitation stars and hobgoblin roses: we had to pass again by the same great Hall by which we entered, under the living leathern canopy of the imminent bats which almost grazed or stuck to our much-enduring bonnets as we passed—so low was the roof in some places.

## THE MAMMOTH CAVE IN KENTUCKY.

And have a thousand burning worlds on high,
And tens of thousands marshaled in the sky,
Scattering their splendor o'er Heaven's boundless plain
Besieged thy gates for ages—and in vain?
Never the gentle Pleiad here hath gazed;
Not here hath ever flashing comet blazed,
Nor keenest lightning sent one arrowy ray,
'Midst these dread strongholds of the night to play,
Nor here the artillery of the thunder even
E'er woke one echo of the Voice of Heaven.
Stars from their spheres have shot—but here unmissed,
Of them this frowning under-world ne'er wist.
Still of the sun unseen, there lives a sign,
His warmth comes even to this sepulchral shrine.
Yet by no change seems the awful gloom beguiled,
Here rain nor rainbow ever wept nor smiled.
Yet oh! the hanging gardens glittering there
Where sunshine laughs not, and no dews appear;
And not a butterfly pursues its flight,
Giving and gaining hues more freshly bright.
Behold the inverted beds of sumptuous flowers,—
That wealth of stony blooms, and frozen bowers,
Those spectral buds, those sparry branches drear,
That pomp of floral petrifactions there,
Those ghostly wreaths—those braids of shadowy leaves,
Which Nature, as in stern self-mockery, weaves,
Roses and sunflowers; tulips rich, and bells
Of sumptuous lilies, where no sweetness dwells;
And sculptured irises, and dahlias pale,
Unknown to spring's bright ray, or autumn's gale,
All in a deadly beauty coldly clad,
A funeral pomp, bewilderingly sad.
How sweet—how exquisite compared with these,
The lowliest hedge-flower, touched by dew and breeze!
How dear, compared with such stark frigid shows,
The wan and withered ruins of a rose,
That once has looked on day's bright star, and grown
Something that seemed a stray smile of his own
True, 'tis most beautiful, most wondrous too,
This tranced—this spell-bound nature, calm and new;
But yet this mockery of earth's heaven-born things.
Though fair, though glorious, but despondence brings.
'Tis like Death's palace with his cold white show,
Of all that most should smile with life's fresh glow.
For me, I long to leave these precincts drear,
Shun this cold ghost of Nature reigning here,
(So fixed, so fate-like, life and motion seem
Near this, the fleeting fictions of a dream),
And once again the glad Creation hail,
That tells with thousand tongues the eternal tale.

Give back the world! the changeful hues and forms,
The hurrying shadows of its very storms.
Oh! for a mountain-scene to lift me now
On high; as 'twere to climb near Heaven's sweet brow;
Give me those scenes, fresh, moving, breathing, free,
Where even midst gloom, a thousand glories be.
And sound, ye clarion-tones of winds, which make
The stately forests to their centres shake!
Give even the quivering darkness of that Night,
Which heaves and hovers as 'twere taking flight!
And give the change of seasons and of hours,
The strife of elements, the shock of powers!
And life-like shiftings, and awakening signs,
True, quickening tones from Nature's thousand shrines.
Give me, for these cold vaults, and these bare halls,
The glistening smile of streams—the roar of falls;
The startling wonders of the restless deep,
The towering headland, and the cloud-capped steep;
Glaciers for stalactites, keen moons for spars,
For these dull gauds Heaven's galaxies of stars;
Nay, humbler be the yearning, less the prayer,
Give any scene of outward Nature fair,
For th' awful mysteries of this solemn cave,
Give but a breath, a cloud, a flower, a wave;
For all the dreadful splendors that it boasts,
*One* mirrored ray from yonder starry hosts!

## CHAPTER XVIII.

A Conversation in a Coach—A loquacious Gentleman—The other Passenger—His Appearance—An American Argument touching the Potency of Money to make a Gentleman—An Exhibition of genuine Feeling—A Kentuckian's Notion of England—The slight Value set on human Life in America—The Duel—Pigs paramount in Louisville—Herds of Swine on the Alleghanies—The Hotel-Keeper and the Kentucky Cave—Danger attending a Visit to the Caves.

I CAN not refrain from giving a conversation which I heard as we came by the coach to Louisville. One of the speakers was a very agreeable and apparently well-informed gentleman, who seemed to have seen a great deal of the world. When he first entered the "stage," it would seem it was with the benignant intention of giving a sort of *conversazione* in the coach, in which after a few preliminary interrogatories to the various passengers (as if to take the size and measure of their capacities), he sustained all the active part, not calling upon them for the slightest exercise of their

conversational powers. He varied the entertainment occasionally by soliloquizing and monopolyloguizing; and ever and anon it appeared as if he addressed the human race generally, or was speaking for posterity in a very elevated tone indeed, and seemingly oblivious of that fraction of the contemporaneous generation who were then largely benefiting by his really most animated and amusing discourse—for he was thoroughly original and very shrewd and entertaining.

Where had he not been? What had he not seen? what not met, tried, suffered, sought, found, dared, done, won, lost, said? The last we could give the most implicit credence to, no matter how large the demand. Now he told us, or the ceiling of the coach, how he had been eighteen months in the Prairies (which keep very open house for all visitors), shooting herds of buffaloes, and with his cloak for his only castle, and all his household furniture, and how he had been all this time without bed or bread: and he described the longing for the last, much in the way Mr. Ruxton does in his account of Prairie excursions; and now—but I will not attempt to follow him in all his wondrous adventures.

Suffice it to say, Robinson Crusoe, placed in juxtaposition with him, was a mere fire-side stay-at-home sort of personage, one who had never left his own comfortable arm-chair, in comparison. In short, the adventures were marvelous and manifold, and all told in the same agreeable, lively, Scheherezade-like sort of a manner—so agreeable, indeed, that I am sure had Judge Lynch himself had any little account to settle with him, he would have postponed—*à la* Sultan of the Indies—any trifling beheading or strangling, or unpleasant little operation of the sort, to hear the end of the tale.

After these narratives and amusing lectures had been poured forth continuously for a length of time, it chanced that a quiet countryman-like person got into the coach, bundle and stick in hand. After a few questions to the rustic wayfarer, our eloquent orator left off his historic and other tales, and devoted himself to drawing out, and "squeezing the orange of the brains" of this apparently simple-minded and unlettered man. The discourse that ensued was a singular one—to take place, too, in the United States between Americans.

The new-comer was a Kentuckian by birth, who had not very long ago gone to settle in Indiana. He called himself a mechanic—these facts came out in answer to the queries put to him by our unwearied talker—but he had, as I have said, much more the appearance of a respectable country farming man—and indeed,

I believe, mechanic means here, in a general sense, a laborer. He seemed, a fine, honest-hearted, straight-forward, noble-spirited son of the plow; and his lofty, earnest, generous sentiments were spoken in somewhat unpolished but energetic and good language; and what particularly struck me was a really beautiful and almost child-like simplicity of mind and manner, that was combined with the most uncompromising firmness and unflinching adherence in argument, to what he conceived to be right.

His features were decidedly plain, but the countenance was very fine, chiefly characterized by great ingenuousness, commingled with gentleness and benevolence; and yet bearing evident traces of strength, determination, and energetic resolution. It was rather a complicated countenance, so to say, notwithstanding its great openness and expression of downright truth and goodness.

After opening the conversation with him, as you would an oyster, by the introduction of a pretty keen knife of inquisitorial questions, the chief speaker began to hold forth, capriciously enough, on the essentials and distinguishing attributes of a gentleman. He declared, emphatically, that one qualification alone was necessary, and that money only made a gentleman, according to the world, and, above all, in the United States (quite a mistake is this, I fully believe). "Let a man," said he, "be dressed here in every thing of the best, with splendid rings on his fingers, and plenty of money to spend at the ends of them, and he may go where he will, and be received as a gentleman; ay, though he may be a gambler, a rogue, or a swindler, and you, now, *you* may be a good honest mechanic; but *he* will at once get into the best society in these parts, which you would never dream even of attempting to accomplish—"

"But he would not be a gentleman," broke in the Kentuckian, indignantly. "No, sir; nor will I ever allow that money only makes the gentleman: it is the principle, sir, and the inner feeling, and the mind—and no fine clothes can ever make it; and no rough ones unmake it, that's a fact. And, sir, there's many a better gentleman following the plow in these parts than there is among the richer classes: I mean those poor men who're contented with their lot, and work hard and try no mean shifts and methods to get on and up in the world; for there's little some 'ill stick at to get at money; and such means a true gentleman (what *I* call a gentleman) will avoid like pison, and scorn utterly."

"Now that's all very well for you to talk so here just now; but you know yourself, I don't doubt, that *your own* object, as well as all the world's around you, is to make money. It is with that object that you work hard and save up: you do not work only to live, or make yourself more comfortable, but to get money: and money is the be-all and end-all of all and every body; and that only commands consideration and respect."

"That *only*, sir, would never command *mine*, and—"

"Why, how you talk now! if you meet a fine dressed-out gentleman in one of these stages, you look on him as one directly—you don't ask him did he *make* or *take* his money—what's that to you?—there he is, and it is not for you to busy or bother yourself to find out all the private particulars of his history; and if you find him, as I say, well dressed in superfine, and he acts the gentleman to you, he may be the greatest rogue in existence, but he will be treated by you like a gentleman—yes, even by you."

"Yes, sir, that may be while I know nothing of him—while as you say, he acts the gentleman to me; but let me *once find out* what he is, and I would never show him respect more—no! though he had all the gold of California."

"Ah, California! just look at *that* now—look at people by scores and thousands, leaving their families, and friends, and homes—and what for but for gold? people with a comfortable competence already; but it's fine talking. Why, what are *you* taking this very journey for?—why, I can answer for you—for gold, I doubt not; and every other action of your life is for that object: confess the real truth now."

"I will, sir—I am come here from Indiana, for though I'm a Kentucky man, I live in the Hoosier State. I'm come here to see a dear brother; and instead of *gaining* money I'm *spending* it in these stages to get to see him and 'old Kentuck' agin. So you see sir, I love my brother—I do more than money, poor man as I am; ay, and that I do too."

"Well, I dare say you do; but come now, just tell me—haven't you a little bit of a *speculation*, now, here, that you're come after, as well as your brother—some trifle of a speculation afoot? You know you have now. You *must* have. Some horse, perhaps—"

It was quite delightful to see and hear the indignant burst of eager denial which this elicited from the ingenuous Kentuckian.

"No, sir! *no*, I have *not*—none whatever, indeed I have not:" his voice quivered with emotion; the earnest expression of his countenance was more than eloquent. If his interrogator had accused him of a serious crime he could hardly more anxiously and more earnestly have disclaimed it. To him, I thought the bare suspicion seemed like a coarse desecration of his real motives, a kind of undervaluing even of his "dear brother," to suppose he must have had a "little speculation on hand" to make it worth his while to go to see *him.*

He went on in an agitated, eager tone:

"And look ye here; I am *leaving off* my work and money-making for some days on purpose—only for that, and spending money at it, too!"

His somewhat case-hardened antagonist looked the least in the world discomfited, for that angry denial was a magnificent burst, and uttered in a tone that actually seemed to give an additional jolt to the rough coach; and I might say it had really a splendid theatrical effect, but that I should hesitate to use that expression with reference to one of the most beautiful natural exhibitions of deep feeling and generous sentiment I ever witnessed.

"Where are you going to?" at last inquired the other, apparently about to commence a little cross-examination.

"About twenty miles beyond Munsfordville," replied Kentucky, in his simple, direct manner, "to—" I forget the name.

"Why, you're come by the wrong stage, then," exclaimed the other, "you should have waited till to-morrow, and then taken the stage to ——, and then you would have gone direct."

"Well, yes, sir; it's true enough, sir; but you see—in short, I couldn't *wait*—no, that I couldn't. I was so anxious, and I felt so like seeing my brother; and I was in such a mortal hurry to get to him."

"Hurry, man! why how will you see him any sooner by this? Why you might as well have walked up and down Main-street till to-morrow; it would have advanced you just as much on your journey."

"You're right, sir, I know that; but I really *couldn't* wait: I wanted to feel I was going ahead, and getting *nearer* my brother at any rate; I got so impatient-like. No, sir; I couldn't have staid till the morning any how you could fix it."

"You'll have to walk for your folly, for you'll get no conveyance this way, I tell you."

"I'll have to walk the twenty miles to-night, I suppose," said Kentucky, with the most imperturbable smiling composure; "but never mind that! I shall be getting near my brother, then. Ha," he said, after a pause, "you see I *do* love my brother, sir, and I don't regard trouble for him. I'll have to walk the twenty miles to-night with my bundle, I dare say, and spending money at that, too, perhaps, for a bit of food; but I couldn't have *waited*—no! not another hour at Louisville—I felt so like getting *nearer* to my brother."

At the end of the argument about money-making being the all in all, one or two of us signified briefly that we thought Kentucky was right. You never saw any body so surprised. He had evidently entertained a deep conviction that all in the stage-coach were opposed to his opinions, and that he stood alone in his veiw on the matter. He replied he was glad any body thought as he did, and reiterated with strong emphasis to his opponent:

"I'm sure, sir, I'm right; it is the principle, and the manners, and the mind, and *not* money that makes a gentleman. No, no; money can never make half a one."

I shall feel a respect for "old Kentucky" forever after for his sake.

This high-hearted fellow-passenger of ours seemed to know very little of any country but his own. He discovered we were English, and exclaimed—"That England may be a good country, but I could never bear to live under a king: a man's life must be miserable there! I couldn't bear their laws neither."

"Why, they're pretty nearly the same as here."

"You don't say so!" exclaimed the other, much astonished; for he seemed, like many others, to have an idea that we could not do any thing, or move from any place to another without the sovereign or the army giving leave, or, *vice versâ*, and condescending to regulate all our domestic affairs.

After that true "Nature's nobleman," the Kentucky "mechanic," had vanished from the scene, the same gentleman began talking to a neighbor in his loud, clear voice, on another subject—the little value set on human life in the United States. He said,

"The other day, while I was at ——, two men had a quarrel," and he mentioned their names, which I do not accurately remember, "the one told the other to meet him in the market-place, and to prepare his mind; he did so, and a pistol also: the other had a six-shooter; they fired, and neither fell. Then the one who had the revolver coolly put six bullets into his antagonist, and left him stone dead; and this was in the market-place with numbers assembled, who formed round in a ring," said this gentleman, "to see the horrible spectacle, without one interfering to prevent it. One can not begin to imagine how indifferent the people here are to life in general."

The talkative gentleman told other anecdotes of the same nature, but one will be thought enough, I have no doubt, though it was interesting to hear them related, for he was a capital narrator, all life and spirit; and one could not help paying amused attention, though, it must be confessed, his small talk was chiefly of murders, duels, executions, terrific fights with Indians, encounters with grizzly bears and such small deer—in fact conducted on the principle of Madame Tussaud's "Chamber of Horrors;" a kind of verbal conversational Reign of Terror.

I have already said what a very nice town Louisville is—city, I ought to say, for all large towns have that rank here: yet one thing a little detracts from its general appearance, and that is the preponderating population of pigs that in all directions perambulate its handsome streets. I had observed this with surprise, and was amused at a corroborative paragraph in one of their papers here lately, saying that really the pigs are becoming masters of the place; they push the two-legged citizens into the streets, occupying the side-walks, and taking the wall of them. So things begin to look serious here, and we are prepared any day for a *pronunciamiento* of the pigs, they carry their snouts so high already, and seem so bristling with importance.

In crossing the Alleghanies it was quite a curious sight to see armies of these animals driven along—a perfect stream of swine, rejoicing in all the fat of the land, certainly. It is said to be a wonderful spectacle to see them slaughtered, and almost as magically turned into lard and lard-oil, as if the latter article had been ordered for Aladdin's lamp by his first genie gentleman-in-waiting and equerry.

I must not forget to speak of a rather whimsical but thoroughly obliging, hospitable, and, I believe, excellent old gentleman, at whose hotel we were staying on our way to and from the Mammoth Cave. Singularly enough, he has lived for nearly half a century within a few miles of the cavern, but never has visited it. "Time enough," he growled, in a voice that might have sounded from the subterranean depths of the cave itself, and would have rumbled at Echo River, like a discharge of Satanic artillery, "Time enough to go under ground when I'm dead;" and we almost agreed with him, after we had all gone a-caving, and come back feeling so subterraneanically sepulchral, and with such a dreary antediluvian fossil-like sensation, perfectly convinced of the hollowness of the world in general, and of Kentucky in particular. Indeed, we rather envied Mr. Bell his superficial views and his never having been buried alive, or trodden underfoot by half a quarter of the inhabitants of the State.

One of his female slaves told me, ladies return sometimes from their cave expedition half dead, and keep their beds for "a many days," and occasionally have received severe injuries from stumbling on the rugged sharp-pointed rocks. This negress was one of the most good-natured beings I ever met with: she voluntarily undertook the task of rubbing off from some of our clothes the dust of the cave: she scrubbed away with such zeal that soon her arms became a sort of faint cream color, and her thick crop of wool was so densely powdered as to assume the same tint, together with her smiling gentle face. She appeared to compassionate us profoundly; and, perhaps, imagining, in consequence of her master's prejudices against that mighty cave, that no one of their own free will would visit such a dreadful place (to come back in such a fearful plight), she appeared to entertain an opinion that travelers in general had to go through this ordeal; and, peradventure, were thus naturalized and made real children of the soil, after carrying so much of it away about their persons and habiliments. The claim would be well *grounded*, at any rate.

Mr. B——, the English gentleman who visited the cave at the same time we did, has just arrived here: he called a little while ago and told me that a poor young lady, who was very ill at the Cave Hotel while we were there, died the day before he came away. She had caught cold in coming out of the cave only a few days before, after being much overheated by walking there, and neglecting to put on a shawl: inflammation came on, and she had thus fallen a victim to this slight imprudence.

## CHAPTER XIX.

The Steamer from Louisville—The Passengers—The Lady in the Turban, and her refractory Charges—A Family of another Description—The Liliputian Liston and his Model Grandmamma—The Sonnambula of a Stewardess—St. Louis—Ravages of the Cholera in that City—Rapid Growth of St. Louis—Vast Number of German Immigrants—Progress of American Civilization—Prairie Hunting—Frequency of Steamboat Accidents on the Mississippi.

We left Louisville in a steamer with rather indifferent accommodations, but commanded by a most obliging and courteous captain. There were several families on board, who were removing to remote parts of the Union; slaves, children, chattels, cattle, accompanied them; they were, in short, domestic Atlases carrying their own little world on their shoulders—farther *west* of course—which is quite the way of the world hereabouts.

This was one of the very roughest sets I had ever been among. They lived entirely with the first-class passengers, so no doubt they had paid first-class price. Some were from the heart of old Kentucky, and none of them were emigrants; they all comported themselves very quietly and well, except one family of children, belonging to some hard-working back-woodsman, to judge from appearances. They were awfully spoilt, and led their parents miserable lives; scratching and beating their mother, and boxing the ears and kicking the shins of their (little) respected papa, and knocking cruelly about the only person in the family who had the sense to control the imps a little, in the shape of a gaunt tall grandmamma, resembling a retired grenadier, "in" a turban, with a short pipe—the last evidently the consolation of her soul, and the former ingeniously constructed of some light-colored handkerchief, or handkerchiefs, and apparently built upon her head by her own hands, in a fantastic fashion, having a little appearance of a fortification for defensive purposes, which was rendered necessary by the violent attacks of the undutiful brats before alluded to. Had it not been erected with considerable engineering skill, this poor rustic Cybele with her tower-like turban would have been left defenseless and bareheaded by these little furies.

She was wont to confide to me her troubles on this head—enough to have turned *her* head and turban too, besides other subjects that "worrited" her "pretty considerable." We were great "friends together," and she was quite benignant and patronizing in her manner toward me. Sometimes (smoking her short pipe the while) marching up to me and laying her huge heavy hand on my shoulder, she would exclaim, "Wal, them children of ourn *are* bad children—mighty bad, mighty bad; it wears and worrits a body, I guess, properly: and, my! I feel so skeary-like too, for I've never been aboard one of these steaming boats, nor never *seen* one afore."

This surprised me "considerable," for I should have thought no one could live in the States without seeing them. This I expressed.

"No, I haint; where I live to home, these don't come none on 'em; and they're mighty queer boats, I guess, and I don't like them, and feel proper skeary, too, aboard on 'em."

Then she pensively puffed away at the short pipe, till the roaring of some of those young rebels demanded her presence as "head pacificator;" when, telling me (to console me for her temporary absence) she should soon be back, she, and pipe, and turban, would vanish for a while in the distance. For the benefit of those who like to study various fashions of dress, I may as well remark that the attire of this worthy dame, altogether was a costume somewhat resembling the war-dress of Abd-el-Kader, engrafted on the pacific garments of a Dutch skipper's wife; but no description can do it justice.

I took quite a liking to the worthy soul, and pitied her much for being, as she was alternately, a sufferer from "skearyness," and from the kicks and cuffs of those insubordinate grandchildren of hers. But occasionally she would make a dash at them, like a charge of Napoleon's Old Guard, and retire, crowned with victory, to smoke the short pipe of peace. On one particular day several pitched battles were obstinately fought, besides numerous slight skirmishes. The intrepidity of grandmamma, the Invincible, and her desperate charges, ultimately won, however, the field, and decided the war in favor of the party of order; but the squalling, kicking, biting, and scratching, were alarmingly vehement. The passengers in general preserved a sort of armed neutrality, prepared, however, if the disorderly little enemy attacked them, to drive them back ignominiously with unbrellas, parasols, canes, and other weapons of the kind.

There was another rather large family on board, the very antipodes of these, utterly unlike them in class, manners, appearance, every thing. The mother was a lovely Spanish-looking lady, with beautiful jet-black hair, and delicate regular features: she was exquisitely but simply dressed, and a Spanish mantilla of black lace depended, with exceeding grace, from her small statuesque head. Her voice was "sweet and low—an excellent thing in woman," especially on board a crowded steamboat, where there is always a hurricane of noises. And what a refreshing contrast it was to that sheikh-like dame's tones, which would have drowned the town crier's.

The eldest child of this family, a little girl, was one of the loveliest children I ever saw, and with very charming and pleasing manners, neither loud nor forward, nor too shy nor too bold—just what a child of her age should be, and like a child—which is not always the case here. The youngest child was one of the dearest little pets I ever saw: he was about three or four years old, and a perfect embodiment of fun, mischief, and merriment—the very soul of sauciness and drollery—an infantine Polichinello, a baby Flibbertigibert, with such endless quips and cranks and "mops and mows,"—methinks such a comical little darling Scaramouch was never beheld before! He seemed a duodecimo Grimaldi, a Lilliputian Liston. He was like a supply of laughing-gas to the whole cabin, but he seldom laughed himself. There was a sort of quiet, profound intensity of fun diffused over his whole childish countenance and figure, that was irresistibly comic; his eye, cheek, nose, chin, seemed all twinkling and winking together, and he had a little way of putting on a despairing look of mock pathos, that was marvelously amusing.

His usual dress was a sort of tiny blouse; but, the morning of his departure he was attired in a kind of microscopic pea-jacket (he was a very small child), with a mighty knowing-looking hat, stuck jauntily on the side of his unspeakably comical little noddle; and, as he strutted up and down the cabin, with his infinitesimal little "pattes" stuck in the pockets, or the wee short arms a-kimbo, it was "*impayable*" indeed.

The grandmamma in *this* family was quite a model grandmamma. She must have been a person of the most wonderful force of character, and of remarkable greatness of mind; something (not in person) like the strong-minded Madame Mère. It will seem incredible, but she actually did not spoil little George! I have even seen her look grave when thinking, perhaps, he was verging on the bounds of pertness, or exhibiting signs of incipient insubordination—grave and remonstrant, when every one was convulsed with laughter round her.

But she was a model grandmamma in other ways too: such care of the children as she took; so nicely she made them behave; and on the morning of their disembarkation, at a place whose name has slipped my memory, she shone forth in full glory. It appeared they had expected to arrive very early indeed at this place, but, owing to a fog coming on they did not. Well, up she got in the dark, and dressed herself as neatly as ever, and then she lighted the fire—for the colored stewardess in this steamer happened to be particularly lazy, and, I believe, also, poor woman, she had a great deal to do. Then the active old lady called all the children, and dressed that darling little monkey, George, and helped the other children to dress—poor little things! all half-asleep; and called her daughter (in vain, and no wonder at that hour of the morning). She then gave the youthful travelers some biscuits for their breakfast, and next began, most sedulously, to pack about two dozen carpet-bags and a score of boxes, while the stewardess went slowly somnambulizing about, laboriously yawning, stretching herself industriously, and diligently doing nothing.

How so evidently superior a family came to be without servants, I know not; probably they preferred traveling independently without them. So it seemed, at all events. Little George's departure was universally regretted; he left quite a broken-hearted boat behind him.

This same sonnambula of a stewardess was a very handsome person. Her mouth was too wide, but, excepting this defect, her features were very fine; her eyes magnificently large, reminding me a little, both by their size and lustre, and their languid expression, of the great dark orbs of the women at Constantinople. She had a straight classical line of nose. I think she must have been a Quadroon, from descriptions I have read of their personal appearance. Her hair had not the slightest wooliness or even curl about it: it was very black, and parted in the straightest possible bands on her forehead. But there was a whisper in the boat, that these Madonna-wreathed bands on the fine forehead of the Sultana-like stewardess were not of native growth; that, in short, her own hair being afflicted with a ripple, or a frizzly infirmity, she wore a wig. If I was required to make affidavit of the fact, I really could not, and am rather disposed to doubt its being a fact at all. This languid and somewhat indolent stewardess was an exception to the general rule. They are usually a most active, obliging, quick, and attentive set of people, and perform their duties admirably.

We find it very cold at St. Louis, but we are in a very comfortable hotel (Monroe House), the rooms of which are kept delightfully warm. It will doubtless be known in England how dreadfully this large, busy, noble city suffered lately from fire and cholera; the last almost depopulated the city for a time. A third of the inhabitants were carried off by the pestilence; and great numbers fled in dismay, panic-stricken, with their families, to settle in other and, as they thought, less dangerous localities. I was told here, the other day, that though it is only a short time since this appalling affliction had befallen the city, yet so great had been the influx of emigrants, that the gap which had been made by cholera was quite filled up. "So," added my informant, with not uncharacteristic indifference, "the dead are not at all missed; not in the least, you see."

Merrily were huge houses going up in all directions. From our hotel windows we had a long view of gigantic, and gigantically-growing-up dwellings, that seemed every morning to be about a story higher than we left them on the preceding night: as if they slept during the night on guano, like the small boy in the American tale, who reposed on a field covered by it, and whose father, on seeking him the following day, found a gawky gentleman of eight feet high, bearing a strong resemblance to a Patagonian walking-stick.

This city is considered the commercial emporium of the West: it is not the capital of Missouri (Jefferson City claims that honor), but is the largest city in the State. It was founded by the French in 1764; for a long time it was little more than a village; it is now an immense and fast-spreading city. There are a good many (American) French still resident here, and a great number of Germans. They tell me the German immigration this last year has been truly enormous. A gentleman observed the other day, the Germans, or the "Dutch," as he called them, are "eating up the West," and sometimes driving the Americans out of their own towns. "The greater part of the West," he said, "will actually be in their hands soon."

This is the chief dépôt of the Great American Fur Company.

We are going to try and see a prairie. The Looking-glass Prairie, I fear, is too far off to attempt to go to in this cold, bleak, unpropitious weather; and I am much afraid there is none near enough; for civilization hereabouts walks with no mincing, graceful, dancing-master-like steps, but great, seven-league boots, and sprawling, earth-shaking strides, and goes swinging along at such a pace that it is all the horizon can do to get out of her way in time, and if once she caught it napping, it might go very hard with it.

I shall not try to embark on the great Grass Sea to-day; besides, from what I hear of the extent to which inclosing has been carried on this year, I doubt much if even the Looking-Glass Prairie has escaped being framed in, and broken up into small pieces.

We were a long while getting here from Louisville, in the steamer; very nearly as long as we were crossing the Atlantic to New York. The nights and mornings were generally very foggy, and the captain appeared to have an amiable, unusual weakness in favor of that trifle, called human life: a pleasant trifle enough sometimes. Ah, if some of the poor victims of fast boats and reckless competition could make their voices heard, would they not seem to parody that well-known *refrain*, that brief speech, "I'll thank you for that trifle, Uncle Sam!" Particularly careful was the good captain of the good steamboat Hindoo, and we had not a single accident of any sort or kind all the way to St. Louis; and it is a very difficult navigation; for the Mississippi, sullen and sober as it looks, is one of the most variable of rivers. Its sandbanks are perpetually shifting, and then there are the "snags and sawyers." In the papers you will often see whole columns, headed, "Snagged," containing a melancholy list of boats that have had that unpleasant and unnecessary operation gratuitously performed upon them: frequently they are materially damaged. Then follows, sometimes, a list of "boilers burst." There has just arrived news of a tremendous explosion on board a new and magnificent steamer, "The Louisiana." Hundreds of lives are said to be lost. But this does not alarm me in connection with my projected voyage to New Orleans. I think the safest time is always directly after a great accident, for people are naturally just then more careful.

## CHAPTER XX.

The Mississippi—Its Impression upon the Author—Its Banks—The immense Forests seen from it—Its varied Scenery—The Mississippi by Night—Hosts of floating Trees—Steamer "snagged"—Visit to the late President's Cotton Plantation—His Slaves—Interesting Negro Children—Shanty of Mr. Taylor, the President's Son—An aged Slave—His extreme Politeness—The black Valet of Mr. Taylor—The immediate Slave Abolition Question—Instances of Ill-Treatment of Slaves—Persecution of Musquitoes.

I AM now at New Orleans. We have had a most successful and enchanting tour, and our late voyage I found extremely interesting.

I have been most agreeably disappointed with the Mississippi, which has, in general, the reputation of being monotonous and wearisome from its usually flat banks, and long lines of almost interminable, dense, unvarying forests. I am, on the contrary, quite delighted with it, and watched and gazed on it, day after day, and hour after hour, with ever-newly kindling interest and admiration. These very forests themselves were to me sources of ever-fresh wonder, and the mighty current of that marvelous river, sweeping on like the flow of unpausing Time, carrying all before it, I thought sublimity itself.

That the banks are flat for hundreds and hundreds of miles, I own; but those forests are so grand, so boundless—the breadth of that astounding river is so imposing—its bends and curves so glorious and beautiful—that I could not find it at all monotonous. And then its islands, creeks, bays, branches, and reaches, are so numerous and interesting, and its many magnificent tributaries are so diversified and so splendid, that it did not seem to me in the least degree wearisome or dull.

Besides these, there is the busy hum of life at various places on the shores. The landing-places, wharves, the plantations (toward the south), the rising and risen villages and towns, the scattered huts of the wood-cutters, the long rows of slaves' habitations (called "quarters"), and all the openings—the clearings in the old mighty woods, where the settlers' cottages are cheerfully sending up their blue smoke to the sky, the germs, probably, of future mighty cities —and then those innumerable flat-boats and rafts with small hamlets of houses on them, some wearing the look of a little nautical village; and all kinds of strange craft, from the roughest and rudest, that almost look as if the "snags" and "sawyers" had determined to join company, and had linked themselves by some natural process together—to the magnificent steamer "Autocrat" —one of those "floating steam-palaces," which look really like some of the wondrous fleeting creations one sees every now and then in the clouds. This "Autocrat," they say, is the largest steamer on the Mississippi, and is about four hundred feet long, and gorgeous as an enchanted castle inside. The one we came in to this place was nearly that length, and decorated with costly magnificence. And then there are the poor trees, twisting and twirling, and tossing about in the rapid stream (sometimes roots uppermost), which form the dreaded "snags" and "sawyers" of the Mississippi voyagers; and the countless flights of birds that frequently make the air alive with their myriads of hurrying wings, sometimes looking like the moving folds of gigantic serpents.

How, then, can these stirring and wondrous scenes be insipid? They are certainly not; and I think any one who can find it monotonous and tiresome (unless they had pictured to themselves a totally different scene, and expected a sort of exaggerated Rhine, or magnified blue Guadalquiver), must be somewhat devoid of heart, mind, and imagination, and especially the first time that one steams down it. I can imagine it might become a little tedious, a little wearisome or so, the one-and-twentieth voyage or thereabouts; but the first time! I can not comprehend it. No! the first time it is all change, wonder, novelty, matter for speculation and food for reflection, an object of ceaseless interest, and of ever-recurring astonishment and admiration. We saw it under a vast variety of aspects and change of climate, and even seasons; and often did its whole appearance seem altered. The captain of one of the steamboats observed to me, the other day, that after long years spent in navigating that wondrous river, he could truly say he "had never seen it in any two voyages alike." There are so many different "stages" of water—the banks are so perpetually changing, the sand-bars are so incessantly shifting their position, besides other alterations, that I could indeed readily believe him.

I have seen it up in the northwest, amid snow, hail, ice, rain, and clouds, and storm, and in the burning sunshine of the south, and under its clear and unshadowed skies, by night and by day, in the gale and in the calm, flowing through its almost interminable mighty wilderness of forest in solitary grandeur, or watering a thousand teeming plantations with its turbid swelling waves, receiving its splendid tributaries (the Ohio, Arkansas River, &c.) as if they were so many dew-drops, and sweeping on as if with a magnificent unconcern and disdainful indifference, apparently wholly unaltered and unaffected by these immense and majestic accessories to its might and greatness.

The breadth of this ever-broad river is scarcely visibly changed, though the depth is of course very often greatly increased, as stream after stream rolls into its great waters. In the very absence of change here, is there not something sublime? In every way it is unlike every other river I ever saw, and appears to be a sort of molten flowing world in itself.

By night the scene is one of startling interest and of magical splendor. Hundreds of lights are glancing in different directions, from the villages, towns, farms, and plantations on shore, and from the magnificent "floating-palaces" of steamers, that frequently look like moving mountains of light and flame, so brilliantly are these enormous river-leviathans illuminated, outside and inside. Indeed, the spectacle presented is like a dream of enchantment. Imagine steamer after steamer coming sweeping, sounding, thundering on, blazing with these thousands of lights, casting long brilliant reflections on the fast-rolling waters beneath; (there is often a number of them, one after the other—like so many comets in Indian file!) Some of them are so marvelously and dazzlingly lighted, they really look like Aladdin's palace on fire (which it in all likelihood would be in America), sent skurrying and dashing down the stream, while, perhaps, just then all else is darkness around it.

I delighted, too, in seeing, as you very frequently do, the twinkling lights in the numerous cottages and homesteads, dotted here and there; and you may often observe large wood-fires lit on the banks, looking like merry-making bonfires. These, I believe, are usually signals for the different steamers to stop to take up passengers, goods, and animals. I recollect, on one occasion, our captain was hard-hearted: the steamer was overflowing with passengers already, and continued on her course, notwithstanding there was a perfect conflagration for a signal on shore, to induce him to pause. There must have been some person or persons extraordinarily anxious to be taken up, for the hubbub made on shore was surprising: there were furious shouts, waving of hats, a hurricane of cries and gesticulations, and people running with great perseverance along the banks, yelling and squalling like maniacs. In vain—on we went, and our imaginations might fill up this mysterious outline of circumstances as they pleased. For me, I felt sure cotton was at the bottom of it, somehow.

I heard, however, afterward, that there had been lately bands of disorderly emigrants, who had got taken on board the steamers thereabouts, and who had made themselves very disagreeable company while on board, and yet who thought the benefit of their society was sufficient payment for their passage. Some of these gentry were probably the bawlers and bonfire-makers we had left behind us, stamping and handkerchief-hoisting.

It is quite curious to see the hosts of floating trees, agitated and restless, and ever-tossing about in the rapid current, and occasionally rolling and writhing in a little whirlpool. They look sometimes like a hundred sea-serpents at a blow! Who could believe that birds had ever built and sung in their branches? or that they ever were appareled in the sweet livery of spring? they have become such black, mummified monsters, and look so hideous and forlorn, drifting helplessly along, in the giant steam.

We were badly "snagged" twice. Once was really a very severe snagging, though we survived it; but I assure you the shock might give one a faint idea of being blown up. The first time a large tree was stuck in such a manner through the left paddle-box that the wheel couldn't move, and a great deal of delay was occasioned by our having to stop for the hands to extricate the wheel from its disabling situation.

The most serious of all our snaggings (for we were favored with a great variety of samples) was once in the night. We were asleep in our cabins, when we were suddenly woke up by an immense stunning shock, and the steamer stopped immediately, quivering, so to say, in every nerve of her huge body. There were a great number of horses and mules on board, and they became dreadfully frightened, and commenced rearing, kicking, plunging and snorting furiously, and the noise and uproar really, altogether, sounded most frightful for a time—for, of course, there was no lack of shouting, yelling, and rushing backward and forward. After a little while, on went the powerful steamer again, plunging through the thick darkness with the great blunt arrow that had struck her so sorely, fast in her poor wounded side; but, this time, it had just missed the wheel.

Another snag subsequently hit her in the opposite side; but the wheel fortunately escaped that also; so away she went, something like a savage *belle*, of whom I have lately read, with wooden skewers in her two ears. When morning came, eager was the rush of all to see the extent of the damage inflicted. There stuck the grim snag right through the paddle-box, as fixed as fate, and there we left it when we left the steamer. I believe, however, it was then in process of extraction.

Besides these very severe hurts, the unfortunate steamer suffered a long succession of bumps and thumps (as well as her passengers) from a whole series of snags, almost through the whole night. They would not let one repose for a quarter of an hour together in peace. The vessel went, jarring and jumping along in as disagreeable a manner as it is well possible to imagine; very much as if she was playing at leap-frog, or hopping on one paddle for a wager. The poor mules and horses uttered a most vigorous kicking protest against such rough treatment, and that additional hubbub did not improve the quiet or comfort of the bipeds.

I was very glad when we arrived at Natchez (built, I suppose, on the scene of Chateaubriand's lovely work "Les Natchez"). From thence we availed ourselves of the President's kind invitation, to go and see his cotton plantation, and it was a truly interesting sight to us.

The late President's son was there, and received us with the kindest hospitality. The slaves were mustered and marshaled for us to see; cotton was picked from the few plants that had survived the late terrible overflowing of the Mississippi; and the interior of one of the slaves' houses was exhibited to us. As to the slaves themselves, they were as well fed, comfortably clothed, and kindly cared for in every way as possible, and seemed thoroughly happy and contented. The dwelling-house we went to look at was extremely nice: it was a most tastefully decorated and an excellently furnished one; the walls were covered with prints, and it was scrupulously clean and neat.

V—— expressed a great wish to see some of the small sable fry, and a whole regiment of little robust, rotund, black babies were forthwith paraded for her especial amusement: it was a very orderly little assemblage, and it can not be imagined how nice and clean they all looked. Such a congregation of little smiling, good-natured, raven roly-polies, I never saw collected together before. One perfect duck of a child was only about three weeks old, but it comported itself quite in as orderly a manner as the rest—as if it had been used to give parties and assemblies, and receive any quantity of company, from every nation on earth, all its days, or rather hours. It was as black as a little image carved in polished ebony, and as plump as a partridge (in mourning). These pitchy-colored piccaninnies differed from white children in one essential particular, for they were all perfectly quiet and silent; all wide awake, but all still and smiling.

After the main body had departed a small straggler was brought in (whose mother, perhaps, had lavished additional cares upon its state toilet); and it alone, apparently alarmed at finding itself thus unsupported and insulated, testified its disapprobation at the presence of English visitors by a very mild squall. We saw an older child afterward, who was very nearly white, with lovely features and fair hair; the mother was a mulatto, and the father almost white.

V—— was delighted with the whole company of little inky imps from first to last, nursing and fondling them in high glee; and it may be readily conceived that the mothers stood by equally enchanted at having their little darkies so appreciated—and not a little proud; showing their splendid glittering teeth almost from ear to ear.

All the slaves were evidently taken the kindest care of on Gen. Taylor's plantation. Men, women, and children all appeared to adore Mr. Taylor, who seemed extremely kind to them, and affable with them. He informed us he sleeps always in his own rustic shanty, surrounded by the slaves' quarters, without bolt, bar, or lock of any description on his doors, and that the negroes were not fastened or shut up in any way. This shanty was a very nice wooden building, with a colonnaded promenade in front, looking on the river, and had a capital sitting-room, very cool and pleasant. The overseer's house was at a little distance.

The principal mansion boasted, too, of a good and large collection of books, among which Mr. Taylor showed me an illustrated Mexican "Don Quixote." He had brought it with him from Mexico, and added, that it was said to be the first work ever illustrated in that country. The engravings were well executed, and the designs were spirited and clever.

We saw an aged slave, a hundred years old, and apparently quite hale and hearty. He did not seem to be the least deaf or decrepit, or to have lost his faculties in any way: he had quite polished and graceful manners, something like an old French marquis of the *vieille cour*. He really reminded me a little in his courteous salutations of dear old Marquis de l'Aigle, who used to tell me at the Château d'O—— of his dancing minuets with poor Marie Antoinette. He came daintily forward and treated us to most

Chesterfieldian bows and reverences, with multitudinous respectful inquiries after our health and well-being.

"What do I owe you for those chickens you sold to me a little while ago?" asked the President's son of the old slave. "One dollar and five bits," replied the centenarian with the most unhesitating accuracy and promptitude. The money was immediately paid to him. Mr. Taylor had told me before that he always bought his poultry of this old man, who was allowed *to rear them on his own account*, "and who, I assure you, invariably charges the very highest prices for them," added he, laughing.

I took an opportunity of offering this sable Sir Charles Grandison a trifling *backsheesh* to reward him a little for his walk to the lodge to see us (though, by the way, we were told it was no unusual exertion for him, as he very frequently came there); the bowing increased to almost *ko-tooing*, and he went on his way rejoicing and bowing still, like a self-acting porcelain Chinese Mandarin, "nid-nid-nodding."

We brought away a *tiny* bale of the President's beautiful white cotton, just as it came off the tree.

When the slaves were collected together in front of the house for our inspection, they had each, as a treat, some tobacco given them, which is what they dearly love. This they afterward proceeded to smoke to our healths, to which I had no sort of objection, provided they did not wish me to hob and nob with them. They were generally fine stout-looking people, and had not at all a stupid air. One very remarkably intelligent-looking youth was Mr. Taylor's valet; and the latter informed me that this young negro had *taught himself* to read and to write. For some time Mr. Taylor had remarked that he sat up very late, and after observing this repeatedly, he resolved on watching him, to see what object he had in maintaining these lengthened vigils. He thus discovered the fact. The poor aspiring darkie had saved every candle-end he could find, and deprived himself of sleep night after night to accomplish his design. Might not such a one become a Toussaint l'Ouverture in time?

Alas! there are too many interests involved—even those of the slaves themselves—to permit the immediate extinction of slavery. I am quite aware that on plantations such as the one I have been writing about, one sees entirely the *couleur de rose* of the business; but I believe it is very rarely the negroes are ill-treated, except, as I was told by an American, occasionally by small farmers, emigrants, who have never had such power before, and who are often led into abusing it. The French are said to be very severe masters, but I was constantly assured the worst of all are the *colored* people themselves. This will appear less astonishing when it is recollected that these people are universally ignorant and uneducated, without any proper moral training to teach them to restrain and subdue their naturally violent and inflammable passions and tempers.

I can not but think, too, that sometimes when the proprietor himself does not live much on his estate, or personally superintend his colored laborers, they are harshly used by the overseer. One must guard against believing all the exaggerations and prejudiced statements that one hears; but I have been told some painful things relating to this, that seemed certainly from unimpeachable authority.

Mr. —— told me at New Orleans that an overseer had actually offered to flog one of the negroes under his charge to show him how it was done, and this in the most careless manner, as if it was quite a common-place proposition. I can hardly help thinking the man had been piqued by some remarks of Mr. ——, and said this as a sort of bravado, to show him he defied his opinion. The other story is, I fear, more *vraisemblable.* An overseer was talking of the idleness and carelessness of the negroes being sometimes very irritating and provoking—as no doubt they may be—and, said he, "when that rascal did so and so, I shot him, that's a fact, for I got so mad I couldn't do nothing else." I have heard, not overseers, but other persons say the same sort of thing frequently, as an excuse for very intemperate and inconsiderate conduct toward others, and they seem to think this exonerates them from all blame, as if they were really not responsible agents at the time. A gentleman conversing with me some time since in the West, on the subject of some new regulations on board one of the steam-boats, said that the black waiter, on bringing him some beefsteaks and hot potatoes that he had ordered for luncheon, required payment down before the savory and smoking refection was tasted. Highly indignant, the gentleman remonstrated, nay recommended the ebony-complexioned waiter to "*absquatulate,*" without loss of time. He remarked he was above all suspicion, and while he was getting out his purse and counting out the coin, the beefsteaks would be very fast deterioriating in value. Poor Pompey declared the captain's orders were absolute, and that all were required to submit, and again reiterated his request for immediate payment. "I got so mad at this," exclaimed the narrator, "that I took up the whole tray and flung it and the contents in his ugly face." I am afraid there is generally method in this pleaded madness of a moment, for its victims are commonly the helpless and unresisting.

Mr. —— had gone to see the jail, and he remarked some singularly ferocious-looking men, who proved to be Spaniards. "Ay, they are right desperate chaps, them," exclaimed the jailer or turnkey who accompanied him; "I reckon them furriners 'ud think no more of murdering a man right slick, nor you would of walloping your nigger." But I am saying more than I intended on this theme; and of all people in the world, the English have the least right to find fault with the Americans for retaining still the legacy which they had from England, that melancholy and dangerous keepsake that was her gift—a gift forced on their acceptance too.

I must confess one sees very original advertisements in their papers sometimes. The other day this one caught my eye:—"To be sold immediately, a negro woman, and a case of damaged Marseilles soap:" and often you see mules, carts, wheel-barrows, negroes, and farming utensils, all huddled up together in a comprepensive advertisement. How comprehensive, alas! They do not seem to think; but of one thing I feel quite certain, from many observations I have made, if you had the power to liberate all the slaves in the United States, you would find not a tenth, not a twentieth—perhaps not a hundredth part of them—would accept their freedom from your hands.

I have had an almost sleepless night of musquito torment. The housemaids assured me that the musquitoes hardly ever bite now,—that their *gay season* was over, and that they were living very retired lives; occupying their leisure, I suppose, in improving their minds. If they would but learn to have a little philanthropy! But they would perhaps answer, they "already like man very much indeed." Ah! it is quite a platter affection, a cupboard love.

Hearing the satisfactory report I have quoted above, I left my net rolled up last night, and was almost eaten up alive. I could hardly sleep a wink the whole night, and passed its long hours chiefly in the pleasant occupation of violently boxing my own ears, in ineffectual attempts to deal death and destruction at those unpitying tormentors. They are the most ubiquitous little monsters in existence, and the most unkillable: you give yourself a blow that might knock down the "Mammoth horse," and, though sorely hurt, rejoice in thinking you have pulverized the foe, and you feel him instanter biting away at the very hand which hit the blow, or, laughing at you (and stabbing at you, too), perched on the top of your own nose.

These Liliputian lancers came on like the clouds of irregular Cossack cavalry that so harassed the French in their direful Russian retreat—they are here, there, and every where, their terrible "hoorah," and deadly dreadful little war-whoops, freezing one with horror. In the day-time it is hateful enough, but at night far worse. However, at night, one has the happy resource of the "bars," as they call the net apparatus here, but none in the day. It would perchance lengthen one's life a little, or at any rate spare one's self from sore anguish, to adopt Cromwell's plan, and wear a coat of mail under the outer apparel, but soon would these clever little assassins, these "Thugs" of domestic life, find a joint in one's armor; and then should one not be like those ancient warriors, who, by a cruel device of the enemy, found themselves closed up and imprisoned in cuirasses almost red-hot?

## CHAPTER XXI.

The St. Charles Hotel at New Orleans.—The Swedish Waiter and Jenny Lind.—Oppressive Heat in December in New Orleans.—Vast Quantities of Cotton.—The probable future Aspect of the Banks of the Mississippi.—Commerce of New Orleans.—The City.—Its Port.—Its Inhabitants.—Its Churches.—The City subject to Inundations.—Places of Sepulture above Ground.—Wreck of the Louisiana Steamer.—Wonderful Capabilities of the Valley of the Mississippi.—The Americans not extravagant when they describe the Resources of their Country.—Alligators.—The Red River.—The artificial Embankments of the Mississippi at New Orleans.—Their Insecurity.

We are quite suffering from the heat of the weather here, and we are told it is unusual to be so oppressively warm at New Orleans in the month of December.

We are at a very splendid and comfortable hotel, called "the Verandah;" it reminds me much of a Parisian one. The St. Charles is the largest of all the hotels in New Orleans, but it is much crowded, and we were recommended to try this, as it is quieter, and thus pleasanter for ladies. The St. Charles looks a little like St. Peter's at a distance—it is surmounted by an immense dome; it boasts, likewise, of a splendid Corinthian portico.

It is said to be the largest in America. The attendance at this Verandah hotel is admirable, and all the arrangements excellent. But the charges are much higher than usual in the States.

We are waited upon by a little Swede almost fresh from Jenny-Lind land; and he asked me at dinner yesterday, in an anxious tone, whether I had ever heard his gifted countrywoman sing. I replied in the affirmative. "Then I come from two miles of her in Sweden—I am from two miles of her" (from where she lives in Sweden).—"Indeed!"—"Yes, and I have known her from a little child. She is very good and fine, oh, very fine; and I hear in England they much like her." I assented, and, eloquent in the praise of his northern land's nightingale, he continued, "She sings so beautiful; she is a wonderful singer! Nothing like her, very great—very fine and great"—and then, by way of crowning all his praises, he exclaimed, with prodigious emphasis, "Oh, she is *very neat, very neat.*" I was not quite sure what particular form of encomium was intended to be conveyed by that expression, but, nevertheless, signified my concurrence unhesitatingly, as it was evident he considered this a "clincher," for he spoke quite "in italics."

The quantity of shipping here seems to be enormous, and the quays and the levee (as the great promenade which interposes itself between the Crescent City and the Mississippi is called) were so covered with huge bales of cotton (though it is far from a productive year) that the ground was literally strewn with little lumps of it, fallen from the plethoric bales in moving them. It almost looked as if it had been snowing in large flakes. I think one might drive a tolerably profitable trade as a gleaner by picking up the scattered cotton, collecting it, and making it up into a few second-hand bales. You might almost glean enough to freight a small ship—or stock a little warehouse.

Once or twice in our Mississippi voyages (for we stopped to see various places, and thus our voyage was performed in separate divisions, and by different steamers) we found ourselves in vessels that appeared to eyes inexperienced in such matters to be alarmingly overladen by the heaped-up cotton bales. I recollect on disembarking from one steamer, that she really seemed, as we watched her from the wharf where we had landed, to be all but submerged. She looked as though she went along her course making the most profound courtesies imaginable into the water, and how she kept her head above the element in question I know not.

We have luckily got large and airy apartments in this same

Verandah Hotel; for if they were not so I know not how we should endure the heat. It is now evening—considerably past the middle of December—and we are sitting with broad immense French windows wide open, and, of course, we have no fire, and yet it is suffocatingly hot, and we are gasping for breath; but as the New Orleanists themselves are grumbling and scolding at this weather, as unseasonable and insufferable, I presume we may expect a speedy termination to this frying-pan temperature.

A very agreeable and charming French Louisianian lady, who had traveled with us across the Alleghany Mountains called to see me the other day. She assured me she was suffering much from the great heat, and seldom remembered it so oppressive. Madame V—— had just returned from Paris. She was traveling in company with her mother, husband, and several friends of theirs, forming altogether a very large and agreeable party. Among them was a Greek gentleman, who had lately settled in New Orleans, and a M. ——, who had traveled a great deal, and was a remarkably well-informed and pleasing person.

Almost whenever we look out of the window, we behold cotton in vast quantities, carried through the streets in rather awkward-looking carts or drays, which recalls to us that we are in the Crescent City—the City of Cotton *par excellence*. It is called the former name from its semicircular conformation, following the sweeping curves of the Mississippi shore. It is built on the left bank of that mighty stream, and is about a hundred miles from where it mingles its far-traveled waters with those of the Gulf of Mexico—far-traveled indeed! In its irresistible flow, through how many climates and latitudes has it gone, sounding and sweeping on, in its majestic breadth and more awful depth, and its haughty power, and gigantic features—more like a long sea than a mere river—a drawn-out Adriatic—an attenuated Mediterranean.

Campbell's fine line would apply to it lengthwise, as to the ocean:—"The lightning's wing sinks halfway o'er thee like a wearied bird."

I shall want a microscope when I return to England; so miserably small and petty will seem its rivers, its hills—all its features. Magnifying glasses might save one's patriotic vanity a little, till we get used to the miniature scale.

The Mississippi springs to life amid the chilly glare of everlasting snows, and it ends its mighty career beneath a burning sky, ay, almost under the flaming heavens of the tropics. Nothing gives one a better idea of the immensity and greatness of this sublime river, than the reflection that a vast space, comprising about to millions of square miles, pours its surplus waters into this king of rivers. It is indeed a Long Sea. Then not easily can one forget, in looking on those wonderful waters, what change another hundred years will almost certainly have produced on the vast scenes which they lave. What very nations of men will crowd on its busy shores, and throng its immense valley! What a world of wonders will be presented to the future voyager! What industry, what prosperity, what splendor, what yet undreamed-of attainments of civilization, and triumphs of science, and achievements of art!

Already you see the beginnings of all these. The desert is gradually blooming, the forest is retreating, the habitations of men are rising in all directions, fleets of steamers and other craft are covering the face of the river; thousands of enterprising settlers are setting foot on the shores, and advancing further and further into the beleaguered wilderness—but a hundred years hence, nay, fifty! Imagination almost fails to paint to herself what shall then be unfolded and displayed in broad day to the gladdened vision.

In a commercial point of view, New Orleans stands in a preeminently advantageous position. The Mississippi, with its numerous fine tributaries, lays at its feet the products of about twenty-five thousand miles of navigation (only reckoning streams navigable for large vessels), through regions of almost unparalleled fertility, and of still greater promise; and it carries back the varied and extensive contributions of nearly every country and every climate. The city proper is built in the form of a parallelogram; its whole length (including the incorporated fauxbourgs) is said not to be less than five miles parallel with the river. Some of the streets are extremely handsome, but present a very foreign appearance. There is one enormously wide street, or "place," with trees in rows down the middle of it, something like Eaton-square.

There are a good many villas in the suburbs, surrounded with gardens, in which orange and other beautiful trees abound. I should think the best possible view of New Orleans, is the one we saw on our arrival from the river. It is indeed magnificent, seen from there; and what a noble and busy aspect did its fine port present, crowded with vessels of all sorts, descriptions, sizes, nations, and appearances; splendid steamboats by hundreds, and a multiplicity of river craft, rafts, barges, flat bottomed boats, &c.

The inhabitants of New Orleans, consist chiefly of Americans, and French and Spanish Louisianians. French is the language generally talked in the streets, in short, the prevailing tongue; but there are some of all nations.

There are many churches in New Orleans, some antique-looking, and others apparently of a very recent date. We attended a Protestant one, lately finished, of admirable architecture. The cathedral, or Church of St. Louis, in the Place d'Armes, is a venerable looking edifice.

Whenever the Mississippi overflows in the least, the streets of New Orleans are inundated; but the levee (designed chiefly for the purpose) prevents the great body of the swelling waters from entirely annihilating the place. Not long ago, there was a very serious overflow. The *crevasses* were fearful, and some alarm was entertained for parts of the city. Boats were the only means of conveyance in the streets, and windows the ways of ingress and egress. It must have been like Venice, but an impromptu sort of Venice, without the needful contrivances and conveniences.

New Orleans has several peculiarities of its own, even when it is not thus unceremoniously entered by the Mississippi. For instance, the cellars and graves are above ground. With regard to the cellars, the basement story of the houses is usually raised very considerably above the surface, the hall door being reached by a flight of steps. The graves are also elevated. The dead are buried in sepulchral houses, which are termed here "ovens." These often contain three or four tiers. Those belonging to the wealthy are frequently very handsome, and built with marble walls. There are walks leading to different parts of this singular cemetery, paved neatly with shells. Were they to attempt to dig into the marshy ground, they would drown the remains of their lost friends and relatives, and write their loved names indeed in water.

There was something very melancholy in the appearance of the cemetery, that we saw. Altogether, the damp swamp of the unwholesome-looking ground, the low, flat, gloomy inclosure, with its cold and sombre houses of death, and the carelessness and neglect visible, I thought, in general, made it a very mournful spectacle. I believe it is not considered prudent to stay long in this sad place, which may account for its seeming rather deserted and uncared-for. Certainly, in general, however little value America may seem to attach to life, before Death, in their magnificent cemeteries, they usually spread a "feast of roses."

While speaking of melancholy subjects, I can not resist repeating an anecdote I heard the other day from Mrs. ——. Soon after the horrible catastrophe of the Louisiana steamer, the numerous unknown, unclaimed bodies were laid out on the levee, for their friends or relatives to identify and remove them. A friend of Mrs. ——, a young man of rather delicate health, wished, out of curiosity, to see this appalling spectacle. His friends remonstrated with him, and earnestly sought to dissuade him, telling him that, in his state of health, and subject as he was to nervous depression of spirits, he should carefully avoid such a frightful scene; but he disregarded all their representations and entreaties, and decided on going. He went, and on beholding the ghastly sight, the hideous rows of mutilated bodies, some mere trunks, and all in the most awfully dreadful condition, he was seized with shivering and fainting; he was quickly conveyed home, but never rallied from the shock; and, after lingering a few days, he died.

The noise of the terrific explosion of the "Louisiana" was heard at a great distance, and fragments of the boiler flew in different directions very far. A mule, in one of the streets, was cut completely in two, by a fragment, and on the levee, numbers of persons were killed.

We saw the other day, from our windows, an immense procession of Freemasons—at least, such I imagined them to be. They were very handsomely attired and decorated; but one of their number was a most ferocious-looking personage, with a tremendous beard—such a beard! An extravagant humorist might say that a fox-hunter would be fain to draw that cover for a fox, with a probability of success. You might think, in looking at him, that he at least might bear a charmed life among bursting boilers, railroad collisions, and such disasters, and dangers, and fatal accidents; for if Death stared him in the face, poor Death would surely run off, frightened to death himself.

One can not but think what a wonderful place this same New Orleans will probably become in the future. It is calculated that the Great Valley of the Mississippi, now only containing, comparatively speaking, a mere handful of inhabitants, could easily sustain and comfortably accommodate one hundred and fifty millions of people. Now the population is about ten millions. What a future! what a country! and what a noble people, to work out its grand destiny, and to fill up magnificently the magnificent designs of Nature. It is all petty malice and jealousy which make people talk of their exaggerated expressions and ideas. A man must have imagination indeed, must out-Shakspeare Shakspeare, the myriad-minded, and the very lord of imagination, to deal in hyperbolical extravagance here. What would be exaggeration in other countries, is here the simplest moderation, and in all probability lags behind the reality. The fact is, they feel their destiny, and their country's destiny, and they would be stocks and stones if they did not; and if, in England, we are disposed to think they "greatly daring" talk, we should remember a little what a prospect lies before them. Nature, their present, their future—all is in such an exaggerated mood here, all on such a stupendous scale! For them to have little views, and entertain trifling projects, or hold petty opinions, with regard to their mighty country's advancement and progress, would be as absurd as to see a party of giants in go-carts or in pinafores, and playing at "Tom Thumb" and "Goody Two Shoes."

People take different views of things. Our little Swedish waiter seems to think America was especially designed and provided by Nature as a vast receptacle and a sort of asylum for destitute or somewhat needy Swedes; a kind of country of ease for Sweden in particular, who kindly allowed her advantages to be shared by a few other refugees from a few other nations. Regarded in this rather modest light, it appeared to give him tolerable satisfaction, on the whole; though on some points he seemed inclined to think, a little change would be beneficial, such as having a Swedish president here, and trifles of that sort. However, he was an excellent waiter, and labored most zealously in his vocation; always at hand, always active, attentive, and in good-humor: he must be invaluable to the master of this busy hotel.

We have a great fancy for tasting and trying all sorts of unearthly, half-supernatural dishes. We had found bear excellent in the West; sometimes a wild buffalo capital. Had it been the country for such animals we should have ordered hippopotamus-pie, or a leg of camelopard, or chimpanzee chops, or a few slices of rattlesnake, with orang-outang sauce. As it was, we asked for wild turkey, and wild geese, and wild raccoons, or "possums." I believe these things (I do not know about the last) are accounted very good, and it amused us trying and experimentalizing on them. The *recherchée cuisine* of the hotel did not admit of such "curiosities of cookery;" so very frequently, and with regret, our poor little Swede was constrained to bring us tame beef and mutton, and other such common-place dishes instead. However, he did his best, and brought, triumphantly, the other day, *wild ros bief* (buffalo); and, in short, dubbed any thing wild that could possibly be called so. According to him we tasted various very savage fish, and soup manufactured from particularly uncivilized turtle. We should have liked to taste alligator much, but, however, failed in so doing: it is said to be pretty good. There are very few, if any, left in the Mississippi; the numbers of steamboats there have crowded them out, and frightened them away. The Red River, with its shore, is called, I believe, the cotton-planter's paradise, and it is also the alligator's, if the account I hear of the quantities there be true. In the Mississippi they abound only in the creeks and small branches.

The Red River rises in the Mexican Cordillera, and debouches into the Mississippi about two hundred and forty miles from New Orleans: it is navigable for thirteen hundred miles above its union with the waters of the great river. But what is that compared with the united navigable channels of the Mississippi and the Missouri, which in length actually exceed three thousand miles! I have heard it stated to be exactly three thousand four hundred and twenty miles.

The artificial embankments, or levees, that I have already alluded to, commence on the east bank, sixty miles above New Orleans, and continue to extend down the river more than one hundred and thirty miles. On the west shore the embankment commences one hundred and seventy-two miles above New Orleans; some, however, think that, instead of a protection, these artificial levees will prove a means of aggravating the dangers apprehended. By a natural process the river, it appears, is continually raising its channel by a continued succession of deposits, and also elevating its own banks; but whether the banks are raised by Nature or by art, the result will be equal; for by either it would seem unquestionable that the process of upheaving the bed of the river is accelerated (as the river can not there deposit the extra material on the neighboring surface), and, perhaps, the more so, as the velocity and force of the current are considerably weakened and diminished as it advances toward the sea.

The tremendous *crevasses* of this year have greatly alarmed many people. The poor Crescent City already *looks up* at high water to the awful river, and with very tearful eyes too sometimes, and I am not at all sure, on second thoughts, that her commanding commercial position is so very favorable and enviable a one. There is also some chance that she may find herself some day a "fair forsaken," for it is not at all unlikely that the great potentate and papa of rivers may one fine morning run off altogether.

In Mr. Mackay's "Western World" this is perfectly explained. New Orleans then would have no chance but to put herself upon "rollers," and rush after it, taking up a new position somewhere on its banks.

The electric telegraph is established on an enormous scale in America. The whole of the Western, Northern, and Southern States now hold frequent and uninterrupted communication through its instrumentality. The great line was completed in September, 1848. The other day at New Orleans they knew what had happened at Paris twelve days before—so at least I was told.

---

## CHAPTER XXII.

Mobile—Lake Ponchartrain—An Indian Encampment—The Indians and their Squaws—Chumpa Girls—Some Account of Mobile—Its Harbor—Festival of the New Year—Rival musical Processions—The Magnolia Grove—Manner of Life of the Indians—Manifold Miseries attending waiting for Steamers—Madame L—— V—— —Mr. Clay—Preparing to start for Mexico—Madame L—— V——'s old black Slave—Her Remembrance of Washington—Verses on Madame L—— V——'s deceased Children.

In the month of January, 1850, we came by Lake Ponchartrain, in a very good steamer, to the Gulf, and so to Mobile.

Before we embarked on the lake we had to go by railroad a distance of about six miles; and as we were waiting in a curious circular sort of car, we saw an interesting procession of Indians—an Indian encampment on the move. The men seemed a magnificent-looking set, splendidly rigged out in very brilliant and picturesque habiliments. At a little distance, at first sight, I thought their costume looked very much like that of Highlanders in their *grande tenue*. They stalked along with extreme dignity, and their haughty walk reminded me of the theatrical, yet bold strutting march of the Albanians, the finest steppers I ever saw.

They were as upright as their own arrows, or the tropical palms; but not so their unlucky squaws, who followed after, bowed under the weight of papooshes, lodge-poles, pots, pans, kettles, all sorts of luggage and lumber, live and otherwise. They looked bent all manner of ways, and old—no wonder—something like a party of nomadic nut-crackers or itinerant notes of interrogation. Poor creatures! how wearily they seemed plodding along after the ungallant gentlemen of the party, who had burdened themselves with nothing but their guns.

We had a charming little voyage over Lake Ponchartrain. I made acquaintance with a particularly nice Louisianian lady on board, who had the misfortune to have a child afflicted with a sad deformity: its little arm was a mere short stump, with something like the rudiments of a hand attached to it. It was a most engaging, charming little child notwithstanding, full of life, good-humor, and spirits. The mother appeared to adore it, and so did the black nurse.

I was much struck with the great mutual affection this nurse and the child showed to each other, and particularly by the negress's constant and extreme attention to the child when the lady was not there. I mentioned this to her, and also that I thought this nurse had a remarkably good and gentle manner with the child. "Yes," she replied, "but at first she was very rough, and spoke so strangely, that I could hardly understand her." I asked her the cause of this, and she proceeded to tell me that, for some reason, being obliged rather hastily to find a fresh nurse for her child, she had sent for one of the *field hands*—her husband owned a sugar plantation—who were in general rough and rugged to an inconceivable degree; and that, if translated from the field to the house, they were almost insupportable for a short time, but gradually acquired the gentle manners and the quiet ways of speaking of the house servants, and entirely left off all their uncouth and almost savage habits. The blacks, it would seem, then, like all of us, more or less, are the creatures of circumstances.

We saw a most magnificent moon on the Gulf of Mexico the other evening. It appeared of enormous size, and of the most beautiful fire-color—in short, more like a rising sun than a moon.

The weather here is deliciously cool and fresh after New Orleans. This morning we had a visit from two Indian chumpa girls. They are called so from carrying little fagots of pine-wood for sale for the fires, and they generally quietly march into your room without the ceremony of knocking, uttering the magic word "chumpa," which they seem to consider a sort of "Open Sesamé." They belong to the remains of the great Choctaw tribe, and there is a large camp of them not far from Mobile. The Cherokees have lately been removed.

This place, at the mouth of the Mobile River, has become the seat of a very extensive trade, and it is the principal outlet of the commerce of the State of Alabama; and enormous quantities of cotton and other staples are brought down by the different rivers from the upper districts, and also from the western portion of Georgia, and from the state of Mississippi, to this point. Next to New Orleans, this city is the largest cotton market in the Union; it has a beautiful view of the Bay, from which it receives pleasant and health-giving breezes. Near the town are numbers of pretty and substantial villas, with delightful gardens.

Mobile has a good harbor, and is well-defended by fortifications. Indian names are in the ascendant in this State: Alabama itself, I am told, means "Here we rest." Then there are the Tallapoosa and Coosa Rivers, the Cahawba and the Chattahoochee (this river united with the Flint, forms, I believe, the Apalachicola, which runs through Florida). Then there is the town of Tuscaloosa, on the Black Warrior River, Tuscumbia, &c. The Bay of Mobile is thirty miles long and twelve broad.

The city was founded by the Spaniards in 1700, but did not become a place of importance or wealth till the Americans captured it in 1811. Some time ago it belonged to Florida, and it may be seen there still in a not very antiquated map.

There were some marvelous processions last night to celebrate the New Year. These appeared to be representations "of all the world and the rest of mankind," and a little besides this tolerably comprehensive catalogue, for Olympus was there; and, by the way, ran rather foul of another Celestial empire, China, that occasioned some trifling discord, which soon passed away. Pig-tailed Mandarins, pagodas, and colored lanterns on poles, clashed with tridents, chariots, and mythological divinities. But the most trying part of that unlucky rencontre was, that each had a good large noisy band of music, and these bands, with unfaltering intrepidity, came sounding and marching on, nothing daunted, though an harmonious, or, rather, an inharmonious collision was inevitable. "Tweedledum" marched from one end of the street, and "Tweedledee" from the other; and Tweedledum puffed and blew, and twanged and flourished, and Tweedledee fiddled and squeaked, and grunted and groaned.

"The plot thickened;" demi-semi-quavers were fluttering convulsively in the air, and all sorts of queer crotchets seemed in the heads of the musicians. Infuriated drummer-boys, from the central flowery-land, rub-a-dubbed madly against the "rataplan" of their opponents; either opposition empire came on, as bold as brass and catgut could make them: the fiddlers of snowy Olympus played the sublimest of jigs, and the most thrilling of polkas; the Celestial trombones "Yankee-doodle" and "Old Virginny," with electrical effect. On they came still—would either give way? No: louder, and louder yet. The basses and trebles, and flats and sharps, and livelys and maestosos, were jumbled together into one most horrible hash and clash of music. Where would it end? Now comes the tug of war. Messrs. Neptune and Mars, and their myrmidons, advance against Chang-fo and Co.: the wind instruments were distending their cheeks almost to bursting, the drums were beaten till they were quite beat. All the notes seemed entangled together in inextricable confusion—a grand hodge-podge of sounds. And now one Mandarin shoulders poor Minerva and her owl into the gutter (as if she were an outer barbarian); another apostrophizes the solemn ancient Pluto, with "Go long, there, clear off, you old critter—wake snakes, will ye," and other impressive expostulations, and even the bands of music are utterly confounded and commixed. All, however, comes right at last, the two comets have met without serious damage, and each was seen pursuing its way in its own separate orbit.

I can not describe to you the beauty of a large magnolia grove near this place. This majestic wood reaches nearly down to the beautiful blue bay, and the trees are unspeakably magnificent. Madame L. V—— tells me that when all the splendid flowers are out in their full beauty and fragrance, their odoriferous enchantments are beyond all expression. I am told their delicious scent is so powerful, that ten miles out to sea, the air is filled with the rich perfume!

We have several times visited the Choctaw camp in company with Madame L. V——, and in her carriage. These Choctaw Indians are a singular people. As to civilization, poor creatures! I can not think that theirs extends beyond wearing old second-hand coats when in full dress, and in drinking the hateful "fire-water." They have adopted its ugliest points, and its vilest; but what know they of its advantages and benefits? Their mode of life in that camp seems pretty nearly as savage as it can be, except—and this is, indeed, an improvement—that they no longer go out in their horrible war parties, nor do they now depend entirely for their subsistence upon the chase. They have in general a certain nobleness of look, and the women are, many of them, very handsome. One day an Alabamian, who was not a disciple of "the Mississippi of men, the Father of Waters" (Father Mathew) came lounging into their camp. His fiery and inflamed visage, and ruby nose, contrasted strangely with the calm, stately, finely-tinted features of the Indian. The savage, being sober, had then, really, the superiority. *Apropos* of tint: if one had been asked to point out the red man, I think the rubicund pale face would have been selected. I did not know till I came here that the Indians and negroes mutually hate each other. The Indians say the Great Spirit made first, Indians, then white men, then dogs, and then niggers.

We have been detained here a long time waiting for the "Royal Mail" steamer, which has not made her appearance. Many people, besides ourselves, have been watching for her arrival with equal anxiety, for the same cause, namely, intending to go to Mexico as passengers in her.

Lately it has been particularly disagreeable, living this life of suspense and looking-out; for, as the steamer was so very much after her day, it was expected she would stay the shortest possible space at Mobile Point, and the intending passengers were earnestly recommended by the "Royal Mail" agents to be quite prepared to start at any time, and in no time. She might arrive in the night, and in that case a little more time was to be allowed; but a mere fraction. One was to sleep weasel-fashion with one eye open and to keep one's self, as it were, packed and stowed, and locked and corded, and carded, all ready for almost instantaneous departure. This became, in fact, a life of perpetual packings and unpackings; for anticipating with horror the confusion of a possible night departure, we had every thing ready every night in case—and then all the indispensable things had all to be got out again in the morning; and almost regularly these were found to have gone burrowing down to the bottom of the trunks and carpet-bags, after the wont of such indispensable things in general.

There were constantly flying reports of the steamer being actually arrived, and the confusion that ensued then was indescribable! By some strange contradiction it appeared as if every thing was so ready that nothing could be found—in short, the discovery was made that nothing really was ready at all, but the "Royal Mail" steamer; so when this alarm was over, all was to be undone and done over again more systematically. The former had been, so to say, only playing at packing—a mere rehearsal of preparation, but now it must be taken seriously in hand, and you may guess the privation of those days. Talk of journeys over deserts—of dreadfully severe quarantine regulations—what were they to this

Tantalus-like state of trial—this slow starvation amid plenty—not a book could one allow one's self to take out of the trunk, because they were, of course, at the bottom. Writing materials were denied one—watches were a luxury not to be thought of; not even an innocent pair of scissors, or a harmless little pincushion. Utterly useless would it have been to have purchased other books, &c. They must have all submitted to the same despotic necessity, which knows no law (not even Lynch-law), and must have been without hesitation or commiseration made pitilessly "*ready*," crammed into groaning boxes, and choking trunks—in fact, we were (or we fully believed we were) utterly packed.

In short, I should have had a most uncomfortable visit to Mobile but for my charming friend, Madame L. V——, who is one of the most delightful people in the world, and with whom we drove out almost every day, leaving directions to send all sorts of scouts after us in case this truant vessel should arrive. Madame L. V——, and her mother, Mrs. W——, are intimate friends of Mr. Clay, and I have heard many very interesting anecdotes of him from them. A grand-daughter of Mr. Clay is at the Roman Catholic convent, near Mobile (she was placed there for her education), and, to his regret, she has lately declared her intention of taking the vail. I believe Mr. Clay takes great interest in her (her mother, his daughter, is dead), and is much grieved at her taking this step.

Madame L. V—— has a very charming daughter, who is a nice companion for V——. Two other lovely children Madame L. V—— had the misfortune to lose, and she has not yet recovered the severe shock of their death. We went with her one day to the cemetery, where repose her darlings. It is a totally different one from that at New Orleans, and very prettily situated.

I have at last a prospect of going to Mexico. The new United States Minister to that Republic (whom I have made acquaintance with at Madame L. V——'s house), having written to Washington, and represented the inconvenience to which he is subjected by this long delay, and the length of time that has elapsed without his being able to assume his diplomatic functions and conduct various important negotiations, the authorities have ordered that a war-steamer shall be "detailed" from Pensacola to convey him and his suite to Vera Cruz. He has obligingly invited some of the detained passengers to accompany him, and among others ourselves. Madame L. V—— advises us to accept this courteous offer, as most likely the English steamer that has been over-due so long will not call here at all now, and I am disposed to do so myself.

We have had a delightful drive again to-day with dear Madame L. V——, and saw numbers of the chumpa girls returning from the pine woods (which are a good many miles off) so laden with the chumpa (pine) that they could hardly move.

One of Madame L. V——'s slaves is a capital old woman, and apparently quite an original—"qui ne se desoriginalisera pas," I should think now, as she must be hard upon a hundred. She perfectly remembers Washington, having seen him once driving out in a carriage on some great occasion in full dress. "E mighty fine man as ebber I seen; his head berry white (powder probably), he sit up *so* in de carriage," straightening herself and looking dignified with all her might, "just like so; and old Massa he in same carriage, dressed up fine too (he was one of Washington's family, Judge W.). I member all berry well, for little child dying, and I ran out o' house and left it, just berry little while, cause eberry body say 'Go see great General Washington' and *amost* pushy me out for to go see him: little child dying, but I just ran to seen him, and people all halloa and shout berry loud." She gave us all this information in the most elevated tones, a speaking-trumpet voice. She had a white turban on, which showed off her jetty ancient countenance very picturesquely.

There are two portraits of Madame L. V—'s lovely lost children in her drawing room. They suggested the few following lines.

Bright lovely beings!—on each imaged face,
More of the angel than the child we trace—
More of the immortal than the mortal see,
In each mild aspect's pictured purity.

Sweet mother, check thy deeply mournful sighs,
Grieve not to spare these Seraphs to the skies.
Ah! not for them need flow the bitter tear;
How bless'd their sunny fate, both *There* and *Here*.

Oh! not for them should sorrow's drops be shed,
We scarce can dream they died, scarce deem they fled.
Around them seemed to smile, all fresh and fair,
A happier world's serener, clearer air.

'Twas scarce a change—'twas scarce a second birth,
More of Elysium knew they than of earth?
From Love to Love, from living Light to Light,
How smooth the transit, and how short the flight!

And what to them was Death's pale kiss of Peace,
That bade the flutter of life's pulse to cease?
Though swift the stroke, though brief the warning given,
'Twas but a step from *such* a Home—to Heaven!

I believe, besides ourselves, Lord Mark Kerr, (who is lately come from Canada, where he is aid-de-camp to Lord Elgin), and Mr. P——, United States Consul at Mazatlan, a friend of Madame L. V——'s, are going in the war steamer with Governor L——. It is expected to arrive very shortly here, and we are all quite ready to start, I hope and trust, having subsisted almost without the barest necessaries of life, for a period of about three weeks, in a high state of preparation. The weather has been rather unsettled and rough, but looks just now a little more promising for our Gulf voyage.

But before I beg the reader to accompany me in my departure from the United States, I must detain him with some further remembrances of Boston and New York, to each of which cities, I propose devoting a brief chapter.

---

## CHAPTER XXIII.

Boston as a Commercial City—Its Wharves—Its Shipping—Its Trade—The India Wharf—American Boys—The Present and Future of America—The Fashionable Quarter of Boston—American Ladies and Gentlemen—Young America—Boston the Metropolis of Railroads—Gallantry and Patience of American Travelers—Fresh Pond—Wenham Lake Ice—Mr. Prescott's Town House—Library, and Literary and Philosophical Institutions in Boston—Its Periodical Literature—Its Charities—Its Patronage of the Arts—Power's Sculptures—Frequency of Fires in American Cities—General Appearance of Boston.

Boston seems one of the busiest cities in the world; a brief visit to the commercial quarter will fully satisfy the visitor as to that fact.

Beside its wooden wharves (some of which have durable stone fronts) are innumerable vessels of all dimensions and devices, and of every variety of build and rigging. The water is very deep, and large ships seem almost leaning (as if tired, after their long tempest-tossing, perchance, and weary wanderings), against the warehouses and ranges of substantial and solid edifices, reserved for commercial uses—for some of the slips run a little way into the land. Great numbers of these warehouses are crowded along the shore; the packets from Europe have a convenient slip especially set apart for their accommodation, and exclusive occupation. Mr. Cunard's steamers have a one thousand feet long wharf. Altogether, the sight is an interesting one; the eye is almost bewildered with the heterogeneous and ever diversified scene.

The coasting trade is said to be three or four times as great as that to foreign ports. There is an extreme difference perceptible in the "naval architecture" of the crowded coasting craft. There are stout-looking schooners, which ply between Boston and New York, a devious and difficult voyage, and some rather Quaker-looking brigs, somewhat formal and precise, and punctilious in appearance, that are preparing to run a starched and stiff course, if the weather will permit them to do so, to drab-suited Philadelphia. Pass on, and you will see the less elaborately finished craft, which are bound for the Carolina shore, and for the trading and wealthy cities of far off Alabama and Louisiana, "'way down south." Then there are the fairy, knowing-looking Baltimore clippers, their graceful masts clustered together like a whole dense plantation of tall slim walking-sticks for young giants. They are for the Monumental City.

Then immense steamers are to be seen, bound for various places, that look so light, despite their large size, that a strong puff of wind might, peradventure, lift them "right away" out of the water, to continue their voyage in mid air. If you entered, you would find their furniture and appointments such as might have tasked the most skillful looms of Persia, and beggared of their costliest materials the marts of furthest Ind.

And that brings me, without further digression, to what is called the "India wharf," which is nearly a thousand feet long, and about two hundred and fifty feet wide. The richly freighted ships from distant Hindostan, and jealous China, bring here their many treasures: and those vessels, too, that are bound for these favored lands, with innumerable wares for their different markets. Wherever you turn, on all these wharves you find the bustle of business. It would be a difficult matter to describe the profusion and superabundance of rattling and lumbering drays and carts, and barrows and trucks, the crowds of porters jostling each other, and the throngs of the busy dealers and clerks, and superintendents and assistants, and consignees on every side, or the strange chaos of commerce seemingly heaving all around you. What is there? nay, what is there not? Salt, sugar, molasses, cotton, calico, marble, leather, silk, flour, coffee, fruits, oil—stowed away in bales, barrels, boxes, bags, hogsheads, jars, casks, chests, sacks, and cases, till there seems enough to feed, and clothe, and supply half a world for a century to come, piled before you.

I shall beg the reader now to seat himself on Prince somebody's carpet, as in the fairy tale, and taking leave of these busy scenes (there are, by the way, about two hundred docks and wharves altogether, surrounding Boston), fly over some zig-zagging streets of huge warehouses, which streets are grim and gloomy enough, but of no great length, and over the noisy, reeking Irish quarter, which I am told intervenes, and the carpet shall stop the way, for a time, in the centre of the city. I have mentioned before, how that the sidewalks were turned into counters "of ease," for the overflowing, crammed shops; and how they looked as if it had actually rained silks and calicoes, and cottons, or as if some of the richly-laden ships, had by some magic, been carried into the heart of the town, and wrecked almost on the door-steps of the stores.

But look at these newly-arrived hurrying Yankees. They stalk over these piles without casting a look to the right or left, with their curious boots turned up at the points, something like Turkish cimeters (these are not the dandies of Boston, but haply speculators in some of the ten thousand and one lines which people speculate in, throughout these busy regions); they have an eager, onlooking, straight-forward stare, and a rather vacant, and yet anxious look, as if they had sent their minds on before them, and their bodies were hastening after, and trying, at least, to keep these very go-ahead *avant couriers* in view—in short, running after them as well as they could. And sooth to say, these personages are rather cadaverously complexioned; as is the wont of bodies no longer tenanted by their spiritual occupants.

Look at that boy, that mannikin, with his hat so knowingly on one side, and the Turkish cimeter-like boots and all; he is "a dreadful bright boy," that. You would see him chew and smoke, if it was not forbidden in the Trimountain City, and hang his nether limbs out of a railroad car (if you met him in one, and if he could by possibility lengthen them, so as to contrive so to do); or he will tell you, perchance, with his tiny squeaking voice, "We air a great people, by thunder, the greatest on the airth, and can do all things double first-rate, from blowing up a universe and a half, if it misbehaves, to blowing half a soap-bubble. Now; we'll put the Atlantic and the Pacific in our side-pockets any day, and reduce all Europe to no whar and a grease spot," and so forth:

and very soon not only this species of boasting, but other ungraceful bragging (which, though not so broad, is yet sufficiently extravagant) will be entirely confined to this very young America.

As this people progress and advance more and more, they will gain more the humility of true greatness. They will feel more the vast responsibilities that rest upon their Titanic shoulders; they will weigh more what stupendous steps they have yet to take—what almost incomprehensibly-great destinies are slowly unfolding before them; and these most momentous and grave considerations will gradually produce their effects, and at length impress continually their views, opinions, works, and even words. They will feel more and more that their past and present colossal greatness does not make future improvement and progress—as Napoleon's renown was said to do of all future fame—impossible, but imperative—absolutely indispensable. Nature has done so much for them, that to be commensurate with her, to keep pace with their giant opportunities, they *must* act as giants.

And we must be just, too; for, verily what would be boasting and hyperbolical rhodomontade with others, is the mere simple truth often with them. Nature speaks to them in such grandiloquent strains that she sets the example of "tall talking." But I must return to "*mes moutons*."

We will take a glimpse at the fashionable quarter of the town. Near the Common are a number of very handsome mansions; and in driving or walking along the streets in the neighborhood of it you will see many splendid equipages of the merchant princes and princesses of old "Shawmut." You will often meet a group of graceful ladies (perhaps going to shop in Washington-street), not only beautiful, but with countenances of the most intellectual expression. From all I hear and see, I believe the Boston ladies are particularly accomplished and amiable.

The gentlemen look like gentlemen—not because they have lemon-colored kid gloves, or Parisian boots, but from their whole air and manner. As to being merely well-dressed in the cost-and-quality-of-material sense of the word, that almost every body is. A mob in the United States is a mob in broad-cloth. If we may talk of a rabble in a republic, it is a rabble in black silk waistcoats (the favorite wear among certain classes in America) and well-brushed hats. Therefore, to look really like a gentleman in the United States, depends in nowise on the clothes, but entirely on their wearer; and the tailor has less to do with manufacturing a gentleman here, than in perhaps any other part of the world. For in all other countries you are a *little* assisted to the conclusion, unwittingly, by the dress; but here not in the least, and you must judge wholly by *l'air noble et distingué*, or the reverse, of the individual.

It is very seldom you see any equestrians in these northern cities. Every body chooses either to walk or go in carriages. The Common is a very agreeable place for promenading; and there you will see a great deal of *little* America in the shape of pretty fairy-like children, enjoying the fresh air with their Irish nurses, or their graceful mammas.

Little America is unhappily, generally, only grown-up America, seen through a telescope turned the wrong way. The one point, perhaps, in which I most concur with other writers on the United States, is there being no real child-like children here. The little creatures, looking all the time every thing that is infantine and unsophisticated, will read novels and newspapers by the hour together, and the little boys will give you their opinions dictatorially enough occasionally; and the little girls "talk toilet," and gossip, and descant on the merits of the last French novel, or the elegibility of such a *parti* for a husband for such a lady; or on the way Mrs. So-and-So misconducts her household affairs, and spends money at Newport or Saratoga Springs; and so far this is not pleasing to our English tastes.

But, nevertheless, there are many very good, and perhaps sufficient reasons assigned for the necessity that exists in this country at present for bringing up their children with a thorough knowledge of the world. The boys have all an active part to play in the mighty drama of busy life on which they are entering—nationally, politically, socially, or commercially. No drones are admitted into the great Transatlantic hive. There is no time to spare; they must be ready, as soon as possible, to take their places and run in the great race, or they will be distanced by their more agile and precocious contemporaneous competitors, and see prize after prize borne away by those who had learned their A B C with them, or after them.

The girls are generally married early to husbands in business, and have to take care of themselves. They ordinarily live (till a competency is acquired and a house bought) at the enormous hotels that abound in the State, while their husbands are at their desks or counters all day.

What quantities of omnibuses and hack carriages are plying backward and forward from the railroad dépôts! The trains seem going and coming incessantly, for Boston is a sort of metropolis of American railroads: it is the centre of the whole railroad system of New England, and from it the iron lines radiate to all parts. The star of Massachusetts is an iron star, and its rays shine with the far-searching light of progress and power. Canals and roads give it countless other additional facilities for intercommunication and self-accommodation.

The New England railroads are in general exceedingly well-managed; but they are not as fast as ours. They have no express trains running sixty miles an hour; but in a few years they will, I doubt not. (As to the electric telegraphs in the United States they put us entirely to the blush). It has happened to me on these railroads to look out of the window, when we have stopped very suddenly, and to see a lady, lounging as slowly as possible, parasol in hand, across the rails, evidently rather enjoying thus keeping the train waiting till it suited her to dawdle out of the way.

As to the cows, they seem to think the iron road was especially intended for them; but their constant habit of getting in the way, and the "cow-catcher," which adorns every train—invented in order to convince them of their error—has been so often mentioned, that I will not dwell on the subject. I have heard that the railroad sometimes takes a short cut across a church-yard in this country, but I never saw an instance of this, nor should I believe it. They treat and brave death lightly enough certainly here; but *the dead* are uniformly respected and honored.

We stopped one day in the "cars" (as they usually call the train) about a quarter of an hour, for a newly-married lady, whose husband, by some strange absence of mind, thought she had entered the car, and jumped in just before the train started. He paced up and down, looking for the gentle bride, in vain. At last the sympathizing conductor, on being informed of the mistake, had the train stopped, and the gentleman ran back and brought the lady to the cars; the passengers all waiting with the greatest patience, and acquiescing unmurmuringly in the gallant conductor's decision; indeed, many hardly looked up from their newspapers, as if it was the most every-day circumstance that had happened.

I have invariably remarked that, eager and go-ahead as they are, the Americans are the most philosophically patient travelers in the world. You are kept waiting for a cow, or a pig, or another train coming, or a forgotten wife, and they betray no symptoms of impatience or indignation. The *contretemps* is borne with the most inexhaustible stoicism and the most unvanquishable good temper. How an Englishman would fume and fret!

When we were at Cambridge the other day, we went with Mr. and Miss Everett to see Fresh Pond, which in reality supplies, as we were told, England and other parts of the world with the far-famed Wenham Lake ice. The water is like liquid diamonds, so transparent and sparklingly pure. The scenery around is worthy of being mirrored in it. I am told, in the winter it is one of the gayest scenes in the world. During the time of the ice-cutting, innumerable sleighs assemble on the spot, and the *beau monde* of Boston are all to be met there. The clear polished ice is cut into blocks, about two-and-twenty inches square, for which operation a machine expressly constructed and invented, is used (called the ice-cutter), and it is then covered with saw-dust, packed, and sent to all quarters of the earth—India and China among others.

We went to see Mr. Prescott's town-house the other day—a very handsome and spacious one, with a large library. He has a number of good pictures and busts; among the former, some fine ones of Spanish monarchs. Framed and hung up in one of the rooms, we saw a portion of the rich lace that adorned the shroud of Cortez.

Boston is, I think, very rich in libraries, both public and private. It contributes very largely to the prosperous advancement and reputation of native literature, and it has a remarkable number of literary and of philosophical institutions. It has some of the most valuable periodicals and journals of the country. I have just been informed there are fifty weekly newspapers in Boston, besides sixteen daily ones; but this is only a small part of the periodical literature of Boston.

This mightiest city of New England, therefore, seems to advance with simultaneous progression in every varied walk. Unsurpassed—nay, hitherto, in some respects, unrivaled—in material prosperity and practical development, she sedulously devotes her unwearied energies also, to cultivating to the highest point all the mental faculties. The intellectual studies of her inhabitants are pursued with ardor and vigor; and on all sides you see evidences of this truth, in the numerous and excellent educational establishments and admirable scientific institutions.

The instruction of the people is a paramount consideration in the public charities, and among the crowded seminaries and schools are several most munificently endowed by some of the public-spirited citizens of the Granite City. The arts, too, seem to flourish and improve here, and to keep pace with the ceaseless march of knowledge and erudition. Music, painting, and sculpture here exert their exquisite influence and weave their magic spells. There is a gallery of sculpture, in which Power's matchless works are exhibited; and though some of the less initiated and refined may call the "Greek slave" (as I have read in some jocular account of it) "the greatest piece of whittling in the world," they appear most sincerely and earnestly to admire it and the other beautiful works of art in the saloons. Music, too, is making great progress.

It appears to me that refinement and elevation of taste are advancing here as rapidly as science, knowledge, wealth, and prosperity. Those who wish to indulge in any invidious and vituperative observations respecting America had better make haste, or they will find themselves absolutely compelled to praise and admire instead. Not only in Boston but universally in New England the habits of the people seem daily becoming more and more polished and refined.

Boston just now is not very full: the greater part of the wealthy inhabitants are gone to the watering-places. I find it is a custom here sometimes, on going into the country, merely to turn the key in the lock of the house-door. No domestic is left in charge of the vacated building, but it is left to take care of itself.

This city is well lighted. Speaking of lighting, however, I must say in America the fires, so frightfully frequent, render gas almost a work of supererogation. If you arrive at a town at night, you may be pretty sure you will find it illuminated by a convenient conflagration; and though they do not exactly intend to burn down their houses to light travelers the better through their streets (as extravagant a mode as Charles Lamb tells us was adopted in some wild country for pig-roasting before cookery was known), yet it really has that effect, as we found from practical experience. Boston and the other towns in New England are all lighted by gas, but I think the lighting arrangements sometimes are a little neglected, and, in some few towns, rather insufficient.

State-street is a very busy and wealthy-looking street in Boston, and Tremont-row, hard by our hotel, is a particularly handsome one. But this is altogether a very striking town, although its streets are not so regular and wide as those of many smaller towns. Boston was planned in old times, when much irregularity prevailed in the system of city building. Besides this, it is very much circumscribed, from its situation on a rather vandykeing Peninsula, with a surface far from regular, joined by a mere narrow strip of *terra firma* to the main land. In short, the city proper is in confined and straitened circumstances. It wants some territorial acquisitions to increase its accommodation for building-ground, ornamental space, &c. If M. Agassiz would set his coral insects to work, to enlarge and spread the available land around, he would confer a signal service on the city, which, nevertheless, is, all things considered, a very noble capital.

Towns and villages in numbers have started up around it, to relieve it of its superabundant population, but these offshoots hardly add to the stateliness of its appearance. Notwithstanding this, it is a "great place," as they say here; and, as a lady, who is not a beauty, often takes more care of her personal appearance, and endeavors to rectify and to compensate for the mistakes and niggardliness of Nature, by additional attention to various little arts of pleasing—so Boston, disadvantageously situated in some few respects for imposing architectural show and symmetrical display, makes amends for these inconveniences and unfavorable conditions by the most scrupulous order and cleanliness, and the most finished propriety and exquisite management. This is one reason, I believe, why it reminds me of a promoted Amsterdam—that is, hoisted on a hill—and other towns in Holland.

The houses are of granite and brick, and a flight of marble steps often conducts you to the hall doors of Boston's hospitable mansions.

## CHAPTER XXIV.

Bustle in the Streets of New York—Trinity Church—Wall-street—The Park—The Shops in Broadway—Traffic in Broadway—Irish and German Emigrants—Wharves of New York—Its Shipping—The Astor House Hotel—The Exchange—The Custom House—Theatres—The City Hall—The Chair of Washington—Churches—Benevolent, Literary, and Scientific Institutions—Squares, Mansions—Foreigners in New York—Sympathy between America and Russia—Those two Nations—Anecdote of an American in Russia—Pearl-street—Military Companies in New York—The Militia—The Firemen—The Electric Telegraph in America—The Battery—The Halls of Justice—The Bowery.

New York is certainly altogether the most bustling, cheerful, lifeful, restless city I have yet seen in the United States. Nothing and nobody seem to stand still for half a moment in New York; the multitudinous omnibuses, which drive like insane vehicles from morning till night, appear not to pause to take up their passengers, or it is so short a pause, you have hardly time to see the stoppage, like the instantaneousness of a flash of lightning. How on earth the people get in or out of them, I do not know: the man behind surely must sometimes shut a person half in and half out, and cut them in two, but neither he nor they have time to notice such trifles. You see them thrust, and shoved, and pushed, and crammed through the hastily opened door, as if they were the merest "live lumber."

Empty or full, these omnibuses seem never to go slower. I have seen dozens upon dozens of them go by perfectly empty, but just as much in a hurry, tearing and dashing along, as if full of people too late for the train.

You almost wonder at the houses standing still in New York, and begin to think them rather slow and behind the age. You feel surprised they are not built on wheels. I did hear, indeed, of whole suburban streets being removed, the other day, to a more eligible situation on rollers, or something of that kind—but I will not vouch for the fact.

New York has been so often and so minutely described, that I shall not dwell on the details of its plan, situation, or appearance. I will only mention a few points that struck me. Perhaps the building I was the most pleased with in New York is the Trinity

Church. I do not profess to understand ecclesiastical architecture, but if one of its perfections be the raising the thoughts and contemplations from earth to heaven, then must Trinity Church be deserving of the highest commendation. Its spire is unspeakably beautiful (three hundred feet high), and almost seems to pierce the sky, like a flash of retorted lightning. It is situated on the western side of Broadway, exactly opposite the entrance of Wall-street into it. Wall-street is the busiest street in New York, and answers to our Lombard-street in London.

The park is pretty, but too small for such a city as New York. It has a beautiful fountain, and is splendidly illuminated at night by thousands of lamps. There are numerous superior shops in Broadway, but the most pre-eminently magnificent is "Stewart's;" it is one of the finest structures I ever saw, its front being composed entirely of white marble. Mr. Stewart is going to add immensely to this splendid store, and it will occupy almost as much space as the Palazzo Doria at Rome.

Crowds of carriages, private and public, are to be seen in Broadway, passing and re-passing every moment, filled with ladies, beautifully dressed, in the most elaborate Parisian toilets. Among the thousands of fashionable promenaders who are thronging the side-walks, there is often to be seen, a group of Irish or German emigrants, just as they have come from the crowded packets, the latter looking very picturesque, with their national costume. I saw the other day, a large party of these poor people. They looked like Bavarian peasants, and they, as well as several pudding-like children who accompanied them, seemed struck with utter astonishment, at the noise and incessant bustle of animated Broadway. The carriages scampered by as if all New York was going to turn out and leave them in undisputed possession. They looked so bewildered, that I fancied they were perhaps come from some of the quiet hamlets I have seen by the side of the Danube, where time and the river seem to flow by with equal calmness.

But look a little beyond that German group. From what part of the world do those most extraordinary masqueraders come? One has got only half a hat, another, two joined in one, and their habiliments are marvelously grotesque. Their hair, in some instances, hangs nearly on their shoulders, in others it radiates away very respectfully from the skull, as if controlled by some mysterious centrifugal force of the brain within. In the name of fortune, whence are they? They look intelligent, resolute, self-confident —in the name of fortune, indeed! for perhaps these men, at the moment you are half pitying them, half wondering at their forlorn and destitute appearance, are worth millions of money, and to-morrow, they will shine out in all the splendor of a New York exquisite's toilet. They are returned Californians, just landed, come to enjoy in "the States," the golden fruits of their toils, their perseverance, and their industry.

The wharves of New York, during the business season, are densely lined with the shipping of every maritime country under the sun. Merchantmen of every size are there, and for at least three miles, they present an uninterruptedly continued forest of masts, and cordage, commingling, apparently, with the chimneys of almost innumerable steamers. More than a thousand sailing vessels, nearly a hundred steamers, about eighty tow-boats, and two hundred canal-boats, may usually be found in the noble harbor of New York, during the busy time of the year. In the severest winter, this harbor is never obstructed by ice, so that vessels are not inconvenienced on that account.

I have already mentioned the magnificence of the New York hotels, but must just add, that the enormous Astor House not only is said to be furnished with its own private printing press for striking off the diurnal bills of fare, but it also makes all its own gas. However, it does not yet, I believe, manufacture its own linen or plate!

The Merchants' Exchange I was much struck with. It has a glorious portico, formed by a towering and imposing colonnade, the shafts of whose noble Ionic columns are separately composed of enormous blocks of granite. We entered the great room, and were amazed at its magnificent proportions. It is a rotunda, and of vast diameter, adorned with high marble Corinthian columns.

Beyond this, at the corner of Nassau and Wall-streets, is the Custom House for the port of New York. It is two hundred feet long, ninety feet wide, and eighty feet high, and is constructed wholly of superb white marble: the form is that of a Grecian temple of the Doric order of architecture. The front looking to Wall-street displays an immensely broad and lofty flight of steps, also of white marble. I understand it has a second similar front on a street at the back, which runs parallel to Wall-street (Pine-street, I believe). Each front has a noble portico. It is made fire-proof throughout, huge slabs of marble covering the whole roof.

The great hall of business is a rotunda, sixty feet in diameter, with recesses and galleries, making it eighty feet. It has an elaborately stuccoed dome, supported by sixteen Corinthian columns.

The Custom House is built on the site of the Old City Hall, in the open gallery of which Washington was inaugurated first President of the United States.

There are numerous theatres in New York. We visited none of them, so I can not describe their internal appearance and accommodations. One, called the Park Theatre, is exactly opposite the Astor House. Not far beyond the Park Theatre stands a rather gloomy and unattractive building: it is called Tammany Hall, and is the place where the Loco Focos are (or were) wont to assemble. Still a little further up, and within the area of the Park, stands, beautifully situated, the City Hall. Its front elevation is of white marble, and is ornamented with pilasters and columns of the Corinthian, Ionic, and Composite orders, rising one above the other in regular gradation. In the Common Council Room is a chair (which is still used by the President), that Washington sat in when he presided over the first American Congress, which assembled in New York.

From the cupola that surmounts the building, a view of the whole vast city is commanded; and in this there is a clock; and there is also an apartment constantly occupied, night and day, by a watchman, whose office it is to keep a perpetual look-out for fires, and to give the alarm, by striking an enormous bell which hangs in a belfry in the rear of the cupola, and which is exclusively used for this purpose. By this bell the man watches with a hammer in his hand, ready to give the necessary notice when he observes the least indication of fire. The sound can be heard from one end of the city to the other, and is almost instantaneously responded to by a hundred others in every direction. The number of strokes indicates the particular ward.

There are nearly three hundred churches, I believe, in this city. There are a considerable number of excellent Literary, Benevolent, and Scientific Institutions. Some of the squares of New York are very handsome. Washington-square is prettily laid out with walks, and shaded with flourishing trees. Union-square has a fountain in the centre, and is inclosed with a handsome iron fence. St. John's Park is also embellished with a fountain, and adorned with trees.

Some of the private mansions in New York have quite an imposing and palatial appearance, and are very magnificently furnished. All the States have their representatives in the crowded and ever-animated thoroughfares of this populous city—nay, I might say, indeed, so have almost all the nations of the earth.

The French appear to muster numerically stronger than any other people, but this arises from the fact, that nearly all the New Yorkers are accoutred in Parisian costume. Their very hair is cut and combed, and their beards trimmed and clipped strictly *à la Française*, which does not in general improve their personal appearance. Looking merely to the people, you might often fancy yourself in the Boulevards, instead of in Broadway. *Au reste*, Germans, Swedes, Poles, Italians, and hosts of others meet you at every turn. There are but few Russian visitors here it seems; but I am very much struck by the apparant *entente cordiale* that exists between Russia and the United States. There seems an inexplicable instinct of sympathy, some mysterious magnetism at work, which is drawing by degrees these two mighty nations into closer contact. Napoleon, we know, prophesied that the world, ere long, would be either Cossack or Republican. It seems as if it would first be pretty equally shared between these two giant powers.

I can not resist dwelling a little on this interesting subject.

Russia is certainly the grand representative of despotic principles, as the United States are the representatives of democratic ones. How is it that these antagonistic principles, embodied in those two mighty governments, allow them to be so friendly and cordial toward one another? In the first place, the Emperor Nicholas is a very far-seeing and astute politician; he keenly feels all the benefits that may accrue to him from cultivating the best possible understanding with the United States. He has deep and profound motives for this, which if he lives long enough, time will gradually develop, to the astonishment of many, perhaps, who ought to be more alive to the signs of the times than they are; and in the second place, there *is* a sympathy between those apparently dissimilar countries.

Russia and the United States are the two young, growing, giant nations of the world—the Leviathans of the lands! They enjoy extraordinary advantages; the older nations seem to have paved and prepared the path before them. Around the footsteps of either living and far-striding colossus, science and knowledge have shed the most surprising light; the most astounding and marvelous and momentous discoveries have been made; the most useful triumphs achieved. Man almost seems a second time to have been hailed master of the creation—civilization has penetrated the uttermost corners of the earth—time and space and the lightning are his familiars and his servants. With all these advantages, those two grand young nations are strong to the race, and fresh to the glorious contest. Far off, in the future, centuries and ages beyond this present hour, is their culminating point. What to other nations may be work and labor, to them is but, as it were, healthful relaxation, the exercising of their mammoth limbs, the quickening of the mighty current of their buoyant and bounding life-blood, the conscious enjoyment of their own inexhaustible vitality.

There is much similarity, in short, in the position of those two vast powers. The extraordinary increase in the United States of wealth, of territory, of population, and the wondrous opening of fresh avenues, and new approaches incessantly to mightier dominion, greater influence, and vaster resources, are known to all; but though assuredly not even remotely approximating to the United States, in the advancement of mental energies and intelligence, or in commercial enterprise and facilities, or manufacturing capabilities, or even in the thousand practical manifestations of civilization, and internal improvements, and progressive material prosperity and development, yet Russia is making immense strides, too, on her part. Her population has increased to sixty millions; she is beginning to develop her gigantic resources; her physical power is stupendous and paramount; her internal condition flourishing and apparently stable. She is strong in her geographical position, protected to the rear by Nature herself—by inhospitable wildernesses and world-wide barriers of ice—thus she can unhesitatingly afford to fling her whole Titan strength and force into the van. Her foreign policy is most energetically administered, as well as most skillfully and successfully conceived.

She has plenty of time, too, before her—she can watch and she can wait. She is conciliating those who would seem to be her natural enemies; economizing, for the present, her interference; consolidating her energies and means; improving her opportunities, and placing herself, move by move, in the most formidable attitude, both for offense and defense, and playing the mightiest and the most magnificent game that perhaps has ever yet been played on earth.

Still there is, undoubtedly, the greatest possible difference between her and America. The former is constantly watching other nations, adapting herself to meeting and confronting their policy, waiting to snatch, to seize, and to conquer. Her chief energies seem to have an outward tendency—an outward direction. In America, on the contrary, those noble energies have a more central action. She is ever occupied in incalculably important internal improvements; her glorious task is of a more domestic kind. In her own vast regions are her giant powers perpetually at work, advancing, perfecting, enriching, and strengthening! Her internal intercommunications, her extension of navigation and commerce, her expanding manufacturing industry demand the most incessant attention. The most carefully finished touches are sedulously given to the comprehensive machinery by which is regulated, in various modes, to a certain extent, the momentous schemes and enterprises of that speculating, industrious, active-minded community. All that concerns their privileges, their well-being, their personal rights, attracts the most deep and unwearied interest; while reforms, skillfully adapted to the spirit of the age—such as measures for the attainment of a more speedy and efficient administration of justice; the revision and amelioration of divers laws and systems; the establishment of harmony between conflicting and antagonistic interests; and, above all, increased provisions for the happiness, through munificently-enlarged opportunities for the enlightenment and education of the people, have occupied, and do occupy, her indefatigable politicians, administrators, and citizens.

She has nothing to do with, or to gain from intrigues of diplomacy and Machiavelian machinations of policy. Her stupendous work is at home, but her influence is felt to the furthest ends of the earth, and her shadow is spreading from pole to pole. Like a colossal tree, she *stands*, and firmly stands, while she grows and spreads, and her roots are deepening while her branches are expanding.

Nay, she is framing additional supports, new stems and trunks, like the Indian banyan, so that, while uprearing her glorious bulk and stature in height, she is ever multiplying her props and her foundations.

Russia is anxious to foment contentions and jealousies between other nations, for her own ulterior purposes and profit. America would merely incline toward a constitutional propagandism, and that chiefly from a generous desire felt by all her people, from her loftiest statesman to her lowliest citizen—that others should participate in what, with a thorough straightforward conscientiousness, they firmly believe to be the most precious of benefits and advantages—their free institutions and popular forms of political organization.

If Canada (and that is certainly not a very unlikely event) should be annexed at any future time to the United States, the latter and Russia would be adjoining countries. The two grand extremes would meet. Despotism and democracy would shake hands over a rivulet, and smile at each other across a footpath.

Russia is determined to be on the best possible terms with the United States at any rate, and I have been over and over again impressed with that conviction, since I have been in America; and that the latter takes her flattery—her complimentary cordiality, and gentle insidious advances very kindly, is most plainly evident.

The empire of the Czar is wonderful certainly; but how much it seems dwarfed when compared with America! Its progression is chiefly or wholly in physical advancement; but that of the United States is in both material and mental aggrandizement. Russia will leave no methods untried, to attach the United States to her interests—to insure at least her complete *neutrality*, in the event of contingencies, which her telescopic view steadily contemplates, and her mighty hand ever labors to bring about. She has no desire whatever to try her strength against the rival young giant—to wrestle (like the mighty athletes of old) with that tremendous competitor, in the Amphitheatre of Nations, for the edification of the world. She knows the prophecy, and has some faith in it, but is bent on substituting (for a time at all events) "*and*" for "*or*." The world may be shared, may be Cossack *and* Republican. She positively will be modestly content, for a season, with only half a world. A Cossack hemisphere may hob and nob in a friendly manner with a republican one, over the conquered empires of earth and of the ocean.

I have spoken of Russia watching; America watches too, but unlike the contemporaneous colossus, it is more the powerful pulsations of her own mighty heart that draw her regards. If all is right *there*, the future is at her feet and she knows it. And she has occasion to watch, for more reasons than one; for there are symptoms of grave disorder threatening there, and strange signs of the dissolution of the great federal compact. Nothing more convinces the uninitiated stranger of this fact, than the incessant denunciations thundered against disunion, the accumulated protestations and manifestations and deprecations, all to the same effect. I think they exaggerate the evil that would arise, in the event of dissolution, but the subject is too deep for discussion here.

After this long prose, I can not resist repeating an amusing anecdote I heard the other day, relative to an American in Russia. This gentleman had a great wish to see the Czar, and asked

G*

the United States minister to procure him an introduction; but the public receptions were over, and the minister told him it was impracticable. Somewhat indignant, and resolved to test the assumed impracticability, the traveler addressed a letter to one of the Emperor's aids-de-camp, I believe, and solicited an interview with his Imperial Majesty, as he had "brought some acorns from the grave of the great Washington, expressly to lay at the Emperor's feet, well knowing how the character of the mighty liberator was appreciated," &c. Success crowned his efforts; he had the interview he desired, and not only that, but he dined with the Czar, and the following day was invited to drive out with him, and had the pleasure of passing the United States minister while seated by the side of the mighty Nicholas, and of making him a very patronizing bow as he dashed by in the imperial carriage; so runs the story.

Pearl-street, a labyrinthine street in New York, which is said to have been originally built by the Dutch, along a cow-track, is a very zig-zagging thoroughfare indeed. One would really almost think the Dutch cows had taken to drinking draughts, *not* of water "as deep as the rolling Zuyder-zee." It is very narrow, and the houses are very high, like those in Old Edinburgh; waves and billows of merchandise of every description and denomination seem pouring over from the brimming stores and warehouses, into the inconveniently narrow street. If you were in Paris, you might think the street had been purposely obstructed with stubborn barricades; but there are no *enfans de la patrie*, with pikes and muskets to oppose your progress behind them. So if you can climb like a cat, or twist yourself about like a serpent, or a slippery eel, you have every chance of surmounting those costly and peaceful obstacles to your progress.

Look at those two tall Kentuckians, with their tufted chins, somewhere about seven feet "above snakes;" they can take a few of the interposing calico-mountains and cotton pyramids in their stride, but at last even they must stop and scramble over or through with difficulty and exertion. Like Damocles' sword too, over your head, are suspended from high cranes threatening loads, that would soon pulverize you out of your difficulties, and reduce you to very convenient dimensions, if they chanced to tumble upon you.

There are a great number of military companies in New York, and some of them are really very martial-looking indeed. I am told there is a company of Highlanders, formed by the sons of far

Caledonia; and there are German, French, Italian companies, &c. There are a number of target companies, each known by some particular name—usually, I believe, that of a favorite leader who is locally popular among them. Others take their appellation from some celebrated historical character, and others from any thing that happens to occur to them, it would seem.

A few of them are "The Washington Market *Chowder* Guard" (chowder is a famous dish in the United States), "Bony Fusileers," "Pea-nut Guard," "Sweet's Epicurean Guard" (surely these must be confectioners), "George R. Jackson and Company's Guard," "Nobody's Guard," "Oregon Blues," "Tenth Ward Light Guard," "Carpenter Guard," "First Ward Magnetizers," "Tompkins' Butcher Association Guard," "Mustache Fusileers," "Henry Rose Light Guard," "Atlantic Light Guard," "Junior Independence Guard," and multitudes of others.

The militia numbers about one hundred companies, which comprise six thousand men. The Target Companies are said not to fall short of ten thousand men. I am informed that the passion of arms is beginning to manifest itself very much here, and the youths are not happy till they are enrolled in some of those bands. It is said that thousands of the boldest spirits in the Mexican campaign, who were ever in the van, and at the post of danger, rushing to the cannon's mouth with fiery valor, and storming, with irresistible intrepidity, the strongholds of the enemy, were those who had figured in such "Target Companies" as these.

Generally a target, profusely decorated with flowers, is carried before the company, borne on the stalwart shoulders of a herculean specimen of the African race, to be shot at for a prize, or for glory, and the "bubble reputation" alone. On its return from the excursion and practice, the target will display many an evidence of the unerring skill and markmanship of the young and gallant corps. I remarked before, that it is supposed that the love and desire of military distinction is increasing. In corroboration of this, I find it observed in one of their papers, that the American boy, after delightedly firing off his pistol or his minature cannon, on "Independence Day," or other national anniversaries and festivals, in commemoration of particular events, rests not now on his budding laurels till he becomes a member of one of these Target Companies. Fired with youthful patriotism, and glowing with a boyish ambition, he desires ardently in some way to distinguish himself among his fellow-striplings; and, once admitted as a member, he strives hard to attain the post of lieutenant or captain among his companions in arms. Subsequently he aspires to join a more regular militia corps ; but it is said, there are many instances where their devotion to the Target Company, which originally inspired them with military enthusiasm is so strong, that they will not desert its ranks for those of the most brilliant and best-appointed militia company in New York. There are so many of those enrolled bands, that they and the omnibuses share the honor of filling, and rousing the echoes of busy Broadway.

I hear that some of the best and finest of their organizations are formed out of the fire companies, who thus take upon themselves a twofold responsibility, the protection of the property and lives of the citizens from a most formidable and merciless foe, and the rendering themselves capable of discharging the patriotic duty of crushing any enemy to their institutions that may threaten the country, either domestic or foreign. Nowhere, on the earth, I should think, are such numerous and splendid bodies of firemen ; and in no place under the sun, or moon, I honestly think, have they such extensive, incessant, and unlimited practice. And what men in the world ought to make such admirable warriors as firemen ? At all times, but especially at the dead hour of midnight, forced to leave their homes at a moment's notice, to start from slumber, after, perhaps, a day of wearying toil and harassing vexations—to confront the direst extremes of cold and heat—to brave the "pitiless pelting" of the storm—to face the raging element, that is their remorseless and tremendous antagonist—to dare almost every imaginable peril without the prospect of reward, or of promotion, or even of renown and glory—they should certainly make heroes, when fame and victory beckon them proudly onward.

They are trained, too, to strict discipline ; taught to obey every word of command of their superiors, and to act together in concert, and it may be imagined they would prove gallant candidates for glory in the field. Often the lieutenants and captains of the Target Companies are artisans, laborers, clerks, and mechanics. The companies elect their officers, and constantly without the least favor—I borrow the expression of an American writer—shown " to class, or rank, or wealth." The man who is most distinguished by these advantages, frequently shoulders his musket as a private ; and yet he may most largely subscribe to the company's expenses for yearly "excursions," and other contingencies and needs.

I have already mentioned the number of the electric telegraphs in America. I must just add, that on one particular occasion the New York Herald (on the 5th of January, 1848), contained ten closely printed columns of important matter, that had all been received during the preceding evening and night over the wires. The entire length of the electric lines in the United States, which, indeed, bring within speaking limits nearly every portion of this vast Union, is stated on fair authority to be ten thousand seven hundred and twelve miles, of which three thousand and six hundred miles are traversed by double wire; but while I am writing, more are probably completed. Indeed, if it is not an Irish bull, I should say, that in order to keep pace with what is going on in this indefatigable country, this unparalleled hive of industry and intelligence, you should go *far ahead;* and if I had boldly said fifteen thousand miles, perhaps I should have been nearer the truth by the time my words are read.

The Americans, from what I hear, are remarkably expert operators on the electric wires—those slender threads that are, without doubt, charged with the mighty task of revolutionizing and incredibly elevating the intellectual and mental condition of the whole inhabited world.

One of the most charming appendages to New York is the Battery, which is close to Delmonico's Hotel (where we are now staying). It is situated at the commencement of Broadway, that lengthy Mississippi of streets; and it is adorned with a profusion of noble trees, some of very large size, and is laid out in broad graveled walks, commanding a charming view of the harbor, and its very ornamental islands, of the almost innumerable vessels constantly arriving and departing, and of the adjacent fair shores of New Jersey, and of Staten, and Long Island. There are grass-plats in the Battery, all of which are intersected with paths and walks, and overshadowed by trees, that look like veterans of the primeval forest. It is not a very fashionable promenade, but this arises probably from its being so far from the fashionable streets and squares of the city.

When the first steamer that ever crossed the Atlantic arrived at New York, the Battery is said to have presented a most heart-stirring and majestic spectacle. The "Sirius" was the name of this precursor of all the magnificent steam Leviathans that have followed in her triumphant path. The moment it was reported that her shadowy flag of smoke was seen floating in the direction of the Narrows, the hundreds of thousands of citizens of New York, aroused and excited to the utmost by the announcement of an event so congenial to their energetic natures and zealous, enterprising temperaments, rushed with simultaneous impetuosity to the Battery to greet the triumphant stranger. Instead of the "Sirius" ascending the East River directly to dock, she passed the thronged Battery, as in graceful and grateful acknowledgment of the sympathy and breathless interest shown in her success, and swept grandly past it again, close to the densely-lined shore, while the air was literally rent by the enthusiastic shouts and deafening hurrahs of thousands and thousands of people, proclaiming how a noble victory had been gained—a victory without bloodshed, or suffering, or loss, or sorrow, to any single being, but of profit and incalculable benefit to the whole race of mankind, and the unborn myriads of the most distant posterity. May these be the victories that in future may blaze with all the pomp of glory, and all the festive splendor of success—victories that, instead of severing nations and people, shall unite them in bands of universal brotherhood!

There is no frowning artillery here to make the Battery agree with its warlike name—no mighty walls, no upheaved mounds. It was once, I believe, applied to the use its name points out, but has been entirely dismantled, and looks the very abode of peace and repose. So in due course of time may all the earth witness one grand disarmament and dismantling of all her warlike strongholds, and Reason and Justice reign paramount!

Speaking of justice, there is one very gloomy-looking building in New York, called "The Halls of Justice." The architecture professes to be Egyptian, and the edifice is built of a rather dark-colored granite, quarried at Hallowell in Maine. Its architectural ponderous massiveness, combined with the sombre hue of the material, gives the building a truly prison-like aspect, and has caused it to obtain the *sobriquet* of "The Tombs." It occupies a square, bounded by Centre, Elm, Franklin, and Leonard streets.

New York, as a whole, strikes one as unlike every city ever beheld before. The cosmopolitanism of her citizens, the extraordinary stir and bustle and tumult of business going on perpetually—the heterogeneous compounds, and kaleidoscopical varieties presented at every turn, bewilder and surprise the traveler.

Besides the ever-teeming tumultuous Broadway, there is another street that deserves, perhaps, especial mention in any description of New York, and that is the Bowery, a complete business street, which also traverses longitudinally the city. This street has been aptly named the Holborn of the empire city of the West. It runs parallel to Broadway, and changes its title of street for the more rural appellation of "Avenue," when it leaves the town behind it.

I have mentioned the East River, and ought perhaps to add, that it is a continuation of Long Island Sound on the east, uniting it with the estuary of the Hudson, and separating Long Island from New York. It is of scanty width, but deep, and at particular states of the tide it has a very heavy current. Long Island Sound (or one part of it, I am not quite certain which portion) is called the Hell Gate, which name is a corruption of the old name, Hurl Gate.

---

## CHAPTER XXV.

Vera Cruz by Moonlight—The "Walker" Steamer—The new Minister to Mexico—Lord Mark Kerr's exquisite Drawings—Scenes on Deck—Love of Music of the Americans—The Aspect of Vera Cruz—Effects of a Norther—Sopilotes—Their Functions and Appearance—The Castle of St. Juan D'Ulloa—The Harbor of Vera Cruz—Its Commerce—Its Foundation—The German Housekeeper—Her polyglot Stories—The Alameda—Vast Number of laden Mules—Departures for Mexico—Vera Cruzian Watchmen—Dresses of the Vera Cruzians.

We landed at Vera Cruz by the most magnificent moonlight I think I ever beheld. A huge arch of dazzling silver sparkled overhead, and all beside seemed floating in one vast silvery sea: any place must have looked beautiful so deluged with splendor, and certainly Vera Cruz did; her defects were really dazzled away, and her beauties all glorified and increased a hundred fold.

We had a very rough passage of about ten days in the surveying steamer "Walker," of the United States Navy. She was very foul, which prevented her making a rapid passage, and the weather was against her. Every thing was done to render us as comfortable as possible. We had a charming and large cabin, and a delightful collection of books was placed at our disposal. The "Walker" is reckoned the most rolling vessel in the whole United States Navy, and she gave us during our voyage a great deal more than a touch of her quality.

Our kind and excellent friend Governor L——, the minister to Mexico, had never been at sea before in his life, and it was not to be expected he should find this tremendous tossing about very pleasant. Naturally enough he was constantly thinking we were all showing, like Falstaff, a marvelous alacrity in sinking; he suffered much too, from the horrible *mal de mer*. But, notwithstanding all this, his unalterable good-humor never failed him, nor his wish to see every body comfortable around him, however uncomfortable he was himself; and very seldom did his almost inexhaustible good spirits forsake him. Sometimes when in the midst of one of his entertaining stories, laughing and making all laugh, the frolicking steamer, as if enjoying the joke, would seem to be contemplating standing on her head, he would suddenly regain his gravity in one sense, while he lost it in another. But generally he was the life and soul of the ship: though it must be confessed the "Walker" did not exactly fly, the time did.

We had Lord M. Kerr's magnificent drawings to look at, and his richly-stocked portfolio beguiled many an hour. He is not only a most gifted but a most industrious and indefatigable amateur artist; many of his drawings are most elaborately and exquisitely finished, and their number and variety are prodigious. Here you might luxuriate among the magical beauties of queenly Granada, and bask in the sunny and fairy-like courts of the matchless Alhambra; and there the snowy winter scenes of Canada would make you almost feel the freshness of the keen clear air, so exquisitely delineated were they; and there again you had the glowing tropical scenery of the West Indies to feast your eyes upon.

The weather, after the first few days, began to be exceedingly warm. The passengers spent almost all their time upon deck, for most of the cabins below were very close, and hot; ours was an exception to this; we had a very large sky-light, which was of course, always wide open when possible, and the magnificent American flag was thrown lightly over the opening to shield us from the intense glare of the sun.

On deck, what scenes tragi-comical are ever going on! To be sure, all decks in rough weather present pretty nearly the same spectacles; yet, like the fun of Punches and puppet shows, it seems an untiring species of drollery. Look at that tall gentleman; he appears trying hard to learn to walk on his own nose, which is certainly, though not otherwise than a handsome one, quite sufficiently pointed perhaps, and projecting; but he does not wish other people should do so too—no, that would be expecting quite too much of the poor nasal organ aforesaid. But that very stout gentleman seems to intend it nevertheless, nay, to be very seriously determined on doing this; but stay! the nose rolls suddenly one way and the very stout gentleman the other; the threatened feature is safe for this time. Then they go bouncing along by fits and starts, and performing insane *ko-tooings* to nobody, and catching tight hold of nothing, and swinging round sometimes in a wild partnerless waltz. A reel is of cosmopolitan constitution on board ship, and the Scotch can claim no monopoly of it—all are dancing it like mad in general.

Governor L——, when not incapacitated by the *mal de mer*, zig-zagged about to the utmost capacities of the "Walker," and nothing daunted, boldly attempted to walk whenever there was the least possibility of performing that most extraordinary of all imaginable feats, on board a rolling vessel on a rough sea. He wisely caught hold of every thing to steady him that happened to be nearest, and made handles and temporary sheet-anchors, of heads, ankles, benches, bonnets, boots, heels, hats, cabin-boys, carpet-bags, throats, ringlets, wide-awakes, elbows, and chins, and in short, whatever came handy, dragging himself on thus with the most philosophical indifference as to whether he had griped hold of your nose or your shoe. He held on like grim death, for the nonce, "and no two ways about it."

As I said before, he was very amusing and pleasant, and had an immense flow of spirits: it was diverting to see him occasionally, when a sudden terrific lurch came, upsetting furniture and philosophy, pathetically turning down one corner of his mouth with a lachrymose and rueful expression, while he had not had time to dismiss the merry curl on the other side. He was particularly anxious to know, on such occasions, how long the vessel might be supposed to have a chance of going on before she foundered.

One day we sprang, or carried away, our jib-boom, and the main-stay sail came down, and great was the confusion and alarm; for I think one or two on board were not much better sailors than the excellent minister. I believe, if the truth had been told, there were several who would have thought it an improvement if the ship could have accommodated a select few of the Royal, or any other Humane Society to restore us to life, after any extent of drowning we might be subjected to. However that might be, it was a gallant and goodly company on board, and pleasant was it to hear them singing in merry chorus in the evening, when the water was comparatively calm (very much *comparatively*, I assure you), "O Susanna!" which rather whimperingly-inclined lady seems really to be the "undying one," and also the universal and ubiquitous one; for go where you may, you will hear her invoked. I am told they harpoon whales to this cheering tune in the Antartic regions.

Then there was a right jovial parody about "Californy," too, and no end of "Uncle Neds" and "Mary Blanes," &c. But among them, however—which was a great want of taste in these songsters—was *not* the good old ditty with the impressive words, beginning—

> "Come all ye Continentallers, I'd have ye for to know,
> That for to fight the enemy we're going for to go."

The Americans, I think, are a very musically inclined people—far more naturally so, it strikes me, than we "Britishers." They have a very pretty custom (and they have so many, it is strange that those which are of a contrary description should ordinarily alone have been dwelt upon by travelers), and this is, of calling each other by the names of their respective States. If there be more than one from a State, I suppose by a kind of subdivision they resort to the names of their towns. If this be the case, what grandiloquent denominations some of them might come in for. "Here Constantinople, young Ninevah wants you;" and "Pekin, call Carthage and Mesopotamia to help Alexandrianopolis and little Herculaneum." As it is, through our skylight, we heard constantly some of their beautiful State names shouted out. "Indiana, come give us a song right away, and Alabama will join." "No; it is Louisiana's turn any how." "Where's Texas? is *he* coming on deck?" "Wall, I jist calc'late he ain't a-going to do nothing else; there he comes, too, with Michigan and Arkansas."

We arrived at Vera Cruz in the evening; but it was some time before we were able to land. The getting out of the "Walker" into the boat was a work of difficulty, so rough was the sea. At last, ourselves and carpet bags were dropped in, the former by some ingenious sleight of *foot*, very creditable to our activity. His Excellency and Mr. P—— had already gone on shore, and we found Mr. P——, and some other of our fellow-passengers waiting on shore to receive us and escort us to the hotel. The American Consul at Vera Cruz was so good as to take us on shore in his boat.

The glorious Orizava was only dimly visible in the distance, owing to some slight mist. The town, I thought, looked beautiful from the sea. It is the fashion to abuse Vera Cruz (no doubt its situation and climate are odious), but its sixteen grand domes and cupolas, its battlements, and picturesque buildings are very striking.

The hotel we are in is in the great "Plaza," almost close to the fine old cathedral, and opposite to the former palace, now partly used as a prison. On the other side are seen handsome houses, bearing severe marks of the bombardment of the city by General Scott. We found it very hot when we first came here, but rejoiced much at the speedy prospect of a norther. It came, indeed; but, alas! though to some extent we were benefited, it was at the expense almost entirely of light and liberty.

Thus it was—instead of windows, except one tiny pane in the door, there are, as it were, large wooden gates, or very huge clumsy rough doors opening on to the indispensable balcony: when the norther blows at all severely, it is absolutely necessary to close these great portals, or your room would be full of sand; and, besides, you would be blown out of it. Therefore, we were made melancholy prisoners of, and taken into close captivity by ourselves; and, in spite of all our precautions in the night, our balcony-doors blew open, and my little girl and I were almost blown away, beds and all.

There are an enormous number of "sopilotes" here—a kind of turkey-buzzard, vulture, or carrion crow, or cousin-german to all three; and these are the feathered scavengers of the place. "I calc'late" they have no sinecure office, and so they occasionally appear to opine themselves, for you see the omnivorous black creatures looking very grave and contemplative, sometimes motionless and quiet as a row of mutes, solemn and gloomy as a congregation of undertakers, and you look upon the dismal sight, and begin thinking of sextons and "black jobs" (as I have seen funerals described in matter-of-fact England); when suddenly up goes one undertaker with a whizz, and away goes another with a whirr, to make room for a fresh set.

The castle of St. Juan d'Ulloa, which commands Vera Cruz, is built on the little island bearing the same name, about four hundred fathoms from the shore: it is said to be a strong citadel. Its northwest angle supports a light-house, with a splendid revolving light, nearly eighty feet above the sea.

The harbor is reckoned a very insecure one, the anchorage so bad that the vessels are not considered safe unless made fast to rings of brass, which are fixed for the purpose in the walls of the castle. Still, however disadvantageously situated, Vera Cruz may boast of considerable commercial importance, although, of late years, Tampico, with rather a superior port in a less unhealthy part of the coast, has been rapidly springing into consequence.

Vera Cruz was founded about the latter part of the sixteenth century, on the very spot where Cortez first landed. There had, however, been a small town there before that event, which by Cortez himself was called " Villa Rica de la Vera Cruz." Philip III. bestowed on it the titles and privileges of a city in 1615. A French squadron took the castle in 1838, but shortly afterward abandoned it and restored it to the Mexicans. The Americans again captured it under General Scott, and it remained in their possession till the ratification of the articles of peace.

While the foreign trade of Mexico was carried on exclusively by the *flota*, which sailed from Cadiz periodically, Vera Cruz was celebrated for its " fair," held when the ships assembled at its port; but, in 1778, the abolition of this system of regular fleets put an end to this fair, as also to the yet more famous and splendid one of Porto Bello.

The houses here seem all built in the ancient Spanish or Moorish style, ordinarily inclosing a spacious square court, with broad covered galleries. They have commonly balconies in front. The foot-paths are usually under the shelter of arcades, which is very pleasant in hot, sunny countries.

This hotel, where we meet with great civility and attention, is kept by a Scotchman, very considerably Mexicanized—(poor man, he is in very bad health, and the climate seems to be slowly poisoning him). The housekeeper is a German, and she, on the contrary, appears to be more intensified in her nationality by the process of transplantation. She seemed perpetually in a high state of saur-kraut, and utterly Teutonic. She was very kind and good-natured indeed to us, although frequently she had declined altogether, we were told, the felicity of lodging ladies in the hotel.

She explained to me, in a remarkably intelligible mixture of Mexican-Spanish, English, French, German, Indian, Scotch, and any thing else that came into her head, leaving it to me to unravel them, her reasons for this occasional indisposition on her part to receive guests of her own sex.

" Mexican ladies mit ther airs muy desagradables. Von Señora, wife of a General, come here, sehr cross, sulky. No canny, I tink, head. Gone, loco. Order comida for she and de General, husband Muy buena it was; I help cook it. Todos good, when she see it, no taste it, take it all todos up, and troze it all at cook's cabeza! There! wat you tink o' dat? The Señora got no comida, nein—soup, frijoles, chickens, todos she trowed in cook's cara, mit her zwei hands! And O ciel! dere was dinner, disshes, and tódos on floor. De General, husband, poor man (he blind) hear noise—came to mich, say 'Muy schlecht, me can't help, he a'most cry, pobecity! lose him dinner too. Hoot awa, a bonny Señora dat, madame."

But, if her languages were wonderful, so were her gesticulations. Impressive indeed they were. While her voice was pitched an unusual height to suit and make up for the Babel of languages in which she was constrained to utter her sentiments, she spoke with great rapidity. Suddenly she changed the scene from Mexico to Hanover, where it appeared she had been housekeeper to a gentleman who was an acquaintance of our late kind Duke of Cambridge.

"The English Herzog Cambridge," she exclaimed, "wat von good prince dat! Come von day, all out, tous, Madame, come to mich, Cambridge did—" (I think the good frau did not intend any disrespect to the royal Duke by thus familiarly speaking of him, but, not knowing what Herzog was in English, when she did not use the German word she was quite at fault). "Well, Cambridge say, tell the family I comes, eh? Ha, ha! he laugh, sehr. Good nature prince—oui, madame, ja, always smile and laugh. O! how unlike cross lady mit General husband!"

She then proceeded to tell some wonderful stories about the Herzog, and cows and fresh milk, and a party and a country-house, *hacienda*, but the extraordinary patchwork of languages defied all comprehension—patchwork?—nay, it was more like silks of mixed colors: German, shot with French, and that shot over again with English, and crossed with Spanish. She seized my hands every now and then as if about to give me a lift to assist the understanding, but I was in a hopeless state. There was a whirl of *haciendas* and Hanoverians, and generals, and chickens, and herzogs, and cows, &c., in one's brain; a human windmill, a living telegraph, making signs at the rate of a million a minute before me—and all was confusion and mental darkness. She continued, however, fast and furious; and the chief actor in this scene was evidently perfectly satisfied; she was exceedingly diverted, and intensely interested by her own tale. Now she seemed almost on the point of cheering herself with hearty bravos, and now she successfully melted herself almost to tears, speaking

in the most pathetic accents, with clasped and wrung hands. We, not having the most remote notion at this juncture what particular form of human grief she was representing, were at a loss to console her.

As a housekeeper she was very superior indeed, and most kind and obliging did we find her. She kept the hotel in admirable order, and seemed to be running about from morning till night. If any of the *Criadas* or *Mozos* neglected their duties, there was the detachment of Hanoverian light horse after them *instanter*—trot, trot. She had, however, an unpleasant custom of keeping part of the broad galleries that ran round the house in a perpetually flooded state, from the gigantic scale of washing operations that seemed always going on there. At times the soap-sud breakers ran so high, it was a matter of great difficulty to pass them with safety, and a small life-boat was quite a desideratum.

We walked in the Alameda, yesterday evening, for a short time, escorted by the American Consul here, who is a gentlemanlike and well-informed person. He served in the Mexican war, and told us many very interesting anecdotes respecting it. The Alameda is pretty enough. At the further end a fandango was going on: the music sounded rather pleasing in the distance.

Not far from this spot is the beginning of a railroad, which, say the Americans, may perhaps be finished in five hundred years: it is intended to be carried on to Mexico. The streets here are wide and handsome, and clean too; thanks, probably, in great part, to the solemn scavengers, I have before mentioned.

Now that the *norte* is gone, we almost live upon the balcony. From thence we saw an enormous train of packed mules the other day. It seemed almost never-ending, as it came into the Plaza: the whole place appeared alive with them, when they stopped and were collected together and unloaded. The mules looked strong and well fed; they appeared to have a few little affairs of honor to settle with their comrades on their arrival, for a variety of kicks were interchanged; and it was some time before the "party of order" gained the ascendant.

We have made acquaintance already with a number of tropical fruits, through the kind care of our German friend. As yet I like none of them much. There were sapotes, bananas (those however were old acquaintances), Grenaditas di China, as they called them—mamey, and others. The living at this hotel is extremely good (though of course the cooking is Mexican); and we have certainly on no occasion thrown the repast at our Mozo's wild Indian head. He is an extraordinary genius, this same Mozo who usually waits on us; for he actually comprehends my Spanish, and except a few very trifling mistakes, such as bringing me a jug of boiling water instead of ice, or clearing away all the things, when I ask for a few more, we manage quite capitally. I am perpetually asking him for bread, and potatoes and other vegetables, and milk; for at sea we were deprived of all these pleasing articles of food, and the two latter are very good here. He seems satisfied in his own mind, as he brings fresh *pápas*, and more *leche* and *pan*, that we came from a country where cows are unknown, vegetables ungrown, and bread wholly unheard of, and that we are duly delighted with our new Mexican fare.

We have received several visits from the English Consul and his son. Mr. Gifford is good enongh to give us all the necessary information with regard to our journey to Mexico, and to lend us a couple of small trunks in the place of our large ones, which he advises, for several good and sufficient reasons, should be left behind at Vera Cruz. We have been detained about a week here in consequence of the diligences being so full, it was impossible to get places. After considerable difficulty, our *asientos* are now secured. Our kind friend, the American minister, started some time ago.

The *cortège* had altogether an imposing effect. Eight stout mules were attached to the huge carriage, and a large escort of dragoons, drew up before the front of the hotel. These, I believe a short time before the diligence started, trotted off to wait for it at the gates.

The diligencias always leave Vera Cruz about ten o'clock at night, for the heat of the day would render the journey almost insupportable, especially to the poor mules, who have to drag the unwieldy vehicle through the hills of sand which cause the first part of this journey to be very wearisome and disagreeable.

We were on the balcony when the United States minister took his departure. With him was Mr. P——, a walking arsenal, and a movable powder-magazine, determined no *ladrone* should annex his goods and chattels. He said laughingly to us, "I have just thirty-seven shots to give them, if they attempt to meddle with me."

His Chilian servant did not look quite so light-hearted as his master; he marched gravely behind the bushy bulwarks of his own enormous mustaches in rather a darkly contemplative mood. However, I believe (like his nation in general), he is a right brave man, and probably, if he entertained any apprehension, it

was of the gunpowder magazine inside the diligence blowing up, as such an explosion was not impossible, taking lighted cigars into account; and it would have been an unpleasant and unprofitable way of quitting existence—on the road to California too! which he and his master were.

Mr. P—— told me, he has always had Chinese servants at Mazatlan, this Chilian being almost the only exception. He says they are the best servants imaginable—quick, obliging, attentive, and trustworthy.

Lord M. Kerr started, very shortly after his arrival here, for Mexico. He rode part of the way, in order to be able to stop when he chose, to sketch: a Mexican guide accompanied him. He thought of taking the diligence from Jalapa, I believe, and after going for some distance by that, perhaps riding again.

The bawling the watchmen make here, is astonishing and alarming. They seem to be in the habit of perpetually frightening people to death, to assure them that they are safe. Imagine all the dogs of Constantinople in profound affliction and pain, and you may form some idea of the howling of Vera Cruzian *serenos*. They have that pretty name, not certainly from the state into which they have suddenly aroused, and horribly startled the unfortunate slumberers, but because in the Mexican climate in general, the state of the weather (which they have to report), is cloudlessly fine, and so they are constantly crying a yelling tempestuous *sereno:* the rest of their terrible hollabulloo, I believe, consists of the hour, and "Ave Marie purissima."

We have seen some very picturesque Mexican peasants and horsemen. The women's dress with the flowing *reboso* is very graceful. These *rebosos* are long, colored scarfs, and are crossed about in some peculiar manner, which has a pretty effect. The men wear enormous hats, with silver cords twisted round them, very wide trowsers, which are slashed up the side of the leg, and splendid *serapes* of many hues, which are tossed about in every imaginable shape and manner:—it seemed to me as if no two were ever worn alike. Their horse-furniture is generally handsome, and their profusely ornamented saddles are (Dominie Sampson would say) "prodigious."

## CHAPTER XVI.

The Mexicans—Climate of Mexico—Luxuriance of its Vegetation—Beauty of its Flowers and Birds—Jalapa—The Journey from Vera Cruz—The State of the Roads—The Diligence—A formidable-looking Passenger—Cornish Miners in Mexico—The Inn at Perotè—English Hardware in Mexico—Hacienda of General Santa Anna—General Scott and the Passage of the Chapparal—Puente Del Rey—The Mountains of Mexico—Orizaba—Its magnificent Height—Cathedral of Puebla—Mexican Spurs—Rio Frio—Popocatapetl—National Character of the Mexicans.

WE have had a delightful journey from Vera Cruz, excepting always the frightful roughness of the roads. I believe, since the days of the Spanish dominion, they have never been repaired or touched. General Scott's artillery could have done them no good; but there they remain unmended. Formerly, it is said, this road was the finest in the world. No doubt the standard was not very high in those days: Macadamization had not seen the light, and the French *pavé* had. But from the very ruins of the road you can form an idea of the former excellence of it. The loose stones lying about, over which you bound with such excruciating jolts, were originally part of a fine pavement, which every now and then, indeed, for a very short distance, you roll over, and which has withstood ruin, rain, revolutions, and that old gentleman with the sharp scythe, who, though supposed to fly, continues to leave very deep footmarks wherever he treads—and where does he not?

If the Mexicans, instead of manufacturing their three hundred revolutions since their independence, had spent the time and money devoted to these topsy-turvy, useless pursuits, and busied themselves in improving their internal communications, developing the natural resources of their magnificent country, and advancing the education of the people—what might Mexico be? What might it not be at this moment? If a calculation could be made, and they could ascertain what they might have accomplished with the money and means and misdirected energies that they have applied to such worse than idle purposes, would they not regret their folly? No, not a bit, I dare say; though, but for their many internal sources of weakness, in all probability they might have successfully withstood the Americans, and remained in possession of California, and, in course of time, discovered what

that possession implied. This might have been better and more patriotic in the end than playing at revolutions, unhinging the whole country, and upsetting every thing, as if this were really a desideratum and advantage to a nation.

As to the extreme natural beauty we beheld during the almost magical journey from Vera Cruz to the capital, no words, I feel, can adequately describe it. We passed through every variety of climate, each with its own peculiar productions, with splendid snow-topped mountains crowning the scene, themselves crowned by the gorgeous magnificence of the resplendent tropical heavens. Such mornings! such sunrises! heaven and earth seemed meeting, as it were, and mingling in glory without end. Such nights! heaving and blazing with stars. Those glorious masses of stars seemed almost coming down on our little world: nearer and nearer they seemed to shine, as if drooping under the weight of their immense glory and majesty, and sinking toward us! You know what the Neapolitan embassador said to George the Second: that the moon of the King, his master, was far better than His Majesty's sun. I wish he had seen the stars of Mexico, which I think are not very unlike Italian moons; and her moons like great white suns, and her suns like the skies on fire. Certainly the heavens in the tropics are marvelously glorious—but earth is so beautiful here, too.

One morning, at sunrise, coming from Puebla, we saw the great mountain, Orizaba, reflecting the light of the rising luminary, and looking as if it was literally made partly of gold and partly of fire, so gloriously was it beaming back those dazzling splendors from its huge crest of glittering snow. Between Jalapa and Peroté, and still more between Vera Cruz and Jalapa, the astonishing prodigality and unutterable magnificence of the tropical vegetation is perfectly overpowering! I could not have believed, without beholding it, that such a Paradise remained to this world! Such colors—such blooms—such forests of flowers! Such inconceivable luxuriance of foliage and fruit! You can not for a moment "begin to imagine" the glories of these scenes—their inexhaustible variety—their indescribable exuberance—their extraordinary and matchless brilliancy of coloring!

Nature seems like a perpetual miracle there. It made us think of the sumptuous Sultana in the "Arabian Nights'" tales, who changed her regal dress twelve times a day. Just try to fancy in those marvelous regions endlessly-spreading colossal bowers, under a green overhanging firmament of uptowering trees, and such

bowers too! Myriads of flowers of a hundred colors, crowding coronal upon coronal; and these again intertwined and overtwined, and round and through, and sub and supertwined with others, and others still! It seemed as if there was really going to be a flood of flowers, and this was the first flow of the dazzling deluge: a gorgeous deluge indeed that would be—its own rainbow. There were innumerable roses, interwreathed with convolvoluses, flowering myrtles, aloes, cherimoyas, floripundias (a magnificent sculpture-like, bell-shaped flower), the verdant liquidamber, jessamines, and others, with creepers and parasitical plants, festooning and trailing themselves about with the very wildest luxuriance, so that often the coiled and heaped-together boughs and branches appear to bear hundreds of different sorts of leaves and flowers at once!

One of the most magnificent flowers I ever saw, grows on a tree of considerable dimensions (if, indeed, it is not a parasitical plant), and looks, with its multitudinous clusters of large, gorgeous, and vivid scarlet blossoms, like a pyramid of planets in a blaze, or a candelabra of comets, with forty thousand branching flames in all directions. These were most beautifully contrasted by the snowy white lilies I have spoken of before, which literally lined the road-side in many places.

In short, altogether, it was quite bewildering. One felt that one would fain have ten thousand eyes to see with, and ten thousand senses to admire, appreciate, and realize (I must go back to the United States for the right word) all the immensity and variety of those wondrous royal realms of Nature. I have said that the leaves, branches, flowers, fruits, stems, seemed all confusedly intermingled, and matted, and massed together in beauty. There were heaps of cactuses garlanded with wildernesses of roses; there were floripundias coiled about with creepers that seemed almost moving in their wild life-like grace; besides countless other labyrinthine complications.

But I have said nothing of the splendid birds, that like animated rainbows and winged sunbeams were darting about amid these transcendent scenes. But it is quite useless to attempt to describe these unimaginable regions—one might as well strive to convey in words a glorious strain of the most exquisite music.

After leaving Puebla, we mounted up so high, that it became quite cold; and at Peroté, too, where we slept one night, we should have been glad of a little fire! There the vegetation was chiefly confined to pines and firs. We had extremely hot weather for the first day's journey; but we had a delightful and most refreshing rest at Jalapa, which is a place of enchantment—a little Cashmere of delights—a very kingdom of roses. The climate is reckoned very good, and the poor Vera Cruzians fly there to take refuge from their terrible *vomito* (the dreadful Vera Cruz fever).

I think this lovely Jalapa is unlike any town I have ever seen any where: its houses and streets do not seem to take away the country air of every thing belonging to it. In those garden-beautified, quiet, picturesque streets, you feel as far out of the hard, and stale, and work-a-day world, as if you were in the midst of a vast savanna, or the shadowy recesses of an untrodden forest. I can hardly tell why it is so, but so it seemed to me. Diligences seem to rattle there, and busy travelers to congregate in vain: all, still, appears quiet, all peaceful, and holiday-like at Jalapa. It seems, as it were, consecrated by its own beauty.

And Nature has so much to say there! Her flowery treasures fill the streets and courts with their odoriferous delights. Her glorious mountains and hills look upon you there in a hundred beauteous shapes.

We found a delightful hotel in that exquisite town—all galleries, and balconies, and arcades, and courts; and to breathe the delicious air of balmy Jalapa alone, is a pleasure. Is the reader aware, that the not delicious medicine, whose name closely resembles that of this fair town, is produced from a root, which grows in great profusion near it? From this place it takes its name; and as this association is not particularly charming, I prefer spelling the word in the old way, "Xalapa." What a fall from roses and floripundias, to tumble down to this nauseous drug! But I believe the flower of this same plant, is a very beautiful convolvulus. Very useful it is, no doubt; and, in this utilitarian age perhaps, more to be thought of, than poor Flora's daffydowndilly treasures, and roses and posies.

The dreaded first stage from Vera Cruz, I did not find so dreary as I expected. Our escort met us at the gates of the town and our eight mules went gallantly on, till the deep loose sand reduced the gallop to a trot, the trot to a walk, and the walk even at times almost to a stand-still: some parts of the way we went washing the wheels of the cumbrous diligencia actually in the sea. There seemed to be no regular road, just there, or if there was, the coachman evidently disregarded it, for it could not be supposed it led through the sea.

Afterward we came to a very heavy part of the road; it seemed all the mules could do, to tug us through, and a great deal of time was consumed in this slow battle with the sand.

We stopped to breakfast at a very nice pavilion-like place. There we were ushered into a very pretty airy room, where the breakfast was already prepared, on a large round table. Señor N——, a friend of the English Consul, who had been introduced to us by him at Vera Cruz, was one of our fellow-passengers. He is a member of the Mexican Congress, and appears a highly-informed person. He speaks French and English very fluently. He was exceedingly obliging, and did the honors of the diligence and the hotel admirably for us.

They have a very pretty plan in some of these country "fondas," of putting up windows of dark blue glass, which shed a delightfully cool light through the room. This, however, is rare, for ordinarily there are no windows at all, only the great doors I mentioned before.

From Jalapa, we had an American coachman, who drove extremely well; but the road was frightful. The diligences, and the hotels that they stop at, all belong to one person, a rich and enterprising Mexican gentleman, who has done much to improve the communication between Vera Cruz and the capital, and, I believe, between Mexico and Guadalajara as well, which line also belongs to him. But there is much room for further improvement.

Some of the stages are a great deal too long—above all, on such infamous roads; and while several of the hotels are exceedingly comfortable and well-conducted, others are of the most primitive description, and amply furnished with—nothing; at least, nothing that you can profitably and pleasantly make use of.

The roads are horrible. Every now and then came an unearthly jolt, that tossed us all up like shuttlecocks to the ceiling, and made one think really some drivers, in despair had left their foundered wagons on the way, or General Scott some broken cannon, which we in our frisky diligence had taken a flying leap over. Our involuntary flights to the ceiling and back, were like the short, fluttering, up-springings of the poor pigeons of Loo, which I used to commiserate so much when hawking there: they were thrown up to attract the hawks, and then jerked back again.

At other times we felt we were droping into a chasm, that seemed desirous of emulating the mammoth cave in dear "old Kentuck." We found we had our own heads "in chancery" sometimes, pretty nearly, and the whacks and thumps that all got, were tremendous.

At length, the much-abused diligencia came to a dead stop, heart-broken—or spring-broken at any rate, as we discovered; and this accident revealed to us the astounding fact that these diligencias, actually pretended to have springs, which otherwise we should not have dreamed of. We were all requested to descend, while the huge vehicle was raised and the injury temporarily repaired, by the united efforts of the coachman and an American gentleman. who was an outside passenger, on his way to California. At last we mounted the high steps, and were placed on the wheels, or "the *wheel*," again.

The spirited proprietor of these coaches, should arrange that an "experienced surgeon" should accompany them in their journeys. It might be useful practice, too, for a few young beginners—as good as walking the hospitals.

We saw a beautiful waterfall in the distance, on the way to Peroté, which Colonel A—— (a friend of Señor N——) first pointed out to us, saying it was a "Cataráta," like Niagara: the first it was, and a very pretty one; the last I must beg to be excused from admitting.

We had a steep hill not far from this place, long, but not tedious, and so just the reverse of that sermon, Canning characterized as "tedious, though not long." The road on both sides was bordered with the most enchanting natural gardens of flowers of all hues. Hesperides (and of any extent) for hedges, or instead of them! Colonel A—— gathered us some delicious flowers, and our great barge on wheels looked as cheerful as the Russian treillaged cages in which ladies at St. Petersburgh used to sit (I know not if the fashion continues) in their drawing-rooms, playing at summer and the south.

We drove on merrily, with our gallant escort galloping and prancing by the side of the stage, the flags on their lances fluttering gayly in the wind (and themselves all *sarapes* and mustache, showing only the point of a nose, and two dark eyes in addition), and with our curious collection of articles within, such as roses and revolvers, convolvuluses and cigars, books and bowie-knives, escopétas and oranges, gunpowder and sugar-plums, fans, parasols, and pistols. I forgot to mention how our kind Hanoverian housekeeper loaded us with generous gifts of tea and sugar, and fruit, and cakes, which she good-naturedly insisted on our taking. It was rather perilous, however, to have loose parcels in the vehicle, as they were flung about in all directions; and you stood a chance now of having a tea-canister in your eye; now a huge packet of sugar struck you on the nose; and now the basket, but not the oranges (these were acting the part of cannon-balls, and knocking people about right and left), was on the point of trying to go down your throat.

Frightful present dangers make one forget remoter perils; and the alarm occasioned by these active missiles, and also the serious terror with which we contemplated our brave defenders, made us think but little of robbers—but this requires explanation assuredly. It must be told that the passengers were superabundantly armed —they frequently declared no danger was to be apprehended in consequence of their having such a heap of firearms among them, from which I begged leave to differ. Now imagine an old "escopéta" loaded, and frequently pointed at your head during the mad jumps of that lumbering and eccentric vehicle, that seemed playing with an invisible skipping-rope, and constantly catching its feet in it; a large covey of pistols performing curious circuits in the air, occasionally in the hands of their valiant owners, and various other similar murderous instruments of defense, which were enough to make your hair stand on end, considering the position they placed themselves in with reference to your brains, during the plungings and prancings of that wild-colt like coach.

At one of the "ventas" we took in a gentleman who looked like the Tower of London on its travels, such an arsenal had he hung round his belt. At the first glance you might have taken him for the commander-in-chief of all the brigands in Mexico, but you would have been widely mistaken. This was a most pacifically disposed and pleasant English gentleman, Mr. G——, a superintendent of the far-famed Guanajuato mines, who had been in Mexico about twenty years without losing a jot or particle of his English manners, way of speaking, or appearance, although it is by no means the existing fashion in Hyde Park, or even on the Northwestern Railway, to hang your waist round with pistols, and other such belligerent ornaments. He told us the mines of Guanajuato (which place, we were told, the Cornwall miners who work there pronounce invariably "Go-and-a-quarter") have been extraordinarily productive during the last year, they having yielded, in 1849, 8,400,000 dollars, which is above half a million more than they did last year. New mines have been opened, and the improvements in the methods and machinery are said to be very extensive.

Mr. G—— told me, on the whole, the preference was perhaps to be given to native workmen over those from Cornwall, in consequence of the latter being so addicted to drinking, and to quarreling with one another—at least in Mexico. Already round Guanajuato there are more than a hundred mines, and nearly eighty thousand workmen are employed.

When we arrived at Peroté, I was rather terrified at the first aspect of the *méson;* but presently reflected it was of course only the mules' stables we saw, and I felt consoled for a brief space of time; but on descending from the diligence, what was my consternation to find that those rough-looking stalls, which I was rather compassionating the poor mules for having to inhabit, were destined to be our apartments! They were almost exactly in size and every thing else like rudely-built loose horse-boxes, the chief difference being that there were small beds instead of straw in them, and a very little table fastened against the wall, with a couple of mouldy-looking chairs. Window there was none of any sort or kind.

Notwithstanding the rugged appearance and appointments of our quarters, they gave us a very good dinner (after stoutly refusing to let us have any thing unless we went to the public table which I declined, and almost while still reiterating "Nada, nada! no es posible!" they brought it), and a very civil *muchacha* waited on us. All the plates and dishes at all the *mésons* we stopped at on our way from Vera Cruz to Mexico, have the eagle and nopal (the arms of Mexico) on them, and inform the hungry traveler, in very conspicuous characters, that they belong to the service of the *diligencias generales*, and all of them are made in busy England, expressly for this line. That sweet little island of ours, as we know, likes to have a finger in every pie and pie-dish!

We saw an immense *conducta* during our journey. A vast number of mules were carrying silver from the mines to the coast. It was a very gay, and pretty, and interesting sight. It seemed as if there was a whole regiment of soldiers escorting the specie-burdened mules.

Peroté is reckoned a sort of metropolis of the *ladrones.* It is said the diligence has on several occasions been pillaged at the very gates of this gloomy and wild-looking town. We came at a very fortunate time. About a week before, a diligence had been stopped and plundered, and the brigands were taken and suffered capital punishment. This had, of course, struck terror into the rest for the time, and, with a strong escort, we felt very secure, except from the six-shooters and escopétas of our friends.

The specimen we had of the latter weapon might have figured

in a museum, as an antique, with credit to itself, and less danger to others, than loaded and in a loaded diligence: it looked horrible, really, in the hands of a raw, inexperienced Spanish youth, who, with his brother, had just arrived from Spain, to settle in Mexico —with some relation, I believe. It probably dated from about the time of the great Spanish Armada.

It appeared to me they allow the diligencia travelers any amount of dawdling-time that they require. Sometimes, when the mules were all ready, the greater part of the passengers would be lounging about with their cigars, keeping the rest of the "gentle public" waiting: when it suited their pleasure, the agreeable sound "vamos, caballeros" was heard, and, ere long, we were off. I must confess, however, it is very likely at these times the stage may have been a little before its time, and this was the reason the "caballeros" were allowed to stretch their cramped limbs for a little longer period.

I ought to have mentioned before, that we passed a fine-looking *hacienda*, or *quinta*, that belonged to General Santa Anna. It had a deserted, melancholy appearance; but whether it still is his property or no, I know not. It is between Vera Cruz and Jalapa; and, I believe, many other *haciendas* between these two places are, or were, his. We also came by the famous battle-field of Cerro Gordo.

The American whom I mentioned before (and who was a very gentlemanlike, intelligent person, with very quiet manners, though bristling with arms like a fortress) pointed out to us the field, on which he had fought. He gave us an animated account of the battle; and so near the spot, and described *vivâ voce*, it was very interesting. So well too did he tell his tale of war that we were fain to shoulder our very parasols in martial sympathy. He told how General Scott had cleared the passage through the Chapparal, making a circuit of a few miles, and thus gaining the side of the hill that looked to the northeast, the most easy of access, and which it appeared, was not so well defended as the rest. The hill has two peaks.

General Scott gained one, and the American forces charged down the slope and up the steep in front of them, "even where the deadliest of War's death-bolts showered" from the thundering batteries of the foe. The battery was taken, and the cannons played against the retreating Mexicans, who, broken, and disordered, fled impetuously through the Chapparal. Santa Anna with some difficulty effected his escape.

Cerro Gordo itself is a mere Indian village, of transparent-looking cane huts. Paul Pry need not "drop in" to such dwellings to see all that is going on in the household.

We passed by the ruins of a very fine stone bridge across the river, near Plan del Rio, another assemblage of bamboo huts, which was burned by Santa Anna on the advance of "Los Yankees." This bridge, we were told, the Mexicans blew up, hoping thus to stop General Scott's artillery. Others say, it was to hinder the passage of an American specie train, *en route* from Vera Cruz. In six hours after this destruction was completed, Los Yankees had, with their usual quickness and ability, made a capital road across the chasm, which not only answered their purpose at the time, but which remains to answer that of ours, and all other travelers; for the sacrificed bridge has never been restored by the Mexicanos.

Puente Nacional, formerly "Puenta del Rey," is in a savagely beautiful glen, through which the river sparkles and dashes in its passage to the Gulf. Rivers are very rare in Mexico, and there are no large ones in the country.

I have said nothing yet of the Coffre di Peroté. It is 13,514 feet high, and its crest is distinguished by a mass of rock, that is shaped much like a chest, from which the mountain takes its name. I did not very much admire this same Coffre di Peroté: what is it, compared with glorious, unmatched, unmatchable Orizaba? In Mexico you become quite *difficile* about your mountains; you pick and choose, select, reject. The ten-thousand-footer on this side seems like a mere upstart mushroom of a mountain, and the eight-thousand-feet-high hobble-de-hoy on that side is really a ridiculous little molehill, a Tom Thumb on tiptoes, looking tall with all its might, but a poor dwarf, after all. As to the clouds upon it, they must be mere grovelers of clouds, very much addicted to low company, to hover so much about it: mountain indeed! We will perhaps allow it to be something like the lofty artificial garden-mounds in a Chinese picture, which the lady, with her little club foot slightly raised, is going to step over with such careless ease.

But now, Orizaba, come into court; let us have a look at you. Majestic Orizaba, thou art indeed magnificent! What is there in the world like thee? standing alone, and thus in thy "single blessedness" towering to thy mighty height of seventeen thousand eight hundred feet! (Some writers give it eighteen thousand feet. It is said to be the only mountain of equal height on the earth that thus rises detached and apart from all others in its lofty solitude, communing with only heaven). Thou "star-mountain," with the dazzling summit of perpetual snows, so pure, and cold, and bright, in the face of the burning sun of the tropics! How beautiful are the girdling forests of cedars and pines, and other trees that adorn the giant sides of that consummate Orizaba.

At Puebla I was sorry not to see the inside of the Cathedral; which, to judge from the exterior, must be well worth a visit. It is considered by the Pueblanos to be partly of angelic architecture—and well did the celestial stone-masons do their work.

Puebla was called on this account "Puebla da los Angeles." The mortal workmen must have felt a very mortal jealousy of these winged laborers; but history says not whether in consequence of diminished wages, there was any strike. Naturally (or supernaturally), the immortal builders left their earthly competitors far behind, both in the rapidity and perfection of their work. This superstition is, of course, chiefly confined to the Indians.

We were too much charmed with the peace and quiet of our hotel to stir out that evening. Certainly the luxury of not bounding about like an India rubber ball, banging your head against the hard coach, and wrenching your hands almost off in the vain effort to steady yourself, can only be appreciated by those who have been tossing on the stormy surface of that great highway from Vera Cruz for some days. Puebla is a very large town, and a handsome one; it has an immense population of spurs, cloaks, sombreros, and rebosos (for we could see but little of the enveloped wearers), which perpetually paraded the streets.

We saw some most beautiful spurs of wrought silver for sale at one of the places we stopped at: the workmanship was exquisite. The spurs were not quite the size of a wagon-wheel (without the rim), but might, perhaps, on a pinch, serve in that capacity. The would-be sellers of them brought them to the window of the diligence, to tempt us. We admired them very much—not their size, but the extreme beauty of the designs, which were most delicately executed upon them. All praised, but none purchased: peradventure though a present of sharp spurs might have been a good hint to the worthy gentlemen who sometimes deign to interest themselves in the temporal affairs of travelers (and to relieve them from the troublesome charge of that plague, baggage—a good hint that they were welcome to use them and make themselves scarce at their earliest convenience), yet it would have hardly been worth our while to encumber ourselves with these huge articles, in order to lay them at the feet, and fix them on the heels, of these gallant gentlemen.

The name of the place where those beauties were offered us for sale has slipped my memory ; but well do I remember the road which followed. Indeed, it was sufficient to have jogged any memory in the world. To this day it is to me a mystery how we ever arrived alive at this city of Montezuma. Instead of being a road to this beauteous place, it would seem to be a succession of barriers and obstacles expressly designed to keep you from it.

When the tribulation of jolting had a little subsided, and people began picking up their parcels and packages, a fresh trial awaited us : it was a sort of dust ordeal now that we had to pass through. " Hombre ! que polvo ! dispense, V. Caballero, sirvase V. levantar los vidrios." " Si, Señora, con mucho gusto," and up went the windows on both sides, but soon to come down again, for it was too hot, full as the carriage was, to keep them closed long, Oh, what a dust was that! Methinks I shall never hear people talk, or see them write of the dust of their ancestors with patience again—it will seem so disrespectful to compare them to such an unmitigated nuisance. Such dust, and such quantities of it! Had it been gold dust, we might have become very valuable freight before we drove into the court-yard of the Casa di Diligencias here. As it was we might have had a good crop of Magveys in the " coche," or any thing we pleased, for we had become quite landed proprietors of the soil, so deeply spread was it over our large light shawls and various habiliments.

Rio Frio was the last breakfasting-place we stopped at, and here it began to rain, while the travelers were devouring their rice " guisados," "frijoles," and chocolate. Presently out rushed Mr. —— in great haste, leaving his " Almuerzo," with a huge umbrella opened, and consternation in his countenance ; but it was not to protect from the rain yonder *muchacha* with the black streaming hair, nor certainly that decrepit old dame with the tattered *reboso*. No : it was for the precious pistols exposed on the box-seat (or rather what is called the *pescante*) to the storm ; having carefully placed the big umbrella upon these sweet little pets, he returned to his repast, with a clear conscience. The welcome drops began to patter down fast ; however, soon it became rather too much of a good thing, and the day became chilly and clouded. It is said, though, at Rio Frio it is always cold, and almost always windy; it was both that morning.

I trembled for the view—the " hermosissima vista"—of Mexico

and its vast valley of enchantment—that glorious valley, which is about a hundred miles in extent, and a whole world of beauty and magnificence, and fertility in itself! We had seen a splendid sunrise, and had a grand view of Popocatapetl, this morning, but, *l'appetit vient en mangeant*, and we were longing to gaze at sundown on the valley of valleys, with its stupendous guardian chain of encircling mountains, its majestic capital, with a thousand domes, and towers, and terraces, in the centre; its lakes like glittering sheets of silver; and all the glories that those among our fellow-passengers, who had been there before, described with great and vehement enthusiasm and rapture.

In mentioning Popocatapetl, I ought not to have neglected the other grand volcano, Iztaccihuatl, for they are not very far from each, and do not affect a surly solitude like that sturdy old bachelor, Orizaba. "Iztaccihuatl," or the "White Lady," might seem to be the fair and gracious bride of stately "Popocatapetl."

Not a word have I said about Malinche, another but a smaller volcano. It is said to be about thirteen thousand feet high, and is a very majestic mountain. The name is the Aztec alteration for Marianna, the beauteous Indian wife of Cortez. Then, of Cortez himself, and of his battle-fields, I have said naught, nor of the wonderful Pyramid of Cholula, with its splendid and Titanic terraces marked out against the sky—that marvelous work of the marvelous Aztecs.

One word of the people in this loveliest of all countries, or that vast accumulation of *sarapes* and whiskers, which I presume to be the people. They would appear, to judge by the outward man, or rather the outward mantle and mustaches, to be a ferocious and mysterious set of personages, but I believe they are neither one nor the other; a little treacherous, perhaps, and a little choleric occasionally, fond of *pronunciamentos*, and *pulque; au reste*, full of contempt for all foreigners, whom they call disdainfully "Los Gringos" (except their first cousins, the Spaniards, who are nicknamed "Los Gachupinos"), and superlatively so, it strikes me, as far as I have yet seen, for their conquerors the Yankees. They—that is at least the prouder and richer classes of Mexico, appear generally to mention them with a kind of sneering shrug, which seems to say "hombre! we *could* have beaten them; *but*, only in short—the stars were more in fault than we!"

I think the Americans have done good to the country and the people in some respects. I should be inclined to believe that there is now a greater craving for education, a deeper sense of its desirableness and necessity, than before the war. I am told great numbers of young Mexicans of good family go to the United States now to be educated, and they will come back, of course, with vastly enlarged views, and developed powers of intellect.

---

## CHAPTER XXVII.

Mexico when First conquered—Cortez and Montezuma—The musical Gentleman—Mexican Plants and Flowers—The Cathedral in the City of Mexico—Arrival of the Diligence at the Hotel—The Passengers—M. de Zurutuza—Appointments of the Hotel—Mexican Pronunciamientos—The Mexican Lady and her Flowers—The Form of Government best suited for Mexico—The Streets of Mexico—The Passengers and Vehicles—The Shops—Rebosos and Sarapes—Picturesque Costume of the Mexicans.

It was not possible to roll along the broad causeway leading to Mexico—that causeway made, if I am correctly informed, by the ancient Indians, and not think of the days of old, when along that magnificent road marched the hosts of Cortez in their pride and power—the gallant Spanish chivalry—while before their wondering eyes rose the city of ten thousand enchantments, the unspeakably beautiful Tenochtitlan, like the capital of the Eastern King of the Genii, spreading over and covering its beautiful islands, with its palaced streets, that swarmed with gay canoes—its temples, its groves, its floating gardens, its crystal seas, covered with barques (those majestic lakes which are now so diminished and reduced), and all its unimaginable beauties of art and nature—all that unrivaled valley-world which, shut out from the rest of earth, scarcely seems to belong to that earth—fenced and walled round by its glorious giant mountains, leaning their snowy-helmed foreheads against the stars, and reflecting themselves in those silver waters, as if they repented of leaving such a scene of enchantment, and thus returned and haunted it ever.

What a vision must this have been to the eyes of the Spanish conqueror, and those of his adventurous followers, when, too, they saw the splendid procession advancing from the gates of the glorious city to meet them—the mighty monarch of the Aztecs, the imperial Montezuma, surrounded by his court, his richly appareled chieftains; in short, as says one of the old Spanish writers, about two hundred nobles of the royal blood, "vestidos di libréa con grandes penachos conformes en la hechura y el color......descalzos todos y sin levantar los ojos de la tierra, acompañamiento con apariencias de procesion;......y se vió á los lejos una gran tropa de gente mejor adornada y de mayor dignidad en cuyo medio venia Montezuma sobre los hombros de sus favorecidos, en unas andas de oro bruñido," &c.! Montezuma himself, with "el semblante magestuoso con algo de intencion. Su trage un manto de *sutilisimo algodon*," finest cotton!—though there were no Manchester mills in existence, and not a spinning jenny to help them. "Trahia sobre si differentes joyas de oro, perlas, y piedras preciosas en tanto numero, que servian mas al peso, que al adorno," &c.

This probably the Spaniards thought, and kindly in their own minds resolved to relieve him of such a cruel weight, and any of his friends and followers who were similarly inconvenienced. Then on approaching nearer, they saw the mighty Emperor of the Aztecs descend from his resplendent palanquin (canopied with glittering and many-colored decorations of feather-work) and advance to meet the Spanish commander, leaning on the arms of two of his relations, the Lords of Tezcuco and of Iztacpalapan.

In coming from Vera Cruz you do not enter Mexico by the most beautiful approach, and we had unfavorable weather; at least the enormous volumes of dust, like the columns of sand in the Desert, hid the greater part of the sublime prospect from our eyes. Still, here and there we had glimpses of its almost supernatural beauty, and of the majesty of those mountains, which seem so jealously to surround it, and shut in all that fairy land of loveliness, that seems a "locked, and guarded, and a treasured thing." Around those giant heights clung light fleecy clouds. As to the exceeding enchantment of what even those glimpses revealed, it is indescribable; yet M. de Lamartine *might* do it justice (he only has portrayed Constantinople in fitting, living words), or Eōthen.

Every body seemed intensely delighted to be at last near this Queen of Cities. One cigar-loving Mexican gentleman, who seemed very pensive all day, and reduced by the awful shaking and jolting, and the dust, and the after-storm of mire, to the merest remains of a powder-puff, a jelly, an expiring whiff of tobacco, and a splash of mud, suddenly picked himself up, and put himself together again, and began actually to sing for very joy (it was a very quavering strain, I confess, as if the voice had not got over the rough treatment it had received): he was very like a musical box tuned up and set a-going mechanically, for he never ceased this strain for a moment—the time was unaltered, the expression the same, or rather the non-expression; and this long series of *shakes* continued, neither lower nor higher, quicker nor slower, uninterruptedly to be poured forth till we stopped at the hotel.

I with my little party had been fortunate in one respect, for we had had one side of the *coche* secured comfortably to ourselves. I heard an amusing answer to a remark that was made one day—that our danger was greater from within than from without (with a glance at the loaded blunderbusses), "No tiene V. cuidadoly, no hay *mucho* peligro!"—"Do not fear; there's not *much* danger."

I admired exceedingly, as we drove along, the beautiful Arbol de Peru, with its graceful branches, and some very singular cactuses, called, I am told, *organos* from their remarkable resemblance to the barrels of an organ. These were formed into extremely beautiful hedges, most artistically arranged, so as to grow in the shape of gigantic festoons, the tallest being very high. They make a formidable fence too, thickly set with prickles, almost as good, or as bad, as a *chevaux de frise.* There were some Brobdignagian aloes too (the Maguey), with leaves about a dozen feet long.

In coming to the hotel, we drove past the majestic old cathedral, situated in a most magnificent plaza, and another fine church, on crutches, as it were, so was it propped and held up, while its huge form seemed leaning over the street very threateningly. This was the work of the sharp earthquake which had nearly destroyed the city some years ago. People say, that, if it had lasted two minutes longer, all Mexico would have toppled over. (So it really must have been a little worse than our diligencia-quakes.) We saw other traces and symptoms of that terrible visitor, as we rolled heavily along, behind our handsome team of large powerful Yankee horses, who quickly dragged us through the noble and populous streets, over which, already, the shades of evening were beginning to settle; and soon our fortification on wheels rolled into the courtyard of the Casa di Diligencias, and capitulated at discretion.

The doors were thrown open, we made a movement to get out—huge volumes of dust rolled out of the doors—hidden awhile from mortal eyes and each other in these floating shrouds, we descended like so many Apollos and Minervas from the clouds, and still enwrapped *in* them. The living musical box, enveloped in mystery, seemed suddenly to come to the end of its mechanical melodies, and, clapping on its huge sombrero, gave a jump out of the vehicle, that must have broken all the springs and works in its body, and vanished. (*Nota Bene.*—This same musical box was pleasing and well-bred, and a very good specimen of a polished Mexican.) The different passengers evaporated different ways, and we found waiting to congratulate us on our safe arrival, by the side of the diligence, our friends Lord M. Kerr, and Mr. P—, the latter buttoned up to the chin, not without some reason, for the evening air was chilly; and I have found since, the mornings and evenings are a little coldish in Mexico—at least at this time of the year, yet not assuredly nearly so much so as in the spring in England. In the day-time it is quite warm.

I found Mexico so fashionably full, that we could get no room of any sort or kind at the Casa de Bazar, where I had intended to go (it having been recommended to me), but we are very comfortable here. This hotel is the property of the Diligence-king of Mexico, who is master of about a hundred or more, I suppose. M. de Zurutuza is immensely rich, and has lately, I understand, purchased a magnificent estate, for which he gave an enormous price, but he still keeps on his hotel. Of course the superintendence of it is entirely given up to a Prime Minister, who administers the affairs with great zeal and discretion.

There is a capital housekeeper too, who showed us a splendid suite of apartments the other day (M. de Zurutuza being away) which are reserved for the proprietor. They are luxuriously furnished: some are hung with pictures, others with very fine French and English engravings. There is a superb piano-forte there, on which we were graciously invited by the *femme de charge* to play whenever we liked.

Mr. —— called the day after we arrived. He apologized, as he ought to do, for having no pretty little *pronunciamientos* to show us just at this moment, which seems extraordinary, as there is, it is well-known, usually a running revolution going on in Mexico—perhaps they are taking breath a little, after the American war.

This national sport is generally not quite so dangerous as steeple-chases or fox-hunting, and far less so than bull-fighting. It is described as an amusing little *divertissement* enough, and the pop-gunning and cannonading must have a lively and festive effect.

Altogether, the political horizon seems to be very calm and clear just now, though there was a very pretty and promising little rebellion got up at Puebla about ten days ago, which was blighted in the bud, and one here about the same time, that burst like a bubble, or a " biler" on the Mississippi. The one at Puebla broke forth rather tamely, and came to an untimely end—it committed suicide, perhaps, with a precocious squib, or an inconsiderate cracker.

It really seems to be the native land of revolutions, there having been about three hundred and thirty, large and small, since the War of Independence. Here the doctrine of compensation is apparent; people can not be allowed to live in such a paradise for nothing. We may go on and enjoy our jog-trot peace and quiet at home in our misty little island; we have to keep our windows shut to exclude the fog and chilling dropping rain: it would be hard to have them broken open by drizzling cannon balls, and rather expensive too, though glass is cheap. We want a good roof over our heads, to prevent rude Boreas from visiting us; to have it summarily blown off by a shell would be a double hardship in our bitter clime. So we have the blessings of order, as maintained by our metropolitan and rural police; and of britannia warming-pans and coal-scuttles: and the non-blessings of fog, ice, snow, clouds, east winds, and unripe gooseberries. They have glorious suns, and balmy airs, and mighty mountains, and dazzling stars, gold and purple skies, a silver earth, and insurrections of every pattern and species, a large assortment always on hand, agreeably diversified by numerous little stabbings and killings, by undisciplined amateurs; for the regular *pronunciamiento* must be quite a profession in Mexico, by all accounts, and is conducted on principles of high art.

However, it is liable to abuses, as every thing else is, and they say if the little boys want to rob an apple-stall they get up a small *pronunciamientito*, and call, "Viva General Santa Anna," or any body else, to strike terror into the soul of the *Manzana*-seller, and, as they hope, to make President Herrera shake in his chair, and then they rush on to the charge, and divide their apples of discord in peace. Such a Brummagem *pronunciamiento* as that, it would not be worth while to see; but as there are so many English and foreigners in the city, the Mexicans really should get up scientifically this characteristic little national spectable for their amusement and edification—though, perhaps, a spontaneous growth is better: forced, like early asparagus, these interesting little insurrections might be possibly insipid.

Talking of revolutions, I was told a tale of a lady at Puebla, who had some beautiful flowers on her balcony, and who neglected them during the civil war, a week ago (we came through as it was dying off, I believe, but we were rather sleepy and did not find it out at all). She left them for nearly three days, and then, afraid that they would be quite spoiled, in spite of the peppering balls that fell round faster than usual (the popular tempest, just going to clear off perhaps for a few weeks or so, was expending its last strength fitfully), out she stepped, on her fair balcony, armed with a watering-pot—not so bad a weapon after all, if it could have held enough—and proceeded to refresh the unlucky flowers, some of which had had their heads carried off by bullets, while several were bearing scars like the very flowers of chivalry. She watered them pretty fast, you may be sure, but before she had done, bang came a great ball, and cut in two the body of a flower-pot. That was enough; away ran the lady at once, thinking that the flowers had better be killed than herself.

Some contemplative persons would say the people would be happier than they are now, under a mild, paternal, unmistakable despotism, and it is rumored that the army and the church would have no objection to furnish them with the said despotism on reasonable terms. But then each individual general and priest would patriotically wish to serve the public in the capacity of autocrat, and take the trouble off his fellow-creatures' hands. But I am against all plans of this sort, and any thing that might disturb that just equilibrium of compensation I have adverted to. The people would be too happy, positively; they would all turn to musical boxes, like my diligence friend, and go whistling and piping away all their lives, too full of ecstasy, perhaps, to work or think—crazed with very bliss in this Eden of the earth.

If you were to give them the mighty Nicholas, and his firm, strong, temperate government—for such it is—the consequences might be frightful. A whole people, perhaps, light-headed from very light-heartedness, too happy for any thing; a nation in a long delirium of joy; intoxicated with felicity. Besides, they would be the envy of the whole world (with their climate, their country, all their advantages, and no daily battles), and thus hated of all. No; they *ought* to have a little share of the trials of mortals, or the inhabitants of the rest of this earth would feel it unfair indeed! The Presidentship, held for a short term of years, must be a fruitful source of jealousy and quarreling in general, except in the United States; but they are an extraordinary people, there, and it will not do to step in a giant's footsteps, unless you are somewhere about the same size, and with a nearly equal length of limb; unless this is the case, there is a great chance of the one who makes the attempt coming upon his nose.

I should think that the good people here (who, without being as capable of self-government as the calm, thoughtful, shrewd, resolute Yankees, are intelligent and sensible) would be far happier if they would first take care to get a very good President, and then take care to keep him as long as he lives; and instead of changing state-postillions at relay-stations only a short way apart—go on (as Eōthen, I think, says of marriage) Vetturini-wise along to the end of their journey—at all events as far as *he* can take them—and the next generation may find a new one.

The streets here look wonderfully gay, almost always, like Naples on a holiday, so crowded, and so brilliant, though the people are generally, I think, more serious and taciturn, from the little I have seen of them, than the Neapolitans. But there are such multitudes of them, and such quantities of carriages of various kinds, from the London Brougham or the Paris britska to the most charming original, aboriginal, indescribable, huge nondescripts, drawn by astonished looking mules, that do not so much seem to be trying to drag them, as attempting to race away from them with might and main, utterly scared; * and they really look as if they were about to topple over, and crush every thing near them. *Gare!* get out of the way, ye very mountains, for the runaway old globe seems taking a gallop—a world on wheels.

In the days when Montezuma or Guatamozin was emperor, the Lord Mayor of Tenochtitlan might have gone to his Guildhall in such an awful equipage, in his full dress, thatched all over with feathers, and with a couple of Aztec Gogs and Magogs standing behind as footmen. However comfortable and convenient as a carriage, a Brougham or Clarence may be, it looks almost like a dapper piece of impertinence by these time-honored, venerable vehicles. But, Shades of all the Aztecs, what comes there? A New York omnibus, as large as life. Retire, gentlemen shades, at once, as I should have done, from the window, had I had one, and had I seen the sight from there. As it was, it was from the glass of Mr. ——'s handsome English Brougham that I beheld it, and altogether I could hardly believe in Aztec chiefs or Indian emperors any more that day. An omnibus with "Fourth Avenue" on it.

The streets, as I have said, are the gayest in the world, perhaps. They are generally very broad and clean. The *portales* are charming inventions: you have a wide corridor supported on handsome stone arches, with very brilliant shops on the solid side,

* Since I wrote this I have seen the same idea in Mr. Taylor's charming book, "El Dorado:"—he must forgive the apparent plagiarism. It may, perhaps, serve to show how exact was his description.

and the spaces between the supporting pillars are gayly filled with a vast variety of stalls, where you may buy little trays, playthings, dazzling sarapes of all colors, flowing rebosos, mangas, tortillas *ad libitum*, tilmas (Indian cloaks), dulces (sweetmeats), pictures, little figures of saints, prints, shoes, and many other miscellaneous articles.

The fruit-sellers exhibit their tempting piles of zapotes, cocoa nuts, and all sorts of fruit, from the Tierra Caliente, at the corners, and they display too an immense number of glasses and cups filled with cool and refreshing beverages to arrest the steps of the passer-by, heated, perhaps, by walking in the sun, before he came under those delicious places of refuge from sun, wind, or rain; the first the most frequently making those portales desirable promenades. As I have seen them do at Naples, in the busy and stirring Strada Toledo, so in Mexico do the various tradesmen constantly pursue their occupation in the open air—that is to say, open here—save and except the umbrageous shelter of the covered porticoes. Of course, here are to be seen innumerable *rebosos* and *sarapes*, kaleidoscopically diversified in both patterns and colors; a marvelous and almost endless variety of both, and also in the manner of draping them about the person. Look at that little urchin of perhaps six summers, with about a mile of glittering *sarape* wound around him, like a long, huge shining snake wreathing about his small person; not, however, having caught that strutting little six-year-old in its gleaming coils, but being scornfully clutched and grasped and scotched (not killed—for it looks living in its spiral, serpentining grace—as living as the snake wound round Laocoon, which is saying a very great deal!) and, in short, tossed and thrown about at his will and pleasure; and *how* he stalks, *how* he attitudinizes, how he haughtily paces along (stepping like a young panther) with his splendid prey and prize; how he gives the brilliant folds another proud toss over his shoulders—and methinks now he has chosen *his* fashion and mode and manner of wearing the magical *sarape*, for ever and aye uncopied and uncopiable. A Mexican and his *sarape* seem one and indivisible, like the ancient Centaurs and their horses—inseparable and the same. The whole dress is very graceful; what a horror is a swallow-tailed coat in comparison, and the crown of all the hideousness of modern European dress—the tight black hat; how frightful is it by the picturesque sombrero, with its delicate silver cords and hanging tassels. They sometimes have the cord fastened by some little silver wrought bird or animal, exquisitely finished.

## CHAPTER XXVIII.

The Cathedral of Mexico—The Grand Plaza—The Palace—Importunity of Beggars—Site of the Cathedral once occupied by the Grand Aztec Temple—Description of the Temple by old Spanish Writers—The Interior of the Cathedral—The Calendar Stone of the Aztecs—The Stone of Sacrifices—The Aztec Priests and their Victims—The Idol worshiped—The National Museum—Colossal Statue of Charles IV. of Spain—Armor of Cortez and Pedro de Alvarado—"El Salto de Alvarado"—Ancient Map of Mexico—Beauty of the City—The Shops and their Multiplicity of Articles—Mexican Horse Furniture—Mexican Houses—The Plaza del Toros.

We started to see the magnificent cathedral, wearing as usual, our *gringos* bonnets; Mr. P—— told us we should haply not be admitted in that head-dress; but being already accoutred, and inclined to think he was possibly in error, we continued on our way, resolved to try our fate.

When we came into the Grand Plaza, a little doubt and hesitation came over us. What streams of *rebosos* and mantillas were going in and out of the building—not one bonneted head any where! Should we go on or turn back? One must have something on the head—simply unbonneting would not do. In deliberating mentally on the difficulty, and giving it due earnest consideration, I was disposed to believe, that our wearing bonnets, or no bonnets, then and there, would scarcely be regarded in the light of an ecclesiastical subject, or occasion an ecclesiastical controversy; that Protestants like us, if once allowed the enjoyment and free use of our abominable heretical heads, might, without doubt, put any thing upon them we chose; and that if an Inquisition had still existed, and we had been given over to its tender mercies, the bonnet question would have easily been put to an end, by the heads that wore them being "put down" at once by the inflexible Sir Peter Laurie of that stern tribunal. So the bonnets were retained, and we leisurely and calmly crossed the stately Grand Plaza, one of the finest I ever beheld in Europe, Asia, Africa, or America.

The whole of its vast space is uninterruptedly open, save by the twofold avenue of orange-trees in front of the cathedral. The noble equestrian statue of Charles IV. at one time stood in the centre, but, since the Independence war, it has been taken from its high position, and placed in the court-yard of the Museum, where, in these revolutionary days, it might have a select society of statues of deposed kings to accompany it, and have a friendly ride together. The splendid national palace covers nearly the whole of the eastern side of the Plaza (it has a princely frontage of five hundred feet); while the vast cathedral, with a very handsome church contiguous to it, which has a beautifully sculptured front, occupies the northern side: it is said they are going to pull this church down. Around the other sides a Cortal runs, whose noble arches exhibit an immense profusion of heterogeneous articles for sale.

We were assailed by many beggars and *léperos* near the Cathedral. I had not then learnt the recognized and proper method of dismissing them, if you are not inclined to encourage their laziness, by giving them any *reales* or *quartillos*. This is by saying, "Perdone V. por Dios," or "Perdone V. Hermano;" but I improvised a very efficient substitute in my own sturdy Anglo-Saxon, which, after a few repetitions, I can recommend as answering the purpose thoroughly. "Pray go away, I've nothing for you,"—a thousand signs and gesticulations, to make me understand he wants money. "You had better go away,"—he mutters something: looks perplexed;—"Don't stand there in the pathway,"—he can stand the strange gibberish no longer, and moves away discomfited. The effect is very lasting, too! I don't think the same *lépero* ever attacked me again. They seemed to have a sort of fear that the heretic might have been pronouncing some dreadful words of sorcery or witchcraft, and in short, that they had better avoid any further communication.

How beautiful the Plaza looked that morning in the glorious sunshine, with its picturesque crowds of monks, priests (with their enormous shovel hats, over the spacious brims of which you might almost drive a carriage and four), soldiers, country people, vailed señoras, Indians, *forçats* in chains, horsemen, laden mules, &c.! It was impossible not to be struck with the scenes and living actors grouped and lounging about it.

The cathedral is built upon the site of a portion of the ruins of the grand Aztec temple, that vast pyramidal edifice which was supposed to be founded by Ahuitzotli. This was the enormous idol-temple, which so astonished the Spanish conquerors by its size and magnificence. Its various piles of buildings, and courts, and sanctuaries, and halls, occupied, according to their statements, the whole of the ground on which the cathedral now stands; and in addition, part of the Plaza, and even the circumjacent streets! The old writers expatiated on the wonderful assemblage of five hundred dwellings within its inclosure—on the mighty hall constructed of stone and lime, and adorned with dreadful serpent-forms, writhing and hideous, in stone. There were four huge gates, facing the four cardinal points of the great court, paved with stone; there were grand flights of stone stairs, and splendid sanctuaries, which were dedicated to the dreadful god of war. Then there was a vast square for their mystic dances, and educational establishments for the priests, and "genteel Ladies' Seminaries" for the priestesses.

There was a temple of mirrors (which for the sake of their studies we should, perhaps, hope was not adjoining the latter structures), and another of fair shells, and a frightful and terrible one, whose door was a giant serpent's great gaping mouth (possibly to frighten the priestesses away from the pavilion of looking-glasses next door—*quien sabe?*) Then there were beauteous fountains, where consecrated waters glittered in the sun, making sweet music; and richly-colored bright starry birds, such as abound in radiant Mexico, kept for sacrifice: and there was the house especially designed for the emperor's devotions; and the lovely bowers and gardens for the "holy flowers"—the scarlet manitas, I suppose (the centre of which is formed like a hand with the fingers slightly bending inward), and, terrible transition from the fairest and sweetest things in nature to all that is most ghastly and loathsome—there, too, stood the grinning Towers of Skulls.

Yes! there rose the horrible skull-towers, actually built of that portion of the skeletons of the victims sacrificed to their monster idols. In that stupendous temple, they tell us, chanted night and day, at least five thousand priests in the service of their barbarous false divinities, who were anointed three times a day with perfumes of the most precious and costly description. They tell us, too, that the most devout of these priests were dressed in garments of sable hue, their flowing locks stained deeply, with some sort of ink, and their persons carefully bedaubed with a rather curious kind of cosmetic, made of the ashes of burnt scorpions and spiders. Whether this was done to improve or disfigure, I know not: if it had been in Tierra Caliente, I should have thought it was, perhaps, a cunning "dodge" to keep musquitoes away.

Imagine their horrible god of war, Megitli, being born with a shield in one hand, an arrow in the other, a great plume of pea-green feathers on his villainous pate, his visage dyed a sort of true or garter blue, and his left leg adorned with—not the insignia of the Order of the same Garter—but with a luxuriant crop of feathers: the monster's colossal statue thus represents him. It is supposed that somewhere about fifty thousand human victims were sacrificed every year in Mexico alone to their different idol demons! The knowledge of this takes away very much from one's interest in the Aztecs, and even (less justly) one's compassion for poor ill-used Montezuma. Surely they must have been a cruel people originally to have had so cruel a religion, but, of course, individually, may be entirely exonerated from such a charge.

The cathedral covers an immense space of ground, has two lofty white ornamented towers, and its interior is inconceivably rich and splendid. There is a very costly balustrade, that occupies the centre of the church, which is composed of a metal brought from China, through the Philippine Islands. It is called from this circumstance, "Metal de China:" it is supposed to be a composition of brass and silver, and is very massive. It is said to have cost an immense sum, as it was actually paid for by the weight in hard dollars, and some say it contains so much *gold*, that a rich silversmith in Mexico offered the bishop a new silver rail of exactly equal weight, in exchange for the old metal!

On the hallowed pavement of the cathedral stood or knelt a large number of persons, and we discovered that a funeral service was going on there. Beside the coffin on the bier, which was placed rather near the entrance, were priests chanting dismally and very nasally. A number of lighted candles were disposed round the coffin—holy water was thrown on it, and soon after the corpse was carried out. It appeared to be the funeral of a poor person, as the mourners were miserably attired. Subsequently, and with only a brief interval, another coffin was brought in, and the same ceremony repeated. The nave, with its arch resting on pillars of a partly Gothic character, and the high altar at the extremity, with its magnificent pile, resplendent with burnished gold and solid silver, and costly marbles, formed a very imposing spectacle. The many shrines along the side aisles were adorned with different pictures, and on all sides were beheld the glitter of gold and the pomp of almost inexhaustible treasure. Some of the railings and the lamps are said to be of solid silver. There was a long row of female penitents kneeling at the altar, with immense lighted candles in their hands; they turned round and stared our *bonnets* entirely out of countenance, smiling as they did so, and I am afraid nudging one another; we relieved our poor shamefaced bonnets from their embarrassment, by removing them quickly from their gaze.

After quitting the interior of the cathedral we threaded our way among the Señoras and Señoritas, léperos, rancheros, Indians and begging children (who are terrible little torments in Mexico, and pursue you sometimes mounted upon each other's shoulders, like the posturing Arabs), and went to see on the outer wall of the building the famous calendar stone of the Aztecs. It is fastened on the wall, and is a very large circular stone of basaltic porphyry, covered with curious hieroglyphical figures, by which the Aztecs used to designate the different months of the year, and which it is thought formed a perpetual calendar. This immense sculptured stone, with its astronomical signs, gives one a more favorable idea of the people than the horrible idolatries I have spoken of before.

We have lately been to see the National Museum, which is extremely interesting. Mr. D—— was good enough to be our cicerone.

Let me give the reader a slight idea of the dreadful Stone of Sacrifices, which, however, at once puts to flight all the better opinions that the great calendar might have induced one to form of the ancient lords of the land. It was upon this that their hideous human sacrifices were performed, those with which the great Temple of ancient Tenochtitlan was so fearfully disgraced and defiled. This stone is in excellent preservation, and bears its silent but eloquent and terrible testimony to the horrors and barbarities of their so called religious rites and ceremonies. It has a hollow in the centre, into which was inserted a piece of jasper, and upon this were stretched the miserable victims, while their hearts were deliberately cut out by the pitiless priests. There are little canals or grooves, which slant toward the edge, for carrying off the blood of the unhappy sufferer. Hard by is the hideous idol's shrine, in whose honor these detestable sacrifices were performed. The extracted palpitating heart was laid at the grotesque monster's feet, after being inspected by the high priest, and subsequently introduced into his open mouth. The tongue projected; and in the hollow thus made, the revolting offering was thrust, being pushed in with a spoon of gold by the chief priest.

We are told that the unfortunate wretches were held down by six priests, while the appalling operation was performed. The collars have been preserved (and were shown to us) which they put on the necks of the helpless victims to keep them quiet, while the abominable murderers "stole their hearts away," in this most atrocious fashion. Alas! to think there was no ether and no chloroform in those days—not that those merciless demons would have used it, though.

During the ghastly tragedies above mentioned, those half dozen assistant executioners, it appears, were wont to be clad in red garments, with waving crests of green feathers on their heads; in their ears were hung rings of green and gold, and blue stones were cunningly fastened in the upper lips. What beauties must they have looked! They had actually devised a costume more outrageously ugly than that of our parish beadles, or even than the old Windsor uniform.

After the devoted hearts had been extracted (the poor victims would have found it very difficult to retaliate on their tormentors—the heartless barbarians!) they cut off the heads of the unfortunates, and used them in adding to the Tower of Skulls; then they devoured some portions of the bodies, and consumed the remainder, or flung it to some of the wild animals that were confined and kept in the palace precincts. Some speak of that foul idol as a goddess;—what a vile representative of a Queen of Hearts!

After that sight I shall not scowl again at a New York omnibus, or any other evidence of human progress and civilization. I should not feel shocked—not much—if I saw that horrible old gaping idol thrust into a modern deal packing-case (supposing it were less huge), and addressed,

"To —— MONTEZUMA AND GUATAMOZIN, ESQS.,
In the SHADES (of the Cypresses),
Chapultepec Gardens.

Per omnibus,
To be left till called for.

If the case were directed to those sanguinary priests, it would be asking the omnibus to go a little *too much out of its way* to leave it for them.

The idol in question is the hugset and most hideous of all the abominable objects scattered round the great sacrificial stone, heterogeneous combinations of human figures, with those of animals and reptiles. The presiding genius of the place—this horror of horrors—the Aztec god of war—rejoices in the euphonious name of Queatzalcoatl (which sounds somewhat like the quacking of a duck, and sometimes like quizzical), is about fourteen feet high, with four faces, and pairs of arms and legs in proportion. (I hope I have not confounded this with the other respected gentleman,

Megitli, and that in reality this old "quizzical" is the god of the air). His chasmy mouth seems angrily yawning for its awful accustomed banquet. One almost felt inclined to pin a paper, in mockery and revenge, deaf-and-dumb beggar fashion, to its breast, with "starving" written thereon.

The remainder of the abominations scattered on the pavement around, were, some of them like Chinese inventions of deformity, and others peculiar, I think, to Aztec conceptions; such as serpents in a full dress of feathers, and other incongruities. Queatzalcoatl might be presented to the Peace Congress, methinks, as a very fair representation and embodiment of the terrible genius of war.

These hateful and yet painfully interesting relics of antiquity, are collected in the court-yard of the Museum, and railed round. We were admitted, however, inside the fence, and so had an excellent view of them. In the centre of this court-yard stands the famous colossal equestrian statue of Charles IV., executed by the Mexican sculptor, Tolsa. It is very highly praised by Humboldt, and in general is said to be the finest work of the kind in the New World. It is of bronze. The horse (modeled from an Andalusian charger, I believe) I could not admire: it looked clumsy, I thought, and without any symmetry. It has spirit, however, and its royal rider looks animated and life-like. The attitude is fine and striking, and altogether it is a very noble work. Lord M. Kerr took a capital sketch of it.

In the interior of the Museum we saw many interesting remains of the ancient Indian possessors of the country, and also mementos of the earlier Spanish race. Here are preserved the coats of mail of the great Cortez and of Alvarado. Cortez, judging from his armor—helmet, cuishes, and breastplate—must have been a man of about the height of the Duke of Wellington (a height much in fashion for heroes in all ages), and of a powerful frame. Pedro de Alvarado, who performed the celebrated leap, on the far-famed night which obtained the melancholy name of the *Noche Triste*, apparently was slighter and rather taller than his great chief. The measure of this wonderful leap is still shown on a walk near the spot, while the fosse, crossed by a little bridge (it is, however, I believe, filled up now), retains the denomination of "El Salto de Alvarado."

This *Salto* took place on the 1st of July, 1520, when the Spanish invaders were compelled to retreat from Mexico to the heights of Tepeyayac. On this mournful and memorable occasion Cortez commanded the troops to march in silence. The vanguard was led by the intrepid and invincible Sandoval: the valiant Pedro de Alvarado brought up the rear. It was indeed a melancholy night —a *noche triste* in every sense. The rain poured down in almost sheets of water; the heavens were obscured by black clouds; the splendid moon and stars of Mexico were invisible—all was quiet—the dreary echoes of the splashing rain alone drowned the measured steps of the retreating Spaniards. A wooden bridge, to enable them to traverse the moats or canals, was borne along by a number of the soldiers, and on they went, full of determination and energy, under their renowned leaders. The first canal was passed in safety—the hostile sentinels, who guarded it, were overpowered; but the sound of the almost momentary struggle had aroused one or more of the watchful priests. The consecrated trumpets were loudly blown—"To arms!" was the cry; and the suddenly awakened city sprang from its peaceful slumber. The retreating forces of Cortez were rapidly hemmed in, and surrounded by water and land. They had just reached the second canal, and there the hideous conflict raged fearfully: the canal was literally bridged over with dead bodies, and along them the rear guard passed. Cortez performed prodigies of valor, and poor Alvarado of jumping; yet not against him be this recorded. Alone by chance on the border of the third canal to which he had fought his way, with intrepid courage, his horse being killed, and himself encircled by merciless enemies (perhaps with the pleasing idea of Queatzalcoatl before him) against whom it was hopeless for him to contend single-handed, he, with prompt decision, planted his lance firmly in the bottom of the canal, and lightly leaning his weight against it, sprang into the air, and vaulted over with an agile bound safely to the opposite shore, leaving the Indians gaping and gazing with uncontrollable admiration and wonder at the tremendous feat. A contemporary author says, when they beheld this surprising leap they ate earth by handfuls. To bite the dust, it appears, was to express approbation in those days—a disagreeable mode, we should think, of elaborating a bravo. How expensive a way it would be in California! (Had they had Jenny Lind in those days, small landed proprietors would have eaten their whole estates bodily.) But the reader will be tired of "Alvarado of the Leap," whose leap I have certainly not skipped over.

Mr. D—— pointed out to us, among other things, the fine map of Ancient Mexico, which was actually given by Montezuma to Cortez. There was a vast assemblage of antiques on every side—

Indian idols, amulets, and ornaments (mostly cut in obsidian, I believe). Many of the idols and figures bear a striking resemblance to Egyptian images.

Among ancient curiosities were some modern ones—eastern mirrors and Chinese nondescripts, and some marvelously well-executed figures, made of rags by the modern Mexicans. An old woman, who is dying they say, is the only person (except a daughter of hers, whom she has taught) who knows how to make them now. There are wax ones that are also clever, but they are very common, and not to be compared to those of this "Ragged School" of Art.

At one end of the room there was a little plant of the manita flower; there are but three trees of the Arbol de las Manitos (*Cheirostemon platanifolium*), I am informed, in Mexico: it grows to a considerable size. Two are to be found in the Botanical Gardens, and one is in the Toluca Mountains.

I was introduced in the Museum to an English gentleman, who has lately arrived here from a sojourn of two years in Siberia—a voluntary exile. He then left Kamtschatka in a Russian merchant vessel, visited Polynesia, and subsequently the interior of South America. He had just come from the western coast of Mexico, and intends going from Vera Cruz by the next packet, on his way home. What an extensive and interesting tour!

After the stillness and seclusion of the Museum, and the grim company of so many grinning idols and dusty relics of the past, the gay streets, overflowing as usual with pedestrians, horsemen, and carriages, seemed doubly exhilarating and amusing; not that I did not appreciate those memorials of the olden time, and wish there were many more of them, unspoiled and unshattered: for well says the old Mexican, Ant. de Gama, "Quantos preciosos monumentos de la antiquedad por falta de intelligenza, habran perecido en esta mañera."

I wish I could give any adequate idea of the beauty of Mexico, it is so unlike any other place in the world. Humboldt says, setting aside its very peculiar situation, that it is one of the very finest cities ever built by Europeans in either hemisphere, being only inferior to St. Petersburgh, London, Berlin, or Philadelphia, as respects the regularity and length of its streets, as well as the extent of its public places. But then to make these compare with charming Mexico, you must widen and adorn those streets with those gay covered colonades, the *portales* (the despicable and discarded Regent-street covered way gave not the slightest idea of them), pour into them the picturesque and streaming population of a Neapolitan holiday, give them a sky overhead yet clearer and more exquisitely beautiful than that of fair Parthenope herself, enthrone everlasting spring upon their terraces and gardens, and then place the whole in such a paradisiacal valley as this, with its giant wall around it, of the snow-crowned Cordillera.

Fancy coming at the end of Bond-street or Park-lane, to a view of sublimer Alps, and more colossal Pyrenees. On looking down any of the principal thoroughfares and streets of this capital, you behold these grand mountain forms towering into the sky, clearly defined against the lucid lustrous cerulean of the heavenly arch, and sometimes almost as if they were within a stone's throw, so marvelously pure is this atmosphere.

I wonder if the shops and stalls are always so abundantly provided as they seem to be now: perhaps they are particularly full, as it is so near the Carnival. In many of the shops are the most beautiful materials for ladies' dresses, shawls of all the colors of the prism, scarfs of all the shapes and patterns which Proteus, or Mrs. and the Misses Proteus could have by possibillity desired. You might ransack your imagination in vain for a quarter of the multiplicity of articles which greet the eyes at every turn.

What is there not to be found here? Look round; here are sombreros, mantillas, rebosos, satins, silks, silver, gold, china, pictures, mats, and twenty thousand things besides, all close at hand; and just look at those splendidly embroidered cloth-mangos for gentlemen, with a circular piece of colored velvet in the middle to act as a sort of masculine necklace. Here are wax figures, most elaborately and exquisitely finished, faithful representations of every class in Mexico, a perfect population in themselves, and, it is asserted, not given to the melting mood, which you would have suspected. Here are spurs, like merely moderately-sized windmills! that weigh, some of them, a pound and a half, and the rowels of which clatter along the pavements when the wearer happens to walk, like a traveling tinker's store on an uproarious and kicking donkey. And here are gold and silver ornaments in lace, and aerial flounces and furbelows, and artificial flowers, which it is said —but I can not corroborate the assertion by having witnessed any thing of the sort—are made by men; and that you may there see a whole regiment of stout, active Mexicans, who ought to be quarrying stone, or working in the mines, or mending their abominable roads (which must destroy a large proportion of ill-starred travelers annually, we should think), with enormous mustaches, and desperate looking *cuchillos* at hand, actually employed in mincingly manipulating delicate decorations for ladies' dresses, trimming fairy caps, and artistically twisting and pinning bows of ribbon.

Would the reader like to give two hundred dollars for a cheap pair of Guadalaxara stamped leathern boots, wrought all over with silver? and a saddle for about double that trifling sum? Would he admire more those *lassos* or *sarapes*, or beautiful Mexican hats with their tassels and broad rolls of shining silver, fastened with little lions, serpents, and other devices? Or has he any fancy to pay away a small fortune for a complete set of horse furniture, and a full riding dress of the country to match? It is a most beautiful costume altogether; and one can not help hoping the Mexican *caballeros* will not give up their magnificent and appropriate costume and splendid horse equipments, to adopt the ugly fashions of Europe.

I heard English saddles were becoming very common here, but I am unpatriotically happy to say I have seen but few of them. But let us go back to the shops. There are the costly *anqueras*, stamped and gilt, or otherwise curiously and ingeniously wrought, and terminating in a fringe of multitudinous little bells or tags, of silver generally, but sometimes of brass or iron, which jingle merrily as the sledge bells of Russia or Canada. These *anqueras* are sometimes of fur, embroidered richly with gold and silver in large stripes. And, close by, are the gold-embossed jackets; then there are piles of large silver buttons, which are necessary for the adornment of different portions of the dress; there are trinkets, slippers, wares of all sorts, little images, all kinds of cotton and woolen cloth; in fact, every thing, and all things, and a great deal besides!

All the houses here are of stone. In the most distinguished portions of the city, I believe two sorts of hewn stone are used, porous amygdaloid and porphyry. The gates and balustrades are generally of iron and bronze. The houses have flat terraced roofs and large court-yards (*patios*) with colonnades running round them, and are often profusely adorned with plants. We are told the interior is often decorated with beautiful mosaic and arabesque. Few windows, in general, look out upon the streets.

Some of the fronts are enriched with glazed porcelain or beautifully carved and ornamented, and there is usually an imposing-looking arched gateway, in the centre, leading to the colonnaded *patio;* and through them you may occasionally catch delightful Arabian-night-like views of the splendid interiors. They often reminded me of the princely palaces of Genoa the Superb, of whose enchanted courts you may frequently catch similar peeps in driving along the streets, and which, seen in this rapid and partial manner, seemed like the aërial visions of a gorgeous dream.

Through the Mexican gateways you see sometimes a beautiful fountain, sparkling against the sun, beds of flowers, or bowers of orange-trees, and the corridor's light and sculptured arches. Some of the buildings are tinted with rich and delicate rosy hues, like the soft reflection of the rising or setting sun, and some have the faintest *soupçon* of a tinge imaginable, like a fairy's blush (if Queen Titania and her handmaidens ever do blush), and some are completely covered with frescoed arabesque designs.

Mr. D—— has taken us to see the Plaza del Toros, the amphitheatre for bull-fights. It is an enormous circular inclosure, in a very dilapidated condition, in consequence of which such exhibitions are at a stand-still here, for it is supposed not to be safe—so the poor bulls *are.* There is an immensely great national manufactory of tobacco in the southwest part of the city, which is said to supply the entire legitimate demands for *cigarros* in the Confederation.

## CHAPTER XXIX.

Mexico—The Viga—The Chinampas—Floating Gardens, Fields and Orchards of the Aztecs—Abundance of Flowers in Mexico; and of Fruits—The Fruit-stalls—The Meat and Poultry—Tortoises, Salamanders and Frogs—The Population of the City of Mexico—Its numberless Vehicles Its Environs on Fête-days—Defective Police Arrangements—Frequent Robberies in Consequence—Mexican Chocolate—Victoriana, the Waiting-maid.

We are more and more enthusiastically charmed with this peerless Mexico. What a climate—what scenery! What a brilliant and busy city—what beauties and wonders on all sides!

The Viga I am quite delighted with. It is an enchanting promenade, with a canal running on the side of it, half-overshadowed by lovely trees. The Arbol de Peru (Peruvian pepper-tree) was conspicuously graceful and striking among them. There were crowds of Indians in their flat canoes, almost lost among heaps of flowers, and fruits, and vegetables.

We visited the celebrated Chinampas, formerly the floating garden of the Aztecs, now stationary. They have taken up their permanent abode at a little distance from the canal of Chalco. The metropolis is principally supplied with vegetables from them still. There are flowers sprinkled here and there. The old chroniclers tell us that in 1245, after many persecutions, the Aztecs, wandering from place to place, left Chapultepec to establish themselves in an island group to the south of Tezcuco Lake. Oppressed by Tezcucan chieftains, they sought refuge in Tezapan, where, having assisted the princes of that land in some insignificant wars, they were allowed to establish themselves, in freedom, in a city, which they named Mexicalsingo. But they were commanded by some oracle to transport themselves and their families from thence, to some islands to the eastward of Chapultepec, and to the western side of the Tezcuco Lake.

Long before this, an old tradition was popular among them, to the effect—that in whatever place they should see an eagle seated on a nopal, with its roots fixed in a rock, on that spot, they should hasten to found a city. They first hailed this sign in 1325, and there (in one of the islands in the lake) they founded the first house of their gods—the great Mexican temple, called, in their tongue, Teocalli. This history seems to me to bear a faint and perhaps merely fanciful resemblance to that of the modern Mormons, now settled in their flourishing city of the great Salt Lake.

Through all of their Arab-like wanderings, wherever they stopped, those Aztecs were wont to cultivate the earth, and where they were then settled, frequently encircled by barbarous enemies, as they were, in the midst of a great lake, where fish were remarkably scarce, they devised the ingenious expedient of forming floating gardens, and fields, and orchards, on the surface of the tranquil waters. These they framed skillfully of the woven-together roots of aquatic plants, wreathed and intermingled with various boughs and branches, and twigs, till they had secured a foundation strong enough to uphold a soil, formed of earth drawn from the bottom of the lake. Their corn and chili, and different plants required for their sustenance, were sown on this.

It appears that these gliding gardens, were ordinarily elevated about a foot above the surface of the water, and were of an oblong shape. Soon afterward, these insulated and raft-like fields were adorned with lovely beds of countless flowers, which were not alone cherished by the people (who were great lovers of these luxuries of nature), but were employed in the worship of their idols, and were a favorite ornament of the palace of their new emperors. These famed Chinampas, along the Viga canal, are now attached to the mainlands, on the grounds that lie between the two great lakes of Chalco and Tezcuco. Little trenches, filled with water, appear to divide the gardens. There are small bridges, thrown across the water, to keep up the communication with the mainland. The Indian proprietor has generally his humble hut in the garden, but no longer can he (if desirous of removing for a space, his "location"), seated in his canoe, tow along his fairy and flowering island to another part of that fresh, silvery, glistening sea.

Whether in gardens floating or fixed, flowers never fail them in their bewitching climate. Their roses are all *roses des quatre saisons* (so well rendered by Lord ——'s gardener "quarter sessions roses")! From March to June the flowery sea almost overflows, and its many-colored waves, and sunny tides bury all in their beauty. We are told that, on the *dias di fiesta*, even the very humblest classes, are nearly smothered in roses, and crowned with variegated garlands of carnations, poppies, sweet-peas, jessamine, and other gifts of the munificent Flora of Mexico.

If the inhabitants of this favored land rejoice in myriads of flowers, they have an equal good-fortune with respect to fruit. All climates and seasons contend in Mexico to please the natural or acquired tastes of the epicures of the land. The name of their fruits is Legion. Within a very few leagues you may have in Mexico the greatest imaginable variety of climates; in short, from the united influence of its peculiar geological structure, and the way in which heat is qualified by the differences of elevation in every portion of its extensive territory, t combines every conceivable production, and is unparalleled in these particulars on the face of the earth.

The fruit-stalls are veritable natural curiosity shops; the treasures of Pomona seem indeed here innumerable; from the north, the south, the east, the west, they appear to be gathered together in inexhaustible profusion; chirimoyas, bananas, chicozapotes, pine-apples, pears, oranges, apples, grenaditas de China, melons, cocoa-nuts, black and white zapotes, capulin (the Mexican cherry), dates, mameys, mulberries, plums, shaddocks, pomegranates, mangoes, citrons, walnuts, strawberries, and thousands of others. The consumption of these, and of vegetables, such as tomatoes, potatoes, plantains, cauliflowers, garbanzos (a small bean, much in favor), gourds, cabbages, &c., is stated to be quite enormous in proportion to the population. I should think such articles of food, were much wholesomer, in this climate, than meat; but I believe, the city markets are also well supplied with the latter. Turkeys, and poultry in general, and a very great variety of wild water-fowl are abundant, and at very reasonable prices; and also rabbits, hares, pigeons, &c. They have besides, a choice selection of rather singular articles of diet, which the lower classes are said to patronize extensively: tortoises, creatures they call salamanders, and frogs. I have sometimes eaten the latter at Naples, and found them excellent when fried; very like a delicate little spring chicken; but here I have never seen them brought to table.

There is also a plentiful supply of good mutton, beef, and pork, but veal is said to be prohibited. The necessaries of existence ought to be cheap enough here, one should think, but in other things Mexico is reckoned a very expensive place to live in.

The population here in general is of a mixed character, perhaps one half being Creoles (or descendants of the Spaniards), one fourth Mestizoes, half castes between Europeans and Indians, and nearly another fourth copper-colored Indians; with some Blacks and Mulattoes, and from six to seven thousand Europeans.

Many of the grandees and magnates here (frequently successful speculators) are possessed of enormous wealth, but the masses are commonly lazy and indigent. Great numbers pass their time in lounging about the streets, portales, markets, church porches, and various public buildings, asking charity of the passers by, and appealing usually to what they imagine to be the most lively feelings of the persons they address. "Señor, by the love of the most blessed Madonna!" and, "Madrecita, by the life of the little one!" and so forth. They seem a happy set of people, enjoying their *far niente.* My *châtelaine* always drew their most attentive regards, and I was almost afraid one day it would suddenly be snatched away from its ordinary sphere of being; but they contented themselves, like good children, with looking and not touching.

The white Creoles are said to be distinguished for courtesy, gentleness of manners, kindness, and hospitality; and, from the very little I have seen of them, I can readily believe it.

Carriages seem literally to swarm in Mexico; every body appears to possess one or more. I believe the señoras here consider it the most indispensable of all necessaries. There are *carratelas,* and French open carriages, and English closed ones, and *volantes,* and I know not how many more species; but they are multiform and multinominal, and multitudinous; and in the evening they appear in shoals, filled with beautiful señoras, and señoritas, their large black eyes flashing out like lamps designed to dispel the gathering dusk.

The environs of the city, too, are said to be generally gay and crowded in the evening, especially on *fête* days, and to present a joyous scene of bustle and animation. Hundreds of light canoes, of different sizes, mostly with awnings, and crowded with Mestizoes and native Indians, are to be seen gliding along in all directions on the shining canals, generally with an indefatigable guitar-player among the company, and some of the festive party singing or perhaps dancing.

Mr. D—— says, however, from defective police arrangements, or other causes, it is dangerous to go out of the city after dusk without arms. Some persons incautiously doing so, have been lassoed and plundered, and every body who is compelled to go should go well armed—more penalties for living in such a paradise! They say these gentry who are so free with their lassos are mostly of the mongrel sort, part native (Indian), part Spanish, and part Negro; and that the gangs of guerillas and robbers, which annoyed the American armies during the war, were chiefly formed of such tricolor individuals.

Last night we found it a little too cool in our skylighted windowless apartment, and I asked for a *brasero*, or *braserico* (a kind of chafing-dish). After a little delay, one was brought, but the warmth it afforded was barely sufficient to warm the tips of our fingers—however, fortunately, but little more is needed. I find the air here very delightful, and none of us have experienced, during our very short *séjour* here, the remotest inconvenience from the rarification of the atmosphere in this elevated region; but Lord Mark told us, the other day, he found occasionally an unaccustomed oppression and shortness of breathing on running up stairs, or ascending a hill, since his arrival in Mexico.

I wish the reader could have a glimpse of the damsel who especially waits on us. She is named Victoriana. Her long jet-black hair flows and "wanders at its own sweet will," sometimes waving overshadowingly above our chocolate cups in a rather alarming manner; but she usually contrives with a little twist and toss of her head to prevent its sweeping away the deep foam from that richest of beverages.

And here I must quit Victoriana for a while, to rave a little about Mexican chocolate. It is nectar and ambrosia at once, and I think would spoil us for every thing every where: tea in China with the ethereal flower in it, which will not bear keeping or carriage; coffee at Mocha would surely seem nothing, or positively nauseous, in comparison. I believe the plant from which it is made is the natural growth of Mexico—and Olympus, perhaps. When the jetty-locked Victoriana brings it in the morning for *desayuno*, with a most excellent sweet roll (an improvement on an English bun), if Messrs. Mars, Phœbus, and Mercury, and Mesdames Juno and Pallas dropped in unexpectedly through the skylight, we should be able to provide them at once with their usual food, the "best entertainment" for gods and goddesses.

Victoriana has one of the merriest of countenances, and appears clad at all times in the simplest of dresses, the throat, shoulders, and arms bare, and the drapery altogether very cool and airy, the damsel's own abundant hair playing a large part in it. She is a great chatterbox, and talks rare gibberish and *patois*. She has found out that we are exceedingly fond of milk, and good-naturedly exerts herself to bring us a large supply of it—sometimes, I think, leaving the good people at the *table d'hôte* with a considerably diminished quantity. This milk is delicious; it is brought in a kind of huge caldron, holding about a couple of pails, or thereabouts.

In my own mind I am perfectly convinced that Victoriana is Indian—(she is of a tolerably near approach to black: it may be an invisible green, which sombre coloring is lit up by blazing bright dark eyes and white teeth)—but she will not hear of such a thing for a momnet. No; oh no! "Soy Mexicana!" Yes, that of course; but of the Indian race partly? Oh, quite out of the question. "Vaya una idea!"

V—— did a little portrait of her, which she seemed to admire prodigiously, and called one of the *galopinas* in to look at it. They both praised the performance highly, and at last Victoriana suddenly snatched up the drawing and ran off with it. We ran after her, begging her to restore it (as we wanted to keep it); but she concealed it somewhere, and then returned, looking very demure, as if nothing had happened. "Como dice Vm.? Me habla Vm.? No entiendo bien lo que Vm. dice!" (which was just possible!) "Vaya vaya el retrato, el dibujo?" "Si, el retrato, es muy bonito." After ineffectual attempts to make her refund it, another was done, which she served in exactly the same way. Off she scampered with it, like a mouse carrying off a morsel of cheese to its hole to devour it at leisure. It was useless to draw her any more, as it was evident if one hundred and fifty were sketched they would all be carried off and hidden in a similar manner.

If other travelers should take the fancy to sketch her too, what a gallery of portraits she will have, and all of herself! She looked so enchanted, however, with her own *beaux yeux* on paper, that I think she intends distributing these little representations of herself among her relations and friends, to show them how handsome she is, of which fact she might think they were not sufficiently aware, and, therefore, designs impressing it on their minds duly.

There is a very splendid bedstead here, most beautifully inlaid with mother-of-pearl: the workmanship is exquisite.

---

## CHAPTER XXX.

General Herrera, the President of Mexico, and the American Minister—Chapultepec assaulted and taken by General Scott—Enormous Cypresses in the Garden of Montezuma—Dona Mariana, the Aztec Wife of Cortez—View from the Summit of Chapultepec Castle—Impressions caused by it—The Mountains Tacubaya and Toluca—Tanks and Baths of Montezuma—The Opera-house at Mexico—The fat comic Actress and the brilliantly dressed One—Beauty of Mexican Ladies—Madame Bishop—Payments in Kind for her Singing—Beautiful Appearance of the Stars in Mexico—View of dusty Victims alighting from the Diligence—The Brother of M. Arago the Astronomer—The Volcanoes, Popocatepetl and Iztacchihuatl—Patio of M. Arago.

THIS morning we had a visit from our excellent friend, Mr. L——, who was presented to the President in due form yesterday, and delivered his address extremely well.

He told us he had never been accustomed, in his own country, to so much form, and pomp, and state, and ceremony as is observed by the Mexican President, and that—owing to this circumstance—and being rather taken by surprise in these particulars, he felt a little nervousness and trepidation which, however, soon passed over. By the account he gave us of it, the President of Mexico must assume much of monarchical state. Mr. —— said General Herrera was seated on a sort of throne raised on a platform at one end of the hall, under a splendid canopy, with many ministers and officers around him, the latter dressed in very costly and magnificent uniforms. "Such splendid and bedizened-out uniforms, to be sure; and," he added, laughingly, "I thought it must all look just like Solomon on his throne, with his great courtiers round him." Mr. —— had been offered the choice of coming to this country or going to St. Petersburgh. I think the grandeur and splendor of the Czar's court would have struck him a little more than General Herrera's republican royalty.

He seemed much pleased with the President and his reception, and appears altogether to like Mexico, which, charming as it is, is a compliment to it, for I believe he had never left home before: under these circumstances it is very common, as well as natural, to feel a little of the *mal du pays*. He is looking for a house, as he expects Mrs. —— will join him in May.

We have had a delightful visit to Chapultepec: this fortified castle was taken by the American forces in the late war, under General Scott. It is the most haunted by old Aztec memories of all the traditionary and interesting localities which Mexico can claim. We had a charming drive.

Chapultepec is an isolated volcanic hill, rising in the centre of the great plain, about three-quarters of a league from the capital. The Indian name for it may be interpreted, I believe, the "Hill of Grasshoppers." Its position is singular and remarkable; it shoots up boldly in the heart of the valley, precipitously steep on all sides; the zig-zagging road has still the *adobe* embankments (*adobes* are sun-dried bricks), and the little corner batteries which the Mexicans threw up in anticipation of the American attack, and there are almost innumerable traces of General Scott's cannon balls, from Tacubaya, and from the elevated ground to the rear of Molino del Rey; these are to be seen in all directions. The poor Mexicans had a too plentiful peppering for their *frijoles* on that occasion.

But before I say more of the fortress of Chapultepec let me do homage to the great cypresses in what is still called the Garden of Montezuma. We drew up to within a short distance of them in the carriage, and Mr. D—— then proposed that we should alight and walk toward them, which we did through a tangled wilderness of yellow flowers. They are the most glorious trees I ever beheld. The largest of them all was said, by Humboldt, to be forty-one feet in circumference; but I am told it is actually forty-five feet. It certainly looks yet more than this. The vast trunk seemed to me like a noble tower shooting toward the sky, and lost in its own far-spreading and mighty cloud of deep green foliage, where half an army might have hid—*à la* "King Charles in his oak." Soft streamers of thick gray moss depend from every bough, which gives these trees a doubly venerable and patriarchal appearance.

The cypress which is second in size to the huge one I have

mentioned, is little inferior in any respect; and indeed by some it is thought more beautiful and graceful. There are several others of dimensions almost similar. Would not Michael Angelo, that poet-sculptor, have thundered at them, as he did at his own Moses, though with a different feeling, "speak!" Think what they could tell, had they tongues (and brains and memories into the bargain, by the way). Venerable were they when Montezuma was a puling infant, and a mischievous hobble-de-hoy! and they looked on in unaltered unshaken majesty, while the gallant Scott thundered, with his conquering artillery, against the strongholds of the descendants of Montezuma's Spanish conquerors; while the echoes of the world-overspreading Anglo-Saxon tongue thrilled through the branches of those thousand year-old monarchs of the forest, and may have rejoiced the shades of the avenged Aztecs.

The opening onset of the gallant and ever-victorious Americans, when they stormed Chapultepec, was made under cover of these mammoth trees. Perchance these stately survivors of empires creeds, triumphs, wars, and a hundred changes, may still stand in their solemn pride and lordly majesty, when a hundred other changes may have transformed all around but themselves and their mighty comrades, the mountains.

It is whispered by the voice of superstition, that these scenes are haunted by Malinche—not the mountain but the maiden, though a walking mountain might stalk under those trees—in short, by the spectre of the celebrated Doña Mariana, the beauteous Aztec love of the great Cortez. If such be the case, she is a ghost of taste, it must be owned; and one can not wonder she snatched away the heart of the gallant Cortez—not in the way her countrymen, the red-jacketed cannibal priests were wont to accomplish such operations. She became, as it were, a sort of counter-conqueror, and ruled rather despotically over the great captain of the age.

The true name of these cypresses is Ahuahuete (*Sabino ahuahuete*, or *Cupressus disticha*). The chief of these is called Montezuma's cypress. At the village of Atlixco, there is said to be a cypress (they are not like what we in England call by that name) seventy-six feet in circumference, and which is supposed to be one of the oldest of vegetable monuments on the face of the globe, if not indeed the *most* ancient.

But this is not all. At a village called St. Maria del Tule, ten miles to the east of the capital, there is an immense trunk of the same species of cypress, measuring one hundred and eighteen feet in circumference, though by all accounts it would appear to be three stems, closely, almost imperceptibly, joined together. It must be like the great "Boabab" of Asia; but the suspicion of this latter one being a treble tree, renders it less interesting. I confess, in one of the mighty Ahuahuetes that I saw, I detected something that looked as if a similar process had taken place. There is certainly a suspicious line along the trunk; but I am assured I am wrong, and by those likely to know better than I do.

After admiring this giant grove for some time, we crept, feeling very microscopical and mite-like, back to the carriage, which had assumed considerably the appearance of a nut-shell drawn by the "industrious fleas," formerly in vogue in London, by comparison with these colossal suzerains of the vegetable world. We intended to drive up the precipitously steep (but zig-zagged) ascent on which stands embattled the castle, but the fates willed it otherwise, and we had not gone many yards before the harness broke, and our gallant grays (fine-looking American horses) were relieved from the trouble of dragging us up. The Mexican *cochero* indulged in some vituperations against the American harness; the horses took the whole affair very philosophically; and we, anxious to see the beauteous view which we knew the elevated summit of Chapultepec must present, left Mr. —— to superintend the *criados*, and the reparation of the damage, and climbed up the hill.

It was rather toilsome work, but we felt a great reward was awaiting us; we pushed on vigorously, and, at length, found ourselves on the height, and on a broad graveled terrace fronting the entrance. Trumpets were sounding cheerily, but we staid not to ascertain why or where, intent upon taking, not the castle, but the best possible position for seeing the *hermosa vista*. The commandant—as we afterward ascertained he was—came forward, and very courteously asked if we would like to see the view from the *azotea* of the castle, and observed we must be much fatigued by climbing the precipitous ascent. I informed him of the accident that had occurred, and that we had come with the *Ministro Ingles*, who was detained at the bottom of the hill by the misfortune aforesaid. He immediately said he knew the *ministro*, and scarcely had he pronounced the words, before Mr. D—— appeared on the esplanade, having scrambled up by a short cut, I believe, and a still more steep and far more rugged path than the one we followed. Indeed, it looked pretty nearly perpendicular. Mutual civilities were exchanged, and we forthwith hurried to the flat roof of the castle.

What a Paradise world we saw! the different and greatly diversified scenes were all mingled and mixed in beauty without end. How surpassingly grand was the apparently illimitable and gigantically-castellated amphitheatre of heights! The sun shone gloriously, and the stupendous mountains, especially the magnificent Popocatepetl and Iztaccihuatl, seemed joining earth and heaven, yet with their mighty foreheads turning pale at their own audacity, blanched as they are by interfulgent snows.

To particularize the separate glories of this unparalleled panorama to one's self at first seemed impossible; all appeared to be blended together in one magical unity. After long, long gazing, till that ocean of beauty seemed to spread over the whole mind and spirit, and leave every thought bathed and streaming with its splendors, one began to know that this vision of magnificence was composed of various parts—some earthly and material parts too: but still it was—oh, how glorious! and from that height all below was so still, so calm; shining, too, in such a blaze of dazzling light, that the earth around you seemed no more the common earth. Some mighty change seemed to have taken place—you gazed on dreamily, and the scene seemed to grow more and more awful in its beauty—Nature's apotheosis, as it were; a world divided from the sinning, struggling world without. The grand mountains seemed not so much like vast masses of earth towering up and heaving their giant forms toward the cerulean firmament, as stooping, downward-leaning heavens themselves—immeasurably vast stupendous stalactites, depending grandly from the unimaginable heights of an overarching Celestial Universe above; in short, all kinds of wild fancies entered one's mind—for really it was as if the loveliness and majesty of a thousand worlds were concentrated here.

But it is not, after all, so much the scene itself, as the great and boundless glory the imagination ever lends it; for the soul once awakened, and stirred and thrilled by the sight of that magnificent scenery, makes it ten thousand fold more glorious. She heaps far other mountains of more transcending height upon those visible ones; and it is she who clothes them with a heavenly awfulness, and it is she who kindles the firmament into most unutterable splendor above, as if it were all made of the moving brightness of angels' blazing passing shadows; and it is she who brings the stars in their mid-majesty as suns, as worlds gorgeously shimmering down upon that paradisiacal prospect; for she unites it with all that the immense and glorious universe, without a shadow of a limit, hath of the majestic, and of the lovely, and of the terrible.

Perhaps it might be thought that the view of the city of Mexico would detract a little from the visionary appearance of this world-wide prospect; but, indeed, it does not. Its glittering towers, its many churches and convents and domes, looked almost spiritually beautiful at that distance, with that exquisite sunlight beaming upon them, and making them sparkle like silver and crystal, as beautiful as if they all (like what is reported of Puebla's cathedral) were built by angelic architects, and of supernatural materials.

The valley itself looks matchlessly lovely from Chapultepec; and if there are some symptoms here and there of a lack of care and cultivation, the few uninhabited *haciendas*, partly dilapidated, with patches of earth around them, left to the wildness of Nature, were the more picturesque, and lent more variety to the scene. There were vast tracts covered by the silvery-gleaming plantations of *magueys* to be seen, great fields where herds of cattle were pasturing; exquisite gardens, rainbows of the earth, shadowing *paséos* near the city, and groves of many-foliaged trees.

Then how endless appeared all the beauteous shapes of the nearer rocks and hills; and how the fertile variegated valley of enchantment flows far in among the mighty mountains in some parts, which seem to fall back before it, and so the ever-waving lines are beyond imagination varied and lovely.

In one part the rocks and heights are far off in the horizon, and in another they are almost running into the valley, like rugged promontories and capes frowning and peering down on its tranquil scenes.

But the sparkling canals must not be forgotten; nor the stately aqueducts, with their open tops and noble lines of a thousand arches; nor the sapphire-tinted lakes; nor the romantic villages, with their clustering masses of trees; nor the lordly avenues of bright-leaved poplars and shady elms leading to the city; nor the wonderful skies above, that looked clear, brilliant, fervid, and glowing, as if they were all of blue flame, burning more and more brightly every moment. Only fifteen miles beyond Tacubaya tower the mountains of Toluca, and Guadaloupe's apparently insulated hills are not much further on the opposite side; but, in the other directions, the valley spreads its sea-like surface between fifty and sixty miles before it reaches the everlastingly-planted feet of the mountains.

Tacubaya lies near Chapultepec, with her gardens of flowers, and her pomp of sumptuous palaces. The shrine of "Our Lady of Guadaloupe" stands on the brink of a mountain promontory, which sallies out toward the lovely Lake of Tezcuco. To the north is Tacuba. The tops, I might well say the great *domes* of foliage of the gigantic cypresses were at our feet to the left. Among the hamlets, scattered about to the southward, are those of San Augustin, San Angel, and various others.

We then went and looked down the steep rocks over which it is said the unfortunate Mexicans, after having given up all further thoughts of defense, flung themselves in despair, and fell crushed and mangled at the base. While we were there, a little *commandantino* ran out of the castle, in the shape of the Colonel's pretty boy, a charming little fellow, with a sword by his side, the most soldier-like strut, and the blackest and merriest of eyes.

After thanking the obliging commandant for his civility, we descended, and went to see the tanks and baths of Montezuma. One could not but look back, again and again, on the colossal Ahuahuetes, that had overshadowed, perhaps, in the olden time the imperial ruler of the Mexicans—and what a presence chamber would that glorious grove have been—what a hall of audience! If powerful kings had come to visit the Aztec monarch, could he have received them in a nobler state chamber? What a canopy more than regal, over his head, fretted with the diamond and golden dews of evening! Mr. L—— might have thought of Solomon's glories, indeed, under such circumstances, and still more of those wonders and triumphs of Nature—of her prodigal riches of vegetation, that excel him "in all his glory."

The castle of Chapultepec was built by the viceroy Galvez, the last representative of the Spanish monarchy in this country. The vice-queen was a famed beauty, and was exceedingly popular in Mexico; and he was wealthy and magnificent. It was supposed to have cost the Spanish government three hundred thousand dollars. Chapultepec was said to have occasioned great jealousy and suspicion to the Mexicans. Though thus originally built as a mere summer palace, its commanding and excellent position, fortified and strengthened with walls and parapets toward Mexico, with moats and underground vaults to the north, which were sufficiently large to contain an immense supply of provisions, rendered such a distrust and suspicion not unnatural. It was something like the deception practiced concerning the fortifications of Paris; only it was pretended there, that they were built to guard against the possible attacks of a foreign foe, and here, that there was no fortification contemplated at all, only a summer mansion with a beautiful view for the innocent delights of the *Villegiatura.*

One thousand and fifty bombs fell on this devoted fortress, during the late hostilities, before the assault. The head-quarters of General Scott were in the palace of the Bishop of Tacubaya, which place is clearly visible from Chapultepec, and said to be actually within the reach of its guns. Though Chapultepec was well defended and manned by artillery and infantry, it is not considered that it can use cannon to advantage when the attacking forces have approached the base of the rock.

We paid a visit to the great square tank, from whence, we are told, the grand aqueduct is supplied. Its water is of the clearest sparkling crystal, and of the most exquisite transparency. The "Koh-i-noor," the "Mountain of Light," can hardly be brighter. There is a cave too of no great dimensions.

One more look at that glorious grove, at those hoary and wondrous trees, and, above all, at the stupendous giant of them all, standing there in its mighty greatness, so solemn, so placid, so darkly and silently sublime, with its own vast shadow making an eclipse, and an evening twilight, and shedding a gathered gloom and a dense duskiness around—in itself a wood—and then back to lovely Mexico.

We rolled through the gates, and went on at a fair pace, till our harness gave way again, and caused a little delay. At last we gained the *paséo* in safety, where our rope-repaired tackle could not have shone very brilliantly; but we little minded that, and rattled steadily on to the Hotel de Diligencias, when, after bidding good-even to Mr. ——, we went to dinner, with our thoughts full of giant cypresses, mountains, Montezumas, Malinches, and fortresses.

I must now say a word or two about the Mexican Opera-house which we went to, though the opera company is not here now; but plays are performed there. It is a very handsome theatre indeed, and the box of the *Ministro Ingles* is capitally situated. We had a Spanish comedy. A señora acted, and very well too, who had formerly, I believe, been a celebrated beauty; but she was too fat to permit the *beaux restes* to vouch much for her previous perfection. Without being absolutely like the lady whom a friend of mine compared to a "feather bed in spectacles" (that lady wore glasses), she bore a faint resemblance to a very liberally stuffed eider-down quilt. She, however, was full of life and merriment, and the very dimples on her broad elbows seemed to laugh, ha! ha! as she shook with the severe exercise, which the employment of the risible faculties was for her, when occasionally during some droll passage of the performance, she indulged in it.

Another señora on the stage was very brilliantly dressed, as a Madrileña (a native of Madrid). Whether the costume was correct I can not say, not having been in that part of Spain. It was one of the costumes, I imagine, of the middle classes. The dress was of white satin, with very bright full scarlet flouncings, and a large black lace mantilla, most gracefully and coquettishly disposed, with a single flower, I think, on one side of the head, fastened on the splendid ebon braids of hair. The wearer of the dress looked extremely pretty in it, and the costume itself had altogether a very pretty and graceful effect, though the description does not sound promising.

My attention being a little taken up by looking at the house, and having the different occupants of the boxes pointed out to me, I could not very satisfactorily follow the speakers on the stage; but even when I did not perfectly catch the point of the remarks and repartees, those merry dimples aforesaid, on the fat shaking elbows and shoulders—those dimples laughing so heartily (till they, and all that was visible round them, turned to a scarlet, almost as bright as the Madrileña's flounces)—those dimples almost in hysterics, made one laugh just as much as if one had thoroughly understood the joke.

Diamonds were in profusion; some of the ladies were very beautiful, and seemed extremely well dressed; they had the usual dark flashing eyes of Mexico, and the graceful Spanish manner of playing with their fans. I saw no smoking among the ladies—there may have been a little, but I am inclined to think not.

Madame Bishop has lately been singing here, and was exceedingly admired and popular in Mexico. She went into the provinces also, and I hear, at some of the theatres there, her sweet sounds were sometimes paid in fighting-cocks and cigars; to such an extent, indeed, that she was obliged to advertise in the papers that she could receive no more payments in "crowing Chanticleers" or prime "Havannas," and that none would be taken at the doors.

There was a little *divertissement*, an Andalusian dance, &c. On coming out of the theatre, I was almost rooted to the spot by the marvelous beauty of the stars. I never saw them so glorious before any where—so large, so lustrous. The Persian idolater might have found a thousand suns there to worship; they literally gleamed with the different colors of the rainbow. One had a crimson, another an emerald tinge; a third shone on the deep, blue, glorious sky, like cerulean fire on cerulean air. They sparkled, and quivered, and blazed, and *lightened* in their splendor, till the heavens seemed all stirring, and breathing, and living. When we remarked this diversity of colors to Lord Mark afterward, he laughingly exclaimed, "So even Mexican stars wear the national *sarape*," which idea amazingly amused V——.

We have a broad balcony running all round the interior of this hotel, on the floor on which we are. On the lower story are *almacens* (warehouses). The dining saloon on this floor runs out far across the court-yard like a glass promontory, for it is more like a conservatory than a *comedor* (dining-room), and seems to try and make up by its vast profusion of windows for the deficiencies of these agreeable additions to a house, elsewhere in the hotel. When we were, by chance, occasionally a little tired of the sky prospect afforded by our *claraboya* (skylight) in this cloudless climate, one sheet of blue, with hardly the least little vagrant cloud to diversify the view, we wandered forth on to the balcony (sooth to say, perpetual sight-seeing has left us but little time in which to grow tired of our sky-peep), as this balcony commanded a splendid view of dusty diligences, and various vehicles of that kind. We were often amused at the comical sights presented when the door was opened, and the cramped wretched passengers rolled out on the pavement.

Frightful is the deeply-rooted wickedness of the human heart. We rather rejoiced than otherwise at the spectacle of sufferings we had ourselves undergone, and, as if with mocking exultation, watched the unfortunate occupants of the *coches* by slow degrees exhibiting signs of life. At first, perhaps, when the doors of the dungeon were opened, apparently a very large brown paper parcel would tumble down the steps, and stand miraculously upright in the court-yard. Then you would see it, as it were, suddenly galvanized, and displaying every appearance of life. Indeed at length this rather uncommon brown paper parcel would be seized as with an ague fit—a vehement shaking from head to foot—when, lo! a huge quantity of dust, almost amounting to land enough for a little Italian principality, would fly off, and a *reboso*, with a gown, would become visible; and, finally, a señora appear, looking wild and haggard from fatigue. What is that, too, which descends the steps like a white formless mist—like the smoke which the eastern fisherman saw come slowly out of the vase in the Arabian tale! Gaze steadily, and after a while you will see that nebula resolved into two starry eyes (and perhaps a diamond-luminary or two sparkling on the fingers) as a once light and graceful señorita, lamed and bruised by the jolting she has suffered, limps away, settling her *reboso*, and coaxing her hair into a little order. Sometimes one would see the newly-arrived shampooing themselves vigorously, and extending their arms very tenderly and carefully, not to clasp them around the necks of cherished objects waiting to welcome them, but that the poor wretched objects themselves may ascertain whether or no these members are sound and unbroken. Hark! there thunders in the Puebla Diligencia! Behold that vast violoncello-case, all travel-stained and dusty, which can with difficulty be pushed through the coach-door. Hush! a groan! the last of the bass-strings must be broken! What a mighty instrument; what a size! the very Lablache of double basses! But, stay! that *peon* has run against it, a cloud of dust arises, and—strange metamorphosis—lo! a jolly *padre*, immovable from cramp and weariness! He stands in every body's way; the great American horses shove by him on this side, the bustling *cochero* on that. "Fuera! padre"—at last he totters off.

We have been to see the two magnificent volcanoes this morning, accompanied by Mr. P—— from the *azotea* of the Casa de Bazar. This hotel is kept by a brother of the far-famed M. Arago, the distinguished French astronomer and statesman. I mentioned to him that a friend of mine was acquainted with his celebrated brother. "Ah, madame, vous voulez dire mon frère l'astronome?" I said yes, and he told me it was very long indeed since he had seen that famous brother of his, and that he himself had been so long settled in Mexico, it seemed easier to him to speak Spanish than French. He is said to be very like the astronomer in appearance. He was particularly courteous and obliging, and accompanied us up to the *azotea*, which was a splendid one of great extent.

Language can not depict the majesty and beauty of Popocatepetl and Iztaccihuatl that morning. The atmosphere was remarkably and peculiarly clear, even for Mexico, which was the reason of our little expedition. I had received a hasty note from Mr. ——, early in the morning, stating this fact, and recommending that we should lose no time in repairing to the *azotea*, to see the volcanoes in their fullest glory. We found, to our dismay, that this house was *azotea*-less, but were advised by Mr. P—— to go to M. Arago's hotel without delay; he offering to escort us there, being acquainted with M. Arago. We lost no time, and I am indeed glad to have had so favorable an opportunity of seeing, in its greatest splendor, one of the most sublime scenes in creation. Though the sun was terribly hot there, we could not for some time tear ourselves away from the contemplation of all that august magnificence of Nature. It must be remembered that Popocatepetl far out-towers Mont Blanc.

Before we went down stairs, M. Arago asked me to look down upon his *patio*, which is really beautiful, with superb fountains and corridors, the loveliest and most graceful, and a vast profusion of large gayly-colored Chinese lamps, or lanterns, which are lighted every evening, and must produce the most magical effect, reflected by the sparkling waters of the clear fountains. Trees, covered with flowers in all seasons, overshadow costly tables of marble, and guard from the hot sun, in the day-time, the visitors to the Café de Bazaar adjoining the hotel. The hotel is crammed with guests.

In returning, we were pestered with beggars, especially Liliputian *léperos*, mounted like monkeys on each other's shoulders, and keeping up the most inharmonious din. The hair of one was like a huge gooseberry-bush, and she would most pertinaciously follow us, though there was hardly room for us and her shock of hair on the broad pavement: it stuck out at the sides like two great black wings, so that I was constantly coming in contact with that unpleasant hair. A little brother or sister was perched on the girl's shoulders, and helped to do the whining work. I think this spread-out forest of tangled locks was partly designed as a defensive wall to the head that seemed lost in it; for you see tormented pedestrians frequently dealing rather desperate blows at the crowns of these indefatigable persecutors—altogether forgetful of the more gentle "Perdone V." They certainly plague one out of patience. I have not seen any of the deformed *léperos* mounted on the shoulders of porters, or *peons*, that Mr. Ruxton describes—perhaps that portermanship is out of fashion.

## CHAPTER XXXI.

Intention to cross the Isthmus of Panama—The Carnival at Mexico—Magnificence of the Cathedral during that Festival—Throngs of picturesque People in the Streets—The Masks—A grotesque Equestrian—Carnival Quiz on English and French Horsewomen—The Mexican Riding-dress—Mexican Eyes—High-pacing of Mexican Horses—Mr. Parrott instrumental in securing California to the Americans.

I FIND we can not, without great inconvenience and undergoing many hardships, visit the shores of the Pacific from hence. As I am most Pacifically inclined, I shall follow the advice of several of my acquaintances here and take a trip across the Isthmus of Panama, which is said to be much easier. This is a good time for going there, as the rainy season has not yet commenced.

I shall, however, proceed there as soon as possible, as before very long the beginning of the unfavorable season may be anticipated, and this will considerably, and to my great regret, curtail my visit to matchless Mexico; for if we do not go from Vera Cruz by the next British steamer, we should be detained here so long that the bad weather would probably be set in by the time we got to Chagres, and, as there is no steamer direct to Chagres, we have to go round by the Havana, from whence I shall go probably in one of the American steamers to the Isthmus.

Here the carnival is now going on, and we have been escorted by Mr. P——, to see the cathedral in all its pomp: it was astonishingly magnificent. The quantity of gold and silver and gorgeous jewels, and ornaments of different kinds was prodigious, and the brilliancy of the whole scene was almost too dazzling. All around the great altar it seemed to have *snowed* miraculous brightness and sparkling splendors, for every thing was draped with spotless white satin, and glittering with spangles and embroidery, and with solid silver.

Some very fine music was pealing through the vast church, with a noble and impressive effect. There were many priests officiating, who seemed scarcely able to move under the weight of their sumptuous dresses; crowds of people in holiday dresses were in the cathedral, and the odor of incense was delicious.

The great square was very gay. There were throngs of women in various dresses; some with china shawls of half a hundred colors; some in country costumes, among whom shone conspicuous the brilliantly-attired Poblanas (women from Puebla), sombreroed *caballeros*, blanketed Indians, priests, children, friars, *soldados*—it was quite overflowing.

The *léperos* mustered as strong as usual, but were far too much taken up with gazing at my *châtelaine* to importune me seriously; they came to beg, but they remained to stare; so the *châtelaine* made a capital diversion. Perhaps they thought it was a choice assortment of weapons to ward them off with.

I must now speak of our drive in the *paséo* to see the masks. There were a goodly number of soldiers there to preserve order and prevent any carriage from breaking the line, and creating thereby a confusion, which, no doubt was necessary, as the crowds of carriages were extraordinary; they appeared innumerable, and so did the horsemen. It was not dull, for the masks and costumes were capital, and the variety was almost bewildering; but it was the very quietest carnival I ever saw.

One or two groups of extraordinarily-dressed individuals were much followed and shouted after, but, in general, a great silence prevailed, and the pedestrians who thronged the promenades on each side of the drive, merely just by a bright smile, which displayed commonly a brilliant set of teeth flashing like the driven snow in the sun, expressed their pleasure and mirth. One grotesque mask, who seemed a great favorite, was a capitally represented, enormous black *bear* on horseback (no such wonderful phenomenon after all), holding the reins in the most delicate and dandy-like style, in its huge paws; and caracolling about to the great edification of all, the little boys especially, inthe place.

There were some masked ladies riding, with immensely long habits trailing along (they were men dressed up), floating vails, and jaunty riding hats and whips; these were a quiz upon English and French equestrianesses. There were some pretended ladies also *driving themselves* in a light sort of pony carriage, *à l'Anglaise*, with bonnets and doll's parasols—these were excellent. There were, of course, a vast number of Turks, Moors, knights, cavaliers, &c.

Of all the dresses, the most beautiful was the Mexican full dress (the riding costume) itself. The *sombreros* most profusely ornamented with the brightest of silver; the splendidly-embroidered jackets, with hanging buttons of silver; the trowsers, also embroidered and thickly adorned with similar silver buttons (these are slit up the leg and display an under pair, of the whitest linen beneath); and the spurs delicately and richly ornamented, and about the usual *unusual* size, were superb. Occasionally the gold-embroidered *manga* would be gracefully worn, and they sometimes display a kind of winged shoe. The horses seemed to me almost without exception beautiful; their trappings were very sumptuous and picturesque.

Among the lookers-on, we saw very many fine faces, with the almost perpetual houri-like eye—large, dark, and lustrous—till you got rather tired of it, and might even think the pink variety (such as the ferret's, or the albino's) pleasing, by way of a change. The blue, of course, is quite a relief. Not that I mean to disparage Mexican eyes, they are magnificent; but at least one thinks a little variety would do no harm. Human nature is so fond of novelty in all countries, save perhaps France (which is so constant to ceaseless change it is quite remarkable how that surprising and consistent people retain their tastes, and seem never tired of that old game of theirs—pulling down and setting up constitutions). I must say, however, on the promenade we saw some lily-white *güeras* (*blondes*, fair women), most likely Germans, Americans, or English, with very blue eyes, flaxen hair, and light skins.

The quantities of splendidly-colored China crape shawls upon the shoulders of the women who lined the sides of the road were astonishing. One would think they must have bought up half the manufactories of China.

Tired of the scene, at length we wished to return toward home, but found we must go back the whole length of the drive first; for the soldiers would not hear of letting any body break the ranks. It was rather tiresome, and I was only consoled by watching the beautiful horses, mostly high-stepping *Brazeadors*, that went prancing along, looking as conceited as any Christians, and twice as handsome. I have been positively assured that they teach them to raise up their fore-legs immensely high (which they almost all do) by putting on them magnifying spectacles when they are young, by which means the stones on the road are made to appear like large blocks in the way, and they lift up their legs in order to step over them, and so acquire the habit. I dare say the reader will laugh incredulously, but I tell him just what was told me as a fact, and I am further informed this is constantly practiced in South America.

We got home at last; but driving through the streets of Mexico just now is a trial to the skill of most coachmen; for there is a new order come out, that no one must drive within a certain number of inches of the pavement. The Mexicans themselves laugh at this curious regulation. Mr. —— said he was stopped the other day on this account, and mightily offended the official by saying he had forgotten to bring a yard measure with him, but would hang it to his carriage-wheel in future. The man was furious, and said his order must not be turned into ridicule. The muzzle of a pistol then peeped out in answer, and ended the controversy.

Victoriana came to have another portrait done of her, for her egotistical gallery, and brought another *muchacha* belonging to the house, to participate also in the benefits of a paper-and-pencil immortalization. But the amateur artist who had sketched the two previous stolen portraits, was not much in the humor to do a third, and still less to delineate the form and features of the damsel who accompanied gentle Victoriana. For the former had certainly less charms to boast of than her patroness had ; and when I state that that twice-pictured damsel herself bore a rather striking resemblance to an individual commonly known as the Knave of Clubs (and to that gentleman, too, only when afflicted with the mumps—his personal charms being by no means overpowering at any time), it will not excite so much surprise. It perhaps may be conceived that Sir Peter Lely might have felt a little hesitation with respect to admitting this new candidate for pictorial honors into his gallery of beauties (had she lived in his day), and it is a melancholy fact that the amateur artist before alluded to, looked particularly blank at the not very charming prospect before her.

Victoriana, notwithstanding her likeness to the knave of clubs, *en petite santé*, had at least a very pleasing and gay good-humored countenance, but her poor friend was the most forlorn and doleful-looking damsel you ever beheld (so it was mumps and dumps); and with her on one side and Victorina on the other, V—— looked like Garrick between Tragedy and Comedy, and ought to have done the whole group, thus including herself, in these characters.

To please them, at last she did two little rough sketches, sufficiently flattering to both these mulligatawny-complexioned nymphs. Then the merry one looked contemplative and absorbed in dreaming and delighted thought, as she gazed on her own picture : and the dismal one turned merry. In short, Tragedy looked very comic, and Comedy rather tragic and serious ; perhaps the latter was secretly plotting how to run off with both sketches for her private collection in some corner of the scullery devoted to high art.

We had a farewell visit from our friend Mr. Parrott, who is to start on his return to California almost immediately. I have heard, not from himself, but from others, that it was owing to his energy and promptitude that California was secured to the Americans. He sent an express to the American commander-in-chief of the squadron in the Pacific announcing the war, when there was an idea that Great Britain would attempt to take California under its protection—an idea arising from the circumstance of there being a large British force concentrated near, and indeed at anchor off the port of Mazatlan at the time. Notwithstanding there was considerable difficulty in forwarding this express, Mr. Parrott contrived, with great adroitness, to send it through safely in five days, the usual time being ten days. This delivered the first news of the war to the United States forces in the Pacific.

Very shortly afterward California was occupied, without any opposition or resistance from us, by Commodore Sloat, and the force under his command. He had hardly planted the American flag in the territory, when our eighty-gun ship, the "Collingwood," (admiral Sir G. Seymour) ran into the harbor of Monterey; but if any designs were entertained of frustrating the plan of the Americans, the time was already past, when any obstacle could successfully be thrown in their way, and the "Collingwood" almost immediately (when the state of affairs was ascertained) took her departure.

Of course I can not answer for the entire correctness of this account, but I believe it is substantially true. Mr. Parrott, during part of the Mexican war, acted as volunteer. He told me he had never enjoyed better health than when undergoing all kinds of hardships and privations, and subsisting entirely on rations of fat pork; but then the charming Mexican climate, must be taken into account.

## CHAPTER XXXII.

Departure for Vera Cruz—Threatened Accident to the Diligence—Last Look at Mexico, and its early Stirrers—The Little Peñon—A magnificent View—Passengers by the Diligence—Splendid Sombreros—The Escort of Lancers—Mexican Robbers—Of what Class composed—Some of their Exploits—Escorts alleged to be sometimes Robbers—Arrival at Rio Frio —Mr. and Mrs. G—— —The Plain of Puebla—Malinche—The Pyramid of Cholula—Its early History—Its Height and Appearance—Chamber discovered in the Pyramid—What it contained—Arrival at Puebla.

We were both quite unhappy to leave beautiful and most enchanting Mexico. Even our parting with good-natured, kind Victoriana, was quite affecting! After telling us how much she *siento'd* our departure, she flung her arms and hair about us most affectionately—those mahogany arms, and that ebon hair almost strangled us.

We left Mexico at about half-past four o'clock in the morning. I found, during the time we were there, that one attains a great proficiency in the art of sleeping, in that clear, elastic air, and on that morning we dressed and prepared for our journey, between dreaming and waking. While I saw the trunks and packages, busily vanishing one after the other, I remained in such a state of "masterly inactivity," that I scarcely cared, and could hardly rouse myself, even when those dreadful sounds, "the diligence is ready," broke upon my ears. However, awake or asleep we must go, and we hastily passed along the deserted corridors, a dreary procession, in a state of semi-consciousness, mechanically following our cherished carpet-bags, and well-beloved boxes.

Having seen their "old familiar faces" looking down upon us from the mountain heights, of the diligence summit, we clambered into that imposing vehicle. The companion coach was ready hard by, and off we started, but soon stopped again, with a jerk that almost, or quite severed soul and body, but, fortunately the second jerk, on starting once more, brought them together again.

In the mean time, we felt naturally a little bewildered and confused. What had happened? Surely the *ladrones* had not lassoed the *cochero* on the box of the diligence, in the very streets of Mexico. Or had that careless functionary, driven the wheels within the quarter of an inch prescribed by law? And were we all about to be summoned before some dread tribunal, to answer for our hair's breadth scrape (not '*scape*)? We knew not, nor did we ever know, for on we plunged in the half lamp-lit darkness (they have huge swinging lamps swung from corner to corner), and away we trotted as merrily, as before this little incident, which remained clothed in impenetrable mystery. It served thoroughly to awaken us, however, so that we took our last look of queenly Mexico with very wide-awake eyes.

How quiet seemed those streets, generally so alive with busy thousands! The *sereno* was about to make his exit from the scene, and the coal-seller, the *carbonero*, his entry: he would probably be soon followed by the *mantequilleros* (lard-venders), and the *lecheras* (milk-women), the *carnicero* (butcher), Indian *cambista* (exchanger), *tortilleros*, and the tender duck-venders, whose cry is "Oh, my soul, my soul! hot ducks!" (but I believe this is an evening cry), *buhoneros* (peddlers), the honey and *requeson*-sellers, and *aguadores*. A remarkably picturesque class, are these last. They are water-carriers, and have great earthen jars, slung at their backs by a strap, which passes like a *bandeau* across the forehead. Then a mere trifle of a jar, as they seem to consider it (we should find rather weighty and unwieldy), swings carelessly in front, to balance the bigger one, by a band put over the top of the head.

The sunrise was lovely, and when we looked back at the valley of Mexico in the golden light of morning, the prospect was indeed, all that one can dream of the beautiful and the sublime. It was enough to electrify a mummy, or an oyster with admiration.

I forgot to say, when we reached the barrier of the city, we found an escort of soldiers waiting for us, who immediately ranged themselves on either side of the *coche*, and cantered leisurely along with us. It was after quitting the shores of fair Lake Tezcuco, that we turned to the south, and after changing horses at a place called the little Peñon (a hill standing in a solitary position between the Lakes of Chalco and Xochimilco), we continued our course to Ayotla.

At this point it was that General Scott's army quitted the main road to Mexico, and turning round the Peñon Grande to the south of the city, followed the opposite shore of the Chalco Lake. It was near this, at the base of the soaring Peñon, that we bade adieu to the glorious valley, and began to toil up the ascent of the mountain.

We had a fresh relay of horses, at a flourishing-looking *hacienda* of considerable size, on a shelf of the mountain, and it was looking back from that spot, that the prospect of the unrivaled valley, which we had lately left, was magnificent. Looking towards Tenango and Ameca, we beheld a vast plain, where stretched fields of verdant corn, and shone out stately *haciendas*, and the white walls of populous hamlets. Chalco spread its many-glittering waveless waters beneath us, and through some chasmy opening in the surrounding hills, you marked Tezcuco, holding its sparkling mirror to the morning. Onward and upward then, till that earthly heaven, the valley, opened all its apparently world-wide scene before you—while the cloud-belted giant mountains—some with their foreheads dazzling as very constellations with perpetual snow—seemed placed there expressly to draw the glances of mortals to the skies, lest they should haply forget them among such endless glories and such bewilderment of beauty around.

Not long after this exquisite view we got deep into the cold pine forest, which, I suppose, is the beginning of the tract called the "Black Forest;" and we were glad to draw our cloaks well around us; the air felt very sharp. We reached, at length, those savage looking defiles, which are said to be the places most haunted by robbers, of any in all Mexico, except, perhaps, the country about Perote. Our gallant little squadron of lancers took occasionally, some short cuts in the hilly pine woods, but kept, however, within hail. We watched them with some little anxiety; and the party, in general, was observed to be rather more cheerful, when their gaudy, and gracefully-wreathed *sarapes*, and long lances, with streaming scarlet pennons, were very close to the sides of the carriage.

I have not mentioned, on coming to Mexico we had passed a tree under which a whole set of robbers had been shot the week before. I did not observe it on our return, but it was somewhere, I think, in this forest. Our diligence was nearly full: we occupied one side, and besides ourselves there was an agreeable and very *poli* old French gentleman; a Mexican, with his son, natives of Puebla, and returning there from a visit to the capital; and a young Mexican gentleman who had been educated at New York, spoke English remarkably well, and seemed imbued with much admiration of "The States," which he in courtesy called the *United* ones.

(Forgive me, my dear American friends, but just now, when you are so fiercely quarreling, it is allowable to say this, is it not? One of their printers the other day unintentionally *anagrammized* the word, and printed it "*Untied* States." However, the Americans I have seen in Mexico seem to think, in general, all these vexatious disagreements will blow over.)

The French gentleman and two of the Mexicans were carefully nursing on their knees splendid *sombreros*—to be sported on high-days and holidays, I suppose. They took off the covers which protected their treasures from dust and dirt, and they were extremely handsome, of the most delicate materials, and exquisitely decorated with silver. One had the costliest little silver dog on it possible, as an ornament, to join the silver band, if I recollect rightly; it was so beautifully executed it almost looked alive, and yet was only about the size of the famous little dog in the fairy tale that, couched in a nut, betrayed its whereabouts by a sharp little "Yap, yap." After exhibiting them to our admiring view (I believe they thought our curiosity was excited by the mysterious way in which they were folded and enwrapped), they—especially the Frenchman—kept up a very animated conversation, in Spanish, about the theatres, the great carnival-ball, and so on. How happy the Frenchman seemed, talking of ballets and operas, and of his seeing Cerito at Paris, and Carlotta Grisi, Marie Taglioni, and half a hundred more!

A Parisian is a Parisian every where, and always; for, except occasional visits to France, it appeared this gentleman had been settled in Mexico twenty or thirty years: but he was, notwithstanding that, apparently as much a citizen of Paris as if he had never penetrated into the country further than the Bois de Boulogne. Every now and then they stopped in the middle of an *entrechat* (that is, the description of one), or left poor Carlotta Grisi balancing herself, with great grace, and twirling upon one leg in a very difficult *pas* and posture, to throw a sidelong glance out of the window to see whether those who were riding so close to the carriage were lancers or *ladrones*, and, after this brief investigation, resumed their discourse, till higher and more rugged rocks, and a deeper and ever deepening gloom of crowding pines, caused another reconnoitring look, and many an uneasy after-peep, cast "slantindicularly" out of the loop-holes of our traveling fortress.

One of our lancers was a negro; another seemed to have entirely run to mustaches; a third, of a light copper-color, had swathed himself up in his cloak like an Egyptian mummy (evidently suffering from the cold severely); a fourth seemed to consist chiefly of lance and spurs, and the point of a bluish nose—the points of the one and the other equally sharp. The fifth was a splendid cavalier, whose spirited horse curveted about in the most graceful style—but I will not go on particularizing. Suffice it that all were *sarape'd* up almost to the eyes, and that altogether they had a most imposing effect, and a highly picturesque appearance.

Their uniform was multiform, and of all the colors of the rainbow: their complexions varied almost as much, and their horses were not behindhand in variety of hues—grays, blacks, *alazans* (sorrel-colored), piebalds, *priétos* (dark brown), and others. I believe, in addition to their lances, they are armed with holster-pistols and *escopettes*.

With regard to the robbers, we are told they are usually very humane and often courteous. If the accounts we hear of them, from even *Mexicans*, be true, they ought to be so, as they are frequently persons belonging to good society, who having gambled away their property, "take to the road," temporarily, as a means of recruiting their shattered fortunes. Gambling is the curse of Mexico.

These distinguished marauders appear to consider this a sort of guerilla warfare, which is not derogatory or degrading—a singular delusion, to say the least of it. A colonel in the army, we were told, was shot a little while ago for heading a desperate troop of brigands who plundered a diligence, and this is said to be by no means an isolated case; but that, after all, may be an exaggeration. One thing appears certain; they are generally exceedingly civil and considerate toward passengers who at once give up their money and valuables.

We were told that they have occasionally robbed a party of priests; and then, having ordered the poor fat *padres* to lie on their rubicund faces in the dust—*la boca á tierra*, while they ransacked their trunks—they have insisted on the panting, puffing ecclesiastics giving them absolution for their sacrilegious sin. One day, it seems, they attacked a large party of actors and actresses returning from a visit to Mexico. They seized their heterogeneous wardrobe, and were perfectly enchanted at the gorgeousness of the dresses, glittering with tinsel and spangles. They could not resist the delight of dressing themselves up in their brilliant costumes; and while one accoutred himself like a Roman senator, hanging the false flowing beard (which he should have tied to his ell-long mustaches) behind like a dragoon's horsetail to his helmet, another attired himself in the graceful costume of the Sylphide, with a wreath of white roses stuck on the top of his great bushy head, and the little gauzy wings, fastened on to the herculean shoulders, so that he looked like a vast cherub booted and spurred—at any rate, we may imagine such mistakes were made. A party of dragoons galloped up, rescued the heroes and heroines of the buskin, and seized for summary punishment the Sylphides and senators.

We passed numerous crosses on our road through these gloomy regions, which indicated where murders had been committed; but these might be relics of the olden time. As for us, we had immense, unbounded confidence in the lances and mustaches, which had so warlike an appearance, galloping at our side. They seemed a gallant set altogether, and determined to put to flight any number of *ladrones*. They were very active and vigilant, and spied about for brigands, as if they would rather have liked a little skirmish than not.

Travelers, however, have sometimes told me in Mexico, that they do not place much dependence on them. They say, in the first place, when not employed as escorts, they themselves become the robbers. That trifling circumstance matters not at all, I think, or is rather favorable than otherwise; for they must know the haunts and habits of their sometimes comrades particularly well. And then it is so seldom now that travelers carry any real valuables with them on these dangerous roads, that their pay and gratuities as protectors must be in general a more certain source of livelihood to them, than their booty as banditti. Besides, occasionally travelers must be allowed to go safely, otherwise they would more and more restrict themselves to a mere change of linen and a few cigars. And then it is the interest of these *soldados* to keep up the confidence of *viagéros* in escorts, for thus they are always sure of some employment and emolument, either as defenders or defiers of the law. No; I am resolved that nothing shall shake my full dependence on these red pennons and purple points of noses.

At last we drew up at the door of the *posada* at Rio Frio, which is situated a short distance below the summit of this uncomfortable pass, without having seen the slightest *soupçon* of a robber, to my great delight. The *Almuerzo* was already prepared, and we had wherewithal in our purses to pay for it to boot. There was a complete hurricane at Rio Frio.

In the companion coach were Mr. and Mrs. G——, and all their children (Mr. G—— had been a traveling companion of ours to Mexico). His wife is a French lady, very pleasing-looking, and extremely fair, with light-colored hair. She traveled *à la Mexi-*

*caine*, without any bonnet, but, however, not with a *reboso*—in short, with nothing at all on her head: this must have been unpleasant in the clouds of dust that were whirling about. When they got out to go to breakfast, two or three little blue-eyed children were blown away like feathers, and the poor nurse was running after them in dismay, and waltzing with the wind in the wildest fashion. I remained in the diligence and breakfasted on biscuits. I had rather have had *bear* for breakfast, as we had sometimes on the Mississippi.

Before we started, Mr. G—— flew (the wind being favorable) to the side of the carriage, and told me they were going to Puebla, where we should all stop for the night, and I anticipated the pleasure of making Mrs. G——'s acquaintance there; but fate decided otherwise. But now, the horses being to—*vamos*, the *coche* thunders along amid the roaring of the wind, and soon we enter another somewhat perilous and rugged pass—but this opens on the fair and fertile table-land of stately Puebla.

Boldly stands the peak of Malinche alone upon the plain, and it is the first spectacle that presents itself (and a very noble one too) on quitting the shade of the woods. The table-land over which our road then led, descends very gradually to Puebla, which is a distance of about forty miles. It is covered with maize and wheat; but there does not seem to be any division into hedged fields. Here and there you see *haciendas*, and churches, and gardens, and ruins. These last struck us much when we first came from "The States," where such a thing is as rare as a Cape jessamine would be at the North Pole. Popocatapetl looked awfully beautiful and magnificent from there, and Iztaccihuatl did not yield much to it in grandeur.

I believe one of Cortez's great battles was fought very near this volcano of Malinche; but I get a little puzzled with the number of volcanoes and mountains, and the Aztec and American battles—Cortez and General Scott, "El grande Emperador Montezuma" and gallant "Old Zach."

We soon came in sight of the wonderful and huge pyramid of Cholula, built by the Aztecs; it is supposed as a *Tcocalli.* A temple to Queatzalcoatl formerly stood on it; but now it is crowned by a Christian chapel dedicated to the Madonna.

Some antiquaries have conjectured it served for a cemetery, as well as a sanctuary of religion. It is thought by Humboldt to bear a striking resemblance to the temple of Belus, and some other Oriental edifices. It is believed by the Indians to be hollow; and they have a curious tradition that while Cortez remained at Cholula, a number of armed warriors were concealed in it, who were to have attacked, suddenly and unexpectedly, the Spanish army. It appears to be true, at any rate that Cortez, having some cause for distrust, or some secret information of such an intention, assaulted in a very unlooked-for manner the inhabitants of Puebla, and put six thousand to the sword.

Humboldt says the base of this mighty pyramid is almost *double* that of the great pyramid of Cheops in Egypt; its height, however, is not so great. It is said to be constructed most exactly in the direction of the cardinal points. It consists of four distinct terraces or pyramidical stories, and is entirely built with alternate layers of clay and *adobes* (sun-dried bricks).

The pyramid is partly covered on the eastern side by the spontaneous growth of vegetation, some prickly pears, and different small shrubs, giving it at a little distance, rather the appearance of a *natural* abrupt conical-shaped hill. It seems to equal in its elevation which is entirely *artificial*, and in noble form, the range of hills that stands in the front of it, or the height of Tlaloc that towers behind it. You ascend to the platform on the summit by a flight of about one hundred and twenty steps.

When the present high road was made from Puebla to Mexico, the first story of the Cholula pyramid, it is said, was cut through, and a square chamber was brought to light, which had no outlet, and which was supported by beams of cypress, and singularly constructed, each succeeding course of bricks passing beyond the lower. In this square chamber were found two skeletons, some basaltic idols, and a few painted vases varnished in a curious manner.

It is said, also, that there are fragmentary masses of *adobes* and clay in the immediate vicinity of the pyramid, in one of which, that bore the aspect of an old fortress, were found some bones of men, earthenware, and warlike arms of the Aztecs. Plantations of aloes, corn-fields, and lovely gardens, and cultivated grounds environ Cholula. Formerly there was a great Aztec city of Cholula.

With regard to this extraordinary pyramid, I think the people who could be bold enough to become mountain-builders within sight of those stupendous volcanoes, Popocatapetl and Iztaccihuatl, and so many other mighty mountains, deserve much praise for their almost sublime audacity. The very idea was amazingly grand and daring; but when you add to this that they succeeded in leaving to future generations a work that is strikingly noble and magnificent, even in so trying a position, it must be conceded that those barbaric tribes have some claims on the admiration of posterity. I hope when we arrive at Vera Cruz to see a drawing of the pyramid by Lord M. Kerr. He intended to devote some little time to making a sketch of it.

We lost sight of Cholula at last, and crossed the Tlascala River, and then drew near to the many churches, and towers, and domes, and convents of populous Puebla. Just as we were about to enter the town, we passed the second diligence, whose huge form loomed almost like another Cholula on wheels, in the dusk, with its rather tapering load of trunks, portmanteaus, baskets, and carpet bags. We imagined they had stopped to have the harness adjusted, as we thought we saw some shadowy figures standing by the horses. However, our *cochero* stopped to make no inquiries, nor to afford any assistance—on he drove to the hotel.

There were a good many promenaders, probably just returned from the Alameda, in the streets, and some cavaliers—I believe masked—for the carnival was not over; but the light was not brilliant enough for us to see well. The magnificent cathedral seemed heaving its giant frame to the sky, till you might almost fancy that those angelic visitants, who were supposed to be its builders, were lifting it from the earth to a more blessed region. We drove through the Grand Plaza, and soon found ourselves dashing into the busy court-yard of the hotel.

We asked for *quartos* immediately, and were informed they had but one for our whole party. While I was talking to the superintendent, a person came up to me, and began speaking to me in a language that appeared to me a very strange one indeed. I concluded it might possibly be Poblano-Spanish, with perhaps a slight mixture of some Indian dialect, and I began to reply in Spanish, to the best of my ability. But my new acquaintance shook her head, and made a fresh trial, and I then discovered this unknown tongue was intended for—English!

She was a German (and, by the flickering lamp-light, I saw she was very fair and light-haired, and Saxon-looking), and had come to Puebla to meet Mrs. G—— there, to whom she had rerecently engaged herself as housekeeper. She was in great trepidation at their non-arrival, and feared some accident had happened. I told her all I knew, and we agreed that they would probably soon arrive.

Another *coche* came rattling in, and down rushed the poor German, hoping the belated travelers were in it; but she soon returned, looking very disconsolate, saying—"dat not dem." Brief as Bem's letter to, or of the Ban—"Bem Ban baum!" Shortly afterward, I ascertained that they had sent to the hotel to say their diligence had broken down, and to beg some sort of carriage might be dispatched to bring them and their luggage immediately.

In the mean time, I had secured *quartos*. Mr. C——, an English gentleman whom we had met in Mexico, most obligingly gave up his room to us, which was a good-sized one, and got a small den somewhere. The maids were left in possession of a scrambling-looking apartment, that had been destined for all of us, and finding the poor German housekeeper (who was not in the least *like* a stately functionary of that description in looks, for she appeared rather *svelte*, and delicate, and pretty) had no apartment, they invited her to share theirs.

We were not sorry to see a good dinner make its appearance, which was soon followed by its disappearance; for we were very hungry. After dinner, foaming chocolate was brought, and after chocolate we would gladly have sought repose, but we felt anxious to see Mr. and Mrs. G—— and their children arrive in safety, and remained up for some time; but still there were no signs of them. So V—— went to bed, and I a little while after, as we had to be up *very* early in the morning. I was unfortunate enough thus to miss making acquaintance with Mrs. G——, who, I was told in Mexico, is a very nice person indeed.

Just as our door was closed for the night, hasty steps were heard on the stairs, and in the broad, half-open gallery, sounds of voices speaking French and English were distinctly audible. They had, then, arrived. My maid told me, the next day, that she had seen them, and that they had been detained so long in consequence of there being no conveyance at hand to send for them. I believe they walked to the hotel, and regretted not having done so at once; for the first messenger Mr. G—— sent, never took the message at all, and the poor children were naturally wearied out with waiting so long after their fatiguing journey. I believe, however, they were to rest a little at Puebla, before they proceeded to their new home; for, if I remember rightly, Mr. G—— has given up the superintendentship of certain Guanajuata mines, and undertaken some not far from Xalapa, for which he is to receive a much more liberal salary.

## CHAPTER XXXIII.

Departure from Puebla—Acajete—El Pinal—Alarm of Ladrones—Discomforts of rough Roads exemplified—Pulque—Its Taste—The Plant from which it is extracted—Mode of extracting it—Monde de Pizano—Arrival at Perote—Coldness of that Place in Winter.

On the following morning we had to rise before three o'clock, and so were obliged to give up visiting the Celestial Cathedral of Puebla.

Away we thundered through the deserted streets, and suddenly came to a dead stop. A little alarm, lest we had "come to grief," like poor Mr. and Mrs. G——, was quickly dispelled by discovering the *cochero* had dropped his cloak; so the conductor had to go with a lantern, hunting in the streets for it. The horses fidgeted, the passengers grumbled, the time (as it has a habit of doing) sped on; but presently the conductor arrived, and brought with him the lost treasure, and off we rattled again to the east to meet the morning.

We rolled along on the elevated table-land, feeling a little cold, and particularly sleepy. We arrived at last at Amozoque, which is said to be swarming with robbers; but we were so fortunate as to see none. From this place you ascend by a very gentle inclination, to the summit of the separating ridge beyond Perote. Boldly and proudly towered the great mountain walls of the table-land.

The next relay was at Acajete. At one of these places we tasted some spring water, said to be wonderfully fine, but we did not think it so very remarkable. It is reported that a large gang of *ladrones* conceal themselves often among the ravines and *barrancas* of the Acajete mountains. I am happy to say they did not leave their ambush. We drove on pretty rapidly past thickets, and shelving rocks, and frowning precipices, and stopped to change horses at El Pinal, on the northern side of the mountain, a large and fine *hacienda*, and then rattled speedily along to Nopaluca, where the *diligencia* breakfasted.

I do not remember accurately where, but *somewhere* not very far from this, there was an alarm of *ladrones* given in the diligence. A number of mounted horsemen, apparently well armed, made their appearance; and one, who looked like a chief or captain among them, galloped tolerably near, and seemed to be busily occupied in reconnoitring our carriages, the passengers, and the possible booty.

The French gentleman seemed convinced they were—"Les voleurs! oui, ma foi, les voilà, tenez, il faut—Mais, non—attendez, voyons un peu. Eh, oui! c'est le même;" and elevating his voice, leaning half out of the carriage, taking off his sombrero, and waving his hand, he called, "Como! Señor, quién se lo hubiera imaginado? Se lo hubieran esperado? Pardiez! Me alegro de ver á V.! Celebro mucho ver á V. Me atreveré á pedir adonde vá V.?" Many compliments passed between them, and after a number of mutual civilities and salutations, and a perfect lightning flash of brilliant teeth, shown by the gracious smiles of the caballero, away he dashed from the side of the carriage, still bowing to the señoras, and being joined by his companions, was soon lost to sight. The French gentleman told us, he had met him accidentally somewhere, and been enabled to show him some trifling kindness and civility, and that on recognizing him so luckily, he reminded the caballero of it, and for his sake were thus saved our watches and coins.

By this time we were shaken almost out of all knowledge; one of our bonnets looked like a small coal-scuttle in convulsions; a wretched Mexican had his sombrero almost smashed into his face; another had his visage knocked about with many whacks, pleasingly diversifying his olive complexion with patches of black and blue. When we attempted to talk, it was very much like speaking in *entrechats*, our poor words had to cut such extraordinary capers in our throats. The unhappy Monsieur seemed at one moment like an Indian juggler about to bolt a sword, scabbard and all, or a boa constrictor preparing to swallow its victim, and beginning with one limb at first. The poor man had only got his neighbor's elbow in his mouth, which another jolt almost sent half way down his throat.

Our conversation was necessarily fitful. "Mais où donc est mon chapeau? Cette voiture fait danser tout d'une maniere—Oh! je vous en prie—Ne vous derangez pas, Monsieur." But Monsieur just at that moment was very much "derangé;" he was tossed as in a blanket to the highest roof, and down again, and probably alighted upon the identical *chapeau* they were looking for. "No le incomoda á V. este paquete, Señor?" And "este paquete," at the same moment of time, lodged itself unscrupulously on the nose of the civil questioner. "Hombre! verdaderamente los caminos no son muy buenos, pero, qué hermosa vista! Qué magnifico pais! Parece . . . . ." But the poor wretch just then had his hat jammed over his eyes, which stopped his rapture. Shortly after, you must imagine an immensely polite conversation going forward. The French Monsieur discovers that the Mexican Señor is going to Xalapa as well as himself, and he is charmed. "Tendré el placer de gozar de su compañia de V., porque yo tambien . . . . ." And while thus saying, even, the Señor hits him such a terrible whack, by an involuntary butt with his head, that the wretched victim is doubled up for half-an-hour by it.

At last we learned to watch for the coming jolt, when the horses or mules were all at full gallop, and the road rather worse than usual. At the first symptoms of plunges and shocks, conversation would be generally as suddenly stopped, as if the whole company had unexpectedly been gagged: and some would screw their mouths into the tightest of button-holes, others open theirs wide (the wisest plan, which I can safely recommend, as it saves your teeth from being jammed together in lock-jaw fashion, or played upon like castanets), gasping "like a cat-fish with a sock-dolager hook in its mouth," but all exhibited countenances of intense horror. We almost felt sometimes as if our heads had been jolted off, and re-jolted on again, happy if each got his own head back: what a shame it would have been if one person had acquired two, and aped Austria's double-headed eagle!

We tried some *pulque* for the first time, when changing horses at one of the *posadas*, during this journey: the first time I ever saw others drinking it, I thought they were draining large draughts of new milk (for it looks exactly like it), and admired much the teetotalism of that knot of *arrieros*, and *rancheros*, and *mozos*. Then and there I was informed it was the famous *pulque* they were so industriously imbibing.

I had not at this time courage to taste it, for I heard an alarming account of it; but on our return we all tasted and sipped. H—— and W—— thought it like indifferent small beer; I thought it like nothing exactly, but that it stood "alone in its glory,"—matchlessly horrible. But I can just imagine that you might get used to it in about a hundred and fifty years, and in a hundred more learn to like it: but, on second thoughts, I think this is a little exaggeration, and you might by possibility become an earlier convert. I must also add, to give the stuff its due, that we were told that this was very inferior *pulque*, and therefore we must not condemn universal *pulque* after tasting such a bad specimen. It is said to be but very little intoxicating, and exceedingly nutritious, so it deserves well of its country; and its countrymen have reason to prize it, and sing and say, as Mr. Ruxton tells us they sometimes do—" Viva nosotros y pulque."

The Maguey (*Agave Americana*), from which this beverage is extracted, is an aloe, and is very extensively cultivated in Mexico. The most famous plantations of it are in the vicinity of Cholula, and also those in the Llanos de Apam; there are many places besides celebrated for excellent *pulque*, as the valley of Teluco, where the *pulque* is supplied from immense Maguey grounds near Lerma, and numerous others. The plant grows wild in every part of Mexico, but is not cultivated or milked, *i.e.* drained of its precious sap, except in certain districts. I should imagine, however, the cultivation of it is fast spreading, as the consumption appears to be perfectly enormous. We saw immense fields of it in many parts during our journey.

The process of preparing for the supply of *pulque* is curious. When the central shoot, which would naturally produce the flower, is on the eve of making its appearance, it is anticipated, and rather harshly nipped in the bud, by a deep incision being made, and the whole heart being taken out, as one of those most savage and merciless barbarians of civilized life, called dentists, extracts a tooth, by the roots. This operation is generally performed by the Indians, whose forefathers had a little knack of doing a similar service to human subjects, but not with such beneficial results. Having thus extracted *el corazon*, only the stout outside rind is left, which acts the part of a natural cistern, or large basin, both deep and wide, into which the sap, which dame Nature designed for the sustenance of the immense central shoot, oozes perpetually in vast quantities. Then comes the experienced Indian (athirst already, and fired by thoughts of coming *pulque*) and hacks away the leaves on one side, so as to make a regular breach in these vegetable battlements, and thrusts in a long gourd (*acojote*) whose lesser end is finished off by a horn, while a small square orifice is left at the other extremity, to which his mouth is applied, while by the force of suction, he extracts the sap, which sap, before fermentation takes place, is named *agua-miel* (honey-water), and, in accordance with its name, has an extremely sweet taste, and is quite destitute of that extraordinary smell (not much unlike that of eggs in the sere and yellow leaf of their existence) which appears afterward to form one of its peculiar charms. The sap is allowed to ferment for about fifteen days, when it becomes what they term *madre pulque* (the mother of *pulque*), and this is distributed—but only in niggardly quantities —among the troughs which are to receive daily accessions of *agua-miel.* It acts as a kind of leaven, fermentation immediately begins, and in about a day the *pulque* is ready for drinking. "Viva nosotros y pulque!"

From this plant is also prepared a horribly strong brandy (which we have *not* tasted) called Mexical (or Mezcal or Aguardiente de Maguey), which is but too highly approved of in general in this country. A more interesting subject in connection with it, is the use the Aztecs made of its leaves in manufacturing the paper on which their hieroglyphics were written, some fragments of which have survived. They now make of the more fibrous portions, a stout thread, or twine, called *pita*, which is formed into ropes, and made use of in the mines, and as cordage for ships on the Pacific coast: it is said to be very strong and lasting. In short, the Maguey seems to play an important part in Mexico altogether.

There were a few rocky peaks not far from our road; but dreaming of the Tierra Caliente—the world of flowers and beauty we were soon to see—we did not care much to gaze at the inhospitable looking landscape, save where afar the Coffre de Perote (whose Indian name is Nauhcampapetl) gleamed out, and mighty Orizaba raised his refulgent crest.

We came at length to La Venta de Soto, near which towers a huge pyramidal peak of rock of perhaps three thousand feet high —Monte de Pizarro. From its gloomy clefts and hollows and hiding-places, it is reported *los ladrones* often start to terrify and rob passengers. We afterward entered into that lonely rugged volcanic region, which had struck us much in coming, but which looked particularly wild, bleak, and gloomy by the evening light, which was beginning by slow degrees to fade off.

The black frowning lava scattered in broken and confused beds, as if earthquakes had helped in those olden convulsions of Nature, to produce wilder confusion, looked dreary indeed. Somewhere in Mexico, it is said, a whole population was buried alive (as at Pompeii, I suppose), and this might well be the spot; for many of these huge blocks of lava look like giant tomb-stones. There were a few dilapidated *cabañas*, or *chozas* (huts and cottages), left to decay, as if their inhabitants could no longer endure the oppressive gloom of this stern and savage region. Acheron should flow through these melancholy congenial scenes. I believe it is called "mal pais" (the bad country).

After a dismal drive across this cheerless territory, with only the grandeur of the Coffre de Perote to admire, we arrived at the town. The fortress, where the commandant is our friend, the Coronel Aguado, frowned down upon us, and we soon galloped into the court-yard belonging to that well-remembered collection of dens and cellars, which is called an hotel in Perote. I must not omit to mention, that we had passed innumerable crosses, each showing where some poor wretch lies buried. The people here, as before, refused us a separate dinner at first, and afterward relented, and sent us a very good one. Before dinner, one of our *compagnons de voyage*, Mr. C——, knocked at our immense barn doors, and wanted to know if he could be of any use in sending us dinner. I went out to speak to him, and was surprised at the metamorphosis the bleak air of Siberia-like Perote had wrought in him—he was of a tint hovering between azure and Prussian blue, and his teeth were literally chattering in his head.

After dinner we had some delicious chocolate. We had a most obliging and good-natured woman to wait on us, with very sweet and pleasing manners, quite too good and amiable for such a wild, bleak, drear, robber-haunted place. She seemed like a disguised princess in Perote. If so, she was the most condescending one in the world, for she ran to and fro with the greatest alacrity, bringing us all sorts of dishes, stewed, and fried, and boiled.

I was half asleep when she came to clear away the things and bring chocolate. I told her I was horribly tired (for a wonder, for I very seldom am so with traveling). "Y con razon, Señorita—" (you must know every body here is called *señorita*—no matter if she has a hundred children, and is a hundred herself, she is still called miss and child, *niña*. You may hear sometimes a little beggar girl entreat a decrepit, toothless, bent-double *child* of seventy, to give her *caridad*,) "con razon, los caminos son tan malos, tan detestables."

She told me she had sometimes been to Puebla, and was always half dead after it. I asked her if it was not terribly cold at Perote in the winter; "O si, muchissima." She said the snow was often very deep for a long time together. I glanced round the room and thought "poor travelers!" in order to have any light in the day-time, they must have their door open; and there is no stove or provision of any sort for giving warmth to the desolate dens! She told me they kept themselves warm in the kitchen; but altogether a Perote winter must be a dreary affair.

After a little more conversation, she went to find a lamp for us, and returned speedily with a very promising-looking one. She begged us then to lose no time in going to bed, as we should have to get up at about two o'clock in the morning; therefore, in her soft musical voice, she counseled us to retire immediately, "Se lo suplica á V." We took her advice, and slept well till a terrifying rat-a-tatting at our prison gates aroused us from slumber, and we hastily dressed by the light of the lamp and a *véla*, which our kind friend, the disguised princess, had left us.

My maid told me there was an immense party last evening at dinner, for a great number of Priests and Sisters of Charity had arrived, and there were hardly tables and dinner enough to accommodate them all. She said these Sisters of Charity appeared all healthy, stout, hard-working people; and their rough, coarse hands seemed to be accustomed to somewhat severe labor. She understood from an American there, that they had just come from Spain.

## CHAPTER XXXIV.

Departure from Perote—Magnificent Views from the Heights—Impressions caused by them—The Beauty of the Approach to Xalapa described—The Mirage—Appearance of inverted Houses—Hotel de Diligencias—Visit to a Church—Negotiation with the Mozo touching the Sarape and the American Blanket—Numbers of Friars and Nuns from Spain—Arrival at Vera Cruz—A curious Fact in Relation to Dr. Gutzlaff, the Missionary to China—Arrival of the Steamer for the Havana.

Bitterly cold was it when we took our places in the diligencia, the morning we bade adieu to scowling Perote, after having a *desayuno* of coffee and chocolate, and a small roll, brought in compassionately by one of the *mozos*, for, of course, our poor *princesa* was still locked in slumber.

We rolled heavily through the gloomy, lifeless streets, which echoed with the tramp, tramp, of our eight mules. Most magnificently shone the stars, like so many diamond moons; but they looked almost as cold as ourselves. On we went, through the starlit, piercing, chilly atmosphere, between ten and eleven thousand feet, or thereabouts, above the sea.

At last the pale gray of morning became visible, and soon after up rose the glorious welcome sun, and showed us that we were on the heights of the pass, and about to descend through the woods of shadowing pine. Now then, for all the climates of the world, "succeeding each other in layers," to use Baron Humboldt's well-known expression in describing Mexico. For the visitor to this Land of Marvels, the traveler in these magical regions, in the course of a couple of days (and it is possible to do the same thing in a far less space of time—perhaps in some parts in a couple of hours), may cast his eye over the whole scale of the earth's varied vegetation, from the Tropics' gorgeous and dazzling parasitical plants, to the sombre firs and pines of the Arctic Circle.

Our descent was not at all a precipitous one at first; but after a time we journeyed along quite on the extreme brink and edge of the mountains, so that by leaning far out of the carriage, one could catch the sublimest views conceivable of all that intervened between their towering summits and the sea. The high mountain chain to the north of the pass turns eastward, and is continued on to the Gulf of Mexico, in parallel lines of ridges, on the heights of which the traveler's eye looks down; and that eye might also see confusedly, beautiful, wild, and solitary dells among the hills, and the sombre black region of lava and dwarfed and ragged pines, that he is leaving, and wilderness after wilderness of beauty that he is approaching nearer and nearer to; and from the crest of some of the hills, looking to the south, the awful majesty of the Mountain of the Star (Orizaba), its dazzling brow crowned with unchangeable resplendence, till it seemed to have a brighter daylight of its own. Let him look behind him, and see the white frost like a faint sprinkling from the snows of the Coffre, blanching the funereal foliage of the solemn branches of pine and the beds of gloomy lava; and let him look before him, and mark the groves of oranges, the corn-fields, the gardens of roses, and the palm—daughter of the sun—and thrice ten thousand flowering and blooming trees!—*There* laughs a leaping brook, lustrous, fresh, and clear, as if all the roses had shed all their diamond dews to form its fairy stream, and it rolled, tinted and blushing with their reflections. And here a forest of labyrinthine bowers makes a warm and glowing darkness of flower-shadows—zones after zones, regions after regions, expanse after expanse, are stretching at his feet.

Not the world, but many worlds seem to be outspread in boundless magnificence before us, for it is so seldom you think of the single Earth, mingling in one transcendent unity—one conjunction of almost antagonizing elements and properties, all the diversities, all the conflicting extremes it possesses, that when you behold them thus displayed in one overpowering consummate burst of triumph, and in the most stupendous and imposing array, you seem entering on a new state of existence, on a fresh stage of being, and can hardly believe that these wonders, crowded, heaped, precipitated, and concentrated—(each separate beauty, each different display of grandeur, gaining so much by such juxtaposition—such surprising contrast, that each seems far more beautiful, and far more majestic)—can indeed be the same to which the eye, or the tutored thought, or the imagination has been accustomed. These varieties, so accumulated and agglomerated, seem to be new varieties; this creation, with all its choicest and selectest wonders and glories, so combined and united to each other, seems a vision of many creations, and the boundary—which, however seems no boundary to all this gorgeous magnificence, but only a continuation, along which the dreaming, straining eye appears to travel into eternity—is the all-glorious immeasurable ocean!

With such a spectacle spread out before him does the traveler dash downward—only too fast—to beautiful Xalapa. Spring and summer seem flying on wings of the rainbow and the rose to greet him; and every odoriferously-breathing zephyr is an *avant-courier* of the floral delights that await him. Miles before you are whirled into the bowery, flowery, country-like town of Xalapa, you rejoice in the far-floating odors of its crowding orange groves; and, what a scene enchants you: Fields of living emerald and chrysoprase; woods bathed in the beauty of myriads of blossoms (the starry orange bowers emulating the snows of glittering Orizaba); lovely slopes, the most graceful picturesque hollows; and, built on the smiling brows of sunny hills, lordly-looking *haciendas*, with their white walls sparkling like spotless alabaster; and tangled mazes of vernal delights, and startling phenomena of vegetation; such as stems that seem bearing all the flowers of one zone together, so crossed and mingled are the blossomy treasures—(indeed in some places it seemed like solid masses of blooms). And what fairy glens and gorges, and glittering hamlets, and sequestered homes, and half-ruined convents glimmering through many-colored thickets, and vailing streamers of a thousand-tendrilled blossoming vines; and tortuous paths, and silvery winding rills, and soft acclivities, seemingly intersecting and as it were overlapping each other, as if to conceal some more precious treasures of mystic beauty—if that were possible! And in some parts, afar off something that almost looks like a pageant of gorgeous sunset clouds fallen to earth, and melting in multitudinous splendor—it is but a variegated heap of the all but endless growths of Nature in these regions, billowing over some rising grounds, swelling with softest undulations, while the whole resounds with the joyous notes of singing birds.

But all this time I have forgotten to tell of the beautiful mirage we saw among the mountains: it was pointed out to us by M. de ——. It was hardly possible to believe it was not lakes of shining water we saw: the illusion was extraordinarily perfect, and some in the carriage obstinately refused to believe any thing but the evidence of their own fallible senses, till the scene gradually changed, partly before their very eyes, sufficiently to convince them of their error. We were told it was of very unusual occurrence in those parts.

There was a marvelous appearance also of some inverted houses, which were at a great distance in reality: and besides that, we beheld, before we left the mountain, a singular phenomenon—an immense white stratum of clouds, spread out exactly like a vast ocean of snow, concealing, for a short time, the magnificent view beneath. This vanished as the sun gained power, having made its appearance during the morning twilight.

But now we must enter the charming "calles" of that pearl of cities, Xalapa. Again we admired its single-storied, terraced, and balconied houses, smothered in the loveliest of gardens, and many of them quite as large and handsome as the glazed-porcelain houses of Mexico.

We descended the steep streets to the Hotel de Diligencias, where this time we had much better rooms than the last; we had a very pretty, large, and airy apartment, decorated with a profusion of gayly-painted arabesques, in fresco, and opening on to a broad balcony on one side, and on another to a large wide gallery communicating with a beautiful covered sort of half conservatory, half corridor, enchantingly pretty, adorned with plants, and from this branches the large balcony that runs round the sides of the inner walls of the house, overlooking the great court-yard, which balcony was rather a favorite promenading place when the huge diligencias were heard dashing in from various parts.

Before we went up-stairs to take possession of our *quartos*, a very pretty little fair-haired boy came running into the court-yard, in great haste. It was the little son of M——: he was duly introduced to us, and appeared to be a charming little fellow; the day was beautiful, but cold; and as we were to stay at Xalapa till the morrow, owing to the arrangements of the diligencias, we went out walking, to see some of the old churches. Mr. C—— escorted us.

We climbed up the steep street, and arrived at a handsome-looking church, which was said to be beautiful within, and to have great treasures of *plata* (silver). After a little difficulty we effected an entrance. There was a great deal of dazzling silver certainly: but my attention was painfully arrested by some large wooden figures intended to represent our blessed Saviour, and which were truly shocking; they were most extravagantly painted. We afterward walked a little way to see some of the beautiful views of this charming place, past the gardens, with their wild profusion of clove-carnations, roses, jessamines, and orange trees.

As we strolled on we heard the sweet sounds of a harp suddenly struck very near us. We were just passing a large, handsome house, and without intending to be uncivil, on the impulse of the moment we all looked into the large lofty ground-floor room from whose enormous open but iron-barred windows were pouring the echoing strains: we saw a black-haired though fair señorita, apparently just taking her music lesson; for a grave music-master-like señor was standing by her, and, as it seemed to us, marking the time, and explaining the nature of the aria.

The señorita, having looked up, caught sight of us immediately, and blushing deeply remained in the attitude, and wrapped in the silence of a painted St. Cecilia, suspended in mute surprise. It was evident that the good Xalapenos were never in the habit of giving way to such indiscreet habits of impertinent curiosity; so reluctantly we passed on, and soon after the melodious strains recommenced.

After returning to the hotel, I gave a commission to Mr. C——, to find me a *sarapé*, such as are worn here. A *mozo* brought in a goodly number for me to choose from. Now it happened there was a deep-blue immense American blanket, which I wanted to get rid of, and as I had brought the least possible money with me (for not wishing to enrich the coffers of the robbers, I had the rest by bills on Vera Cruz), it was decided it was better to throw that blanket into the bargain (since after Perote's chilly regions it was no longer needed), and the wonderful bewilderment of the poor *mozo*, at this proposition, was highly diverting. He said in piteous accents, his master had told him exactly what to do: and as the master had, naturally enough, not contemplated the circumstance that had by chance arisen, he had not tutored the *mozo* on this particular contingency; so that he seemed at his wit's end to know what to answer.

"Well," said I, in my choicest Spanish, "go and ask your master; then you will be sure to be right."

"But how can I go?" said he, "till I know what the lady has bought?"

"I shall buy this one, if your master will let me have it for—" (I forget the sum)—"and take this blue one—and you can leave this and take the rest."

"Oh, no! no es posible."

Well, then, he might take them all (mine included) to his master, and bring back that one, and I could then pay for it.

"No, no, that would not do: 'Dispense V. Señorita,' that is quite out of the question."

"But why?" and here he talked so fast, and as it seemed to me in such a curious *patois*, that I could not quite follow him; but yet it appeared to me he wished to leave the chosen one. We offered all sorts of arrangements, but nothing would do. At last Mr. C—— was called in to try to clear up the matter; he could not, and Señor Novarro was at last applied to—whom, by the way, we found here just where we had left him. He soon made all clear; he heard the man's story (who spoke in the most impetuously rapid way, so that none but a native could have well understood him), and he laughed much, and said that stupid man declared he did not know for his life what to do.

"For," said he, "I can not arrange any price for the blue blanket, for my master gave me no directions about it. I can not leave the *sarapés* here to go and ask him, because they are not paid for, and if one was paid for in full and I left it, I can not take the rest *with* the blue blanket, to show, because the lady will have no security for my return, and I can not take—"

But here Señor Novarro interrupted him, and said that he was sure the lady wouldn't mind, and then he explained the difficulty. The shopman and the *sarapés* were sent off, and he soon returned, saying what his master would allow, and the mighty bargain was speedily and satisfactorily closed for all parties.

Soon after, a diligence came thundering down the street, and we repaired to the great balcony to see the new arrivals.

A huge diligence, full of friars and nuns, made its appearance; and Señor Novarro told me the enormous number of these gentry that had lately arrived, filling every public conveyance, had been the cause of his detention at Xalapa, for he could not get a single place. I asked him to what he attributed this immense influx of *padres* and nuns from Spain, and whether he thought it was owing to the alarm occasioned by the late spread of revolutionary doctrines. He had heard no cause assigned, but believed such was the case. It is certainly a curious fact, that, though we never traveled with any in the stage coaches ourselves, we had seen crowds of diligences constantly crammed with these reverend emigrants.

We left Xalapa very early the next morning, after a fruitless search for some keys which H—— lost a little while before we had to start. The sleepy *muchacha* gave us a candle with a snuff of alarming length, and I asked for *despabiladéras*, snuffers, which takes a certain time to pronounce, and by the time the said *despabiladéras* were found (which seemed to have gone on a party of pleasure for the day, with the keys), it was already the time to start, and after we had a very hurried chase—quite a quick thing, but we could not catch our keys—and put on our *sombreros* (which ladies' bonnets are called, as well as gentlemen's hats), it was rather late, and we had some reason to think the American coachman was somewhat indignant at the delay, though he amiably waited for us. Cerro Gordo's *varrancas* perhaps put him in good-humor again.

When we arrived at Vera Cruz, we found the steamer had not arrived. She was very much after her time. Unluckily for us, we found the Casa de Diligencias quite full, and were obliged to put up at another hotel (kept by two Frenchmen), which was not nearly so good. I stupidly forgot to send M. Surutuza's letter, obligingly desiring that rooms should be found for us, and every attention paid us; and, indeed, without that, Mr. Bell sent word soon after we were established in this hotel, that he would contrive to give us apartments; but as the steamer was momentarily expected, and as the proprietors of this *méson* try to make us as comfortable as they can, I did not avail myself of his obliging proposition.

Among other people whom we recognized as having either formed part of our *compagnons de voyage*, on board the United States steamer "Walker," or as having been here before, was Mr. ——, who had come over in the "Walker," for the purpose of bringing back from Mexico the body of his brother (who had died there from the effects of wounds received during the Mexican war), and conveying it to Indiana for interment.

There was an objection to the corpse being taken on board the

"Walker," I believe: at any rate Mr. —— was still at Vera Cruz, not having yet accomplished his melancholy mission, but is about to sail, I think, in a packet ship. He is English by birth, but has been so long settled in the United States, that he has become quite an American, even in appearance.

This reminds me of a curious fact I have heard stated, namely, that Dr. Gutzlaff, who has been so long a missionary to China, and is lately returned, has contracted quite a Chinese *cast of features*, as well as a Celestial gait, countenance, and manners. The latter one can easily imagine, the former seems somewhat of a physiological curiosity.

The British Consul has just been to see me, and tells me they have a great deal of specie arrived to go by the steamer, and an immense mail. He says the steamer will probably arrive to-night, and he and his son must sit up all night to get the letters and papers in readiness for her. We almost live upon the balcony, for the heat inside the room is nearly insupportable. Good news! The English steamer "Thames" has just made her appearance.

---

## CHAPTER XXXV.

Arrival at Havana—Passengers on Board the "Thames"—Affecting Story of an American Merchant's unforeseen Calamity—An American Grinlin Gibbons—The enterprising political Organ-grinder—First Glimpse of Havana—The Harbor—The Morro Castle and the Puntal—The Cabanas—The City of Havana—Volantes—The Paséo—Ladies of Havana—Their Dress—The Gentlemen—Usages of Gallantry at Havana—The Military—Reviews and Music—Anxiety of Spain to retain Cuba—Cathedral of Havana—The Ashes of Columbus—His Bust—How his Ashes have been removed from Place to Place—Worshipers in the Cathedral—The Bishop's Garden—Rare and beautiful Trees and Flowers—Hurricanes at Havana—Volantes in universal Use—Where bestowed sometimes—Havana Houses—How furnished—Social Customs in Havana—Fruits.

We arrived here (at the Havana) after a ten or eleven days' voyage—three days, however, of which we were detained at Tampico; for the sea ran so high, the little steamboat that was to bring out the specie could not get over the bar sooner. The bar was *cross*, they said!

We found the "Thames" a charming ship; so clean, and cool, and large—and we had several very agreeable passengers. Among them were Lord M. Kerr and Mr. Bayard Taylor—the author of some beautiful poetical pieces, and of a work entitled "Views A-foot." He performed a pedestrian tour nearly all over Europe. He was then returning from California, and is, I believe, on the eve of publishing a work—already prepared for the press—relating to that country, which, I should think, would be exceedingly interesting. He is a very gentlemanlike young man, and appears full of intelligence and information.

Mr. Hill, an English gentleman just returned from a lengthened tour, was also on board. He had been living between two and three years in Russia and Siberia (the last *not* involuntary!), having latterly come from South America and Polynesia. He had sailed from Kamtschatka, in a Russian merchant ship, and while in South America, had made several excursions inland. His account of the poorer classes in Siberia, (where the peasants are not serfs), made one think they must form almost the happiest and most flourishing peasantry in the world. It appears they have not only plenty to boil in the pot, but they have the pot boiling almost all day long: in short, plenty of fuel, and plenty of food and clothing. Very unlike the poor *Californians* of olden days. It is probably known to many that on that very soil, now found to be teeming with the golden treasures of earth, the former inhabitants, in a state of the most abject poverty, were wont to subsist on grasshoppers!

We stopped at Mobile point, on our way hither, to land and receive passengers and specie, and came-to among the crowded shipping at the anchorage there; but, in consequence of our long delay at Tampico, the "Thames" staid as short a time as possible, and I had not an opportunity of seeing my dear friend Madame L. V——. Mr. Bayard Taylor, who landed there, was good enough to take her a note from me.

There was a very melancholy circumstance connected with our brief stay at Mobile. Mr. ——, an American merchant, who had been to Mexico on business, expected to receive at Mobile, letters from his wife, to whom he had written from Mexico to say he should go by way of the Havana to New York, on such a day, by one of the American steamers (they are generally very punctual), and as they ordinarily arrive in the evening, he begged her to have tea ready for him.

He appeared a very pleasant, amiable person, and was extremely popular in the ship. I had not made his acquaintance; but one could not but remark his liveliness of manner and flow of amusing conversation. He was in the highest spirits that morning—poor man! compassionating Mr. Taylor for not having to look forward "to tea prepared ready for him," and evidently full of joy and happiness.

The last time I saw him, he was leaning over the rail of the steamer, most merrily talking and laughing with those passengers, who were transferred to a small high-pressure freight-boat, that was to take them to Mobile (as soon as the fog would graciously permit)—Mr. Taylor, Mr. C——, &c. We soon after continued on our course, and I went down to the cabin to read a little before dinner, which was very shortly afterward ready. I was rather surprised not to see the captain in his usual place, and soon every body was shocked to learn the cause of his absence.

He had to break to poor Mr. ——, the news of his young and lovely wife's almost sudden death! The electric telegraph had brought rapidly succeeding accounts, respecting her from New York, the first announcing her sudden and dangerous illness, the second to say she was worse, and the third to announce her death. This sad news was only brought on board a little before we started, and Captain A—— was charged with the painful office of breaking the heart-racking tidings. As the news of the death and illness were brought at the same time, there had been no previous preparation, and the captain vainly attempted at first to disguise the fatal character of the announcement he had to make. His trembling voice, and tell-tale looks betrayed him, and the unfortunate bereaved husband divined at once the whole extent of his misfortune.

Captain A—— told me, afterward, the scene was a most trying and terrible one. The wretched man stood as if petrified with horror, his eyes glaring and glazed, and fixed as in a trance. After he had stood rooted to the spot for some time in agonized silence, he repeated the word "dead" in the deep, hollow voice of the most profound despair; and it was the only word he uttered, or sign of life he showed, during the remainder of that day. Nor did he move his eyes, that constantly were fixed, with a wild, dreadful stare, on vacancy.

The captain said it was a most piteous sight to see, and he began to be really alarmed for his reason, when it became apparent that nothing could rouse him, and he still repeated, as if mechanically, at intervals, "dead! dead!" in the same tone of frozen horror. He was not left alone for a single moment, day or night, so alarming did his state appear.

This sad and utterly-unexpected misfortune cast quite a gloom over the ship. Poor man! he appeared to be a very devoted husband, and Mr. —— said he had seen a beautiful miniature of the deceased wife, which the unhappy man had always carried about with him, and that it was the portrait of a very lovely person indeed. But I will not dwell longer on such a melancholy theme.

There was on board a very ingenious American—I think, but am not quite sure, a New Englander—(it is the New Englanders that the Americans themselves call "Yankees"), who made, during the voyage, out of a common bit of wood, merely with his pen-knife, the most lovely and delicate little wooden chains imaginable, and other curiosities requiring the greatest skill and nicety of handling.

There was among the deck passengers an enterprising organ-grinder, who had resolved on being the pioneer of his profession in Mexico, and who expected to "Oh! Susanna-ize" and "Yankee-doodle-ize" the whole country. His speculation failed; and I was told he complained bitterly of the lamentable want of love for street music in the Mexicans, to which lack, on their part, he seemed to attribute the generally revolutionary state of the country, and their backwardness in the art of self-government. A deliciously hideous monkey accompanied him; but whether his diverting tricks—for he had of course, received a distinguished education—were equally unappreciated, I know not; or whether, if so, the musical speculator thought this indifference also helped to explain many defects in the working of the Mexican constitution, I can not pretend to say.

We had a rapid run from Mobile to this place, and arrived here about two hours after noon, in the most brilliant and beautiful weather imaginable. Every body was on the tiptoe of expectation when we passed the handsome lighthouse (La Farola) with General O'Donnel's name (under whose administration it was built), in immense characters on it.

The first glimpse of the Havana, from the entrance to the harbor, is remarkably picturesque, beautiful, and striking. The colossal palm-trees (the magnificent "Palma real") that tower majestically in the back-ground on the hills (seeming to gaze down like a guard of giants over the splendid city) form a glorious verdant sort of outer and partial frame-work for it, while the eye rests with delight on the nearer objects, especially on the crowded and beauteous harbor, so covered with shipping from every part of the civilized world, with the flags of every nation streaming on the soft breeze, and reflected on its calm and silvery waters.

The Morro Castle is exceedingly striking and imposing. This strong and formidable fortress is built on the solid rock, and almost appears to form a part of it, so steadfast and enduring seem its massive towers and walls and battlements, looking stern and gloomy as an old northern feudal fortress, notwithstanding a few light, plumy cocoa-nut palms cast their delicate shadows on the grass-covered banks near the stately castle.

The harbor is one of the very finest in the world, sufficiently deep for the largest vessels, and capacious enough to accommodate a fleet of a thousand ships, or more. There is a narrow entrance to this splendid harbor (from whose magnificence the city received the name of "La Havana"—as the harbor, *par excellence*, I believe—and yet I think the *present* Spanish word for harbor and haven is "puerto"). This entrance, indeed, is so narrow that only a single ship can enter at once, and it is fortified the whole length with strong works, platforms, and artillery. Opposite to the Morro Castle there is another fort, called the Puntal. This is connected with the city to the north. The Morro is built in a triangular form: it is fortified strongly with bastions, and mounted with many pieces of cannon, which are almost *à fleur d'eau*. The city itself stands on the western side of its noble harbor, and is extensively surrounded by ramparts, bastions, and trenches. In addition to the fortifications already enumerated, it is surmounted with works, which are all of them supplied with a vast profusion of artillery. I hear that they have been lately strengthening and improving the various formidable fortifications, in anticipation of a threatened visit from the Americans. The large fortress, called the Cabañas, stands near the Morro Castle, and covers a great deal of ground; numbers of soldiers were seen clambering up, or half-sliding down its steep sides.

We found the British steamer, bound for Jamaica, waiting for the "Thames." It was nearly evening before we landed, and found ourselves in a very comfortable American hotel, kept by Mr. Fulton, of New Orleans. We found Mr. Kennedy, who is now acting as consul in the absence of Mr. Crawford, obligingly waiting to see us. He told us Lord Durham was here, and very ill, having caught a fever at Jamaica; but Havana itself appears to be quite healthy just now. The heat, however, is very great and oppressive, though we are in one of the coolest and freshest houses within the city. We are very near the entrance to the harbor, and constantly a delightful refreshing breeze blows on our broad balcony, and through the enormous window-gates that open upon it. It is a pretty and interesting sight to watch the ships almost constantly entering or leaving the harbor.

I shall stay here a little while, I think, and see something of the Havana, in case any thing should prevent my return here after we have left our cards with the Pacific. It is an extraordinarily gay-looking town. Of course in the heat of the day no one thinks of stirring out who can help it. But when it begins to be cool, the city seems almost to shake with an earthquake of carriages, going in different directions, whose fair occupants are visit-paying, shopping, and so forth, usually ending with the *paséo;* and beautiful and fairy-like these carriages mostly are. They are called *volantes*, and are generally drawn by mules, driven by a postillion in some splendid livery.

We went out the other day, and I went a little way into the country—a very pretty drive, indeed. It was along a broad smooth road (what a luxury to us, after the road to Mexico!), bordered with a lovely hedge of roses and flowering pomegranates in their greatest beauty. We then went to the *paséo*, where carriages—multitudinous as musquitoes in Havana—swarmed in double lines, and all seemed like a fairy tale in action. Those graceful, aerial-looking, gayly-painted open *volantes*, like cars fit for Queen Mab, and the ethereal-seeming beings within, crowned with flowers, with no other covering on their gracious heads than these delicate blossoms, and their own massive braids of superb black hair—for very seldom did they even wear the mantilla, and when they did, its exquisitely-disposed folds seemed little else than the light shadow cast by those abundant waves of silky sable locks—all was enchantment.

How gracefully waved their fans, with which they fluttered light pretty salutations to each other!—those glistening feathery fans, like the wings of sylphides: and their dresses!—surely Arachne herself must have spun them, and Iris colored them! I will try and paint, in words, three of these fair daughters of Cuba, as they recline in their luxurious *volantes*. One is in a dress of the most sky-like azure; another in a diaphanous dreamy sort of robe, of the most gossamer texture, and of the softest yet brightest tint of rose-color; and the third (who sits forward in the middle) is in spotless lily white: and these dresses float light and full as very clouds about them. They are all *décolletée*, and with very short sleeves, and all are snow-pale, with statuesque features and magnificent hair.

There seem to be hundreds and thousands of these carriages,

with equally fair and fairy-like *damosels* within, and clad in every hue of the rainbow—lilac, emerald-green, the faintest strawy-yellow (that admirably suits with their generally jet-black locks), and various delicate tints and shades of all colors. The carriages themselves look like enormous butterflies glittering in the rays of the descending sun, with their innumerable, bright, varied colors.

Then, how beautiful are the long double rows of trees on either side of the *paséo*, and the flowers, and the exquisite sky above, and the splendid fountains, falling into sculptured marble basins; and how charming is the delicious temperature, and the soft breeze from the neighboring sea!

You do not see here, as in Mexico, hundreds of superbly-mounted *caballeros*, making their steeds champ, and prance, and *caracolear*, till their weighty silver ornaments flash like lightning on the eye. Here the gentlemen are generally pedestrian promenaders, if they are not lounging, stretched out in their luxurious *volantes* themselves. They walk leisurely and gently along, smoking the fragrant weed, and gazing at the fair Habaneras who are passing in their fairy coracles on wheels; and they tell me it is the fashion here, when a gallant señor sees some particularly lovely young doña, for him to exclaim—"How beautiful—how lovely!" and for her to reply, with a slight gracious inclination of her little stag-like head —"Gracias, caballero." I was not a little surprised, at first, at the answer the ladies make to the universally-employed salutation —"A los pies de V. señorita!" "Besos los manos de V. caballero!" (I am at your feet, madam!—I kiss your hands, sir!). But the dignified gentleness with which they say it, seemed to take off from the too great condescension apparently expressed. It was as superbly gracious as the bending of a crowned head in acknowledgment of a subject's homage.

There seems a great deal of alarm just now about the expected American invasion. It is rumored—but very likely falsely—that some of the troops are disaffected; and I am told that most of the troops sent here are from the dregs of the population in Spain, convicts and marauders of all kinds. The cavalry, however, are said to be a very fine body of men: as far as outward appearance goes, they *all* would seem to be so. The foot soldiers strike me as being much taller than our infantry regiments, and are exceedingly clean-looking and well-dressed.

There are reviews going on almost every day now, and military music abounds in Havana: it is rare not to hear the roll of drums and the flourish of trumpets. A military band plays every evening on the Grand Plaza. The best I have heard here is, I think, the Artillery band; but they all are good.

They have a large number of troops already in Cuba, and I believe they expect more very shortly. Rumors of every kind are rife, but one can place no faith in any of them. I believe only that Spain is most sincerely desirous of retaining this magnificent possession of hers—and well she may be. Not only its almost unequaled fertility and natural advantages, but its position, renders it a place of the very highest commercial and political importance. Its situation, commanding the entrance to the Mexican Gulf, and also the communication between North and South America, has caused it to be named "The Queen of the Antilles," "The Sentinel of the Mississippi," "The Key of the Gulf;" and its great beauty and luxuriance have acquired for it the denomination of "The gem of the American Seas." "The Beautiful Antille," "The Pearl of the Islands," and other admiring designations.

When we first arrived here, how natural seemed the loving exclamations and remarks of returning "Habaneros," who, bending over the guards of the steamer, uttered ejaculatory expressions of delight as we neared the enchanting shores:—"O! que escenas tan hermosas. El cielo sin nubes, y la mar tan serena, y el sol tan brilliante." "Si! y las florestas tan deliciosas! Y esa verdura eterna de la hermosissima isla." "Mira V. que multitud de barcos, bergantines y goletas y fregatas y paquetes y—hombre, que multitud!" "Si! y mil banderas y banderolas de variados colores y de todas las naciones! Y que vista tan hermosa ofrece la ciudad desde el puerto. Mire V.! á fé mia, no se ha visto cosa mas bella!" and so on.

We have been to see the cathedral here, which is extremely interesting, from being the burial-place of Columbus. It is not as magnificent as the cathedral in Mexico, but it is a noble building. On the right side of the grand altar is an urn, containing those precious ashes: it is inclosed in the wall. A fine basso-relievo is placed before it, of the bust of that mighty Discoverer. This bust is the size of life, and under it is read the following inscription:—"O restos é imagen del grande Colon, mil siglos durad guardados en la urna. Y en la remembrancia de nuestra nacion." There is a small, but very interesting and beautiful painting opposite to the tomb, which is said to represent the Pope and the Cardinals of that day, celebrating High mass previous to the departure of Columbus from the shores of Spain, on his first adventurous and momentous expedition in his humble "caraval."

Columbus has not had as much rest even in the grave as falls to the lot of most mortals; for his relics have been moved from tomb to tomb. He died in Valladolid, in Spain, in the year 1506, and a tomb was there erected to his memory, and inscribed thus:—"A Castillo y a Leon Nuevo Mundo dio Colon" (in Spanish he is called "Cristoval Colon"). The place in which the body was deposited was the Convent of San Francisco, in Valladolid, and the funeral ceremonies were celebrated with great pomp in the parochial church of Santa Maria de la Antigua; but in 1513, his remains were removed to the convent of Las Cuevas, of the Carthusians, at Seville, and they were deposited in the chapel of Santa Christo. It was in the year 1536 they were transported to Hispaniola, and they were there inhumed near the grand altar of the cathedral of the capital city of San Domingo; but they were not destined to repose there in uninterrupted peace. After Hispaniola was ceded to France in 1795, the Spanish government came to the resolution of carrying off these venerable relics to the Island of Cuba; nor can one feel surprise at such a determination when reflecting on all that Spain owed and still owes to that wonderful man. They may well feel proud of these precious relics, connected—as Washington Irving says, in his highly interesting "Life of Columbus"—"with the most glorious epoch of Spanish history."

Let me transcribe a little of his impressive account:—"Accordingly, on the 20th of December 1795, in the presence of an august assemblage of the dignitaries of the Church, and the civil and military officers, the vault was opened beside the high altar of the cathedral: within were found the fragments of a leaden coffin, a number of bones, and a quantity of mould, evidently the remains of a human body. These were carefully collected and put into a case of gilded lead, secured by an iron lock. The case was enclosed in a coffin covered with black velvet, and the whole placed in a temporary mausoleum. On the following day there was another grand convocation at the cathedral. The vigils and masses for the dead were chanted, and a funeral sermon was preached by the archbishop. After these solemn ceremonials in the cathedral, the coffin was transported to the ship, attended by a grand civil, religious, and military procession. The banners were covered with crape. There were chants, and responses, and discharges of artillery, and the most distinguished persons of the several orders took turns to support the coffin.

"The reception of the body at Havana was equally august.

There was a splendid procession of boats to conduct it from the ship to the shore. On passing the vessels of war in the harbor, they all paid the honors due to an admiral and captain-general of the navy. On arriving at the mole, the remains were met by the governor of the island, accompanied by the generals of the military staff. They were then conveyed, in the utmost pomp, to the cathedral. Masses, and the solemn ceremonies of the dead were performed by the bishop, and the mortal remains of Columbus were deposited in the wall on the right side of the grand altar, where they still remain."

It is hardly possible, I think, to avoid feeling profoundly interested and affected on looking at the spot, that little spot, where the ashes of the mighty man repose who gave the vast world of the wild far West to the East; and to the West—Heaven: for he bade the great Star of the East, the star of holy religion and blessed Christianity, to shed its glorious rays on that benighted and unconscious West.

There were but a very few people in the cathedral to disturb or distract the deep feeling of reverence with which we regarded that hallowed tomb. One or two kneeling figures of women, silently and fervently praying, only added to the solemnity of the scene. It is a touching and sweet custom in Cuba for all, without the least distinction of color or class, to kneel together on the floor of the churches. You will see a fair señora, splendidly dressed, kneeling on her piece of carpet (carried to the church by her little negro page), and by her side, perhaps, a negro bends his head, grizzled with age, in prayer; or a negress, attired in the most gaudy colors of scarlet, blue, and yellow, uplifts her jet-black hands in silent supplication.

We have been to see the bishop's palace-gardens, now belonging to the Condé de Peñalver. The Condé is restoring them to all their pristine beauty, for they had lately been much neglected. There are great numbers of fine mangoes here, and pleasant is it walking in the shadowy alleys which they form. There are also some beauteous bread-fruit trees, whose large and deeply indented leaves I most particularly admire.

A splendid India-rubber tree attracted our attention much. Mr. C—— (Lord L——'s brother), who went with us, broke off a branch, and the liquid India-rubber oozed out plentifully, and covered his hands, sticking his fingers together in an uncomfortable fashion, as if he had been washing his hands in a jar of treacle.

An unfortunate crocodile pines in solitude in these gardens, that is to say, without any of his own kith and kin to soothe his weary hours. Various animals—some rare ones—are confined in that part of the grounds; there are some ornamental pieces of water there, covered with splendid lilies of a beautiful rose color; and the glorious ceiba, and the fair royal palm of Cuba, stand like rival monarchs of the vegetable world. The flowers, of course, were almost without number in this beauteous place.

Besides this delightful possession, the Condé has a splendid house in the city, in which, I hear, there is a *boudoir* representing the apartment of a mandarin and mandariness in far Pekin, which is declared to be in the *Chinesest* taste imaginable, and more Pekinish than the Chinese junk itself.

We have seen several traces of the last violent hurricane here. The most complete ruin is that of an unfinished opera-house of the most magnificent dimensions: it remains there still in its fragmentary state, encumbering the ground, waiting for an enterprising speculator to repair the damage and finish it, or perhaps for another hurricane to act the part of squatter, and make a complete *clearing*. It is a superstition among the more ignorant classes in Havana, that in consequence of turning a church dedicated to San Francisco (who, it seems, is the patron saint of hurricanes) into a tobacco warehouse or something of that kind, the island will be visited by a succession of hurricanes, the last of which will destroy Havana entirely, and sweep it from the face of the earth. It is said several have already taken place on San Francisco's day.

The streets are exceedingly narrow here, and the *volantes*, with their immensely long shafts and enormous wheels, turn in them with the greatest difficulty, but luckily they do not easily overturn. In the suburbs the streets are wider. A single *volante* stopping will sometimes block up a whole *calle*. The *calesero* is urged, perhaps, by some other driver behind to let him pass, but it is not always this is conceded by the fair Creoles in the carriage; at least so says La Condesa de Merlin, in her amusing "Viaje á la Habana." Often, she tells us, is a feminine voice heard from the depths of *quitrin* or *volante*, crying, "No te muevas, Juan, no te muevas por nadie!"

They keep, in rich families, one *volante*, at least, constantly waiting, all ready, at the door, in case any of the members of the family should take a sudden fancy for a little drive; and in many, wealthy establishments, each daughter—nay, each child—has her own *volante!* Among the poorer classes (and poor they must be, indeed, if they do not indulge themselves with one carriage at least) it is constantly the custom, from want of the necessary space and building, to turn a corner of the drawing-room into a coach-house. In fact, I was told they consider a handsome *volante* (and rather than not have a handsome one they would half-starve themselves on a little chocolate and a *cigarito*) a really great ornament to their not otherwise much-furnished rooms. It looks very conspicuous and very stately with its gigantic wheels, and it is occasionally used, I am informed, as a sort of elevated and sociable arm-chair by two, or perhaps three, of the ladies of the house when the rooms are particularly full; and thus, raised as it were on a silver embossed throne above their guests, they chat with them condescendingly, and survey them complacently from an advantageous position.

I have never witnessed this little domestic enthronization myself, but we have frequently seen the *volante* standing like any other piece of furniture in the drawing-room, as we walked or drove by. It is impossible not to see into their sitting-rooms: they are on the ground-floors. Havana houses are generally extremely low—I suppose on account of the hurricanes—and in the less magnificent mansions such a sight, as I said before, is quite common.

These apartments, in general, have a great resemblance to each other; large, cool, and with little furniture except a number of rocking-chairs, which are called here *butacas*. On these, softly balancing themselves backward and forward, will be seen usually the ladies of the family, their perpetual-motion fans in their white hands—those never-to-be-forgotten or dispensed-with fans, which they agitate *cadenciosamente*, and with the utmost grace.

It may perchance be a *tertulia* that you look upon: the great doors are thrown open *de par en par*. Numerous lights are blazing in beautiful candelabras of glass or alabaster; flowers are profusely scattered about in lovely vases of porcelain and silver, and enormous *faroles*—a species of splendid lantern, which sheds the most dazzling light—are illuminating the recesses of the spacious apartments, and the broad corridors, and large balconies, where groups of men may be seen talking together, or admiring the beautiful array of ladies seated in the grand *sala*.

They seem to have a pleasant custom here of rising from the dinner-table after the *segundo servicio*. And during the time occupied in making a complete change of decorations, they take a *paséo*—a little promenade—for a quarter of an hour or some minutes, in the enormous galleries (furnished with green *jalousies* to exclude every ray of the sun, and in which, during the hottest season, they usually dine) or in the beautiful gardens under the shadowy coolness of the interlacing bowers and avenues.

On their return to the banqueting-room, they find an immense profusion of crystal, alabaster, or porcelain vases, and *canastillas* (small baskets) of silver, loaded with a vast variety of fruits. "Mameys" which, says Madame de Merlin, are "Alimento de las almas bienaventuradas en los valles del otro mundo, segun la creencia de los habitantes de Haiti," and the "zapatillas suaves," which she declares have a "gusto silvestre." Then there are *tunas*—a very handsome fruit of a lovely rose-color, about the size of a small pine-apple, the inside of which is excellent, and all of it eatable: it looks like the most delicate royal ermine—with the tiniest little black tags—whipped ermine!—almost beaten to a soft creamy froth. This fruit is reckoned remarkably wholesome, and is so good that the "almas bienaventuradas" would do well to add it to their *mameys*. Then there are *guayavas*, and hosts of others.

Besides fruits of almost innumerable kinds, and sizes, and shapes, there are crowds of light silver dishes, and *bandejas* or *dulces*—which mean all kinds of sweets (*dulces variados hasta lo infinito*); and the table, the borders of the dishes, even the glasses, are wreathed, and covered, and almost buried in flowers. This change is like the work of magic: the most delicious perfumes chase away even the faintest smell of meat, and the eye reposes itself on a rainbow-colored wilderness of blossoms mixed with the most tempting and the choicest fruits. Enormous doors, or rather *puerta-ventanas* (doors and windows in one), are opened on the balconies, and gigantic windows besides, perhaps lightly draperied with muslin (and during the day-time shaded with *persianas*—Venetian blinds) to exclude the tropical sun's scorching beams, are thrown wide open, and through them the soft zephyr passes, and the refreshing, cooling sound and sight of the glittering fountains.

The best time for flowers in Cuba is the winter—if winter it can be called. They then abound in all their richest beauty. In the summer the intense heat of the sun withers them up.

## CHAPTER XXXVI.

Performance of a Military Band in the Grand Square—The Diversified Company—Description of Havana Nights—The Opera-house—The Singers—Exhortation to Spanish Ladies to preserve their National Dress—An Execution—Material Prosperity of Havana—"Jesus del Monte"—Dinner with the Captain-General—The Company—Escort of the Conde—Preparations for the Isthmus Journey—A Tertulia—Miss M——'s exquisite Playing and Singing—The Environs of Havana—The Paséo of Ysabel Segunda—Environs of Havana in the Evening—"Guagiros"—Description of their Houses—Customs and dress of the "Guagiros"—Chinese Laborers in Havana—Anecdote of Chinese Thieves—Preparing to depart for Panama.

We went to hear the military band play last evening in the Grand Square: it was a splendid band, and played several opera airs beautifully. Many ladies were walking up and down, generally attended by *caballeros;* but the greater part of the *distinguées Habaneras* were in their *volantes*, each fair señorita looking like the *Reine des fées*, crowned with flowers. The *muchedumbre* (mob or crowd) were standing about, evidently enjoying the music; the negroes, and their sable dames and damsels, especially appear to delight in it. The whole scene is one of great beauty and enchantment: the lovely trees in the Grand Plaza, the magnificent crystal sun of the night—that crown of glory—(which is so unlike that tame somewhat half-a-crown-like silver lamp, we call the moon, in our little northern nook), the flower-crowned ladies in those fairy chariots, sparkling with silver—the splendid liveries of the postillions—the gay military uniforms—the picturesque-looking negroes and negresses standing about (or sometimes dancing in their glee to the exhilarating tunes that are played), the negresses occasionally in white dresses, scarlet satin shoes, yellow turbans, and blue scarfs, and various other such fantastical combinations of colors, with their great flaming eyes, *á la flor de la cara*—all unite to form a delightful and singular picture.

How true is this description of an Havana night by a charming writer: "La noche es aqui tan deliciosa!—qué transparencia! qué grandeza en este cielo resplandeciente de estrellas y de meteoros!—cómo penetra en los poros abiertos por el calor el soplo tibio de la brisa de tierra embalsamada con todos los perfumes de la vegetacion. El aire fresco de la tarde reemplaza al calor sofocante del dia bajo un cielo tan claro como si el disco de la luna lo ocupase todo."

We have been to the opera, which is very good here indeed. The Tacon Theatre (the Opera-house) is beautiful. Mrs. T——, with whom I have had the pleasure to make acquaintance here, was so good as to invite us to go with her. Her box was an excellent one, and we saw and heard to perfection. The interior of this theatre, which is very large, is exquisitely light and graceful, and beautifully decorated: the boxes are only separated by a slight railing, and there is another gilded railing in front of them. The whole has the most cool, aerial, and brilliant appearance imaginable, and reminded me a little of a vast and most magnificent saloon I had seen in one of the palaces of the Sultan at Constantinople

The opera was the "Huguenots;" it was admirably got up and put on the stage. Steffanoni and Bosio were the chief female singers, and the men were Salvi and Marini, &c. Salvi sang quite splendidly. After the opera, Signora Bosio came on the stage, dressed like a "Madrileña" (it was her benefit), and sang some Spanish airs exquisitely, in the true piquant Spanish style: the songs were interrupted by spoken remarks, and almost convulsed the audience with laughter. Among other things, she appeared (in a pretty *patois*) to be recommending the Spanish mantilla and dress to universal use, and to be abusing the French fashions most unmercifully, in the drollest and quaintest manner, her arms akimbo, and yet looking as graceful as possible.

And how right the "Madrileña" was! What can be so beautiful as that loveliest of costumes? The Spanish ladies should take care what they are doing. If there are to be "no Pyrenees" in the matters of dress, will not "the ladies of Spain" lose their greatest, most characteristic, and peculiar of charms? Such a macadamization of costumes to one insipid sameness, as seems ever to be gaining ground, in defiance of the difference of climate, customs, and other regulating circumstances, will make the world a trifle more trite and stupid than it is at present; but I hope the masses will generally have the good sense to retain their beautiful old dresses. What an unintentional dissertation! "Annotations and reflections" on Signora Bosio's lively sóng! By the way, both at Mexico and here, the mere appearance of the beauteous Spanish costume was alone enough to draw forth ardent applause!

The Habaneros seem to form an enthusiastic audience, and to

be possessed of great good taste and discrimination. The fair Habaneras look particularly well at the opera: we saw some extremely handsome ones, with the whitest of skins, and the blackest of hair. In these light gilded boxes they look like hundreds of Peris in magnificent cages, fluttering their fans, as though about to escape. This incessant movement of nearly innumerable fans makes the vast airy house seem as if it was hovering on ten thousand waving wings, and on the point of soaring away to mix among those *gigantescas nubes* (huge clouds) so well described by the authoress I have already quoted, when she says, "Como se balancean en el aire las nubes gigantescas adornadas de ópalos y de rubies," when from time to time large gauzy splendid luminous vapors float on this resplendent atmosphere.

We drove to the opera, and returned in an open *volante* (one of Mrs. T——'s). The air was so deliciously warm, yet fresh and not suffocating, that on coming out of the house it seemed to be hotter than it was within. Soldiers are stationed round the theatre to keep order, and the crowds of *volantes* rush off with the utmost regularity.

There was an execution here the other day. The criminal was a Spaniard; the crime, murder; and he has confessed, since his detection and imprisonment, a large number of assassinations that he had committed previously. He made a public declaration before he was *garottéd*, stating that all his wickedness was caused by the early desertion of his parents, and his total want of education. Mr. C—— went to see the execution. We passed the place by chance where it was to take place, the evening before, and there was already a large throng of persons collected to see the dreadful spectacle; so they seem as fond of such horrors in this land of flowers and sunshine, as the citizens of smoky, dusky London.

Havana is brilliantly lighted with gas: when there is a moon, however, the gas is not lighted, as it would be indeed quite a work of supererogation. There are American omnibuses that run regularly to the Cerro, and the other suburbs. The Americans (they tell me) take the lead always in commencing these improvements, and after being for a while in leading strings under their tuition, the citizens of Havana take the management of these affairs into their own hands.

No city can well give one an idea of greater material prosperity than the Havana. The numbers of beautiful shops, teeming with every article of luxury, grace, and convenience; the magnificent palaces and *quintas* (country houses) in the neighborhood; the splendor and opulence visible on all sides; the brilliancy and costliness of the countless thousands of equipages, hurrying hither and thither on errands of pleasure and business—all make this appear, as I believe it is, one of the most flourishing and wealthy cities in the world.

As to the carriages they seem literally running over one another. I have before said that I had heard every daughter in a rich family has her own special *volanta*, and I see this is more than corroborated by the Condesa de Merlin. She says, "acqui cada individuo de la familia hasta los ninos, tiene su volanta."

We went up to Jesus del Monte, the other day, to see Miss Inglis, sister of Madame C. de la B——. She appears to be a charming person, and is much liked and admired here: her blonde *chevelure* and blue eyes, make her a great contrast to the dark-eyed Habaneras in general. She is staying with a cousin at Jesus del Monte (it is a sort of suburb of Havana, and is situated on a height, with beautiful views and cool country air). They have a delightful house there, and it is an easy distance from the capital. The road to and from this place is lovely, bordered on each side with roses and pomegranates.

We dined with the Captain-General and the Condesa de Alcoy, the other night. With the exception of Mr. K——, the judge, and Mr. C——, the guests were all Spanish and Habanese. The Conde speaks French fluently, but the Condesa and her daughter know no language but Spanish; so I was obliged to talk Spanish as well as I could, which is very indifferently indeed. The banquet was very splendid.

The palace is magnificent. There is a large full-length portrait of Queen Ysabel Segunda, in one of the enormous lofty rooms, which represents her as very interesting-looking and pretty: the Condesa says she is exceedingly improved in looks lately. During the dinner an immense number of slaves waited behind the guests' chairs (here they did not rise between the courses, as we are told they do in Creole families); and when the dessert was over, all rose at once, and repaired to the large balconied drawing-rooms for chocolate and coffee. Behind her chair, at dinner, the Condesa had a little Chinese page-in-waiting, attired in the complete dress of the scorners of outer barbarians. This costume was made of the richest materials, and looked extremely handsome.

After dinner, a kind of reception, or *tertulia*, took place. The ladies were all ranged in a formal semicircle. I sate next to the

Condesa; and a French lady, who could not speak a syllable of Spanish, sate on the other side of her. However, the Conde and some of the gentlemen who spoke French, conversed with her, and the evening passed away very pleasantly altogether.

We returned home, as usual, in an open *volanta*, after staying a little while in the Grand Plaza, to hear the band. When the Conde drives out, it is always with a gallant escort of lancers. He has an open carriage that looks like one of Parisian manufacture, and the Condesa and Mademoiselle de Roncali always appear in bonnets that seem fresh from Paris, thus discarding the beautiful Spanish *mantilla* entirely.

General C——, the American Consul here—a very gentlemanlike and distinguished person, whose acquaintance I have lately made—has kindly offered to arrange about my passage for me, and I am busily preparing for our Isthmus journey. We have to take provisions, get riding-dresses, &c., and as the steamer stays a very short time when she does arrive, it is necessary that we should be *quite* ready.

To-day it is very hot, and the least exertion fatigues one; notwithstanding, there is a charming breeze from the sea, and this hotel is in a very cool situation. I can not describe how enchantingly cool the palace is: with its enormous galleries and corridors of white marble, and immense halls and *salas*, I should think they could never find it too hot there. In the hottest day it must be like those *ice-caves* where Winter reigns, while Summer is reveling in all her splendor within a few feet of him. I was so sorry when I heard, after we had *left* New Haven, that one of these extraordinary caves is to be seen very near that city. There is another, I believe, in Georgia.

We have been to a little *tertulia* at Mrs. M——'s. The flowers there were inexpressibly delicious and lovely, and so was the music. I never heard such magnificent playing on the pianoforte but once, as Miss M——'s. Her execution is perfectly prodigious; but in addition to that she seems to have a soul at every one of her fingers' ends—and a seraph's soul to boot. The strength and power with which she touches the instrument is wonderful. The whole performance indeed is quite magical, and when one looks at the delicate, *svelte*, sylph-like figure of the young lady, you can hardly believe it was she who called forth the volume of sound that you heard.

Miss M—— sang a French song afterward, beautifully: but, in consequence of a delicacy of chest, from over-exertion of the voice in practicing, she is not allowed to sing often, and only songs that do not try the voice much. The exquisite feeling, grace, and marvelous delicacy of execution with which she sang that little *romanza*, made one regret deeply that imperious necessity forced her to abstain from further exercise of her charming vocal powers. Miss M——speaks but little English, and that with a pretty French accent, though her father is English. Her mother is French. I believe, from living at Havana, she speaks Spanish like a native.

In the large Creole houses here, that I have seen, I observe in the chief *sala* a sort of canopy over a sofa at the head of the room, where the mistress of the house sits with perhaps one or two distinguished guests. The rest are seated on chairs, either in a semi-circle, or in a double line, like a living human avenue.

We had a delightful drive the other day in the environs of Havana. We first went to see Mrs. C——, the lady of the American Consul. Their house is large, and very pleasant; the marble floors, with here and there a pretty mat, look charmingly cool. We then went to see different views of the city, which are all beautiful. We drove through the lovely Paséo de Tacon, and admired its immense length, and splendid fountains, and statues.

The Paséo of Ysabel Segunda, is also a very charming one; and ladies and children are sometimes seen promenading under its umbrageous and flower-besprinkled alleys, which is rare in Havana, for hardly ever does a señora's foot—the lovely Spanish "foot of fire"—touch the earth in this be-carriaged and luxurious place. The different roads around the capital, in the evening, are generally alive with people hurrying on business, or driving leisurely and loungingly along, enjoying the *dolce far niente*, which is indeed to be indulged in to perfection at the Havana. Now you meet a *quitrin* or *volanta*, or two and three together, filled with ladies, and now a *hacendado* (planter) returning from his estate, perhaps, near the capital, *cigarito* in mouth, and looking as if life was as full of sweets for him as his land is of sugar; and now it is a knot of *guagiros*, or *monteros*, coming on some errand to the city or the suburbs. These are a peculiar race in Cuba, and it is said, retain many of the distinguishing characteristics of the ancient Indian race, to whom Cuba once belonged. His humble but picturesque house is probably exactly what, in former times, was that of the aborigines. Light trees of the same height are driven fast into the ground, and form a perfect square. But the following description is excellent: "Y formando un quadrado perfecto sustentan por su extrémidad una especie de red de bambues que colocados transversalmente crecen y son atados á los arboles con lianas ó enredaderas, el techo se cubre con hojas de palmera, y se llama guaño."

These palm-leaf-covered roofs are very light and cool, and they look truly graceful. For the work of building this primitive habitation, the *guagiros* call in the assistance of their neighbors, as they do in erecting the log-houses in Canada (which they call summoning a *bee*) in a day at the longest: it is done with the help of the *vecinos.* They then have a rude house-warming (which sounds terrible, however, in Cuba!) A sucking-pig is cooked, and the feast is devoured right merrily.

Afterward, "forman por medio de tabiques" (these light thin walls are formed of canes), "tres habitaciones iguales, la de en medio es la sala en las otros dos, duerme la familia. Los tabiques se cubren de corteza de palmera, que destinada á este uso, toma el nombre de *yagua.*" The house is finished entirely in two or three days. There are two *puertas,* but no windows. These *puertas* are also formed of the bark of the palm trees, *yagua.* "Y," continues the account, "no estan unidas al edificio sino por la parte superior, de manera que se abren perpendicularmente, y permanecen suspendidas por medio de una vara de hierro que las sostiene en el aire durante el dia." At night this bar of iron serves to fasten the doors with.

Generally, in front of this picturesque and rural abode there is another *cabaña,* of two departments, one of which is used as a kennel and stable during the continuance of the rainy season, and the other is the kitchen—a very simple one. If you go in you will see a confusion indeed, "en el fondo de la cocina y puestas junto á la pared, estan colocados tres enormes piedras que sirven de hornillas encima una olla—y alrededor del fuego bananas buniatos y papas en profusion." Besides, there are chairs, stools, cups of the humblest materials, earthen dishes, dogs, birds, chickens, people reposing on the rough table or floor, birds'-nests full of eggs depending from the bamboos, and a tremendous mastiff, that growls frightfully, and shows his teeth threateningly, if a leaf falls.

This rural lodge is surrounded by magnificent trees which a king might envy, loaded with the most exquisite fruits, some of enormous size—the *papayo* and *plátano*—with their huge leaves, the *alcanforero,* and the beautiful *arbol del pan,* that might feed a whole regiment in a time of famine; the odoriferous *vanilla,* and thousands of cactuses in flower, coiled and *enlazados graciosamente*, with a profusion of hanging plants, that unite the roofs of the *cabañas* with the stately trees, and shut out the piercing rays of the dazzling sun.

These *establecimientos de los guagiros* are not ordinarily destined for a long continuance. They frequently abandon the spot they had thus selected, and transport their *penates* to some other place. They again construct a rude but graceful habitation in a few days: *y siembran en seguida las legumbres;* and wherever they fix themselves they find the same marvelous riches of Nature ready to surround and adorn their homes. However simple their *cabañas* may be, the *entourage* is worthy of an imperial palace.

Sometimes the *guagiro* takes a piece of ground that belongs to nobody, and in general he prefers this; but if he is particularly pleased with a bit of land that already has a *dueño* (a master), conditions are then entered into, as in Europe. I should think, however, he must have less and less opportunities of doing this in this highly cultivated and flourishing island. The *cosechas* (crops) are wonderfully abundant, and, with very little care, this fertile soil will produce *muchas cosechas* in the year. The beasts in Cuba are generally fed on *maloja* (I think this is exactly the same as Guina-grass), and on maize; and the *guagiros* generally provide this for the great proprietors and planters.

The wives and daughters of the *guagiros* make "sombreros de paja y de las cuerdas de majagua," and this forms their chief or only occupation. They have always a slave, however moderate may be their means, to do all the household work. They say these *guagiros* are very chivalrous husbands, and may often be seen carrying themselves the *tapete* (small square carpet) to church, for their wives to kneel upon.

The *guagiro* is quite a *dandy* with regard to his appearance. His mornings are generally passed at the cock-fights—which are as popular here almost as in Mexico—and his evenings in dancing or singing to his guitar, if unmarried, generally before the *estancia* of his lady-love. He is, in his own way, a poet and a hero too; and if by chance he should encounter a rival *guitarrero*, singing sonnets to his *querida*, a duel with their knives, takes place on the spot. If he receives a wound, he springs on his gallant horse, and darts through the *cañaverales* (the cane-plantations), and hurries away to seek a chirurgeon, that he may appear next day at the accustomed spot again, to defy his rival, and prance and *caracolear*, guitar in hand, before his *amada*.

The *corcel* has his bridle generally adorned with numerous knots of bright-colored wool, and the *frontil* has the same ornaments. He himself has a *sombrero de paja*, with an immense brim. A brilliantly-colored scarf is tied round his waist, with the ends floating, *zapatos de tafilete* (morocco leather shoes) of some gay color, with silver spurs: from his beautifully-embroidered *cinturon* (belt) hangs his *machete*, with a silver hilt encrusted with precious stones, and there, too, is his dagger with its ebony handle. When on business he is not ashamed to carry a sack fastened to his shoulders, and when on a pleasure-excursion, on the saddle of the horse you may spy the *guitarra* and the *quitasal* of his fair *señorita*, the amiable *guagira*.

On his business-expeditions he goes from place to place, to *Ingenio* and *Cafetal*, to sell his fruits and collect his money. Then he returns to eat an excellent dinner, and to smoke the most exquisite "cigarros elaborados por so mujer ó por su querida. His horse and his *machete* (after the *querida* and *mujer*, we will hope) are his greatest treasures. The *machete* is not only an indispensable weapon of defense against robbers, rivals, &c., but is the article in which he exhibits his chief luxury and splendor, and his *corcel* is also very necessary to him in this *vida vagabunda* in which he delights, and is often an object almost of adoration to him. But the reader will be tired of *guagiros*.

There are many Chinese laborers here now, and they are said to work very hard and well. Why do they not try them in Jamaica? It is said the Coolies have failed there. I was amused at an anecdote concerning the Chinese, that Captain A——, told me the other day. It occurred when he was on the coast of China in a merchantman—I think at Canton. The ship was constantly robbed at night, by very expert—not house-breakers, certainly, but ship-breakers, I must call them. The weather was exceedingly hot and close, and it was necessary to leave the port-holes open for air. The cunning Chinese *ladrones* availed themselves of this circumstance, and introduced themselves into the apertures by night, very adroitly and silently. Their toilet, it appears, was of the most primitive possible description, and consisted wholly and solely of a copious supply of oil to lubricate their bodies. They thus made themselves as slippery as eels, and if detected, eluded the grasp of the victimized mariners, and plunged back into the water. Their long tails (which would otherwise have afforded capital handles) were abundantly provided with fish-hooks, sharp knives, pins, nails, &c.—in short they were made quite a *chevaux de frise* in order that any one seizing them should rapidly let them go again.

One of those *sharp sharpers* paid a visit one night to the cabin of a young officer, who woke, and despite of oil and fish-hooks, took a good gripe at the interloper and held on like grim death with one hand, while with the other, armed with a stout cutlass, or some weapon of the kind, he actually inflicted the grim death aforesaid on the rascally son of the flowery central land, who thus like a celéstial Paul Pry, had dropped in literally in the cool of the evening. The officer flung the body into the sea, and it was found afterward by the indignant Chinese, and a mighty hubbub was raised. It was discovered by some means, or at any rate shrewdly suspected, that the act had been committed on board the merchant ship, and the mandarins insisted that the offender should be given up to them. It happened that the butcher of the ship, at this juncture, committed suicide. They bethought themselves of dressing him up in the officer's clothes, and formally exhibited the body to the mandarins, who were invited on board—peacock-feathers, buttons, and all. The mandarins were informed that the unfortunate officer, struck with remorse, had put an end to his existence. But our good friend, John Chinaman, was not to be thus easily imposed upon. He declined putting any faith in the outer barbarians' bare assertions, and proceeded to examine the corpse. Immediately that the mandarins noticed the hands of the deceased Knight of the Cleaver, they exclaimed that those were not the hands of an officer, and demanded that the real offender should be forthwith produced. With great difficulty the young man was secreted, and his life preserved from the vengeance of the Celestials.

I intend to leave a trunk here, with all the things I set most value on, for fear of accidents on the Isthmus, and to take as little luggage as possible, as on such expeditions it is very inconvenient: "Ojalá hubiese empezado antes ésta reformá." There is a report that the "Georgia" is in sight. I shall not see much of the Havana this time, but I hope to visit it again on my return; it is so interesting and beautiful an island.

I must go and take leave of my American acquaintance, Mrs. ——. She is going with her husband and little girl back to the United States. They have taken passages on board the "Ysabel Segunda," and they fear she will be very crowded, as they find the Italian operatic company are going by the same steamer, on their way to New York, where they are going to perform. Mrs. —— is in very delicate health, suffering from that fell disorder, so common in the United States, consumption. She came to Havana by medical advice, and great numbers of Americans come here annually on the same account. I hear that many go also to Jamaica and to Santa Cruz. Mrs. W——, another American lady who was staying at this hotel, and with whom I have become acquainted, is just gone to make a tour of the island. She sings beautifully, and her little daughter is extraordinarily handsome; she has lived a great deal in Europe, chiefly in Italy. I have heard since her departure, that she is anxious to introduce some improvements in the railroads here, which are of *her own* invention.

The "Georgia" has arrived. We shall have but little time now to make any further preparations. *Tanto mejor*, for as long as one has time one fancies something may be better arranged, or is requisite. General C—— has kindly called to tell me he is going on board the "Georgia" this morning, and will do all he can to arrange for us to go, but she is expected to be very full. She is a magnificent vessel of about three thousand tons.

When these enormous American steamers first came to Havana, there was a report that it was doubtful whether they could get in through the narrow entrance to the harbor; however, that was found to be of easy accomplishment. The "Georgia" is said to be a very fast vessel, with excellent accommodations, and a most gentlemanlike captain. We take leave of this delightful hotel with regret. Mr. Fulton, the excellent proprietor, has spared no pains to render us as comfortable as possible. Chloe is very unhappy to part with the "lilly missy," as she calls her in her broken English, and her picturesque jet black daughter (a girl of about fourteen), whose name is "Lily," is very sorry, too, for V—— and she were great friends, and equally devoted to a huge and very magnificent macaw (which, however, I think is more like Madame Calderon s description of the Huacamaya than a macaw). This splendid creature Lily is constantly seen carrying on the top of her sable woolly head, like a most stately and dazzling helmet: a very uncomfortable head-dress, I should think, inasmuch as it was perpetually biting at her wool (that did not matter, it was so thick), but her forehead came in sometimes for a snap; and then the *cap did not fit*, and occasionally the creature half fell, and struggled on again with many flutterings and clawings—but Lily only laughed the more, and showed her lightning-like white teeth.

## CHAPTER XXXVII.

Arrival at Panama—The "Georgia"—Kindness and Attention of Lieutenant Porter—Deficiency of Fresh Water—An Alarm on Board—Its Cause—Bustle of Preparation to land at Chagres—The stout Lady and her Trunk—Arrival at Chagres—Polished Manners of American Gentlemen—The Bar of Chagres—Difficulty of landing and of procuring Lodgings—Apartments at Señor ——'s—General Aspect of Chagres—The Castle of San Lorenzo—Its present Condition—Population of Chagres—Adventurers to California—Start for Gorgona.

We have arrived at Panama in perfect safety, and the glorious Pacific, that mightiest world of waters, is at this moment rolling its majestic waves under my windows as I write. I must give an account, as well as I can, of our voyage and journey.

Through General C——'s kind offices every thing was most comfortably and delightfully arranged for us on board the magnificent steamer "Georgia," and through his considerate attention and kindness I had also the advantage and comfort of an agreeable acquaintance with an amiable American lady on board, who was going with her little boy to join her husband in California.

This steamer is commanded by an officer of the United States navy, Lieutenant Porter, son of the celebrated Commodore Porter. It is impossible any where to meet with a more perfect, high-bred, and finished gentlemen than Lieutenant Porter. He seemed indefatigable in his kind endeavors to render the passengers comfortable, and his courteous attentions to all could not be too highly praised. There was an immense number of passengers altogether, chiefly deck passengers, *en route* to California (report said thirteen hundred, but I believe that was a little exaggeration), and yet every thing was conducted with as much order and regularity, and the ship was as perfectly quiet as if there had only been thirty. Our cabins were large, and exceedingly commodious and particularly nicely furnished. Muslins embroidered with different rich patterns and colors, formed the blinds and curtains to the berth; they had a very cool and pretty effect. There were also green *jalousies* to the windows. We had a capital Welsh stewardess, a most civil and attentive one; and the steward was the very person for that arduous office.

The first day we dined in the saloon; but it was very hot, in consequence of its being necessary to have lighted candles there, even in the broadest day-light. The rest of the time we dined in our cabins, where it was very pleasantly cool, considering the state of the atmosphere. An acquaintance of Mrs. H——, a very stout lady, seemed to suffer much from the heat of the weather, but did not appear to become in the least thinner in consequence; and yet she seemed to live only on air, and that air was only what her fan procured for her. She was a very good-humored and pleasing person; and must be one of great energy and resolution, for she is on her way to California, having determined on going there, and making a fortune for her grand-children—so she told my maid. Though very stout indeed, I should not have thought her old enough to have such relatives; but I am sure they ought to be both proud of, and grateful to their enterprising and go-ahead grandmamma. I think I never saw a more benevolent and amiable countenance.

We had an excellent voyage to Chagres; the only drawback was a short supply of water. The captain had waited a long time at Havana for an additional provision, but from some dilatoriness or neglect of the natives, it came not, and he was obliged to start without it. Sea-water and soap go very ill together. How would the reader like to cleanse his face by rubbing it against a grindstone? I think the salt-water and soap seem pretty nearly as rough. It is still more disagreeable to rinse the mouth with it; but those were very trifling disagreeables, and of little moment.

Our voyage otherwise was uninterruptedly agreeable, except one little alarm which, perhaps, may amuse the reader, and I will repeat it for his edification. A day or two before we arrived at Chagres, there had been a little excitement among the deck-passengers—we were told, in consequence of one of them losing some money, and I believe his watch. Suspicion fell upon one of his companions. They were all going to California, where from the mixed state of society, the vast assemblage of people from all parts of the world, and the not yet thoroughly organized system of government at the mines, &c., the most uncompromising severity, and rigid laws against all similar offenders were rendered necessary. There had been threats muttered of Lynch law, we were told, but I did not place much reliance on these reports, as the passengers seemed so well-disposed, respectable, and orderly a set of persons. This little anecdote will partly show how philosophically Americans will sometimes take matters where their interference would be utterly useless and hopeless.

At the dead of night (an ominous beginning !) I was awakened by an immense noise on deck, like a furious stamping and pushing, and as I fancied, shrieks and expostulations. On the promenade that goes all round the ship, several mattresses were placed every night for the accommodation of some of the passengers, for whom there was no room elsewhere. The night was suffocatingly hot, and the cabin-windows were partially opened so as to allow a passage to the outward air through the closed blinds. As I have very quick ears, and the alarm made one more than usual on the *qui vive*, I heard one of the passengers call out to another something like this :

"What in thunder's the matter up there, sir ?—do you hear that infernal noise ?"

"Yes, sir ;—guess they're throwing that man overboard they talked of lynching to-day."

"Wal, sir, I do suppose that 'll be it."

"Yes, sir."

"Good-night, sir !"

"Good-night to you, sir !"

For my part I felt pretty sure all was over, for the tremendous scrambling and struggling and yelling had suddenly ceased. No doubt the poor victim, maddened and desperate, had fought like a demon for life for a brief while, but overpowered by numbers, had been plunged into a watery grave.

I rushed into the cabin where the two maids slept, anxious to impart the dreadful news, and horrify *them* at least. I found them already listening horror-struck, to the noise, and in great fear that the terrible event alluded to had happened. Presently, in the now deep stillness, I heard a loud pattering of rain, it came louder and louder, and there was another (though not so violent) rush and struggle on deck. I then almost instantly guessed what the real state of the case was. A shower of rain had come on suddenly, and all had been hurrying for shelter, and trying to shield themselves in various ways from its pitiless pouring. This, in fact, was the real truth, thank Heaven ! and I do not think the idea of lynching had ever been seriously entertained.

A little while before we arrived at Chagres, the bustle and stir in the ship were prodigious ; and I am sorry to say, the captain was taken very ill, and was confined to his cabin part of the day. At last Chagres came in view, and before long, the hubbub in the steamer became more "fast and furious." Every body wanted their trunks and portmanteaus, and every body in their hurry, got hold of some body else's. My poor stout friend, who seemed in the greatest and most imminent danger of melting away altogether in the heat, and whom I shall call Arethusa, was *minus* a large trunk, which seemed to be all the world to her. Her patience and good-humor were inexhaustible, but she was evidently in deep perturbation about it. She described it in a panting, breathless "hue and cry," *de vive voix*—"it might be known among a million;" it was a veteran trunk, covered with conspicuous scars, each well patched over with tin; its shape and size, too, were particular. Every sort and kind of trunk, case, box, &c. came up but that. Every body seemed to feel for, and with her, she was so good-natured, gentle, and amiable.

The poor lady fanned away, *almost* frowned, and watched that yawning grave, the hold, disgorge from its capacious maw, legions of boxes, chests, and packing-cases, till even half a forest of trees appeared to view—an American Birnam wood on the route to California. (Perhaps the transplanter imagines that these trees in their new soil, will produce fruits of gold, and that he will have a true Hesperides there). The anxious Arethusa, almost in despair, called "*Hold*, enough!" At last there were some tidings of the missing trunk having been seen somewhere, and the poor lady breathed again—by the help of her faithful fan.

The rush into the different boats, canoes, and *dug-outs* that were ready to convey passengers to the shore, which was about a mile off was tremendous; each was anxious to get the first canoe at reasonable prices, and for a short time, the scene beggared all description. We looked on at the little civil war that was raging, in peace, from our cabin windows, and I was very glad to take the advice the captain sent me, to remain quietly till the afternoon, when the bustle and confusion would be over. I had a letter from Messrs. —— at Havana, to Seoñr ——, requesting him to see that every thing was arranged satisfactorily for us, and to engage a canoe for us, &c. Mrs. H——d was so kind as to take charge of this note for me, and as without loss of time she had gone on shore with her friends, I had no fear but that we should have a good canoe secured for us.

In the afternoon the captain was good enough, ill as he was, to come to the ladies' saloon to take leave of us, and give us all the advice he could respecting the journey across the Isthmus, which he was well acquainted with, having very lately gone over it. It is impossible for any one to have been more courteous and obliging than the distinguished commander of that leviathan steamer was, and his counsel was invaluable to us. He took care that we should have a most commodious and safe boat to take us on shore, and sent an officer with us, to see us established in comfortable quarters, till the canoe should be ready, on the following morning, to proceed with us to Gorgona or Cruces.

Truly grateful for all his solicitude and attention, we took leave of him with the most sincere wishes for his restoration to health. I have before this been convinced, that no manners on earth can be more thoroughly distinguished, noble, and gracefully polished than those of a high-bred American gentleman; nay, I doubt whether any can quite equal them, except some of our own gentlemen—it is the truth, and therefore I will say it. I never saw a truer exemplification of this, than in the gentleman I have just spoken of.

There is no shelter at Chagres whatever for ships, and when the sea is at all agitated, the communication with the shore must be exceedingly difficult and perilous: there is an extremely dangerous bar with but little depth of water.

Our boat rejoiced in the name of "Jenny Lind," and the proprietor of it, an American, Captain Taylor, who is settled at Chagres, and owns a goodly number of boats, which ply on the river Chagres, and who seemed well-known to the officer of the "Georgia," who was with us, told me he was a relation of General Taylor, and that he had served through the whole of the Mexican war. When he found we had lately been in Mexico, he asked many questions with great interest respecting the present state of the country, and was anxious to know if we had seen different battle-fields in which he had borne part, and suffered, and which he commented on with much animation.

When we reached the landing-place, we found it a matter of difficulty to transfer ourselves from the boat to the shore: there was a huge quantity of slimy alluvial mud to be traversed, with nothing but the rudest and most distant apology for a wooden pier, consisting of a few half-rotten planks laid on some stakes. It was not without some exertion that we scrambled on to the solid ground.

Mr. —— then accompanied us to the abode of Señor ——, as I was anxious to know if the letter had been received, and a *cayuca* secured. Señor —— was away, "up on the hill," said some of the retainers, with the characteristic laziness and *nonchalance* of the natives. When would he be back? "Quien sabe?" At length, however, we found a more intelligent Grenadian, who told us the letter had been received at the house, in the absence of Señor R——, agent for the Royal Mail Steam Company, and that it was awaiting his return, which would probably take place very soon. This civilized being then begged we would accept a seat while measures were taken for securing us a comfortable domicile for the night.

The officer of the "Georgia," whom I before mentioned, immediately went over to what is called the American town, where almost all the Americans take up their abode, and where, I hear, there are some very fair hotels (one called the "Crescent City Hotel") but before long he returned, and strongly recommended us to remain in the native town, as, contrary to expectation, many of the lately arrived travelers, having been totally unable to provide themselves with *cayucas*, in consequence of the immense demand, were imperatively compelled to wait till the morning's dawn at Chagres. All the best accommodations were consequently engaged.

In the mean time, Señor —— returned from his excursion, and after reading the letter from Havana, entreated us to remain there, instead of attempting to go to the American town, and it was finally arranged we should do so. A capital room was given us, and one for the two maids close by: we had our own provisions, and therefore required but very little. Our apartment was charmingly cool. We had to ascend by a ladder to it; but once there, it was very pleasant: two large windows without glass, but with shutters, admitted a delightful current of fresh air. This large airy apartment was open to the roof, which towered at a great height above us, and there was on one side only a sort of high parapet wall. Ours seemed to be the only room on that floor; we had thus the view of the whole of the enormous and lofty thatched roof, and if we leaned over the wooden parapet, that of an immense space, something like a great warehouse, filled with a heterogeneous assemblage of countless articles, while on a sort of gallery inside, that ran partly round the walls, were festooned strings of onions, whose fragrance would have been rather overpowering to our olfactory nerves, but for the quantity of fresh air that circulated through the large rambling building.

By the way, Señor —— told me a dreadful fire had lately consumed a fine house he possessed here, and which he had occupied only a short time previous to our visit. We saw from our windows the blackened remains of this mansion, which had all the appearance of having been very extensive, and part of the crowded heaps that encumbered the clay floor of the building we were in, was the rescued but injured furniture belonging to it. Señor —— told us he had quite lately also lost his father, and a child, and that his wife was ill. Under these circumstances I felt loth to stay, but he insisted on our so doing.

There were two little couch-like beds in our handsome loft, with pretty pillows covered with muslin, and trimmed with lace: some very good-natured smiling mahogany-colored damsels came to offer their services. I thought they were domestics belonging to the establishment, but found afterward they were relations of either Señor or Señora R——. They took our chocolate to prepare, and soon returned with cups, &c., and the chocolate hot and foaming, of which we partook, and in a little while we went to rest.

I have as yet said nothing of the appearance of this much-vituperated, and I think often misrepresented place. Of course the ground is low, immediately on the river; but at a little distance beyond, it gradually rises till it presents the appearance of picturesque and beautiful wooded hills, giving a romantic variety to the scene. Certainly, where the Americans have betaken themselves, there is a low and marshy flat, that in the rainy season (which lasts here about ten months!) must be a sea of mud: it is said by the Americans, that the summits of the highest hills afford hardly any security against mud, at that extraordinarily "juicy season."

There is only one church at Chagres—of course a Catholic one —and in its construction it is as unpretending as the bamboo houses of the people. These houses, which are nearly as light as so many balloons, mostly consist of bamboo canes, which are thonged and fastened to some slight frame-work of more substantial timber, all covered over with the leaves or the limbs of the cabbage palm, or the cocoa-nut. They have no chimney at all. They all assume to a foreign eye a very strange and fantastical, but I think picturesque appearance.

The town proper—the Chagres of the natives—lies on the north bank of the river Chagres, about a hundred yards or so from the open sea, and contains about a hundred of these huts, screened by their profuse coverings of palm leaves. A sudden bend in the river and a tongue of land running out into the sea, have caused the town to assume the shape of a semi-crescent, and the former almost entirely vails it from view as you enter the mouth of the river. On this point of land stands the fine old castle of San Lorenzo, built by the conquering Spaniards, and in olden days stormed by the celebrated and oft successful buccaneer Morgan, who scaled it and leveled it, after a conflict, in which all but thirty-three out of three hundred and sixteen defenders were killed.

This fort in the time of its strength commanded the entrance to the river and the town, and to all appearance ought to have entirely locked up the Isthmus from an invading enemy. It must have been a majestic castle before it sank into the melancholy state of ruin and neglect in which we now beheld it. It still bears the outward show of great strength and extreme durability; and if it should ever fall into the energetic hands of our noble transatlantic brothers, it is still susceptible of being made an exceedingly strong and important post. It is surrounded by high ramparts in which are mounted perhaps nearly thirty brass guns; there are bomb-proof casemates, and capacious store-houses, large enough to store provisions for the garrison, which might last them for a long space of time. But on whatever side you look, Time, the conqueror's conqueror, seems to reign triumphant: every where his obliterating foot-marks are to be seen, and the castle seems a morunful mockery of its former stately self.

The precipitously steep and inaccessible rock protects it from all assault on every side but one, and on that it is guarded by an outwork flanked by tottering towers at the angles. This is provided with cannon, in a rusty condition; indeed, the whole is in a dreary state of dilapidation: this outwork is commanded itself by the interior fortifications. What a contrast it must present now to its former state when the proud Spanish grandees and hidalgos of old had rule over it! The Americans say this is entirely owing to the indolence and supineness of the "blackre publicans." They seem in general to look upon these as hardly a degree removed from the negroes. Certainly this Castle of San Lorenzo presents a truly melancholy appearance.

I am told the guns, some of brass, and others of iron, instead of standing in their former threatening attitude, have been allowed almost to tumble down. Some of these guns are very fine ones; a part of them bear the date of 1703, and others are much older. Thousands of pounds of powder remain in the magazine, in a lamentable state of ruin, and the magazine is fast shrouding up, and destroying in its decay all evidence of its existence.

The castle is connected with the before-mentioned outwork by a drawbridge, and another connects this with the approach from without. Enormous water-tanks, guns, powder, balls, stores, and every thing necessary during a long siege, indeed, are there to be found, except provisions, and these doubtless have long ago been appropriated and dispatched by the natives, rendered indolent by their climate, and apt to depend almost entirely upon the abundant yield of tropical productions for their livelihood. The crumbling walls of this once stately stronghold seem now to be the favorite promenade, the chosen " Alameda" for the agile wild goat, and that scavenger-general (in these parts of the world), the unprepossessing buzzard.

Notwithstanding the state of neglect in which it is now, it is easy to imagine that this fortress was formerly (as it is said to have been) one of the strongest erected by the Spaniards along the whole of their coast; for it still bears striking witness to this fact, despite of its ruined entrenchments and its rusty guns, its dilapidated watch-towers, its tottering walls, its crumbling battlements, decayed magazines, and damaged powder.

At some distance from the works stands a detached battery, on the height which commands the town and river of Chagres, but it is destitute of communication with the castle. Some superannuated-looking and miserably appointed soldiers are to be seen loitering about the neglected works. Once more, what a change would take place if this were transferred to the hands of the Americans—what a flourishing city would shortly be seen here; and how would this decayed castle regain all its pristine power and more!

Speaking *cosmopolitanically* and philanthropically, I feel one ought to wish the Americans to take to themselves, not only this, but many other portions of this vast continent: but as an English woman, I suppose I should not give utterance to the wish. Yet, if all illiberal prejudice and antagonizing influences and unfortunate jealousies could be annihilated, and the United States and England would fairly go hand-in-hand in the work of regeneration—or rather creation—what might not such a co-operation effect—what would, or could withstand them?

But England is too calculating; beginning now—not to decline, I do not think or believe that—but to lose some portion of that vigorous and restless energy, which *must* advance—and to be more anxious about retaining than gaining; and her object is, perhaps, yet more to check and interdict others from snatching at coveted prizes, than to seize them herself. But if this policy should become habitually hers, it will ultimately prove vain—the Americans will eventually triumph; and if they are wise and liberal themselves, and allow the forms of government under their general sway to be adapted to the nature and habits of the different people, they will yet rule and govern all this hemisphere *at least!* But this is not a subject to be superficially treated.

As to the population of the town of Chagres, I suppose the permanent inhabitants may number about three hundred—nearly all of these are black, or, at least, of the very blackest bronze it is possible to imagine. We were much amused in watching some of these people, especially the women, whose costume (and particularly their *coiffure*) is very unique. Their jet black, strong, coarse hair is sometimes made to stand out on each side of their heads, like huge heavy black wings, frizzled to the last degree: one would almost think the great vultures, besides being scavengers, are the fashionable hairdressers here. The ladies have a *cigarito* occasionally in their mouths, and sometimes behind their ears, ready for use: a little cotton drapery completed their costume. Crowds of children, looking like little Chinese idols, and not at all remarkable for symmetry of shape, having rather a dropsical appearance, rolled about in the sun till one thought they must be baked to dumplings.

Every now and then some California-bound Americans would make their appearance among these sauntering groups. It would be impossible to imagine any human beings more the moral antipodes of each other than the eager, bustling, rapid, impatient Yankees, and these quiet, peaceable, deliberate, and inanimate natives. It is said, however, when roused or irritated, they can be energetic, and as brave as lions.

The Californians are wildly impatient to get on to their destination, and afraid of missing the next steamer to San Francisco. They are almost always to be seen impetuously gesticulating, imploring, threatening, or encouraging the lounging boatmen, who are employed generally unconcernedly re-thatching with split palm-leaves the awnings or coverings of their primitively-fashioned canoes. These boats were to be seen the preceding day by hundreds beached on the oozy mud, and made fast to stakes or pegs in front of the habitations of the various proprietors. On the second day, comparatively few were left, and for those few large prices are naturally demanded. All who were able seem willing to close with any terms; but those who were not, were of course earnestly remonstrating and arguing the point, and the vociferations and gesticulations were all in *italics*.

For our canoe, which underwent a lengthened course of preparation and re-thatching, I found I should have to pay seventy dollars. This was engaged to take us to Gorgona, and I paid to Señor

R—— forty dollars more, for a respectable person to go with us, as far as that place, who understood the habits of the natives, and the best places for stopping at, and who also would engage mules for us there. We waited hour after hour in vain expectation for our boat, with our bonnets on; fortunately the day was not very sultry. As to the swamps we had heard so much of, where we were we saw nothing of them, and while thus waiting we sate at an open window in our cool, lofty apartment, inhaling a deliciously fresh breeze.

At last, to our joy, the thatching was pronounced complete, and we sallied forth, expecting to find an awning of considerable dimensions, and of the most elaborate workmanship, from the time that had been employed in its construction. What was our dismay to find one of the smallest proportions imaginable, and which it was next to impossible to crawl under, or when that was accomplished, to remain beneath long without being cramped like poor Mrs. Noble, in the cage she was carried about in, in China! But no time was to be lost, and, indeed, we were all impatience to see the beautiful Isthmus, remembering the glowing descriptions of Mr. Bayard Taylor and others of its extraordinary natural attractions.

## CHAPTER XXXVIII.

The River Chagres—The Boat—The Rowers—Their Peculiar and Vociferous Songs—Gatun and Millaflores—Exquisite Beauty of the Scenery on the Banks of the Chagres—Innumerable Flowers and radiant Birds—Strange and Prodigal Intertexture of Parasitical Plants—Enormous and brilliant Butterflies—Las dos Hermanas—Accommodations at that Place—The Hostess and her adopted Daughter—Americans bound for California—Scenery during the Progress of the Voyage—San Pablo—An Accident—The Lady with her immense Coiffure—Monte Carabali—Arrival at Gorgona.

Ours was a light and graceful-looking craft, and we soon discovered she was one of the speediest on the river.

After taking leave of Señor R——, we shot off at a merry pace, sitting under parasols and umbrellas and vails, which tolerably screened us from the burning sun, and taking it by turns every now and then to squeeze ourselves under the apology for an awning, where we found it comparatively cool, but, from the necessarily cramped position which one had to maintain, it was not so pleasant otherwise as the outside. We had no seats but our trunks; however, the boat progressing rapidly, soon bore us into scenes of such incredible enchantment and beauty, that all minor inconveniences were pretty well forgotten. We seemed transported to a new world—all was so indescribably wild and beauteous around us. The astonishing excess and superabundance of the gorgeous chaos of vegetation on all sides, even outdid that of the Tierra Caliente of Mexico, and it is difficult to say more.

The sun raged like a blazing tempest overhead, pouring down cataracts of golden flame, as it were, over all these matted masses of flowery and leafy luxuriance, without being able to penetrate their dense and intricate foldings. Our native rowers plied their broad paddles vigorously and swiftly, singing incessantly, and sometimes screeching like a whole flock of peacocks, with a hundred-horse power of lungs, Indian songs, with Spanish words; one of which songs was rather remarkable, inasmuch as, instead of being, as usual, full of the praises of some chosen fair, it was nothing but a string of commendations on the beauty and grace of the singer. "I have a beautiful face," "I am very beautiful," &c.

When we passed any boat—and in our flying craft, with our light luggage, we shot by immense numbers—the yells of triumph, I suppose, of our boatmen, and a sort of captain they had (who was clad in very gay-colored garments with a splendid scarlet scarf or sash to denote his rank, I conjecture) were literally almost deafening, and the beaten rowers were not slow to answer them, with shouts and shrieks of merry defiance, reproach, or mockery. It seemed to me on these occasions they interrupted the usual tenor of their songs, and entered mutually into a marvelously rapid impromptu description of their respective passengers, of their country, and their destination. Each sentence ended with an unearthly yell, that might have frightened all the furies, and quite electrified the lazy caymans that we saw taking their after-dinner nap in the ooze, as we darted by them.

On these occasions, Señor ——'s respectable colored clerk, inspired by the ear-piercing strains, joined with all his might and main; and I am not sure his respectabilityship did not make the most noise of all, or at any rate, the most delirious attempts so to do. The extraordinarily rapid powers of utterance of these wild men of the wood and the water, would have astounded Mr. Charles Mathews himself. Such a volley of volubility, I think, I never heard—it was the most distracting, bewildering, vocal velocity conceivable.

But they did not neglect their rowing for their singing. We sped on wondrously, and many an American who had started long before us, but was dragging along in a heavily-laden canoe, or clumsily-built dug-out, looked with envy on our little light craft. "Wal, now," I heard one cry out, lugubriously, with a melancholy shake of the head to his companions, "we did ought to have had that boat; that's a fact." Poor people, they were in a lumbering, huge canoe, that crawled and crept along at a snail-like pace, but then they had vast piles of luggage, which would have swamped our little *cayuca* in no time.

From the intense heat we soon became very thirsty, and were going to dip our calabashes in the water and drink, when we were stopped by our black troubadours, who said the water was bad there, and we must wait for some little time till it was sweet and good. However, they soon stopped where there was a hut or two, and got us a couple of calabashes full of wholesome water from a spring. A poor anatomy of a dog came limping toward us, looking imploringly for something to eat; he was quite a *squellette vivante*, and fell upon some biscuit we threw him with the greatest avidity. As to us, we fell upon the water almost as eagerly.

Gatun was the first settlement we stopped at: it was a miserable assemblage of cane hovels. Here our rowers rested awhile, and then went on to Millaflores, which name suits the scenery all along this miraculous river. I have said little about it yet, but be prepared, reader, for a great deal of garrulity on this never-ending ever-beginning topic. Oh, what magnificence of Nature! What overpowering and ineffable glory of magnificence! Your very thoughts seemed crushed beneath a whelming weight of splendor. All we could do was to stare and gaze, and utter broken exclamations of ecstasy. What a maze and mystery of unspeakble loveliness it was! the soaring hills of all imaginable shapes, bathed and buried in beauty, and crowned with majestically-luxuriant woods to their very topmost summits. And such woods! it was a perfect blaze of vegetation, bewildering and half blinding one.

The gorgeous countlessly-variegated trees of those woods were literally swathed and draperied over with dazzling scarlet and gold, the most vivid and refulgent! This, I believe, was occasioned by the innumerable multitudes of orchideous, and other parasitical plants, especially the former, which flash and glow with the most resplendent and glorious colors, and wreathe and wind around the highest tops of the gigantic trees, completely covering them with showery vails and lustrous canopies of flowers, crimson, purple, intense scarlet, gold, blue, and all conceivable and inconceivable colors. Earth seems like a sun—a living sun—sparkling and quivering with all the beauties of the whole creation.

I never imagined any thing so lovely as the exceeding superfluity of the blooms and foliage, and verdure here. As to describing it soberly, it is impossible. The enormous variety and inconceivable profusion of queenly palms was beautiful beyond expression. And then *such* birds! like flying bouquets of jewels, or rainbows, on wings, painting the fervid sunshine around them ten thousand colors: and in the evening the fire-flies made a most magnificent and tremulously-stirring illumination, till all life seemed light, and all light life. As to the stars overhead, they shone out like little suns.

The river Chagres itself is beautiful: it winds and twists about like a brilliant serpent, most gracefully and changefully. The prodigious masses of vegetation pour down upon it, and seem as if they flung their glittering many-colored chains on its bright waters to arrest its progress. In many places, enormous curtains and thickly-woven tapestries of foliage swept down, broidered and blazoned all over with sumptuous blooms, into the blue water; and in other parts the most fantastically-variegated and fairy-like garlands, festoons, and streamers quivered just over its surface, reflected therein in all their beauty. Wherever you turned, there was a sweeping, heaving, and gorgeous ocean of flowers and foliage; wherever you caught a passing glimpse of the inner depths of this world-within-world of beauty and glory, you saw wildernesses of creepers and parasites, in thousands of mazes and convolutions.

Some of the latter flowers, on these blossom-embroidered banks, had a most marvelous effect, apparently "doing business on their own hook;" for they seemed to be standing alone perfectly independent of any support. But I suspect, in reality, they were wreathed and re-wreathed, and piled and crowded over and around some irregular stumps of old trees, or chance block of stone—but in such unimaginable and luxuriant profusion that they often formed as it were, enormous towers and gateways, thus standing by themselves, of immense thickness and height. In short, they displayed all kinds of shapes, most fantastically diversified and varied.

Sometimes they appeared like huge triumphal arches, and sometimes of slenderer proportions, like soaring Turkish minarets;

occasionally like the domes of Oriental mosques. At other times, there was a lovely vision of vast avenues of flower-garlanded bowers, vista beyond vista. In several places the sparkling river was almost bridged across by radiant blossomy boughs, a magic bridge of flowers, and rainbows, and meteors. It hardly seemed as if this abounding wealth and deluge of blooms could have sprung from earth's bosom, but as if the very firmaments, "fretted with golden fire," must have rained down these superb and dazzling splendors from their own treasure-houses of starry glory, or poured part of themselves away, molten, over this over-illumined planet.

Through these gorgeous piles and masses of luxuriance flit not only the many-colored birds I have mentioned, but colossal, dazzling, sumptuous butterflies, belonging only to the tropics, and nearly as large as birds—go fluttering and glittering like showers of precious stones, tossed about by invisible genii.

These glorious forests are so thickly matted together, that not even the lightning can pierce them. I have just been looking at my little companion's description of the exquisite creepers, and all the wondrous effects their elaborate loveliness produces, and I see she likens them to quite different objects to what I have done: but such is their apparently inexhaustible profusion and pomp, and prodigality of growth, and variety of form that a hundred people might very probably describe them all differently. I think *I* was most struck with the extraordinary triumphal arches and columns and castellated towers that they formed so exquisitely in their spontaneous, enchanted, flowery architecture, and *she* with the way in which they almost smothered the loftiest palms with their brilliant shrouds of colored light, and streaming festoons and coronals, and then continually passed on to others, linking them together in beauty and enchantment.

We saw a good many Americans camping at a place, whose name I do not remember. The current began to run very strong, but our light boat still got on pretty fast. At last the rowers seemed to become exhausted, and it was late in the evening when we arrived at a settlement called *Las dos Hermanas.*

It consists of a small number of straggling scattered huts, built on a brow of a headland that overhangs the stream just where the river takes a considerable sweep. Señor R——'s lieutenant went on shore immediately to get us as good accommodations as the place afforded, and we were soon ushered into an Indian hut, of which the proprietress was one of the most obliging and kind-hearted beings in the world. She showed us into a very comfortable room (always considering what Isthmus accommodations generally are said to be). The bamboo walls she proceeded very expeditiously and neatly to cover over with thick mats and hides, and a delightful little tent-like apartment she made of it.

She was accompanied by a smiling girl, who, she said, was her adopted daughter, and that her name was Pantaleone. Her own name, she told us, was Arquellina; so I could not but call them Harlequin and Pantaloon. Poor Harlequin was of a preposterous size, though amazingly active; Pantaloon did all the staring for her, and after we were gone, I think could have described us accurately enough for the "Hue-and-Cry" at least.

I can not agree with the Americans about the natives. Not only here but almost every where else, we found them most good-natured, kind, inoffensive, and hospitable people. They are naturally slow, but with a little humoring, and good-tempered bantering, or gentle beseeching, they will make all the haste they can. For instance, the way in which our unwieldy Harlequin bustled and ran about for us was "a caution." She puffed and panted with the unwonted exertion, but looked the very picture of good-humor all the time. In fact, she seemed to grudge no trouble to make her foreign guests as comfortable as possible. She gave up a very snug room close to ours for the *femmes de chambre*, with two good hammocks in it; then she cooked our provisions for us capitally, and, till we retired for the night, kept up an incessant chattering, in which was mingled many an expression of kindly welcome and good-will.

In short, she was the very best Harlequin in the world, not as regards rapidity and lightness of motion certainly, but in more solid qualities; and after she had affectionately bade us good-night, I looked forward to a very sound sleep on the little couch she had so carefully prepared. But in that I was disappointed. Quantities of insects, chiefly ants, that appeared without end, tormented me the whole night, and it was only just at break of day that I fell into a little doze—(V—— happily slept well); but when morning dawned it was time to start, and after repeated rappings at the barricaded outside door, that would not have disgraced May Fair or Belgravia, and confused cries heard without, of *es muy tarde*, and *ya es hora de levantarse*, we got up, and fat Harlequin busied herself in preparing our *desayuno*, and brought us a delicious bowl of milk, which was very welcome and refreshing.

When I asked her what there was to pay, "Nothing," she said, "*Nada, nada.*" I told her that was quite out of the question; and after a little amicable altercation on the subject, she said, whatever little trifle I liked to give. I presented her then with a "*gratification,*" for which she thanked me heartily, and insisted on accompanying us down the steep bank to our *cayuca.* This poor, dear, plumpest of all imaginable Harlequins! how she waddled along down the abrupt descent! Once more I begged her not to trouble herself to come all the way, and she then took leave of us most kindly; and so did Pantaloon also, who was industriously continuing her occupation of staring, till her eyes seemed inclined to leave her head. Her mouth was wide open; and if she had partaken of the nature of the curious air-plants of China she would have thriven much that morning, I imagine, from the quantity of that element she must have imbibed.

After re-arranging our trunks a little, so as to make tolerably comfortable seats (of course without any backs to lean against), we started, and waved our last adieus to our kind Harlequin and Pantaloon. We passed numbers of canoes filled with Americans: a great many of these boats were manned by Negroes. Some appeared to move so slowly, as to be almost stationary, others were "snagged." Some of these, it appeared, had been all night on the river. Our boatmen, like the rest, had rejected their broad paddles, and taken to *palancas*, or poles, and our progress became slower and slower. We ran under the widely-overshadowing boughs of enormous trees, that bent their stately heads over the water, and made perfect tents with their far-spreading branches; and at such times we seemed inclosed in a large hollow sphere of emerald; all looked green within its leafy circle.

The current was exceedingly strong, and many of the heavily-freighted, clumsy boats we passed, seemed hopelessly fighting with it. The *palancas* splashed us terribly, and the boat had a quantity of water in it, but we got to the *rancho* of Palo Matida in very fair time.

The water of the river, we found, had long been sweet and wholesome, and often did we dip our calabashes into it, and drain a refreshing draught. The vocal performances of the crew became "fine by degrees, and beautifully less," as the toil of poling against the rapids grew more severe: a doleful quivering drawl, something like the tone of a superannuated parish clerk, took place of the wild shrieking songs that had made the woods and groves resound the day before.

Most beautiful was the scenery still, though its character was gradually becoming altered. The hilly peaks were higher; at some places, from the highest summits of the hills to the water, swept down a perfect cataract of trees—you almost wondered the solid hills did not come crashing down with them into the stream. They, and their curtaining superincumbent mass of blossoming parasitical plants, together with wild roses, and lilies, and other exquisite flowers, were wedged and welded together in one heaving, dense, and almost massive pall of sheeted tapestries. From this still, silent, but glorious cataract of vegetation, shot, here and there, what seemed pillars of quivering, leafy, bloomy mist, delicate sprays, that appeared all made of rainbow and sunshine, and, in their turn, these were diversified and adorned by stray gauzy films, and floating shreds of gossamer-resembling and lightning-like shoots, many-colored, and light as painted air, glancing like forked tongues of serpents on the sight, and seeming instinct with life; while with a rapid darting flight, resplendent butterflies, birds, and various insects, ruffled their surface.

In many parts these huge piles of vegetable growth looked more like thick, hardened incrustations of leaves and boughs, which no storm even could ever stir or pierce, than actually growing products of the soil. Altogether, Earth's great heart seemed to have overflowed here, and poured forth all its hidden treasures, blended, overcrowded, precipitated, and combined into a rich concentration of preciousness, without form or order.

We passed several encampments of Americans and settlements of the natives during the day. Among the latter, was Peña Blanca, a small assemblage of huts, which huts sometimes look like immensely tall gawky mushrooms, of most ephemeral construction, apparently. At one or two of these places we asked in vain for a draught of milk, though we caught a glimpse, we thought, of cows every now and then near the *ranchos*, tended by a little *vaquerillo*. As we went on, we overtook more and more boats, till the river seemed alive with them. Occasionally, the voyagers in them broke out into a cheery shout of "Ho! for California!" and sometimes called to us to know if we had come in the "Georgia." Most of them were hard at work, helping their boatmen to stem the stream, and urging them to go ahead.

We passed various other *ranchos*, and at one of them stopped for some time, that the little crew of the *cayuca* might rest and eat their dinner. We went by Agua Salud and Varro Colorado, and, still battling vigorously with the racing current, struggled past Palanquilla, and, as we advanced, we saw many marks of cultivation. Here and there were clearings—not very extensive indeed—but enough to admit of fields of Indian corn and *arroz* (rice), and plantain-walks. There were some beautifully shaped hills to be seen rising near the river-banks. One seemed particularly high: it was, as all the rest are, like the rising sun, steeped in molten gold, and panoplied in a pomp of exuberant growths, among which were seen gloriously towering trees, all over-canopied and buried under hanging gardens in the air, of myriad-hued flowers, quite disturbing the quiet, sultry atmosphere with beauty. But, partly in consequence of our boatmen having spent an unconscionable time at their dinner, partly arising from our not having started as early as we should have done, owing to my extreme sleepiness after the night of torment the ants and musquitoes had given me, we were late: the evening began to grow dusky, the splendid living illumination of fire-flies commenced, and we were told it was necessary to stop at San Pablo, which was not a very prepossessing-looking place.

We were collecting together our carpet-bags, calabashes, and lighter luggage, when V—— forgetting for a moment how easily these *cayucas* are upset, though we had repeatedly been cautioned to move very carefully (and the boat had as nearly as possible been tilted over before, and had been almost filled with water),* jumped up very suddenly, and over went the boat. It righted, however, again; but she fell in the water, which was luckily not deep there, and, after a little delay, she scrambled into the canoe again, being helped by an American gentleman, who, seeing what had happened, instantly rushed to the spot, and, plunging into the water, rescued her. The danger was not of drowning, but of alligators.

We clambered up the steep precipitous bank which led to the collection of hovels called San Pablo, looking as we followed the clerk and others to the little village, like a damp procession of naiades learning to be amphibious—for the boat had been completely deluged with water. The huts were very poor ones, but we succeeded in getting a pretty comfortable one, detached from the rest, and where the good people lighted us a fire to dry our clothes. We were very glad to have a little supper after this, and disposed ourselves for rest, after receiving a visit from the mistress of the huts, who was attired in a singular fashion. She had an immense shock-head of hair, grizzled till it seemed powder-

* An officer of the English navy, Capt. Foster of H. M. S. Chanticleer, was drowned here by such an accident. The boat was, however, of course, in the middle of the river.

ed over, and like twenty judges' wigs in one—nay, so enormous was this *coiffure* that it looked more like a wigwam than a wig. She seemed to have run to head entirely.

Two of us reposed on buffalo hides, and two on chairs (I was one of the occupants of the latter). All became quiet and still, except the monotonous but pretty cry of the bird that repeats "Bohio" as plainly as possible. But presently, through the interstices of the canes, I thought I saw a figure moving stealthily near our hut. I looked closer through the bamboos (ours being a hovel of some architectural pretensions, they were woven pretty closely together!): certainly an extraordinary form was creeping slowly toward us. It looked like a haystack stuck on a pole, or a colossal chicken-coop hoisted on a post, and by some magical means perambulating the grounds. However, on more attentive inspection, the mystery was solved—it was the proprietress of the huts, in her curious costume, which seemed more extraordinary than ever. Perhaps to scare away all other intruders, during the night, she had added to the formidable dimensions of her head-dress, where there seemed really a rather roomy loft to let. Her *chevelure* stuck out like a huge balloon of horse-hair round her head.

She crept slowly on and on, and pushed at our fastened door. I went and opened it, and after some difficulty she introduced her vast head, with all its outer works, into the cane shed. I asked her what she wanted? "Only to have a little talk!" I thought it an unseasonable time, but did not like to say so, therefore I answered her queries as well as I could: "Where did we come from? Where were we going to? Did we like the Isthmus? Surely we would go on to California? All the *estrangeras* who visited the Isthmus always went to California! or perhaps to Lima? Was this finer than my country?" So she ran on, in a whisper, lest she should disturb the sleepers; and at length, to my great relief, the balloon slowly rose, not exactly into the air—I almost secretly wished it might be carried up into the clouds! However, it took its departure, and the door was again re-barred and fastened; and nothing was heard but "Bohio! bohio." So I fell asleep, in peace on the rickety chair I had taken possession of.

In the morning an American lady, who slept in the other cane cottage (both belonging to the same people, and like detached apartments of the same house—there were very likely more of them), came and knocked, and asked if we would like to start with her and her party. I was awake, but the others were sleeping, and as I knew it was now only five hours to Gorgona, I declined, and wishing her farewell, had a little more rest, though very soon the bustle and stir incident to many departures from an encampment not far off, and from the village, roused me completely up, and my companions also. We made our arrangements for starting, and before long had a visit from the lady—the head personage in a double sense, who appeared to act the part only of a subordinate appendage to her own giant head-dress. She seemed hanging to it, like a tiny *parachute* to an immense balloon, such as I have before mentioned. She came with many kind salutations, and a welcome bowl of milk in her hand. But alas! when this milk was tasted, it was found to have a terrible flavor of the strongest garlic. We therefore had some chocolate made, and soon were ready to start.

While tying on our bonnets, I was amused by accidentally hearing, a lively conversation, in Spanish, between two of the native ladies, as to whether I was a princess or a countess; one inclined to the first, the other to the last. Words ran rather high; over and over again was repeated "Princesa—Condesa—si no! si," &c. I began to think I ought to enlighten them with some red-book explanations, and inform them I was not a princess, though my father is a prince, and so forth. But it is time to start, and away we go, hurrying down the precipitously-abrupt bank, and hastily taking our seats in our *cayuca*, but not before one of the maids had received an invitation from the lady, not in, but *under* the balloon, which she so perseveringly carried about with her—to pass her days with her, in these bamboo cages of hers—"Gusta V. quedarse conmigo?" She received no answer but a laugh, not being understood; but when I translated the request, an energetic "No" was returned, with an eloquent glance at the buffalo-hides, and walls of sticks and leaves. The good señora stared, with much incredulity and astonishment, at this rejection of her offer, but retained her good-humor notwithstanding.

San Pablo, this village of cages, is very picturesquely situated on its steep bank. The beautiful Chagres makes a graceful sweep and bend here, and there is a clearing behind it extending to some distance; but this clearing is not formal and bare. There are lovely groups of trees left around the cane-sheds of the settlement, and among them some very lofty and umbrageous palms, and acacias of superb dimensions.

The *palancas* were again in requisition, and the current seemed extremely strong. About midway between San Pablo and Gorgona, rises the stately hill, called Monte Carabali: it is a towering peak, and is said to be the only hill in the whole province from whence both oceans, the broad Atlantic and the grander Pacific, can be beheld at once.

Monte Carabali, like all the other heights here, was enrobed in the most effulgent forests, of which every colossal tree seemed clad in a lustrous armor of precious jewels of every hue. I am not sure that it was on this hill or another, that we saw one gigantic tree on the very summit, sheeted so with the most dazzling profusion of scarlet flowers, that it looked like an immense and high-soaring obelisk of fire, sending its intense blaze far into the glistening blue of the resplendent sky, and, as it seemed, scattering around sparkles and sheets of flame.

We had not gone very far on that day, before the hitherto brilliantly clear arch above us, showed at one point a threatening frowning cloud, which soon sent down upon us a tremendous shower. It appeared as if millions of wings were stirring among the many-sounding leaves that echoed the fast thick droppings of the rushing rain. Our canoe shot speedily under the tent-like shelter of an enormous tree, and we crept as well as we could beneath the ruins of our awning of palm leaves which afforded us still some screen against the storm. In fact, the tree did not allow much of it to pass through its wilderness of boughs and leaves. Had it not been for my determination in insisting on the awning being left, we should not have had a shred of protection remaining, from it, either against the drops (of considerable size, I assure you) that found their way through our leafy canopy above, or against the burning sun that succeeded to the storm.

The evening before, finding, I suppose, the awning a little in their way, and that it made the boat somewhat heavier, the head man had relentlessly seized it, and began tearing it down: I stopped these unwarranted proceedings, desiring him in a rather authoritative manner to desist. He grumbled out it was *preciso* to get rid of it; I retorted it was *preciso* it should remain. He then ceased to contradict, but not to claw down the poor awning. I called out my auxiliary force in the shape of the colored clerk, and he, after first siding with the enemy, on seeing I was determined to cut down all who opposed me—of the *aguardiente*, for which they kept a bright look-out—returned to his duty, and issued the most imperative orders in my name and that of Señor R——, and of the central government of New Granada to boot, for aught I know

—that the palm-thatch should be left intact. But it stood in a tottering and precarious state, and required every now and then bandaging and propping up a little by a skillful hand.

When the storm cleared away, we started again, and beautiful were some of the long reaches of the shining river, where we floated between living walls of sculptured emerald—formed of trees, embossed with myriads of variegated, gem-like blossoms; and every leaf hung on those innumerable hosts of boughs and branches was quivering with the liquid diamonds of the rain-drops, and sparkling and glancing in the golden sun, till really this world seemed too lovely almost, for a temporary abode, and the sense of its stupendous beauty grew painful. For not only close at hand were these countlessly varied masses of luxuriance and splendor, but beyond rose hills on hills, all like insulated paradises soaring back again to the glorious heavens they seemed to have come from!

We arrived at Gorgona under an intensely burning sun. This place is about half a dozen miles below Cruces, but I had decided on riding from thence, in preference to going on to Cruces, in consequence of advice given to me at Chagres.

## CHAPTER XXXIX.

Gorgona—Immense Numbers of Americans at that Place—The Native Hotel —The Host and his Daughters—A Fiesta—The Women's Dresses—The truant Clerk in his Splendor—His Glory checked—Hunting for Mules—A projected Railroad through Gorgona—"Sammy," the Servant at the Hotel—Some Account of his Duties, and how they were performed—His Appearance—Spread of Fever in Gorgona—Mode of lading Mules—Departure of Friends for Panama—Pedestrian Travelers to California—Stanzas suggested by seeing them.

Gorgona looked all alive, and seemed to be rather a considerable place, for the Isthmus. The palm-thatched houses of the natives looked very picturesque there, many of them towering to an immense height, and appearing not unlike pictures I have seen of the great African Baobab tree (only higher and more tapering), with slight cane walls running up all round to meet the outward edge of the circle of its widely spreading and high-reared boughs.

This Isthmusian town is situated on a very high and steep bank, up which it is rather hard work to climb under the scorching sun, for our disembarkation there was accomplished under one of the most broiling skies I ever encountered. Close to the river were encamped immense numbers of Americans, who were waiting for mules, or reposing themselves, after perhaps working their way up the river, or who, from neglecting sanitary precautions, were suffering from the fever.

A Frenchman came up to me, and said he belonged to an excellent *posada* here, which he recommended, but I found it was much crowded, and did not go to it. The American Hotel of Mr. Miller, I heard was quite full, and I ultimately decided on going to a native hotel, which was kept by a Gorgonian, who rejoiced in a family of twelve daughters and I do not know how many sons. The dozen of daughters, as far as I saw of them, were very good-natured and very indolent, and had, like our gentle Pantaloon, a great talent for staring.

The house being full, they overflowed into a broad wooden gallery that surrounded it, and a few into the road, even. When the burning sun drove them in, they were always in the way, standing in the porch and the narrow door-ways, and always busily engaged in some toilet offices, such as putting up their long, jet-black hair, fastening flowers into it, and decorating themselves in various ways. I found it was a fiesta, and there was going to be a grand ball in the evening, where all the fashion and aristocracy of the place were to assemble.

It may be imagined that the fair residents of Gorgona looked necessarily very picturesque, when I tell you that they nearly all had a profusion of natural and beautifully-disposed flowers in their hair, which was sometimes amazingly luxuriant and occasionally gracefully braided, or with long jetty streamers flowing down almost to their feet. Their dresses of a light and delicate texture, were generally either snowy white or of a lovely rose color, and on some occasions the white and rose colors were blended : around the corsage were very deep falls of lace ; the arms were bare.

One of mine host's twelve daughters, is particularly pretty, and the arrangements of the flowers in her hair, and different little decorations superadded to her attire (which important performances took place on the step of a door opposite), seemed to be an object of interest to half the city ; and the amiable Gorgons—which name I give them, not because they are ill-favored—quite the reverse—but because they inhabit this same Gorgona—crowded officiously round, all suggesting and talking together, and apparently disinterestedly desirous that the beauty of the place should maintain her position as fairest of the fair. Match me that magnanimity of the mind feminine in the capitals of the Old World.

As the following day was Sunday, I determined on not starting from Gorgona till early on Monday morning; but it was necessary to secure mules for that day. I placed full reliance on Señor R——'s colored gentleman, but the afternoon wore away and he did not make his appearance. A loud beating of numerous wooden drums and sundry twanging of guitars and violins, announced that a fandango had commenced; I began to fear our knight of the ledger was twirling in the waltz, or threading the mazes of the Spanish dances in the bamboo Almack's, or on the smooth sward before the principal huts; but I thought it best to wait, having inquired concerning his whereabouts. I could not engage mules, with the chance of his having already secured some.

In the morning of the second day, we saw from the aperture in our mud-floored room, which did duty as a window, the apparition of the highly respectable truant, mounted on a caracoling *mustang*, and evidently mightily proud of himself and his prancing steed. Yes, it was certainly himself, in utter full dress, astonishing the weak minds of some of the inhabitants of Gorgona by his splendor, and having apparently breakfasted on a poker, other provisions being scarce, so upright was he, and assuredly having forgotten there were such humble animals as mules in creation. Without further ceremony I indignantly called to him, and requested to know what bargain he had made respecting the mules for our journey to Panama. This was a little unmerciful, as it recalled to the bold *caballero* on his curveting charger unpleasing reminiscences of the counting-house and the pen. As to the mules, he had not contracted for any. No! he had made no "bargain;" and as he pronounced, with immense disgust, the unpalatable word, even his shoulders contracted, and his brow contracted, and all symptoms of a poker-breakfast suddenly disappeared.

I was in high wrath, and demanded to know why he had not done so? He had not thought about mules. There were none to be had; *los Americanos* had taken them all, and he glanced at his fiery steed proudly, as if he would say, "to expect *me* to think of such a plodding animal, indeed!"

"Well, then, horses—have you secured horses for us?"

"Tampoco, los Yankees had all the horses, too."

The man was evidently bewitched by his own unwonted finery, possibly purchased by my forty dollars. I told him I was informed at the hotel, there were mules to be had, and I begged he would *instantaneously* make it his business to find them. He seemed to take my words, "au pied de la lettre," for he turned with a discomfited look to the nearest passer by, who was dawdling along the road half asleep, like a somnambulizing snail.

"Do you know of any mules?"—"No."

He turned hopelessly to a little toddling urchin without any clothing, who was disporting himself hard by:

"Where can mules be got, Señor?"

"Quien sabe."

He then turned to another, who, with characteristic *nonchalance*, shrugged his shoulders and went on.

It was difficult not to laugh at the dismal expression of despair this *caballero's* face assumed, thus checked in his new career of glory down the main street of straggling Gorgona, "You see, Señora Miladi, it is quite in vain; I have inquired every where." He seemed to think it would be almost wicked to try any more, as opposing the laws of destiny; and really the man looked so completely stupid in his unaccustomed state and splendor, that unless extreme measures had been resorted to, and the poor soul pulled off his horse and dispossessed of his fine neckerchief, and his refulgent waistcoat, there was no chance of his returning to the full possession of his senses.

"*Muy bien*," I said, "but it is abominable, very, and exceedingly *disagradable*," and so inly resolving to rely on my own resources, I closed—not the window, because there were none to close, but—our conference, and made preparations, forthwith, for summoning my best Spanish to my aid, taking as a guide, poor Sammy, the Hindoo Mozo at the hotel (of whom more hereafter), and having a mule-hunt at once myself.

Out we sallied, and soon came to a mule proprietor's abode, who took us to see his animals; but they were more the shadows of mules that had been, than actually existing mules, in substance and truth. He acknowledged, after a little cross-examination relative to their endurance and strength, that they were *enferme*, and he had given them physic. On we went, and I thought it would be a judicious step to go to Mr. Miller's hotel, and ask him if he knew of any mules which we might engage. Mr. Miller was very civil and obliging, and roared out a courteous answer to the requests which I shrieked vehemently in his ear. If this surprises you, know, oh, gentle reader, that a ball was going on in the next house, and that the noise of drums, violins, guitars—and gongs, too, I believe—was almost deafening. However, through an interchange of shouts, rendered necessary by the aforesaid din, I became aware that there were still several places where I might hope to get mules, and at the first one I visited, I saw some very fine animals indeed, but the proprietor put the most extravagant price upon them.

As I had taken care to have only money with me sufficient to defray my expenses on the road (for fear of robbery), and as these owners of mules demanded prepayment, the preposterous demands of this individual would have left me quite penniless, so I attempted to bargain with him, but he would hear of no reduction. Therefore I prosecuted my search further, and at length made a very satisfactory bargain altogether, which was not, however, finally concluded till the mule-owner had seen our trunks, and till I had made some inquiries respecting him, of the master of the hotel where I was staying, who assured me Señor —— was a very respectable and honest man, and he and his mules might be thoroughly depended upon.

The mules were to be at the hotel door at a very early hour in the morning; indeed, I allowed, in naming the time, for about two hours' dilatoriness, and we then went to enjoy the beautiful view from the edge of the bank, near a large, half-finished house, which promised to be quite a palace of sticks. It was a lovely prospect: splendid hills rose in front, and the American encampment beneath, by the river, with its snow-white tents scattered about under wide-spreading mimosas and umbrageous sycamores, had a very pleasing and striking effect.

An open-air fandango was going on at a distance, and with a considerable space between us and them, the drum and the guitar did not sound unpleasing. All the inhabitants who were not dancing, seemed promenading about, and the wreaths and bunches of natural flowers in the hair of the women, and their light, aerial-looking dresses, gave an air of festival gayety to the whole place and scene: it really seemed a sort of Fairy-land.

One almost foolishly shrinks from the idea of a railroad coming through such a lovely, idle, flower-crowned, unsophisticated place; but we hear it will do so in the course of a few years, and as we came to Gorgona, we passed a number of rails, and a small mountain of wheelbarrows and tools, on the bank of the Chagres, in preparation for the commencement of the work. The insalubrity of the climate seems one great obstacle to its accomplishment; but by careful precautions and perseverance, I dare say its difficulties will be overcome.

N*

It was some time before we could tear ourselves from the contemplation of this lovely view, but at last we returned to our hotel, and begged the almost ubiquitous Sammy to prepare our chocolate, and bring us some bread.

And now I must tell a little about this same marvelous Sammy, who was one of the Coolies imported into Jamaica some time ago, from the East Indies. His Jamaica master, being, like many others, smitten with a wish to seek the new El Dorado of the world, came to the Isthmus with the intention of proceeding to California as soon as practicable; he, however, fell a victim here to the Chagres fever, and left the unfortunate Sammy in a strange country, hardly speaking a word of English (which, from the vast numbers of Americans crossing the Isthmus, would have been very useful to him), and not a syllable of Spanish. He was taken, however, as a servant-of-all-work in this hotel, where, I believe, his master died, and he certainly had no easy place; the cry was "Sammy, Sammy," from morning till night.

It was amusing to peep out into the great *sala*, and to see poor Sammy incessantly scrambling in and out of his beloved hammock, whence he appeared never to move, save on compulsion. That hammock—one among many—seemed to him the garden of Eden, the concentrated essence of all happiness: but, poor wretch! he was no sooner in it than he was out of it, and if you watched for five minutes, you would be apt to imagine he was performing the feat of jumping in and out, so rapidly, as hardly to touch the swinging litter, for a wager. "Sammy!" he was half-way in, and down he tumbled again: "Plate of boiled rice, Sammy!" That done, away he posted again, hammockward; stopped in mid career, "Some roasted bananas, Sammy!" off he stumped: these brought, he accomplished a triumphant jump into the hammock; "Sammy, Sammy!" out again—so that he rushed about incessantly, a most compulsory harlequin, and between every separate service, vaulted, or a half or a quarter vaulted, as the time allowed him, into the tempting bag again, thus performing the most extraordinarily active feats of agility unceasingly.

And, indeed, the immense amount of exertion he went through, by thus running backward and forward, to and from the couch in mid air, was inconceivable, and by far the greater part of this labor was for the sake of repose and rest! He worked like forty dragons in order to be idle. He did pretty nearly every thing, that he might do nothing—just that he might do nothing—and as soon as he began doing it, he had to leave off, and work as hard as before. It was a sad sight to see him snatched back again twenty times in three seconds from his hanging nest of peace. Frequently he had to make a demi-vault in the air and spring round, and often his head would rest for a moment, while his legs still quivered in the atmosphere, as if they heard the call which the sleepy head did not. As to pedestrians walking a thousand miles in a thousand hours, what was that to poor Sammy running, and jumping, and plunging ditto?

But a curious part of this singular exhibition was, that the poor Coolie always retained, in the midst of the most hurried exertions, the same placid, lazy expression. He looked the very incarnation of all idleness while he was laboring most severely. He seemed at such times a sort of galvanized mummy—or a puppet, with its eyes half shut, pulled furiously by wires—or Morpheus himself forced to dance a jig and hornpipe by the German magic fiddle. So sleepy a countenance one never beheld, perhaps, as poor Sammy's. It was all leaden laziness; he looked as if he could do nothing indeed, *thoroughly*, and more nothing than any body had ever done before!

Sammy was rather ancient, but had very fine features. I do not know what tint Coolies are exactly in general, but Sammy's complexion was much the same as that of an anthracite coal. His jet black nose was quite Grecian; he had large black eyes, that always looked half asleep, and splendid teeth. His costume was rather remarkable. Poor Massa's black hat was perched on the top of his large snow-white Hindoo turban, like a chimney pot on a China soup tureen. The rest of his dress seemed a mixture of East Indian, Spanish, West Indian, South American Indian, Yankean, Californian, English, and of his own invention.

I asked him how he liked the Isthmus. He made a piteous face, and after pausing a little to muster his best English, replied in this strain: "Lookee, Madras berry nice, Jamaica so so nice, and dis no nice at all." With that he vanished to cries resounding and reduplicated into one grand chorus of "Sammy, Sammy!" What was not wanted? dinner, breakfast, luncheon, supper, all according as the hours of travelers varied. But he would turn by habit to the hammock first, make a desperate spring and bound, and then plunge back again, as the cries of "Sammy" increased.

A sort of book-keeper and superintendent of this palm-roofed Astor House was a native of Jamaica, who had a wooden leg; and whenever Sammy heard the stump of the wooden leg, he tumbled out of the much-loved hammock in no time, for one of its chief occupations was routing out unfortunate Sammy. He seemed principally to have been engaged for that purpose—in short, as a whipper-in to Sammy.

But a delightful scene took place on one occasion, when one of the native boys, lounging near the door, saw the hammock (so dear to Sammy) unoccupied, while that gentleman was cooking, laying dinner, and waiting, all at once—as it seemed to ordinary eyes—in darted the boy, and was ensconced in the hammock in a half-second. If the reader could but have seen Sammy's speechless rage and fury when on returning from one of his busy cruises, he had almost effected an entry into his port and haven of rest, and found it occupied by that intruder! A lion returning to his den, and finding it in possession of a monkey, or one of his own jackals, could not have been more fiercely indignant; but his rage and his jump were both cut short. "Sammy, pork-steak. Sammy, have done snoozing there." Poor Sammy snoozing, indeed! If ever he *had* been wide awake in the world, old or new—in either hemisphere—he was so then, in his unspeakable rage. With an infuriated gesture of menace at the boy, he darted away to get the steaks, set them down with a slam, which scattered the gravy like spray about, and cutting half a dozen insane summersets anticipatory, in the air, before he reached the hammock, began as soon as he got there (with a final bound that almost sent him over the other side), to knock the boy about with all his strength, muttering profuse Hindostanee compliments to him. The little rascal ducked and dived skillfully. He was lithe, and slippery as an eel in its teens, and Sammy's first and second blow seemed to fall on the air. "Sammy, Sammy," was the cry. Away he bounded, with the arm yet upraised to strike; and whether the blow, which he probably could not stop from the force of its own impetus, fell on the owner of the wooden leg, or on the head of one of the California-bound wayfarers, I know not.

I was truly sorry to be obliged to look after mules on Sunday, but the fever was spreading fast at Gorgona, and I did not like remaining there any longer than was absolutely necessary. We had seen several suffering from its attacks; and the poor wooden-leg caught it. The following morning I saw him with his face perfectly scarlet with fever, and his blood-shot eyes almost starting out of his head, looking as unlike the sallow, quiet, composed person he had been the day before, as possible. Sammy actually snatched a whole nap of one minute and a quarter "by Shrewsbury clock," on that eventful morning.

When we took our little promenade in Gorgona, we had seen

here and there a wretched-looking sickly object; and on asking what was the matter, were always told it was the consequence and remains of the fever. One emaciated creature was almost a skeleton, with a ghastly death's-head, bandaged round. I suppose he had been shaved; he was quite a shocking spectacle. I asked if that, too, was the fever. "Si, si." And yet Gorgona is said to be a healthy spot; but I suppose these people bring the fever from Chagres, or some other insalubrious place they may have visited.

We were up very early on Monday morning, but had to wait a long time for the mules. I began to think I ought to have ordered them to be at the door the night before, to have insured their being there in the morning early. At last they arrived, and after a great deal of talking and loitering about, they began to pack the animals.

This is a curious sight, and interested us, though we had seen much the same thing in Mexico, but not so near. They appear to have the same *apparejos* and *alforgas* for the mules, and while drawing the fastenings tight, they plant one foot firmly, in the same way, against the side of the animal, and pull with all their might. The mule is blinded during this process. As soon as the packing is finished (which takes a long while in the dilatory way in which they set about it here) the bandage is taken off the eyes, and the mule trots away to rejoin her companions, sometimes with a reproachful snort, as if she would say, "This load's too much, *parole d'honneur*."

On Sunday morning we saw our friends, Mrs. H—— and Arethusa start for their *jornada*, to Panama, riding sideways on men's saddles—as we also had to do; but Arethusa (who I must say, so far from having melted away, looked more substantial than ever) almost entirely concealed her mule, which, whatever might have been its actual size, appeared comparatively diminutive beneath its voluminous rider. (Forgive me, kind and amiable friend, I would fain say, and I know you will, for you are good-nature itself.) Nothing, in short, of such an animal as a mule was clearly visible, except a pair of long ears and a tail.

After the lapse of a considerable time, we saw Mrs. H—— return alone, apparently in haste. We looked for the ears and the tail, but *they* were not to be seen. I imagined Mrs. —— had forgotten something, and returned to find it; but I afterward learned she had lost her little boy, who had strayed a short distance from the mule-path, gathering flowers, and had become bewildered among the dense intricacies of the trackless forests. She had returned, thinking he might have found his way back to Gorgona, and if not, with the intention of sending people from thence in different directions, to look for him. We heard of his safety subsequently.

Our room, with its solitary aperture, commanded a view of the commencement of the road to Panama; and many an interesting and curious sight did we witness from it. One that is very characteristic of American go-aheadishness and independence, I will relate. A spare, eager-eyed "States' man," had loaded an obstinate-looking animal with probably all his worldly goods, and was starting, or rather attempting to start, perfectly alone on his road to Panama, for the animal resolutely refused to budge, and he was dragging at it by an immense long rope with all his might and main, he at one end of the rambling street, and it at the other, and shouting out in English to the sauntering natives by the roadside, "I say, which is the road to Pana*maw*?" Another was stepping on deliberately, his bundle under his arm, and a huge umbrella, like that you see represented in Chinese rice-paper drawings, over his head, following the first path that came in his way.

We saw numbers start along this road (which was the right way) almost all with the same frank, free, earnest bearing—and one felt they do not go only to gather up gold in the rich mines of that far land, now a part of their glorious country—they go to help and assist in raising a mighty empire on those teeming shores of the great Pacific, to carry progress, order, and civilization in their train. I have attempted to express this in the following lines:

Beneath the Tropics' blaze of lustrous day,
The nation-founders take their glorious way;
Not solely for the vulgar thirst of gold,
Pass hurrying on the adventurous and the bold.
They haste to bear unto that distant soil
(To flourish soon beneath their patient toil)
Law, order, science, arts—and all that springs
Beneath civilization's sheltering wings.
   Pass—nation-makers! onward go!—
   All earth shall yet your triumph know!

*Here*, their inspiring and momentous march,
Seems under one august triumphal arch,
By Nature raised, as though to greet and grace
Their conquering progress to the Chosen Place.
She shows her vernal pomp—her rich array,
And with her silvery voice she seems to say—

"Forget not *me*, and all I bring of joy,
Blest hoards of pure delights that can not cloy.
On! nation-founders! bold and free—
But keep your souls still true to me!"

And not alone her outward charms appear,
The wanderer's wearied sense to soothe and cheer;
But all her gentlest influences seem,
Away from home—to call up home's sweet dream.
The breath of flowers—the stir of leaves—the breeze
Whispering soft music through the embowering trees,
Seem still to speak of home, with tenderest tone,
And bid them still that pure dominion own.
On!—nation-framers!—do and dare—
Home-prayers shall bless you here—and *there!*

A thousand generations hence shall own
Your power—your influence, felt from zone to zone;
A thousand generations hence shall bless,
Shall praise you for their homes—their happiness!
Yours is a kingly mission, brave and high;
On!—in the name of Truth and Liberty!—
'Tis a right royal progress!—round ye wait
The guardian powers that watch and guard a state.
Long ages needs your task?—away!—
Enough is Freedom, and a Day!

Treasures ye seek, but treasures too ye take,
To yon fair shores, which *ye* shall glorious make;
Treasures that globes of gold could never buy—
The wealth of Thought and Heart and Memory!
Generous affections, quenchless zeal and skill,
To mould, and rule, and conquer at your will!—
On to your task!—with mind resolved, and soul
On fire to seize the prize—to reach the goal.
Wide be your Flag of Stars unfurled,
Ye workmen, that shall build—a world!—

Wide be your Banner of the Stars unfurled,
And on, ye workmen—that shall build—a world.
A host of nations, wreathed with power and pride,
Have rushed to glory, flourished, changed and died;
And history bears them to your gaze; behold!
High towers her pyramid of nations old.
Plant the sublime foundations of your own
On those chief heights of elder lands undone.
*Begin* with all they had of best,
And Heaven inspire ye with the rest.

The noblest heights that others have attained
(What time o'er earth with sovereign sway they reigned)
Shall be the lowliest step—the humblest base
Of your bright state, in eagle pride of place.

There shall be felt through all its movements free,
The heavings of eternity's great sea.
No dull stagnation e'er shall check its powers;
Like rounds of th' angel's ladder, all its hours
 Shall higher lead, and higher still,
 Till Time his measured march fulfill.

## CHAPTER XL.

Arrival at Panama—Hospitality of Mr. —— —His House—Coral and Pearl of the Pacific—The "Espiritu Santo"—Departure from Gorgona described—A refractory Mule—The Cerro Grande—Alleged View from its Summit—A magnificent Forest described—A Forest on Fire—The American's Admiration of the Trees—The Flowers in the Forest—Difficulty of proceeding on the bad Roads—Enormous Loads carried by the Natives of the Isthmus—Attire of Travelers to California—Female Inhabitants of the Isthmus—Their Dislike of Americans—Arrival at the Half-way-house—Mrs. H—— and her Child—The American Character exemplified—The Journey resumed—Escapade of a Mule—A Halt—The Indian Hut—Its Inmates—Noises in the Forest.

I CONTINUE (being now at Panama) my narrative of our transit across the Isthmus, from where I left off at Gorgona. But first, let me observe that we are under the hospitable roof of Mr. P——, where he and his daughter most kindly have arranged every thing in their power to make us comfortable.

The house is charming, and commands an enchanting view of the majestic and mighty Pacific; and almost perpetually, the most delicious and the coolest breezes blow in at the immensely large windows which open on broad balconies with wooden balustrades, some of them ornamented with rare and lovely plants.

There is a little green paroquet here, which is an immense favorite of V——'s, and a great amusement to her. She has undertaken to tame it, and as it is the most savage little beast of a bird I ever met with, it will task her powers to the utmost, and she will be the Van Amburgh of birds, if she succeeds. It already begins not to bite her quite as hard as it does other people.

From the windows we see immense numbers of palm-trees, growing to the very shores of the great ocean, and we can almost fancy the fairy bowers of roses, and of myriad blossoms we have been so enchanted with lately, are continued, and mixed with the labyrinths of coral and wealth of pearl under these placid, translucent, silvery-glittering seas of music and of peace. But coral grottoes and pearl are poor compared to the pomp of the tropical flowers.

While I am speaking of flowers, I must tell of a most lovely and exquisite one here, called I am told, *Espiritu Santo,* which sacred name is given to it from its perfect resemblance to a white dove. It is not in blossom now, so I have only heard of, not seen its beauty; but I am assured the likeness of this snowy flower to the bird above-mentioned is quite extraordinary, and its loveliness consummate. There is another beauteous flower very common here, that seems to have long silky tassels hanging from it.

On the day of our departure from Gorgona, we had to wait—it seemed to me a most unconscionable time—while they were lading the mules; but patience is a virtue that is pretty well exercised on the Isthmus. At last, all was declared to be ready, and the saddle mules were led up to the wooden piazza of the hotel. My little girl was very anxious to ride one that was handsomer and looked in sleeker condition than the rest; I had no objection. Our guides (of whom we had a good escort, and who were said to be *hombres muy respetables*) had no objection either, and we all mounted and started. We had not gone far before V—— disapproved of her mule being led, for one of the Mozos held its rein very carefully. I remarked then that they had not taken off a bandage that covered its eyes, and this circumstance, coupled with the fact of its being the only one they attempted to lead, made me think it was not so quiet as the others. However, on being questioned, they said it would go very well, and at her urgent request let it go loose, and it seemed perfectly sober and steady.

We saw an absurd spectacle, though not an amusing one to the unlucky person concerned, who might have been a loser thereby. A mule, laden with numerous articles of luggage, was playing the most extravagant antics a little way from us, galloping along the valley, that was cleared here and there, with his heels generally cooling themselves in the air: *jets d'eau* of plethoric carpet-bags and divers bundles rained gracefully around him, and the unfortunate owner of the property rushed wildly after, shouting, and extending his arms, which only seemed to make the creature dance his *bolero* without castanets, more wildly, as if he took these demonstrations for "thunders of applause." At last, as if to punish us for smiling at the creature's extraordinary performances, it neared our quiet procession, and our own baggage-mules showed signs of joining in a general *contra-danza* or a Highland fling. When we saw the cherished carpet-bags of our souls, and darling packages of our hearts exposed to such fearful danger, we shook in our stirrups (horridly clumsy things they were), but the danger passed over; the rebel mule was secured. The grief-stricken owner held in his arms his shattered bags and bundles, and with much emotion proceeded to examine the mutilated remains of various treasures, such as travelers only know how to prize (not pearls and diamonds, nor any such trash, but haply a jar of pickles, or something of the kind, invaluable, unreplaceable), and we went on our way, condoling with him, however, on his misfortunes.

I must not omit to mention that to the west of Gorgona is a hill called the Cerro Grande, and some maintain that from *this* (and not Monto Carabali), which is one of those heights forming the ridge which divides the Isthmus longitudinally, both oceans can be seen at once with a glass, and from this alone. Doctors differ, and they set the fashion to all the rest of mankind. I could not find that any one had ascended this hill lately to try the truth of the statement: the path is said to be extremely rugged and abrupt, and the heat of the weather affords an excuse for avoiding such a fatiguing expedition.

After we had crossed this valley, we entered a magnificent forest that appeared to become thicker and thicker, till it almost shut out the intense light of a tropical day, and thoroughly screened us from the piercing rays of a tropical sun at its zenith! It was indescribably delightful. A cool emerald-tinted twilight surrounded us on every side, and still, as we rode on, we seemed more closely encircled and more completely canopied by the pleached and heaped together branches. It was a ceiling and walls of foliage and flower-enameled greenery.

When we got still deeper into that mighty forest, it seemed like a vegetable Mammoth Cave, and as if one was miles below the surface of the earth; for it appeared difficult to believe that otherwise, in the blazing noon of the Tropics, you could be so entirely sheltered from every ray of the sun, with only boughs and leaves above you. The rich underwood mingled its countless shoots and trails with the dense down-hanging garlands of parasites, as stalagmites meet stalactites in earth's cavernous recesses.

We heard a shower of rain at one time above us, like the tramp, tramp of a thousand fairy legions: but hardly a drop reached us (it was not a very heavy rain, of course). We saw scarcely a living creature in the forest (though we heard many), except insects, and by them we were much assailed, though at the time we did not suffer so much as afterward from their attacks. Besides the alligators, we had seen on the banks of the Chagres the ugly armadillo and various lizards, and had heard a loud roaring, which I thought perhaps proceeded from the puma, or South American lion, but was told it was the sound made by a large black monkey that frequents the Isthmus. The forests are said to be inhabited by the jaguar, black tiger, wild cat, ocelot, panther, and a variety of monkeys, who may often be heard chattering away briskly with their numerous comrades.

We have generally been pretty fortunate in seeing interesting sights in the countries we have traveled in, and during this ride to Panama we, for the first time, encountered that grand spectacle, a forest on fire. We rather suddenly found ourselves almost enveloped in a dense smoke, and presently the ground over which we were riding (it was a very narrow mule-path through that apparently illimitable and interlaced forest), and all the surrounding trees—trunks, boughs, branches, leaves, and creepers—became of a brilliant, intense, glaring sort of red orange color (something like the hue of the ripest and richest of Maltese oranges inside), and the most deliciously odoriferous scents pervaded the whole air, as if a thousand phœnixes were expiring at once in their burning spicy nests. In short, the forest was on fire at a little distance from where we were riding. The guides called out to us to push on, but not to be alarmed, for they said there was scarcely any danger, as the trees were so enormously large, and so thickly crowded and jammed together there, that it burnt very slowly, and also, there was very little if any wind (and that was, it appeared, in our favor). The trees, too, had been a little moistened by a late shower; so altogether we felt but little fear, and observed the majestic spectacle with feelings of tolerable security. There was, however, a very loud crackling of branches, like an advancing fusillade, and the sparks and ashes fell fast on us, covering us from head to foot.

We rode steadily on, and before very long emerged from those thick clouds of fragrant smoke which seemed redolent of frankincense, and of all the odorous breathings of "Araby the blest." We emerged, I say, from that perfumed atmosphere, and lost sight of the vivid scarlet and orange-colored reflections of the flames, passing once more into the dazzlingly bright golden sunlight of the Tropics, for just then we came upon a little clearing. We were glad to breathe freely, and shake the remaining ashes from our clothes, which were, happily, of very incombustible materials.

We soon plunged again into the giant woods. And here I wish I could convey to the reader the faintest idea of their astonishing beauty, and of their peculiar characteristics; so gigantic, yet so wondrously delicate in detail; vast, colossal bowers hanging over other bowers festooned and twining together in twenty thousand wild romantic shapes, and with that gossamer net-work of light creepers flaunting here and quivering there, as if the rainbowed spray of myriads of fountains had suddenly been arrested and hardened by magic into permanent forms. Then *such* trees! studies in themselves; some like vast columns of burnished silver, with the most smooth brilliantly white bark you can imagine, and a dome-like top of magnificent foliage; others with glorious leaves, like great green stars, or rather three-quarters of a star, shining like sculptured emeralds; then a majestic kind of wild cotton tree (the silk cotton, I think), with its beautiful product, hanging like feathery snow from it.

A couple of Americans, armed to the teeth, and carrying large knapsacks, passed us (they sometimes carry huge umbrellas, looking like parachutes turned topsy-turvy); and I heard one address the other; "I've seen a many and a many trees in the States, to be sure, but I never saw a *single one* of these here before in my country" (a pretty widely spreading country too), "not one on 'em; it beats all natur, I swarn; it's all new to me, though I've seen lots of trees in my time; wal, I *have.*"

Another inexpressibly lovely tree is the bamboo, which grows to an immense height here, and looks like heaps of gigantic green ostrich feathers. In some instances (on the bank of the Chagres) I saw it forming a most perfect Prince of Wales's Plume, of the most colossal dimensions, and yet of the most aerial and delicate lightness imaginable. Then there are the beautiful plants of the "Spanish daggers," and the coffee trees, the cocoa-nut palms (with the huge cocoa-nuts hanging so temptingly from them), and the zapote, with its large, splendid fruit; the mango, the calabash tree, and the ceiba, and multitudes of others.

And then there are the superb Titanic lilies, and the immense bananas, which, whenever exposed to the scorching sun, have their giant leaves cracked and divided by the heat, and which are sometimes split by the wind; and there are literally roses wedged with roses, ever-lovely, and heaped in such close, inextricable coils, that they almost seem a single mammoth flower; and wildernesses of hot-house plants (I mean hot-house plants in *our* country, with its coal-fire sun), hiding the soil with their lavish luxuriance, and almost forming, one with another, an indistinguishable mass, where the crowded dyes seem to shift, and change, and melt into each other, like the hues of diamonds by lamplight. It is indeed the poetry of vegetation. Yes! it is a mighty poem, written by the living sun on the earth, caught up by the elements and vibrating, as it were, through the beating heart of eternal Nature, that is brooding, like the mother dove, mighty in love and loveliness, over her own offspring of beauty and beneficence.

Sublimely fair, however, as the scenery was, that we might not be deluded by the dream that it was Elysium, we had a road that might have better befitted Tartarus—a road that might well have been designed to torture the wandering spirits of flagitious mules—and of mule-riders too. Sometimes the descents were so precipitous that the creatures almost half tumbled, half slid down them; at other times they had to go stumbling about in break-neck holes of frightful depth, as if they were about to seek in a subterranean passage a solution of the difficulties of the road!

Another disagreeable circumstance was, that the strong thorns belonging to various prickly shrubs, which encroached on the narrow path, caught our riding dresses, which were too long for this rugged expedition, and often nearly dragged us off our saddles. Mine, particularly, which was of very strong stuff, several times as nearly as possible drew me off; for the mule had a terribly hard mouth, and disdained the most vehement pullings of the rein, as my riding dress did the clawings of the stubborn shrubs. On one occasion, just as I hung between shrub and saddle, it kindly tore, and I somehow managed to find myself in the saddle again; but as to stopping the mule it was hopeless. Talk of "Patience on a monument," think of Patience on a *mule!*

At rare intervals a small clearing would let the sun come suddenly down upon us, like a thousand flashes of scorching lightning in one; but we had doubled thick handkerchiefs, and tied them over our bonnets, so that we did not suffer much from the powerful rays. We gathered the leaves of the fan-palm, too, and made additional head-screens of them; but in general the light and heat were mellowed and softened by the over-arching roof of trees I have described.

We met or passed immense numbers of natives, carrying often enormous loads, which they bear, apparently, in general, without fatigue. One man, especially, was burdened by a huge deal case, which looked as if it contained a frame house, at least, on its way to California; and it very likely was one, and an *iron* house "at that!" He did look tired, poor fellow; and the house, or whatever the mountainous load was, had slipped, and he could not get it rightly on again! He rested against a tree, and some of the good-natured California-bound emigrants, who were seated in a group hard by, eating their luncheon and reposing themselves (for almost all we saw walked from Gorgona to Panama, frequently making two days of it), went to help him. They gave him, at his request I believe, a calabash full of water, and assisted him to place the gigantic case (with a small hotel probably inside it), once more firmly and comfortably (!) on his back. It was with some difficulty he made room for our party, especially our baggage-mules to pass.

I have seen the porters at Constantinople carry most enormous burdens, but I think I never, or hardly ever, saw so unwieldy a load on the shoulders of mortal man before. Some of the Americans exclaimed on seeing him, "It *must* be only an empty case;" but that was not at all likely, and the fatigue he exhibited proved it was much beyond the average weight they carry, for we saw others laden with large trunks, strutting on as if they had nothing but a feather on their backs.

I have written of a man thus perhaps carrying a house on his back like a two-legged snail; I must speak, as a "pendant" to this, of an account in an American paper of a man being run over by a house—a curious accident. "A young man at Bath, Maine, met with a dangerous accident; a house ran over him, breaking his ribs, and injuring his lungs. They were moving the tenement, and he was caught by one of the rollers." We ourselves met a mansion taking a walk last summer, I recollect; or, I believe it was resting on its oars at the moment we passed by. This was on the borders of Canada.

The Californians, all with their gay scarlet flannel shirts (which they universally wear), were scattered about the forest on all sides, and their brilliant attire was glimpsed through the woods at intervals; so they looked something like dismounted fox-hunters, thus reminding us of Leicestershire a little, though it would be difficult to find any thing less like that highly respectable county than this wild, gorgeous wilderness-forest of the South. Would not a Vale of Belvoir farmer think poor nature had gone mad, and required a strait-waistcoat here and a pair of handcuffs? Cheerily sounded the emigrants' friendly greetings to one another, and their inspiriting watchword; "Ho! for California!" I could almost have fancied the "Tally" added before the first word, and the last two suppressed.

We had to ford numerous streams of water, and were glad to drink at these from calabashes we carried at our saddles, hob-and-nobbing with our own thirsty mules. We were now approaching the half-way house, where we were told the Americans had erected a large tent-hotel; and now V——'s mule showed signs of his disagreeable temper, by quietly sitting down in one of these streams, and thus intimating his resolution to proceed no further. Of course this could not be allowed, and after a great deal of persuasion had been apparently thrown away upon him, he suddenly bounded up and banged himself against the trees with considerable violence. It was, therefore, necessary he should be led, and as soon as we arrived at the tent, it was decided he should be favored with a load of baggage, and one of the pack mules saddled in his place, one of these being remarkably docile, and only not ridden because his superior strength rendered him peculiarly fitted for carrying the trunks. This ill-tempered individual thus got well punished for his impertinence and contumacy, by having to bear a heavier burden than he had before.

Besides the male natives (who were almost all carrying heavy loads), we met great numbers of the female inhabitants of the country, generally on the backs of mules. We frequently wished them good morning or afternoon in Spanish, and they returned these greetings always most courteously and kindly, with a native grace that was very pleasing. They often wished us a happy journey, and added various compliments on our riding dresses, which they thought *muy bonito, O tan hermosa,* and so on. I think there can not well be a more simple-hearted and kindly-dispositioned race; and they seem as thoroughly happy, too, as they are unsophisticated, though certainly their happiness is not of an elevated or intellectual kind.

They appear, I think, to dislike the Americans in general, and the influx of the vast numbers of intruders, that have almost driven them out of their own homes since the discovery of the California gold mines, seems to be a subject of sore dissatisfaction with them. I verily believe their chief reason for disliking the Americans is, that the latter give them some trouble, which they abhor—and small blame to them, in their delicious do-nothing climate, where Nature serves them as the slaves of the Lamp did Aladdin, in the Arabian tale! And then *Los Yankees* hurry them, and can not endure those slow lingering ways, so little suited to their own ultra-Anglo-Saxon habits of punctuality, dispatch, and business. When the natives took us for Americans (as of course they did, till we told them we were not so, but *Inglez*) they would sometimes address us, as they evidently thought and intended, very sarcastically, mimicking people in a great hurry, and saying breathlessly, *vamos, go-ahead!—ho! poco tiempo, poco tiempo.*

We were not sorry, after going up and down more ravines, and gullies, and slippery and swampy passes, than I can recount (sometimes, that we might not tumble over their ears, leaning back till we almost touched the tails of our mules), to reach the half-way house, and stop at a canvas hotel built by an American speculator in a small clearing where the sun burned with ferocious rays. However, there were some splendid trees near, which afforded shelter for the mules while they rested.

We got some very nice lemonade and orangeade here, and had the satisfaction of learning that Mrs. H——'s poor little boy had, by a lucky accident, found his way hither after a long and weary wandering in the forest; and his mother had come to claim him, having fortunately heard this fact as she was prosecuting her disconsolate search not far off. The poor little fellow fell fast asleep as soon as they laid him on a rude couch here, and it was thus, wrapped in slumber, she found him. The generous-hearted American who told me the touching tale, could hardly repress his emotion as he described the intense feeling of the poor mother, as she clasped her recovered treasure to her heart.

But such is the American: while he will affront with the utmost carelessness all kinds of hardships, dangers, and privations, and display under the most appalling circumstances the firmest presence of mind—as if, like Nelson in his boyhood, "he had never seen fear," and could not understand what it meant—his noble feelings will thrill at a tale of the sorrow of others, and his heroism fails him when some affecting incident appeals to his unselfish and generous sympathies. If the true hero-nature lives any where it is in the American: *if* the age of chivalry is *not* past—though Burke declared it was, in the Old World of Europe—if, in short, chivalry still exists on earth, it is in the great and mighty West. I think I see a satirical smile on the reader's lips, although so many thousands of miles divide us; and I know if I were in a London drawing-room what a chorus would be raised of "dollars and cents!" &c., but I boldly write what I most conscientiously believe: and how absurd it is to keep harping on one fault (and it really seems almost their only one), as if either a nation or an individual could be absolutely perfect!

I heard another adventure of poor little George here. The proprietor of the hotel apologized very courteously for not having a wholly unoccupied room to show us into, as a poor sick gentleman was sitting down in his principal apartment; and he proceeded to tell me Mrs. H——'s unlucky child had fallen into the Chagres, having leaned over the boat and overbalanced himself, and that this gentleman had plunged into the river, and at great risk and with considerable difficulty, had saved him from perishing. But, during his generous exertions he had become, by some accident, jammed in between two canoes, and had had several ribs broken, and was otherwise much injured. On arriving at Gorgona, however—it appeared, contrary to advice—his gallant spirit impelled him to proceed, though in a very suffering state; and assuring Mrs. H——, who was naturally anxious on his account, after his noble exertions on behalf of her little son, that the hurts he had sustained were very immaterial, he started for Panama, but became so ill and exhausted before he arrived at the canvas *posada*, that he found it indispensably necessary to remain till his recruited strength should enable him to proceed.

He came to speak to us, and seemed anxious Mrs. H—— should not be distressed or alarmed on his account, saying it was nothing, and we must tell her, when we saw her, that in a day or two he should be all right. But he looked exceedingly ill and haggard, and seemed to be suffering much. He was, I believe, no acquaintance of hers, but was accidentally passing by at the moment.

The guides and Mozos took a terribly long time here to unpack and transfer the baggage of one of the pack mules to the one who had such an "ugly" temper. At last we rejoiced to find it was all ready, and, without further delay, we jumped into the saddles, anxious to lose no more time than had already been unavoidably sacrificed, in continuing our journey to the Pacific coast. Off we went, and off nearly went all the boxes, provision-cases, and *valises* that had been transferred to the unsafe keeping of that evil-disposed mule.

There was a very steep hill to slide down almost directly after leaving the half-way house, and it was an excessively narrow path. We had barely got beyond the entrance to this, when the infuriated mule in the wildest rage at having these unwonted burdens packed on his back, attempted to dart past us, and, in so doing, nearly knocked one of the riders off her saddle. Great was the consternation among us: we contrived by some means or other—I have not the least idea how—to make our mules clamber up the least steep precipice-like acclivities of the banks, which rose on either side of the narrow pass, and we had a capital view of the long-eared delinquent tearing down the steep hill like a crazy thing, sending the other poor baggage-mules right and left (who happily declined a kicking-sweepstakes), as if they were of no more account to their unnatural brother than our despised carpet-bags, which he was throwing about as a juggler does balls.

What a sight to us it was to see those two scornful heels sending our innocent *valises* in all directions; it was a frightful spectacle, and alas! the provisions! Heels, in place of hands, presenting refreshments—so awkwardly, backward, too—it was unendurable. To see one's dinner a quarter of a mile up in the air, and one's supper a quarter of a mile down in a swamp, was not exhilarating. It would not have been surprising, as the kicking-mule careered onward, had we been struck by Parthian drumsticks, or rained upon by portable soup (only there was none of the last). At length this disreputable quadruped was caught, and the packages were collected, and the whole process of packing had to be gone through with again. There we sate, watching that seemingly interminable arranging of boxes and bags, and wondering whether the cantankerous animal would play at ball with them all again, or get up any other little extempore *divertissement* for our amusement.

After waiting for an immense time, we were once more able to proceed; but the mules were no longer as brisk as they had been. They had been out a long while, and had had very hard work; and while we were more anxious to hurry on to make up for lost time, they were more desirous of loitering on their toilsome way. Poor things! one could not wonder at it; but it was tiresome, and, besides this, we had not got rid of all annoyance from the rebel. It appeared quite out of place in its new situation, and was avoided by common consent, being clearly not on speaking terms with the baggage-mules, who considered it a mere interloper. It was sent to Coventry by the saddle-mules, too, whom it had disgraced.

Restless and irritable, I think it must have been a poet among mules—or genius of some kind: it would lag behind, and then suddenly, probably driven on by the guides, rush forward like a maniac, and half stab us with a sharp corner of a pormanteau, or thump against us one of our own unconscious carpet-bags. We found these visitations so unpleasant, that we resolved not to allow the animal to play us such tricks any more. We therefore insisted on his being kept in front, and the moment he showed symptoms of delaying on his way, we set up with one accord the peculiar sound the Mozos make to encourage or threaten the mules; and this vocal melody, which was assisted by the powerful arguments and voices of the guides (who probably performed an *obligato* stick-accompaniment to the chorus), had fortunately the desired effect. But, no doubt, the creature, not accustomed to being a pack-mule, became really fatigued, and paused frequently, not with evil intentions, but to rest. However, such bugbears had our own tame boxes become to us (and driven against you by a headstrong mule, they are formidable weapons), that we continued to urge it to go on before us by the cries we had learned from the guides, and our voices had but little rest, any more than the foolish mule had.

It was almost constantly "stopping the way." We had no sooner driven it on than it paused again: it was like one of those great buzzing, teasing flies that, toward the end of summer, perfectly haunt you, and if expelled from your hand, are found on your face, and so on. Now we found our friend sticking on a bank, threatening to tumble down on us if we went on, like an avalanche of mule and *mangas;* and now just standing across our path: and now again he would turn short round, as if to dare us to single combat, and sometimes would play at bo-peep behind the trees—in short, he was the dread and horror of us all, and a cry of "here he comes!" was sufficient to send us all helter-skelter.

A weary American trudging on alone under an accumulation of afflictions, in the shape of blankets, bundles, cloaks, and knapsacks, whom we overtook, had compassion on the poor naughty mule, and humanely interfered in its behalf. "Indeed, ladies, I think the creature's nigh tired out: better let him rest a little." But we had lost so much precious time by these various unforeseen misfortunes, that we could not stop, and we knew by experience what allowing the four-footed culprit to loiter behind would bring on us, and the horrible nudging of trunks and elbowing of boxes, to which we should subject ourselves, probably to the demolition of our ribs. So we declined this; and the state of the case was explained to the humane traveler, and, as he looked almost fagged to death beneath his mountain pile of luggage (and as a reward for his humanity to our tired tormentor), I begged him to put part of his heavy load on one of our lightly-laden mules, which he gladly did.

We were now at a more open part of the road, but soon again we plunged into a thick forest for a short time, and then arrived at a partial clearing. The daylight now was beginning to wane, and I was surprised to see one of the leading mules taken by the guides out of the road along a smooth path to the right. The rest of course followed, and on inquiring what was the reason, the head guide came and said, in consequence of the unfortunate delay it would be safer to wait at an Indian village in the wood till morning, as the road further on was very rough and bad, and the forest so impenetrably thick that it would be very dark; also, that one of the guides with the baggage-mules had hurt his ankle very badly in scrambling among some stumps and blocks of stone, and that it was absolutely necessary he should rest.

After a little parleying and demurring, I consented to remain at this Indian village till the moon rose (when, as it was full, it would be a little lighter than most days in England); and wishing good-night to the weary American traveler, who was "bound" to join some of his companions at an American encampment a little way beyond, and who did not seem much to like the prospect of threading the dark mazes of forest alone without the protection of our escort, we pursued our way to the Indian village.

We found one or two of our mules already unpacked, and the poor guide who had hurt his ankle, evidently in much pain. I told the head man we were expected at Panama, and must positively start when the moon rose, and then we proceeded to examine our quarters. But we found this hut by far the most horrible of any we had yet seen any where. It was entirely full of a dense suffocating smoke, and there were I do not know how many old women and squalling children, and dogs, and rats, and toads, and mice, and probably ducks, and pigs, and turkeys, and chickens, besides, of course, an unlimited allowance of entomological curiosities.

The chief old woman, who was very good-natured and kind, compassionating the horror with which we regarded the accommodations of this cane-caravansary (that seemed a Noah's Ark on dry land), brought us out, at our request, a comfortable bench, and we seated ourselves there, not feeling very sleepy or tired, and exceedingly interested by the spectacle of the tropical forest by starlight. But such a noise as there was in that same forest! It seemed a perfect Babel of brutes, and birds, and insects, and reptiles: there were roarings, and howlings, and barkings, and hissings, and yellings, and jabberings. Whether a fashionable tiger-cat held a *conversazione* that evening, or some learned monkeys were imitating the ways of man, and making interminable speeches in a congress or parliament of their own, I know not; but it seemed to me there never was such a collection of chatter-boxes got together before. Poor *dumb* beasts, indeed! it was a perfect "clatter *versus* patter," which almost drowned the squalling of the children, and chiding of the women inside the hut, and the growling remonstrances of an old man who interposed his paternal authority every now and then, and ordered them all to sleep immediately.

But not for long! The clamor outside, it seemed, re-awoke them; and if the denizens of the forest seemed inclined to nod, the din of the huts roused them again—so they appeared to keep each other always awake.

I wonder if any thing could have composed them to a nap. If one had preached them a very long sermon, or recited to them an extensive speech of Mr. Anstey's in our House of Commons, it *might* have lulled them to sleep. Let this gentleman pardon me, for I do not mention his as exceeding others in heaviness—only in length. As to which is the dullest among all the speeches delivered *there*, the powers forbid that I should have to decide: for "in that lowest deep, a lower deep," &c.

At length the moon rose in her glory, and a beautiful sight that moon-rising was. I, vigilant and wakeful, without loss of time, went round to the back of the hut, and called up the guides, who after a proper quantity of dawdling, excuses, mule-losing (I think they had left one unpicketed, on purpose), and sauntering, sat down again composedly by a little fire of sticks they had kindled, and said sleepily the mule would come (I make no doubt it was our long-eared torment of the previous day)—the mule would *find herself;* they must have a little breakfast. And they accordingly breakfasted on a cigar each, and then began saunter the second. At length, to our glee, the truant was found, the packing completed, and off we started for Panama.

## CHAPTER XLI.

The Journey to Panama resumed—Beauty of the Moon-light—The paved Causeway—First View of the Pacific—The American's Opinion of the old Spaniards—And of the present Natives of the Isthmus—Arrival at Panama—The City—The Grand Plaza—The Bay—The Cathedral—Jesuit Church and College—Ruinous Condition of Panama—Americans in Panama bound for California—The Climate of Panama—Breezes from the Pacific—General M—— —Insects and Reptiles in Panama—The Fire-Beetle—The Family of Madame H—— —A social Custom in Panama—Half-starved Horses and Mules—Panama becoming Americanized—The Carriages in that City.

It was moonlight when we resumed our journey;—and such a moon—earth, air, and sky were all swathed up like costly treasures in glittering cloth of silver! it was resplendent. We had much admired, during the night, the glorious Southern Cross, and another lovely constellation, also very much in the form of a cross: all was so beautiful, that heaven and earth seemed almost contending for the palm of loveliness.

We rode silently on, overwhelmed with admiration, and after going for some time through the thick forest, which made the moonlight appear like a soft illumination through an emerald-colored glass or transparency, we suddenly emerged from the woods on a clearing; and so dazzling and glorious was the flood of light that poured down upon us, that I exclaimed to V——, that we must have been mistaken in the hour, as it was broad daylight. But a glance overhead, where the triumphant suzerain of the night was riding in her zenith, pouring, I may say *snowing* down rays of intense white light on every side, undeceived me. It was truly splendid: the air seemed all powdered crystal, or shivered diamonds. The heavenly arch looked so high, and so clear, that the eye seemed to see for a million of miles, up and up, and the air appeared all One Star; verily, the glory sank and melted into the very soul.

Some of our mules had become very lazy. I do not think they had had enough food when we stopped, and our lame guide limping slowly on, caused our cavalcade to journey at a very gentle pace. At length, the morning dawned, the sun rose, and we began to look out with intense anxiety for the mighty Pacific; but the intervening hills still screened this king of oceans from our longing gaze. The road was extremely bad and rough, but we were too eager to mind that very much.

The mule in disgrace was almost forgiven, but the *pas* was still scrupulously given to her—no question of precedence was ever attended to with more rigid etiquette. We did not at all agree with Lady Macbeth, "Stand not upon the order of your going;" our very mules, so taught and trained by us the day before, seemed inclined when their treacherous comrade lagged a little, to make a sidling courtesy, and wait till she resumed the lead. She was still sent to Coventry; and if it was she who was lost in the forest that morning, it was doubtless owing to her going to have a chat with some wildcat or monkey, who did not know what *mauvaise odeur* the creature was in.

At last the rugged causeway seemed a trifle better, and we met numerous groups on foot and horseback, and felt we were getting near the coast. This paved causeway is said by some to have been made by the buccaneers when they were in possession of Panama; by others, to be the remains of an excellent road left by the old Spaniards. As to its state in some parts now—like that of the pack of hounds described by a boy some years ago, as wanting nothing but new horses, new huntsmen, and new hounds—it only requires new stones, new paving, new workmen, and a new road.

Soon after we had to cross a savanna, and we still kept our eyes fixed on the horizon, forgetting even the kicking mule, who took the opportunity of waiting behind, and coming up again with one of her peculiar Chifney rushes, after which, she and the Pacific contended for our anxious regards and attention, and they ran a rather severe race, the majestic Pacific (a splendid bay) winning at last only by a nose—so nearly was it a dead heat.

And now our guides stopped at a hovel near the road, and dandified themselves prodigiously. I suppose they have a dépôt of *sombreros* there, and of handkerchiefs and various toggery. The poor lame Mozo stopped at this place; he could proceed no further; so, with a diminished escort, we prepared to enter into the city. At last the glorious Pacific came in sight, and magnificent it looked; but so long had I looked forward to this happy moment, and dwelt in fancy on the pleasure of beholding this mighty ocean, that it seemed more like hailing again an old friend, than meeting a new one.

Somewhere near that part of the road, we crossed a handsome, though rather dilapidated bridge, over a stream. An American was sitting down to rest there, and as I passed by, drew my attention to it, saying it was almost the first mark of civilization, he had seen in the country.

"And it was built by the old Spaniards," he said, "the natives tell me, as every thing else was that they have that's worth showing. The old Spaniards did nobly by the country; but they won't even keep their works in repair. Some are gone, and some are going, and these niggers get more and more like savages."

The compliment to old Spain I fully agreed in, but not in his sweeping censure on the natives of the Isthmus. Though idle they certainly appear to be, I think their government may bear great part of this blame. A republican form of government is not, can not be suited to people so utterly unprepared for the onerous task of self-government, unfitted by nature, and unaided by education.

It was not long before we were trampling along the streets of the old picturesque city of Panama, among groups of natives, and scarlet-garbed Americans, who, as we passed, asked us a question that had been put to us frequently along the road, always with the greatest civility.

"You're one of the 'Georgia's passengers, I think, ma'am ?"

"Yes."

"Have you seen many parties still on the road ?" &c.

I was much struck by the first sight of Panama, ruined and neglected as it appeared. The suburbs, however, were even less imposing than such parts of a city usually are, consisting of tumble-down Indian huts, squalid and poverty-stricken, some patches of cultivated ground, and some antiquated *ranchos*. Afterward we crossed the line of the old fortifications (strong walls and ramparts still surround the town); and we immediately came to some noble edifices, proud and princely, though in a ruined state.—Their sad condition is almost vailed, and their decay beautified, by the profuse and brilliant vegetation that has poured over them—as the sea closes, with its bright and flashing waters, above a wreck.

We rode through the Grand Plaza, which was then thronged with people, among whom were crowds of Americans; and we passed an extremely noble church, and an old convent of great architectural beauty, ornamented with very handsome pillars, with Corinthian capitals.

Panama is beautifully situated. The lovely bay has been often compared to the famous harbor of Rio Janeiro. The city stands upon a tongue of land that runs far out to sea, ending in a sharp point that is partially overflowed at high tide. Its many decayed but stately churches, its venerable dilipidated monasteries and mouldering convents, boasting many architectural perfections, and crowned with the picturesque vegetation of the Torrid Zone, wherever time has made melancholy rents—its noble stone buildings, terraced and balconied—its ancient fortifications, and broad *plazas*, and, in the vicinity, its numerous gardens and flourishing orchards, villas, and *ranchos* and *haciendas*, and grounds for pasturage, and groves of palms, all render it striking and highly interesting. The longer I stay, the more I admire its situation, which at the base of this range of beautiful hills, with the Pacific washing three sides of its tapering promontory, is very grand.

One broad and verdant mountain, deluged in vegetation, uprears its graceful crest close behind it; and a chain of other noble mountains, crowned with forests, beyond the southeastern shore of the bay, appears perpetually enveloped in soft vapory clouds, which make them, perhaps, seem higher than they are in reality.

We had the other evening a delightful walk on the ramparts: they command an enchanting view of the bay, and a series of green and fertile islands, among which Taboga is the most beautiful. The towers and churches of the fine old town, so picturesque and touching in its decay (at the foot of those indestructible hills, appareled in the undecaying pomp of tropical nature), nearly a hundred miles of fruitful shores exposed to the vision, which takes in the grand curve of the gulf, and the miniature bays and creeks fringed profusely with the feathery palms, and those beauteous islands and forests, and the mountains afar, and the mighty ocean rolling its foamy surf, with its solemn, measured march, high up on the shore, all united to make the scene one of consummate beauty and grandeur.

The venerable cathedral here is a very fine building; and what is left of the ancient Jesuit church of San Felipe is extremely imposing. The magnificent arches spanning the nave are wreathed and crowned by a forest of wild vines and luxuriant shrubbery and these rich masses of foliage form here and there a partial roof for the otherwise uncovered building. A stately college, which had never been completed, looks on one of the plazas. Its pillars and pilasters are splintered and decaying; but Nature has stepped in, and thrown her own mantle of glory around the fading beauties of her sister, Art. There are some Franciscan and Augustinian monasteries here in tolerable preservation; but, altogether, I certainly never beheld any thing like the desolation and decay to be witnessed during a short walk in Panama.

In almost every street may be seen several ruins; had I not been prepared for the general state of dilapidation in which this once prosperous city is now, I should have thought, on the first glance, a succession of dreadful fires had lately taken place here, from the dreary multitude of yawning chasms on all sides, where edifices of different kinds have been.

Nay, at the *fonda* where we first were staying, we needed not to walk out to see ruins, for in front of the hotel was a gaping space, lumbered with tottering, roofless walls, and overgrown by shrubs, bananas, and a hanging wilderness of climbing plants. On the old ramparts, with their massive, frowning battlements, may still be seen some antique guns of Old Spain: they are said to be made of the beautiful and costly bronze of Barcelona.

As a fortified town, Panama, notwithstanding its being girt by strong and solid walls, can not be said to be placed in a favorable position. It appears to be entirely commanded by the hill behind it, which is easy of access, and planted on which, the artillery of a foe might completely batter and destroy all its—ruins!

We live very quietly here, and I hear but little of California; but I was told the other day, there are about ten steamers lately gone, or on the eve of going there, from hence. Still, vast numbers of Americans are detained here, unable to proceed to their destination. A little while ago, they say, there were between two and three thousand here. Most of them encamp near the town, and some, I am afraid, suffer many privations and hardships from the delay they are exposed to.

I have just heard, since I wrote the above, that nearly a thousand Americans started yesterday, in different steam vessels, for California. They are generally a superior class of emigrants that come this way, as it is an expensive route, and the "rough lots," as they often term them, ordinarily go across the plains with their wagons and tents, or by the tedious way of Cape Horn. Tickets have been at a tremendous price, and it is said great impositions have been sometimes practiced on the more inexperienced or easy emigrants.

Yesterday I was suffering much from that odious hay asthma again, which I had last spring. But for this, I might be returning now, or very shortly, to catch the English steamer at Chagres; but I fear I shall not be able to do so just yet. It is at this time of year, only, one is subject to these attacks, and if I were at sea now, or in the heart of a city, or on a desert plain, I should no doubt entirely escape this infliction; but in the midst of the munificence and luxuriance of Nature here (for this seems a city and garden, and forest in one), trailing her glorious masses of foliage to the very shores of the Pacific, and flinging her living *earthly* beauty—clad in those royal robes—almost into its majestic waves (her grandest watery empire), I am thus victimized and tormented. Were I seeking for poor Sir John Franklin now, amidst the barren Arctic ice, probably this vile enemy would keep at a respectful distance; but here, where a mighty Pacific Ocean of streaming flowers and foliage overflows into the sister Pacific of pearls, and shells, and rolling billows, and flashing waves, it pitilessly assails me.

Not so, however, in equally beautiful Mexico; but that is, I think, a most peculiar and matchless climate, the Elysium of the world; bracing as England, beautiful as Italy—nay, *far* more so and blazing with the unutterable glory of the richest and rarest tropical splendors. Mexico really seems hardly of the earth, and the high-sounding name the Chinese claim so presumptuously for their country, would scarcely appear to be a figure of speech, if applied to lovely, matchless Mexico,—"The Central Flowery Land, the Celestial Empire."

Perhaps the people may not be quite worthy of it—what people on earth could be? but they appreciate and love it, I think, deeply; and for a traveler they are just the population for it! They may want, to a certain extent, energy, enterprise, solidity, habits of business, and even, in some respects, patriotism; but they are, I think, the most splendidly picturesque people (not excepting even the Greeks—that is, the *Albanian* Greeks) in the whole world. They dress their country well! they become and grace that beauteous land, and do its outward aspect justice, by thus adorning it appropriately with their romantic-looking selves, and their magnificent drapery-like *serapés*.

We had some splendid singing and playing here the other night from a young French gentleman (partly of Spanish origin), M. de M., who is on his way to Valparaiso and Buenos Ayres, from Paris. He is staying with Monsieur Le C——, the agreeable and amiable French consul. He sang admirably, and his instrumental performances were extraordinarily fine (there is an excellent piano-forte in the drawing-room here). M. de M.'s musical memory appears to be prodigious: he seems to know almost all the modern operas through by heart, and his singings out of the

"Prophète," "Beatrice," &c., were magnificent. Miss P. sings extremely well, and she accompanied him very charmingly in some duets.

There is a delicious breeze blowing to-day through my wide-open windows from the Pacific, and it almost carries away my paper as I write. The breeze seems getting stronger (it is too hot to shut the window), and my writing stands a considerable chance of being wafted off to the "Grand Ocean," as they call the mighty Pacific.

I went a little time ago to see my amiable acquaintance, Mrs. H——. I found her at home, and Mrs. —— also, who is at the same hotel. I saw the poor little boy who had had such narrow escapes; he has hardly yet recovered his terrible and fatiguing walk. His mother tells me, when she first saw him, he was much altered in appearance, and his throat was frightfully swollen —she thought from over-exertion and frequent exposure to the sun; but it appears to me probable, he may have eaten something injurious during his weary march, that may have produced such an effect. Poor little fellow! his chief distress seems to have been the anxiety and alarm that he was aware his mother must be undergoing during his prolonged absence. Mrs. H—— hopes to start for California in a steamer that goes in a few days, and I trust she will arrive there without any further annoyances and trials.

General M——, formerly President of New Granada, dined here last night. He seems a highly-informed person, who has traveled much in Europe, and who would be extremely agreeable, but from a painfully difficult articulation, in consequence of a severe wound received in battle, in his mouth and jaw, which has left a terrible scar. It is said the ball passed completely through his mouth, cutting his tongue in twain in its passage. It was impossible to avoid thinking of the self-same process (though by the instrumentality of a different weapon), to which are subjected magpies, or ravens, or both, in the Old World, to improve their powers of pronunciation—it certainly has the diametrically opposite effect on the human biped.

General M—— appears to be a most public-spirited man, and to have the good of his fine country much at heart. His attention is greatly occupied just now by the contemplated railroad from Chagres to this place, and he is said to be busily engaged in transporting slave laborers from one of the States in the interior of New Granada to work upon it. This is a free State.

Insects and reptiles abound here. It is necessary to shake one's gown well before putting it on, in case a scorpion may have taken a fancy to the garment. Miss P——'s maid shook one out of hers the other day. A few evenings ago Mr. P—— had a passage of arms with a gallant knight-errant, in the shape of a chivalrous centipede that was boldly wandering over the wall close to where some of us were sitting. The meandering reptile, on being attacked by a huge paper-cutter, kept up for some time a persevering running fight. The assailant brandished his weapon of attack vigorously; but when your foe has so many legs wherewith to run away, it is difficult to catch him "any how you fix it." After sundry desperate stabs at the wall, which the centipede with great celerity and dexterity avoided, the poor reptile was partly caught, and his tail docked, but the rest of him ran off, putting all his best legs foremost, and evaporated. Nothing was left as a trophy of victory but the poor fellow's tail, and a select few of its many legs. I was sorry for this *dénouement*, as I can not bear to think of the mutilation and pain of even a reptile; a prompt and speedy death is so far préferable! However, I am not sufficiently read in entomological history to know whether centipedes, as some other reptiles are said to do, can laugh at such mutilations, and grow together again; if so, probably the following morning he would return to look for the missing portion of himself, and neatly patch himself up in no time.

A magnificent fire-beetle was caught in the *sala* last night; the illumination it cast was splendid. It shone with amazing brightness through a cambric handkerchief that was used as a temporary prison for it: one might almost have been afraid that it would commit arson unintentionally, and burn its transparent dungeon. Its incarceration did not seem to diminish its glorious lustre at all. I was afraid it would be hurt, but it literally made *light* of every thing. Miss P—— afterward held it to her ear, and it is impossible to express the effect this beauteous living ornament, this animated diamond produced: it would have made jewels of the first water look dull and dim near it. It cast a splendid glittering glow on Miss P——'s beautiful dark hair and delicate cheek—it was really exquisite. It afterward flew up to the loftiest part of the immensely high roof, and settled there: it flung a lovely fairy-like light over the rafters, and seemed like a star that was shining through the roof.

We have made acquaintance here with a very amiable and accomplished family, one of the most distinguished in the place, that of Madame H——. She is a delightful person herself, and her daughters appear highly educated and exceedingly pleasing. One of her sons is more like an Englishman than a cavalier of the Spanish race, and so perfect are his accent and manner of speaking our language, that I could with difficulty believe he was any thing but genuine Anglo-Saxon. They are of pure Spanish descent.

They have in the rich native families here a charming custom, especially for hot countries. After dinner, all the company rise and adjourn to another apartment, fresh and cool, where the dessert is set out, and the fruits are mingled with the loveliest flowers. Of course, all odor of dinner is thus entirely left behind. I think it is even more refined and pleasant than the Havana custom I have spoken of before.

We escape under the consul's hospitable roof one source of great annoyance to us, and that is, the sight of numerous poor half-starved horses and mules, that we used to see from the hotel, and which seem to make a practice of promenading the streets for food. They eagerly ate any morsel of old crust thrown out to them, and were evidently in a famishing state, trying with their poor noses on the ground to pick up something, in vain. The fact is, I believe, that some time ago, these then deserted streets were covered with grass, and it was the universal custom to turn animals loose to graze there, as in a meadow. Now the busy trampling feet of thousands of Americans have destroyed that formerly abundant street-pasturage; but the inhabitants, mostly averse to innovation, continue the practice, and the wretched creatures often starve to death in the streets. Their carcasses are dragged down to the beach and there they are left to poison the air; and the horrible odor is often plainly perceptible in Mr. P——'s residence, so that it is necessary occasionally to shut the windows, and almost endure suffocation from heat, in order to escape the sickening effluvium.

The city in some respects seems becoming Americanized, but not in important particulars, as the foregoing statements will sufficiently prove. But when you take a little promenade in the roughly-paved plazas or streets (walk you must, for there are no carriages), you will hear "Oh, Susanna," on your right side, "Uncle Ned," on your left, "Hail Columbia," from the balcony over head, and the "Arkansas Hunters," from the shop at your side. I make no doubt, from what I hear, that shandy-gaff, and hail-storms, and mint-julep, are constantly kept in readiness for any that require them.

But imagine what a change it must seem to us, not to see a carriage of any description ever in the streets of Panama, having so lately left the Havana, which certainly, if any place can be so, is almost too full of rolling equipages—in short, from the most over-carriaged town in the world, we came straight to the most under-carriaged one. I asked some one the other day, whether there was not even a one-mule chaise in Panama. "No," was the reply; "but Señor —— *has* a cart"—evidently that was thought to be a great march of improvement. A single cart (for it *is* the only one) in the chief town of a country, where soon a railroad is expected to be laid down!—it will be a jump, indeed!

---

## CHAPTER XLII.

Monarchy and Democracy—England's Treatment of her Colonies—The Greatness of America—Her Tendency to Propagandism—Anecdote of a Paroquet—The Pearl Fishery at Panama—The Captain and his Crew—General Rosas—Beautifully scented Woods in Panama—The Rose Fever—Theatricals in Panama—Hostility between Americans and the Natives of Panama—Fair Children in Panama—The would-be Englishwoman.

New Granada, from accounts I have heard, would not object much to giving up the Isthmus to the United States, but France and England, from various reasons, no doubt would! Education, and many other advantages, doubtless, would accrue to the people under the enlightened rule of the Americans; but, after all, it seems a republican government is not suited to these South American nations: it becomes a tyranny or a nullity with them. The genius, character, and habits of the people tend toward monarchical institutions in general. Old Spain has left her mark upon them; she trained all her colonies in her own spirit; she deeply imbued them with her own principles: this has grown with their growth, and strengthened with their strength; and though, when they threw off her yoke, and asserted their national independence, the example of the most flourishing and powerful nation in this hemisphere was, as it were, instinctively followed (as if the mere resemblance in the form of government, without any similarity in character, traditions, or habits of thought, could effect equal results), yet the people, it would appear, have generally retained the impressions that the mother country sought always consistently to give them.

In vain the letter is altered; the spirit is still there. A monarchy herself, she educated and trained her colonies in monarchical principles, as did Portugal also; and the consequence is, that though by the overwhelming influence of the example of the mightiest people of the New World they mostly are republics in name, it is in name only. Look at Mexico; look at her eminently aristocratical church and army; see how in society counts and marquises retain their titles to this very day, and how in a thousand other things the real tendencies of the people break forth. How differently does England treat her colonies—with what care, apparently, does she lead them, and teach them, and tutor them to be republics in time. Monarchy is a sort of distant vision—a myth to them: they are seldom reminded of it; it is a shadow and a name. and democracy seems the substance. Monarchy is a rare and holiday visitor; democracy is their every-day comrade and friend: it comes home to every man's bosom and business there; it is with him in the market-place, with him in the street, it is part of his every-day life, it is with him in all his social intercourse; and if in the settlers from the old country, habits previously acquired and sentiments originally instilled into them should retain *some* dominion over them, fainter and fainter indeed, but still not wholly eradicated —in the next generation, when no such antecedents have left a shadow behind, it is entirely annihilated.

It may be objected that, notwithstanding Spain through all her widely extended colonies consistently and perseveringly carried out the fundamental principles of her laws, and unvaryingly caused them to participate freely and fully in all the spirit and forms of her own institutions, yet these colonies were not deterred from separating themselves from the mother-country. That they did so —true; but the circumstances under which they asserted and won their independence had nothing to do with their being monarchical, or democratical in their internal policy. Other and more cogent reasons determined them on their course; and although the metropolitan country acted wisely with regard to her dependencies in particular instances, in a number of important matters she committed the most flagrant errors. Heaven knows we manage our colonies ill enough in most matters, and we have ingeniously superadded to our shortcomings and weaknesses the great fault of doing all in our power to make them not only quite indifferent *to* us now, but utterly different *from* ourselves in government and political organization, whenever in the fullness of time (and that time is probably not far distant, and will, we must undoubtedly feel, assuredly come) they sever themselves from us, as the dependencies of Spain did from her, and establish themselves as independent nations, for it will be doubtless as—republics.

Then, instead of having the great tie of a close resemblance in all political institutions, and that wide sympathy which must spring from an identity of all the forms of constitutional administration and of organization, we must take leave of them, and lose them indeed! for they will naturally and spontaneously cling to those governments which have the greatest similarity to their own, and feel that the same act which has disjoined them from a state of government so little analagous to their own selected one, has, as it were, connected them with those that are formed on the same model and established on the same foundations.

It is a great compliment to our mighty transatlantic brethren, without doubt, that we should be moulding and forming all our colonies to tread in their footsteps and follow their example; but it is a very bad compliment to our own institutions; and in the course of time will tend, if persevered in, I am persuaded, very greatly to endanger them. Two great principles will divide the world one day or the other: democracy and monarchy, and one or the other will ultimately have the ascendency; and as we should not think it wise or prudent of our republican brethren to sow every where, from the largest to the smallest of their states perhaps, the seeds of absolutism, or of sovereignty, so neither can it be discreet in us to sow broadcast over our own vast transmarine territorial possessions, the seeds of republicanism and democracy. "Qui se ressemble s'assemble;" and we are actually training and disciplining troops for the future political warfare of the world, that must and will necessarily range themselves in hostility against our professed and declared principles and sentiments.

It may be that our statesmen care not for the future—*après moi le déluge:* it may be that they have a secret leaning toward the wholly popular forms of government themselves; but on this I have nothing to say, neither am I arguing in the least as to the relative perfections of this or that form of government. I only say, *if* we think our own constitution and institutions are good—are the best (and *if* we do not think so, certainly no time ought to be lost in changing them, as far as reason and prudence will permit), then we ought to do our duty, and consistently act, so as to extend this system, and these advantages, to those over whom we have so much influence for evil or for good.

Surely no one can doubt for a moment what Australia would

become, if she established her independence now; and every year that passes over our heads adds more to the strength and vigor of her popular principles. As year after year sees the older settlers more alienated, by the state of things around them, from the once-venerated traditions of their fathers and the character of their ancient relations, associations, and prepossessions; and as the accumulation of democratic elements naturally and necessarily (without any antagonizing, or at least counteracting influences) continues to increase, as hosts of humble emigrants, and few but humble emigrants, pour down upon the shores of that grand and promising colony—how can it be otherwise? Representatives of *all* our different classes and orders should be encouraged to go there, by all legitimate means; another spirit would be quickly infused; and instead of a gradual, but certain alienation from the forms, character, and tone of our institutions, the reverse would be the case, and the manners and all the usages of the society of the older world would be insensibly introduced, adopted, and preferred; and if we aided the development of those inclinations by a strict adaptation to the colony of all the various agencies and accompaniments of a form of government like ours—those co-operating circumstances that have proved so instrumental in our own country in the establishment of a monarchy, and in securing that monarchy's permanency and consolidation—there is no more reason that, in the event of Australia becoming independent of England, she should frame a republican constitution, than that Belgium should have done so when separated from Holland.

We should have a peerage in all our colonies, whose honors should be distributed with perfect impartiality and justice—orders of knighthood, rewards, distinctions, and every thing else that the mother country herself has; and it would soon be found not only that the aristocratic element would be largely infused into the plebeian, but also that a spirit beyond that of mere money-making would be more generally and preponderatingly introduced.

It may be said, and very truly, that the people of the United States are as enlightened, chivalrous, and noble a people as can exist, notwithstanding that the love of money-making certainly largely enters into their composition. Granted, and more than granted; for I have a most sincere admiration for the true nobility of nature of the Americans in general; but their past position was widely different from that of our colonists at present. The history and cherished traditions of their race, the examples of all the mighty countries of the world, *at that time*, tended to inspire them with a deep respect for monarchical constitutions, and the time-honored customs and ordinations belonging thereto; and though their own form of government, chiefly through the decision and habits of thought of some of their principal men, and the local tendency to republicanism that we had encouraged and established among them, became after the separation a commonwealth; yet they instinctively turned for models of greatness and perfection, glory and grandeur and success to the Old World absolutisms, or constitutional sovereignties, and thus combined much chivalrous sentiment and hero-magnanimity with other tendencies and characteristics.

But it is a far other case with the inhabitants of our present important and noble dependencies; they have shining chiefly before their eyes the material prosperity, and fast increasing power, and stupendous greatness of their elder, but liberated brother. All that can attract, dazzle, fascinate, and inspire with the deepest admiration, is to be found in that magnificent and giant nation; and to follow in their footsteps well may be the ambition of every young and independent state. But still Mammon there *is* too much worshiped, and in *that* will their example probably be most faithfully followed.

Do we, or do we not, wish to counteract the democratic tendencies of our colonies? If we do, no further time is to be wasted; and if we do not, we are certainly doing all we by possibility can, short of giving those colonies the *name* as well as the nature of republics, to promote the rapid establishment of such a system of government in all of them. Surely according to the basis of our own constitution—so should the superstructure be *throughout*.

Forgive, reader, this digression. Many things I hear, many circumstances that have transpired under my own eyes, have led me to think much on these subjects; subjects that may seem of little consequence in the present moment, but which will prove of such enormous importance in the future. The Americans are the greatest political propagandists imaginable, and believing their own singularly successful and admirably administered form of government to be the most perfect in the world, who can censure them for being so? They are too clear-sighted, and too desirous that their own democracy should ultimately overshadow and control all the nations of the earth, not to rejoice at the way in which we are playing into their hands.

. . . . . . . . . . . . .

But let me now tell, by way of a little variety, a curious circumstance relating to natural history that has lately occurred. I think I have mentioned a little cross-grained paroquet that V—— took under her especial protection soon after we arrived here. Not being fascinated by its manners, and having an objection to being sharply bitten whenever I approached too near the little wretch, I declined as far as possible the honor of his acquaintance, and never took the slightest notice of him, nor he of me, for he found I would not submit to his biting attacks generally, and therefore he turned his attention to others, who were either more afraid of him, or who by such devotion as V——'s won him over by constantly offering him "dulces" and fruit.

One afternoon I was very busily employed in writing or reading, and it happened I was quite absorbed and wrapped up in my occupation, and hardly knew that my little cross-patch of a paroquet had been left to amuse himself on the balcony, as was sometimes the case. Presently he began making a tremendous and piercing noise, screaming far louder than I had ever heard him do. I took no notice at first, but the sound increased, and I thought was pertinaciously addressed to me—I can not describe what a deafening din the little animal contrived to make, evidently to attract my attention. At last I looked up, and beheld it to my surprise posting directly toward me, as fast as it could waddle, for its gait was something like that of the Turkish or Tunis women, in their tumble-off slippers. It had to cross a great part of the immense drawing-room to get to me; but with its eyes fixed on me in the most supplicating manner, and almost starting out of its little poked-forward head, it hurried on, making right for the place where I was sitting. Surprised at its unusual conduct, and compassionating the poor little creature's evident perturbation and uneasiness—though in what originating I knew not—I put down my hand for the bird to mount on the finger, as it commonly did; it lost not a quarter of a second in so doing, fluttering with anxiety, and half-dead with terror. The moment I took it up, it hid itself, as well as it could, in the folds of a shawl I had on.

I felt there must be some enemy at hand, but what, and where? I glanced round the room. In a corner near the balcony, which was comparatively dark, I perceived a cat, who was all ready for the fatal spring, but had possibly been arrested by the same instinct that had taught the sensible little bird to hurry and clamor so loudly to me for protection. Puss was so grievously disappointed at the loss of her anticipated repast, that she actually seemed almost inclined to dispute with me the poor little trembling paroquet, who was, as nearly as a bird could be, in hysterics of fear. He shook with terror, and seemed as if he would fall into a fit.

I drove the cat away; and after a great deal of soothing and encouraging, the poor little paroquet was restored to composure, and after a long time, showed his convalescence and his gratitude by hints that he began to feel himself in biting trim again. However, I think since this affair he has not bit me, when I have ventured to approach, quite so savagely or so often as before.

To turn from this little ex-demon, to a totally different subject. I was reading in my room the other day, when I was called to see a pretty sight. On hurrying out of our suite of rooms, what should I see but a little winged angel on the stairs! This was a child of Señora ——, who was dressed to perform her part in a religious procession that was going to take place. The little creature looked lovely, covered with resplendent diamonds and pearls, and furnished with bright little silvery wings; but it had a sad expression of countenance, the effect of which was very touching. A sort of star, of magnificent jewels, was gleaming on its bosom, and it seemed almost oppressed by the weight of gems it had to carry.

This angel visitant was accompanied by a nurse, who appeared very proud of the little glittering thing, and of the profusion of costly jewels with which it was so superbly adorned. The pearls were wonderfully splendid; but this is a native land—or rather native water—of pearls, for there is a regular pearl-fishery established here.

These treasures of the deep are abundantly found around the adjoining islands, and prove a profitable source of employment to a considerable body of men, who follow the laborious occupation of divers. It is said, that Messrs. Rundell and Bridge, some time ago, paid down a sum of money for the right to monopolize the trade, and they sent out from England a diving-bell, which it was anticipated would materially tend to increase the supply of pearls from these oyster-beds; but the attempt was a vain one, in consequence of the rocky nature of the bottom of the bay, together with the very heavy ground-swell, which is so frequent here. The trade was, therefore, again transferred to the natives, who sell all they find to the resident merchants, for the jewel-cases of the fair Panamanians, as it is said not many are exported to the Old World.

The cook here (who, by the way, is an excellent one) sent up to me, the other day, a number of lovely pearls, which he had purchased, I believe, from the divers on speculation. They looked tempting enough, as they rolled one by one out of the long tubular case in which they were deposited, shining with extraordinary lustre—so fresh from the great Pacific that all the snowy whiteness of its eternal surf seemed sparkling on them!

But I would not purchase any; for, while traveling and voyaging about, it is far preferable to have nothing that is valuable, as far as it can be avoided. I had left every thing I brought with me of any value in the British Consulate at the Havana, Mr. Kennedy having given me permission so to do.

A day or two ago, I had a surprise, which was occasioned by a very different being from the pretty winged angel, mailed in jewels, and with a little halo of splendor around it. I was returning in the afternoon from the drawing-room to my own apartment, to arrive at which I had to traverse several rooms; the first a sort of sitting-room, which opened on one side to a chamber generally appropriated by Madame Jenny (the French *femme de chambre* of Miss P——) for the safe-keeping of various stores; and on the other side there was a door, which conducted to the room which H. and W. inhabited, who were then both out. When I reached the large gate-like doors which led to the outer apartment, I was much astonished to see them shut, and still more to see them opened suddenly, and a man in a sailor-like garb rush out in a horrible condition!

He had evidently been subjected to shocking bad treatment; his head and face seemed a mass of bruises and wounds, and he appeared considerably agitated, not to say alarmed. He informed me, in a hurried manner, that he was the captain of a merchant-vessel, then at Panama, and had had a mutiny among his men; had escaped with difficulty, was pursued by them, and dreadfully ill-treated; he had rushed into the Consulate for refuge and safety, and was watched by the disaffected crew, who had stationed themselves at the gates of the Consulate, not daring to penetrate further, but intending to attack him, if he ventured to quit its sheltering roof.

Mr. P—— was out at the time, but was momentarily expected home. A chair was brought by Madame Jenny, and placed near the office-door, where the poor man waited till the Consul arrived, to tell his piteous tale. Mr. P—— told me afterward that such cases are of very common occurrence here now. The crews, in general, it appears, are all anxious to get to California (and when there, to go to the mines); besides, they have constant opportunities of getting higher wages, and are continually in a state of discontent.

We have no Consul, I find, at San Francisco, which seems very strange, when it is considered how many English merchant-ships there are now at that port, and what an important place it has become.

There is a family of distinction here, from Buenos Ayres, and as it seems General Rosas makes all his followers, male and female, wear his colors, red and all red: in whatever part of the world they may be, they are forced, on the most broiling day, to go about like land-lubberized and boiled lobsters. The great Dictator, it is asserted, has spies in multitudes in all parts, and no one dare infringe his rules, as they would certainly be detected. Thus these Buenos-Ayrean travelers are condemned to this perpetual blush of "celestial rosy red" from morning till night, and, for aught I know to the contrary, from night till morning also, in the shape of vermilion night-robes.

I believe they do not very often leave their habitation, but whenever they do—no matter how sultry or sunshiny the day, so near the equator—they are necessitated to make their appearance like locomotive bonfires, or beef-eaters of private life, or demons (amiable social ones, however), such as strutted formerly in the hideous *auto-da-fé* processions, painted all over with crimson flames—or perambulating poppies, or peripatetic scarlet-beans, or as if they were burning themselves in effigy (for red in this blazing sunshine seems to roast one); in short, they were, as a French friend of mine once designated a married lady and gentleman of my acquaintance, who were remarkable for rubicund complexions, a regular *ménage carotte.* It would be awkward for them to meet a *vaquero* driving a herd of bulls accidentally, for the fury aroused in these animals by the sight of scarlet is well known.

General Rosas is said to be extremely civil and obliging just now to the English. We have had a tremendous thunder-storm here; it was necessary to close all the windows, and the crashing of the thunder was terrific. The rain came down like a temporary deluge, but the air seemed very sweet and fresh after it, though I do not think it was made much cooler.

Almost every evening we hear fandangoes going on, *al fresco* among the natives, and mulattoes and negroes, who seem passionately fond votaries of Terpsichore. The sound of their guitars, drums and flageolets, with the accompaniment, I believe, of some hollow gourds, in which they rattle a number of pebbles, is pleasant enough at a distance, mingling with the chiming, solemn roll of the ocean.

Madame H—— came to a little *soirée* here the other night. She was sitting by me on the sofa, and as we were conversing together, I was charmed by a perfume on her handkerchief, the most exquisite it is possible to imagine. I could not resist asking her the name of it, and if it was a Panamanian perfume. She told me it was the scrapings of a highly-scented wood that grows in the forests of the Isthmus. These little shavings of wood, the odor of which I think is incomparably delicious, are laid among the handkerchiefs, and give them an intense fragrance.

Madame H—— was kind enough to say she would send me some of these scrapings, as I admired the scent so much, and accordingly a little packet arrived the following day, but of another kind of wood, Madame H——finding her stock of the first was exhausted. This is very sweet, but does not at all equal the wood that had previously so much charmed me.

A French lady at the Havana, the wife of a medical gentleman from Paris, begged me, when I came here, to ascertain whether there was any opening for a French physician here, they having been ruined by the French revolution (not because it improved the general health, though). I consequently made inquiries, and found there were at least two established here, who are much liked. There are American doctors here too, and an English one also. The latter has attended me; he is a clever person, most highly recommended, and has almost cured my hay-asthma. By the way, this complaint is known in the United States, and is called there, rose-fever.

I am strongly recommended, instead of returning at once across the Isthmus, to proceed to Lima in one of the English steamers, that regularly run from hence to Callao and Valparaiso every month. The sea voyage would do me a great deal of good, and drive away, probably, all remains of the indisposition; and I think Lima would, independently of that, be well worth a visit, now that we are, comparatively speaking, so near it. I have almost recovered from the attack, but I dare not venture out at present.

Miss P—— went last evening to the theatre with Madame H——. I believe it is an enormous building, quite unfinished, and not originally designed for the purpose it now serves, it is without any roof whatever, so the spectators sit there *à la belle étoile*, happy indeed if the stars *do* shine, and no storm of rain, such as we lately had, comes down to wash them out of their seats. The performances are said to be very fair. "No toca a la reina," from the French play, "Ne touchez pas á la reine," was given the other night, and, I hear, very nicely acted.

The Americans, many of whom do not understand Spanish, got up some opposition theatricals a day or two ago in one of the hotels, the *sala* of which was fitted up as a theatre; but this failed, the company not meeting altogether with the approbation of the audience—at least so it was rumored. It happened that the evening was oppressively hot, and I think the actors must have found it hard work to please a large number of people, crowded together in-doors, in a comparatively small room. In such an atmosphere as must have prevailed there, they could not have attempted much exertion themselves assuredly, unless they had been salamanders, and applause too, so necessary to stimulate actors, must have been wanting. Certainly the *cooler* roofless theatre must, under these circumstances, bear away the palm and win the *palms*, from the very fact of its being so.

A sort of riot took place here a little while ago, I believe in consequence of some suspected robbery. One man supposed, among others, to be implicated, was chased a good distance by the aggrieved parties. Mr. P——, returning from a ride he had taken into the country, met this hunted man running near the entrance to the town, and he rather coolly asked Mr. P—— to lend him his horse, which proposition was respectfully declined.

It is said there is a great deal of ill-feeling between the Americans and the Panamanians: the former accuse the latter of thieving and cheating, and the natives indignantly retort. One reason, I believe, why the Americans do not agree so well with the natives as the English, is that they are accustomed to look upon all colored people with great contempt. They call all the Indians and half Indians by the general name of Niggers, and treat them as such; and that offends these people much, who, though good-tempered and gentle, are very high-spirited.

Whatever pilfering goes on is laid to the natives by the Californian emigrants; and the natives say, "No, it is all among yourselves." Then revolvers and knives are very apt to make their appearance; and as these articles are not exactly philosophical pacificators, the fray is often begun in right earnest, and sometimes ends in bloodshed.

We have tolerably fine weather here now, with only an occasional deluge; but we hear that in the interior of the country the rainy season has rather earlier than usual almost regularly commenced. A young lady who has lately arrived at Panama from England to take the place of governess in the family of Mr. L——, the Vice-Consul here, said that three times under the most violently pouring rain her clothes had been thoroughly saturated with water in the course of a few hours, and as often entirely dried again by the intensely powerful rays of the burning sun.

Her little pupils are half South American and half English, as Mr. L—— married a lady of New Granada. I saw a pretty little boy of his the other evening; he brought a message from his father to the Consul. I spoke to him in English.

"No hablo Ingles," said the little fellow, with a half-apologetic shrug of his pretty shoulder.

He looked like a little Anglo-Saxon, however, being exceedingly fair, with a delicate *blonde* head. One of Madame Hurtado's children is also very fair indeed, which is singular for a Spanish South American; but every now and then such rare instances are seen, and generally are much admired; as, for example, the famous Mexican beauty of former days, "*La Güera*," *par excellence*, the admired of Humboldt—La Güera Rodriguez, who bewitched even that paragon of philosophers. Would that her influence, or any other influence, could have persuaded him to simplify their difficult language of technicalities and names, and condescend to a little unscientificalization of their terms! not that the truly great Humboldt, however, sins particularly in that respect. What a chattering there is in the outer room, as if an improvised tertulia were taking place; let us look in and see what is the matter.

An amusing scene! A quantity of things are just brought in by the washerwomen, and two or three other native women have lately come in on divers errands. A few of them are most gracefully reclined on the floor, being fatigued by their walk under the burning sun. It is the height of picturesqueness, their coal-black hair streaming around them, and their attitudes most sculpture-like. They are all talking together, with that slightly metallic-sounding voice which seems one of their characteristics. The principal washerwoman claims me as a countrywoman, and with a patronizing inclination of her woolly head—she is black as the blackest raven—informs me graciously she is an Englishwoman:

"I Ingles, tambien; I 'long to England; si."

England! Did she come out of the Durham coal-mines, and had she never used soap and water since? She quickly solved the mystery, by saying she was born in Jamaica.

## CHAPTER XLIII.

Intention to go to Lima—Dinner to Ex-cannibals—Theatricals in Panama —Taboga—The French Tailoress—The "Happy Ship"—Roman Catholic Procession on Good Friday—A mischievous Trick—California thoroughly Americanized—Californian Adventurers and the Steam-boat Agent—The dead Negro—British Subjects buried in Panama—Tone of American Papers in Panama—Spirit of Enterprise of the Americans—Old Panama —Reptiles and Insects in Panama—Morgan and his Buccaneers—The Pirates and the Spanish Fleet—Wealth said to have been buried by the Buccaneers—American Love of intellectual Progress.

I HAVE decided on going to Lima. I find I shall thus have an opportunity of seeing several other places—besides that interesting and famous city—on the western coast of South America, and the steamers are said to be tolerably comfortable.

Captain F——, of H.M.S. "Daphne," dined here last night. He is, I believe, just come from Realejo, and was before that at the Fejee Islands. He told me he had invited the king of these islands, a reclaimed cannibal, to dinner, with his entire court. The invitation was accepted, and His Majesty and courtiers behaved very properly. It must be rather a nervous affair having a party of ex-cannibals to dinner. Suppose your viands should not be to their taste, and in consequence haply a sudden re-action of old habits should take place, and the knife and fork should be plunged into the hosts instead of into the mutton and turkey!

Captain F—— tells me nothing has transpired that gives any hopes of poor Sir John Franklin being found.

Mr. Catherwood, the eminent artist, who executed the splendid drawings which illustrate Mr. Stephens's celebrated work on Central America, is daily expected here; but his non-appearance for a length of time, during which he has been "due" at this place, begins to create some slight uneasiness respecting his safety and well-being. He is, I understand, surveying the country—for the American Railroad Company, I believe.

I have heard a very different account of the American theatricals here since I last spoke of them, and begin to think my informant was over-fastidious. The company are said to display a high order of talent, and much experience in the histrionic art. It is said they played "The Maid of Croissy," and "The Swiss Cottage," exceedingly well. Mrs. Thorne is reported to be a very good actress.

Besides these theatricals, the detained Californians have to beguile their time a little with divers other public amusements; such as tight-rope dancers, and stilt-waltzers (or still-vaulters) from Carthagena. What the last are I know not; but they are supposed to exhibit much skill and grace.

I am afraid I shall not see Taboga while I am here; but we shall pass close to it, I believe, in going to Buonaventura, the first place we shall stop at on our voyage to Peru.

A Mr. Frique, who lately kept a French hotel here, has just opened a similar establishment in the island. He informs the public, in an advertisement in one of the Panama-American papers (of which there are several, "The Star" and "The Echo" very good, and well conducted), that his new hotel is situated on the Plaza; and that, among other delectable treasures, it will have "Cigars of the most *recherché* brands;" but M. Frique will not reign alone monarch of all that is to be surveyed and purveyed in that place.

A Captain Forbes intends to build a rival posada there, I see, in the newspapers; "a hotel which is now on its way round the Horn." Perhaps they have made a little mistake, and it is on its way across the Isthmus in that huge deal case we saw on an Indian's back.

Taboga is said to be a charming place: the town consists of about a hundred cabins, with a number of stone houses belonging to the *millionaires* of the place; and there is an extremely picturesque old Spanish church. This town is built along a beautiful beach, which is said to be half covered with the remains of former buildings, and where a whole fleet of canoes may often be seen laid up. A lovely mountain stream comes dashing and sparkling down a gorge of the hills at the back of the settlement, and crosses the middle of it, on its course to the bay. This clear stream furnishes water to all the ships that visit Panama, in addition to supplying the wants of the residents. The Americans, it seems, are going to build a great many houses at Taboga, in the course of time; "and," says "The Echo," "like New York, Panama will then have a Staten Island and New Brighton."

I have not mentioned the singular sight I saw the day when I went to call on Mrs. H——, to take leave of her before she went to California. Hard at work, in a tailor's shop, which of course was wide open to admit all possible air, was an apparently delicate-looking young Frenchman, stitching away at a coat. This was a French demoiselle, or dame, who, for some reason, a little time ago, perhaps at the mines of California, temporarily adopted this costume, and has since continued it. She looked, I thought, a quiet, gentle person, and was remarkably industrious, stitching away with most praiseworthy vehemence, though the thermometer might be at 100°. Her hair was cropped very short, an advantage in so oppressive a climate.

Europeans here complain of the climate ruining both their hair and their teeth. You hear sometimes quite young ladies say they have lost almost all their teeth here, and have scarcely a solitary ringlet left. The native women, however, seem to have a vast abundance of the latter ornament.

Several of the servants here are natives, and I think they appear to make very good ones. (The head servants are French and Italian.) One, a young Indian girl, rejoices in the soft name of Ramona. She is, of course, excessively dark; but is very pretty, with delicate, regular features. She has a soft, low voice—"an excellent thing in woman," whether white, black, or brown.

An English gentleman has just arrived here from California, the son of Sir ——. He went to San Francisco in a yacht, I believe, the joint property of a number of friends; but this long voyage tried the tempers of these friends, it seems; for, on relating his maritime and other adventures, we were surprised to learn that at almost every port they stopped at, a duel came off. "What a miserable party you must have been?" said a lady, who was listening to the disastrous account. "Oh, no; it was a very happy ship." "How could that be?" "Well, there certainly were a great many duels fought, but it was a very happy ship, indeed!"

If this gentleman had ever made a voyage before, it must have been in a floating Pandemonium; so that this seemed felicitous by contrast.

Monsieur le C—— has called, and brought me some letters for Lima, one to M. de F——, the French commodore, whose frigate is supposed to be now at Lima. He is married to a young lady of Irish descent, who is said to be a very charming person.

Would the reader like a brief account of a Catholic religious procession in this city on Good Friday? The skies were of the most cloudless azure; the weather most glorious, and not insufferably hot; and the moon poured a sea of silver light over every thing. A large number of Americans were collected in different groups, anxiously watching the proceedings. They appeared to gaze with deep and intelligent interest (not a mere empty curiosity—a far more intellectual feeling) on a solemn pageant so new to most of them, and which was naturally associated, in their inquiring and cultivated minds, with all the mystery, the religion, and the history of the past, and which appeared to their imaginations linked with all the powerful memories of those dark, and mighty, and wondrous ages, when the whole civilized globe trembled at the awful thunders of the Vatican—they thought of the time when all the mightiest powers of Poetry, Harmony, Architecture, Oratory, Sculpture, and Painting—all that influences and impresses the mind, all that quickens the sympathies, all that electrifies and elevates the imagination—were used with such overpowering effect by those who then swayed and directed at their will the whole Christian World. That crowd of spectators formed in itself an impressive and significant sight: it was the Young World gazing on the Old.

The first part of the procession was composed of men and children, carrying long and large candles, burning. These were followed by penitential banners and a Cross. The procession moved to the sound of sacred music; and in due order came the civil and military authorities, some of them in very magnificent uniforms, and bearing the flag of New Granada. Then came a representation of the Holy Sepulchre: it consisted of a pyramidal structure of four floors, on each of which were placed large lighted candles, in glass shades, ranged as nearly together as it was possible to be, and all encircled and decorated with a profusion of brightly-colored flowers and glittering ribbons. The effect was very brilliant, and borne after this were several other splendidly-illuminated structures of less symbolical importance, but almost equally resplendent and superb. Then followed a number of lovely señoritas, clad in the deepest black, and each bearing a lighted taper in her hand. In different parts of the procession were to be seen religious enthusiasts and devotees, both male and female, who were shrouded in sable drapery; the former of whom continually scourged themselves with great apparent earnestness and frightful severity. Accompanying these were priests, and chanters, and choristers, I believe; and as the loud sound of the musical instruments died softly away, and the sweet melody of the chant, and the breath of the incense charmed the sense, the scene seemed more imposing and touching than before.

Ten magnificent tombs were erected in the ten principal churches of the city; some were decorated in a style of eastern splendor at night, and made resplendent by myriads of candles. In front of them, and on the altar, were illuminated vases, groves of artificial and natural flowers, &c. During all the evening, numbers of men and women went from one church to the other, reciting prayers for the heavenly welfare of the strangers in the city.

I have taken a good deal of this account from one of the American papers, but am sorry to add that the writer, in the middle of his narration, flies into uncontrollable raptures with the delicate hands and fairy feet of the Panamanian Señoritas. It appears, besides, that at the close of the grand procession, from the Church de la Merced, a disagreeable incident arose. The spectators, and all there, were alarmed and disturbed by a creature rushing among them at a furious pace, and making what the Americans call a regular stampede. Some mischievous person, it seemed, had caught a donkey, and attached a dry buffalo hide, with diabolical ingenuity, to the elongation of his spinal process, and he conceived he might rid himself of the inconvenient appendage, by making a sudden and terrific descent upon the procession.

It accomplished this, and the speedy dispersion of the crowd at the same time. The culprit was finally "comprehended as a wagrant," and the procession again moved on. But it seemed the *prestige* was gone after this unlucky donkey-as-trophe, and the deviser of this vile trick rejoiced in its full success. Was he an emissary from Exeter Hall?

One of the sad consequences of carrying fire-arms always about the person, occurred here a few days ago. A man named James Parker died of a gun-shot wound inflicted by a companion of his; the poor man survived the wound more than a fortnight, most of that time suffering great pain. So ended the golden dreams of California for this unfortunate sufferer.

Glancing at the newspapers here, you might almost imagine you were in one of the busy cities of the model republic. I see an announcement that the "New York Hotel is situated here in the main street, in the very centre of trade." In anticipation of the promised Railroad, I hear they are already about to erect a "Railroad Hotel" at Gorgona; in short, wherever there is an American, there is America: he carries his country about with him, and his unremitting industry and perseverance subjugate all around him.

California by all accounts, is almost thoroughly Americanized, notwithstanding the large number of settlers from other parts of the world. But in a Californian newspaper, it is very common to see a strange mixture of American and Mexican terms "Ayuntamientos," and regulations about "the polls," "Independent tickets," and "Pronunciamientos," "alcades," and "justices of the peace," all mingled together. I hear there are now, notwithstanding the late departures, three thousand Americans in Panama. However, a great many are going off in sailing vessels, as well as in steamers.

A little time ago, a large number who had through tickets for the "Tennessee," were awaiting that steamer here, and she did not make her appearance till long after the time that she was due. This caused great inconvenience, and consequently immense dissatisfaction, although generally the Americans take *contretemps* like this very philosophically—but they suspected some foul play, it seemed. Large meetings were held, and committees appointed to wait on the agent of the Pacific mail line of steam-ships (American) here. The agent promised to do all he could; but that proved to be nothing, and the malcontents became more indignant and more furious still. Some of these were for seizing the steamer "Panama" (which was lying at Taboga island), *vi et armis*, and instantly proceeding to San Francisco; others were for marching on the agent's office, and taking possession of all the old inkstands, desks, books, and spy-glasses belonging to the company, and "holding on to them" as collateral security, for the supposed damages sustained.

The whole town of Panama was in a state of uproar, and the graphic chronicler of these events says: "And now the tide of indignation began to swell and heave mountain-high, every stream sent its torrent, every rivulet sent its rill, and lo! the avalanche, the grand climax of desperation, was at hand!" On Tuesday, the disappointed passengers had a grand meeting in the Great Plaza. Gloom and wrath sate "in mirrored armor," says the poetical narrator, "on the brows of the desponding." Every thing looked threatening and angry, when suddenly a low rumbling noise, increasing as it rolled on, till it was like the roar of a "young earthquake," in long petticoats, bib and tucker, announced the "Tennessee!" "Has she arrived?" "Well, she has." "Thus they still repeated the reverberating sound, and on the glad tidings flew like a streak of flogged lightning:" and soon like a great leviathan of the Pacific, the noble ship came careering along, toward the anchorage of the bay. As she neared the place of mooring a deafening huzza shook the air, almost like a broadside, and loudly arose the chorus of that spirited song:

"Away down in Tennessee,
A li, e li, o li, u li."

All then became calm and serene, and they went home, singing: "Corn cob, twist your hair—cart-wheel surround you," or some such merry ditty.

The grave-yard of Panama is a melancholy place: it is surrounded with walls, in which the interments are made. These walls have apertures in the shape of an oven to admit the corpse; and when after decay the bones become dry, they are removed to make room for new bodies. The tops of the walls of the gloomy inclosure are constantly strewn with skull-bones, and the corners of this melancholy burial ground are crowded with the relics of mortality.

Also outside the gates are graves. An American editor says, he saw there the other day a horrible sight—the arm of a dead negro protruding about ten or twelve inches out of the ground in a state of advanced decomposition. The writer says he could not judge whether this was done designedly, or through carelessness, or whether the poor wretched negro, recovering from some swoon, came to life after he was buried, and weakly thrust his arm out thus for help, to rescue him, from what the relater rather mildly calls "his unpleasant situation!" It is said the arm has since been covered over.

I suppose from this, the negroes here are not buried in consecrated ground, as the frightful spectacle was beyond the gates. The burial ground where foreigners are interred is a short distance removed from the native cemetery, and is a small inclosure walled in, and shaded by some noble trees. There are several large tombstones there.

The late British Consul, I believe, built this small square, and occupies a place in it: a stone slab is erected to his memory. There is a tombstone, with an inscription to the memory of "Leonard Childers, one of the Secretaries to the British Legation at the Congress of Panama, who died at this place of the yellow fever, July 16th, 1826, aged 21 years;" and another "Sacred to the Memory of John James Le Mesurier," who came to Panama, also as "Secretary to Mr. Dawkins, Commissioner from the King of England to the Congress of Panama. He had not been here a fortnight when he was seized with the fever of this country, and died at the age of 18, on the 14th of June, 1826, cut down like the promise of a flower half-blown, while others live to weep him." It is said, three weeks after their arrival they fell ill and died.

The American editor of "The Echo" indulges in a very noble strain of feeling in dwelling on this subject, and recapitulating these melancholy details. He says: "After reading the above, though an American, we felt proud that we were the descendants of British ancestors. Wherever she finds her subjects in foreign climes, England throws over them the mantle of protection" (not Protectionists' protection!); "to the living, she points to the lion and the unicorn, and the Cross of St. George, as the shield of defense; and to the dead, whose memories deserve memento, she erects tombs and monuments to perpetuate their deeds and worth. The country which produced such a poet as Gray, knew well when and where to erect a 'storied urn or animated bust' to the memory of her departed sons. We honor the man who loves the land of his birth, and we admire and respect the government which cherishes the valor and renown of her warriors and her civilians.

"But to proceed. A little further on, we saw several newly-made graves—the final resting-places, doubtless, of some of our adventurous countrymen. A number of them had no board to indicate their name, or state from whence they came! Those that had an inscription on their headstones we give below." (Then follow the names of a few of the writer's countrymen.)

To have a thoroughly good and most extensive view of the bay, the ocean, the islands, the forests, and a hundred miles of shore, the visitor to Panama should ascend the bold steep called the Cerro Lancon. About five in the morning, before the intense heat commences, is the best time. I have not been able to attempt it in consequence of this "rose-asthma" I have had.

There was a robbery the other day at the Western Hotel (about 1200 dollars were stolen). A man was suspected, and he, finding himself about to be arrested, ran off, but was closely pursued, and near "Theatre-lane," he threw a watch over the walls. He was secured, and the watch was found, with the glass broken, of course: it is said it was stolen from a passenger at the hotel about three weeks ago. When charged with the robbery, he acknowledged he had stolen the gold watch, but denied any knowledge of or participation in the recent theft of the money. When it was made apparent that he had stolen the watch, the crowd "were for Lynching him on the spot, and but for the intervention of Mr. Vinton," says the journal, "would have accomplished their purpose." He was committed to jail to await his trial. A reward of three hundred dollars has been offered for the detection of the robber or robbers and return of the money, or two hundred dollars for the restoration of the money only.

Nothing can be better than the tone in general of the American papers established here. They are the sworn enemies of all disorder and demoralization, and the consistent advocates and supporters of justice and right. I see in the papers that Lynch law is most uncompromisingly condemned. Earnestly do "we deprecate such a course of procedure; it is subversive of all law and the most sacred rights of the citizen; it should be frowned down by all well-thinking men."

What a wonderful people the Americans are! One finds oneself continually repeating this mentally, when hearing of, or seeing their indomitable determination and force of character. What a wonderful people, individually and collectively! Some time ago, many left Panama, Mr. P—— informs me, in old whale-boats, in the "dug-outs" of the natives, which they converted into a rough kind of schooner, and in iron boats. One of these iron boats was dragged across the isthmus by fifty or sixty men, and went safely, I believe, to San Francisco; but they put out to sea in many wretched vessels, entirely unseaworthy. When Mr. Bayard Taylor was here, he said many small companies of men started in the miserable log-canoes of the natives for El Dorado, and after a forty days' voyage, during which time they only reached the Island of Quibo, at the mouth of the Gulf, the greater part returned: the remainder had not been heard of.

Old Panama, built by the conqueror Pizarro, is at some distance from the comparatively modern town; it is further up the coast. The present city was built in 1670; but when I look at its extraordinary state of decay and dilapidation, it is really difficult to believe it is not far older. In how much better repair is Pompeii!

There do not seem to be many pleasant walks or rides near the city, by all accounts. When you have passed through the neighboring orchards and gardens, begin the dense woods, through which there are some narrow mule-paths, and of which the embowering, entangled, and thickly-accumulated underwood is completely impenetrable to the outward air. There is a malaria, too, arising from the always enormous quantity of decaying vegetable matter, so you may stand a chance of being asphyxized or poisoned.

Then the reptiles and insects are too endless for me to attempt any enumeration of them, beyond the more familiar names of musquitoes, garrapatos, centipedes, scorpions, poisonous spiders, tarantulas, snakes, ants, and jiggers. The ants, by the way, eat away the houses here; when once they have effected a lodgment, the beams quickly crumble away under their virulent attacks.

There are others that destroy paper, and others, again, that *make* it. There are great numbers of *winged* ants here—such little torments! They seem to be constantly devising different ingenious methods of worrying you, for they fly about your head and face, and when you think you have succeeded in driving them away, they suddenly drop their wings entirely, and follow this up by dropping themselves on your book, and rapidly crawling all over the open page. If you are drinking a glass of lemonade, you find it suddenly covered with floating ants' wings, that stick in your throat and half choke you. If the little wretches would consult their looking-glasses, they would save us that annoyance perhaps, for they are tolerably well-favored insects with wings, and frightfully ugly little plagues without.

Here comes a shower of wings on my paper. Are the little rogues turned poetical? and do they mean figuratively to bid the letter "haste, haste, post haste?" a sentence our good old forefathers were wont to write on their scrolls; they who did not know what haste meant! when very Time seemed to have dropped his wings, like these identical ants, and to go limping along with a crutch and a gouty shoe. Their world, indeed, stood on a tortoise, as some of the eastern nations say.

The American population resident here, and in the neighborhood, are talking of organizing a police of their own, to prevent brawls, burglaries, and street-fights. All kinds of strange accounts come in from California: among other things it is said a man was actually starved to death in a place called the "Happy Valley." He was found quite dead, after having literally gnawed and eaten the flesh from his own arms in the desperate struggle with the icy King of Terrors. There are a great many terrible stories of suicide and madness, and horrors and misery of all kinds there.

I believe the settlers suffer a great deal in going there, very often, too. Mr. P—— says some time since a small ship, or rather boat, started, so crowded with emigrants to California, that it bore the greatest possible resemblance to a human bee-hive, and that literally the unfortunate, half-suffocated passengers might be seen seated in a long row on the edge, with their legs and feet dangling in the water, thus attempting to keep themselves cool.

There are a good many shops here, but articles in general seem very dear. House-rent appears to be enormously high, and Mr. P—— pays as much or more for his house, unfurnished and unfinished (for he had to do almost every thing to it short of building the walls), as is demanded for a first-rate house in one of the most fashionable parts of London.

I have already mentioned that Old Panama was destroyed by the buccaneers in 1670, under the noted Morgan. In 1685, a vast number of Filibustieros, or Buccaneers, in three companies, came from Mantanzas (in Cuba) and from the Caribbean Sea, and shaped their course to this part of the continent, and after encountering immense difficulties, and experiencing fearful hardships, they crossed the land in about a fortnight, and arrived at the Pacific shore. One of these companies was formed of one hundred and twenty Englishmen; the second of one hundred and seventy Frenchmen; the third of two hundred and sixty persons, who were also French.

They arrived at a bay called Bocachica, and there they found two canoes, which had been sent to meet them by the allied buccaneers, French and English, whose fleet was cruising in the vicinity of this city. After a little repose they started for some islands called the King's Islands, about ninety miles from Panama, where they met the fleet, which was now composed of ten vessels—two frigates, four ships, three barques, and one brig. Out of the ten commanders, eight were English, one French, and the other Dutch; this last was the Admiral, and he was called David. The number of men in the vessels was eleven hundred. Most of these vessels had been taken by some Englishmen under command of David, and brought through the Straits of Magellan to the Pacific Ocean.

The chief now resolved to attack the Spanish fleet, which at that time of the year usually came from Lima to Panama; the first expedition they made, however, was to seize on the city of Seppa, about twenty-one miles east of Panama: five hundred men were engaged in this expedition, who embarked in about two-and-twenty large war-canoes. Seppa was taken, but it contained comparatively little treasure; so that the disappointed pirates looked on this expedition as a serious loss of time, with very little profit. In May they left Seppa, and returned to their ships, which were waiting at a little distance from the town.

Then the fleet weighed anchor, and started to the westward, along the coast toward Panama. They passed on the 8th of May in sight of the ruins of Old Panama, which had been destroyed by Morgan, and a great number of the very men who were then actually in this fleet in the later expedition. They shortly afterward reached the present town of Panama, and went down to the island of Taboga, which island, says the chronicler of these events, seemed to them a perfectly enchanted spot, so admirable was the beauty of its vegetation, and so splendid the edifices constructed there by the wealthy inhabitants of Panama. The pirates, on the 9th and 10th of May, were anxiously employed in watching for the appearance of the expected Spanish fleet.

At last, on the 17th of that month, seven noble ships were seen coming toward the buccaneers, with the royal Spanish flag nailed to the mast-head. The fleet of the Filibustieros rejoiced heartily at this sight, exclaiming that their hopes were about to be realized, and that the great struggle was at hand. None but those who have either gazed upon or participated in an ocean battle, can paint to their imagination the tremendous scene which shortly after was exhibited on the great Pacific, when those two hostile fleets met " in concerted array," on the foam-crested billows. For the desperate and lawless corsairs, it would either be a victory that would place them almost at the summit of their proudest hopes, or a complete annihilation of their powers and their terrors. Like the pirate-scourers and sea-bandits of the Gulf, their flag displayed the ghastly death's head and bones, and they were doggedly resolved to a man, to sink or swim under their almost worshiped piratical banner. The admirals of the two opposing fleets, with their forces drawn up in the order of fight, were met to dispute the sovereignty and supremacy of the great South Sea; for, indeed, at that period few vessels, save those of the Filibustieros and the Spaniards, cruised in the Pacific Ocean.

The battle was long contested, and at one time the Spaniards had the decided advantage over their opponents, and would have had a most complete triumph; but unfortunately for them they lacked a skillful and experienced commander to direct their operations, and this proved, of course, a most serious drawback to their cause. The pirates had their vessels greatly injured, and found themselves obliged to fly in all directions, and land on divers points of the coast, to repair their armament. But although overcome in the first skirmish they were not destroyed, and without considering their material and numerical inferiority, they sailed again on the 26th of June for Panama, recruited in spirits, confident in hope, and with all their vessels repaired. The Spaniards in the interim had fortified the city, and with their vessels in good order were waiting, thoroughly prepared to encounter their deadly and relentless foe.

But the cunning Filibustierios, seeing they had no chance of then overpowering their adversaries, or attacking them with the faintest prospect of victory, abandoned for a time the enterprise, and went on smaller expeditions along the coast, assailing and sacking cities, and plundering vessels wherever they could find any treasure worthy their attention.

Among these lesser expeditions, one of the most important was directed against the city of Realejo, 795 miles west of Panama. Realejo was taken and burnt down in October, together with a considerable number of towns and villages in the vincinity. At the beginning of the year 1686, the buccaneers with their fleets, directed their course toward the city of Panama, and, as they had previously done, made Taboga their head-quarters. After having made their dépôt secure by strengthening and fortifying it as well as they could, they resolved on losing no time in making an onslaught on the city; and they obliged the President of Panama (as a preliminary measure to their operations) to surrender all the prisoners the Spaniards had taken in the previous ferocious engagements on these waters. They then seized all the provisions in the place, to sustain them in their lawless career; and after that, they made a further demand on the President, insisting on his paying six thousand dollars; to which demand, backed by so formidable a force, the President submitted.

Emboldened by their success, the freebooters, with their usual audaciousness, again made a levy of ten thousand dollars on the President, to which the Spanish chief magistrate, though with reluctance and deep humiliation, was compelled by circumstances to submit. The buccaneers, having extorted these sums of money, returned, well pleased with their success; and they proceeded up the Bay of Panama.

The pirates during the years 1686 and 1687 haunted the seacoast of Central America, and successively seized on all the prosperous and flourishing cities which the Spaniards had built in that part of the world. Realejo, Acapulco, and Tequilla were taken and plundered by them. A party of the Filibustieros sailed in one of their vessels, and went as far as California, where they found some Spanish settlements and missions already established. But the El Dorado of the present time was then not known to possess such golden attractions; and as the promise of plunder and booty in those regions appeared to be small, they resolved to abandon the now far-famed land, as not presenting sufficient charms or guerdons for their bold exploits and intrepid achievements.—It was said of old, the inhabitants of the "Eureka State" were so poor, they lived upon fried grasshoppers.

The buccaneers, wherever they presented themselves, were commonly successful: but at length the Spaniards, becoming more accustomed to their peculiar mode of warfare, fortified their cities, and increased their defenses; while the pirates, from leading a rough, roving, and irregular life, exposed to countless hardships and privations, were being diminished day by day; so that, toward the termination of their wonderful career in the Pacific, a mere skeleton of this once-powerful banded force of ocean brigands was left as a small nucleus, around which to muster and rally their marauding and piratical forces. Whenever there was a city destroyed by these corsairs, the Spaniards immediately reconstructed it again, fortified it with the strongest-walled barriers, and furnished it with guns of the heaviest calibre.

The buccaneers, having succeeded in accumulating immense hoards of treasure, tired of their life of lawless enterprise, and with their best leaders growing gray and superannuated, resolved at length to abandon their pillaging and piracies of the Southern Seas and the cities of the coast, and to return home, leaving their extraordinary deeds and works behind them, for the wonder, the admiration, or condemnation of after ages.

In the year 1688, they returned to the shores of the Atlantic, directing their footsteps across the Isthmus of Panama, by the same route they had taken in their unhallowed pilgrimage westward. The terrible piratical flag of the death's head and bones never more streamed in hideous ascendency over the mighty waters of the Pacific, as if the King of Terrors himself were watching for his prey, determined that the bright waves of the Southern Seas should vie with the graves of Earth in concealing the mouldering remains of mortality.

This is a brief sketch of the last famous voyage of the buccaneers in the Pacific. It appears to be very commonly believed that they did not carry with them (when they abandoned their life of peril and plunder) all the vast, the almost unbounded riches they had accumulated, by perpetually pillaging vessels, and sacking flourishing and wealthy cities.

Many historians and narrators have thought (and it is said that a great number of persons in Panama believe it) that they deposited an enormous amount of wealth (specie and heaps of jewels) underground, in some of the islands which were their usual places of rendezvous, in the intervals of their daring expeditions, which costly treasures they did not, from various reasons, dig up from their hiding-places. These islands are situated between Panama and Realejo, all along the coast. In late times some exploring parties have been organized to seek in these localities for the spots where it is supposed some of these valuable treasures were hidden. No satisfactory discoveries have been made as yet; no precious jewels, no heaps of gold, no chests of silver bullion, have shone forth, to reward the treasure-hunter's toil. To this hour, it appears, the earth, to whose keeping the gathered spoils were confided, has guarded the wealth in her secret recesses.

There are a great many difficulties in the way of the explorers; but, if the tale be true, I have no doubt that, sooner or later, the indefatigable hands of Americans will succeed in disemboweling the treasures, and giving back to the light of day the precious spoils that rewarded the intrepid enterprises and fearless adventures of the famous and powerful Filibustieros. There are, however, nobler objects for the Americans to direct their minds toward accomplishing.

Bolivar, though doubtless he in some respects, revolutionized the minds of the people, and made them friends of liberty, yet did little more for their advancement or their enlightenment. He left behind him nothing, here at least it would seem, that could contribute either toward the intellectual elevation of their minds, or to the enlargement of their stores of knowledge. It is said there is an educational institution here, not much superior to an infant school in England. The industrial pursuits of peace are but poorly and scantily developed, and the Americans may, and I doubt not will do much in time by their enlightened example and assistance in awakening the dormant energies of the people, and improving their intellectual condition generally. Wherever an American goes, there springs up his free press—the constant accompaniment of his footsteps.

It is asserted that during the Mexican war the Americans had newspapers constantly printed to amuse their anxious and weary hours, animate and lighten their labors, and reconcile them to hardships and privations of all kinds. An American looks upon his daily press and his daily bread as equally necessary to his existence.

## CHAPTER XLIV.

The probable Future of Panama—South American Railroads projected—Gold-seekers in Panama—Large Importation of Fruit-trees into California—American Improvements in Panama—Alleged Ill-treatment of Emigrants by Ship-owners—The Green Mountain Yankee—The Indians and the damp Gunpowder. The Government of New Granada—Its recent Policy.

WHAT will be the future of Panama, it is impossible with any precision to say. Situated as it is about midway between Patagonia and the United States' possessions up to the confines of Oregon, it is most favorably placed; and its commercial facilities in this central position, are almost unrivaled by any port on the western side of this great continent nearer than Valparaiso in the south, or San Francisco in the west.

If it ever has a railroad or a canal connecting the waters of the two oceans, terminating at this point or in the vicinity, it would be scarcely possible to exaggerate the enormous magnitude and amount of the trade, which would follow the completion of either of these means of transit and oceanic intercommunication. What an immensity of traffic would necessarily centre here! How would this wretchedly dilapidated city spring up from ruin and decay, and more than regain its pristine splendor! how would it extend its dimensions; recruit its impoverished finances, and probably become at no very distant period the capital and the commercial metropolis of a wealthy and wide-spread empire.

The products of China and Japan, and the innumerable fabrics of eastern climes and lands, would assuredly seek this as the easiest and most direct communication with the United States and with Europe; and the route of Cape Horn, so tedious and perilous, would be entirely abandoned. How would the flags of all the nations of the world be reflected on the waters of this beautiful bay!

The government of New Granada appears to be a very liberal government, on the whole; and from all I can collect, it seems to be nearly the best of the South American republican governments altogether. The President, in his message last month, was able to say: "New Granada is at peace with all the neighboring republics, and the great Powers of the North, and of Europe. While the other republics of South America are still disturbed by internal troubles, New Granada presents the spectacle of peace and happiness."

I believe the same steamer in which we are going to Lima will convey to Callao in Peru and to Chili the engineers who are engaged to superintend the formation of the first railroads ever constructed in South America. An American company is going to commence a line in Chili from the port of Caldera, on the Pacific Ocean, to Copiapo, in the mining district of that country, about fifty-five miles from the sea-board. The chief and most active directors of this company are natives of the United States, who have been for many years resident in Chili, and have justly acquired a very considerable influence there by their character for enterprise, their liberality, and public spirit.

Copiapo, in the province of Coquimbo, is above 500 miles north of Valparaiso, in one of the most productive of the mining districts of Chili. It is said to be about 1100 feet above the Pacific, and the road will be 55 miles long, with descending grades from that point to the coast, the grades not to exceed fifty feet to the mile in any part. The engines are made by Messrs. Norris, of the United States, and the cars, and turn-tables, and the entire equipment of the road, are made in the United States. The iron for the rails, I believe, came from England. The other line is much shorter, being only from Callao to Lima, about eight miles.

These, the first two railroads in South America, are almost certain to be successful, and will introduce, under favorable auspices, to this vast continent, one of the most prominent features of modern civilization and prosperity. It is an era, indeed, for the people of these regions.

Americans still keep pouring into Panama; for steamers are continually coming to Chagres, bringing large parties of emigrants. We hear that several have lately lost their way in the dense forests of the isthmus. It often becomes indispensably necessary to lighten the ascending canoes (overloaded as they frequently are) about six miles below Gorgona, and the passengers are required to find their own way as best they can to that place. They usually try to take a path across the country; but as it is exceedingly difficult to do this, they often miss their way, and many of them acquire, unwillingly, a great deal of topographical knowledge from having to pass a weary night among the woods and hills; but it sometimes ends seriously.

Mr. Montague, an American gentleman, told me the other day he had heard some dead bodies had been found in the forest, which, there was too much reason to suppose, were the remains of some of his unfortunate countrymen.

We begin to like much the style of living here, and especially the cool, light architecture of the houses: the rooms are invariably high, and the windows and doors very large. In these hot countries, in general, by the way, it seems the heights of the natives' houses might serve as a kind of thermometer, to inform the traveler of the average degrees of heat. It appears that the temperature instinctively, to a certain extent, determines the elevation. Where there is great heat, the habitations are enormously high, and where the atmosphere is subject occasionally to chilly damps, or the place is exposed to winds more or less violent, the roofs are proportionally lower. They generally build their houses, in the native villages, on a raised bank of earth.

In all the warm regions the invaluable bamboo furnishes "the uprights" at the angles of the proposed edifice, and the jambs of the doorways; and when the heat is uninterrupted and uniform, mats of the palm usually, and other easily-appropriated materials, form the slight partitions within and without (in most of the houses there are only the canes for walls). Every where the thatched or tiled roof presents a spacious veranda, an open colonnade, which surrounds the house (of enormous dimensions in some of the better houses), which veranda is in fact a continuation of the sloping line of the roof beyond the upright partitions, and either a lengthening of the rafter-like timbers of the roof resting their terminations on a line of perpendicular posts beyond the wall of the house, or an addition made after the construction of the simple edifice.

I hear that for several days past a number of the detained Californians have been washing with bowls and tin pans the earth and sand near the breaches in the ancient wall on the south side of Panama. There were rumors that some sparkling dust had been observed by persons accidentally wandering in that vicinity. The eager emigrants (hoping they had detected a rival to the mighty gold-dust-bin, California!) instantly began to dig out the vast mass of rubbish scattered about in that neighborhood, thinking any thing that glittered on the Pacific coast must be gold; but on carefully testing the produce of their day's zealous labors, they found they had got nothing but the scorious refuse from some Spanish bell-casting or cannon-founding of olden times.

I mentioned that we had seen emerge from the cavernous hold of the "Georgia" a small forest of trees, as if from that "oak leviathan" were sprouting numerous younger branches. It appears probable that they belonged to a Mr. Booth, of New Jersey, who is taking with him to the El Dorado about thirty thousand fruit-trees. What a benefactor is this orchard-planter to all the future little school-boys of the Gold State! Who does the most good, the leader in wars and insurrections, or the public-spirited individual who benevolently adopts means to provide posterity with the blessings of pumpkin-pies, or seeks to lighten the labors of learning by affording the cheering consolations of apple-dumplings? Apples, too, grown in such a soil! Must not every pippin be a golden pippin, and indeed every apple equal to the one for which three goddesses disputed?

The El Doradians are too good-natured to be angry with me for a little Californian epitaph I made the other day:

Friends! but let me for awhile in this auriferous soil remain,
Then, when changed to gold-dust, dig me up, and take me home again.

We are informed that American improvements are thronging fast in upon the Panamanians. A genuine Yankee hand-cart has been seen in the Plaza, the first vehicle of the kind ever witnessed here—at least within the memory of man. There is an ox-cart, besides, just established for heavy goods, drawn by a solemn-looking pair of oxen, particularly dilatory in their movements, who are tugged along by a *mozo*, by means of a rope in their noses. "Clear the track!" cry the Americans, who are charmed at these signs of coming improvements, and hail the innovations heartily.

Several of the steamers over-due have not yet arrived, and much discontent continues to prevail. Some of the poor passengers have not hesitated to say they considered themselves swindled out of their money; others declare they have already submitted to cruel hardships and impositions. I hear that many of them protest they were shown a diagram of the ship (a most perfect model) they were to take their passage in, and the exact position of their berth was pointed out to them; but they were soon lamentably undeceived: they were thrust, they say, into a different quarter from that which had been shown to them, and instead of a berth, an atrocious invention of the enemy called a "standee" (a miserable thing, made to be just put up at night for the *dis*-accommodation of the unlucky martyrs) was substituted. Yet they all look as good-humored as ever, when by chance you see them sauntering about, and trying to do nothing, which seems very difficult to them—a herculean task, indeed!

I must give the reader, for his edification, an account of a son of the Green Mountains, in the United States, during a storm at sea: in the papers it is headed, characteristically, "It takes a Yankee, it does!" During the last trip of the noble steam-ship "Ohio," from New York to Chagres, and while the terrific gale which she encountered was raging at its very highest pitch, and half the passengers were on their knees, expecting the vessel to go to the bottom every moment, and the other half standing aghast, and gazing horror-stricken at the awful abyss of foaming water yawning hideously before them, a tall, Green Mountain Yankee, from Vermont, with a white hat stuck knowingly (and how it stuck on at all in that gale must ever remain a mystery!) on one side of his head, was observed pacing the deck, deeply "calc'lating," and soon he was heard inquiring whether there were any "Californy" tickets for sale—he was willing to give one half and would run all the risk! The newspaper account thus ends: "That chap is now in Panama, and sails hence for San Francisco, in the 'Oregon.' We rather 'guess' he will find a prospect in California!"

There are ten steamers now anxiously expected here that are coming round the Horn, or through the Straits of Magellan, one of which is a river steamer, called the "New World," intended to run on the Sacramento River. This is the second river steamer that has ever been sent round.

I must repeat a tough story that is now in circulation relative to the natives and their unsophisticated simplicity. A number of kegs of gunpowder, it is asserted, were placed upon the backs of the "men-mules" (who would be, were it not for the opposition-trains of their less numerous four-footed rivals, in almost the position of the camel—the ship of the desert), for transport across the isthmus, with the strictest reiterated directions that they should be kept perfectly dry; but unfortunately a most violent shower of rain overtook them before they got half-way across. The powder they had much reason to fear, had become wetted by the superabundant fluid.

In this predicament they kindled a good fire, and an attempt was instantaneously made to dry the combustible compound of saltpetre and brimstone; when, alack! it ignited, exploded, and went off like a tremendous sky-rocket, shaking the ground, and blowing the unhappy Indians into the air, and shivering them into twenty thousand pieces.

I have said that the Government of New Granada seems one of a really liberal character; and the news lately arrived from

Bogota would seem to corroborate that statement. The Secretary of State has just presented a law to establish immediately the freedom of *the press*. The ministers, I see, have lately presented a projected law for the decentralization of the financial administration of the Granadian Republic. This seems a hazardous experiment; for if it receives the national sanction, it will doubtlessly tend to weaken much the Federal System here.

If each of these provinces (as they are called) has the management of its own financial affairs, the political power of the country will most likely fall into anarchy. This country requires, I should think, as much consolidation as possible; and any thing that tends to overthrow the unity of government would materially injure its prosperity.

They have a Vice-President here, after the example of the United States, and his election, by late accounts, was just about to take place. General Obando is the new "Designado." If the President and Vice-President both should die, the "Designado" at once assumes the supreme power of the government, and is immediately recognized as the head of the nation. In short, he is another edition of the Vice-President, a second "en cas;" so that New Granadians would seem to be very careful not to have a chance of being left without a supreme governor for a moment. They must, I suppose, be aware that they are terribly flighty mice, and sure to play when the cat is away, since they seem so anxious to provide a number of "deputy-provisionary-vice-sub-supernumeraries."

## CHAPTER XLV.

Arrival at Lima announced—Embark on the "Bolivia"—View of Panama from the Sea—Buenaventura—The River and City of Guayaquil—Horses' Dread of Alligators—Native Boats and their varied Freight—Parrots, Macaws, and Paroquets—Ponchos—The Guayaquil Ladies—Grass Hats—The five Productions of Guayaquil—Payta—Its Population—Its Salubrity—Its Market—Scarcity of Water at Payta—Former Wealth of that Place.

We arrived at Lima in perfect safety a few days ago. I should not at all repent of the resolution I had taken to come here, were it not that I shall thus be longer without my English letters, which will be awaiting me at Jamaica.

I must console myself by thinking I am on my way home, though by a rather lengthened *circumbendibus!* I was so afraid of missing my letters altogether, if I attempted to arrange for them to follow me, that I preferred the chance of their accumulating, and waiting for me at some given spot; and besides, I originally calculated on being at Jamaica long before this: it is very difficult to arrange satisfactorily about letters at such a distance.

The sea voyage hither has done us an immensity of good, and also the delicious climate of Lima. We suffered terribly from the intense heat, however, during part of our voyage; but I have now got rid of the remains of that hay-asthma, which incapacitated me so much from going about for nearly a fortnight at Panama.

We hear that the cholera, which is said never to have passed the Equator, is now within three leagues of Bogota, and apparently gradually creeping on. The people here say it will stop at the Line—*nous verrons!*

The morning we left Panama was not very hot, fortunately for us, for of course we had to walk to the beach (at about the hottest time of the day, too), as it was the only way of getting there, unless we had ridden on mules, which was not worth while, or gone in the famous hand-cart. Behold us, then, on our sultry way, after having taken leave of our lovely and amiable young hostess, escorted by our thrice hospitable host, and with Pio (not "Nono," the Pope, unless *again* in disguise, but that secular individual who filled the office of head-mozo in the Consular establishment) superintending the safe conveyance of our luggage, carried by peons. We were introduced to the captain of the "Bolivia" on the shore, who subsequently very obligingly made every possible arrangement for our comfort and accommodation on board the steamer, and we were soon rapidly gliding along toward the vessel among the snow-white pelicans.

When we got pretty near the English steamer, we saw a boat alongside, from which people were, it seemed to us, ineffectually attempting to raise some huge dark object into the steamer. This was an immense bullock, which we for some time thought was dead, but after awhile he showed that he was very alive, kicking and struggling tremendously: he floundered about, half in the water, it seemed, more like a young whale on four legs than a respectable land animal, accustomed to the progress of civilization, and the society of domesticated cattle, and about to be devoted to the service of some of his cousins and namesakes. At last the poor bull was hoisted into the vessel in safety.

The view of Panama from the sea is lovely. When we had steamed along about an hour, we came to Taboga, after passing several other hilly and volcanic-looking islands. Taboga is very lovely. Down to the beach grow the rich groves of orange and of tamarind. Beside a clump of cocoa-nut palms is the town, sheltered and shaded; and the hills rise, as they so often do in these delightful regions, in a beauteous semicircular amphitheatre of natural terraces, enriched with the most exquisite vegetation to their summits. Some of them may be about one thousand feet high. Various species of palm, and banana, and lemon, and orange, and tamarind trees cover the ground in a thick mass, till, on the beach, they almost dip into the water.

It is said—I know not with what accuracy—that this is the only place between Cape Horn and San Francisco, where a dry dock is practicable, and that here it would be very easy to construct one. The Indian houses here seem to be thatched with grass, and there is a curious fashion of arranging gourds on the roof, divided in two, to preserve them from rain.

At dinner, we met Mr. and Mrs. Campbell, and a sister, I think, of that lady's. Besides us the two latter were the only ladies on board. Mr. Campbell is the chief superintendent of the American engineer corps for the projected Chilian railroad. He was accompanied by two resident engineers, and several first-assistants; and there are a number, besides, of artisans and sub-assistants.

The chief engineer of the Anglo-Peruvian railroad was also on board, with a considerable band of associates and assistants. The first place we stopped at was Buenaventura, which was a miserable-looking town. Whether it had ever seen better days in the time of the Spanish dominion, and has become impoverished and half depopulated since, I know not. The coast was rugged and bold, but nobly wooded.

Buenaventura is the port of Bogota, on the Pacific. Those who go by this route to the capital, generally follow the course of the river Cauca to Cartago, from whence they ride along a dreadful road to Bogota. The time occupied altogether by this journey is usually about three weeks. The country, we were told, is splendid. The Atlantic and Pacific are thought to be connected through a communication between the Cauca and the Magdelena.

From Buenaventura we proceeded to Guayaquil. Soon after crossing the Line we found the heat intense, and so it continued till we got near Callao. We were much amused by one of our fellow-travelers in the morning rushing into the cabin to know whether we would not go on deck to see the Line, as we were very near it.

Before entering the Guayaquil river we passed the singular rock called by the English Dead Man's Island ; by the Equadorians, El Enamortajado (corpse). We thought it looked very much like a gigantic fossilized Egyptian mummy ; a most colossal corpse laid in state on its boundless ocean bed, with its face upturned to the everlasting sun and stars. Noble sepulchral lamps, indeed !

There is a story in reference to its sombre designation of terror, of some men having been forgotten there and left to perish during a Guayaquil Pronunciamiento ; but its extraordinary formation is sufficient to account for its melancholy name. After that we passed a large island called Puna.

The river of Guayaquil is a noble, deep, large stream. While we were ascending it we felt almost suffocated with the heat, which was terribly oppressive. Guayaquil is eighty-five miles from the mouth of the river. When the heat of the sun moderated, we went on deck.

I thought some of the scenery on the banks lovely ; in many parts they appeared to me to assume a particularly park-like aspect, with charming openings between the groups of trees, that made one long to land and explore a little there—please the musquitoes.

We tried in vain to catch a glimpse of grand old kingly Chimborazo and the great Cotopaxi. There was a floating canopy of clouds to be seen, and that was all. Before we reached the river there suddenly came on thousands of bright, beautiful flashes of lightning, like winged suns darting about with bewildering rapidity—most exquisite meteorological pyrotechnics they were—and with their dazzling reflections they sometimes almost made the Pacific one sheet of flame. The southern constellations—and conspicuously beautiful and interesting among them the Cross—looked magnificent when the lightning partially ceased.

At length we arrived at the town of Guayaquil, the chief seaport of Ecuador. There has been a serious rebellion going on (and that *is* strange, for one really wonders how they can go on with their petty revoltings and revolutionizings without laughing), and the city is actually in the hands of the wrong man, whoever that may be. I heard his name but forget it, which is as well, for he may very likely be the right man by this time. There were no signs of any thing being altered or disordered in any way by this pronunciamientical state of things.

These outbreaks seem a part of the constitutions of these new Southern republics generally. "Sweet chasing sweet, joy overtaking joy." I am told that in Peru, the election for the President regularly produces one, or rather *is* one. Law and order are entirely set at defiance; rebellions and massacres are then merely pardonable ebullitions of enthusiasm and patriotism, and are quite amicably committed, and, as the Frenchman said when he killed his wife, innocently done in a *petit moment de vivacité*. In short, revolution seems almost the normal state of things. No wonder Guayaquil looked so gay and contented.

I know not whether there was any extra lighting of the town to express their joy at being in such delightful circumstances; but I must say, I have seldom beheld a more magnificently-illuminated city than Guayaquil. As you ascend the river the town is on the left-hand side; broad quays of immense length, and splendidly lit-up at night, adorn the city greatly, besides being eminently useful to the shipping; for, when moored to the rings upon the wharf, vessels of very considerable size may remain alongside of them without touching the ground.

There are said to be immense numbers of very large alligators some miles above the town. They occasionally overset accidentally the slight and fragile canoes of the Indians, who bring in these boats to the Guayaquil market fruit and vegetables (among which are enormous numbers of splendid pine-apples); then woe to the poor boatman! for the moment the alligator sees him in the water, he seizes upon him, and his repast is too soon an accomplished fact.

They say the horses and cattle are afraid of going to the river to drink, and often make use of different stratagems to avoid this ferocious enemy; but, if they unsuspiciously come and stoop down to drink, the alligator, till then concealed, or nearly so, darts at the head of the poor animal, insultingly pulls his nose, and drags him quickly down, depriving him of all power of motion by a blow from his terrible tail. The common belief in the complete impenetrability of an alligator's natural coat of mail is now sometimes disputed; though there is no doubt that he is provided with very excellent armor.

Guayaquil appeared to me an exceedingly picturesque town. The balconied and veranda-surrounded houses have a particularly pretty effect, especially in the brilliant illumination that I have described. Guayaquil looked all alive; but we saw no symptoms of anarchy; numerous promenaders seemed enjoying the beauty of the evening.

It is curious that here, within two degrees of the equator, the ladies are remarkably fair, and, indeed, have almost Anglo-Saxon complexions. They are celebrated for their beauty; and formerly, I believe, in the Spanish days, there were many very distinguished families residing here, possessed of enormous wealth.

In the morning we beheld a very gay and busy scene: the steamer was literally surrounded with native boats of all shapes and sizes, some filled to overflowing with almost innumerable parrots, macaws, and paroquets; pine apples and various tropical fruits in others, piled in perfect pyramids and mounds; and the noise was nearly deafening. Every parrot strained its harsh voice to the utmost, and seemed in the greatest possible rage and fury. Was there a revolution among the ornithological population of the republic, as well as among the human? Was this a parrot-and-paroquet pronunciamiento? No; they were too sensible —they only objected, perhaps instinctively, to a sea-voyage. But what a noise they made! Talk of people being deafened by artillery in a battle, indeed! the sharp edge of these piercing sounds seemed to cut through and through the tympanum like knives.

The little paroquets (some were lovely tiny creatures, with white rings round their necks, and the most charming little turquoise-blue heads conceivable) repeated incessantly, "Perroquito chiquito, blanquito bonito;" and the macaws reiterated, in their hoarse, guttural manner, "Tocar la pata," or something like that, in the hubbub. The poor birds seemed fit for Bedlam at last, for none appeared to like to give in, and the clatter seemed to increase. If the natives wished to find purchasers, surely they should have gagged these ear-splitting creatures.

For a moment a terrible idea floated over my horror-stricken imagination. Was it possible the living contents of these canoes would be transferred to the good steamer "Bolivia?" But no; most of the passengers must have had a surfeit of parrot-talking forever. If there were any amiable English visitors on board, politically inclined, and ambitious of a seat in Britain's Parliament, I have good reason to think that morning's trial and torment has caused them to change their minds; and if any of them should have been elected (as I am told a gentleman lately was) in their absence, they will probably take an early opportunity of accepting the Chiltern Hundreds.

Extraordinary as it may appear, a few of the shrieking chatterboxes were bought. One little blue-headed beauty became a great favorite with V——; but whether, as some thought, the poor little thing had been injured, or whether it never recovered its own small share in the animated debate I have spoken of, I know not; but it died very soon.

The Captain sent me some splendid ponchos to look at, which were of very brilliant colors, and exquisite materials. They were made by the Indian women; and they say these fine and beautifully-finished ones take a great deal of time, and a considerable amount of labor. They were fringed and embroidered, and appeared to be of rich silk; but I believe were formed entirely of the wool of the Vicuna.

I am constrained to confess, Guayaquil is rather a candle-light beauty; not so, it seems, are the Guayaquilenas, with their delicate complexions and masses of magnificent hair and miniatures of feet—Cinderella's glass-slipper would not have fitted many of these South American ladies, for it would have been much too large. The Guayaquil grass hats are very famous: they vary in price from three to fifty dollars: they are extraordinarily durable, and the best require great care and attention in choosing the peculiar grass of which they are made, and subsequently in preparing it; which accounts for the apparently extravagant price asked for those of superior manufacture.

Ecuador, in which this grass grows, I believe, prohibits its exportation. The most delicate of these hats can only be worked upon, it is said, in a particular state of the atmosphere, which restricts the hours of labor upon it (without any interference of our benevolent Lord Ashley) to a limited number during the day, consequently a very perfect and superfine hat occupies whole months in preparation. Of course, the only genuine ones are made at the place whence the hats take their name; but large numbers of a very tolerably successful imitation, though decidedly inferior, are manufactured in the province of Piura in Peru, and exported from Payta.

Gay and brilliant as revolutionized Guayaquil looked, we were not sorry to leave it; for the heat and the musquitoes were altogether almost insupportable. We bade farewell at last to the town, and started, carrying off from those thick-thronging boats full of pine-apples and paroquets, quite a mountain of the former, which are certainly marvelously excellent at that place; they are very large and juicy, and of most exquisite flavor, and the inside is of a snowy whiteness.

We had some Guayaquil beef at dinner, which was exceedingly good; so that five productions of Guayaquil seem to be superlatively fine—beef, hats, pine-apples, ladies, and paroquets.

How we longed, as we steamed down the river—whose heated banks seemed steaming in emulation—to breathe the fresh air of the ocean! Still the pretty scenery of parts of the river kept us at the cabin windows, though the closeness of the atmosphere did not allow us to dream even that we were inhaling that luxury called air.

At length we were once more on the glorious Pacific, on our way to Payta. Chimborazo and Cotopaxi, were neither of them visible; but the ocean looked as beautiful as it possibly could, to console us a little for the disappointment.

Payta is an extraordinary place indeed—a sterile, treeless, waterless desert. It is the port of Piura, the chief town of the province; which large town is distant about forty miles in the interior, and is the first city built by Pizarro, when he conquered the province. It is said to contain about 12,000 inhabitants. The population of Payta amounts to about 4000.

The bay on which it is built, if I am correctly informed, affords the only secure anchorage on this part of the coast. It is difficult to imagine any thing more dreary, wild, and inhospitable-looking than this bleak, arid place.

The houses, with their high, thatched roofs, stand under a barren range of yellow, bilious-looking sand-hills, that seem afflicted with a perpetual jaundice: there is neither tuft nor sprig, nor leaf nor blade of vegetation visible. Most of the houses are constructed of the bamboo, either slightly filled in with clay, or intermixed with a few strips and shreds of hide, and the principal ones are coated with mud inside and outside, and whitewashed: the habitations of the Indians, like those on the Isthmus, are mere cages of cane. It is like dwelling in a Brobdignagian wicker-basket turned topsy-turvy, and with an immense extinguisher-like thatched roof, in place of the bottom of the basket.

Dreary and melancholy as its appearance is, the situation of this town is said to be particularly salubrious: the Indians live to an exceedingly advanced age here. The profession of the healing art has a very bad chance at Payta: a barber and a painter are said to have followed the medical line here, and undertaken to attempt to kill off a few of those long-lived individuals, but unsuccessfully: draughts could not destroy them—pills could not poison them.

Before the yoke of Spain was thrown off, there was a very considerable overland commerce from the Atlantic coast to Panama, on the Pacific: the richly-freighted argosies, heavy with gold and treasure, always put into Payta, on their way to and from Callao —strange as it may seem—for water, as well as provisions. Provisions and water are brought from the interior, and the latter from some distance, for there is not a single drop of fresh drinking water within six leagues of the place: as a shower of rain only falls about once in three or four years, the inhabitants are entirely dependent upon a river six leagues off, for that essential necessary of life. Regularly every morning come in, laden with water-barrels, mules and donkeys, which also bring into the town abundant supplies of vegetables and meat.

These two last are very reasonable in price, but the water is extremely dear. The natives say, in Payta it is far more economical to drink wine; therefore, no doubt they do—whenever they can get it. Let not Father Mathew, or any other preacher of teetotalism come here, for Nature herself seems to oppose their principle in this thirsty place.

The poor mules and donkeys who bring the precious liquid, and the various articles of consumption to the town, are rarely allowed to taste a drop of water until they return to the above-mentioned river, and they are, under ordinary circumstances, driven back into the interior the same night. The musquito, who, alas! is not a water-drinker (would that Father Mathew could make him one!), and the common house-fly, are the only creatures of the insect tribe to be found in this place: no reptile exists there.

The very dogs, during the oppressive heats, have been frequently known to migrate to the banks of the "abounding river," that they might satisfy their raging thirst in peace, thus deserting their masters.

The market is very well supplied, on the whole, I am informed: bananas, plantains, figs, pomegranates, cherimoyas, aguacates (which fruit has several *aliases*, though it seems a respectable sort of natural production enough—they are sometimes called "avocados" and "alligator" pears; the last is sufficiently absurd, for it neither resembles a pear, nor an alligator),* tomatoes, sweet-potatoes, and other tropical fruits and vegetables, are plentiful and excellent. Besides they have poultry, and beef, and mutton.

The Indian women who assemble in the morning in the market-place to sell provisions, have not forsaken their old national costume, such as their ancestresses appeared in, in the days of "the Children of the Sun"—the Incas of Peru, for which I honor them greatly. This costume is remarkably simple, consisting chiefly of a large, flowing, black dress, with very wide, loose sleeves.

The exquisite transparency and clearness, as well as the dryness of the atmosphere at Payta, are very remarkable; but there are no rich twining plants and flowers there to embroider the very air with their high-fantastical, and delicate vagaries: all is sterile and glaring.

But, however dreary and unfruitful the vicinity of Payta may be, the province of Piura has the reputation of being eminently fertile, and rich in many productions, animal, mineral, and vegetable. Great quantities of cotton grown there are among the exports from Payta. It also exports silver, cattle, goat-skins, &c. The cotton generally produces two crops in the year, and grows to the size of a tree. It is of an extremely good quality.

The town is the dépôt still, as it was under the Spanish rule, of the extensive commerce of the interior of North Peru. The best Peruvian bark is found in the valleys of Loxa in the northern part of Peru, and in those of Hualaga in Bolivia.

Some little time ago Payta had actually been totally without rain for ten years. If during three or four years the inhabitants are blessed with a few precious showers, their wild, rugged hills smile with delicate verdure, and it is even of vast pecuniary advantage to Payta.

There are the marks of former water-courses leading to the sea,

* In Jamaica, I hear, they are called "subaltern's butter."

in the neighborhood, now completely dry; but the traces of water having once flowed there, are still, travelers say, perfectly plain and visible in the beds of the now empty channels. It is supposed —and it seems with much reason—that some ancient revolution and convulsion of nature either diverted the course, or entirely dried up the sources of these former torrents; it appears no tradition exists of water ever having been heard of or seen much nearer to Payta than now.

Some of the best houses at Payta have their patios covered over with awnings, which is a charming plan while the sun is in his full power; but when his rays decrease, the more air in these hot regions, I think, the better. But since they have no shade outside their houses at this place, they appear determined to have all they can within!

In former days, I believe, the old Spanish Viceroys disembarked at this port on their way to the capital of Peru! which journey by land might be accomplished in about a fortnight's time.

The riches of this place were formerly proverbial, and often, report says, tempted the cupidity of the old British navigators. When navigation was not so finished a science as it is now, the beating to windward from Payta and from Panama, to Callao and to Valparaiso, was said to be inconceivably slow and difficult.

Near the coast the currents and winds add very greatly to the length of the voyages. It is necessary to sail out to sea, to meet the wind more to the westward; under which circumstances, a good sailer may perform the voyage from Payta to Lima in a fortnight or twenty days.

## CHAPTER XLVI.

Cherimoyas—Lambayeque—The Balsa—Its Use—Numerous Reptiles and Insects at Lambayeque—Curious Mound-tombs—Sepulchral Curiosities found in them—Alleged Imitation of them in Birmingham—Huanchaco—The peremptory Lady—Description of Callao—Its Destruction a Century ago—The frozen Apple.

Just as we were starting from Payta, I received a splendid basketful of cherimoyas from the British Consul. I was not, of course, able to thank him for his thoughtful courtesy, to my great regret, but we shall stop there again on our return.

These cherimoyas were exceedingly fine, and they are so popular a fruit and have so tempting an appearance, that I am quite provoked with myself for not being able to like them; but such is the case, nevertheless.

Our next stoppage was at Lambayeque, where there seemed to be neither port nor harbor: an apparently miserable assemblage of huts and hovels, with a very few houses of higher pretensions, stood on the beach: this is the landing-place for Lambayeque, the town itself of that name being about seven miles in the interior.

The little village on the beach is exposed to the mighty swell of the mile-long waves of the Pacific, that rise far away at sea into huge rolling billows, and then tower into foamy-crested and mountainous breakers, which plunge down on the trembling shore, after a terrific sweep, in surges of long-resounding thunder.

Here, as well as at Payta, they make use of that singular and useful contrivance, the balsa, which is a large pile of logs of some light and suitable wood, crossing and re-crossing each other in layers, and very strongly lashed together. These are secure even in the midst of the mighty waves of the Pacific, when tremendous billows and sweeping surges beat around them, and vast walls and precipices of water threaten, as they roll on with fearful force, to whelm and engulf them. If by any accident the lashing should give way, they are instantaneously lost. Of course there are times when not even the balsa can pass the formidable breakers.

Payta is warranted to be free from reptiles and insects, and from all accounts, they must have transferred themselves and their always large families to Lambayeque, which is said to swarm with them. There is one creature, called the salamanchaca, the bite of which is described as being extremely venomous and dangerous.

Near Lambayeque, it is stated, there are several of those curious mound-tombs of the ancient Peruvians, in which are ordinarily found numbers of those variously-shaped hollow vases and vessels denominated "huacos." These huacos are generally formed into uncouth representations of human beings, animals and reptiles; and the acts and occupations of ancient Indian life are shadowed forth quaintly on them very frequently. They were for the use of the departed.

The greater part of them are constructed of a black earth; but some—no doubt from the tombs of their chiefs—are of silver, and even of gold. Most of them have apertures, which, upon applying the lips to them firmly, and blowing into them, produce a whistling and very strange sound. It is also said, if you put them on the fire, when they are thoroughly heated, they will send forth a sweet and melodious tone; but people do not like experimentalizing thus on them, for fear the poor superannuated musical-boxes should break.

It is necessary to be very careful of whom you purchase these sepulchral curiosities, I am informed, as the eager demand among travelers and visitors, and even among residents, especially those from the United States and Europe, for these archæological treasures has been the cause of their being pretty successfully imitated, it is rumored, in Birmingham, that toy-shop of two worlds! (and which appears anxious for the custom of the Elysian fields to boot). If any one is anxious to procure the real article, he must pay a visit to the old burial mounds, or depute some trustworthy friend or acquaintance so to do.

In the inland town of Lambayeque, the market is supplied, I hear, with exquisite white grapes, as well as a variety of other fruits. A curious currency appears by some late accounts to be in use at Lambayeque—no other than eggs, which freely circulate as small coin; not a pleasant coin to put in your pockets, I should think, however agreeable that operation may be in general.

There, as in other places in Peru, the inhabitants are fond of quaffing a refreshing beverage, called chicha. They have other contrivances, I believe, besides the balsa* for passing the tremendous surf of the Pacific: at these places the inflated hides of animals are used for this purpose frequently, and called "cavallos;" but I fancy this requires a person much experienced in the practice.

We went from Lambayeque to Huanchaco: the coast there was very wild and rocky, and scarcely a trace of man's habitation or handiwork was to be seen in any direction. But among the bold, rugged rocks, in face of the majestic Pacific Ocean, rose, alone, apparently, shedding a heavenly halo over the great solitude, a little Christian church! This being elevated on a peak of rock, was visible when the town or village it belonged to was hidden.

We proceeded from thence to Casma, which I thought very charmingly situated; and then, after a short delay, came on to Callao. At one of the intermediate ports, I forget which, several Peruvian ladies came on board, their diminutive feet *chaussé'd* with the prettiest little white satin boots imaginable, almost large enough for an English doll! Their toilet in general for the voy-

* Some of the balsas have a rough mast, supporting a square-sail.

age was such as in London might be worn at a *matineé musicale* or a very brilliant breakfast at Chiswick, or perhaps even at the Opera, save the lovely mantilla, undulating so gracefully over their luxuriant death-black locks.

I saw one lady who came in one of the native boats with a great many rowers; she was superbly dressed, and appeared to be a person of great distinction there; she was excessively indignant at the difficulties that presented themselves in the way of her getting on board the steamer: the unfortunate craft she was in was plunged and tossed about like a shuttlecock in convulsions by the restless waves; but she scolded the boatmen in the most stentorian of tones, and stamped her little Liliputian white satin foot in a perfect fury. They seemed to be straining every nerve to obey her reiterated and imperious directions, but in vain; and she grew more and more angry with them. She completely ignored the sweeping Pacific, apparently resolved to consider the stupidity of the boatmen the sole and single cause of her not reaching the deck of the "Bolivia" immediately. Supported by two retainers, for she chose to stand up, she continued to give her commands more and more peremptorily: what a Lady of the Lake, or the Ocean, was she! They made a desperate attempt; and the bounding canoe shot up against us with terrific force. I expected with horror to see canoe, boatmen, and lady all struggling in the waves; but no—the little white satin feet were at last seen triumphantly rushing up the ladder as if they had been seven-leagued boots, instead of those baby-shoes! The old blood of Castile and Leon must have stirred in that little form: she looked as if she would have commanded the very elements.

We arrived at Callao at last, and one of the first sights that struck our eyes was an English man-of-war, the "Dædalus," the ship from whence the supposed sea-serpent was seen, some time ago. Since that she has been re-commissioned. Captain W—— came on board the steamer, and was good enough to offer to take us on shore in his boat.

We accordingly proceeded to Callao with him in a beautiful boat, shortly after. In the harbor were great numbers of merchant-ships—American, Peruvian, and English. I must not omit to mention that the boats of the "Dædalus" are adorned with a representation of the sea-serpent, in memory of that extraordinary apparition.

Callao is the principal sea-port of Peru. On entering its harbor, you have, on the right hand, to the south, the steepy island of San

Lorenzo, bare and rugged, without a leaf or blade on it. In front are the white houses of Callao, and its mouldering, but noble castles; and beyond spreads the verdant plain, toward a crescent-shaped range of bleak and frowning hills, which inclose this valley of Lurigancho, through which runs the beautiful river Rimac.

Beyond this fertile and smiling valley, to the left of Callao, and at the foot of the swelling mountains, rise the majestic spires and domes of Lima, the City of the Kings, as it was called in past times, "La Ciudad de los Reyes" (it is sometimes now designated as "El Cielo de los Mugeres, el Purgatorio de los Hombres, y el Infierno de los Burros"). Above all tower in their ineffable sublimity, the summits of the stupendous Andes, whose cloud-capped, snow-crested peaks are awfully magnificent.

Callao is about six or seven miles from Lima. It is a consider able town in itself. Many foreign merchants reside there; and on all sides you see large flourishing-looking warehouses and stores. At Callao the anchorage is very good, and the waters of the bay are rarely visited by a stormy breeze. There is a very good landing, at an extremely-handsome mole of stone, which is inclosed by a substantial iron railing. All is life, bustle, and activity around you.

Captain W—— drew my attention to many enormous heaps of corn piled up in the open air, and told me they left them there exposed always to the weather, during every change of the seasons; so dry is the climate, and so remarkable the absence of rain. Great numbers of Liliputian donkeys were to be seen in all directions, engaged in transporting vast quantities of goods to the various warehouses and stores. A great many rude carts and drays, made of raw hides, also went busily to and fro, loaded heavily with different articles of merchandise.

In addition to the heaps of corn and fine wheat from the flourishing republic of Chili, there were large earthen, picturesque-shaped jars, of an alcoholic spirit, called *italia* (manufactured at Pisco, a little south of Callao, and said to be very popular here); blocks of salt brought from the Sechura mines, and iron vessels of quicksilver used in the mines for preparing the precious metals. The scene was altogether novel, interesting, and very animated.

Nearly all the dwelling-houses at Callao are one-storied structures (the safest in case of earthquakes): they are generally built of adobes, and with flat roofs. The Old Town of Callao was completely destroyed by the terrible earthquake of 1746. The ocean, it is said, then receded to an extraordinary distance, and returned again, as if with increased force and fury, in three successive mountainous waves, which entirely overwhelmed the unfortunate town. One man only, we are told, survived this frightful destruction out of a population of three thousand. His escape was almost miraculous.

He was in a protected situation, in a bastion of the fortress, looking upon the ocean. From this isolated position, he beheld the terrified inhabitants of the town hurry from their endangered houses with breathless precipitation, in the utmost agitation, disorder, and alarm; but ere they could reach any place of greater security, the howling waves of the infuriate ocean, which had previously retired in so extraordinary a manner, returned with the terrific and awful violence I have described, and its tremendous surges swallowed up every inhabitant of Callao, except the trembling wretch in the bastion of the fortress.

Though Callao is now, despite its size, a rather insignificant-looking place, it is thought by some, that when the ancient Spanish custom, of having the chief towns removed from the ports, shall yield to modern notions of practical utility and convenience, the population and the opulence of Lima will gradually find their way down to this port; and already there are a good many very pretty and well-built houses beginning to rear their loftier fronts among the humble dwellings of the town.

Captain W—— was good enough to write and order a private conveyance for us from Lima, instead of our going in the omnibus, which was very full, as there were a good many passengers for the "Kingly" City. We stood a moment at the door of the house whence the omnibus starts, till we saw our luggage arrive safely, part of which I wished to send on by that conveyance.

They were loading the omnibus, and an unfortunate negro who was standing on the roof of the vehicle, pulling at a rope, to fasten some luggage firmly on the top, lost his balance, or the rope gave way, and he fell back down into the street with great violence. He appeared insensible, and his head seemed much cut. He was immediately taken up and carried, apparently with great care and attention, into the house.

While we were waiting for our *coche*, we were invited to stay in the house of Mrs. M——, the wife of an eminent English merchant of the place, who resides at Callao. It was an exceedingly pretty house; and in that, and the house of the agent of the British Mail Steamer Company, we saw carpets for the first time for many months—very handsome carpets they were too, from

England. Mrs. M—— invited us to have luncheon with her. This consisted almost entirely of a great variety of exquisite fruits, and a profusion of cakes.

Among other fruits, there was an extraordinary species of apple, called here the frozen apple. On cutting it in half, the core, and a circular portion of the fruit around it, are like a lump of ice; this is only to be found, we are told, in a particular kind of apple, but yet not all the fruits of this separate species are possessed of this peculiarity.

Mrs. —— has some magnificent old inlaid cabinets, of admirable workmanship, that she bought at Lima, I believe. They reminded me of some I saw at Sir William Parker's, at Malta, which had been presented to him by the present Queen of Portugal. In the market-place here, under temporary booths, we are told, are stationed numerous venders of *piña*, or iced pine-apple water, ice cream, &c., and of fruits almost endless.

At length our conveyance drew up to the entrance of Mrs. M——'s charming mansion; and with much gratitude for her kind hospitality, we took leave of her, and started for Lima.

---

## CHAPTER XLVII.

Site of old Callao—The shouting Inquirer—Approach to Lima—Absence of Rain at that City—The graceful Peruvian Costume—The Poncho—Male and Female Equestrians—Arrival at Lima—The Aspect of the City—Miradors—Multitude of Asses in Lima—London and Lima—Costumes of Lima Ladies—The Bridge over the Rimac—Venders of Cigars—The Cordilleras.

On our road to Lima, we saw a monument placed to commemmorate the spot where a Spanish vessel of war, a frigate, was deposited, at the time of the memorable earthquake of 1746, by the receding ocean. It is about a mile from the sea-shore. By the way, the present town of Callao is not built on the same spot that the old town stood on before its total destruction. It is more removed from the beach, probably to avoid, on any similar occasion, the terrific billows that swept away all of the ancient town which the frightful earthquake itself had spared. If I am correctly informed, Old Callao, indeed, was about two miles to the south of the new town.

There is a rather gentle inclination the whole way from Lima to the coast: a great many public carriages, as well as private ones, are constantly running on this road, and I think there is no doubt the railroad will answer here admirably; and I can not but believe, those who think Callao will take the place of Lima in the future will be mistaken, as the railroad will so materially interfere with such a prospect.

The wealthy merchants will have their magnificent mansions in the city, and their houses of business at Callao: some, if not many, follow this plan now, and with the additional facilities afforded by the railroad, it will become the common custom.

We stopped a short time at a sort of half-way house to rest the horses, of which we had four attached to the carriage; there was an omnibus pausing there likewise, which seemed to be filled with black people and Indian women smoking. A man came to ask us if we would alight from the carriage, and he roared and thundered this inquiry (seeing we were foreigners from our wearing bonnets), in a terribly loud voice, determined we should *hear* if we did not understand Spanish, which reminded me of the favorite custom in my own land, of trying to make an unfortunate foreigner understand and learn our language, by the curious process of first depriving him of his hearing; in short, by deafening him with a perfect volley of shouts, as if he were still in his own distant country, and the speaker or shouter in his; and by dint of hallooing, this last hoped to make up for the space that separated them, though it should be from England to Japan. A poor German Prince was found one day in the hall at —— in a state bordering on distraction, with a footman on each side of him hallooing in his ears.

Not very far from here, I believe, there is a chapel, at which the old and new Spanish Viceroys used formerly to meet when a fresh one was appointed, and the successor arrived in Peru to assume the functions of governor.

For the last few miles near Lima the road is delightful, with beautiful gardens on either side of it. What a situation is that of the City of Kings! Surrounded with these luxuriant groves and gardens, out of which tower so magnificently the domes, and cupolas, and steeples of its many noble churches and monasteries, with the boundless Pacific heaving the majesty of its unfathomable waves at the foot of the gracious and throne-like height on which it is elevated, and above all, in *every* sense, the giant grandeur of the awful Andes soaring behind it to the skies, crowned with eternal snow, and really looking as if they almost overshadowed and overhung the stately city, for they appear far closer than in reality they are. What a situation it is!

An extraordinary canopy of clouds generally envelops the highest peaks and summits of these sublime mountains, as if their awfulness would be too overwhelming were they beheld uncovered, and these clouds seem ever to threaten the beautiful Lima with some unheard-of tempest. Is not Lima the King of Cities as well as the City of Kings? I should unhesitatingly answer yes, had I never seen Mexico and Constantinople.

Notwithstanding the appearance of the thick and sable clouds that hover almost continually over the mighty peaks of the mountains, it is said never to rain at Lima, and thunder and lightning have not ever scared the inhabitants of the plains of Peru. In the mountains, however, fall showers of rain, and occasionally there arise furious hurricanes and tempests. A great deal of dew and of mist in the winter, dropping in the valleys, makes up for the absence of rain; and it is not often the sun is seen, save through a softening vail of vapor. But I can not corroborate the statements of those who say the sun never shines in Lima, as I have seen it already several times pouring forth its most brilliant beams, but not for any length of time continuously and uninterruptedly. The full glory of his tropical resplendence is in the morning (when he does appear): then gradually grows and gathers around him that floating pavillion of clouds which casts a soft and delightful shadow on the earth.

The approach to the city from the port of Callao is a very wide, handsome road, that runs almost in a straight line; and as you draw near the suburbs of the capital, on each side are to be seen numerous immense remains of fine *haciendas*, which have been deserted during the troublous times of civil war and revolution, and still-inhabited villas and cultivated grounds and gardens.

Olive trees and aloes grow along the sides of the road. Where there is an interspace between, the gardens and the distant fields are to be seen divided by rude walls of adobes, and irrigated by means of numerous *acéquias*, or small canals, conducting the fertilizing waters of the silvery Rimac.

Still advancing, you find the road alive with busy passengers, and citizens and ladies of Lima, besides droves of beasts of burden, conveying cargoes of merchandize almost continually to and fro. When any specie is thus transported, the train of animals is usually escorted by a small body of negro soldados, carrying lances with a little bright scarlet flag at the end of each.

It is sometimes stated that an enormous quantity of specie is smuggled away from hence, but I know not whether this is true. We saw a goodly number of equestrians and equestrianesses as we passed along, the former accoutred in the brilliant and graceful Peruvian costume. The poncho, or cloak, is always worn—this I have mentioned before: it has a circular opening for the head of the wearer to pass through, and has generally a gay fringe round the edges. It displays often a great brilliancy and variety of colors; occasionally it is very richly and fancifully embroidered, and sometimes it is of a snowy white, but generally exhibits broad and bright stripes—orange, scarlet, blue, green, or rose-colored, or variegated combinations of these, and at other times different patterns, gayly intermixed and diversified.

The poncho hangs gracefully over the shoulders, and falls almost down to the knees. It is certainly very picturesque and striking, with the ordinary accompaniments of richly-carved stirrups (which stirrups are usually triangular and rather massive-looking blocks of wood, generally ornamented and tipped with burnished silver), and glittering caparisons for the horse.

However, I do not think the poncho for a single moment can be compared with the far more beautiful and more picturesque Mexican serapé; and the Mexican costume altogether is, I think, very much handsomer. The hats worn here, are commonly the white Guayaquil grass sombreros, sometimes with very broad brims, and at other times like small plates; and the windmill-like spurs are perfect masses of heavy metal, very frequently of silver, the enormous rowel standing out four or five inches from the heel, and the spikes being perhaps an inch and a half or more in length.

As for the horsewomen, the greater part of them are peasants (Indian dames, or negresses), who usually ride in cavalier fashion, with an ample balloon-like white muslin dress—which sometimes makes them look like the dome of St. Paul's on horseback—or else the same description of capacious garment in gaudy calico of many colors; a delicate silk stocking and beautifully fitting shoe on a very little foot, which is furnished with a spur, a shawl or fluttering scarf of the most florid designs, and of a hundred hues, an immense Guayaquil hat with broad streaming variegated ribbons, and coquettish bows on whichever they consider the "congregation side of the head," and with the shining cascade of abundant coal-black tresses, carefully divided on the dark forehead, and hanging down the back in long braided streamers. They generally ride at a quiet little jog-trot butter-and-egg-pace, while the gentleman equestrians dash to and fro at a wild gallop, and make the dust fly merrily.

The verdant and flourishing appearance of the neighborhood of Lima is a matter of astonishment to the traveler, till the cause of this is known. It is not only the vapors and dews that contribute to this, but the circumstance, that in all the plains in Peru that lie between the Great Cordillera and the Pacific Ocean, the water is found invariably from three to four feet below the surface, thus compensating for the absence of rain by the facilities afforded to irrigation, a practice which was universally resorted to by the ancient Peruvians, and adopted and continued by their Spanish conquerors. The skill of the Indian inhabitants had literally intersected all the cultivated country with the acéquias, by which the waters flowing from the mountains are divided and subdivided into almost innumerable little channels for irrigation.

But now about a mile from the capital, our vehicle, rolling amid thick clouds of dust, has arrived at the avenue, or Alaméda; and the road runs between straight double rows of tall poplars and willow-trees, with a handsome promenade on each side (furnished with stone benches for all who wish to see omnibuses and donkeys, and enjoy volumes of dust) to the city: from this broad, splendid avenue we pass through an arched gateway into Lima: this gateway admits you within a lofty thick wall, which surrounds the city entirely, and forms its sole defense.

We were in Lima, the capital of Peru! Peru, whose very name seems like a fairy tale, and to mean a world of gold and silver and precious stones. The land of the magnificent Children of the Sun, the stately Incas, who could offer a hall piled with gold as a ransom; whose Spanish Viceroys, in later days, on state occasions, walked on pavements of solid silver! Away we rattled to the French hotel to which we had been recommended, but not on silver pavements, nor very praiseworthy stone ones.

The houses in Lima are, I think, handsome. They frequently consist only of one story (on account of repeated earthquake visitations), though there are many exceedingly fine ones with two stories; but these have very often a deserted air, and are out of repair and dilapidated, in consequence of having been abandoned by their original owners, who took alarm at their loftiness and supposed insecurity—and they now are sometimes tenanted by poorer families. There are, however, very many exceptions to this rule.

The houses in general are surmounted with a flag-staff; they have, I think, a remarkably Moorish air, and I was much struck with the resemblance of their very peculiar balconies to those I remember so well at Valetta, in Malta; although these at Lima are very much longer and larger altogether; indeed, I have lately seen some that form spacious apartments in themselves, beautifully furnished, carpeted, and decorated. But I will briefly describe them.

You must imagine long lines, all along the fronts of the houses, of enormous verandas of wood, many projecting very far over the foot-pavements, from the second stories of the houses (which are called "altos" here). The lower part, probably to the height of three feet, or thereabouts, is entirely closed up along the extended front, and at different parts and at the two terminations this immense, covered wooden balcony is supported on far projecting beams, with sculptured and variously-shaped ends, while from the inclosed portion to the roof are long, light shutters of lattice-work (or glass windows), which are depended, and swung from hinges at the top: if these are required to be open, there is, I think, a long, hooked bar, by which they can be fastened, and kept wide open; but, occasionally the head is used by the fair Peruvians instead, who, with their arms resting on the light, wooden wall of the lower part of the balcony, keep back with that graceful mantilla'd head the light shutters. If the head is pushed out far enough, of course, all in the streets on all sides is visible; but if the Señora objects to this, and is tired of the front scene, she has only to walk to either end, and take a complete side view.

Most of these "miradors" are furnished with glass windows, now, but I believe this has only been done lately. These capacious verandas are not very unlike gigantic and enormously lengthened out opera-boxes, from which the spectator may observe all that the street presents of a "spectacle;" and the very large and handsome ones, provided with delicate mats, or many-patterned carpets, and furnished with chairs and cushioned sofas, form a kind of conservatory-balcony, where the bright human flowers of beautiful Peru, guarded and shielded from wind and mist-like dews, may smile (and sometimes smoke!) in all security and in peace.

The houses in Lima have large court-yards; those in the more distinguished of them, are quite little plazas in themselves—but I will say more of them presently.

We rattled noisily up to the great double-gates of the large French hotel, after passing through a number of busy, populous, looking streets, and soon after took possession of an apartment which, rather to our disappointment, did not look on the street, so that we found ourselves in a large saloon, verandaless and windowless. When the great gate-like doors, that open on a very broad and uncovered kind of semi-patio of stone, which has a staircase ascending from the lower court-yard (for this hotel has two stories, and we are in the "alto"), are closed, we have no light except from a small "claraboya," or skylight, which shuts or opens by means of long ropes, hanging down into the room. The bedrooms have small windows looking on the stone-paved corridor and down upon the court-yard, which court-yard is a thoroughfare.

The immense arched gateway that leads to it in front, opens first into a broad covered passage-way, which in most houses is decorated with some arabesques or with a gaudy painting on either side, representing a variety of subjects, often scriptural, but occasionally mythological. Ours is, pleasantly enough for us, occupied on one side by the ample stall of a female fruit-vender, who has always a most abundant provision of delicious fruits, and who sits there from earliest dawn, I believe, to "dewy eve"—very dewy are generally the eves in rainless Lima.

Without meaning any bad compliment to the inhabitants of this grand old capital, I am constrained to say, I think I never saw or heard so many asses as in Lima: their name is legion, and they bray with a hundred-donkey power. We are anxious to see the gentle Llamas, but it is said they very rarely come into the city. There are hosts of convicts here, and very villainous-looking ones. Notwithstanding dilapidation, donkeys, and convict gangs, however, Lima is a very charming place, on the whole; not gay and glittering as the Havana, nor beautiful and enchanting as Mexico, but with a thousand peculiarities and glories of her own, besides her majestically superb situation. Lima is like nothing but Lima, and as unlike all our mostly commonplace, though wealthy, and utterly civilized European cities as it is possible to imagine any thing to be! Herculaneum, hoisted above-ground, might in some few particulars partially resemble it. Yet no; it would not! Ideal cities of half-destroyed *châteaux d'Espagne* would be most like it!

I can not help smiling to think of good-humored Madame J——, at Panama, who knew but two great cities, London and Lima, and was perpetually talking of the two together, as if they were the Siamese twins of towns. "Ah, at London and Lima I used to go to shops and buy so and so; there's none here;" and, "But at

London and Lima they do this and that;" or, "When one is at Lima and London it is easy to find such and such things." And the difference is so ludicrously vast—they are such complete architectural antipodes to each other, and such antipodes in every thing else.

Lima, which, besides its stately title of the City of Kings, was called proudly the City of a Thousand Towers and of a Hundred Gates, as if it were a nobler Spanish Thebes, is certainly quite the city of churches, steeples, domes, towers, palaces (in decay), verandas, colonnades, piazzas, porticos, patios, corridors, balconies, quadrangles, galleries, lattices, frescoes, arabesques, vestibules, cowled priests, ponchoed cavaliers and saya-y-mantoed ladies.

I dare say the reader may have seen engravings of the latter extraordinary costume of the Lima ladies, which is now very considerably modified, and instead of looking as if they were walking about in elastic, closely-fitting, upright coffins, which they must formerly have had the appearance of doing, they look like very graceful ladies, floating along in an atmosphere of encircling black silk, and closely masked, only showing one bright black eye, as if they were so many fair Cyclopesses.

I know not how it is, but something in the arrangement of this cloaking vail always makes it appear to me as if the eye was in the middle of the cheek. In coming back from Mrs. A——'s, the other day, we missed the turning into our street, and I asked one of these "Tapadaes," as they are called, the way; and while she was courteously telling me, I tried to ascertain what it was that gave it, to me at least, that peculiar appearance. Perhaps it may be partly the extreme fullness of their flashing eyes, that makes the size of the suppressed (and perhaps somewhat *com*pressed) nose seem less, and the exposed eye more prominent, and level with that feature—but I could not make it out satisfactorily at all.

The English minister, and Mrs. A——, are particularly kind and amiable to us. Mrs. A—— is a truly charming person. How I envy the exceeding fluency and correctness with which she talks Spanish. She took us out for a drive yesterday, and we were perfectly enchanted with the views in the vicinity of Lima, and with the town itself.

We crossed a very striking and picturesque stone bridge, thrown across the sparkling Rimac, to go to one of the Alamédas. This bridge is old, having been built in 1610. The carriages enter it by a broad arch across the centre of the street, and there are two lesser arches crossing the two side pavements. Lofty, handsome carved turrets and spires surmount these noble arches, and give the bridge a very imposing effect. They say every stone in this *puente* has been loosened by the dreadful earthquake. The river Rimac dashes boldly and brightly along over a rocky and ragged bed.

This bridge joins the main portion of Lima to the suburb of San Lazaro, which would otherwise be separated from the principal part of the city by the river: it appears a very busy and animated thoroughfare.

There are recesses, semi-circularly shaped, with stone benches, that open from the wide promenades along the bridge, and where often rests the visitor to Lima, gazing on the throngs that pass ceaselessly by, characteristically attired, and intent on their various errands of business or recreation. Beside him, perhaps, are several fair Limanians, in saya-y-manto, or dandy citizens, star-gazers on the one brilliant orb—that eye which is peeping out like a planet from many sable clouds.

Near the entrance to this old, solid, yet fantastic bridge, are stationed sometimes venders of cigars. An old man, I have heard, sells here the cast-off stumps of these articles, arranged neatly on a tray.

The view from this bridge is exceedingly lovely. If the eye travels down the silvery road of the river, its left bank is beheld richly embellished by the luxuriant gardens of magnificent old convents, and of the splendid mansions of the Peruvian *millionaires*. The view ends with the Pacific! Then, if the glance is turned in the opposite direction, we scan the broad, verdant avenues of the lovely Alaméda del Acho; and beyond, the shadowy groves and gardens of the valley, and the glistening turrets of the Pantheon; the entire exquisite scene being bounded by that lower range of mountains which incloses the charming green valley of the Rimac.

But the view beyond this is sublime indeed: the higher range of the glorious Cordilleras, when the clouds admit of that majestic sight, are seen, with their indestructible diadems of perpetual snow, towering on high, mountain behind mountain, summit above summit, crests gleaming between crests, and peaks soaring beyond peaks; an untrodden, undesecrated world between the earth and the spotless skies, shooting up its myriads of rocky spires—like natural conductors of the lightning and storms, as if to interpose that pure and higher part of creation, fresh as it came from the most awful hand of Omnipotence—betwixt the wrath of Heaven and the now sullied, blighted lower Earth.

Vain fancies! We have a securer shelter; and where the humblest church lifts up the lowliest spire (as some eloquent writer once said), there is a better conductor of that awful lightning of wrath from our wretched heads, and from our fallen world!

## CHAPTER XLVIII.

The Great Plaza—The Cathedral of Lima—The Streets of that City—The Silversmiths—The Bells of Lima—Charitable Institutions—Churches and Convents—Handsome Houses—Palaces of the Past—Grotesque Paintings—Well-appointed Carriages—The Limanian Beggar-woman—Particularities of Lima Ladies' Dress—Their Shoes—M. and Madame B——Their Daughter.

The Great Plaza, a principal public square in Lima, is extremely handsome. It has a large brazen fountain in the middle, said to be about forty feet high, surmounted with a figure which represents, I believe, the Goddess of Fame bearing aloft her trumpet

The old palace of Pizarro once stood in this square—on the north side, I am told; but now its place is filled up with a handsome colonnade, which has a great number of shops and stalls under it. This colonnade forms one side of the Plaza. The first stone of the famous old cathedral, on the other side, was laid by Pizarro, and his bones are said to repose in a vault beneath the sacred edifice.

Some people think the cathedral a huge and clumsy mass of tasteless architecture; but allowing that it has an abundance of defects, architecturally speaking, still there is something about it that is both pleasing and imposing. If you can fancy a gorgeous and fantastic temple in the clouds, when sunset casts its fleeting pomp over the skies, adorned with a thousand strange splendors, you may a little paint it to your imagination. There is a profusion of diversified rich coloring, and a mass of lavish tracery, and curious and quaint decorations on the front of the edifice. I intend to visit the interior before I go from Lima.

There is an ecclesiastical building adjoining the cathedral. It is the Archiepiscopal Palace. The Government House is on another side of the square, and the covered colonnades or portales occupy the remainder. Under the portales, which of course open under their large and handsome arches to the Great Plaza, are numerous well-supplied fancy shops, and a great deal of exquisite gold and silver embroidery may be seen there. There are excellent "tiendas" (shops) also in the Calle Mercadéres, which is quite a French street, being almost entirely occupied by French shopkeepers. They display a profusion of handsome and excellent goods, of various kinds.

There is another street where the Peruvian silversmiths congregate chiefly, but they do not make much exhibition of their handiwork. The exquisite silver filagree work, however, is most surprisingly beautiful, and most elaborately and delicately wrought; but the specimens of this highly finished workmanship mostly come from the interior, and are made by the Indians.

I never heard any thing like the sublime tone of the bells of Lima. It is the profoundest and most majestic sound imaginable, and resounds through the air as if the deep vibrations would dwell there, and brood, and never cease, lengthening and deepening on and on—the most unearthly yet most beautiful music I ever heard. The reason given for this extraordinary and matchless magnificence of tone, is the enormous quantity of silver in the bells. There was a large proportion originally, and this was added to, I am told here, during the casting of the bells, by devout persons throwing in, as oblations and offerings, almost innumerable silver coins, of divers weights and values. In short, the contents of half a mine of the precious metal almost are suspended in the air.

The great cathedral bell is surpassingly glorious in its unfathomably deep peal of tremulous silver thunder—nay, it seems a thousand thunders rolling afar! But the other bells at Lima are also very rich and harmonious in their sublime tones.

There are several eleemosynary establishments in this city, among which the Foundling Hospital is said to be particularly well-managed, and a lunatic one particularly ill. There are a great many handsome churches and convents in Lima, and they are the prominent features in all parts of the city. They are mostly enormous structures, crowned by majestic domes, and towers, and steeples, and displaying on their extensive fronts a perfect labyrinth of elaborate painting, complicated decorative designs, statuary, and carving.

I hear that some of these immense churches and nunneries, inclose within their widely-extended walls very spacious and superb squares: the convents often have porticos, piazzas, and covered colonnades, beautifully built and finished, and supported one above another on highly-ornamented rows of splendid arches. Their massive walls are wholly covered with richly-figured, glazed porcelain and fresco paintings, their roofs artistically adorned and carved, and contiguous to them, or even *within* their vast encircling walls, are exquisite gardens of the richest shrubs, and plants, and flowers, with gushing fountains and shadowy walks, from which the busy world is shut out, and where contemplation may dwell undisturbed. I hear that the orders in Lima are exceedingly strict, and that generally no women even are admitted into the principal nunneries.

We have seen here very handsome streets, and some regal-looking old houses. Some of the most splendid, we were informed, are now subdivided and let to a number of families in indifferent circumstances—in fact, forming a little town in themselves. Still as we drove by and caught a casual glimpse through their enormous gateways—their gigantic fountained court-yards, their superb piazzas, and the remains of former gilding, and painting, and elaborate carving, and various showy and costly, though mouldering adornments, made those palaces of the past look like genii structures of the Land of Faery and sorcery, under some evil enchanter's gloomy thrall and desolating spell. They are not in what is now considered the fashionable part of Lima. In the generality of houses here, beneath the covered verandas, there usually is a broad and handsomely-paved entrance to the court-yard, through massive and exceedingly high double gates (which are thickly studded over with strong brazen knobs).

Around this ample court the house is built, and in those that are constructed of two stories, the stables, apartments for domestics, store-rooms and offices open on this court-yard, and are on the same level with it. From thence ascends a flight of broad stairs to the vast galleries above, leading to the different suites of apartments occupied by the various members of the family, the great salas, or reception-rooms, &c.

The entrance is frequently a little shorn of its grandeur and imposing effect by having shops built along it: but when it is not thus disfigured, the line of the street is divided from the court-yard by a thick, lofty wall. The immense gates open into a wide covered passage-way of some length, which is adorned commonly on both sides with frescoes. The window-sills in the court-yards are usually gilt, in the houses of the wealthy, which, with the bright-colored jalousies, gives them a gay appearance.

Occasionally, the handsomest and principal part of the stately mansion crosses the court, exactly opposite to the entrance. The whole of this portion of the building is then adorned by a noble portico, and the front of the mansion is decorated by elaborate iron open-work, brilliantly gilt or bronzed over, and presenting a very rich appearance. These house have ordinarily only one story, and have rooms of very great height and vast size. At the back of this principal or central portion of the house is another lesser court-yard, called the "traspatio;" it is a sort of kitchen and servants' court-yard.

On driving on the Alaméda the other day, we observed a large wall, built along one side of the tree-shaded promenade, and covered all over with grotesque-looking paintings, the color of which seemed as fresh and bright as if just done. I did not examine it closely enough to see accurately the subjects, as we dashed rapidly on, drawn by Mrs. A——'s beautiful and spirited horses; but I imagine it to be one of which I have read a description, and which is called by the natives, "El mundo al revez," where the system of nature is entirely reversed, and dogs are hanging their masters; horses riding on men's backs; and some of the finny tribe, represented standing a-tail-tip, with fishing-rods in their mouths, angling for *ci-devant* gentlemen-sportsmen who are seen nibbling at the bait! In short, all is almost in as great a state of confusion and disorder, as if the whole world, instead of a part, had suddenly become French or Irish, and were altering every thing to their hearts' content; for even themselves, must and do own, that while among the noblest people on the earth, they are certainly the fondest of change and excitement.

In driving through the streets here, we often meet handsome and well-appointed carriages; some remarkably so. We saw a really splendid one the other day, with beautiful horses, that might have been transported to Hyde Park, and admired there. The ladies occupying it were all in Parisian bonnets. I thought they were foreigners. Alas! no; they were Limanians: and they had deserted thus the loveliest of all head dresses—their own matchless mantillas. The saya-y-manto we see, by the way, worn almost in its original quaintness and eccentricity, by an old beggar-woman, who comes sometimes to the great gates of our sitting-room while we are at breakfast, and asks for money, bread, milk, clothes, any thing—every thing.

She has never favored us with a sight of more than her one eye, holding her vail over her face with as much care (before only V—— and me) as I once saw a Turkish beggar-woman bestow upon her coarse yashmack, who when we offered her half a handful of small coins if she would drop her yashmack, indignantly refused, and marched away with the step of an insulted queen.

We should not have guessed the mendicant "tapada" was old but from her shriveled hands, and quavering, cracked voice, so well disguised was she. We were told she had formerly been tolerably rich, but had been reduced by different misfortunes. Her once handsome saya-y-manto was not exactly tattered, but the rich black satin had lost its lustre, and grown dingy with age. The saya is a silken or satin petticoat, stitched neatly in very narrow plaits, and thickly quilted and lined. This used to cling like a web of wax around the form; but now, fitting at the waist, it hangs in full folds down to the satin-slippered feet.

This petticoat, formerly, I believe, was almost uniformly black, but in these days (though frequently it is still of sable hue) it is very often blue or brown.

The manto is a black silk vail, of impenetrable thickness, drawn up from under the waist of the silken saya, and gracefully gathered over the shoulders and head as a sort of hood, very much resembling the Maltese faldetta (and no doubt both have originated from Moorish costume and customs), though so much more concealing the face. All the upper part of the form is thus closely covered and disguised, except the one eye. One hand is occupied in holding this manto firmly across the masked face, and the other from time to time may possibly be allowed to pass through a little opening in the manto, more especially if its fair owner considers it deserving of admiration, and if its small fingers are enriched with sparkling jewels.

The embroidered ends of a many-colored scarf or shawl are permitted to pass through this same opening, generally fringed and flowered. All wear satin shoes and silk stockings, even those in the most tattered, worn-out habiliments. We are told, that the extravagance formerly shown in this article of dress was very great. If a more than usual quantity of dewy moisture had made the streets of the capital as muddy as if a heavy shower of rain had fallen (and this is not unfrequently the case), the ladies would immediately eagerly hasten to make their appearance in the most delicate new white satin shoes, which of course could never be worn again; hoping that by speedily "making hay while the sun shone" (a very inappropriately quoted proverb!), in the morning they might have the good fortune to spoil entirely one exquisite pair of *zapatos de raso*, in the afternoon they might possibly have the superlative felicity (if the inexorable climate did not cruelly disappoint them by drying up the moisture) of destroying another pair, and in the evening even of severely damaging a third.

This refinement of luxury is now rather out of fashion, and the Lima ladies are no longer such empresses of all the Russias, with regard to their *chaussure.* The reader knows, perhaps, that the fair Czarina never wears a dress twice.

Mr. P——, the English clergyman here, called to-day, with his very amiable wife; and also Mrs. B—— (the wife of one of the English merchant-princes here), who is extremely agreeable and pleasing. The next apartments to ours are occupied by a French lady and gentleman, M. and Madame du C——. M. du C—— had the misfortune to break his arm, by a fall from his mule, in crossing the Isthmus of Panama, and he has never recovered it. He is chief Secretary, I believe, to the French Legation here; but as his right arm has suffered, and as the same arm was unfortunately injured seriously, some time previously to this disaster, in a duel, it is feared he will have to resign his situation, and return to France. They have a little fair-haired, smiling daughter, who is a wonderful contrast to the dark-eyed natives, as they pass to and fro.

---

## CHAPTER XLIX.

Signal Instance of the Heroism of a Lady—The Procession of the Oraçion—A Lottery in the Grand Plaza—How conducted—Distinguished Visitors—Chorillos—The Sale of "Almas," or Souls—The Public Museum—Portraits of the Spanish Viceroys—Mummies of Peruvian Incas—Beautiful stuffed Birds—Manco Capac—Who where the first Incas?—The Children of the Sun—Progress in Civilization of old Peru.

We are still at Lima, waiting for the steamer.

The other day I had a visit from an English lady, residing here now, who has exhibited such heroism and presence of mind as perhaps hardly any one ever displayed before, under such peculiarly trying circumstances. It appears that the ship she came out in was commanded by a very incompetent, inexperienced, and weak-minded captain, quite unfit for the situation, and always intoxicated, till at last he became wholly and utterly incapable of managing the ship. Mrs. S—— was in deep mental affliction at the time, but unhesitatingly (finding there was no one in the vessel who could take the command) assumed the responsibility of navigating the ship herself. Every one knows how difficult the navigation in going round Cape Horn is, yet this skillful and strong-minded lady succeeded in bringing the ship safely to Lima, assisted only by a very youthful nephew.

It might be imagined a person who could act thus would be masculine, and rough, perhaps, in deportment and manner. Nothing of the kind. This lady is eminently feminine, has a very mild and sweet expression of countenance, and is particularly gentle and pleasing. She never alludes to the subject herself; but I could not resist one day asking her a little about it, though fearful of awakening melancholy recollections in her mind.

She spoke with the utmost modesty of her own wonderful performance; and said, in speaking of her arrival at Lima (where she came to rejoin her husband, who had left England previously), that, though deeply grateful to a merciful Providence for having so graciously protected her and her children, yet this was, perhaps, the most painful moment of her life.

I mentioned that at the time she took the command of the ship she was in deep grief: she had just lost an adored child, a little daughter, who had gradually faded and sunk from the time of their quitting the English shores. On their arrival at Callao, she and her children were on deck, anxiously looking for the husband and the father; but she knew he would miss the one lost treasure; and when she saw him earnestly gazing with growing anxiety, deepening fast into sorrow and terror, as he scanned the diminished group, she felt her heart oppressed almost to breaking within her.

The sweet simplicity and tenderness with which she related these touching circumstances were most winning—most interesting: how evident was it that that noble heart, undaunted amid terrible dangers, was one of the softest and warmest that ever beat in a woman's bosom! This affecting tale has made a deep impression in Lima. No wonder! How often has conduct not half as extraordinary and sublime been lauded to the skies! What true courage was that she displayed in conduct which demanded so much energy, so much promptitude, decision, and self-reliance, and self-forgetfulness, too!

As we sit in our claraboya'd drawing-room here, we hear frequently a bell ringing in the court-yard just below, which is a thoroughfare. It is the Host being carried to some sick person. The sound of the bell is usually accompanied by a lugubrious and rather monotonous chant. If in the evening, a number of attendants (often Indians or negroes) generally carry lanterns, and walk on either side of the procession. The priest, bearing his sacred charge, walks between these rows of light; a canopy is borne over his head by four boys, and a crowd of people sometimes follows the procession. Every person remains uncovered while it passes, and upon their knees.

There is one moment here, as in most of the South American countries and cities, very impressive, fugitive as it is—it is the moment of the Oraçion, when the great cathedral bell turns all the air to a most heavenly thunder-music. Then every hat is reverentially lifted, and every lip seems to tremble with a whispered word of prayer; then the parent lays an affectionate hand on the little child's bowed head; and all seem, for one brief moment, raised from earth, its cares, and business, and interests. Even the lottery-man, who was hallooing "Suerte, suerte!" stops at the unfinished word, and suddenly pulls up his curveting voice on its haunches! Soon 'tis o'er; and the bells ring again—again —a joyous peal. But impressive as this looks to a stranger, there is too much reason to fear it is a custom only mechanically followed by those who have observed it continually.

We saw a curious sight—to us at least—the other evening, in returning from a drive with Mrs. A——. This was the lottery-drawing, which is very formally conducted, and which takes place in the Grand Plaza, exactly opposite the cathedral. A temporary platform and apartment are erected there, which in front are open to the public. In the forepart of this stage are to be seen several hollow wooden globes, of a large size, painted of a conspicuous yellow color, and turning on the stands which sustain them by means of a crank. Into each ball opens a little door, and by the side of each of the globes the different numbers that are to go into it were exhibited on inclined planes, so as to be exposed to the public view: these numbers were painted upon little flat, circular counters.

Behind all this display and array sit three official-looking persons, the judges, grave as an equal number of Lord Chancellors on the wool-sack; then three venerable old gentlemen are seen who have to turn the aforesaid globes; and there is a triad of little boys (who, we were informed, are orphan children, usually from the Foundling Hospital—a curious education for them—this teaching the young idea how to gamble); and these complete the *dramatis personæ.*

Generally, as the expected hour approaches, the Plaza becomes gradually filled. When we passed through, the crowd was gathered densely around the place where the stage was erected. Armed soldados, shovel-hatted and cassocked priests, friars barefooted, mothers with their children, women in their curious *incognita*, the saya-y-manto, cavaliers with rattling spurs, and ragged negroes with glittering teeth; and numbers of eager, staring individuals, in all kind of dresses, and of many different colors and complexions, stood around.

At the proper moment, the three old Fates who turn the globes, cast the numbers into them, on the one side thousands, on the other tens, and in the middle hundreds. These being rolled backward and forward three or four times, the doors are opened at the same moment, and each of the little fellows appointed to the office takes out a number: he does not look at it, but holds it out with outstretched hand to the crowd. Then the boys go up to the table, and display the numbers to the judges, who record them; and having given the proper information to one of the old worthies who turn the wooden globes, he chants it out, and announces the possessor of the prize to the motley assemblage (who are awaiting the decision of fortune) in a sonorous voice.

Then the numbers are put into the globes again, and the selfsame process is repeated, till the whole of the prizes have been drawn and disposed of. Then the multitude disperses; away flit the sayas-y-mantos, perhaps with a tear of disappointment clouding the brilliancy of the one solitary eye; away trot tatterdemalions on teetotaller-like donkeys, who look as if they had abjured not only drinking this or that, but eating and drinking altogether; and off march dingy soldiers, with a fringe of rags adorning their multiform uniform.

These lotteries belong to a society called the "Beneficéncia," and their profits are bestowed on charitable institutions and hospitals.* The Beneficéncia, I believe, farms the lottery out; and in a single year, the sale of the lottery tickets brought about forty-three thousand dollars. So fond are the Limanians of this species of gambling, that at the shops there are frequently little lotteries and raffles.

Ideas are said to be becoming very much liberalized; and I have heard from good authority that some of the priests even have lately shown a most tolerant and enlightened spirit, and have written and preached in a strain that evinced an extraordinary change in their once bigoted opinions.

* There may be educational establishments at Lima, but I know of none.

I had a visit to-day from Monsieur and Madame F——, and Mr. and Mrs. W——. Monsieur F—— commands the French squadron in the Pacific, and is at Callao in his fine frigate "L'Algérie :" he is an exceedingly gentlemanlike and agreeable person, and Madame F—— is very beautiful and pleasing : she is of an Irish family and is the niece of the celebrated Marshal Bugeaud. She was married at Algiers, and now in her husband's noble frigate "L'Algérie," she intends to go round the world with him. From hence Monsieur F—— seems to think they will proceed to the Sandwich Islands, and afterwards to China.

We dined with Mr. and Mrs. A—— last night. A Peruvian lady and her daughter-in-law came in to visit her; they were dressed much like two Parisians, and with many handsome jewels. The ladies retain their own surname after marriage. They asked many questions relative to Mexico, and were full of grace and intelligence; the younger one spoke French.

We had a charming drive yesterday. The streets seemed fuller and gayer than usual. The Lima winter is now coming on, and the weather is becoming very cool: the fashionable watering-place, Chorillos, is quite deserted. When Lima and Callao happen to be at war, which is not a very extraordinary circumstance, Chorillos is sometimes used by merchant-ships as a port, in place of Callao. During the bathing season it is said a good deal of gambling goes on there, and heaps of gold load the gambling-tables, and large fortunes are risked and exchanged; but Chorillos is now only tenanted by negroes and native Indians, and Lima is full.

Besides meeting numbers of handsome carriages, we were often in danger of running against large droves of donkeys, who are so loaded and covered with heaps of fire-wood, fagots, and immense bundles of clover, that they look like self-moving stacks, and fill up nearly the whole street. The foot-passengers have to hurry out of their way at the cry of the negro-drivers, who shout "Ciudado," as they drive on their little moving mountains of sticks and grass; then there are various salesmen and saleswomen, the milk-venders and water carriers, and all carrying their goods on the backs of donkeys.

At the corners of some of the streets may be seen certain pictorial devices, to hint to survivors and mourners their obligations to those who have gone before them to the grave, and are supposed to be suffering the pains of purgatory. Representations of the head and upper part of the human figure are exhibited, done to the life—or death—surrounded by flames of fire. They call these mournful pictures "Almas," or souls, and they are intended to display the actual state and position of the unassisted and unrelieved departed friends of any of the passers-by who may have neglected this duty.

These unpleasant fancy-portraits might produce lasting uncomfortable impressions if there were not means at hand by which the situation of the persons represented could be ameliorated. Fortunately all this has been considerately taken into account: a small mysterious box stands near for the reception of any sum the survivors may like to introduce into it for the relief of the "Almas."

What crowds in the streets, and what many-colored crowds too! The Negroes, the Mestizos, the Indians, Zambos and Cholos, and some of the more humble of the olive-colored descendants of the old proud race of Castile, all go peaceably donkeying on together, and occasionally a fair North American or Anglo-Saxon, like Mrs. P——, with her blue eyes and light-colored hair, goes vision-like by. Verily there is a great deal of variety on all sides.

There are so many of our fair countrywomen, and of the lily-browed American ladies to be seen from time to time at Lima, that I think the makers and inserters of dolls' eyes may venture boldly to send some blue-eyed ones to South America. I see the "Morning Chronicle" tells us that none but black-eyed puppets can be imported here, because the black orbs are universally the wear in these regions; so those with azure peepers would be looked upon as unnatural monsters.

We have been to see the Public Museum, which we found interesting. Madame F—— was there, accompanied by one or two of the French officers. In the room you first enter, the eye is struck by a large number of old portraits, the size of life; these are the likenesses of the forty-five Spanish Viceroys, beginning with the far-famed Pizarro: his countenance was rather striking. They show in the vaults beneath the cathedral, a mouldering corpse, supposed to be that of the Great Conqueror of Peru; but it seems extremely doubtful whether it is so or no.

The Viceroys are dressed in different old Spanish costumes, showing the rise, progress and change of fashions. From black habiliments, with lofty, starched-up ruffs, they advance into rich and flourished embroidery, thickening till it is almost a golden armor. After a while the tide of this lustrous embroidery ebbs a little, and only besprinkles lightly the extreme borders of the vestments.

But there is a more touching and melancholy sight than this to be seen in the Museum. Under cases of glass are placed, in a sitting or crouching posture, certain mummies, exactly as they were taken from their ancient sepulchres. Their legs are crossed and bent: their stiffened arms crossed over their lifeless breasts, with the elbows placed as if resting upon the knees, and the beardless chins are supported on the hands: their teeth—though some few, if I recollect rightly, are missing—were splendid still—large superb rows of glittering ivory (just what Sir J. C—— would have called a magnificent dinner-set), and a little rusty straggling hair yet adhered to their scalps.

These mummies are asserted to be those of the ancient and much civilized Incas of gorgeous Peru. Well may they grin with that sardonic expression, after all they have witnessed! Since the overthrow of their own noble race, what change, what perplexity, what wars, what dissensions!

But Peru is beginning to feel the vitality of the mighty spirit of the age; and if she, and the other South American countries, can learn in time the difference—the vast difference—between real liberty and license, all may yet be well with them, and Nature may not in vain have thrown all her choicest treasures at the feet of these, her spoiled children.

There are a great number of huacos (or images) and earthen vases, aboriginal antiquities, and other curiosities taken from the old Indian graves, and some sepulchral vessels of solid gold and silver, collected here. There is a library in the same edifice, containing nearly thirty thousand volumes, among which are some books of great value. They are exceedingly well arranged.

There were stuffed birds in another room of the museum, to go to which we passed between two of the Indian mummies, who, with their brilliant teeth exposed, seemed grinning with a sort of cadaverous civility, and appeared like mournful guardians of the display of some of the natural glories of their country. Stuffed birds of the most dazzlingly splendid plumage are beautifully arranged here. All the most vivid hues of the rainbow strike the eye, and a few colors, it seemed, over and above that. One bird was quite preternaturally resplendent; its wonderful blaze of feathers seemed like concentrated essence of sapphires, diamonds, carbuncles, and all kinds of precious stones. There were some colossal albatrosses. These enormous birds on the wing must look a little like flying elephants dressed in white muslin.

After spending some time pleasantly in examining the different objects in that interesting room, we took leave of the sumptuous birds and the preserved Incas, and went to pay one or two visits.

The first of the Incas of Peru we have some slight grounds for claiming as a countryman; and to him Peru owed its prosperity, its remarkable advance in civilization, and the development of its industrial energies.

Before the establishment of that religion, of which Manco Capac was the founder, the Indian tribes of Peru were living in the same state of savage barbarism as the other nations of this race. They subsisted entirely on the products of the chase, and of their rude fisheries: the vanquished, in their sanguinary combats, were torn to pieces by their ferocious enemies when made prisoners. They worshiped the most hideous and hateful animals, and also lightnings, storms, gloomy caverns, and frightful precipices. Sometimes they would kneel in abject adoration before the trunks of giant trees, and at other times fling themselves down in terror-stricken superstition to worship the burning volcanoes, whose raging fury was tearing up the entrails of the earth, and demolishing their fragile altars and false gods.

At length—according to the story, about eight hundred years ago—a change took place, and a stranger, as they believed, came to them from the sun—but first let us see what the old Spanish chroniclers say of the name of the country. It is pretended, though it can not be known with what truth, that the first adventurers having found a native fishing in a river, asked him what the country was called. The terrified Indian, not rightly understanding them, told them "Baru," and "Pelu," the first, it is supposed, being his own name, and the latter the name of rivers in general: the Spanish discoverers compounded these words into the present name of Peru.

It was very difficult for the Spaniards to ascertain who the first sun-worshiping Incas really were. You know that the old native tradition makes the original Inca, Manco Capac, and his sister, and spouse, Oella-huaco, the Children of the Sun. Historians and philosophers, in attempting to discover for them a less supernatural and more probable origin, have hesitated whether to pronounce them natives of Europe or Asia.

Among conflicting opinions, some have believed them to be descendants of the Scandinavians who first are supposed to have landed on the American Continent in the eleventh century; others again declare them to have been Mongolians of the family of Genghis Khan, brought to this coast by contrary winds and tempests.

Among other stories, the following absurd one is related by some:—An Englishman, about eight hundred years ago, was wrecked on the rich coast of Peru: the chief who was then reigning over barbarous hordes of savages there, demanding who he was, was told in answer by the shipwrecked islander that he was an "Englishman." The Indians repeated the word with a very natural mispronunciation (as the North American Indians are said to have pronounced English "*Yankish*," whence Yankee), "*Incasman*," and they added to this very politely, Cocapac, or most beautiful, and made altogether Inca-manco-capac. Probably the gentleman who was so complimented by the copper-colored barbarians, rejoiced in a profusion of sandy hair, unkempt and uncut after his stormy voyage; for his golden, glittering locks made them think he was born of the sun's fire—he was worshiped accordingly.

Other accounts, which favor the belief that a fair-haired Englishman and his wife were shipwrecked here, state that for a length of time they hid themselves in the mountains, and after a number of years came down to the astonished Indians with their children, whose golden locks flowed luxuriantly down their backs, and proclaimed themselves Children of the Sun, sent by that considerate luminary to reign over them, and teach them many useful arts. They were hailed with reverential joy, and became supreme rulers over the credulous people.

These enlightened chiefs established a firm and stable theocratic autocracy, which bound every individual in the country in the closest (yet not galling) chains; and from whatever source they sprang, there is no doubt that the princely Incas, adored as sacred personages, and obeyed as temporal sovereigns, thoroughly understood the people over whom they reigned, and conferred upon them the inestimable blessings of peace and of civilization. No means were neglected by the Incas which could secure their widely-spread influence, strengthen their eminent position, and perpetuate their power. Not only their own persons were reverenced, but all that was in any way connected with the sovereign dignity, was held in such religious veneration, that any individual having occasion to visit the metropolitan and imperial city of Cuzco, was under the necessity of making profound obeisances to all those whom he happened to meet coming from it. Notwithstanding that too many highly interesting evidences of the progress the Peruvians made under their energetic masters were ruined and destroyed by the unscrupulous and ruthless invaders, yet enough has remained to bear witness to the wonderful strides that wisely-governed people made in agriculture and political science, in arms, in arts, in architecture, and in manufacturing industry.

Defaced though their temples and other noble structures are, still we are told they excite lively admiration, and awaken a pleased astonishment.

---

## CHAPTER L.

Manco Capac and his Wife—Their Instruction of the Peruvians—Old Peruvian Roads—Bull-fights at Lima—Mode of conducting them—Spectators at them—Limanian Ladies—Beautiful Specimens of Peruvian Art and Ingenuity—Silver ornamented Fruits—Lima Burial-places—The Amancaes—The Fiesta of St. John—The Valley of Amancaes—The Flower of that Name—The Streets of Lima after the Fiesta—Concerts given by a French Lady—Fruits of Lima—The Grenadilla—"Italia"—Custom of washing Plates by the lower Orders in Lima—The Gorgonian Servant—"Huacos" and other Curiosities found in Peruvian Sepulchres—The "Señorita"—A Garden in the Suburbs—Its numerous Trees, Shrubs, and Flowers—Enervating Climate of Lima.

I SHOULD like much to go to Cuzco, but I fear it would be too fatiguing a journey for my little girl.

Probably the most striking vestiges of the civilization of the ancient inhabitants of the country are to be found there. Manco Capac, the first Inca, taught the Indians to plow, to sow, and also to irrigate the fields, which so greatly contributed to the fertility of the land. His thrifty Queen Consort, the fair Daughter of the Sun, did not disdain to instruct the female part of the population in the simple arts of spinning, carding wool, and making clothes for themselves and their husbands and children! The rude altars erected to the savage beasts of the field in the forests were demolished; the chase, as a means of subsistence, was abandoned; the earth was carefully cultivated, and peace and content smiled over the now fruitful and happy land. The worship of the sun was made the ruling spirit of all their institutions.

These people were ignorant of the art of writing, but they skillfully preserved the memory of particular events by bold paintings, and by knotted cords of a variety of colors, in which latter art they were singularly expert, and showed great ingenuity. They constructed remarkably fine roads: the route from Quito to Cuzco was five hundred leagues in length, and there was another of the same extent that traversed the lower country, nearer to the ocean.

In addition to these were a great number of other roads, intersecting the empire of the Incas in all directions. These roads are described to be of peculiar construction, and must have demanded much labor. They were raised terraces of earth, generally about forty feet broad, filling up the hollows of the valleys, and forming a regular level way. At intervals along these superb roads were to be seen stately temples, hospices and Peruvian caravansaries (open at all times and seasons to wayfarers and travelers), arsenals, fortresses, and villages.

It is impossssible not to feel indignant at reading the recital of the barbarous conduct of the old Spaniards toward this noble, civilized and inoffensive people. A late Spanish writer has ingeniously attempted (while acknowledging the melancholy facts, which he candidly confesses are too clearly substantiated for him to dispute), to prove that these black deeds were the crimes of the Age, and not of the Spanish nation. There is undoubtedly some truth in this, but not quite so much, it is to be feared, as the accomplished author would fain himself evidently believe.

I should perhaps have been tempted for once to go to a bull-fight here, but none have taken place since we have been sojourning at Lima. They are said to very superior to those at Havana, which are miserable, and only attended by the lowest of the populace; horses of the most wretched description, quite broken down, and staggering from weakness, alone being used there, and the whole spectacle painful and horrible. In Havana, the *élite* of society are too fastidious and refined to tolerate bull-baiting; here, on the contrary, it is generally allowed to be brilliant and well-appointed, for all Lima attends it; and for a few days before it actually takes place, the excitement and state of joyous anticipation into which the Peruvian capital is thrown, is described as being intense.

On the morning of the gala day, a gay procession parades all the principal streets of Lima, exhibiting to the admiring gaze of the multitude the splendid equipments by which the victims are to be adorned when they make their appearance in the ring, and also displaying, for the inspection of the curious, some of the ingenious instruments by which the poor creatures are to be tormented. This procession is accompanied by a band of music, ordinarily consisting of some decrepit clarionets and valetudinarian flutes and flageolets, in various states and stages of infirmity, and one or two superannuated drums.

After these, are borne, stretched out on ornamented frames, the rich coverings of gaudy silk, all glittering with spangles, and foil and tinsel, which are to be thrown on the backs of the bulls; then come, attached to poles, carried by boys, the short, sharp spikes which are intended to be thrust into the bodies of the enraged animals. Each of these is brilliantly decorated with fanciful figures of various kinds, cut out in gilt and bright-colored paper, and ingeniously enveloped in light, airy, net-work balloons. Following these, come the most prominent objects of the procession—three or four figures of the size of life, or larger, which are carried high above the heads of the gaping crowd.

These enormous puppets or images are hollow, and are formed of reeds, with an outward covering of painted paper, and contain a quantity of explosive fireworks. These figures are placed in the arena, and of course are attacked by the bull, and by their explosions, help to increase his rage and fury. Sometimes a negro or mulatto is represented in an absurd attitude, and ridiculously accoutred; sometimes an English cottage-girl, such as you see in old prints, in the pretty costume of past days, with a gipsy bonnet on her head, and a flower-basket on each arm; and occasionally a London or Parisian dandy is exhibited, preposterously caricatured. They sometimes put dwarfs in little pits in the ring, with enormous head-dresses of red and yellow feathers; the feathers dip and disappear when the bull rushes at them, to his great surprise.

Thus are the people wound up to a proper pitch of enthusiastic expectation; and when the day comes, all is animation and delight. The vast uncovered amphitheatre where the bull-fights take place, is at the farthest extremity of one of the Alamédas. It is surrounded with a vast number of boxes and benches, and is capable of accommodating, with comfort and security, many thousand persons.

In the middle of the arena there is a little inclosure of posts. This inclosure is of a circular shape, and the posts are near enough together to prevent the entrance of the bull; while a man, if in imminent danger, can with facility introduce himself between them, and there remain in safety.

When the time approaches for the exhibition, the populace, in dense multitudes, stream toward the amphitheatre, along the beautiful "Alaméda del Acho," beneath whose over-shadowing trees the Indian female stall-keepers sell "picanté," and "chicha," and the native brandy, "pisco."

Ladies are seen rapidly dashing past in their handsome "berlinas," or "volantas;" cavaliers go caracoling along on their fiery steeds, which are decked out with silver-embossed and glittering trappings; and the huge amphitheatre is soon overflowingly crowded with spectators of all ages, sizes, classes and colors, and with a fair sprinkling of inquisitive visitors from distant countries, too; and the boxes are resplendent with thousands of bright eyes, and vividly-colored shawls, and with the rich gold-embroidered uniforms of military officers.

Some saya-y-mantos appear among the lovely crowd of Señoras; the open benches are filled with Indians, negroes, soldiers, peasants, zambos, cholos, &c. Three or four bulls are generally sacrificed, and then the sport terminates; and the crowd—of course greatly edified—wend their way back again to their splendid mansions in the capital, or their rustic "chacras" (Indian cottages) in the neighboring hamlets.

We dined again with Mr. and Mrs. A——, whose kind and friendly attentions are unceasing. After dinner, a Limanian lady came in, who seemed a highly refined and sensible person, and who is considered one of the most accomplished and intellectual of the ladies in this capital. Her complexion was extraordinarily dark; so that indeed I took her at first for an Indian. She is a person of much distinction, and of pure Castilian descent, I believe.

We had several opportunities of seeing the ladies of the country at Mrs. A——'s little *soirées:* they have generally glorious eyes, and their skins are not darker than those of Spanish women. On Sunday, after the service at the little English chapel of the Legation, a number of mantilla'd Peruvian ladies came to pay the fair mistress of the mansion a visit. Among them were two Guayaquil ladies, both very handsome, with very delicate, and exquisitely fair complexions, extremely regular features, and eyes like black suns—if such a simile may be allowed. Their manners were as prepossessing as their appearance.

Mr. Yates, an English gentleman from Liverpool, who is acquainted with one of my brothers, called the other day, and brought a large number of beautiful specimens of Peruvian art and ingenuity, to show us. Quantities of dried fruit were among the articles; these were most fantastically decorated and framed with sparkling silver; some so delicately done, that the still naturally-colored fruit seemed to be embossed with glittering drops of the diamond-dew of morning. Mr. Yates is going to send these curiosities to his daughter in England: he is married to a Danish lady whom he first met at Lima. He is here now on business of importance, which is under the consideration of Congress at present.

The silver-ornamented fruits I have described, it is customary for persons in society to present to one another on feast days, and occasions of rejoicing, a pretty and graceful little attention. The most elaborately-wrought specimens are usually made by the nuns. Among other things, were some exquisitely-finished peacocks and flowers, in whose construction the fair artists displayed extraordinary skill. Mr. Yates and Mrs. S—— have presented us with some of the silver-encased fruits, but I fear the silver will turn black during our journey across the Isthmus, which is at this time of year the reverse of Lima : here there is no rain, and there it is all rain.

Mrs. S—— gave me a sad and sickening account of a visit to one of the burying-places here ; it reminded me much of the horrors of the Campo Santo at Naples. She said in one case, where there was some obstruction to its free passage, the body of a child was cut up, and thrown down into the vile receptacle for the perishing remains of humanity in separate *parcels*, wrapped up in the torn shroud or some old rags of linen : however, so long as we continue our detestable system of intra-mural interments in our own metropolis, and have fetid church-yards in its most crowded haunts (so frequently desecrated when fresh candidates for admission are brought to the reeking soil), we should be indulgent on such matters.

We have been to see the Amancaes, a famous place, and a famous flower, and a famous fiesta. The place is a valley some three or four miles from Lima, between wild and rugged mountains, looking down upon the city and upon the Pacific, and with the towering snow-capped Andes for its colossal back-ground. The flower is a golden-colored species of lily ; and the fiesta that of St. John's Day ; a few days previously to which, and sometimes on the very day, arises and blossoms brightly to adorn the chosen spot, this consecrated flower. It is popularly believed that, although up to the day before "St. John's Day," or even on the very eve of "St. John," not a single flower of the Yellow Amancaes may be discernible, yet on the hallowed morning, the flower will punctually appear to gild these previously sterile regions.

The weather was very delightful, and the Andes gloriously visible in all their majesty, the day that Mrs. A—— was kind enough to take us there in her carriage. Mrs. W—— and her sister also went. Madame F—— was with them in their handsome equipage, which Mr. W—— drove himself, and a small cavalcade of gentlemen joined in the excursion.

The feast being on the 24th of June, is fast approaching now, but we shall perhaps be gone before it arrives. The scene is described as being very singular, and characteristic of the manners and customs of the people: thousands pour along the Alaméda de los Descalsos on the great day of jubilee. At the spot where the road enters into the mouth of the valley, two chapels are temporarily erected, covered with floating streamers and banners, and gay flaunting ribbons, and each is made for the time the habitation of a saint, arrayed in refulgent robes. This is for the purpose of collecting contributions from those whose hearts and hands are expected to be expanded and open under the influence of the joyous time, when the tide of excitement and exhilaration is flowing high, and all is glad emotion and anticipation.

The pedestrians and equestrians, and those who are rolling in their gay carriages to the selected spot, are eagerly surrounded by noisy groups of men, women and children, thrusting little plates toward them, and indefatigably importuning them for money. The celebrated valley of Amancaes, gradually narrowing between the mountainous walls, which are seen abutting irregularly upon it, terminates almost in a point in the upper part. At this extremity, a mile distant or thereabouts, numerous clusters of booths are placed (all decorated with flags and emblematical devices), and these are but too abundantly supplied with the native brandy, and chicha and italia. The lily grows in profusion among the neighboring hills, as well as in the valley; and eager groups of people set out through the day on exploring parties and come back laden with the golden-colored spoils of their adventures.

If none of the yellow lilies are actually growing on the ground, still it is half-covered with bunches and garlands of them, brought from any place where it has happened to spring up; and the flower-hunters are to be seen profusely adorned with the glistening blossoms, while the prancing steeds of many of them are also similarly decorated, and look like moving bowers, their superb caparisons being overlaid with these blooming, glowing gems. The scene must be altogether a very striking one: hundreds of splendid equipages are seen in all directions, filled with the fairest flowers of Lima—who are not by any means yellow lilies; but on whose dark and richly-braided locks the golden flowers show to great reciprocal advantage.

The servants who attend these brilliant carriages are often clothed in very handsome liveries, covered with gold and silver lace, which might a little recall remembrances of the Queen's drawing-room days in London, and the state liveries that then make their appearances in the thronged streets; but the Lima horsemen's saddles and bridles, enriched with real, and beautifully wrought silver, attract more a stranger's unaccustomed eye.

Tapadas are said to be generally very numerous on these occasions, their brilliant rainbowed scarfs, fluttering and gleaming in studied negligence, and the one-gun battery of the single exposed eye, doing great execution. A wild national dance is usually performed here, and a wilderness of guitars is continually tinkling, and sounding cheerily and sweetly.

Hark! Suddenly sounds the vesper bell: like bounding silver balls from silver cannon, with thrilling awful power, come the mighty tones from the peerless bell of the Lima Cathedral. The people stream back through the willow-skirted walks and road of the Alaméda de los Descalsos, on either side of which lights are gayly sparkling through the windows of the houses which look upon it—but the Feast of the Amancaes is over. The preparations for the celebration of this festival were perceptible on the day we drove there.

We remained for some time entranced with the extreme beauty of the extensive view. I had not before seen Lima in its fullest splendor. The day was brilliantly fine, and it looked like an enchanted city dominating the ocean, and with a host of white-crested tributary mountains standing behind its throne. What a noble sight it was: it almost appeared to be a city all of temples and sacred edifices. So innumerable seemed its domes and steeples, pinnacles, and spires, one could hardly believe such things go on within its walls as bull-baits and cock-fights.

Then how glorious looked the blue, calm, unbounded Pacific at its feet! so still, as if it felt the hushing influence of these hallowed temples: its smooth, shining surface looked like the vast floor of a colossal cathedral, whose towers were the giant Andes, and whose roof the purple heavens of the South. Even charming little Gemma, Mrs. A——'s sweet little girl, seemed impressed with the awful beauty of the scene, and her lovely infantine countenance looked grave and thoughtful.

With many a last admiring look at the sublime scene—on one side at the high-soaring peaks of the gigantic Cordillera, and on the other at the almost innumerable towers and turrets and terraces, and spires and steeples, and cupolas and convents of the city, partly embosomed in romantic and beautiful gardens and in umbrageous sylvan groves, and at the ocean of oceans, the wide-spreading Pacific that with

"Soft swelling waves,
A thousand bright islands eternally laves—"

with many a feeling of regret we left that lovely valley of the Amancaes, lovely not in its own self, without the flowery enrobing of its famous golden lily, but for the consummate beauty of the views it presents on all sides; and we drove again through the willowy avenues of the Alaméda de los Descalsos, after passing many flourishing groves, and fields, and plantations of the busy suburbs. The streets looked very gay and animated as we drove back to the French Hotel. We met hosts of ladies taking the air in their carriages; others were sitting in those broad piazzas, which have such a pretty effect with their Oriental-looking jalousies; and crowds of pedestrians—militars, civicos, and saya-y-mantos were thronging the *trottoirs*. Undisturbed by the multitudes, some of the gallianzos were comfortably perched along the sides of the rivulets that flow through the streets of Lima. These birds are the sopilotes of Peru, and they fly about the town unmolested, nay, encouraged, perfectly tame and at home every where.

The running streams I have mentioned are conveyed by conduits from the river Rimac, and flow not only through all the main arteries and chief thoroughfares of the city, but also through nearly all the lesser streets. They must contribute very considerably to the healthfulness and cleanliness of the town. As you drive along the "calles," every niche and nook, and corner and crevice, seem to be occupied by some petty trader, busily disposing of his and her small wares.

Before the bull-fights take place, it is the fashion here, on the day previous to the sport, to suspend immense and conspicuous signs containing programmes of the spectacle, at the entrance of the portales, or arcades; these flourished advertisements are generally painted on linen or muslin, stretched over frames of light wood; and sometimes the approaching cock-fight is announced by pictured placards of equally portentous appearance and dimensions. Boys also are sent round with printed and illustrated hand-bills, and cards of the coming sport; and it is frequently pompously announced that the judge will be the chief-intendant of the police. The watchmen recite a long history here in crying the hour—thus it runs: "Ave Maria Santissima, las doce (or whatever hour it may be) han dado: Vira Peru, y Sereno."

A few evenings ago at Mrs. A——'s, the conversation happened to turn upon the debate in our Parliament on the bill for legalizing marriages between brothers and sisters-in-law. A Peruvian gentleman who was there asked, apparently in much astonishment, if that was forbidden in England: he was told it was. "Hombre!" he exclaimed, "es posible?" and proceeded to tell us a friend of his had married three sisters in succession. They must have procured dispensations from the Pope, of course.

There have been concerts lately given here by a French lady, who has been starring it in India and China, I believe! The place where the concerts are given is so near our hotel that we can hear a little of the strains of the songstress and her assistants, without moving from our chairs: they have failed here, I am told. The opera season has not yet begun in Lima. They have frequently a very good company, I believe, and the "palcos" are thronged with ladies superbly attired, and sometimes glittering with a perfect armor and panoply of jewels, if report speaks truth.

I sent down some days ago to our fruitseller, under the great gateway, for some of those frozen apples we saw at Callao. She sent up a number of apples, that to outward appearance were precisely the same; but on cutting them in two, we found they had either thawed, or had never been frozen at all! We have been told since, that while only one species of apple ever presents this appearance, yet you can never be sure that these will do so till you have opened them: it perhaps depends on the different stages of ripeness in the fruit. The vegetables and fruit here are mostly excellent; the *aguacates* are exquisite; we have them constantly at breakfast: they seem to hold a place between a vegetable and a fruit. Then we have pine-apples, melons, oranges, cherimoyas, grenadillas, pears, and hundreds of other delicious fruits. (Nearly all the tropical fruits however, except aguacates, I confess with deep penitence, I think detestable—too rich usually for hot countries.)

Among the vegetables, are cabbages, yuccas, potatoes (sweet; and Irish, as they call our common potato), tomatoes, pumpkins, radishes, beans, and peas, and numerous others. The cherimoya is a very great favorite here, and I believe I am in a minority of one in not liking it: it is called the queen of fruits. In size and shape it bears outwardly some resemblance to a very large pear; the rind is rather rugged, and of a color between brown and green. It is supposed that this queenly fruit is pre-eminently excellent at Lima: it is commonly eaten with a spoon; the rich pulp is white and saccharine, and not unlike an aromatic and creamy custard. The more I tried to like them the more I abominated them—I can't exactly say why.

The cherimoya is the "Doctor Fell" of fruits for me. Perhaps one reason may be, it has so much pretension about it, that if you are disposed not to approve, your dislike becomes hatred. The grenadilla is better, *selon moi*, and more refreshing; the inside is like a large heap of the ripest interiors of gooseberries. They have raisins brought here from Pisco, as well as "italia," which raisins are excellent, by the way.

Italia is not like the common drink, called "pisco." The italia derives its name from the circumstance of its being made from an exquisite grape imported originally from Italy, and extremely improved by the climate of the new country, or probably by some difference in the cultivation.

The present President of Peru is a Cholo. He was reproached at the time of his election with so being: he is, by all accounts, a firm, strong-minded man, not at all disposed to yield to popular clamor, and brave as a lion. During one of the Pronunciamientos here, he made his appearance in the public square, exposing himself with the utmost confidence to the infuriated people, something à la Empereur Nicholas, and he so charmed and awed them by his gallant and dauntless bearing, that not a finger was lifted against him.

We dined a few days ago with Mr. and Mrs. P——. They have a very pretty and good-sized house in the Calle de Guadaloupe, an immense distance from our hotel; but our obliging host sent for a carriage (a hired one) for us, and we gladly mounted this lofty vehicle, which was gayly decorated with yellow silk lining in the interior, and proceeded at a most funereal pace to the abode of our friend. Whether our driver had a particular fancy for crossing and recrossing the little rivulets in the middle of the streets or whether this carriage was in itself rough, I knew not precisely, but there was certainly a great deal of jolting and jarring—perhaps the driver thought a little exercise before dinner was good for our healths.

Some of the humbler orders of Lima Señoras have a curious little unsophisticated custom of their own, which is decidedly original: it is washing the plates, and glasses, and dishes from their dinner-tables in the gutters of the streets. Now, although the waters of the Rimac are as clear as crystal when dashing over their pebbly bed, they are doomed to experience in their peregrinations through the Lima calles the truth of the proverb that says, "Evil communications corrupt good manners;" and these contaminated currents most abundantly testify to this fact. I should therefore think the flavor of the "caldo," or of their favorite fiery red-pepper sauce itself, can not be much improved by their contact with these gutter-washed platters.

It is quite affecting to hear the ladies in Lima (I mean in general our own country-women) lamenting over the difficulty of keeping any maid-servants here now, as they all go to California, the male emigrants being anxious to provide themselves with emigrantesses: in short, hard-working wives, to cook, and wash, and take care of their homes. Some of the ladies pathetically dilated on their misfortunes, and one told me she had taken care to engage a most undeniable Gorgon, and she expatiated on the poor woman's ugliness, as an admirer might do on the charms of his fair one:

"So exquisitely and deliciously hideous she was! such blubber lips! such goggle, boiled-mackerel eyes! such a squat nose, with such wide, horrible nostrils" (something like the prompter's box at the opera, by her description)! "and such a villainous complexion, and old as the Andes nearly!" And this chosen and selected star and wonder disappeared sooner than the rest.

A handsome young carpenter persuaded the goggle-eyed dame to visit El Dorado as his spouse; and the astonishment and indignation of the bereaved lady knew no bounds. It seems that the emigrants do not care quite so much for looking at pretty faces, in their new distant homes, as having hard-working, industrious, managing wives; good housewives, who will cook and wash, and drudge, and keep their houses tidy and comfortable.

If the lady had tried to find a beauty instead, she would perhaps have acted more wisely, for the *belle* would have been far more *difficile*, to begin with; and would have looked with horror at the prospects of the hardships and drudgery which the wives of miners and adventurers in California have constantly to undergo. It was a mistake, decidedly. I dare say, too, that goggle-eyed Gorgon thought more of her appearance, and was more conceited than a beauty would have been; it is so often the case.

Mrs. S——, whom we went to see a little while ago, has given us some charming old "huacos," which are warranted to be really from the sepulchres of the ancient Sun-worshipers. One of them has strange marks and hieroglyphics on it, and a curious monkey-like little monster on the handle. She also kindly gave me some of the pieces of cloth found in those old tombs, remnants belonging to the shrouds or dresses in which the mummies were found wrapped.

The ancient places of interment were generally vaults, built of adobes. With the bodies are frequently found gold ornaments, and other treasures: the wrappings and draperies of the mummies are found occasionally most splendidly dyed and embroidered, and often exhibit considerable artistical taste and manufacturing skill. There are belts, with balls and tassels, mats, sacks, and other articles, usually scattered about the vaults in great abundance.

I have read a description of one fragment that appears to be an allegorical design. It was the representation of a beautiful butterfly, with its rich wings outstretched, as if flying, or about to fly. The colors were light red, and azure, and white, and a glowing, golden brown, and apparently carefully imitated from nature. This butterfly was displayed on a deep ground of crimson. Surely it was meant to represent the enfranchised soul, in the manner of the classical ancients.

It is said there are some small bags found in numbers in the vaults, that are made of cotton, hair, or wool. Sometimes they are fringed, and otherwise decorated; they are generally sewn up, and inclose often tufts of hair, dark-colored pebbles, and little bunches of parti-colored feathers. The fragment of cloth Mrs. S—— so oblingly gave me, was quite recently taken from a mummy; the colors are still clear; they are brown, figured over with red; the figures are not very unlike some of those hieroglyphics on the earthern vessels I have mentioned. The material is of immense thickness, almost equal to that of a carpet; it is in excellent preservation. There is a curious war-sling, given to me by the same kind friend, which is still in use among the wild Indians in the interior of Peru; it is very strongly and neatly made.

Mrs. S—— has an exceedingly handsome house; a two-storied one, with immense galleries, and covered balconies. These balconies are magnificent; they are furnished and carpeted. They afford such an excellent view, that during "dias de fiesta," they are crowded by the friends and acquaintances of the amiable mistress of the mansion. I have received a kind invitation to come here to witness some of the great religious processions which will shortly take place, and shall certainly avail myself of it, if I am still in the Peruvian capital. In this earthquaking city of Lima this is almost the only two-storied house whose inhabitants I know. There are a profusion of interesting curiosities in the large and lofty rooms here: huacos of all kinds and shapes, formed into various sorts of monstrosities, some very elaborately finished: and there are quantities of beautiful inlaid cabinets—such an "embarras des richesses" in that line, indeed, that the children have some magnificent ones, in which to put their toys and books. Others are used for stores of Berlin-wool and canvas (Mrs. S——'s sister works very beautifully); and, in short, costly and exquisite as they are, they are obliged to make themselves generally useful here.

I think I have not mentioned that the room in which Francisco Pizarro was assassinated is still shown at Lima, and the balcony from whence the unpitying, infuriated Almagros afterward threw his body; but I doubt its being the true one.

"L'Algérie" is shortly to leave Callao; for Payta first, and then probably for the Sandwich Islands. We went to take leave of Madame F—— yesterday. She and Monsieur F—— are staying at the French Minister's. Madame F—— seems to look forward with great pleasure to her extended tour and voyage round the world, and not to regret Paris in the least. She expects to be much interested in China: it is altogether a very spirited undertaking for this young and beautiful lady.

We also went to see Mrs. B——. Her house is remarkably pretty, with a garden like a vision of enchantment. Such flowers! among others, that lovely "variable," the chameleon of flowers, which changes its color three times a day. It is, I believe, pure white in the morning, a soft rose-color in the afternoon, and in the evening a deep glowing crimson. The Peruvians somewhat impertinently call it the "Señorita."

My bird-fancying companion went with Mrs. B——'s little adopted daughter to see two splendid feathered monsters. By her description, I think they must be huacamayas, a rare and huge species of parrot. She says they were of enormous size, and of the most dazzling colors conceivable, but very savage indeed. They were formerly kept in the garden; but the distracting noise they made caused them to be banished to a more distant place of abode.

The garden here is in the patio, and the delicious odors with which it floods the drawing-rooms are charming. Still the luxuriance of Lima gardens can not strictly be compared with that of those of the Havana. I must give a list of the plants and flowers in one small garden there belonging to a villa in the suburbs. First and foremost, the villa itself (which was more like a kiosk at Constantinople than a house, all balconies and galleries) was smothered in the most lavish growth of creepers and climbing plants; and it was most magnificently over-shadowed by a princely bamboo, whose huge giant branches rose to a great height above it to fall in mighty mammoth plumes, such as might have surmounted the head of a Titanic birthday beauty, two miles high, —in the land of giants and ogres. It was also like a vast high-soaring fountain of transparent emerald, tossing skyward its fairy columns, and falling in graceful cascades of feathery, far-spreading, and foamy lightness.

The garden was certainly too crowded with its wild botanical treasures; yet entangled and heaped together as they were in the richest profusion, they all appeared in the most flourishing condition, and those that could find no space below for their exuberant glories and fanciful vagaries shot up above, and hung their enchanted bowers, and spread their mosaiced and rainbowed parterres, in the air, at least so they seemed to do. There were jessamines, hibiscus (called here "mar pacifico"), mignonnette *trees*, pomegranates, floripondias, verbenas, dahlias, "conchitas azules," marivillas of three colors, orange trees, bananas, papayos (papaws), silk sugar-cane (a particular kind of sugar-cane), guanabana, aloes, tobacco plant, espuelas, Peregrina trees, madamas; quantities of different kinds of roses, Alamo trees, diamela, Almendras (almond trees), Almizcle (musk), Tuna (a peculiar sort of cactus), fig-trees, Jupite or astronomia, grape-vines, azucenas (white lilies), Itamo real (tree), Albahaca fina (a kind of sweet basil), yerba Luisa, romero (rosemary), malva real, caña de azucar, violets, mejorana, aguinaldos blancos, cundiamor, Indio trepador, the fine flor del zapota, claveles rosedâns, murallas (trees), the caña brava (bamboo), and others whose names I could not ascertain. Remember, this is quite a common-place and *very* little garden, with hardly any care whatever bestowed upon it.

Delightful as this cool and rainless climate of Lima is, there must, I think, be something peculiarly enervating about it. Notwithstanding the untropical freshness of the air, Europeans complain that they can not take exercise here as in their own countries; and what is strange, the eyes seem often affected with weakness. The complete absence of sun and glare in general ought, one would imagine, to be favorable to the visual organs. I can not say that we find walking fatigues us more here than at other places, but we constantly hear complaints to that effect. To be sure, we have been here but a short time as yet.

I heard the other day two English ladies, who had been out shopping together the previous day, inquiring after their mutual healths, and one said: "I really felt as if I should die when I arrived at home; I lay down on the sofa, and could not move hand nor foot for hours." And the other, "I felt quite ill after the fatigue of going to those shops. I have not recovered it. I have felt so tired and wearied out ever since." From curiosity, I made inquiries as to the amount of exertion they had undergone, and found it was what would be considered a mere nothing in London.

We are going to see some of the churches. The magnificent church and convent of San Francisco I fear we shall not be allowed to enter.

---

## CHAPTER LI

About to leave Lima—The Cathedral—Fragile but enduring Buildings in Lima—The Reason why they are the latter—The Tower of San Domingo—The Chorister of the Cathedral—The Shrine of Santa Rosa—The Inquisition at Lima—The Cemetery—Cemeteries in the United States—Lima Mode of Sepulture—Remains of the Temple of the Sun—Peruvian Politics—Disheartening News from California—Verses on Happiness—Earthquakes at Lima—The Shoes of the Ladies.

We are still at Lima; but an American steamer has lately arrived, and if it is possible to manage it comfortably, I think of taking a passage in her to Panama, as the sooner we cross the Isthmus on our way to Jamaica now (before the roads are utterly turned to swamps and morasses) the better. The rainy season has doubtless set in, but in the beginning it is comparatively easy to effect the transit.

This American vessel is a river steamer. She has come here from New York, through the straits of Magellan, after losing almost her whole crew at Rio Janeiro of yellow fever: fifteen men belonging to the steamer died there, and the captain is still ill from the effects of the severe attack he had of that dreadful disorder. In some instances, it is stated, merchant vessels were left without a single man on board. It began among the shipping, and for a long time did not make its appearance on shore; but at length it burst forth there also, and spread with awful violence.

Mr. Yates has most obligingly volunteered to arrange about our passage to Panama, if the accommodations on board the "New World" are sufficiently comfortable. I have consulted an eminent English Medical gentleman here as to there being any danger of infection on board the steamer, and he positively assures me there is not the smallest cause for any apprehension.

Mr. Yates escorted us to see the cathedral and two other fine churches this morning, as well as the building where the Congress assembles. This is not very imposing, but we could not gain admittance to the finest part. A ragged soldier piloted us about: he had lost a limb in one of the revolutionary battles here. As he led us along a handsome hall, I saw at the extreme end, where immense doors opened on a kind of patio, what I thought was a beautiful garden, and the distant hills and mountains behind it.

This was a spirited, well-executed fresco, on a high wall opposite, so arranged as to fill up the whole space in front of the opened doors: when seen from the hall it has the appearance of being a natural landscape and garden. The court-yards were like open-air panoramas. The people seem to have a perfect passion for fresco-paintings and arabesques.

If the truth is to be told, Lima itself, the regal and the aspiring, is very near being one huge colossal opera-scene. A great number of the princely-looking edifices that rear their haughty fronts as if they would defy the terrible *temblor* itself, are only built of stones and bricks (or often of gigantic adobes) up to the height of the belfries; above this all is lath and plaster, paste-board and rushes, reeds and stucco; a vast accumulation of architecturally arranged whips, and wicker work, and whim-whams, and walking-sticks; but the effect is as splendid as if all was built of granite and adamant. Who would dream, when looking at this city from the Amancaes, that these glorious domes and steeples, so thickly crowding together that one might almost think the inhabitants of Lima all dwelt in churches, or in convents at least, and that no secular habitation intervened—who would dream, I say, that these apparently massive structures were closely akin to a child's house of cards, or the back-ground scenes of a ballet in London or Paris? But Lima is justified in placing her faith on a reed, and in thinking stability, or rather solidity, of construction not literally worth a rush here.

These light and fragile fabrics are the only edifices of any elevation that can withstand the shocks of the devastating earthquake. The reader will remember, I dare say, the account of the earthquake in New Zealand, when all the strongly-built stone houses suffered and sank, and became piles of ruins, and those with slender wooden walls stood uninjured. No lofty structure could survive the assaults of frequent earthquakes, except those of such "leather and prunella," papery composition: *they* bend and quiver like a storm-shaken pine of the forest, but regain and recover their perpendicular position unimpaired.

There is one very high tower, that of San Domingo, where they say the ringing of the bells causes an extreme vibration, like that in the leaning tower of Pisa, yet it is considered safe. As to the private dwelling houses, they are generally, of course, of the same materials; but as rain is unknown here, and wind does not visit the "face" of the fair city ever "too roughly," you might live in a tent of silken taffetta, if so minded, without injury from the elements.

The cathedral has two aisles inside, supported by a vast number of pillars. There is in the interior some very beautifully carved wood; but while we were admiring this, a ragged-looking boy, who had been previously chattering with some urchins of comrades, rushed toward us, gesticulating and vociferating amazingly, and said on no account could the ladies be permitted to remain. Captain W——, who had joined our party, with Mr. Yates, tried to pacify him, and persuade him to allow us to stay.

Suddenly he darted away, and with remarkable rapidity appeared before us again in a change of costume, that had been effected with such celerity, that we should have been disposed to think it was a twin brother of our youthful persecutor, had not our eyes followed his agile movements. He was now a chorister in flowing robes, and with much dignity of deportment he ordered us away: it was "quite impossible that ladies should come there;" but this our presence practically contradicted, so we replied not. He frowned and fulmined at us; probably threatened us with the vengeance of the Pope and the whole College of Cardinals, and sweet Santa Rosa of Lima if we did not depart.

His rage and eagerness prevented his speaking very clearly, and we were really much taken up in looking at the beautiful wood carvings; but we soon told him we would go, and his countenance lighted up a little. He behaved civilly enough when he saw us departing, merely looking as if he would like particularly to have the exterminating of us quietly, without any torturing whatsoever.

We had hoped to have avoided any unpleasant rencontre of this kind; for hearing they were very particular about the head-dress here, we had doffed our already-excommunicated bonnets, and put a "manto" of the moment on our heads, formed of black scarfs; but this young gentleman quickly discovered we were heretics, and treated us accordingly. The shrine of the patroness of Lima, Saint Rosa, was brilliantly decorated. In the fine Murillo at Belvoir Castle, this saint appears. The cathedral formerly was enriched by vast quantities of solid silver, which have gradually melted away, under the unscrupulous attacks of the many different revolutionists and pseudo-regenerators of this fine land.

We afterward went to see the ancient Inquisition : it is now used chiefly as a prison for the meanest criminals. In a large hall we saw a truly beautiful carved ceiling; it was perfectly exquisite, but is quite lost where it is. We were told by a Peruvian gentleman there, that it has long been contemplated to remove it to some more conspicuous and suitable situation. We looked into one of the old dungeons of the Inquisition. Horrible! When the accused was brought from his cell, he did not enter the hall of judgment, or whatever this great gloomy chamber was called, but was led up to a small grated opening in the wall, to hear the sentence.

We were shown the place where an immense crucifix had been formerly attached to the wall at the upper end of the room, above the place where sat the solemn arbiters of life and death. Behind this figure was arranged machinery, by which it was made to nod and shake the head, when appealed to, before the irrevocable decision was pronounced. The Peruvian gentleman enlarged upon the horrors of those olden days in a strain of glowing indignation, till that gloomy old hall of the Inquisition resounded with his eager eloquence.

Mr. Yates, who had most obligingly undertaken to pay a visit to the American steamer, and let us know whether she had sufficient accommodation, has brought us word that the captain will make all necessary arrangements, and that he fully intends to stop at Panama on his way to San Francisco. He says the vessel is beautifully clean, and that we shall have it almost all to ourselves, as there are only three passengers in her now for California. When she gets to Panama, she will probably find crowds anxious to take their passage in her.

I have just returned from a charming drive with our kind friend Mrs. A——, after going to take leave of Mrs. S—— and her sister, and the pretty children, with their flowing English-looking golden ringlets. We drove to the cemetery, a little distance from Lima: we found the great gates locked, and could only look through them. After seeing the most magnificent and beautiful cemeteries in the world—those of the United States—all others look dreary and poor in comparison. Even those glittering, much-adorned church-yards, which I remember admiring once in Bavaria, would, from their petty size, look inferior indeed.

Then in the United States they generally choose a natural

situation of the greatest beauty; and Nature and Art strive together to perform, as it were, everlastingly the noblest funeral obsequies around the tombs of the departed. Statues of angels and weeping mourners stand by the graves among flowers and trees; the air thrills with perpetual hymns of singing birds; silent sermons are preached from changing foliage and varying blooms. All is touching, and beautiful, and hallowed, in that place, which the imaginative Germans so poetically call "God's Acre." And so it should be.

The Old Romans were the wisest of mankind, it is my humble opinion, in their way of disposing finally of their dead; and next to them are the Young Americans! Death is not made unnecessarily and improperly gloomy and repulsive. The pale angel is still an angel, and regarded as the one who, in opening the gates of the grave, throws wide the portals of immortality.

It is the custom in Lima for a large clumsy hearse, drawn by mules, and driven by a postillion, to go round in the morning, and collect the bodies of those who have died in the preceding night. The hearse, called the car of the Pantheon, brings them to the cathedral, to receive the latest offices of the Church. Sometimes the corpses are brought in coffins, and sometimes not. When the latter is the case, a public receptacle is used during the performance of the funeral ceremony, which is made to fit all comers.

On returning from the cemetery, which is inclosed by high adobe walls, we found it quite cold, and were glad to put on additional cloaks. Our hands were extremely chilled. There must be some great difference in the climate or the construction of the houses in Mexico and Lima. We have never found it cold in the houses here (without fires, of course), while in Mexico—in the mornings particularly—we often found it so. In Mexico, on the contrary, I never found it cold out of doors; whereas here, several times we have found it imperatively necessary to put on warm, thick shawls on going out.

I am sorry to leave Lima before the religious *fêtes* take place, for the city, from its many peculiarities, must present a very striking scene on those occasions. From all its nearly innumerable churches and convents are floating then myriads of consecrated banners, and from the houses, too, tens of thousands of "banderas" are streaming with their gaudy hues on the flushed air.

The insides of the churches are adorned with a forest of artificial flowers, and miles of festooning ribbons, and are besides decorated with other ornaments, in almost endless profusion. Processions go through the streets, and music awakens the echoes, while incense from censers of silver thickly ascends in odoriferous clouds, and a hundred splendid pageants appear on all sides.

Just now, serious reflections on such subjects I will not enter into. The spectacle itself, however much there is to be deplored in such exhibitions, must be fine, amid all the picturesque adjuncts of the capital of Peru, where the old Sun-worshipers whilom knelt in rude idolatry.

Speaking of them, I should have very much liked to visit the remains of the ancient Temple of the Sun, about twenty miles from this city. This old edifice is said to have been about three hundred and thirty feet high; some writers state that it was at least six hundred feet above the level of the sea, raised on an elevation which was in part artificial. The ruins are scattered over three grand terraces, rising in regular gradations one over the other. The remains of an ancient and stately town lie mouldering around the fallen temple of Pachacamac, the life-bestowing deity.

The scenery around is reported to be very splendid; the gigantic mountain-views contrasting strikingly with the smiling groves of orange, and the fruitful gardens and fields of the lovely valley of Lurin—quiet hamlets, with their painted churches and soaring steeples; the Pacific tossing its foam in sparkling garlands on the shore, and fading away in the blue horizon; the wild-whirling clouds on the distant lofty peaks; the haciendas hidden in thickets of fruit trees; old earthquake-ruined bridges, and Indian chacras, dotted here and there.

Altogether, by all accounts, it must form a very interesting scene, and assuredly must be well worth going to see; but we found various difficulties in the way; and not thinking of going so soon, I put it off; and that most arrant thief and vagabond, Procrastination, has robbed me of this. Is not that same Procrastination the chief pavior of Pluto, where good intentions were used instead of stone or wood?

I will not enter into any Peruvian politics, my sole intention being to tell the reader what we actually see around us. It would only be the gossip of politics that I could give in these hastily written pages, and would neither amuse nor edify. I will, therefore, merely say, there seems a growing jealousy between civilians and the military. The South American armies, as far as I have seen, seem to be maintained generally not for the purpose so much of fighting the country's battles with foreign foes, as for settling endless disputes among the belligerent factions at home.

Far be it from me to say that the sole movement here has been a "progressive retrogression;" but I am disposed to think, in educational matters, and other things indispensable to successful self-government, there has been displayed a remarkable supineness in high quarters; which "masterly inactivity," in those who desire to lead and autocratize over the people, renders the government, popularized though it is, more a military despotism than a constitutional democracy.

Physical force, I believe, embodies pretty strongly the ruling idea in their vexed politics. If the citizen is jealous of the soldier, let him himself erect the school-house (which acts so great a part in the prosperity of the United States) in opposition to the barracks; and in time, though we may have many a phase of various aspects to witness first, we shall see real improvement and positive progress here; especially if moral training keep pace with intellectual—for the one without the other is a dangerous mistake. Chili, from what I hear on all sides, is the most flourishing of all these South American republics: the people are steady, industrious, enterprising, and temperate; and, it seems, moderately enlightened.

There is an English book-club established here, and they have a number of interesting works sent out from England. I have just read one of them, Layard's "Nineveh." I have not yet mentioned that the steamer we are going in is a river steamer, the second that has been sent round Cape Horn. She is going to run on the Sacramento River, in California.

I have lately heard my English friends here lamenting over some melancholy accounts that have come from that "Eureka" State. A young American gentleman, who apparently was exceedingly popular here, has attempted to commit self-destruction, after a melancholy series of misfortunes. He had not very long ago lost a beloved wife, who was killed by a fall from her horse in California. He was slowly recovering from this dreadful blow, which it is said he most profoundly felt (so deeply, indeed, that his reason, it was believed, was slightly unsettled by the shock), when by some unforeseen calamity—the great fire, I believe—his newly-made fortune was entirely shattered, and he fell at once from affluence into destitution. He attempted to shoot himself, but blew off nearly half his face, and yet remained alive.

The story is a very sad one; but many almost equally heart-rendering occurrences, it is to be feared, have taken place in the golden land since the great emigration commenced. One man went mad from sudden success, and killed himself in a paroxysm of delirium. In short, I have heard so many mournful histories with regard to successful and unsuccessful speculators, that I am reminded of some verses of my own, in a poem written long ago. Here is some of it:

I.

Oh, Happiness! where is thy home?
Say, where dost thou linger and dwell?
Stars and seraphs sing—"*this* side the tomb"—
Dear, impossible Blessing, farewell!

II.

Hence no more—oh, no more—never more,
Come in shadows or seeming near me;
I might dream thou wert clasped to the core,
And but wake to find grief, and not thee!

III.

Did I think I could seize thee when borne
On the whirlwinds of passion and pride,
All my spirit on fire with its scorn—
All my heart like a storm-troubled tide?

. . . . . . . . .

IV.

Say oh! Happiness, where is thy sphere?
Where, where dost thou linger and dwell?
All still seek thee afar and anear,
But, impossible Blessing—farewell!

After seeing the fragility of the materials used here generally in the construction of buildings, I am no longer surprised at what the residents tell me; namely, that if a heavy pattering shower of rain came down, Lima might melt away like a huge heap of Brobdignagian bonbons, or like a confectionary-metropolis—a vast collection of mammoth barley-sugar temples—or else it might be swept away altogether into the Pacific. But in this earthquaking land, it is imperatively necessary it should be so.

Here they pray continually to be protected from earthquakes; the word "famine," in our Church Service, is left out, and "earthquake" substituted. Compensation is Nature's favorite rule, and one she scarcely ever (if ever) infringes.

The charming little child of Monsieur and Madame du C——, has just paid us a visit. V—— was playing with some paroquets, which attracted her into the drawing-room, for of course the balcony doors were wide open. Little Bertha is one of the most sensible children I ever met with: she gave an account of their passage across the Isthmus, and her poor papa's unfortunate fall, in the most touching and pretty language, in a perfectly simple and artless yet animated manner, and then reverted to her *chère* France, where she was so happy, and had so many playfellows and pleasures, and her "*pauvre* papa" was quite well. Though the little darling seemed contented and happy enough at Lima; and it would have been sad, indeed, if at five or six years of age she had begun to grieve for "days lang syne," for they seemed "lang syne" to her.

But the Captain of the "New World" has sent us word he shall be ready to start in the evening. I have got to send back books that have been kindly lent to me from the English Book Club, to write a note of leave-taking and thanks to Mrs. B——, who has sent us a beautiful plant, and to do all the innumerable necessary nothings people find to do before leaving a place; and then farewell to beautiful, dilapidated Lima, mighty in fragility, and refulgent in decay; the most splendid city that the Spaniards ever built in South America, and the capital of the richest of its countries—superb Peru!

Mariquita, our Peruvian female attendant, has just been to take leave of us, and her sister to boot, bringing with them one of the loveliest little dogs you can imagine. Mrs. B—— told me the other day, that in this neighborhood people are occasionally subject to a shortness of breathing, which is very distressing. It is something like asthma, but not exactly: keeping the chest warm is recommended by the faculty, and these little dogs, with their soft, satin-like fur, are used as living muffs or cushions (as in England those silken breast-plates called comforters are used); and in almost all cases these animated canine cuirasses are found to be perfectly efficacious.

Independently of their being employed in this remedial service, these tiny creatures are often seen nestling in the folds of their mistress's gowns, more like doves than dogs. They are wonderfully small, and their wee feet emulate in delicacy those of their fair owners.

One of the *femmes de chambre* went the other day to order some walking shoes, and told me when she entered the shop, she fancied at first it must be a place for babies and children's shoes only, so marvelously small were those satin "zapatos," but they were found to be all ladies' shoes. The only thing that spoils their feet is, they wear their shoes too short even for their diminutive feet, which makes them look (as they are inclined to be the least *soupçon* too broad for their length) a little—a very little—disproportionately short; but in the most refined classes this defect almost entirely disappears.

To return to the canine subject: I hear that at Chihuahua, in Mexico, is a breed of the most extraordinary little dogs imaginable, much smaller even than these, and yet excessively fierce. They make the best and most vigilant guards and watch-dogs possible, dwarfs though they are.

With regard to educational establishments, I believe I have done Lima a little injustice. I have been informed lately there are several.

---

## CHAPTER LII.

The Voyage from Peru to Panama—Farewell to Lima—Guanacos—The Rio Lady in the Omnibus—The Railroad begun—Arrival at Callao—Rodil's defense of Callao described—Polite Attention of Captain W——The Harbor of Callao—The Beauty of the Pacific—Handsome Appointments of the Steamer—The musical Stewards—Mr. Beebe, the Hatter, for California—Arrival at Payta—The British Consul there—Description of Payta—Treatment of Peru by the Spanish Conquerors—Insurrection of Tupac Amaru—The Indians beyond Peru.

I WRITE this chapter at Jamaica. Our return voyage from Peru to Panama was most successfully performed. I have formerly mentioned how much we suffered on our first voyage, thermometrically speaking; but we experienced scarcely any oppressive heat whatsoever on our way back.

We left the city of the land of the Incas in that unromantic conveyance called an omnibus; for we feared we were late, and thought that we should save time by so doing. Mr. Yates was good enough to arrange all for us, and we found the omnibus just starting. The administrador recommended dispatch. We clambered in hastily, and—weak mortals—we thought, when we got in, it was full; but another passenger appeared—an Indian woman, with a little chocolate-colored baby, who looked round with great *sang-froid* on the crammed vehicle, most philosophically indifferent. These Indian infants seem the most stoical little dingy Diogeneses on earth.

At last the omnibus overflowed. A few arms, and heads, and shoulders, and such insignificant portions of the human frame were squeezed out at the rows of open windows, and then, *arré!* On we go, through the Morisco-Spanish streets of the noble old city, on, till we dash through the great gate.

Magnificent Lima, farewell! Like so many Sister Annes, we can soon see nothing but clouds of dust. Would we could have seen flocks—not of sheep, but of the gentle llama, those singular animals which, if they are over-loaded or ill-used, shed tears, look up pathetically and half reproachfully, and then in despair, if not relieved or soothed, lie down and die. I am assured this is a fact; but I will say no more of them, as they are so well known, nor of the vicunas and alpacas.

By the way, the guanacos are by some supposed to be a smaller kind of the large animal, on which the Patagonians were said to have ridden, bearing a resemblance to the mule, and also to the stag or elk. They are not, I believe, used as beasts of draught or burden by the South Americans, though some authors state they are capable of drawing more weight than two horses.

The first day Mrs. A—— landed in Peru, she was lucky enough to see a long string of the interesting llamas, but has not seen one in Lima since.

For the dust, we could but just glimpse the noble trees of the great avenue leading from the town. A young Peruvian gentleman in the carriage, whose poncho was lying like a lady's shawl carelessly on his arm, to save his *casaca* from the *polvo*, quick as thought doffed his sombrero, and popped his head through the poncho, without apparently discomposing a single hair.

A lady seated opposite to me was very communicative. She told me she had only lately arrived from Rio Janeiro, and she regretted exceedingly the imperial magnificence and the court gayeties of that capital. She was a thorough-going monarchist. It was delightful to see the *cortège* of the Emperor and Empress when they went out. At the opera their box looked so splendid; the Imperial Court gave such life and brilliancy to every thing. Lima seemed so dull in comparison. The President indeed! what was that! Nothing at all! "Oh qué differencia, qué lástima, qué disgracia," that there should be no great court here! Rio was infinitely preferable, she thought, and every thing so very flourishing there.

And now, thanks to an intermission of dust, we caught sight of the many-towered capital, leaning, in its haughty beauty, against the everlasting Andes. "Qué maravilla!" "Ah! Lima was very well," but the fair Brazilian reverted to Rio. "Pero Rio!

Eso es superior á todo elogio, hechicero! admirable." "The climate here, however, must be pleasanter by all accounts. "Pero está V. Equivocado."—"It is charming at Rio, a little hot certainly, but it is cooler in the evening; and then there are such diamonds, and all seem so happy there."

The omnibus stopped, and a Peruvian caballero, who was one of the passengers, soon saw a friend of his on horseback, near the door of the "fonda;" wishing to speak to him, he attempted to reach the "portazuela;" but seeing this would incommode us, managed to get out of one of the front windows, really like a very graceful monkey, and climbed in again with equal agility.

As we drove along, some splendidly dressed caballeros galloped past us with their magnificently caparisoned horses caracoling very prettily: but on thundered our great lumbering vehicle, "ciudado! caballeros," for our ebony coachman has had a little tiny taste, it seems, of "pisco." But the beautiful horses were every now and then to be seen through the dust, dancing a pretty little ballet along the gently descending road.

The railroad is already begun! we caught a glimpse of the works as we passed by. An unfortunate accident had just happened, the day before we left, I think. A man was killed, it was said, and others injured: and some of the natives began to shake their heads, and said it was ominous, and the railroad constructed by heretics would not answer, and so on. Last year, I believe, the attempt was made; but the superintendent, a young man of talent, went mad from over-anxiety, and subsequently died here. There appears, however, no doubt now of its succeeding.

We arrived at Callao in excellent time, and by Mrs. M——'s kind invitation went straight to her house. We heard that the American steamer would not start for the present, and Captain W—— had obligingly left us a message to say, he would come at the right time to take us on board in his boat.

I was anxious to take a poncho with me to England, and had not had time to get it at Lima that morning. Mrs. M—— sent for one from a Callao shop, which I bought. Mr. B——, who amiably came to see us off, on looking at my purchase, told me very likely it had been imported from England, where they make them now, to undersell the market here. So my poor poncho was partly disenchanted in my eyes—manufactured at Leeds instead of in the interior of Peru! but I don't quite believe it is the case. I think my poncho has a very Peruvian and anti-Leeds air; so I shall try and console myself.

Callao does not look to advantage after Lima, notwithstanding it boasts some very pretty mansions, like Mr. and Mrs. M——'s, for example. It is said that in some of the by-streets there you will see English signs hung up, such as "The Lively Pig," &c.; but Valparaiso is said to be still more Anglicized in its nomenclature.

I was sorry not to be able to go to see the old castle of Callao, which, under Rodil, during the War of Independence, stood a siege of two years. Rodil defended the fortress most gallantly and resolutely. The blockade was so strict, that the garrison was reduced to severe extremities, horseflesh being sold for a gold ounce per pound, and chickens for their weight in gold. In addition to this, he had treachery and insubordination to contend with constantly within the walls; and he was compelled to maintain his legitimate authority as commander by many terrible examples of severity.

Thus attacked, and hemmed in on all sides by land and by water, with treason close at hand, and war, hatred and rage without, a thousand hardships and privations increasing upon them day by day, and hopelessness casting slowly its heavy shadow over their outworn spirits, Rodil, with a few faithful adherents, "preux chevaliers, sans peur et sans reproche," still were true to their posts, and devoted to their duty, their king, and their country, till a frightful famine forced them to surrender. Here, where the Royalists made their last stand in the country, was the royal flag of Leon and of Castile furled for ever; but Rodil has left a glorious name behind him, which even his enemies must respect.

The round turrets of the dilapidated castle are flanked on each side by lengthened lines of fortifications, by curtains, and bastions, and batteries, and walls, and embrasures. Inclosed within prodigiously thick and casemated walls, are extensive barracks (which at present are turned into useful warehouses for the peaceful customs), magazines, &c. It is thought by some that a very insignificant army, numerically speaking, properly commanded, and well found in siege *matériel*, might have taken the place in two weeks, or perhaps one, instead of two years. This fortress had, however, a proud reputation of yore in Peru.

Shortly after Captain W—— arrived, we took leave of Mrs. M——, and walked to the mole, where we found the boat in readiness to convey us to the American steamer. So, wishing Mr. B—— good-by, who had walked with us to the boat, we were handed in by Captain W——, and soon found ourselves alongside of the vessel. She reminded us of the Mississippi steamers in her appearance. When we arrived alongside we had only one little step to make into the steamer from the boat.

The Captain had not yet come on board, and after looking at our cabins, which were most charmingly arranged and most comfortable, and which were, indeed, beautifully furnished, we paid a flying visit to the "Dædalus," and admired the perfect and admirable order which was perceptible at every step—saw in the chief cabin two splendid engravings of Napoleon and the Duke of Wellington (the latter, uncle of Captain W——), and returned to the "New World" just at the right time, for very soon after we left the harbor. It was smooth as a polished mirror, so protected is it from the southerly winds that generally blow here, by sandy San Lorenzo, and by a slender tongue of land that projects considerably, and by Fronton.

In the harbor were many vessels, chiefly merchant ships, not laden with gold and silver, but guano; not to be despised in this age of utilitarianism, and bringing plenty of gold and silver in its unsavory train. But we quickly lost sight of them, and of the town and fortifications; and adios to the beauteous "Ciudad de los Reyes:" if there was any truth in the old proverb, "El que bebe de las pilas, se queda en Lima," we—teetotallers as we are—should have staid longer.

I may mention that I was told that Callao is sufficiently Americanized to have, in deference to Yankee tastes and prejudices, besides its own italia and pisco, timber-doodle, mint-julep, and such concoctions. Ice is extremely plentiful. It is ordinarily frozen snow from those giant mountains, which are so "convenient" for the purpose.

Again we were on the vast Pacific, and once more under the glorious stars and stripes, which I so deeply reverence, honor, and love. The evening was most delightfully calm, and we were perfectly enchanted with our spacious and beautiful cabins, one of which had eight large windows, and all wide open, with the tranquil ocean lying like a great cloudless sky close to us. Looking on that mighty world of waters of the Pacific, I always feel as if I saw further—much further than on any other sea. Its lovely smoothness, and the sometimes brilliant transparency of the atmosphere, make it seem as if, over its softly-heaving surface, one looked into very Immensity and Eternity. I marvel not that some of the tribes of the ancient Indians imagined, that beyond that cerulean-looking ocean was placed the everlasting heaven-land to which their enfranchised spirits sailed after death. On this account a small canoe was often buried with them, in which they might embark without delay, with a sufficiency of provisions laid in for the voyage. They believed it was a submarine navigation they had to perform.

Of course, I felt this sublime vast effect was always assisted and partly produced by the imagination, and the consciousness that one might look from Lima, for instance, on and on, if physically empowered, to New Zealand in a slanting direction, without encountering a single island of any size or significance between, while from there again it is all ocean!

We had a charming dining, and sitting cabin besides, assigned to us, which had four windows. This was like a beautiful satin tent: the large, long cabin also was draperied with bright-colored satin along its whole extent, and in both there were white marble tables with a profusion of gilding, suberb vases, and other decorations; and the prettiest possible light curtains to all the windows of white muslin, embroidered with a thousand vivid colors (which curtains, I believe came from Germany); and in addition to all this, we had most comfortable berths. You see, on the Sacramento, in far California, they will glide along in a vessel almost as luxurious as Cleopatra's barque of old.

The Captain had thoughtfully ordered a milch goat to be brought on board, which supplied us with excellent milk, which I always think one of the greatest of luxuries on board ship. A charming, little, playful kid accompanied its revered parent, which often paid us a welcome visit in our cabin! We had plenty of books, many of which belonged to the Captain, mostly interesting voyages and travels, which I think interest one more when one is actually traveling than at any other time.

In the evening, when sitting in our own quiet cabin, looking from our eight windows on the Pacific—often itself like a huge melted gold and crimson sun, so dyed with the glories of the departing orb—we heard skillful guitar-playing and excellent singing in or near the neighboring saloon. They were two musical stewards, one particularly so, who sang almost every evening a great variety of South American and Spanish airs. One was a Brazilian—I believe from Rio—who not only played the guitar, but the castanets admirably; the other a German.

One of the passengers was a son, I understand, of the famous hatter, Mr. Beebe, of New York, who had crossed the Atlantic with us from Liverpool in the "Canada" steamer. He was going out to California, I believe for the second or third time, on a great hat speculation. I fancy thousands of those useful articles were on their way to the golden land, so well selected to please all tastes and suit all fashions, that if I am rightly informed, he has reason to hope when he arrives all will take off their hats to him, and—put his on.

After a pleasant voyage we arrived at Payta, and there we saw the French frigate "L'Algérie" at anchor. Presently Monsieur F——, the Commodore, was good enough to come and pay us a visit, and invite us to go on board the frigate. He proposed our first landing to see Payta, which we had not done satisfactorily before. We were soon ready, and took our places in the beautiful French man-of-war's boat. The men were a very fine sailor-like set, and seemed as thorough Jack-tars as even our own John Bulls (or rather *Jack* Bulls); they looked as clean and healthy as possible.

We glided rapidly along, and soon landed on that most barren of shores. M. F—— pointed out to us a number of balsas that were hard by. A young French gentleman was lately drowned there, but I do not accurately remember the circumstances; it was, however, in landing at this place.

I was anxious to go and thank in person the British Consul for the fine cherimoyas he had the goodness to send me when we were here before. I was truly sorry that, as I was not sure the "New World" would stop at Payta, I had brought no fruit or other offering from Lima in return for his thoughtful attention.

We walked through rather a curious-looking street, and before long, after visiting the market-place, found ourselves near Mr. Higgenson's house, who came out to meet us, and we crossed a handsome court, and soon found ourselves in a cool, airy room. It was very early in the morning, and Mr. Higgenson's daughter was not yet up. I am told she is a very handsome and accomplished person, uniting Anglo-Saxon with Peruvian charms; for Mrs. Higgenson was a lady of Payta.

The consul was a little severe on our steamer, for he likened its appearance (he had never seen one of that peculiar construction before) to that of a great dead whale floating helplessly along. After sitting a little while, we took leave of the hospitable consul, who wished us to stay to breakfast there: but we declined, for we had but little time.

Walking a short distance through the town, we saw a great number of animals laden with provisions and water, that had just come in from the country. I can not describe to you the singular appearance of this town, with a desert round it sterile as the Great Zahara ; but the inhabitants are, as I before informed you, extremely well supplied with all the necessaries, and even luxuries of life. My pet aversion, the ambrosial cherimoya, with its comprehensive flavor (according to its admirers) of strawberries, papaus, nectarines, cream and custard, in this neighborhood has arrived at the very climax of perfection. Numbers of Indians from the country were to be seen, attired in their own peculiar costume; the women with long, glossy, black plaits of hair, streaming from under their Guayaquil hats, and sometimes with immense black ponchos hanging considerably below their knees.

How cruelly was this race treated of old by the Spanish conquerors, and after the conquest by those placed in authority over them. And yet the Spanish nation, truly generous and chivalrous, and the Spanish kings were not to blame ; but that terrible and devouring thirst for gold, which seized on all the early colonists, and hardened them, as cupidity and the worship of Mammon only can, till their hearts were petrified, and their natural feelings of mercy and justice obliterated.

It is said that various humane edicts and ordinances, which issued from the throne, were practically set entirely at naught in the colonies. "Los repartimientos," a most unjust system of taxation was established, and pushed to the utmost. In nearly all the districts, the corregidors from Spain had scarcely any settled salary, and lived on what they wrung from the wretched natives.

As far as the Indians were concerned, these functionaries were monopolists of the sale of all the necessaries and all the comforts of existence. The corregidor, when he went his round of visitation to the different hamlets in the part of the country under his jurisdiction, carried with him all such articles, bought at extravagant prices from the Lima merchants, and the Indians were allowed neither to choose nor to remonstrate. These beardless aborigines were compelled to purchase razors; their wives, who desired no vail but their own abundant long hair, which streamed over their shoulders and down their backs, had mantillas forced upon them, and so forth ; and the unfortunate people were obliged to perform a certain amount of work (according to the sum owed) to pay the corregidor whatever price he chose to set on his often utterly useless wares, and a tax for the Crown besides.

The time within which this task was to be completed, depended on the tyrannical fancies or necessities of the corregidors ; and it frequently happened that, wholly unable to comply with the hard conditions imposed upon them, and to fulfill the unmerciful tasks their despotic masters sought to exact from their unequal strength and impoverished energies, they sent deputations to the Spanish Viceroy, entreating him to have compassion on them, and to protect them from their unfeeling oppressors. But long ere their humble plaints could reach the Viceroy's ears, the crafty corregidors had contrived to tell their own tale, in their own way; to exaggerate the non-compliance of the poor natives, and to plead right and custom, and the most imperative necessity, for their unjustifiable extortions. In short, they continually not only escaped all censure and punishment themselves, but artfully managed to have the wretched aborigines severely chastised for presumed insubordination and rebellion.

In 1780 the Indians, driven to desperation by continued despotism and oppression, and seeing no other chance of deliverance from the hateful system that was grinding them to the dust, openly rebelled. Their chief was named Tupac Amaru. The first act of their insurrectionary violence was the indiscriminate slaughter of the justly unpopular corregidors, together with other colonists, whenever and wherever they could accomplish their destruction.

The troops of Peru and of Buenos Ayres were united together to put an end to this unexpected rebellion. A savage war desolated the entire country for three years, during which gloomy period, horrible barbarities, calling forth fearful retaliations, were but too often practiced; and all was fury, rapine, hatred and revenge.

At length Tupac Amaru was taken prisoner, and condemned to suffer death. The fallen warrior was ignominiously dragged to the place where he was sentenced to be executed; and before his horror-stricken eyes, the miserable man was forced to see his wife and children pitilessly butchered. He was then subjected to shameful and inhuman tortures, and finally torn into quarters by four horses.

There was another unjust institution called the Mita, but its operation was chiefly confined to Potosi. Every able-bodied male was forced to labor for the space of a year in the mines, and at the farms the females, in the same manner, were obliged to work to acquire for their masters a certain specified and agreed-upon profit within the assigned period, beyond the sum required for their own subsistence; but, as it too often happened that their strength originally was not equal to comply exactly with the terms of their contract, or that they became enfeebled and incapacitated from severe drudgery, they frequently could not work out the stipulated sum in time, and thus incurred a debt to their master, and were forced to labor on as slaves to liquidate it.

Instead of diminishing, this debt very often was enlarged, and the poor wretches then remained positive slaves for the rest of their natural lives; and if death set them free, the wives and children they left behind them were mercilessly seized, and obliged to go on with the task which they had failed to finish.

The food of these unhappy beings was bad and scanty, more especially in the manufactories; and the over-worked sufferers were locked up from dawn till night, and cruelly flogged if their inhuman task-masters were not satisfied with the amount of the work done, or detected any carelessness in the execution of it.

It is really terrible to reflect on such scenes of merciless tyranny on the one side, and of pitiable degradation on the other: but such was the gentle Mita, and its operation and results. It is easy to imagine that the greater part of those to whose fate it fell to labor thus severely, suffered deeply in health, and in countless cases their strength was utterly worn out, and their constitutions irremediably shattered, by the time their terrible tasks were accomplished, so that probably scarcely one in a dozen survived to return to their humble homes.

The aboriginal population of Peru, at the time of the conquest, was stated to be about six millions. In 1796 a census was taken, and the number was then 608,899. Since then, till the War of Independence, and the Emancipation, the pure Indian population, it appears, gradually continued to diminish.

Those Indians who live beyond Peru, to the eastward of the mountains, are said not yet to be civilized or reclaimed, although in particular places they submitted to the Missionaries and Jesuits; and most of the tribes within the vast empire of the Brazils, with the exception of a small number on the banks of the giant Amazon river, are as wild and thoroughly uncultivated as on the day when Columbus first discovered the Western World.

But I am prosing sadly about the poor Indians. Will the reader forgive me, and even let me have a few last words about fair, beautiful, and far-famed Peru?"

## CHAPTER LIII.

Peru—Her internal Communication—Her Forts and Coast—Peruvian Agriculture—Manufactures of inland Peru—Commerce of Peru—Her Commodities—Her Trade—Her Government—Her Religion—Peruvian Fertility—Mineral Resources—Animals—Cattle—The Face of the Country—The Andes—Rivers and Lakes of Peru—Her Coasts.

PERU labors under very considerable disadvantages, with regard to inland communication.

The elevated plateaux and table-lands, separated by deeply-embosomed valleys, and the gigantic mountains that intervene between the coast and the table-land, render traveling tedious and difficult. Roads and bridges, in many parts, are entirely wanting; and in places where rude and scarcely-distinguishable paths are found, they lie along the perilous edges of overhanging and rugged precipices, perpendicularly steep; and these tracks, moreover, are almost always so dangerously narrow, that the sure-footed mule can alone tread them with any security.

Those travelers who can afford it are usually carried on the backs of Indians: they are borne along in this way often for a fortnight or three weeks together, over paths that lead zig-zagging along, among rocks and steeps to all appearance inaccessible, and through uninhabited wildernesses and unbroken forests.

The means of necessary internal communication, however, are more carefully attended to, in regions that lie lower; and I am informed that the Government are giving their attention—please Revolutionists and Pronunciados—to a general system of road-making. Perhaps, in time—as engineering difficulties are despised and defied in these days, and as the first railroad has already been commenced under Government auspices in the country—the Peruvians will connect their chief cities by means of railroads, and join in the mighty march of the royal progress of nations.

A few rather strong forts protect the commerce of Peru on the seaboard, and perhaps a couple of small war-steamers complete the defensive powers of the nation. As for the standing army, it is generally asserted, by persons of more experience than myself on such matters, to be formed of such materials, and so inferior in discipline, &c., as to be useless in case of foreign invasion, and perhaps worse than useless in case of domestic dissension.*

However ill-provided the Peruvians may be with artificial means of defense against foreign foes, their coast presents powerful natural features for protecting the country. Huge rocky walls, almost perpendicular, and towering cliffs, there stand like Nature's fortresses. All the powers of the earth might be defied with proper management and method. Were the Peruvians in general like the Swiss, they might perhaps keep the world at bay; but where so many of them are composed of the indolent, passive Indian tribes, they are not likely ever to imitate the independent example of these sturdy and hardy mountaineers.

Agriculture in Peru, by all accounts, is still almost in its infancy; and in general the implements used in husbandry are of rude and simple construction. Their system of farming is commonly altogether primitive and unmethodical. They drive their corn and sugar mills generally by means of oxen, overlooking the advantages of wind and water.

The natives of Peru have a good deal of quickness and ingenuity, though their arts and manufactures, speaking in general, are susceptible of very great improvement. There are beautiful ponchos of extraordinary fineness made in the district of Tarma; thick and excellent blankets on the table-lands, as well as other articles. In the valleys, cow-hides are made into traveling-cases, for hammocks, or for beds and bedding; and goat-skins into what are called cordovans; mats used for carpeting are manufactured from rushes, and packing-cords from a native plant.

Inland Peru is celebrated for its exquisite silver filigree-work: this is chiefly made at Huamanca, and is perhaps unparalleled for beauty, delicacy, and durability; but in a general way, the United States and Europe, in the principal towns, supersede with their manufactures, to a great extent, the less-finished productions of the natives; and in exchange for gold and silver or raw material these are plentifully supplied to Peru.

The commerce of the country has lately materially increased, during a temporarily lull of foreign and domestic disturbance. Of

* We left all of our friends at Lima very apprehensive of the riots and excesses of the next presidential election, which is now beginning to be much thought of. They tell me, they generally, on such occasions, have their houses barricaded and closed, and are obliged to imprison themselves strictly the whole time. Robberies, massacres, and violences are said to be of continual occurrence there. I only repeat what I was told, and would gladly believe such statements exaggerated.

the export trade the principal articles are the precious metals, copper, quicksilver, and tin, and other metals. While Mexico was under the necessity of sending to Europe for mercury, Peru boasted of a good supply of her own at the mines of Huanca-Velica, one portion of which for two centuries produced yearly three thousand quintals; but such was the state of affairs in Peru in the years '37 and '38, that the quicksilver sold at two hundred to two hundred and twenty dollars per quintal, while in London, at the same period, it was sold at sixty-five dollars. The working of the mines was then naturally suspended; but now the mining operations have been revived by private companies, and thus some of the richest quicksilver mines in the known world are as productive again as ever.

The ancient Peruvians formerly used vermilion or red lead in their colored delineations, but I know not if it is still found there. Peruvian bark and various kinds of plants for medicinal purposes are also exported; drugs, precious woods, and gums of different descriptions; hides, tallow, &c.; seal, chincilli, and other skins; cotton and wool, and other articles of less value.

Peruvian wool is considered to be equal to English, but it is customary to export it in a very dirty condition, which occasions it to be sold at a reduced price. South Peru supplies the largest quantity, but the vicuna and alpaca are reckoned the best. Cotton is exported from Payta, Islay, and Arica, but the annual quantity is said not to be above thirty thousand quintals.

Of late, saltpetre has become an article of considerable trade. It is said that each successive year now manifests a rather large increase in the amount of exports. The imports into the republic are of great variety, and are chiefly from the United States and Great Britain; France and Germany have, however, of late introduced a greatly increased number of their respective wares.

Probably Peru for some length of time will continue to receive vast quantities of foreign-manufactured goods, more particularly those of the more delicate and finished descriptions, while the different exporting nations in exchange for these will be not disadvantageously repaid through the resources of the enormous mineral wealth of that highly-favored country.*

In the year 1847 the trade between the United States and Peru amounted to the following numbers: exports from the United States to Peru, 192,978 dollars; exports from Peru received in

* The total imports in 1840 amounted to 10,100,000 dollars, the total exports to 9,741,733 dollars.

the United States, 396,223 dollars.—But enough of commercial statistics.

The Peruvian Constitution, established finally in 1839, recognizes distinctly executive, legislative, and judicial functions, which are thoroughly independent of, and separate from each other. The government, as you know, is founded on popular supremacy and democratic principles. The President's term of service is for six years, and to him the executive power is delegated by Congress.

There is not, as in the United States, a Vice-President; but the president of the executive council succeeds to the presidency in the event of death or dismissal from office. This council consists of the ministers and of members of the senate. In a senate and assembly chosen from the people through electoral colleges, resides the legislative power. The representatives are thus apportioned; one for every twenty thousand inhabitants.

Judges are appointed by the executive, and are irremovable except for ill conduct. The Constitution provides for the several subjudiciaries, and nominates justices having separate qualifications for the departments, the districts, towns, and parishes. The operations of the courts are said to be carried on with impartiality and honor. But among the indispensable qualifications of a Peruvian judge, knowledge of the law is said not to rank; and through the want of the necessary learning on the part of the lawyers and the arbitrator, the most grave injuries are not unfrequently inflicted unintentionally on the unlucky applicant.

The established religion is Roman Catholic, and none besides is tolerated. An Archbishop and several suffragans preside over the church. The archiepiscopalian residence is at Lima. The church is stated to be enormously wealthy, and to have amassed vast amounts of property from devout donors.

Literature is generally believed to be in a state of steady, but slowly-progressive development. Enlightened and superior education is limited to a certain number of the whites: the Indians and negroes seldom learn any thing more than the business of their confined and simple transactions demands.

As to the fertility of Peru—independently of its fine and tropical climate, which allows it to be fruitful in nearly all the vegetable productions of the East and of the West Indies—the elevation of its various mountains, as in Mexico, causes the plants and the fruits of all climes and latitudes to grow to perfection within its extensive limits. Rice, sugar, tobacco, cocoa, yams, sweet potatoes, &c., are cultivated in the warmer situations; while in the colder, are wheat, the vine and quinoa (chenopodium quinoa). The grapes are good, but the wine made from them is indifferent.

Maize is cultivated, and forms the common diet of the population. The dried leaf of the erythroxylon coca is much used by Peruvians for chewing, as the betel is in the East. A kind of melancholy madness, Pöppig says, is brought on by its use; but other authorities are of opinion that it produces no deleterious effects. The chinchona, or Peruvian bark, is indigenous and in great abundance: it grows at the elevation of ten or twelve thousand feet and abounds mostly in the provinces of the north.

Like those of Mexico, the mineral resources of Peru are universally believed to be inexhaustible. The entire country is one mighty mound of incalculable mineral wealth; the rivers, and streams, and mountains are glittering and sparkling with gold, with silver, and with precious stones. It is stated that the greater part of the mines actually being worked at present, are situated in the Cerro de Pisco in the Junin department; but I hear their amount of produce has considerably fallen off since the last revolutionary troubles, which left behind them so much anarchy, and such a depressing sense of doubt and insecurity. M'Culloch is inclined to estimate the average annual value of the mines of gold and silver of Peru at from seven hundred to seven hundred and fifty thousand pounds sterling.

Peruvian animals do not differ much from those of other parts of South America. The American lion or puma; the uturuncu (a kind of tiger); a black bear that inhabits the mountains; the skunk; a number of varieties of deer, armadillos, bears, &c., are among the catalogue of Peruvian wild animals, and are hunted by the natives. The llama, vicuna, alpaca, and guanaco, and many others, are either used as beasts of burden, or are prized for their skin and wool. In the rivers are alligators. Reptiles are not so abundant or troublesome as nearer the Equator.

The cattle of Peru are not particularly large, but yet are on an equality with the generality of those in Great Britain and Belgium. The meat is generally tender, well-flavored, and juicy, especially when fed on Lucerne grass. The bones are very small. In the mountains, black cattle thrive well; but rapidly pine, fall away, and die on the low lands of the coast. Mules and horses are usually of an ordinary size, but goats, swine, &c., grow very large in Peru, and are reckoned of a superior sort.

Sheep, of all foreign animals acclimated in Peru, seem to some to have succeeded the best. At an elevation of twelve or fourteen thousand feet above the level of the sea, on the vast commons and pasture grounds of the Andes, they have increased to an extraordinary degree. On the coast but few sheep are bred, but during particular months, vast flocks are driven from the interior, and fattened for the market of Lima. A usual bargain between the drovers and the farmers is to give the lambs for pasturage, the latter calculating on receiving one hundred and fifty lambs from every hundred ewes.

In addition to this increase, which surpasses that in England, there are lambs twice a year, commonly in June and December. Hitherto little care has been taken by the breeders to improve the wool, but this is fast becoming here an increased article of export. More attention, without doubt, will be speedily drawn to the subject.

This fertile country has on the north the republic of the Ecuador; on the south and southeast it is bounded by Bolivia, and on the east by the vast empire of the Brazils, the Pacific being on the west. Its greatest length from S.S.E. to N.N.W. is calculated to be about fifteen hundred miles, and its breadth varies much; at some parts it is six hundred miles. Its estimated area is five hundred thousand square miles.

The whole of the country is traversed by the Cordilleras of the Andes. The eastern range of these mountains approaches to within from thirty to a hundred miles of the Pacific coast. The country is naturally divided into three separate regions; consisting firstly, of the slope between the Andes and the coast; secondly, the mountain regions of the Andes themselves; thirdly, that part lying east of the Cordilleras, forming part of the great basin of the Amazon.

These divisions are all very dissimiliar in character. Between the Tumbez river and the Leche, the coast region is almost a desert—that is to say, where it is not traversed by streams, or is not susceptible of artificial irrigation: in such parts it is principally composed of arid, sandy, and sterile wastes, and is barren and desolate. Immediately upon the coast lie all the principal settlements made by the Spaniards.

The Andes in Peru consist of two main chains or Cordilleras, in different parts connected by intersecting ranges, and inclosing various extensive and splendid valleys. A mighty cluster of mountains rear their lofty crests around Cuzco, occupying probably three times the extent of Switzerland. Around Pasco (in latitude 13° south) is another knot that surrounds the plain of Bombon, thirteen thousand five hundred feet above the level of the ocean, and in which are found the productive and valuable silver mines of the Cerro Pasco.

The loftiest summits of the Peruvian Andes are toward the south, where the Nevada da Chuquibamba reaches to twenty-one thousand feet in height. Several others, surrounding the noble valley of Desaguadero, may also approach nearly to this elevation, indeed some may equal or transcend it. In Peru, the west Cordillera is the loftiest at the mountain knot of Pasco, the Andes separating into three collateral chains, which proceeding northward, divide the basins of the Maranon, Huallaga, and Ucayale. The last range of the Andes to the east, in Peru, extends between the sixth and fifteenth parallels, to a distance varying from two to four hundred miles from the Pacific, and divides the basin of the Ucayale from those of the Yavari, Beni, and other affluxes to the mighty Amazon.

The space called the Sierra, which is inclosed between the colossal ridges of the Western and Eastern Cordilleras, is in some parts occupied by mountains and sterile rocks; in others, by table-lands, on which grows a short fine grass, and by a considerable tract of hilly pasture-ground; and in other parts, again, by fertile and extensive valleys, that formerly supported a large population.

The country east of the Cordilleras, the third region, is still comparatively unknown. It is almost buried in forests, all but impenetrable, and apparently interminable, and can hardly with justice be said to be a part of Peru, being occupied solely by a few devoted missionaries and by tribes of independent Indians.

In the great Peruvian Andes, the mightiest and largest rivers in the world have their source. The Tunguragua, regarded in general as the proper source of that sublime river the Amazon, and its vast and majestic confluents, Huallaga and Ucayale, the latter of which is formed by the junction of the Paro river with the Apurimac, have their sources on the eastern side of the western chain of the Cordilleras, and flow through, with many tortuous windings, in a northerly direction, until they pass the boundaries of the country.

These mighty rivers are mostly navigable, and with the desirable assistance of steam navigation, without doubt, ere a lengthened period has elapsed, they will carry the wealth of this distant region across the continent to the ports of the Atlantic Ocean.

Peru has but few lakes, but boasts that of Titicaca, which is the largest and most elevated lake in the whole of South America. This, however, is partly in the neighboring country of Bolivia, being inclosed by the Cordilleras, south of the table-land of Cuzco. It is remarkably irregular in its outline: a number of head-lands divide it into a main body of oblong shape, and several subsidiary portions. Its height above the sea is about 12,795 feet, and its area 4000 square miles, and in many places it is reported to be 500 feet deep. Many small mountainous islands are contained in it, and the lake takes its name, which signifies the "Leaden Mountain," from the largest. On this island, which is generally uncultivated, though extremely fertile, tradition places the first appearance of Manco Capac.

The remaining lakes in Peru are small, comparatively speaking; but are the sources from whence all the noble rivers that pursue an eastward course take their beginning. As to the rivers of the coast, they are of little account, being, shallow, small, and incapable of navigation.

The coasts are lofty and bold throughout. Some miles of a loose sandy desert intervene in the northern provinces, between the high lands and the Pacific; but generally the lofty cliffs approach close to the shore, which perhaps, in an extent of one thousand six hundred miles, has not a dozen really secure harbors. Of these the best are Callao, Payta, Salina, Sechura, Pisco, Islay, and some few others. Lambayeque and Truxillo have merely open roadsteads. Vessels are obliged to go within a quarter of a mile before they can anchor, and the terrific swell that rolls with unbroken force from the vast Pacific, causes a prodigious and perilous surf.

---

## CHAPTER LIV.

Departure from Peru—On board the "New World"—The nautical Ladies—Chimborazo and Cotopaxi—The Volcanoes of the Cordillera—Crater of Cotopaxi—A narrow Escape—Arrival at Panama—An Amateur Concert—Departure from Panama—Scene occasioned by a dead Mule—Badness of the Road—Arrival at Cruces.

Once more we are in the French man-of-war's boat, taking our leave of balsas, cherimoyas, and the shores of Peru.

Before we started we met a gentleman who informed us the American steamer was going almost immediately; so we gave up visiting 'L'Algérie;' but we went close to her, and beautiful she looked and in perfect order; and then we hastened to our disparaged and maligned steamer, which reminded us, instead of a dead whale, of the river-palaces of the Mississippi, full of life and power.

With much regret we took leave of Monsieur F——, and sent by him a message to say, how sorry we were not to see again his charming wife. I can never forget their amiability and cordial kindness. Indeed having met them will ever be among the most pleasant recollections of my travel.

On going on board the "New World," we found we were going to take a little turn for an hour or two, to give some nautical recreation to two or three Paytian ladies, who were friends of the American Consul's family. Had we known this, we might have staid and visited Madame F—— and "L'Algérie." They all came on board in high glee; but we had not proceeded far ere we heard many dolorous plaints from these inexperienced voyagers: their heads ached with the motion of the ship: they were giddy: "Se maréa Vm., Señoritas." "Es el primer viaje, Caballero!" Soon after they were obliged to confess they did not feel superlatively well, and seemed to wish the Captain to land them at once, though it was not easy, in the middle of the water. "Despáchese V. vamos!" to the Captain. This, however, was also difficult. The steamer had coals on board to serve her as far as San Francisco (Captain W—— said he had never seen a vessel so deep in the water), and her movements thereby were not accelerated.

Finding they must take it philosophically, the ladies of Payta behaved like heroines, rallied one another on their bad sailorship, and laughed away their discomfort. "Qué tertulia tan alegre!" "Si, pero—a fé mia me maréo." "Vaya, vaya, una idea, Conchita!" The Captain, too, assures them it is only fancy—they are quite mistaken. Ah! the "Norte Americanos" are so funny! and they laugh—how they laugh!—in a pretty, silvery-sounding chorus, and then stop to ask the captain if a storm has not come on (it is as smooth as a mirror). But great is the delight when they near Payta again! Then they suddenly feel overwhelmed with the charms and pleasures of their little voyage, though it was so "borrascoso—Ah! habia peligro de naufragar." They don't feel *quite* sure they have not been down to the bottom and back again; the "Capitan" tells them they are perfect sailors; he would ask no better wife than the Señorita Conchita, born to be a "skipperina." Ah, Capitan! our voyage has been charming—"a las mil maravillas! pero—que prodigio!" They never saw Payta look half so beautiful before: the land looked lovely, quite so! paradisiacally charming, positively! (such an Arabia Petrea as it was!)

At last they trip, with their white-satined little feet, into the boat, and I doubt not laughed right merrily during their happy disembarkation. But perhaps after this first trial they will take courage to make a voyage to Guayaquil next time, especially as they so nobly braved such awful terrors and sea-sickness.

And now indeed farewell to Peru. Does the reader remember the curious island I mentioned, not far from Guayaquil, bearing resemblance to a corpse? We were not to stop at Guayaquil, and I had no idea we should go near the land; but by chance looking out of my cabin-window—it was quite early in the morning—I beheld that singular isle not far of, and knew it again instantaneously.

We were then near Guayaquil. Bright and lovely grew the morning, as we sped on; extraordinarily clear grew the air; and, oh! delight! there were the giant mountains. There stood glorious old Chimborazo, once supposed to be the highest mountain in the world, but now a dethroned king, yet very monarch-like still; shining with its never-melted snows, as if, like Shelley's Moon, it was "with white fire laden"—and those white fires seemed to brighten the very daylight around.

I imagine another mighty mountain I saw, that seemed towering almost as high, was Cotopaxi; I have been told, at least, since, that they were both visible that morning. Chimborazo is supposed by some authors, to be an extinguished volcano; if so, perhaps some day the Moon of Snow that crowns its gigantic peak, will be melted by the terrific fires that are pent up in its unfathomable and awful caverns, and the huge mountain will return to its dangerous activity, and recover from its long-continued trance of "suspended animation."

As to their geological structure, the great thickness and extent of the porphyritic and schistose rock, are said to be the only phenomena by which the Andes are distinguished from the mountains of Europe. The crest of the Andes is universally covered with basalts, porphyries, green-stone, and clink-stone. Divided into columns, these rocks look at a distance like vast assemblages of dilapidated and pinnacled towers. Without any admixture, the porphyries of Chimborazo are eleven thousand four hundred feet in thickness; and the pure quartz to the west of Caxamarca is nine thousand feet, and the sandstone of the neighborhood of Cuenca, four thousand eight hundred feet; while granite and primitive limestone in Europe, I believe, constitute the summits of mountain chains.

Some of the volcanoes of the Cordillera throw out scorified rocks, or water, and often clay, with a mixture of carbon and sulphur. The most elevated of the mountains of the Andes from which in late years there have been eruptions, is Cotopaxi. Its height is 18,890 feet. This volcano in 1758, shot its formidable flames to a height of 2700 feet above the edge of the crater. In the eruption of 1744, its roaring was heard in Honda at a distance of two hundred leagues.

The eruption of 1803 was preceded by an awful phenomenon. The snows covering the mountain suddenly melted. For above twenty years no distinguishable vapor or cloud of smoke had risen from the crater; but in one night the subterranean fire had so rapidly done its work, that the outward walls of the cone were heated till they had become bare, and exhibited the black color that belongs to vitrified scoriæ. Humboldt heard at the port of Guayaquil, fifty-two leagues from the edge of the crater, the roaring of Cotopaxi day and night, like almost continual discharges of artillery.

By degrees we began to advance a little quicker, as our coal somewhat diminished. We fell in with the English steamer, and the Captain tried to speak her, but in vain. It was in the evening, and at first we thought we saw lights on shore, and fancied that we must be near the coast, but we soon observed that those lights changed their bearings, and saw that it must be a ship.

Soon after, the Captain sent us down word that it was the English mail steamer. Cosmopolite as I am, to a certain extent —I felt that that steamer looked like a little bit of our "fatherland," sailing as we were on the great Pacific in an American ship—though under the shadow of the stars and stripes I always feel at home, "un poco mas o menos," as the Mexicans so often say.

One morning a huge shark, that had been pertinaciously following our vessel, was caught, but the floundering monster got loose again. We saw a great number of whales another day, spouting up splendid fountains of water: it was a beautiful sight.

We had an alarm, which did not, however, last long, one night. We had been watching the beautiful phosphorescence on the cloven waters, when, on a sudden, the bell was rung sharply and violently, and almost immediately the engine stopped. Soon, very soon after, we saw from the cabin windows an enormous black object drifting by, so close that we fancied it must touch the side of the steamer. It was a ship. She had crossed our track, and a collision was avoided by a mere hair's breadth. I think I have not yet spoken of the extraordinary fog-banks we saw on our previous voyage. Really we could hardly believe that it was not land, an immense island, that we were looking at.

On our voyage we saw one or two huge merchant ships, walking the waters gloriously indeed; one especially of great size, with all her sails set, that looked like a perfect castle of canvas. Then we had glorious Pacific sunsets and sun-risings, and splendid weather almost the whole way.

At length we found ourselves once more in the Bay of Panama. We felt quite sorry to leave our beautiful and comfortable cabin; and I shall always feel grateful to the Captain of the "New World," for his obliging civilities and attentions toward us. We stopped only a day or two at Panama, where, according to a previous invitation, we remained under the hospitable roof of the English Consul.

I was very anxious to get our muling and canoeing over, as the rainy season was becoming worse and worse. I also longed to reach Jamaica, to possess myself of the dear home-letters I expected to find there. Mules were quickly secured; and first Monday, but afterward, from some unavoidable delay, Tuesday was appointed for our transit across the Isthmus.

A pleasant little amateur concert took place at Mr. P——'s, the second evening we were there. We met again our amiable French friends. Some English ladies, and Mrs. L——, a lady of New Granada, married to the English Vice-Consul, were there too; Mrs. L——, with a nice little girl, one of her numerous children, who seemed hardly to understand English. The child appeared passionately fond of music, and remained as if glued to the piano-forte. Madame H——o most kindly lent us side-saddles for our ride, which materially contributed to our comfort.

The morning we were to start, the pre-payment for the mules occupied some little time—no slight affair when you have to pay eighty or ninety dollars in French franc pieces, which we had to do at Panama. After this was satisfactorily concluded (the price, however, having been raised on account of the dreadful state of the roads), we were preparing to start, when Mr. P——, who with his daughter was kindly intending to ride a few miles with us, was hastily summoned to give his advice with respect to a poor sailor, who had just broken his leg in an English ship in the harbor. He was sent, without any unnecessary delay, to the hospital. Poor fellow! perhaps he had gone unharmed through many a savage tempest to meet with so serious a misfortune in the peaceful harbor.

At last we started, and rode gently through the streets and plazas of Panama, which reminded me, among other ruined places, of beautiful Messina, which we saw almost directly after it had suffered from a third bombardment during the last revolutionary troubles of Sicily. Yet was Panama lovely, as if dilapidation became it. We had quite a gay cavalcade: Mr. P—— on a beautiful horse, Miss P—— ditto, young M. H——o, who amiably came also to accompany us a little way out of the city, and M. Santa Maria, to whom the mules belonged, who was to go with us himself the whole way to Cruces.

M. H——o (by his friends always called Pepe, the diminutive, as I am informed, of José) was on a fiery steed, which he was trying, I believe, for the first time. We were all gently cantering on, having just left the suburbs of the city behind us, when his horse became restive, and played all sorts of curious antics; waltzing round without partner or music, and performing many other eccentricities. He was obliged to leave us, which took much from the picturesqueness of our cavalcade, for his wild-looking, plunging, prancing-about courser, that "*caracoleared*" so finely, and his gay poncho streaming from his shoulders, and all the handsome Panamanian accoutrements, that made him look so South American, or rather so like a Spanish caballero merely a little South Americanized—were not a sight to be seen every day.

We were already at a good distance from Panama, and soon after our kind friends, Mr. and Miss P——, said good-by to us; and on we journeyed, finding the sun terrifically hot, and glad to see some prospect of shade ahead, and wondering whether this was really a rainy season (soon we were convinced)! A miserable looking man, on a miserable looking mule, was following the same road we were (to Cruces), Mr. P—— had entered into a little conversation with him, and the poor emaciated being told him he had just come from California, from the mines, where he suffered greatly from exposure, and from standing up to his waist in water often, till it brought on a particular kind of paralysis that is said to be very common at the California mines, and incurable.

We had stopped for ten minutes or so, to take leave of our friends, and the poor, wretched object on a mule, that looked as if it also had been disappointed in California, and was returning in starvation and disgust, with its long-eared head almost bowed to the ground, had got the start of us. Not very long afterward, at a very narrow part of the road, where it ran between two walls of slippery cliffs, this very mule, dead, and obstructing the path, was displayed to the horror-struck eyes of his quadruped relations. "Arré," shrieked the mozos. There was scarcely any room for them to step on one side, and the banks were too steep for the laden mules to climb; but they refused to pass over their fallen fellow-creature. They *would not* trample on their brother, laid low in the dust—O! mule, mule, how unlike art thou to man!

Then ensued a scene that baffles all powers of description. We were first alarmed by the leading baggage-mule charging back upon us, with his eyes starting out of his head, and looking perfectly mad with terror and horror. Then the others caught sight of the dreaded object, and were equally horrified with the fugleman of their party. Again and again the yelling muleteers and mozos strove to drive them over the obstruction; shrieks, blows, shouts, gesticulations, thrusts, threats, all were in vain. Such a *mêlée* of men and mules, legs, arms, sticks, tails, trunks, heels, long ears, shoes, sombreros, and portmanteaus I never beheld, and the scene and the noise were appalling.

All seemed in vain. I don't know which appeared the maddest, the mules or the men; the worst of all, perhaps, was poor Señor Santa Maria—the mozos drove (or tried to drive) the mules, and he drove the mozos. As to the mules, the poor, insane creatures, snorting, trembling, plunging, and half jumping one over the other, seemed as if they could not overcome their terror, and their intense aversion to touch the body of their lifeless companion. The men tried to drag the dead mule up the steep banks, but they could not manage it, so the battle recommenced.

At the beginning of the fray, with the most extraordinary intrepidity, I had—run away. Now if the reader thinks this paradoxical, let me inform him that it required some courage, not being a fly, to clamber up the sides of a perpendicular precipice of glass, for such pretty nearly was the wall of rock on either side of us. I was not alone in this act of glorious valor. We all, by common consent, slipped from our saddles at the same moment, and scrambled up that horrible bank; it would have been perishing very ignominiously to be squeezed flat between two of our own trunks, and kicked out of the world by refractory mules.

As for the mules, they submitted at last: probably, however, they had so lost their mulish senses in the confusion, that they did not know which way they were going. I saw some of them taking a mad flying leap over their poor fallen fellow-brute, and the others instinctively followed. Señor Santa Maria informed us afterward, not a single mule touched the body of the dead one, not even the heaviest laden. There is something very touching, I think, in the respect shown by the poor animals for their fellow-comrade, and for death.

We passed afterward many other dead mules, but none that had died, poor fellows, so inconveniently as that one. It was just in the most narrow and difficult pass of the route. Poor things! that horribly bad road tries their strength so dreadfully! They are generally dragged on one side of the pathway; and, except from the shocking stench, they caused us no annoyance. What became of the unfortunate paralytic Californian we never knew.

At one place where we stopped to let the mules drink—a very wild, romantic-looking spot—there were a number of natives crouched under the trees, talking and laughing. One, who was huddled up all of a heap, appeared as if he had no particular features or form of his own, looking, as uncouth people do sometimes, as if he was merely a fortuitous concourse of atoms; he bore evidently a strong dislike to the Americans. "Ah! Yankis! ah! Yankis! Go-head! Aha! Go! come! ho! head-ago!" he kept calling out, and repeatedly mimicking and caricaturing some one pushing impatiently along. I remember almost the same thing happened on our first visit to the Isthmus.

The road was execrable. Imagine the great wall of China pulled down over it, and scattered in huge blocks and rugged fragments along it, in all possible irregularity and confusion; and occasionally rushing streams swollen by the rain, dashing and roaring across the rocky road, through which the careful mules half-waded, half-swam. At times you have to clamber up and down a curious kind of steep staircase or rocky ladder, half-natural and half-artificial, some short, some long, but all prodigiously rugged and rough, and startling us with their apparent impracticability.

We progressed tediously along from one "pantano" (marsh, or pool) to another. My mule, though a very good one, fell and scrambled up again three times; luckily for me, I kept on the saddle. I generally went first, and thus had to experimentalize and choose the road. The patience and prudence of the mules are extreme. They will stand sometimes in a brown study, pondering over the path, and then seem to feel their way as if their hoofs were hands.

We suddenly encountered at a narrow turn in the road, some extraordinary looking affairs; some like gibbets, others like fittings for a theatre, benches, lumber, railings, posts, &c.; and the men-mules, who were carrying them, seemed sorely fatigued. We saw afterward other parts of the same huge nondescript laid by the side of the path; I suppose temporarily, till the peons had rested. These belonged to a traveling circus of an American (Colonel Somebody, whose name I forget), *en route* to Panama.

As to the rain, I can not give any idea of it: it found its cataract-like way through the thick-woven boughs of the forest, and almost washed us from our mules where it was more open. Do not be afraid of having any long descriptions of the beauty of scenery on the way to Cruces; through that curtain and wall of water, nothing was to be seen. It is like going behind the falling sheet of Niagara, I think, only *there* you are comparatively dry. What a procession of mermaids on horseback—I mean muleback—we were. The holes our poor mules plunged in and out of, are frightful to think of even at this distance! Mine came down into them several times, but extricated himself and regained his legs again. These were not the regular serious tumbles, but only little extra variations and pastimes, *pour passer le temps*.

It was partly a subterraneous ride, such caverns and chasms did we go groping among. Scrambling in and out of these places made us about twice as long as we should have been under other circumstances. Indeed, it pretty nearly doubled the distance; and by the time we arrived at Cruces, it had been dusk about half an hour. Our mules had proved excellent ones; and in taking leave of their civil master, we complimented him much on his animals.

---

## CHAPTER LV.

The Hotel at Cruces—A felonious Cat—The New Granadian Gentlemen—Progress toward Chagres—Lightning, Thunder, and Rain—Arrival at Chagres—The dead American—Quarrels between Americans and the Natives of Panama—Humboldt's Estimate of the Indians—Incredulity of Californian Emigrants—Melancholy Case of two returned Californians—A beautiful Sunset—Arrival at Jamaica—Kingston—Descent of General Lopez on Cuba—Strange Effect of it—Reverses of Jamaica Planters—The Glories of Nature—Creation's Praise, a Poem.

Cruces is overflowing with Americans. Look at that one with (as is often the case) a paroquet on his hat, a monkey on his right shoulder, and a squirrel on his left—surely not all the riches he is going to take back to "the States"—who can doubt his being a true Connecticut Yankee, one of those who have occasionally manufactured "*oak* pumpkin-seeds, so nateral that they actilly sprouted?" These gentry almost invariably ask us, as we pass, what *State* we are from.

The little American hotel at Cruces was quite full, so we passed the night in a native house. The master was very obliging, and so were his family and servants; but the poor old man had become half crazy since his wife's death, which had occurred a short time previously. He swung in his hammock in the state room of the cane lodge incessantly—not that that, however, is any proof of madness, or the white population of South America would all need strait waistcoats; but his speech and manners were incoherent and wandering, though he tried to be civil and hospitable.

The cabin consisted of two rooms, I believe; one, the front room, which served as parlor, dining-room, dormitory, and kitchen, and one which was given up to us. We all passed a pretty good night, though a disastrous adventure happened. We had a cold chicken, which with biscuits and chocolate, was to be the next morning's repast. Soon after we retired to rest a scuffling noise was heard; a plunge and a rattling of paper, in which the inestimable chicken was wrapped, and a confused scramble. Alas! the cat had entered, and carried off at one fell swoop our intended breakfast. Jeremiads were useless. We forgot our misfortunes in sleep, and in the morning got something to supply the place of our lost chicken, which make-shift, though not so good, yet answered pretty well.

No time was to be lost. At a very early hour in the morning I sent to engage a boat, and some owners of canoes, who I learned were very respectable people, came and agreed to take us to Chagres for what appeared to me a reasonable consideration. They promised to be at Chagres that evening, to put up a good awning, and to prepare their boat as soon as possible; I, therefore, engaged their canoe; and, as is customary in the Isthmus, paid down the money.

We waited a good while, and I thought it would be better to go down to the shore, and hurry them a little by personally superintending the preparations. I found them dawdling most industriously; but by entreaties and good words, and patient, though earnest exhortations to them to bestir themselves, I accomplished my object, and soon all was ready. The awning was a far superior one to the vile trap we had before in our Isthmus canoe, and all promised well.

Just before we started, two Granadian gentlemen came running down the bank with some light baggage, to hold a parley with the head-boatman, who presently afterward came to me, and beseechingly and deprecatingly begged me to allow him to set these caballeros down at a village he named, not far down the river: without my permission, of course, he said he told them it was impossible; but they had been disappointed, I think, of a boat they had tried to get, and were anxious to avail themselves of this favorable opportunity.

Would not this much retard us, by loading the canoe so much more, I wished to know? He assured me we should not be a moment longer on account of it, and it would particularly oblige them and the caballeros if I would give my consent. I granted their request, of course as a great indulgence, and off we started, under a broiling sun at first (but that was soon changed for deluges of rain); indeed, while I stood on the shore, superintending the construction of the awning, I thought my bonnet would almost have been burnt on my head by the intense rays of the sun.

The New Granadians soon arrived at their destination, paid the boatmen, and thanked me very gratefully and gracefully for the permission I had accorded; and lifting their light sombreros, and murmuring a profusion of acknowledgments, away they ran up the bank, and away we sped along the winding river.

Our boatmen hurried on in the highest good-humor, and apparently determined I should have no occasion to regret this simple act of complaisance. The rain was terrific.

I said our ride was a sort of subterranean grope—through such holes we burrowed along; and really our little voyage seemed a kind of submarine navigation, pleasingly diversified, however, by several awful storms of thunder and lightning; but, alas! by no coral bowers, no pearly grots—we saw, felt, heard, and were aware of nothing but rain! rain! rain! Umbrellas were a mockery and a snare. They seemed to act like positive cōnductors of the rain-lightnings! The very awning, which at first sheltered us, became a practical joke; water-proof cloaks, tarpaulin, &c., were mere straws for the drowning to catch at.

We felt unresuscitable by all the Humane Societies on earth. They may recover people half or three-quarters drowned; but the utterly melted away—how could they ever restore them to substance and life? Water-proof! why, it seemed to rain into the very brain! Nothing but watery images suggested themselves—Niagaras and whirlpools, twirled mops and twisting maelstroms,

Scotch mists and English pic-nics, doctors' strengthening draughts, St. Swithin and London milk (yclept sky-blue), soup at a French *auberge*, Whig measures, and every thing wishy-washy in the world, till the great globe itself appeared to be one vast moist sponge.

It is, I believe, a fact that a man chemically speaking, is forty-five pounds of carbon and nitrogen diffused through five and a half pailfuls of water, under ordinary circumstances; but travelers in the isthmus, during the rainy season, turn to twenty pailfuls of water, minus the nitrogen and carbon—at least so I should say from appearances. Such wretched, washed-out individuals no fancy can picture. Nature had need to work in fast colors indeed, when she exposes her living handiwork to such pitiless pourings.

On we went, feeling past all drowning, dazzled by the terrific flashes of lightning, and half deafened by the roaring peals of long-reverberating thunder, like a thousand boomings of artillery. Was it not all a mistake? Had we sunk to the bottom of the Pacific, which we were so lately careering over in smiling sunshine, and was a naval battle raging over our heads? Whether the glorious orchideous flowers were in bloom, of course, we knew not, or the other myriads of trailers and climbers. Whether there were as many decayed trees floating in the river as on our first expedition we knew not:—but if so our skillful boatmen avoided them cleverly.

The only serious stoppage we had was coming in collision with a large boat full of returning Americans; our canoe was all but overturned. The Americans and the boatmen called for us to sit perfectly still, which we did. Perhaps at that moment, we thought to be *more* drowned was almost an impracticability. People ought to traverse the Isthmus during the deluge in a diving-bell. I wonder Messrs. Rundell and Bridge's diving-apparatus was not kept for that purpose. Well! we went on as before. However, presently we began to entertain a sort of insane idea that we *might* be more drowned still, for we found the boat was frightfully full of water, and sinking fast. We shrieked to the boatmen, and pointed out the danger; they seized enormous calabashes, and began bailing out as fast as possible. We were so deep that the water of the river seemed all but pouring over the edge of the boat. After that, constant bailing was resorted to, and in due course of time we arrived safely at Chagres.

I had much difficulty in persuading the boatmen to go to what is called the American Town; they declared it was dangerous, as it was already dark. They seemed afraid of the boat upsetting at the mouth of the river. However, on reconnoitering as well as I could, I did not agree with them, and assured them it was quite "preciso" that we should go to the American hotel. After a long argument they consented, and in perfect safety, thank Heaven! we arrived, and found the master of the hotel standing on the bank with a lantern, looking out for boats, as the "Crescent City" was to start the next morning, and passengers were still arriving to go by her.

He promised to do what he possibly could for our accommodation, and finally we were quartered in a very comfortable room, which an American medical gentleman was obliging enough to vacate on our account. We felt almost bound to have the Chagres fever in return for such compassionate disinterestedness—but we really had not time. The room was very nicely furnished, and its four female occupants slept most soundly till it was time to rise and make preparations for going on board the steamer.

When we arrived the evening before, one of the first questions the master of the American hotel, and one or two other Americans, who came to ask for news, put to us was: "Did you see a dead body, tied to a raft, floating down the stream? I said we had observed nothing of the kind—indeed the rain prevented one from seeing any thing. He told me it was the dead body of an American, who had been stabbed in a quarrel with the natives, who refused to bury it, or allow it to be buried where the affray had taken place, but had fastened it to a slight raft, and sent it drifting down the stream. "It will be here at eight o'clock to-morrow morning, we expect," he added, coolly; "and you *must* have passed it on the road." I felt rather glad we had not seen the ghastly object.

Some Americans, who had lately arrived at Chagres, had brought the tidings, and they passed it, I believe, floating steadily down the river. These quarrels, unfortunately, too often occur; and as the Americans are generally armed to the teeth, with bowie-knives and revolvers, and the natives have always at hand the most formidable knives conceivable, about as long as a man's arm, with which they cut their dinner or their foes in pieces, lamentable results frequently take place.

Just before we returned to Panama from Peru, a kind of battle had occurred between the Californian emigrants and the Panamanians. After a little time the natives, who are intrepid to the last degree when once thoroughly aroused, cared no more for the revolvers than if they had been "cigaritos," they watched their opportunities, rushed boldly and rapidly up to their opponents (all with fire-arms in their hands), and plunged their long knives in their breasts. Four Americans, I was told, were left dead, and others grievously wounded. This was very melancholy, but I believe the Americans themselves say it was, in the first instance, the fault of their countrymen. They despise the Indians, and look on *all* colored people as "Niggers;" as they call all Europeans, save English and French, Dutch (the Swiss, Italians, Portuguese, Danes, are all named alike, with *one* exception only—and that is, the Dutch themselves! They call *them* Hollanders). I was mentioning a Dutchman once in the United States, and called him so: I was corrected—"No! *he's* a Hollander."

I think there is much that is interesting in the character of these Indians. Idle, dilatory, and careless, unquestionably they are; but they appear thoroughly hospitable, full of frank, generous susceptibilities and gratitude toward those who treat them with conciliatory gentleness and consideration. Contented and peaceful, but the bravest of the brave when their blood is once up: it would seem the elements of a right noble character are there. I say this from the few opportunities of observation that I have had, not from any prepossession for such "children of Nature" in general.

I think it is in Guiana that Humboldt mentions (in talking of the fancied primitive perfection of human nature) that it is customary, if a child is sickly, to kill it to avoid the trouble of taking care of it, and to prevent its being any impediment to hurried excursions and removals; also, he says of twins, one is regularly destroyed (as it is considered *infra dig.* to be the parents of twins—and something "like rats and opossums.") "Such," exclaims Humboldt, highly indignant, "such is that simplicity of manners, such that boasted happiness of mankind in the natural state. A man kills his son to escape a little ridicule, or to avoid traveling more slowly—in fact, to get rid of a trifling inconvenience."

We had accomplished our journey across the Isthmus in two days, and that in the *rainy season;* and we received many compliments from the Americans on the rapidity with which we had made the passage. V—— was charmed with her ride from Panama to Cruces—perhaps the only person that ever was or ever will be.

The Americans are so astonished at our not having been to California, they positively can not believe it, it appears to them such a pitch of preternatural stupidity. To some it was useless protesting we had not been, and had not intended to go. I convinced one at last; and he said he supposed then we really had not been; we *must* have got frightened, or "sick," at Panama, and that made us turn back. Another, who civilly refrained from contradicting, soon after asked: "And pray, ma'am, did you bring much gold dust? or perhaps you didn't stay long enough in California."

We found it pretty rough getting to the steamer, on the morning of our departure from Chagres, and with considerable difficulty got on board. A yellowish-brown long line of demarkation shows where the Chagres is lost in the clear waters of the Carribbean Sea. We had delightful cabins, with a sitting-room, sofas, tables, every thing charmingly commodious, and comfortable. The Captain, who was as obliging as possible, sent us word we should not start till night, as he had learned many other passengers were on their way down the river.

In the evening after it was dark, there was a sudden alarm. We heard a great scuffling, running, and shouting on deck; and presently, in extreme haste, a boat was lowered and pushed off. We remained watching in much anxiety, fearing that some boat, in attempting to reach the steamer through the heavy surf, had been upset. After some time we were much relieved to learn that no lives had been lost. A canoe coming out to the "Crescent City" had been in the greatest danger of being carried out to the open sea, from the boatmen having unfortunately broken their oars, and the boat thereby becoming unmanageable, and at the mercy of the waves. Had not their cries for assistance (which was so promptly rendered) been heard, they must doubtless have perished.

There were a number of returned Californians on board. From the glimpses I had of them, I should say none looked particularly happy or thoroughly satisfied with their expedition; one can not always judge from outward appearances. There were two very melancholy cases on board. An elderly gentleman, who had gone mad, after losing nearly all he possessed through some ill-fated speculation in California. His nephew was accompanying him home, and taking care of him as well as he could; but from exposure, I believe, and over severe labor in the mines, he was in the last stage of consumption, and reduced almost to a skeleton. In this miserable condition of hopeless suffering, he was doomed to have his last days embittered by the melancholy spectacle of his afflicted relative's malady, and forced to listen to his wild ravings and jabberings, and to have the wearying charge and responsibility of attending on him.

We had a capital stewardess on board the "Crescent City," and I hope it will not be thought I am speaking any treason against British maritime supremacy, when I say I think in general the American steamers have better stewardesses than the English! On board the "Georgia" we had a charming one too, a Welsh woman, rejoicing in the pretty name of Annie Morgan.

We had two very agreeable fellow-passengers on board the "Crescent City," in the shape of a Californian squirrel and a Chagres monkey; two amusing little personages they were. (They belonged to some gentleman just returned from El Dorado). The squirrel, tame as a kitten, was chiefly composed of two great black eyes and a splendid bushy tail. Jacko was the only pretty monkey I ever saw, and not at all mischievous. The little squirrel was extraordinarily fond of warmth: though the weather was almost insupportably hot, it would coil itself round into the very heart of shawls and cloaks (thrown on the sofas or camp-stools) whenever it wished to sleep.

We saw a most singularly beautiful sunset one evening on our passage hither. The sea became of a wonderfully rich color, neither exactly purple, nor lilac, nor crimson, nor violet, nor rose-color, but an extraordinary mixture of all these, a most regal and exquisite hue, which I think must most nearly resemble the Tyrian purple of old. I never saw such a color but once or twice before, I think, in my life. It continued some time without variation, and then softly died away in beautifully fine gradations.*

It was charming, watching this and other lovely effects of morning and evening light, reminding us of our delightful Pacific days and evenings (though this sea was not so smooth or grand). Looking on such fair sights, with the many sea-noises and sea-changes

* We afterward saw at Kingston, Jamaica, when driving one day with our truly kind friends Dr. and Mrs. Stewart, a far more magnificent sunset; one so awfully grand, that I feel it is hopeless to attempt to convey any impression of it. It was after a terrific thunder-storm. Behind the clouds, which were piled in mountainous masses one above the other (and still as if on and on, forever, showing a higher stratum of others between—height above height, glimpse beyond glimpse, vista behind vista), a thousand colored suns of glory seemed flashing, beaming through those wondrous and gorgeous transparencies. *All* hues were there, from the most vivid scarlet and burning crimson and purple, to the softest azure and palest green; every shade of gold and orange, and every tint conceivable and inconceivable.

around, what dreams, what visions, what phantasies visit the soothed yet awakened mind? what a world of wonders is around us! how full seems all of meaning, beauty, mystery, and eloquence —how full indeed! Ay, and if man could suddenly be endowed with a hundred additional senses beside his small allowance of five, he would doubtless find an endless multiplicity of objects around, fitted for their perception only and delight, that he has been unconscious of, as the blind of beauty and the deaf and dumb of music and sweet speech In this life mortals are prisoners in very narrow cells, which are furnished with very few chinks. But I must not even in this trifling degree, ramble from my purpose of keeping strictly to plain narrative and a matter-of-fact relation.

When we arrived at Jamaica I was much struck by its noble outline of mountains. The entrance to the harbor of Kingston is exceedingly fine. The Blue Mountains rise in some places to about eight thousand feet above the level of the sea, and run longitudinally through the island from east to west.

We have as yet seen hardly any thing of Jamaica. It seems to possess lovely and greatly-diversified scenery. The mountains so amphitheatrically encircling the fertile plains on which Kingston is built, we see from our windows. Our old African friend, the date palm, seems to flourish here. There is a fine one in one of the streets close to an hotel, called from it "Date-tree House;" but I have seen no dates. It is probably not the season. Mangoes (of which the best is a sort called commonly "Number Eleven") abound, and are very good. There seem to be various lovely acacias on all sides, calabash-trees, and the pretty lignum vitæ, with its countless heaps of little azure blossoms; the allspice, or Jamaica pepper-tree, and numbers of our Isthmus vegetable friends. But I must wait to see more before I give any description.

When we first landed, I was sorry to learn from the courteous agent of the American Steam Company here, that the Bishop has lately left the island, and that his daughter is very ill.

They seem to have delicious breezes almost constantly blowing here, but lately it has been very dry. Last evening it rained heavily, and as about a hundred windows were open in all directions, in rushed a number of colored damsels in turbans, armed with divers mops, and contrivances of the kind, to wipe up purling rivulets that were meandering prettily about the floor (for the windows had defied our efforts to close them; and, besides, it was suffocatingly hot) and they fastened down some of the windows, but the rain trickled abundantly through, notwithstanding. To our astonishment (who felt something like a party of antediluvians running away from the pursuing Flood; or I should say perhaps, like a set of feminine Noahs, or Noah's doves, or any other inhabitants of the ark, gladly escaping to the dry land), they burst out into joyful exclamations about the rain, congratulating themselves and *us* (on rain!) and the goats and pigs, and ducks, too, methinks, as they looked out of the windows—and snuffed it up as something rare and precious.

One very black, smiling maiden, showing her glittering teeth from ear to ear, could not rejoice enough—or wish us joy enough of this rain (stupendous insult!)—working away very hard all the time to wipe away the little brooks and streamlets. "Berry nice, oh, berry, dis *good* rain." Now that is a disinterested philanthropic, patriotic mortal. The more she had to labor, the more she liked it, for it was for the good of her country and her fellow-mortals! She rubbed and scrubbed, and laughed and smiled, and chuckled and crowed and quacked and chattered, all glee and good-humor, a perfect duck of a woman in two senses. Really the Isthmus St. Swithin had better come here to be made much of.

I have received a most courteous and hospitable invitation from Sir Charles Grey, to remain at the King's House, during my stay in Jamaica. We shall avail ourselves of his kindness, and go there to-morrow.

Kingston does not at all give me the idea of an unwholesome climate. I hear the cholera is committing frightful ravages at the Havana. Here, they say, they are not alarmed at all, as it has never been here, though it has before been in Cuba. I advise them not to be too sure yet. The cholera is said never to have passed the Equator, but this year it has crept very near to it, and may have crossed the line by this time. The last we heard of it, it was near Bogota, and creeping onward, it was said.

I found a very interesting letter here from Havana, giving me the particulars of the late American invasion of the island of Cuba, One singular fact is mentioned in it. I do not know that it has been remarked upon in any of the newspapers, so I repeat it. I am assured that it is quite correct. As soon as the alarm was given in Havana of the landing of General Lopez and his followers, the cholera, which had been raging there with terrible violence, stopped as if by magic. The streets had been crowded with funerals; not one was to be seen. A counter-panic chased away this dreadful visitor for a short space of time. After a few days, when all the alarm had entirely subsided, and no further apprehensions were entertained—when, in short, the island and the city returned to their propriety, the cholera again resumed its interrupted sway. It might have been only a coincidence, but I think there is but little if any doubt that the interregnum was occasioned by that mental counter-irritation: the mind and imagination have so much to do in predisposing persons to take such disorders.

There are numerous coolies here, male and female. These Hindoos are very striking and picturesque-looking people.

Kingston looks as if it ought to be a magnificent place, and had once been so, but has the appearance of being not only dilapidated but depopulated and deserted. The chief streets are still very handsome, with villa-like houses. veranda'd and terraced, running back from the road, and with gateways and gardens generally. The people who knew Kingston formerly mourn over it, and say: "In past times, before our ruin, this main street was the gayest of the gay, the busiest of the busy: an incessant roll of carriages and sugar-laden carts resounded through it."

The last terrible blow at the prosperity of Jamaica was the vile Slave-grown Sugar Bill, which combined in so remarkable a degree the iniquitous with the ridiculous. Poor Jamaica! how deeply she has suffered! I hear that many once rich planters have gone to spend their last days in obscure corners, to starve unknown, and die incognito. Alas! with perhaps a curse on their lips for the unnatural mother-country, who has cut away the last prop and support from under them. If the reader wishes to know where the deepest hatred can be felt against England, let him go to her own ill-used colonies. I sincerely hope something may yet be done for this lovely, unhappy island. How we *must* misgovern—how we must have a very genius for perverting Fortune's best gifts, and for mismanaging those splendid possessions we acquire with so much labor and glory, to injure and destroy (as far as we can), with so much shame. When shall we, for their sake and our own, change our most detestable policy, or rather impolicy? But I will try and turn to the beauties of nature, and not the follies of man, who so often defaces her noblest loveliness.

. . . . . . . . . . . . . . . . . . . . . .

Ever glorious is Nature! What wonders have we lately beheld of her lavish luxury of profusion, her inexhaustible treasury of glories and enchantments, her array of stately triumphs! What gratitude should glow in the heart and spirit of man when looking on all the consummate works of Heaven, scattered with such gracious liberality at his feet, to bless his eyes, to cheer his thoughts, to elevate his mind, and array his path to immortality with that glory which seems worthy of an immortal, making the world like the vestibule of heaven for those whose thoughts draw beauty from beauty, and add majesty to majesty.

But how often, when the mighty mother most appealingly calls on him does he turn away. Mountains and forests, lakes, savannas, clouds, flowers, stars, valleys, lightnings, seas—all mirror one great truth, all breathe one eternal hymn! Nature is a perpetual oratorio!

## CREATION'S PRAISE.

I.

Immemorial gray mountains! up-towering and free,
Like the hierarchs of Nature still seem they to be;
Ah! no Atlases bearing one Earth's pretty weight,
All the Firmament's pride seem *their* burden and freight.

II.

All its Earths! all its Heav'ns! its vast galaxied field,
Where crowned splendors on splendors shine thronged and revealed.
Soar aloft, kingly mountains! ay, fearless they soar,
And sustaining that glory's dread burden, adore!

III.

Yea, they praise Thee, O Lord of those Firmaments!—King
Of the fair worlds around, like fresh fountains that spring;
Their pure crests seem to praise Thee, and each hallowed air,
That awakes, like a breath fresh from Paradise, there.

IV.

Ocean! glassing those heavens, and thus bringing them down
As to blend with our world—nearer Glory and Crown!
Dost *thou* lift not thy thousand-toned voice evermore,
In strong orisons, Ocean! from shore pealed to shore!

V.

Not a murmur, a moan, but where heaven-music dwells,
Haunting *thee*, as thy memory, thine own rainbow'd shells;
Not a wave but hath mirrored the deep-glancing scene,
Where the shadows of Hosts of Immortals have been!

VI.

And ye, Stars! do ye breathe not in light and in fire—
(As though each were some angel-bard's far-beaming lyre),
That bright order, and beauty, and harmony move,
For aye, in the steps of the Source of all Love.

VII.

And *thou* MAN! dost *thou* praise Him by acts and by words?
Dost thou thrill to thy being's own innermost chords?
Doth thy soul to those long "Hallelujahs" reply,
Rolled in thunder and flame through all Earth and all Sky?

VIII.

Man! too oft while great Nature seems proffering her shrine
For the pomp of full spirit-oblations divine;
From her voice, and thine own holiest happiness here,
Thou turn'st back with weak scorn, self-unjust and severe.

IX.

While the darkly-magnificent heavens of the night—
While the morning star, heralding joyaunce and light—
While the storms—while the seas—while the deserts and plains,
Proclaim with eternal Hosannas, "He reigns!"

X.

The One—silent, deaf, senseless, 'midst things He hath made,
Still seems Man! who like monarch of all He arrayed,
O'er whose head He stretched roofs, hung with suns and with flame,
At whose feet *such* a world, his heart's homage to claim!

XI.

Shall the universe one glorious unison be,
All uniting in rapture of worship, save *thee?*
Shall far worlds—severed spaces—strange elements join
In one deep diapason of homage divine?

XII.

And shalt *thou* dwell apart, and thy worship retain,
Perchance for those Works that His voice did ordain,
Perchance for thyself, and the pomps, shows, and joys
Of the swift, arrowy life which a moment destroys.

XIII.

For those Works that are Worships themselves! that point still
Upward—heavenward—the children of His mighty will!
Works that cease not by day and by night to proclaim,
E'en out-thundering all thunder, His praise and His Name!

XIV.

And thyself! while each power that thou vauntest is given
Direct from the o'erflowing rich treasuries of heaven,
And thy fast-fleeting life is but lent thee to lead
To the life everlasting—the true life, indeed!

XV.

Immemorial proud mountains! stoop lower your crest,
Be ashamed for the Earth and its vile human guest!
Billowy Ocean! be silent! roll onward in peace!
Bid your stormy, august "Hallelujahs" to cease!

XVI.

Stoop! thou Mountain! but *not* for the weight or the might
Of the far-stretching firmaments—height piled on height!
Stoop! since ev'n, from earth's floor to heaven's blue glistering roof,
Thou still hurl'st 'gainst mankind thine all-righteous reproof!

XVII.

Hush! thou Ocean! but not that the songs of the spheres—
That the strains of the blest pierce through time's rushing years!
Hush! since each lightest murmur of homage from thee
Seems reproach to thy scornful clay-rulers to be.

XVIII.

Be the contrast less striking—th' upbraidings less stern!—
Pale—ye great crowning Fires of the Firmaments! burn,
Pale and faint!—so be all things less grandly sublime—
Thus *thy* consciousness, Nature, shall crown not *our* crime!

XIX.

Stars!—ye heavens in the heavens!—all of joy, love, and light—
Hide your sovereign, sublime tribulations from sight!
Dare we gaze on your spheres, stirred all over with love,
While ourselves and our brethren thus gracelessly move?

XX.

Thunder, Whirlwind, and Earthquake! ye too—lords of doom!—
Shout the march of His might, midst your grandeur of gloom!
*Ye* too lift up your voices of terror to cry,
"Hail to Him who above all the highest is high!"

XXI.

Old war-chariots of Storm and the Whirlwinds! delay!—
Or bear up thousand hopes of man's soul on your way.
Not a wind on its course of rejoicing but sings
Of Immortal, Transcendent, Omnipotent things!

XXII.

And on trifles and toys still we wander intent,
And few tones with those thousand high tones have we blent!
And we hoard in our hearts, ashy treasures and things,
That drag earthward our souls from the joy of their wings.

XXIII.

Mighty Forests! what strength of devotion is there!
Lo! their countless leaves thrill as with passionate prayer,
While the shadows, the silence, the depths are o'erspread,
With an hundred Great Presences, sacred and dread.

XXIV.

Peace—let *us* only listen, and fling earth's dull cares,
Away from our minds till *they* tremble to prayers;
And the far-sounding chorus shall evermore ring,
Raised in honor profound of Their King, and Our King!

XXV.

Joy—Creation's grand hymn hath ne'er ceased to be sung,
'Tis resounded—repeated—no harp is unstrung;
In yon hollow-voiced thunder it lives and it rolls;
Joy!—if *we* will but listen, 'twill peal to our souls.

XXVI.

Morning hymn of creation! each cadence and word
By the quick ear of Faith is still thrillingly heard,
And new Birth-hymns of later Creations beside,
That we dream not and glimpse not—swell the outpouring tide.

XXVII.

Hark! 'tis "Holy!" still "Holy!" and "Holy!" again;
Worlds commence—worlds take up the Majestical Strain—
Worlds commence—worlds continue the Wonderful Hymn,
Till the skies and their orbs are all perished and dim!

XXVIII.

The Great Truth that shone out with the rays of young light,
It shines out still as clear, with as searching a might;
And can *we* e'er be blind to its splendors intense?
When if we will but look, oh! 'twill blaze to our sense.

XXIX.

Watch the eagle and lark on their proud sunward flight,
Their blue pathways all strewn o'er with gold-bloom and light;
Think ye *they* bear the freight of *their own* joy alone?
With earth's deep soul of prayer and of praise they have flown!

XXX.

From her hills—from her rocks—from her hoarse-sounding woods,
From her free trackless wilds, and her loud torrent-floods;
Fervent breathings of strong adoration are borne,
To ruffle the orient pavilions of morn!

XXXI.

Soaring messengers! hurrying on high to convey
Quick jubilant hints to the blue realms of Day,
Oh! how dead are their hearts who no fair greetings send,
With the punctual, plumed courier's high service to blend.

XXXII.

And not only the Morn and the Noon seem to bear,
A rich, deep weight of worship that halloweth the air;
But the dusk, regal Night, in her mystical sway,
A proud rivalry boasteth and challengeth Day.

XXXIII.

Yea! dark, gorgeous, magnificent heavens of Old Night,
Where Time's self seems Eternity, shown us aright;
*All* thy Suns have their Uriels, and breathe far around
Lofty tidings for souls not in death-trance profound.

XXXIV.

To the Sabaoth of Systems in awful array,
Beleaguering our dull sense—enlightning our way;
Shall Indifference dare still her base weapons oppose,
And confront the confederate Creations as foes?

XXXV.

Glorious Nature! too oft man deals death on his soul—
Thought and mind—wrenched from *thy* solemn, life-full control;
With dim ashes strewn o'er them—vile taints, chains and tears,
Through that dark vale of shadows, where glide our vain years.

XXXVI.

From thy shrine, mightiest mother, they turn, and forsake
All thy haunts—all thy hoards—*thy* great compact they break.
Hollow sepulchres then of themselves e'en they seem—
Ah! no temple of Thee, and no palace of Dream!

XXXVII.

Then high visions forsake them, and splendors of thought,
With immortal delights and rich promises fraught;
Queen!—thy kingdoms, illustrious with treasure!—no more
Then imparadise life with their fresh, boundless store.

XXXVIII.

The Immemorial Gray Mountains are dust in their sight,
And discrowned Constellations seem emptied of light;
Dead lies Ocean!—for *them* Heaven is furled as a scroll,
Nature!—know thine Unbuilder!—a world-stricken Soul!

XXXIX.

Where should be thy throne is thy sepulchre cold,
And not there spread thy banners and pageants unrolled
But a deep funeral darkness, or vapory display,
Of the gauds of a moment—the pomps of a day!

XL.

And the Mountains still point to the Firmaments far—
And those Firmaments tremble with star linked to star;
And still Deep cries to Deep, and the Clouds and the Storms,
All repeat awful tidings—reflect mystic forms.

XLI.

And ten thousand great schemes and vast systems around
In one broad Act of Homage incessant, are bound;
"Dust to dust!" ever darkens our brief earthly day—
Worlds on Worlds ever beckon us upward—away!

XLII.

Wake! O Man! Populations and nations, awake!
Your glad part in the unbounded, dread chorus to take;
They have *ages* to breathe Adoration's high strain—
Ye have *hours*—and thus dare ye unquickened remain?

XLIII.

Join the hymn! swell the unbounded, undying acclaim:
Glory, honor, and praise to the One glorious Name:
While all majesties, powers, thrones, existences tend
To Truth's bright consummation—still world without end.

XLIV.

While on universe—universe heaped and amassed,
Burst and bound to proud being and birth, free and fast—
That yet all, the grand anthem of all, thus may join,
And exalt their great Maker's dread honors divine!

XLV.

Ay! on universe—universe gathered and heaped
To their life of stupendous transcendence have leaped;
Till—(while each lauds His glory, with powers more supreme),
Some New Chaos of very Creations they seem.

XLVI.

Even a Chaos of very Creations!—so blent
In unknown complications, through th' endless extent.
Lord of Lords! Oh! thou God of all Gods! they can be
But the veriest faint shade of a shadow of Thee!

XLVII.

Ah! as far as our frail, fettered senses allow,
Let us gaze on the scenes of their wonders e'en now,
Where the heavens burn with stars—maze thick crowded on maze,
Till All Space to *One Sun* seems to brighten and blaze.

XLVIII.

Oratorio of Nature! Oh, strike our dull ears!
With our souls let us list to your anthems, ye spheres;
Let your sun-blazoned oriflammes lead us on—on,
Till Earth's conflict is o'er, and Heaven's victory is won!

XLIX.

Is't enough? Oh, if not, look, thou mortal, within,
Through those deep mists of doubt—through the dark clouds of sin;
And behold the vast scene of *thine own* awful soul,
To the ken of a hushed contemplation unroll!

THE END.

## The Island World of the Pacific:

Being the Personal Narrative and Results of Travel through the Sandwich or Hawaiian Islands and other parts of Polynesia. By Rev. H. T. CHEEVER. Engravings. 12mo, Muslin, $1 00.

## The Whale and his Captors;

Or, the Whaleman's Adventures and the Whale's Biography, as gathered on the Homeward Cruise of the "Commodore Preble." By Rev. H. T. CHEEVER. Engravings. 16mo, Muslin, 60 cents.

## Five Years of a Hunter's Life in the Far Interior of South Africa.

With Notices of the Native Tribes, and Anecdotes of the Chase of the Lion, Elephant, Hippopotamus, Giraffe, Rhinoceros, &c. By R. GORDON CUMMING, Esq. With Illustrations. 2 vols. 12mo, Muslin, $1 75.

## The Pillars of Hercules;

Or, a Narrative of Travels in Spain and Morocco in 1848. By DAVID URQUHART, M.P. 2 vols. 12mo, Paper, $1 40; Muslin, $1 70.

## Glimpses of Spain;

Or, Notes of an Unfinished Tour in 1847. By S. T. WALLIS, Esq. 12mo, Paper, 75 cents; Muslin, $1 00.

## Sketches of Minnesota,

The New England of the West. With Incidents of Travel in that Territory during the Summer of 1848. By E. S. SEYMOUR. 12mo, Paper, 50 cents; Muslin, 75 cents.

## Life in the Far West.

By GEORGE FREDERICK RUXTON. 12mo, Paper, 37½ cents; Muslin, 60 cents.

## Adventures in Mexico and Rocky Mountains.

By G. F. RUXTON. 12mo, Paper, 50 cents; Muslin, 60 cents.

## Fresh Gleanings;

Or, a New Sheaf from the Old Fields of Continental Europe. By IK. MARVEL. 12mo, Paper, $1 00; Muslin, $1 25.

## A Second Visit to the United States.

By Sir CHARLES LYELL, F.R.S. 2 vols. 12mo, Paper, $1 20, Muslin, $1 50.

## Oregon and California in 1848.

With an Appendix, including recent and authentic Information on the Subject of the Gold Mines of California, and other valuable matter of Interest to the Emigrant. By Judge THORNTON. With Illustrations and a Map. 2 vols. 12mo, Muslin, $1 75.

## The Little Savage.

Being the History of a Boy left alone on an uninhabited Island. By Captain MARRYAT, R.N. 12mo, Paper, 37½ cents; Muslin, 45 cents.

## White-Jacket;

Or, the World in a Man-of-War. By HERMAN MELVILLE, Esq. 12mo, Paper, $1 00; Muslin, $1 25.

## Redburn:

His First Voyage. Being the Reminiscences of the Son-of-a-Gentleman in the Merchant Service. By HERMAN MELVILLE, Esq. 12mo, Paper, 75 cents; Muslin, $1 00.

## Mardi: and a Voyage Thither.

By HERMAN MELVILLE, Esq. 2 vols. 12mo, Paper, $1 50; Muslin, $1 75.

## Omoo;

Or, a Narrative of Adventures in the South Seas. By HERMAN MELVILLE, Esq. 12mo, Paper, $1 00; Muslin, $1 25.

## Typee:

A Peep at Polynesian Life, during a Four Months' Residence in the Marquesas. By HERMAN MELVILLE, Esq. The revised Edition, with a Sequel 12mo, Paper, 75 cents; Muslin, 87½ cents.

## Loiterings in Europe;

Or, Sketches of Travel in France, Belgium, Switzerland, Italy, Austria, Prussia, Great Britain, and Ireland. With an Appendix, containing Observations on European Charities and Medical Institutions. By J. W. CORSON, M.D. 12mo, Paper, 75 cents; Muslin, $1 00.

## Narrative of the Texan Santa Fé Expedition.

Comprising a Description of a Tour through Texas, and across the great Southwestern Prairies, the Camanche and Caygua Hunting-grounds, &c. By G. W. KENDALL, Esq. With a Map and Illustrations. 2 vols. 8vo, Muslin, $2 50.

## Travels in Egypt, Arabia Petræa, and the Holy

Land. By JOHN L. STEPHENS, Esq. Engravings. 2 vols. 12mo, Muslin, $1 75.

## Travels in Greece, Turkey, Russia, and Poland.

By JOHN L. STEPHENS, Esq. Engravings. 2 vols. 12mo, Muslin, $1 75.

## Incidents of Travel in Yucatan.

By JOHN L. STEPHENS, Esq. 120 Engravings, from Drawings by F. CATHERWOOD, Esq. 2 vols. 8vo, Muslin, $5 00.

## Travels in Central America, Chiapas, and Yuca-

tan. By JOHN L. STEPHENS, Esq. With a Map and 88 Engravings. 2 vols. 8vo, Muslin, $5 00.

## Consular Cities of China.

A Narrative of an Exploratory Visit to each of the Consular Cities of China, and to the Islands of Hong Kong and Chusan, in behalf of the Church Missionary Society, in the Years 1844–1846 By Rev. G. SMITH. 12mo, Paper, $1 00; Muslin, $1 25.

## Shores of the Mediterranean.

With Sketches of Travel in the East. By F. SCHROEDER. Engravings. 2 vols. 12mo, Muslin, $1 75.

## Altowan;

Or, Life and Adventure in the Rocky Mountains. By an Amateur Traveler. Edited by JAMES WATSON WEBB, Esq. 2 vols. 12mo, Muslin, $1 25.

## A Summer in Scotland.

By JACOB ABBOTT. With Engravings. 12mo, Muslin, $1 00.

## Etchings of a Whaling Cruise,

With Notes of a Sojourn on the Island of Zanzibar. To which is appended a brief History of the Whale Fishery, its past and present Condition. By J. ROSS BROWNE. Illustrated by numerous Engravings on Steel and Wood. 8vo, Muslin, $2 00.

## Old Hicks the Guide;

Or, Adventures in the Camanche Country in Search of a Gold Mine. By C. W. WEBBER. 12mo, Muslin, $1 00.

## Travels in the Holy Land.

Travels in Egypt, Arabia Petræa, and the Holy Land. By Rev. Dr. OLIN. 12 Engravings. 2 vols. 8vo, Muslin, $2 50.

## Glory and Shame of England.

By C. EDWARDS LESTER. 2 vols. 12mo, Muslin, $1 50.

## A Year in Spain.

By Capt. ALEX. S. MACKENZIE. Engravings. 3 vols. 12mo, Paper, $1 05; Muslin, $1 50.

## Spain Revisited.

By Capt. ALEX. S. MACKENZIE. Engravings. 2 vols. 12mo, Paper, 70 cents; Muslin, $1 00.

## Letters from Abroad to Kindred at Home.

By Miss C. M. SEDGWICK. 2 vols. 12mo, Muslin, $1 90.

## Scenes, Incidents, and Adventures in the Pacific Ocean;

or, the Islands of the Australasian Sea, during the Cruise of the Clipper Margaret Oakley, under Captain Benjamin Morrell. By THOMAS JEFFERSON JACOBS. With numerous Engravings. 12mo, Muslin, $1 25.

## Travels in Europe and the East.

By VALENTINE MOTT, M.D. 8vo, Muslin, $1 90.

## Lewis and Clarke's Travels beyond the Rocky Mountains.

Account of the Expedition of Lewis and Clarke across the Rocky Mountains, and to the Mouth of the Columbia River. Prepared from the Original Edition, with an Introduction and Notes, containing Notices of Recent Travelers, and a View of the present condition of Oregon Territory, by ARCHIBALD M'VICKAR. Engravings. 2 vols. 18mo, Muslin, 90 cents.

# Harper's Library of Select Novels, *continued.*

No.

73. THE ELVES, ETC. By Carlyle. 25 cts.

74, 75. THE STEP-MOTHER. By G. P. R. James, Esq. 50 cents.

76. JESSIE'S FLIRTATIONS. 25 cents.

77. CHEVALIER D'HARMENTAL; or, Love and Conspiracy. By Sue. 25 cents.

78. PEERS AND PARVENUS. By Mrs. Gore. 25 cents.

79. THE COMMANDER OF MALTA. By Sue. 25 cents.

80. THE FEMALE MINISTER. 12½ cents.

81 EMILIA WYNDHAM. By Mrs. Marsh. 25 cents.

82. THE BUSH RANGER. By Charles Rowcroft, Esq. 25 cents.

83. THE CHRONICLES OF CLOVERNOOK. By Douglas Jerrold. 12½ cents.

84. THE CONFESSIONS OF A PRETTY WOMAN. By Miss Pardoe. 25 cents.

85. LIVONIAN TALES. 12½ cents.

86. CAPTAIN O'SULLIVAN. By William H. Maxwell. 25 cents.

87. FATHER DARCY. By Mrs. Marsh. 25 cents.

88. LEONTINE. By Mrs. Maberly. 25 cents.

89. HEIDELBERG. By James. 25 cents.

90. LUCRETIA. By Bulwer. 25 cents.

91. BEAUCHAMP. By James. 25 cents.

92, 94. FORTESCUE. By Knowles. 50 cents.

93. DANIEL DENNISON, &c. By Mrs. Hofland. 25 cents.

95. CINQ-MARS. By De Vigny 25 cents.

96. WOMAN'S TRIALS. By Mrs. S. C. Hall. 25 cents.

97. THE CASTLE OF EHRENSTEIN. By G. P. R. James, Esq. 25 cents.

98. MARRIAGE. By Miss S. Ferrier. 25 cents.

99, 100. THE INHERITANCE. By Miss S. Ferrier. 50 cents.

101. RUSSELL. By G. P. R. James. 25 cents.

102. A SIMPLE STORY. By Mrs. Inchbald. 25 cents.

103. NORMAN'S BRIDGE. By Mrs. Marsh. 25 cents.

104. ALAMANCE. 25 cents.

105. MARGARET GRAHAM. By G. P. R. James, Esq. 6¼ cents.

106. THE WAYSIDE CROSS. By E. H. Milman. 12½ cents.

107. THE CONVICT. By James. 25 cents.

108. MIDSUMMER EVE By Mrs. S. C. Hall. 25 cents.

109. JANE EYRE. By Currer Bell. 25 cents.

110. THE LAST OF THE FAIRIES. By G. P. R. James, Esq. 12½ cents.

111. SIR THEODORE BROUGHTON. By G. P. R. James, Esq. 25 cents.

112. SELF-CONTROL. By Mary Brunton. 25 cents.

113, 114. HAROLD. By Bulwer. 50 cents.

115. BROTHERS AND SISTERS. By Miss Fredrika Bremer. 25 cents.

116. GOWRIE. By G. P. R. James. 25 cents.

117. A WHIM AND ITS CONSEQUENCES. By G. P. R. James, Esq. 25 cents.

No.

118. THREE SISTERS AND THREE FORTUNES. By G. H. Lewes, Esq. 25 cents.

119. THE DISCIPLINE OF LIFE. 25 cents.

120. THIRTY YEARS SINCE. By G. P. R. James, Esq. 25 cents.

121. MARY BARTON. By Mrs. Gaskell. 25 cts.

122. THE GREAT HOGGARTY DIAMOND By W. M. Thackeray, Esq. 25 cents.

123. THE FORGERY. By James. 25 cents.

124. THE MIDNIGHT SUN. By Miss Fredrika Bremer. 12½ cents.

125, 126. THE CAXTONS. By Sir Edward Bulwer Lytton. 37½ cents.

127. MORDAUNT HALL. By Mrs. Marsh. 25 cents.

128. MY UNCLE THE CURATE. 25 cents.

129. THE WOODMAN. By James. 25 cents

130. RETRIBUTION. By Mrs. Emma D. E. Nevitt Southworth. 25 cents.

131. SIDONIA THE SORCERESS. By William Meinhold. 50 cents.

132. SHIRLEY. By Currer Bell. 37½ cents.

133. THE OGILVIES. 25 cents.

134. CONSTANCE LYNDSAY; or, the Progress of Error. By C. G. H. 25 cents.

135. SIR EDWARD GRAHAM; or, Railway Speculators. By Miss C. Sinclair. 37½ cents.

136. HANDS NOT HEARTS. By Miss Janet W. Wilkinson. 25 cents.

137. THE WILMINGTONS. By Mrs. Marsh. 25 cents.

138. NED ALLEN. By D. Hannay. 25 cents.

139. NIGHT AND MORNING. By Sir Edward Bulwer Lytton. 25 cents.

140. THE MAID OF ORLEANS. By the Author of "Whitefriars." 37½ cents.

141. ANTONINA; or, the Fall of Rome. By W. Wilkie Collins, Esq. 37½ cents.

142. ZANONI. By Bulwer. 25 cents.

143. REGINALD HASTINGS. By Eliot Warburton, Esq. 25 cents.

144. PRIDE AND IRRESOLUTION: a new Series of the Discipline of Life. 25 cents.

145. THE OLD OAK CHEST. By G. P. R. James, Esq. 37½ cents.

146. JULIA HOWARD. By Mrs. Bell Martin. 25 cents.

147. ADELAIDE LINDSAY. Edited by Mrs. Marsh. 25 cents.

148. PETTICOAT GOVERNMENT. By Mrs. Trollope. 25 cents.

149. THE LUTTRELLS. By F. Williams, Esq. 25 cents.

150. SINGLETON FONTENOY, R.N. By James Hannay. 25 cents.

151. OLIVE. By the Author of "The Ogilvies." 25 cents.

152. HENRY SMEATON. By G. P. R. James Esq. 50 cents.

153. TIME, THE AVENGER. By Mrs. Marsh. 25 cents.

154. THE COMMISSIONER. By G. P. R James, Esq. 50 cents.

155. THE WIFE'S SISTER. By Mrs. Hubback. 25 cents.

156. THE GOLD-WORSHIPERS; or, The Days we Live in. 25 cents.

## Mount Hope;

Or, Philip, King of the Wampanoags. An Historical Romance. By G. H. HOLLISTER. 12mo, Paper, 62½ cents; Muslin, 75 cents

## The Heir of Wast-Wayland.

A Tale. By MARY HOWITT. 12mo, Muslin.

## The Moorland Cottage.

By the Author of "Mary Barton." 12mo, Paper, 25 cents; Muslin, 37½ cents.

## Yeast:

A Problem. By the Author of "Alton Locke." 12mo, Muslin.

## Alton Locke,

Tailor and Poet. An Autobiography. 12mo, Muslin, 75 cents.

## Jane Bouverie;

Or, Prosperity and Adversity. By CATHERINE SINCLAIR. 12mo, Paper, 50 cents; Muslin, 62½ cents.

## Eastbury.

A Tale. By ANNA HARRIET DRURY. 12mo, Muslin.

## Maurice Tiernay,

The Soldier of Fortune. By CHARLES LEVER. 8vo, Paper.

## Roland Cashel.

By CHARLES LEVER. With Illustrations by Phiz. 8vo, Paper 75 cents; Muslin, $1 00.

## Standish the Puritan;

A Tale of the American Revolution. By ELDRED GRAYSON, Esq. 12mo, Paper, 75 cents; Muslin, $1 00.

## The Shoulder-Knot:

Or, Sketches of the Three-fold Life of Man. A Story of the 17th Century. By Rev. B. F. TEFFT. 12mo, Paper, 60 cents; Muslin, 75 cents.

## Lavengro:

The Gipsy—the Scholar—the Priest. By GEORGE BORROW. 8vo, Paper, 25 cents.

## Home Influence.

A Tale for Mothers and Daughters. By GRACE AGUILAR. A revised Edition, with a Memoir of the Author. 12mo, Paper, 75 cents; Muslin, $1 00.

## The Mother's Recompense.

A Sequel to "Home Influence." By GRACE AGUILAR. 8vo, Paper, 25 cents.

## Godfrey Malvern;

Or, the Life of an Author. By THOMAS MILLER. With numerous Illustrations. 8vo, Paper.

## Vanity Fair.

A Novel without a Hero. By W. M. THACKERAY. 8vo, Paper, $1 00; Muslin, $1 25.

## The History of Pendennis:

His Fortunes and Misfortunes, his Friends and his greatest Enemy. By W. M. THACKERAY. With numerous Illustrations. 2 vols. 8vo, Muslin, $2 00

## Raphael;

Or, Pages from the Book of Life at Twenty. By ALPHONSE DE LAMARTINE. 12mo, Paper, 25 cents.

## Memoirs of my Youth.

By ALPHONSE DE LAMARTINE. 8vo, Paper, 25 cents.

## Additional Memoirs of my Youth.

By ALPHONSE DE LAMARTINE. 8vo, Paper, 12½ cents.

## Genevieve;

Or, the History of a Servant Girl. Translated from the French of A. DE LAMARTINE, by A. R. SCOBLE. 8vo, Paper, 12½ cents.

## Jane Eyre:

An Autobiography. Edited by CURRER BELL. Library Edition, 12mo, Muslin, 90 cents

## Shirley.

A Tale. By the Author of "Jane Eyre." Library Edition, 12mo, Muslin, 90 cents.

## The Children of the New Forest.

A Novel. By Captain MARRYATT, R.N. 12mo, Paper, 37½ cents; Muslin, 45 cents.

## The Bachelor of the Albany.

A Novel. By the Author of the "Falcon Family." 12mo, Paper, 37½ cents; Muslin, 45 cents.

## Now and Then.

A Tale. By Dr. WARREN. 12mo, Paper, 50 cents; Muslin, 60 cents.

## Mary Grover;

Or, the Trusting Wife. A Domestic Temperance Tale. By CHARLES BURDETT. 12mo, Paper, 30 cents; Muslin, 40 cents.

## Wuthering Heights.

A Novel. 12mo, Paper, 50 cents; Muslin, 75 cents.

## The Tenant of Wildfell Hall.

A Novel. 12mo, Paper, 50 cents; Muslin, 75 cents.

## The Peasant and his Landlord.

A Novel. By the Baroness KNORRING. Translated by MARY HOWITT. 12mo, Paper, 50 cents; Muslin, 75 cents.

## Agnes Morris;

Or, the Heroine of Domestic Life. 12mo, Paper, 25 cents.

## Angela.

By Mrs. MARSH. 12mo, Paper, 75 cents; Muslin, 90 cents.

## Lettice Arnold.

By Mrs. MARSH. 8vo, Paper, 10 cents.

## Edward Vernon:

My Cousin's Story. By EDMUND CHILDE. 12mo, Paper, 50 cents; Muslin, 75 cents.

## The Image of his Father.

A Tale of a Young Monkey. By HENRY MAYHEW. With Illustrations. 12mo, Paper, 50 cents; Muslin, 75 cents.

## Model Men, Women, and Children.

By the Brothers MAYHEW. With Illustrations. 18mo, Paper, 50 cents; Muslin, 62½ cents.

## The Fear of the World;

Or, Living for Appearances. By the Brothers MAYHEW. With Illustrations. 8vo, Paper, 25 cents.

## The Green Hand.

A "Short" Yarn. 8vo, Paper, 25 cents.

## The Professor's Lady.

Translated from the German of Berthold Auerbach, by MARY HOWITT. With numerous Engravings. 8vo, Paper, 18¾ cents.

## Adelaide Lindsay.

A Novel. Edited by Mrs. MARSH. 8vo, Paper, 25 cents.

## An Easter Offering.

By FREDRIKA BREMER. Translated from the Unpublished Swedish Manuscript, by MARY HOWITT. Contents: The Light House, Life in the North. 8vo, Paper, 6¼ cents.

## Miss Fredrika Bremer's Novels.

Comprising The Neighbors; The Home; The President's Daughters; Nina; New Sketches of Every-day Life; The H— Family; The Parsonage of Mora. One Vol., 8vo, Muslin, $1 50.

## Life and Adventures of Martin Chuzzlewit.

By CHARLES DICKENS. With numerous Illustrations. 8vo, Paper, 50 cents; Muslin, 75 cents.

## Dickens's Christmas Tales:

Comprising The Haunted Man; The Cricket on the Hearth; A Christmas Carol in Prose; The Chimes; The Battle of Life 8vo, Muslin, 50 cents.

## W. G. Simms's Works:

Comprising Guy Rivers; Martin Faber; Mellichampe; The Partisan; The Yemasse; Pelayo.

## Fielding's Works

The History of Amelia, with Illustrations by Cruikshank; The History of Tom Jones, with a Memoir of the Author, by THOMAS ROSCOE, illustrated by Cruikshank.

## Smollett's Works:

Roderic Random, with Illustrations by Cruikshank; Humphrey Clinker, with a Memoir of the Author by THOMAS ROSCOE, with Illustrations by Cruikshank; Adventures of Gil Blas, translated from the French of LE SAGE, with a Memoir of the Author, by T. ROSCOE, with Illustrations by Cruikshank.

## Georgia Scenes.

With Original Illustrations. 12mo, Muslin, 90 cents.

## Scenes at Washington.

A Story of the Last Generation. By a Citizen of Maryland. 12mo, Paper, 37½ cents; Muslin, 50 cents.

## The Diary of a Physician.

By Dr. WARREN. 3 vols. 18mo, Muslin, $1 35.

## The Vicar of Wakefield.

By OLIVER GOLDSMITH. 18mo, Muslin, 37½ cents.

## Recollections of a Housekeeper.

By Mrs. C. GILMAN. 18mo, Muslin, 45 cents.

## Recollections of a Southern Matron.

By Mrs. C. GILMAN. 12mo, Muslin, 90 cents.

## Love's Progress.

By Mrs. C. GILMAN. 12mo, Muslin, 65 cents.

## Miss Edgeworth's Tales and Novels.

With Engravings. 10 vols. 12mo, Muslin, 75 cents per Volume. The Volumes sold separately or in Sets.

VOL. I. Castle Rackrent; Essay on Irish Bulls; Essay on Self-Justification; The Prussian Vase; The Good Aunt.

VOL. II. Angelina; The Good French Governess; Mademoiselle Panache; The Knapsack; Lame Jervas; The Will; Out of Debt, out of Danger; The Limerick Gloves; The Lottery; Rosanna.

VOL. III. Murad the Unlucky; The Manufacturers; Ennui; The Contrast; The Grateful Negro; To-morrow; The Dun.

VOL. IV. Maneuvering; Almeria; Vivian.

VOL. V. The Absentee; Madame de Fleury; Emily de Coulanges; The Modern Griselda.

VOL. VI. Belinda.

VOL. VII. Leonora; Letters on Female Education; Patronage.

VOL. VIII. Patronage; Comic Dramas.

VOL. IX. Harrington; Thoughts on Bores; Ormond.

VOL. X. Helen.

## Miscellaneous List of Novels and Romances.

ADVENTURES OF A YOUNGER SON: by Trelawney. 85 cents.

ALLEN PRESCOTT: by Mrs. Sedgwick. $1 25.

ANASTASIUS: by T. Hope. 50 cents.

THE ATLANTIC CLUB-BOOK: by Paulding and others. 50 cents.

BERNARDO DEL CARPIO: by Montgomery. 50 cents.

BLACKBEARD: a Page from the Colonial History of Philadelphia. $1 25.

BURTON: by Ingraham. 75 cents.

THE BOOK OF ST. NICHOLAS: by Paulding. 62½ cents.

THE BUDGET OF THE BUBBLE FAMILY: by Lady Bulwer. 90 cents.

THE CABINET MINISTER: by Mrs. Gore. 85 cents.

CALEB WILLIAMS: by Godwin. 85 cents.

CAPTAIN KYD: by Ingraham. 75 cents.

THE CAVALIERS OF VIRGINIA: by Caruthers. $1 25.

CHEVELEY: by Lady Bulwer. 90 cents.

# Miscellaneous List of Novels, *continued.*

CHARLES VINCENT: by Willis. $1 25.

CHRONICLES OF THE CANONGATE: by Sir W. Scott. 70 cents.

THE CLUB-BOOK: by James. 45 cents.

CONTI THE DISCARDED: by Chorley. 90 cents.

THE COUNTESS IDA: by Fay. $1 50.

COUNT ROBERT OF PARIS: by Sir W Scott. 90 cents.

THE COURTIER of the Reign of Charles II.: by Mrs. Gore. 50 cents.

CYRIL THORNTON: by Hamilton. 87½ cts.

DARNLEY: by James. 85 cents.

DEERBROOK: by Miss Martineau. 90 cents.

DE L'ORME: by James. 70 cents.

THE DESULTORY MAN: by James. 90 cts.

DE VERE: by Ward. 90 cents.

DIARY OF A DESENNUYEE. 45 cents.

DREAMS AND REVERIES OF A QUIET MAN: by Fay. $1 12½.

ELKSWATAWA, the Prophet of the West: by French. $1 25.

FALKNER: by Mrs. Shelley. 62½ cents.

FRANK ORBY. 80 cents.

THE FROLICS OF PUCK. 90 cents.

GENTLEMAN OF THE OLD SCHOOL: by James. 90 cents.

GEORGE BALCOMBE: by Tucker. $1 25.

THE GIPSY: by James. 45 cents.

GODOLPHIN: by Bulwer. 90 cents.

HENRI QUATRE: by Mancur. 50 cents.

HENRY OF GUISE: by James. 90 cents.

HENRY MASTERTON: by James. 87½ cts.

HERBERT WENDALL: a Tale of the Revolution. $1 25.

HOBOKEN: a Romance of New York: by Fay. 45 cents.

HOME; or, the Iron Rule: by Mrs. Ellis. 25 cents.

HOPE LESLIE: by Miss Sedgwick. $1 25.

THE HOUR AND THE MAN: by Miss Martineau. 50 cents.

THE JACQUERIE: by James. 90 cents.

JAPHET IN SEARCH OF A FATHER: by Marryat. 45 cents.

JOHN MARSTON HALL: by James. 85 cts

KONINGSMARKE: by Paulding $1 25.

LAFITTE; the Pirate of the Gulf: by Ingraham. 75 cents.

THE LINWOODS: by Miss Sedgwick. $1 50.

LORD ROLDAN: by Cunningham. 45 cents.

LOUISA MILDMAY. .0 cents.

MAHMOUD. 90 cents.

MARIAN: by Mrs. S. C. Hall. 50 cents.

MARY OF BURGUNDY: by James. 85 cents.

THE MAYOR OF WINDGAP: by Banim. 42½ cents.

MELMOTH THE WANDERER: by Maturin. 90 cents.

MEPHISTOPHILES IN ENGLAND. 50 cts.

MERCHANT'S CLERK: by Warren. 45 cts.

MICHAEL ARMSTRONG: by Mrs. Trollope. 90 cents.

MIRIAM COFFIN: by Hart. $1 25.

MORLEY ERNSTEIN: by James. 45 cents.

MORTON'S HOPE: by an American. $1 40.

MOUNT SOREL; or, the Heiress of the De Veres: by Mrs. Marsh. 12½ cents.

MY LIFE: by Maxwell. 85 cents.

MYSTERIES OF PARIS: by Sue. 56¼ cents

THE NEVILLES OF GARRETSTOWN: by Dr. Lever. 12½ cents.

NORMAN LESLIE: by Fay. $1 25.

NOVELLETTES OF A TRAVELER: by Nott. $1 25.

ONE IN A THOUSAND: by James. 45 cents.

THE OUTLAW: by Mrs. Hall. 90 cents.

THE PARTISAN: by Simms. $1 25

PAUL ULRIC: by Mattson. $1 25.

PELAYO: by Simms. $1 25.

PHILIP AUGUSTUS: by James. 85 cents.

PREFERMENT: by Mrs. Gore. 90 cents.

THE QUADROON: by Ingraham. 75 cents.

THE REFUGEE IN AMERICA: by Mrs. Trollope. 85 cents.

ROMANCE OF HISTORY—FRANCE: by Ritchie. 70 cents.

ROMANCE OF HISTORY—ITALY: by Macfarlane. 70 cents.

ROSE OF PERSIA: by Spring. 50 cents.

SALMAGUNDI: by Paulding and Irving. $2 50.

THE SCHOOL OF FASHION. 85 cents.

THE SELF-CONDEMNED. 45 cents.

SHEPPARD LEE: by Himself. $1 50.

THE SKETCH-BOOK OF FASHION: by Mrs. Gore. 50 cents.

THE SMUGGLER: by Banim. 85 cents.

SOUTHENNAN: by Galt. 70 cents.

SPECULATION: by Miss Pardoe. 50 cents.

STORIES OF THE SEA: by Marryat. 37½ cents.

ST. PATRICK'S EVE: by Lever. 6¼ cents.

THE STUDENT: by Bulwer. 80 cents.

SYDNEY CLIFTON: by Strong. $1 25.

TALES AND SKETCHES: by Stone. 70 cts.

TALES OF THE EARLY AGES: by Smith. 70 cents.

TALES OF THE GOOD WOMAN: by Paulding. $1 25

TALES OF THE PEERAGE AND PEASANTRY: by Lady Dacre. 50 cents.

TALES OF THE WOODS AND FIELDS: by Mrs. Marsh. 45 cents.

THREE ERAS OF WOMAN'S LIFE: by Mrs. Smith. 45 cents.

THE THREE WISE MEN OF GOTHAM: by Paulding. 62½ cents.

TWO OLD MEN'S TALES. 80 cents.

THE UNFORTUNATE MAN: by Chamier. 80 cents.

VALERIUS: by Lockhart. 85 cents.

VILLAGE BELLES. 80 cents.

THE WANDERING JEW: by Sue. 50 cents. New Edition, with over 500 Illustrations. $5 00

WAVERLEY: by Scott. 70 cents.

WILD SPORTS OF THE WEST: by Maxwell. 50 cents.

YOUNG MUSCOVITE: by Chamier. 90 cents

## Hannibal.

A new volume of the series projected by the skillful book-manufacturer, Mr. Abbott, who displays no little tact in engaging the attention of that marvelous body, "the reading public," in old scholastic topics hitherto almost exclusively the property of the learned. The latter, with their ingenious implements of lexicons and scholia, will be in no danger of being superseded, however, while the least-furnished reader may gain something from the attractively-printed and easily-perused volumes of Mr. Abbott. The story of Hannibal is well adapted for popular treatment, and loses nothing for this purpose in the present explanatory and pictorial version.—*Literary World.*

## Alexander the Great.

The history of Alexander the Great, as penned by Jacob Abbott, will be read with thrilling interest. It is profusely embellished, containing maps of the Expedition of Alexander, of Macedon and Greece, the plain of Troy, the Granicus, and the plain of Issus; and engravings of Alexander and Bucephalus; Paris and Helen; the bathing in the River Cyndus; the siege of Tyre; Alexander at the siege of Susa; and the proposed improvement of Mount Athos. It is written in a most graphic and attractive style.—*Spectator.*

Full of entertainment and instruction.—*Independent.*

## Darius the Great.

Mr. Abbott's design to write a succession of histories for the young is admirable, and worthy of all encouragement, and the manner in which he has executed the work thus far is most excellent. Let him be encouraged to proceed till he has reached the last volume of history, that the coming generation may turn from the world of romance to that of reality, and learn that what is and has been is as brilliant in character, as glorious in description, and as captivating in detail, as that which the genius of fiction ever created.—*New York Observer.*

## Cyrus the Great.

The style is smooth, easy, and attractive, and the whole preparation of the work is such as will secure a large popularity for the series. The great condensation of facts, and the picturesqueness of the style will commend these books to the young. The illuminated title-pages are very beautiful.—*Southern Methodist Pulpit.*

## Xerxes the Great.

They possess more than the interest of fiction, and yet are replete with solid information. The youth that becomes interested in these glowing pictures will find a growing taste for historical reading generally.—*Christian Parlor Magazine.*

## Alfred the Great.

History, under the pen of Mr. Abbott, discloses its narratives and utters its lessons in a style of great simplicity and intelligence, and, above all, with no danger of detriment to morals. He has selected his field with excellent taste. In their line, these volumes have never been surpassed.—*Baptist Recorder.*

## William the Conqueror.

These historical works by Mr. Abbott have so much merit for the interesting style in which they are written, and the beauty of their mechanical execution, that we place them at the head of the more unpretending histories. We know of no works extant calculated to produce a more salutary effect upon the young reader of history; certainly none where leading historical incidents are communicated in a more fascinating manner.—*Buffalo Courier.*

## Mary Queen of Scots.

The history is here given minute in every point of real interest, and without the encumbrance of useless opinions. There is no sentence thrown away—no time lost in mere ornament. Perhaps no book extant, containing so few pages, can be said to convey so many genuine historical facts. There is here no attempt to glaze over recorded truth, or win the reader by sophistry to opinions merely those of the author. The pure, simple history of Queen Mary is placed before the reader, and each one is left to form an unbiased opinion from events impartially recorded there. One great and most valuable feature in this little work is a map of Scotland, with many engravings of the royal castles and wild scenes connected with Mary's history. There is also a beautiful portrait of the Queen, and a richly illuminated title-page such as only the Harpers can get up.—*National Magazine.*

## Queen Elizabeth.

Full of instructive and heart-stirring incident, displayed by the hand of a master. We doubt whether old Queen Bess ever before had so much justice done to her within the same compass. Such a pen as Jacob Abbott wields, especially in this department of our literature, has no right to lie still.—*Albany Express.*

We have read each and all of them successively in the order of their issue with far more interest than it is possible for us to feel in any work of fiction; and there has been no series of books published in this country that we would honor or more confidently place in the hands of the youthful reader than "Abbott's Historical Series."—*Mirror.*

## Charles the First.

We incline to think that there never was before so much said about this unfortunate monarch in so short a space; so much to the purpose; with so much impartiality; and in such a style as just suits those for whom it is designed—the "two millions" of young persons in the United States, who ought to be supplied with such works as these. The engravings represent the prominent persons and places of the history, and are well executed. The portrait of John Hampden is charming. The antique title-page is rich.—*Southern Christian Advocate.*

## Charles the Second.

A valuable engraving of Lely's portrait of Cromwell opens the book, and there are several illustrative wood-engravings and an illuminated title-page. This is a comprehensive and simple narration of the main features of the period during which Charles the Second reigned, and it is done with the clear scope and finely-written style which would be expected from the pen of Jacob Abbott—one of the most able and useful literary men of his time.—*Home Journal.*

www.ingramcontent.com/pod-product-compliance
Lightning Source LLC
LaVergne TN
LVHW020929110826
845150LV00004B/808

* 9 7 8 1 4 2 5 5 5 3 1 6 6 *